Government and Politics in Britain

An Introduction

2nd Edition

John Kingdom

Polity Press

First edition published 1991
Reprinted 1991, 1992, 1994, 1995, 1996, 1997

This edition published 1999 by Polity Press
in association with Blackwell Publishers Ltd.

Editorial office:
Polity Press
65 Bridge Street
Cambridge CB2 1UR, UK

Marketing and production:
Blackwell Publishers Ltd
108 Cowley Road
Oxford OX4 1JF, UK

ISBN 0–7456–1719–0
ISBN 0–7456–1720–4 (pbk)

A catalogue record for this book is available from the British Library.

Typeset in 10 on 12 pt Sabon
by Ace Filmsetting Ltd, Frome, Somerset
Printed in Great Britain by T. J. International, Padstow, Cornwall

This book is printed on acid-free paper.

Contents

Preface

The chapters of this book represent an exceptionally wide-ranging introduction to British politics. The expectation is that it will be studied over some time (one or two years) and the chapters generally reflect a sense of cumulative development so that, for example, chapter 4 is written on the assumption that chapters 1, 2 and 3 have been mastered. However, it is also the case that each has a clearly discernible focus and assumes no detailed prior knowledge of the topic. Hence the chapters can (under the direction of the teacher/tutor) be studied in a different order without major conceptual difficulty. Each chapter concludes with a summary of main points, a list of key terms and concepts, questions for discussion (which may be treated as essay topics to be completed under various conditions chosen by the teacher/tutor, or used for group discussion) and a guide to further reading.

The summaries and key terms and concepts

The summary of main points is intended to highlight the essential thrust of the discussion in the chapter, providing a means of quick recapitulation and revision aid. The lists of key terms and concepts are intended as a form of self-testing upon completion of each chapter. One should feel able to give concise definitions of all these before proceeding. Usually they are explained fully in the chapter.

The Glossary and Chronology

The Glossary can be used variously as an aid to revision, in essay writing and to provide speedy clarification of a meaning during the course of reading. The definitions offered are necessarily brief and greater clarification should be sought in that part of the text where it is dealt with most fully (as indicated in the index). New terms appear in **bold** type when they are first discussed.

The Chronology will enable you to see at a glance the sequence of the major events in British politics and their relationship to world events. It is often surprising to discover what happened when.

Further reading

The study of politics at an introductory level is essentially concerned with reading and thinking. We are not able to study our subject in a laboratory and we cannot manipulate the real world to conduct experiments. There is of course a real world of political activity, and it is profoundly dangerous to forget this fact, but the amount any individual can find out by direct observation is minuscule and, in the early stages of study, we must rely on accounts from various sources, including the mass media, historians, and academics from the range of disciplines discussed in chapter 1.

The further reading suggested at the end of each chapter cannot pretend to be comprehensive and students should feel free to explore the literature of the disciplines according to their particular interests. The recommended sources are chosen for various reasons: sometimes the work is a classic, sometimes it is controversial, and sometimes unusual. Generally the suggestions are made because they are regarded as of an intrinsically high quality as well as being stimulating.

Material for light relief is not included as a joke. Much literature and drama, light and serious, addresses the big questions of life and politics. It is important to remember that politics is not something outside normal social experience, unable to explain everyday problems; on the contrary, it lies at the very root of our social condition.

Journal articles are not included in the reading because there are so many, though of course references can be found throughout the text. However, for students new to the subject two journals will be of special value: *Politics Review* and *Talking Politics*. Other accessible journals are *Parliamentary Affairs* and *Political Quarterly*. There is also some excellent political reporting and analysis in the quality press.

Since the first edition of this book was published, the growth of the internet has given students another source of information. A number of web sites are mentioned at the end of most chapters; by using a search engine and following hypertext links you will find countless others.

Discussion

Mere width of reading and acquisition of information does not constitute good study practice; it must be accompanied by thought and a search for understanding. It is better to study a limited number of sources thoroughly, so that they are understood, than to try to cover a wider range in order to commit things to memory 'parrot fashion'. The subject requires thought as much as factual knowledge, and we develop this through argument and discussion with others. This was the essence of the method employed by Plato in the Grove of Academos (hence 'academic') in Ancient Greece, and in spite of the breathtaking advances in modern information technology, it cannot be bettered. Talking seriously about politics is more than an academic enterprise, it is part of the process of being a citizen; it is itself an element of the good life (the prohibition of such talk is a sign of oppression). It can also lead to self-revelation: we can better understand the way we are by recognizing the forces which govern our environment. For example, many people (often working class, women, or members of ethnic minorities) blame themselves for various forms of 'failure' in their lives rather than entertain the possibility that they have been subject to greater political forces. However, this possibility of gaining understanding of one's life can be dangerous; it is sometimes better for the powerful if those without power *do* blame themselves for their conditions. You will see throughout this book that much in politics is about power, and the tension between the powerful and the powerless.

Assignments and questions for discussion

The assignments and questions included at the end of each chapter are integral to the study. The assignments ask you to use a wider range of skills than are required for essay writing. They are to encourage you to see in the media a further rich source for understanding the contemporary world. The 'essay-type' questions may be discussed in groups, made the subject of an address by one member to the others or used as the basis of an essay. They are posed in order to address your mind to certain issues of fundamental importance in the chapter. Even so, the more you study the more you will realize that there are many variants upon them and teachers and tutors will provide a never-ending supply!

Topics for debate

These are intended to be controversial and should be used to stimulate sustained argument. The process of taking part in academic argument and debate can (under the stimulus of the adrenalin coursing through our veins as a result of anger, indignation or frustration over the impertinence or stupidity of others) stimulate thought in a way that lone contemplation may not. Of course discussion and debate are empty and sterile if one does not read and think by way of preparation. If people attend your debates without having done this you are entitled to shred their egos with your knowledge and wit.

Acknowledgements

During the preparation of this edition David Held has remained unflagging in his enthusiasm, advice and encouragement. I also owe enormous debts to Howard Elcock and Andrew Gamble for reading the draft text in its entirety, giving encouragement and making numerous suggestions from a profound depth of scholarship. These have materially enhanced the book in many ways. I am equally grateful to Peter Holmes, who brought to the same task the unique contribution of academic turned teacher. Colleagues who have read chapters in their particular areas of expertise and given generously of their time in many interesting discussions include Jim Chandler, Sonia El Kahal, Michael Hunt, Robert Jones, Malcolm Stevens and Royce Turner. In addition, I must never forget Bob Haigh's seminal influence on this book. Richard Allan, MP, from the perspective of a new and ever-inquisitive member of the 'best club in London', read and made many helpful comments on the chapters on Parliament. I am also indebted to the large number of teachers and lecturers who took part in the survey organized by Polity Press. Their comments were both encouraging and helpful and they will find many of their suggestions incorporated in this edition. A more hands-on contribution came from Joanne Bone, with her limitless patience and skill on mouse and keyboard in producing many of the diagrams. Her colleague Andy Goddard provided wide-ranging computer troubleshooting expertise, wrestling valiantly with the software to produce figure 9.8. At Ace Filmsetting, Jim Henretty worked with laser-like speed, going beyond the call of duty with advice on diagrams and layout. At Polity Press everyone has invariably been enthusiastic and accommodating, Serena Temperley enduring the headaches posed by the production of so complex a book. At the heart of the operation has been Sue Leigh, remaining patient, understanding and invariably charming as the shifting sands of politics led to rewrite after rewrite. She managed to remind me of a world beyond politics with her email postscripts on matters horticultural. Last in time but not in importance comes Trish Stableford, who subjected the proofs to the eye of a veritable eagle and managed to identify inconsistencies, infelicities and ambiguities with wit and humour (however, the answer to assignment question 3 on page 79 is *not* 'You get more sand in your mouth on the beach'!). Most of all I thank my partner, Ann Barham, who as an experienced copy-editor and indexer has brought consummate knowledge and expertise to all she has done. She has worked tirelessly as research assistant, copy-editor, diagram drawer, permissions seeker, internet searcher and initial proofreader. She has also compiled the superb index which so enhances the value of the book. Needless to say, all remaining errors and inconsistencies are mine alone (Ann has a suspicion that some could be hers but I remain responsible!).

I am grateful to the following for permission to reproduce material previously published elsewhere. Basil Blackwell and Polity Press for figure 17.5 from John Scott, 'The British upper class', in D. Coates, G. Johnston and R. Bush (eds), *A Socialist Anatomy of Britain*, 1985, p. 45; *The Economist* for the extracts on pp. 141, 164, 331 and 561; the European Parliament for the photographs on pp. 121, 123, 124 and 499; Noel Ford for the cartoons on pp. 249 and 295; Friends of the Earth for the photographs on pp. 2 and 562; the *Independent* for the extracts on pp. 80, 192, 298, 368, 436, 504, 538 and 672; Little Brown for the extract from Ben Elton's *Stark* on pp. 52–3; the Mary Evans Picture Library for the pictures on pp. 57, 85, 183, 232, 271, 356, 382, 404, 440, 479, 581, 608 and 620; Simon Meyrick-Jones for the cartoon on p. 157; Terence Parks (Larry) for the cartoons on pp. 230 and 241; Punch Ltd for the cartoons on pp. 13, 32, 204, 212, 279, 406, 456, 545, 615 and 664; Albert Rusling for the cartoon on p. 595; Harley Schwadron for the cartoon on p. 455; *The Socialist* for the photographs on pp. 70, 207 and 648; Bill Tidy for the cartoon on p. 643; Times Newspapers Ltd for the photographs on pp. 45, 93, 100, 160, 202, 345, 363 and 431 and the extracts on pp. 110, 604 and 636 © Times Newspapers Ltd; the World Development Movement for the photographs on pp. 92 and 510 and the cartoon on p. 95. The Crown Copyright material in the Public Record Office is reproduced on p. 415 by permission of the Controller of Her Majesty's Stationery Office (PRO document reference CAB 65/28). I am also grateful for the assistance I received in obtaining photographs from Emma Brooks of News International Syndication, Clare Joy of the World Development Movement, Ben Rogers of Friends of the Earth, Ken Smith of *The Socialist*, and the staff of the Punch Library and the library of the European Parliament UK Office.

Chapter One

Introduction: Studying Politics

No one is unaffected by politics. Speaking very broadly, it is about the way people organize their lives together in a community. The important collective decisions shaping the very quality of life – concerning wealth, health, education, morality – are all essentially political in their nature. Studying and talking about politics are a necessary part of the good life which we seek. To be denied the right to do this is one of the first symptoms of oppression. This chapter aims to ponder the essential nature of the subject and the terms and concepts associated with its study. These include power, authority, legitimacy, the state, and society. Finally we address the actual study of politics.

What is Politics?

Encountering politics

Human social life is not a tranquil experience. People seem able to argue and disagree over most things – education, nuclear weapons, the National Health Service, race, gender, the European Union, genetic engineering, the north–south divide, the future of Northern Ireland, and so on *ad infinitum*. Differences are voiced in arguments in pubs and clubs and MPs are elected to continue the arguments in Parliament. Even religious leaders enter the fray; the Church of England's 1985 report, *Faith in the City*, was a damning indictment of inner-city decay and neglect.

Not only do people argue, they resort to violence. Today we see demonstrations, race riots, attacks on the police, attacks by the police and bitter strikes. We see blood and death as people fight for their rights, the rights of others or even the rights of animals. Some are prepared to die. In 1913 Emily Wilding Davison fatally flung herself under the hooves of the King's horse in the Derby and other women threatened to starve themselves to death in Britain's prisons

Ben Bradshaw MP and Charles Secrett of Friends of the Earth demonstrating in support of the Road Traffic Reduction (National Targets) Bill, January 1998

Photo: Jennifer Bates/Friends of the Earth

because they wanted the right to vote. In February 1995 animal rights campaigner Jill Phipps was martyred beneath the wheels of a lorry carrying veal calves for export. People, and even the government, will also kill for their beliefs, as planted bombs and shoot-to-kill policies testify. Throughout all, the unblinking eye of the mass media watches, reports and incites.

These widely-disparate patterns of behaviour, involving matters great and small, serious and trivial, originating at home or abroad, involving ordinary people and the high and the mighty, which may be enacted within the great state institutions of Westminster, Whitehall and the Inns of Court, or in streets and factories, share little in common except for one thing: along with countless other such examples they would be recognized as *events in politics*. It is clear that if we are to study this subject seriously it is necessary to make some order of a world of bewildering complexity; to try to distil the essence of the activity known as *politics*. This is by no means easy; scholars continue to dispute the definition of politics.

I hope I will not destroy faith in the omniscience of professors entirely if I now confess that I do not really know what my subject is.

F. F. Ridley, 'The importance of constitutions', *Parliamentary Affairs* (1966: 312)

Politics arises from certain basic facts of human existence: that people generally choose (indeed find it necessary for survival) to live together and that they differ in myriad ways in their opinions as to how the community should be organized and the nature of the decisions it makes. The source of conflict may either be the simple fact that individuals are self-interested and greedy, never able to feel content with their lot, or that they hold differing views on big moral questions. Disputes are inevitable because the world's resources are finite (no one can have all he or she wants) and the range of opinion on moral questions is limitless.

However, when we come to address directly the fundamental question 'What is politics?' we find it impossible to give a simple answer. Politics can be seen variously as concerned with the art of *compromise*, the exercise of *authority*, the acquisition of *power* and as a form of devious *deception*. It is not the case that any one of these categories of definition is correct and the others wrong, but rather that politics is a many-sided concept, only to be understood if viewed from various angles.

Politics as compromise: the 'art of the possible'

Politics as '**the art of the possible**' is a well-known but enigmatic definition (authorship of which is attributed variously) and retains its relevance because it encapsulates a particular view of politics as a process of participating and finding agreement which has been attractive to western minds since the time of the famous Ancient Greek philosopher Aristotle (384–322 BC). Amongst modern thinkers it is most eloquently expressed by Bernard Crick:

> Politics is not just a necessary evil; it is a realistic good. Political activity is a type of moral activity; it is a free activity, and it is inventive, flexible, enjoyable, and human. (Crick 1964: 141)

However, if such a view were rigidly adhered to, there would be little material for political scientists to study in the real world of violence, murder, duplicity and self-interest. Yet this definition remains important for several reasons.

- It defines the pure essence of politics.
- It stands as an ethical ideal.
- It provides a measure against which real-world systems may be judged.

The view of politics as a compromising and conciliatory activity might suggest that it is opposed to the idea of sovereignty and rule by a central authority. This is wrong because differences cannot be reconciled without some overarching authority, even if this is no more than the idea of *agreement* (or contract) reached between the parties. This leads to a second definition.

Politics as authority

David Easton, an influential American political scientist, argued that politics was concerned with the '**authoritative allocation of values**' (1953: 129). **Authority** is the right of some person or institution (king or government) to make decisions affecting the community. A woman with a gun, or a man with a large wallet, may be able to get their own way but will not have authority if those obeying do so with a sense of grievance. Such rule is unstable; those subjected may be expected to revolt when they glimpse their chance. Authority is derived from legitimacy.

Legitimacy When a government enjoys **legitimacy** people will obey because they believe it right to be ruled in this way. This is a key to the success of any political system, and explains why military dictatorships taking power by force are soon seeking the appearance of democratic civilian rule.

The strongest is never strong enough to be always the master, unless he transforms strength into right, and obedience into duty.

Jean Jacques Rousseau (French philosopher and writer), *The Social Contract* (1762)

Forms of authority The great sociologist Max Weber (1864–1920) distinguished three kinds of authority: *rational legal* (bestowed by normative rules, such as constitutions and election); *traditional* (conferred by history, habit and custom – like a hereditary monarchy); and *charismatic* (where the personal qualities of the leader inspire the confidence, and even adulation, of the masses).

Of course, to say that a government enjoys legitimacy does not necessarily imply that it is a *good* government; legitimacy merely resides in popular consciousness. Hence political regimes will devote considerable time and energy not to making policies for the people's education, welfare, and so on, but to the shaping of attitudes – the process of **legitimation**. We shall see that a great deal of British political life serves this end. For example, when Elizabeth II was crowned by the Archbishop of Canterbury the British people witnessed a tradition whereby the monarchs of old sought to present their earthly power as a manifestation of the will of God.

While it is clear that the exercise of authority is part of politics, this presents a rather legalistic and simplistic picture. Governments cannot always expect to possess legitimacy; in a complex society there will be elements opposed to the government of the day, questioning and challenging it and even seeking to destroy it. Governments can aim to maintain themselves by deception of the masses and by force. This leads to an analysis of one of the most central concepts in politics – power.

Politics as power

American political scientist Harold Lasswell (1936) gave the discipline a memorable catch-phrase in the title of his book *Politics: Who Gets What, When, How?* Here the essence of politics is **power**, and those who get most of what is going are the powerful. Power can be defined as the ability to achieve some desired effect, regardless of the opposition. Authority is one form of power, but a glance at the world today quickly reveals that many regimes are based on cruder forms such as wealth, gender, physical might and violence.

> I put for a general inclination of all mankind,* a perpetual and restless desire for power after power, that ceaseth only in death.
>
> Thomas Hobbes (English philosopher), *Leviathan* (1651: ch. 11)

Concentration on pure power takes us beyond the trappings of government into shadowy corners behind the throne. The authority of the government is often nothing more than an empty legal (*de jure*) title; the real (*de facto*) power to get what is wanted, when it is wanted, lies elsewhere. Although some are content to study only the trappings of the state, it should be a central task of political analysis to track down the real source of power, to find the constitutional Mr Big, though the trail can often resemble the Yellow Brick Road to the elusive end of the rainbow.

We will discover later in this book that the most important approaches to the study of politics centre around hypotheses about where real power lies. Does it lie with the people, *some* of the people, a particular race, the male sex, the armed forces, the talented, the wealthy, the aristocracy, Parliament, the Cabinet, the prime minister, the civil service, the mass media, the professional classes, the managers of industry, the controllers of capital, and so on? Alternatively, does it lie outside the state territory altogether with superpowers like the USA, international groupings like NATO, or mighty transnational corporations with budgets dwarfing those of many nations? We shall find that power – like wealth – is unevenly distributed; some people have much while others have little.

Politics as deception

A popular use of the term 'political' denotes devious, shifty behaviour generally aimed at securing personal advantage – usually position or office. Many of Shakespeare's plays dwell on the intrigue in politics so that Enoch Powell could say in a 1950s BBC series: 'The stage used to be called the Court, now they call

---

* The terminology in this and other quotations is not intended to exclude women; it is merely an example of sexist language and in itself a manifestation of male power (see chapters 2 and 7).

> Get thee glass eyes;
> And, like a scurvy politician, seem
> To see the things thou dost not.
>
> King Lear in Shakespeare's *King Lear*

it a Cabinet, but all the characters are in Shakespeare . . . Only the costumes date.' Such activity can take place at the micro level (within government organizations), as well as the macro level (between rulers and the ruled).

Deception in micro-politics It was probably in this sense that the word 'politics' first appeared in English, as a term of disapproval applied to the activities of those engaged in faction, intrigue and opposition to established governments. People who are 'politicking' are usually understood to be plotting against rivals. The term is often applied to the behaviour of individuals in large organizations, where those engaged in politics (from planning to oust the chairman to gaining a larger desk) are unlikely to be contributing to the organization's collective goal. Much activity of this kind takes place within the corridors and tearooms of the Palace of Westminster, and in the clubs and bedsits around about. Indeed the British Cabinet itself was originally a secretive group of ministers scheming together as a *cabal*.

> One has to be a bit of a lowbrow, a bit of a murderer, to be a politician, ready and willing to see people sacrificed, slaughtered for the sake of an idea.
>
> Henry Miller (1891–1980; American writer), *Writers at Work*

This view is often linked with the ideas of the Italian Renaissance thinker Niccolò Machiavelli; to be labelled 'Machiavellian' is usually taken as insulting. However, Machiavelli's essential point was that intrigue and plotting were justified by the greater purposes of government (see chapter 2). In other words, he believed the old adage that the ends justify the means: 'when the act accuses, the end excuses'. This leads to deception at the level of macro-politics.

Deception in macro-politics This is by far the more important in the outcomes of politics and was captured by the great nineteenth-century prime minister

> I have lots of enemies. . . . Hurd has always been against me, told the lady [Margaret Thatcher] not to make me Minister for Trade – which she very splendidly repeated to me on the evening of my appointment. Arsehole. He's looking more and more like Aldridge Prior.
>
> Alan Clark on ministerial rivalries, *Diaries* (1 Feb. 1991)

> The erosion of public confidence in the holders of public office is a serious matter. In so far as a culture of moral vagueness, a culture of sleaze has developed, we seek to put an end to it.
>
> The Nolan Committee on Standards in Public Life, quoted in the
> *Guardian* (12 May 1995)

Benjamin Disraeli in the aphorism that politics was 'the art of governing mankind through deceiving them'. Legitimation itself can be seen as a form of deception. The perceptive English political essayist Walter Bagehot (1826–77) placed particular stress on deception of the masses as a key to successful government (see p. 59). Today, as the term 'spin doctor' enters common parlance, one is presented with a great mist of deceptive activity (including official secrecy) and the attempt to shine a searchlight through it is one of the principal duties of the political scientist.

> Politics is the art of preventing people from taking part in affairs which properly concern them.
>
> Paul Valéry
> (1871–1945;
> French writer),
> *Tel quel*

As we conclude this discussion on the nature of politics, it should be apparent that all our definitions are inextricably interwoven. There is no doubt that society harbours many conflicting interests which must be reconciled, often by the exercise of authority, and the process is clouded by evidence of great inequality of power and much devious behaviour.

What do political scientists study?

Individuals and groups disagree over ends and means in most walks of life. There are countless institutions that can resolve such conflict, including religious groups, trade unions, clubs, schools, universities, business firms, families, and so on. Does this mean that these are political institutions? Some academics do in fact study the politics of small communities, usually taking a psychological perspective, but the particular focus of attention for the political scientist is the **state** – a very special, unique, and profoundly important social formation.

The state

A state is a community formed for the purpose of government. The Ancient Greeks talked of the **city-state** (sometimes termed the **polity**, from the Greek *polis*) and today we speak of the **nation-state,** a relatively recent formation. Philosophers dispute the nature of the state (see chapter 2), the German Hegel giving it a particularly metaphysical significance as the highest expression of ethics; only through allegiance to, and service in, the state could individuals fully realize themselves. Generally the state is taken to be a community with the following characteristics (Lasswell and Kaplan 1950: 181).

- A clearly defined territory.
- A legitimate government.
- Sovereignty within its territory.
- An existence recognized by other states in international law.
- A 'persona', in which name it is able to make treaties and have obligations and rights independent of any actual person. Thus we speak of the state doing this and that: prosecuting people (state prosecution), providing welfare (welfare state), being sinned against (crimes against the state), keeping secrets (state secrets), educating citizens (state education), and so on.
- Perpetual succession – rulers may change but the state continues to exist, with no alteration to its commitments and responsibilities.
- Universality – all those living within the jurisdiction of the state (there are some exceptions for diplomats) are subject to its rules. Unlike other associations (say, sports clubs or a church), members do not have the right to opt out of state jurisdiction (unless they emigrate, though in this case they would soon come under some other state).
- The right to use force and coercion against members. Weber saw this as the most singular characteristic of the state, distinguishing it from all other organizations. If other agencies, say bouncers outside a disco, teachers, or even parents, use force, they may find themselves subject to the law, but the state can legally imprison, harass, and sometimes kill. From this it becomes starkly obvious that operating the state apparatus confers great and threatening power.

Today some argue that a process of globalization (see chapter 4) through economics and technology and the horror of modern weaponry make the concept of the nation-state dangerously outmoded.

The state and society The notion of the state may be differentiated from that of society; the former is constructed and based upon law, while the latter arises naturally from the free association of people (sometimes termed **civil society**). In the state, individual members stand as **citizens** with legally prescribed rights and obligations, but no such conditions attach to them as members of society, where they are constrained more by economic and ethical norms. The same distinction was made by the German sociologist Ferdinand Tönnies (1855–1936), who spoke of *Gesellschaft* (a community formed by artificial, human contract) and *Gemeinschaft* (a community arising from bonds of affection or kinship). The national community is both state *and* society, a fact that is a source of friction. While all citizens are legally equal, as members of society they can be decidedly unequal. When the legal equality of citizenship is markedly at variance with the real level of societal equality, there will be the potential for political tension.

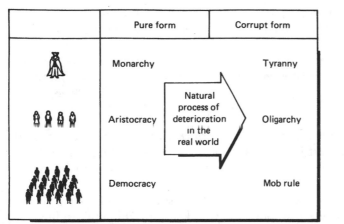

Figure 1.1
Forms of government.

Government

The idea of **government** lies at the heart of political science. Indeed no society has ever been found that did not have some kind of government (Mair 1970). It can take various forms: it may be *constitutional* (limited by laws, see pp. 64–7), *absolutist* (unlimited by laws), *primitive* (a chieftain's rule over a tribe), or *pluralist* (consisting of several institutions sharing the role). Following Aristotle, it is customary to group forms of government in terms of the number of rulers, thus distinguishing **monarchy** (rule by one person), **aristocracy** (rule by an enlightened few) and **democracy** (rule by all the people – the *demos*). However, each of these may be said to tend in practice towards a corrupt variant: **tyranny, oligarchy** and **mob rule** (figure 1.1).

> Politics and the fate of mankind are shaped by men without ideals and without greatness. Men who have greatness within them don't go in for politics.
>
> Albert Camus (1913–60; French philosopher and writer), *Notebooks, 1935–42*

Government and self-interest The fatal deterioration of the forms of government is usually attributed to the corrupting influences of power, which may lead those holding it to act in their own interests rather than that of the community. The historian Lord Acton (1834–1902) observed memorably:

> Power tends to corrupt, and absolute power corrupts absolutely. Great men are almost always bad men.

The selfish tendency of human beings is a hard truth that forms the starting point for much political thought. The key issue is reconciling the common good with the need for government. Scottish philosopher David Hume (1711–76) believed that 'every man ought to be supposed a knave and to have no end other than private interest', arguing that it was crucial for a state to devise a form of government that would inhibit the corrupting tendencies.

> A republican and free government would be an obvious absurdity, if the particular checks and controuls [*sic*], provided by the constitution, had really no influence, and made it not in the interest, even of bad men, to act for the public good. (Hume 1882 edn: 6–7)

The Philosophical Radicals of the nineteenth century (see chapter 2) took the individual pursuit of self-interest as the key to understanding human behaviour. This idea was very influential in shaping many of our modern institutions.

Government and politics Government will necessarily entail politics, even in primitive societies where institutions have taken only the most rudimentary form. In developed societies, politics is often seen as being about the formal working of the **machinery of government** – taking control of it, influencing its decisions, reforming it, changing those in office, and so on. However, it is important to remember that politics does not belong exclusively to the world of institutions. From the boardrooms of industry to the clubs, pubs and launderettes – politics is found wherever people gather and express their anger, hopes and anxieties, and assess their potential to influence events.

The state and the government

The state and the government are conceptually distinct. In the UK, the position of the Queen, who plays no effective part in government yet is head of state, underlines the distinction. For practical purposes the British government is usually regarded as the collection of around a hundred secretaries of state, ministers, junior ministers and their various assistants drawn from Parliament. In contrast, the state can be seen to comprise a much wider set of institutions (the civil service, the Bank of England, local authorities, health authorities, various quasi-autonomous bodies, nationalized industries, the judiciary, the military and the police). Some would go further and include the mass media, the institutions of the capitalist economy and trade unions (Middlemass 1979).

The political and the non-political

It will be apparent that if politics is about reconciling diverse interests it must have many manifestations; indeed no area of life can be seen as intrinsically non-political. Some people find this thought peculiarly disturbing and it is common to hear calls to 'take education (or health, or the siting of power stations, and so on) out of politics'. If something is to be taken out of politics, where is it to go? We have seen that politics is a process whereby differences and conflicts are resolved through conciliation, the exercise of authority and power. However, politics is by no means the only way of resolving such differences; there are three particularly important alternatives.

- The *economic market place* allows the forces of supply and demand to set prices and determine who gets what.
- Through *rational decision-making* experts weigh up the pros and cons of a case to arrive at the 'best' solution.
- *Violence* enables the unsatisfied, dispossessed or greedy to attempt to take what they want by physical force.

All these are present in Britain today, though each has limitations.

The market   The eighteenth- and nineteenth-century classical economists believed the **market** to be a wondrous mechanism for bringing buyers and sellers together at a mutually acceptable price resulting in the optimum allocation of resources within society. However, this raises difficult ethical problems. In the first place it is undemocratic, favouring the economically strong against the weak because it does not *redistribute* resources; it gives only unto him or her that already hath (that is, can afford the price). Thus, rather than taking matters out of politics, it creates a new basis for dissatisfaction and conflict. Secondly, not all allocations can be determined by the laws of supply and demand. Matters such as the level of sex and violence on television, the decision whether to send the task force to the Falklands, the degree of religious toleration to be allowed within society, or the age of consent for homosexuals lie in a territory of value-judgement and morality where the market is quite silent. When governments try to bring the market into areas such as education and health care many people are deeply disturbed. Indeed, because the human capacity to disagree over value-judgements is potentially limitless, there are infinitely more areas of dispute to be settled by politics than by the market.

Rational decision-making   The idea of making communal decisions on the basis of rational criteria seems very attractive; it is the argument for the use of experts (town planners, architects and the like). Organizational theorist Herbert Simon (1947) believed that state decision-makers should arm themselves with all the available information, calculate the outcomes of all possible courses of action, and choose the best policy for the community. However, in practice certain intractable problems beset such processes.

- The principle is essentially elitist and paternalistic, based on the notion that certain people know what is best for the masses.
- It is difficult to decide who the experts should be; obviously election cannot be the answer.
- In reality, experts can never be sure that they have all the information necessary to make the 'right' decision.
- Experts may be tempted to place their own personal interests before those of the community.
- Experts frequently disagree with each other.

War is nothing more than the continuation of politics by other means.

Karl von Clausewitz (1780–1831; German military expert), *Vom Kriege*

Rational decision-making also carries with it connotations of a threatening 'Big Brother' style of bureaucratic rule. Both fascist and totalitarian communist governments can be accused of trying to govern by putting experts in charge, while the call to replace politics with managerialism is ever-present in Britain.

Violence In the real world there can be little doubt that making and enacting collective decisions for communities is often accomplished by various forms of physical force and **violence**. Two world wars, the Nazi extermination of the Jews, the treatment of blacks in South Africa, the silencing of dissidents in Eastern Europe, the brutality of the Tiananmen Square massacre or the ethnic cleansing in former Yugoslavia can leave no one in any doubt of this harsh reality. Historically Britain has been a very violent nation and the Suez invasion, Northern Ireland and the Falklands war have revealed modern politicians still willing to seek violent solutions to political problems. After the Falklands war, Mrs Thatcher employed the language of force on the home front, speaking of the 'enemy within'. This turned out to be the miners, who were to find themselves embroiled in a physical confrontation with the police and security services.

Increasingly guerrilla warfare is chosen by groups wishing to gain their ends or make their voices heard as an alternative to participating in conventional political processes. Today nobody is immune; several thousand civilians have been killed over Northern Ireland, hijacks and atrocities such as the Lockerbie air disaster can occur anywhere and in 1989 the Ayatollah Khomeini set a chilling precedent with his *fatwa* on author Salman Rushdie because his book, *The Satanic Verses*, gave religious offence. However, like the market and the rational decision-making model, violence is not very effective at resolving problems. Violence breeds more violence and, when the fighting has ceased, the parties are obliged to sit around the conference table to seek a durable solution. This has been the case in both the Northern Ireland and Arab–Israeli conflicts, despite the high price paid in blood.

Is there really a world beyond politics?

Man is by nature a political animal.

Aristotle (Ancient Greek philosopher), *Politics*

It will become apparent throughout this book that when reformers believe they are taking an issue out of the sordid world of politics by handing it over to the market or the experts they delude themselves. Similarly, the idea that violence is not part of politics is unrealistic. Hence, in defining what is political we must be guided not by the nature of the issue but by the way people react to it. If we accept that politics is about reconciling diverse interests then it follows that anything can become political. The world that some believe to exist outside politics is a fantasy land, as inaccessible as that discovered by Alice when she went through the looking-glass.

"Maurice has always been politically active."

bond

Political Science

A master science?

Throughout the history of western civilization there runs a great tradition of **political thought** with a pantheon of giant figures who have applied their minds to profound questions relating to politics (chapter 2). The subject is also the stuff of much great drama, literature and art. Aristotle described politics as the 'Master Science' and it is not difficult to see what he meant. All we do in our lives, in society, the sciences and arts, will be influenced by politics; it is through politics that the totality of social existence is orchestrated.

Political scientists do not wear white coats, peer through microscopes or carry test tubes. Is **political science** really a science? Can it produce the systematic, ordered, predictive propositions associated with a subject such as physics? This is not a new question. The work of Aristotle, which involved him in a famous classification of the constitutions of the many Greek city-states, was just as systematic and 'scientific' as his work in the natural sciences. However, the advent of Galileo and Newton in physics led to developments that seemed to transport the physical sciences into new realms of precision, uniformity and prediction.

Yet some social scientists have tried to build a body of **political theory** – laws of society and politics resembling those of the physical sciences. Karl Marx (1818–83) was one of these (see chapter 2). Under the influence of *logical-positivism* (a school of philosophy holding that only statements capable of being disproved

> Every intellectual attitude is latently political.
>
> Thomas Mann (1875–1955; German writer), quoted in the *Observer* (11 Aug. 1974)

> Politics is not a science . . . but an art.
>
> Otto von Bismarck (1815–98; Prusso-German statesman), speech, Reichstag (15 March 1884)

can be meaningful), the post-war era saw renewed efforts by political scientists to steer the discipline towards rigorous theoretical propositions by the use of careful techniques and methods of empirical observation. In this effort to ape the objective observational methods of the 'hard' sciences they sought to ally the discipline more closely with anthropology and psychology. This movement was termed **behaviouralism** and one of its results was a preoccupation with the observable, or more particularly, the quantifiable. The problem with this was that many of the studies (from attitude surveys to voting statistics) were often tedious and sometimes essentially trite. They did not address the really big questions of politics, such as: What is power? Where does it really lie? Why do states go to war? Why do people die of starvation amidst abundance?

Others, including Max Weber, were sceptical of the idea that people and organizations could be studied in this way. Human beings reason and interpret the world, and the proposition that they are best treated as unthinking molecules in a test tube is dubious, if not ludicrous. He argued that the study of human affairs should take account of reason, motives and emotions in order to afford a deeper level of understanding, which he termed *verstehen*.

Today few would deny Weber's argument. Ironically, as the hard sciences push further into the unknown they encounter less rather than more precision and are obliged to construct 'uncertainty principles', 'fuzzy logic' and 'chaos theories' reflecting the vagaries that have long confronted the social scientist. Yet behaviouralism has left a beneficial legacy in that political scientists can no longer allow their minds to dwell for too long in the stratosphere of abstraction and metaphysics like medieval scholastics who disputed how many angels could balance on the point of a needle. Hence, the modern discipline of political science combines many approaches and includes a number of interrelated subdisciplines with various focuses and methodologies.

- *Political theory* examines theories of political institutions, including the law, the state, systems of representation, forms of government, and so on.
- *Political philosophy* searches for highly generalized answers to major questions such as the meaning of freedom, justice, equality and rights. Ultimately **political philosophy** addresses the biggest questions of all: what is the nature of the 'good life' and what must the state do to promote this?
- *Political ideology* is concerned with ideas about the way the state should be organized (see chapter 2).
- *Political economy* examines the state in the economic system. It leads us to the power of economic forces and the working of the global economy.
- *Political sociology* looks more towards the social world for an understanding of politics. It is concerned with how political attitudes are formed and how they are influenced by those with power. It also studies social stratification, including class formation and elites.
- *Political institutions* lead students to the formal machinery of the state, a key site of much political activity.
- *Policy studies* focus on the policy-making process of government and are centrally concerned with the analysis of power.

- *Comparative government* searches for generalizations about politics derived from widespread examination of groups of countries. Conceptually straightforward, it can be immensely daunting in practical terms.
- *International relations* studies the ways in which states relate to each other in war and in peace.

The interdisciplinary perspective

Not only does political science comprise the subdisciplines outlined above, it is itself multidisciplinary; magpie-like, it draws upon a wide range of other disciplines. The social sciences study one single, complex reality and the different disciplines are artificial territories staked out to facilitate microscopic study of particular aspects. However, this can hinder understanding if we adopt a blinkered view.

Hence, while this book is rooted in the territory of political science, it is open to other perspectives. It is, for example, an inescapable fact that many of the forces acting upon the political system are *economic* in origin, whether originating from the stock exchange or the plight of the homeless. To understand the British constitution we require a *legal* perspective, although this must be seasoned with an understanding of the balance of power, which breathes life into the formal constitution. The discipline of *sociology*, concerned with education, culture, class, racism and gender – all of which fuel much political activity – must also have a central place. Underlying all is the *historical* dimension. It is almost impossible to comprehend the present without understanding patterns of development. We do not take an historical perspective by way of neat chronological introduction; we do so because the politics of today is only an ephemeral bloom on the tree of the past.

There is also an important *geographical* dimension to politics. At home there are issues of territorial management and in the world there is a global economy populated by developed and undeveloped countries as well as giant corporations, many of them richer than states. Beyond the world economy is a political order reflecting the balance of military power, political alliances and a global ecological system innocent of national boundaries, underscoring the interdependence of states in the modern world. Only by rejecting the narrow disciplinary approach can the study of politics aspire to the title the 'master science'.

Peering behind the facade

The political scientist must be attentive to the real world before all else and, like Machiavelli, seek to peel away the facade in search of a deeper reality for, as observed above, much in politics is about deception. Writers in the orthodox liberal-democratic tradition betray a tendency to describe what they see as a beautiful stately home. Like overawed paying visitors, they are content to admire the ornate outer facade and the fine draperies and furniture inside but remain too timid to push beyond the red ropes into the living quarters. A central concern of this book is to encourage the habit of enquiry, of looking beneath the surface or, where we are not permitted (and we are talking about one of the most secretive systems in the world), to remain conscious of the limitations of conventional pictures and to be open to those theories about what *might* be there.

Orthodox writing on British politics purports to take an objective position, without a commitment to any political ideology. The cogs and cams of the system are detailed in much the same way as the internal combustion engine might be. The implication of this approach is that the state itself is an apolitical machine, not favouring any particular interest within society, which a government takes over like the driver of a car. This belief is a central plank in the theory of British liberal democracy. However, the idea of the neutral state, easily controlled by anyone in the driving seat, may be contested. To Marxists and others it serves the interests of capital and wealth. Hence, writers implying it to be impartial are actually making a political (anti-left) statement. Rather than peeling away the facade they are contributing to the process of concealment; they themselves are adding bricks to the facade.

Key points

- A common definition of politics is the resolution by compromise and conciliation of the inevitable conflicts in any community.
- Politics necessarily entails the concept of authority, an accepted or legitimate form of power.
- It is possible to speak of politics in the context of any organization but political scientists mainly study the state.
- The state is a community with a territory within which it enjoys legal sovereignty.
- The government of the day may be in control of the state, but is conceptually distinct from it.
- The decisions made through politics can be made by other means but the idea that politics can be removed from life is an illusion.
- The study of politics should be concerned with looking behind the formal facade of government to understand where power lies; to understand who gets what, when and how.

Review your understanding of the following terms and concepts

aristocracy
art of the possible
authoritative allocation
   of values
authority
behaviouralism
citizen
city-state
civil society
democracy
demos

Gemeinschaft
Gesellschaft
government
legitimacy
legitimation
machinery of
   government
market
mob rule
monarchy
nation-state

oligarchy
polis
political philosophy
political science
polity
power
rational decision-making
society
state
state violence
tyranny

Questions for discussion

1 What is politics?
2 'Politics is the art of the possible.' Discuss.
3 Distinguish between power and authority.
4 Distinguish between the concepts of 'state' and 'society'.
5 'Violence is the abrogation of politics.' Discuss.
6 'Power tends to corrupt, great men are almost always bad men.' Discuss.
7 'Education should be taken out of politics.' Why do people say this? How realistic is their suggestion?
8 'Politics is the means whereby the powerful get what they want.' Discuss.
9 To what extent can the study of politics be described as a science?
10 Can the study of politics validly claim to be the 'master science'?

Topic for debate

This house believes with Camus that 'men who have greatness within them don't go in for politics'.

Further reading

Cornford, F. M. (ed. and translator) (1941) *The Republic of Plato*.
Accessible edition of the great masterwork, raising many of the questions and conundrums of the study of politics today.

Crick, B. (1964) *In Defence of Politics* (2nd edn, 1982).
Classic essay on the idea of politics as a peaceful and highly desirable process of conciliation.

Duverger, M. (1966) *The Idea of Politics*.
Classic text by French scholar. Analyses political conflict from its roots in primitive societies to modern times.

Heywood, A. (1994) *Political Ideas and Concepts*.
Perceptive and thought-provoking.

Lasswell, H. (1936) *Politics: Who Gets What, When, How?*
Seminal statement of the power view of politics.

Leftwich, A. (1984) *What is Politics? The Activity and its Study*.
Accessible introduction.

Mackenzie, W. J. M. (1969) *Politics and Social Science*.
Breathtaking 'Cook's Tour' of a wide range of approaches to the study of politics.

Miller, J. B. D. (1962) *The Nature of Politics*.
Stresses the ubiquity of politics; it will always be found in some form or other.

Walles, G. (1948) *Human Nature in Politics*.
Criticizes the idea that people act rationally in politics.

For light relief

Jean Anouilh, *Antigone*.
Highlights conflicts between personal morality and the hypocrisy of a corrupt society, the main character preferring death to compromise.

Anthony Arblaster, *Viva la Libertà! Politics in Opera*.
Uncovers the political dimension and the ideals of freedom in a vast range of operas, from 'The Marriage of Figaro' to 'Nixon in China'.

Bertolt Brecht, *The Caucasian Chalk Circle*.
Who owns what? What is the moral authority for ownership? Brecht's play makes brilliant use of analogy to explore these questions.

William Shakespeare, *Macbeth*.
Intrigue of politics and the corrupting effects of high-vaulting ambition.

L. Niel Smith, *The Venus Belt*.
A sci-fi story about two parallel universes, one with and one without a government.

Anthony Trollope, *The Pallisers*.
The world of the nineteenth-century political establishment, with its intrigue, romance and arrogant power.

Part I

Politics in Context

A central tenet of this book is that politics does not take place in a vacuum; it is enacted against a larger world canvas as well as being inextricably interwoven into the domestic social and economic fabric. Hence Part I of the book aims to set the scene by establishing the context of British politics. Much political debate and action is derived from beliefs about how we should live, what is fair and what is unfair, and chapter 2 explores the world of ideas and ideology. Chapter 3 considers the legal environment in which politics takes place; the constitution laying down the rules of political engagement and giving people the political rights they need to participate. Increasingly our lives are touched by events taking place thousands of miles away in a compelling contemporary development termed globalization. This is examined in chapter 4 on the world economy and world political order. Chapter 5 centres on that sector of the world into which Britain is becoming ever more closely integrated – the European Union. The final two chapters in Part I return to the domestic stage, examining the increasingly important problems of territorial management and the complex of social organizations and attitudes that form the political culture. The substance of all these chapters remains a backcloth to the rest of the book.

Chapter Two

The World of Ideas: Political Ideology

Ideologies are theories about how people should live together in society. As such they provide a central motive force in politics, associated not only with party politics but also with great revolutions and wars. At the heart of such thinking lie fundamental concepts such as justice, freedom, equality, community, rationality, sovereignty, the character of human nature, human happiness and fulfilment; the good life as sought from the time of the Ancient Greeks. People do not easily agree on such big questions, and centuries of debate have generated a body of profound thought, perhaps more important to human survival than any other. Ideas cannot be studied *in vacuo* like butterflies under glass: they are the products of particular times and bound in political struggle and conflict. Hence this chapter aims to introduce not only the ideologies but also the great thinkers and events with which they are associated.

Does ideology matter?

The extent to which ideas influence events can be disputed; sometimes events influence the ideas. Only rarely do thinkers have the joy of seeing their words directly translated into action. Yet ideas permeate the cultural air shaping our attitudes on what is right and what is wrong. When 'men of action' renounce the abstract world of thinkers they delude themselves. When despots hear voices they are often receiving echoes of some cloistered academic ringing down through the ages.

Although **ideologies** are often associated with political parties, even to the extent of bestowing names on them, there is no consistent one-to-one identification. Members of communist parties can espouse conservative values, conservative parties can support liberalism, and so on in a complex square

> [Those] who believe themselves to be quite exempt from any intellectual influences are usually the slaves of some defunct economist.
>
> John Maynard Keynes, *The General Theory of Employment, Interest, and Money* (1936)

dance of changing partners. Indeed, ideologies are not the exclusive property of parties; they inspire political movements and pressure groups fired with ambitions to change the way we live.

A common basis for distinguishing ideologies is in terms of a left–right dichotomy. The distinction originated in the seating arrangements of the French Estates General in 1789, when the nobility (opposing change) sat on the king's right and those favouring change on his left. Never used with academic precision, modern usage tends to parallel the distinction between **collectivism** (members of society work together) and **individualism** (people live competitively,

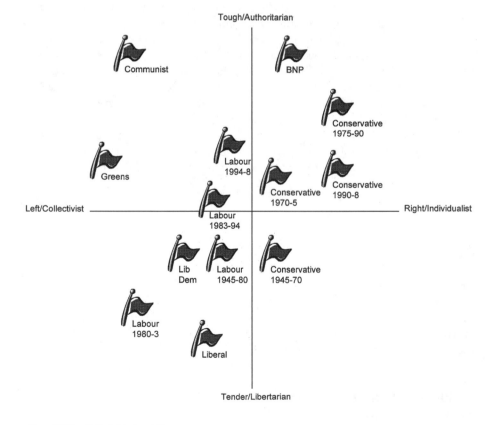

Figure 2.1
A notional two-dimensional distribution of British political parties in the post-war era.

Note: BNP = British National Party.

each acting self-interestedly). A more realistic conceptualization is in terms of a continuum, with an infinite range of intermediate positions, although it is generally believed that most members of the British public are nearer the centre than either extreme. Even this model is simplistic; in addition to substantive policy outcomes there are ideological questions related to means. It is possible to take a tough (*authoritarian, secretive, centralist*) or tender (*libertarian, open, decentralized*) attitude towards government, and these preferences may not coincide with the left–right divide (Eysenck 1951). Fascists, with extreme right-wing views, have taken tough attitudes, but so have communists. This addition creates a two-dimensional matrix (figure 2.1).

Moreover, in the real world ideology cannot be divorced from sectional self-interest. Indeed, Karl Marx saw ideology as a prevalent body of ideas shaping mass political consciousness and largely controlled by the dominant class to consolidate its power and privileges. Accordingly, in considering ideologies we shall pay some attention to the way they serve particular interests.

Ideas, like commodities, can travel. Hence political ideas in Britain have evolved from two sources: the response to domestic society and the response to wider developments within the western world.

Ideology and the Western Tradition

The modern western ideological tradition emerged through a dramatic break with the intellectual habits of past ages. Some momentous events stand as milestones along the evolutionary road, influencing and influenced by the new ways of thinking.

The Renaissance This intellectual rebirth in the arts and literature of the fifteenth and sixteenth centuries was associated with such great figures as Leonardo da Vinci, Michelangelo and Erasmus. Centring on Italy, it entailed a rediscovery of classical learning (buried away in the monasteries during the Dark Ages when free thought was stifled by religious dogma) and a challenge to medieval doctrine and authority. A key political thinker of the period was Niccolò Machiavelli (1469–1527), perhaps the first theorist of the modern nation-state which rejected religion and superstition as a basis for government.

The Reformation The stranglehold of the medieval church under the Pope was further challenged by Martin Luther. In a reform movement sweeping Europe in the sixteenth century he asserted the right of individuals to defy authority and worship in their own way. The ground was being prepared for the idea of individual political rights.

The Enlightenment The seismic intellectual shift that raised the curtain on the modern era was the **Enlightenment**. Seventeenth-century Europe saw spectacular advances in scientific thinking which spread to other areas, including politics and religion. The consequences were to be revolutionary. Although the French Enlightenment (which between 1751 and 1772 saw publication of the famous *Encyclopédie*) is the most feted, the movement enveloped Europe as an intellectual forest fire. At its heart was **rationalism** – a new confidence in human reason – and a conviction that people had both a right and the ability to improve the way they lived. Metaphysical thinking and superstition were challenged, as were traditional forms of authority including the church, aristocracy and monarchy.

The western tradition   These great events, altering the fundamental nature of western civilization, were inextricably bound with a ripening of ideas that together constituted the 'western tradition'. Two ideologies of change were to achieve supremacy in the west – liberalism and socialism – which in turn promoted a powerful reaction under the name of conservatism. Even later came further challenges in the form of feminism and environmentalism.

Liberalism

Liberalism, as the word implies, cherishes freedom. However, this is not as simple as might at first appear. We must ask what we mean by freedom, and from whom or what we are to be free. Contrasting answers to these questions result in various strands within a broad liberal tradition. It is hardly possible to overestimate the significance of liberalism in modern western history. Early thinking opposed autocratic regimes based on royal power, aristocratic privilege, religion and the divine right of kings. It spawned the major revolutions that transformed the world from the ancient to the modern.

Human nature   Early liberal thinkers stressed the essential individuality in human nature. People are seen as separate entities, driven by egotistical desires. However, later liberals modified this view.

The form of government   For classical liberals, the state is not virtuous in itself, as it was for the Ancient Greeks. It is a necessary evil, enabling individuals to pursue their private ends. Good government is minimal government. Hence, in a **liberal democracy** government is limited in scope and power.

The pattern of development

Two key figures in the emergence of this tradition were Thomas Hobbes and John Locke, who wrote against the background of the English civil war. Their method of reasoning was to imagine life in a **state of nature** (without society or government) and logically deduce what the role of the good state should be.

Thomas Hobbes Hobbes (1588–1679) is probably England's greatest political thinker. Writing in the spirit of the Enlightenment, he sought to harness the methods of science to the study of politics. In analysing society he saw the individual as the basic atom, driven by a fundamental instinct of self-preservation. In a state of nature this egoism would prove fatal; it would lead to an unrelenting war of all against all. Therefore they must place themselves under an all-powerful hereditary sovereign (hereditary to prevent fighting over the succession) – a *Leviathan* (the title of his greatest work, published in 1651). This is hardly a liberal conclusion; indeed, it can be seen as a defence of monarchy in the civil war. However, although government is absolute it is not arbitrary; the people enter into a compact with each other to create a sovereign for their common good.

> Solitary, poore, nasty, brutish and short.
>
> Hobbes's description of life in a state of nature, *Leviathan* (1651)

John Locke Another English philosopher has a clearer claim as the founder of modern liberalism. In the second of his *Two Treatises of Government* (1690), John Locke (1632–1704) took a less bleak view of human nature. In a state of nature people would cooperate rather than fight; government should be minimal in order to maximize the freedom and rights to life that nature bestows, allowing people to live in civil society. The state cannot *create* rights; it merely protects those present in nature. Once government exists there is an ever-present threat that it will break its part of the contract and operate in its own interests. Constitutional provisions are needed to prevent this. Hence, Locke approved of the 1688 settlement limiting royal authority (see p. 67) and advocated key principles that lie at the heart of the liberal constitution including:

- a minimal state;
- representative government;
- majority rule;
- separation of powers;
- constitutional monarchy.

> Necessity is the plea for every infringement of human freedom. It is the argument of tyrants; it is the creed of slaves.
>
> William Pitt (1759–1806; prime minister), House of Commons speech (18 Nov. 1783)

Montesquieu Abhorring the absolutist reign of Louis XVI, French scholar Baron de Montesquieu (1689–1755) became an admirer of what he saw as freedom and toleration following the 1688 settlement. In his *L'Esprit des Lois* (1748) he developed Locke's ideas, stressing the separation of powers and distinguishing more clearly between the executive, legislative and judicial organs of government. Liberty is best protected when the constitution renders tyranny impossible.

Rousseau More than any other thinker Jean Jacques Rousseau (1712–78) is identified with the French Revolution. He was concerned with individual freedom,

Man was born free, yet everywhere is in chains.

Jean Jacques Rousseau, *The Social Contract* (1762: ch. 1)

the role of the state, the basis for political obedience, the nature of sovereignty and the idea of contract. Like Hobbes and Locke, he imagined a state of nature but placed a quite different construction on liberty. Submission to a Leviathan 'is to suppose a people of madmen' (1913: 7), while a 'natural' freedom to pursue selfish ends was bondage to the appetites. For Rousseau, people in nature are not selfish egoists but 'noble savages' with compassion for one another. Civilization corrupts this with private property generating greed, vanity, inequality, privilege and envy. The liberal contract is really a trick; the poor are offered protection but what is protected is the wealth of the rich. True freedom in society can only be realized through a communal life where all are equal.

Rousseau pioneered a new conception of popular sovereignty – a social contract whereby people do not forfeit freedom in return for state protection; rather they forfeit rights unconditionally to the community. Because all do so equally, each recovers all they lose. Natural freedom is exchanged for social freedom. Individual wills are unified into a *volonté generale* (**General Will**), something greater than a sum of 'petty self-interest' and the only legitimate sovereign force. It is difficult to underestimate Rousseau's influence, which spread to the arts, literature and education. In replacing the atomized theories with an organic view of the state, he inspired much moral philosophy, his ideas leading to the New Liberalism (see p. 30) that was to lay the foundations of the modern social democratic state.

A share in two revolutions is living to some purpose.

Epitaph of Tom Paine

Tom Paine An Englishman who emigrated to America, Paine (1737–1809) has a legendary fame as a champion of the oppressed. A passionate exponent of Enlightenment thinking, he held much in common with Locke, arguing in his pamphlet *Common Sense* (published in 1776 on the eve of the American War of Independence) that government was a necessary evil. The only grounds for obedience were that it was fulfilling its obligations. However, unlike Locke he was a radical. His *Rights of Man* (1791) used **natural rights** reasoning to defend the French Revolution.

James Madison The American constitution, drafted after independence, reflected much of Paine's sentiment. One of the founding fathers, James Madison (1751–1836), developed liberal thinking into a more coherent theory and political strategy. Like many liberals he feared advancing democracy as a 'tyranny of the majority'. In *The Federalist* (1788) he argued for strong republican government of enlightened rulers regularly called to account through elections. He saw virtue in the large state which increased the possibility of finding good rulers and produced pluralism (see chapter 17), which would prevent domination by any single interest.

That this nation, under God, shall have a new birth of freedom, and that the government of the people, by the people, for the people, shall not perish from the earth.

Abraham Lincoln (US president), Gettysburg Address (19 Nov. 1863)

The liberal revolutions

The post-Enlightenment thinking gave new meaning to the idea of revolution (Gamble 1981: 22). For the Ancient Greeks (particularly the Stoics) it had meant a cyclical process of decay and renewal: monarchy, tyranny, aristocracy, oligarchy, democracy and 'mobocracy'. Life could be understood but not controlled. Christianity had strengthened the attitude; earthly life was to be endured, a better existence would come, but only beyond the grave. However, the new thinking asserted that society could shift onto an entirely new plane from which there would be no return. Major revolutions, in the new meaning of the term, were to usher in the modern age of politics.

The English civil wars and the Glorious Revolution In the 1640s a conflict began in England within the landowning classes, one section (the Whigs) rebelling against royal authority and the other supporting it. The Royalists were initially defeated, Charles I beheaded and a republic proclaimed. Although within little over a decade the monarchy was restored, things were fundamentally different; there had indeed been a 'Glorious Revolution'. In the constitutional settlement the traditional belief that kings enjoyed absolute power by divine right was destroyed.

The American revolution Using the Whigs' language of rights and freedom, the American colonists cast off the British imperialist yoke in the American Declaration of Independence of 1776.

> Men are endowed by their creator with certain inalienable rights; that among them are life, liberty and the pursuit of happiness . . . whenever any form of government becomes destructive of these ends, it is the right of the people to alter or abolish it. (Part of the American Declaration of Independence)

The French Revolution In the history of modern politics the great revolution in France, beginning in 1789, stands as an indelible landmark. The supreme manifestation of Enlightenment ideals, it influenced all modern ideologies. Indeed, it was here that the term originated.

It was the best of times, it was the worst of times, it was the age of wisdom, it was the age of foolishness, it was the epoch of belief, it was the epoch of incredulity, it was the season of light, it was the season of darkness.

Opening lines of Charles Dickens's novel on the French Revolution, *A Tale of Two Cities*

Initially the revolutionaries held the sentiments of the English and American revolutionaries: opposing royal absolutism and ancient privilege. The 1789 *Declaration of Rights* established people as citizens rather than subjects. In 1791 a new Constitution enfranchised a large section of the male population and a democratic spirit began to permeate the cultural air. Political clubs blossomed (the largest being the Jacobins) and popular debate was extended through newspapers and pamphleteering. The momentum was to carry things beyond the middle classes. Government fell under the radical wing of the Jacobins, the Republic replaced the monarchy and the country became more democratic than any previous state. Laws provided for the radical redistribution of property and a bloody Reign of Terror saw thousands of high-born heads roll from the guillotine.

O liberté! Que de crimes on commet en ton nom. (Oh liberty! What crimes are committed in thy name!)

Madame Marie Jeanne Philipon Roland de la Platière (French revolutionary) at her execution in view of the Statue of Liberty (8 Nov. 1793)

However, opposition forces began to regain the initiative. The Jacobins and revolutionary statesman Robespierre were overthrown in 1794 and the nation subjected to a military dictatorship under Napoleon. Yet the old order could never return. The new *Code Napoléon* accepted that sovereignty rested with the people. In Europe it was recognized that a road had been opened that others could follow.

Classical liberalism

A different strand in the liberal tradition came from the new discipline of political economy. Here the justification for limited government lay not in natural rights but in the quest for economic prosperity.

Adam Smith and laissez-faire   A leading figure in the Scottish Enlightenment, Adam Smith (1723–90) argued in *An Inquiry into the Nature and Causes of the Wealth of Nations* (1776) that in a free market, where individuals pursued self-interest, a 'hidden hand' would guide the economy towards the best possible result. The *laissez-faire* principle extended to international dealings, free trade becoming a liberal rallying cry. Though it might appear cruel it was still right. Other classical economists, David Ricardo (1772–1823) and Thomas Malthus (1776–1834), saw poverty, famine and death as an inevitable corrective to over-population. This approach was supported by Social Darwinists, such as Herbert Spencer (1820–1903). Reasoning from the principle of the survival of the fittest, they saw the competitive economy as a means of improving the species, an idea appealing to the rising bourgeoisie who could add to growing wealth a conviction of their own superiority.

Respectable professors of the dismal science.

Thomas Carlyle (Scottish essayist and historian) on the classical economists in 1850

Jeremy Bentham and the Utilitarians   A further strand of liberalism, with much in common with free-market reasoning, was led by Jeremy Bentham (1748–

1832). He rejected the idea of natural rights as 'nonsense on stilts', replacing it with the principle of *utility*. The moral guide for life, law and government was **utilitarianism**: the promotion of 'the greatest happiness for the greatest number'. Generally individuals can best judge their own happiness and should be free to do so. However, it was necessary for the legal and political systems to set patterns of rewards and punishments so that self-interested behaviour would produce the maximum public benefit. Together with the philosopher James Mill (1773–1836), he founded the Philosophical Radical movement which advocated a wide range of constitutional reforms, including frequent elections, a wide franchise, secret ballots, competition between candidates, a free press, freedom of speech, freedom of association and a separation of powers.

However, utilitarianism contained paradoxical implications. Dispensing with pre-social rights undermined the liberal argument for minimum state interference and the intellectual path was cleared for paternalistic state action (Gamble 1981: 81). Indeed, Bentham supported intervention in areas such as education, wage levels, guaranteed employment and sickness benefits. A later utilitarian, J. S. Mill, was to take the reasoning much further.

J. S. Mill With the good fortune, or otherwise, to be the son of James, John Stuart Mill (1806–73) was subjected by his father and Bentham to an intense utilitarian education. After a period of acute depression he resolved to change his life and in doing so changed utilitarianism. Influenced by French thinker Alexis de Tocqueville (1805–59), he questioned Bentham's narrowly materialistic approach, arguing that the freedom that liberals had seen mainly in terms of the economy should extend to other walks of life. This interpretation had radical implications for wider emancipation and a generally more permissive society. Mill's most influential work, *On Liberty* (1859), gave a moral view of freedom.

The only freedom worthy of the name is that of pursuing our own good in our own way, so long as we do not attempt to deprive others of theirs.

J. S. Mill, *On Liberty* (1859)

Mill's arguments for democracy go beyond preventing corruption or maximizing utility. Like the Ancient Greeks he saw participation as a good in itself, necessary for dignity. However, in his *Considerations on Representative Government* (1861) he echoed de Tocqueville's fear of the 'tyranny of the majority'. Hence, while favouring representative democracy he recommended plural voting, the 'wiser' having more (up to six) votes than others (with property the measure of wisdom!). Equality should be withheld until the populace was fully trained in civic virtue. Mill's more sophisticated thinking on individualism, freedom and the role of state were to prove hugely influential.

The industrial revolution Classical liberalism spawned its own revolution, less bloody than previous ones but no less profound in its political effects. It first occurred in Britain, between 1760 and 1860, a product of the new scientific thinking which, when applied to production, was to create an industrial civilization. Driving the new order was a thrusting entrepreneurial class using the freedoms gained in 1688 to create the *laissez-faire* economy. Their escalating material wealth was to challenge that of the landed class and they were to transform economic power into political power with far-reaching consequences. It was this, rather than the astonishing application of technology, that justified the term 'industrial revolution'.

New Liberalism

Persistent poverty, inequality and unemployment mocked the free market's claim to promote the common good. Some liberals began to feel that freedom in modern society was more complex than their classical forebears had believed. In this they were influenced by Hegel, one of the intellectual giants of the modern age.

Georg Hegel Hegel (1770–1831) shared Rousseau's view that the state was not an infringement of freedom but its highest expression. Rejecting the idea of a pre-social state of nature he believed human nature to be a product of social interaction. Rights could only have meaning in a social context and in *The Philosophy of Right* (1821) he asserted that true freedom lay not in a life lived away from the state but in its service. Such an idea could be seen as dangerous; it could lead to a crushing of the individual in totalitarianism. However, in late-nineteenth-century England a group of thinkers leavened this extreme collectivism with a radical form of individualism. They formed the school of English Idealists, under their most notable member, T. H. Green.

T. H. Green An Oxford classicist, Thomas Hill Green (1836–82) believed in the goodness of human instinct. The state was not the all-consuming ideal of Hegel but its essential purpose was to secure the 'common good', something greater than the sum of individual happiness sought by utilitarians. Other New Liberals continued the argument. L. T. Hobhouse argued that, whereas classical liberalism had sought to liberate individuals from the state, New Liberalism used the state to liberate individuals from social and economic restrictions. J. A. Hobson viewed society as a living organism, each part promoting the well-being of the whole. In these terms, *laissez-faire* was a disease requiring treatment.

John Maynard Keynes A hugely influential figure, Keynes (1883–1946) refuted the classical economists' view that the market would necessarily allocate resources in the optimum manner. Left to itself, the economy could reach a point of equilibrium (where aggregate demand equalled aggregate supply) below full capacity, thereby creating unemployment. He argued that cuts in wages (the free-market solution) would further depress the economy; less would be bought and less produced, causing more unemployment in an ever-downward spiral. If capitalism was to be saved, the state could not stand aside; it should take on the job of managing the market, increasing demand through public borrowing and expenditure to maintain full employment. This is the essence of **Keynesianism**.

Essentially New Liberalism saw freedom not as a product of nature endangered by the state, but as a creation of the state. Its influence was felt in the period of Liberal governments between 1905 and 1915 which helped lay the foundations of the welfare state. Indeed, for critics it was socialism rather than liberalism. However, in principle, the individual is given only the *means* to pursue fulfilment; self-help remains central (Simhony 1991).

Neoliberalism

Amidst the transformation within liberalism there remained critics. Isaiah Berlin (1970) saw in the new idea of freedom the foundation of oppression. Perhaps the most tenacious critic was Friedrich von Hayek.

Friedrich von Hayek During his long lifetime Hayek (1899–1992) witnessed both fascism and Stalinism and most of his work was preoccupied with the threat posed by the state. He perpetuated a body of neoclassical economic thought originated by Carl Menger (1840–1921), known as the Austrian School, which admitted only a limited role for the state in offsetting hardship. A fellow member, Ludwig Von Mises (1881–1973), stressed the impossibility of state planning. Hayek's mission was to show modern capitalism as the *sine qua non* of the free society. The market resolves social problems, producing a 'spontaneous order', the outcome of human action but not of human design. Hayek's work is frequently coupled with that of US economist Milton Friedman (b. 1912) and the Chicago School, which again associates the market with freedom and democracy and, in opposition to Keynesianism, advocates an economic policy known as monetarism (see pp. 490–1).

During the 1980s, **neoliberalism** seized the heart of the British polity in a new consensus. First it became associated with thinkers and politicians, including Enoch Powell and Margaret Thatcher, who labelled themselves Conservatives. They formed the '**New Right**' and the term **Thatcherism** entered the ideological lexicon. However, after an initially sceptical response, the Labour Party was to reinvent itself as New Labour and don much of the new garb.

> There's no such thing as a free lunch.
>
> Attributed to economist Milton Friedman

Early liberalism used rationalism and the value of freedom to undermine the claims of monarchy, aristocracy and religion, clearing the way for lasting democratic and egalitarian reforms. However, the principle that governments keep out of private affairs was very much in the interests of those becoming economically powerful through capitalism. The liberal claim that all people were of equal worth sounded a hollow ring in an economic system that created poverty as well as riches (Arblaster 1984: 84–91). While New Liberalism acknowledged the harsh effects of capitalism, it sought to save rather than

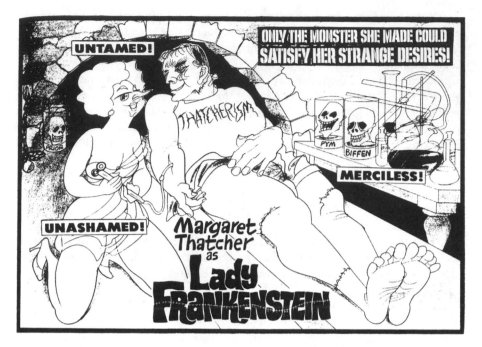

replace it. However, alternative views of the nature of freedom and society spawned two more western ideologies: socialism and conservatism.

Socialism

Socialism stands as the antithesis of liberalism, repudiating its central precepts of individualism, the free market and private property. However, the two share a common core of western assumptions and values: faith in science, belief in industrialization and confidence in the possibility of rationalist improvement.

Human nature Socialists typically view human nature optimistically. People are not isolated individuals but part of a greater society with a sense of moral responsibility towards one another. This cannot be found in some imaginary state of nature; it is a product of society. Liberalism fosters people's worst characteristics while socialism will encourage values such as altruism and fraternity.

The form of government A major misconception about socialism is that it entails a dominant state. On the contrary, some early socialists were libertarians and associated with **anarchy**. However, such thinking was undermined by industrialization and socialism was forced to advocate either a particular form of government within the liberal tradition or an alternative to it. Both models featured in subsequent developments.

The pattern of development: in search of Utopia

Though initially seen as cranks and eccentrics, early socialists set the climate for new thinking. Central to this was the value of a sense of community as opposed to competitive individualism. An important pioneer was French aristocrat Claude Saint-Simon (1760–1825), whose ideas were spread by his secretary, the philosopher and sociologist Auguste Comte (1798–1857). He envisioned a centrally planned industrialized economy administered for the common good, though, with liberal instincts, he had no wish to abolish private property. Another French socialist, François Fourier (1772–1837), saw in large-scale industrialization not progress but impoverishment. Like Rousseau he valued a simple unsophisticated life, arguing for industry based on small craftsmen and farmers living in cooperatives (*phalanstères*) of fewer than 2,000. Though rejecting *phalanstères* as rustic fantasies, Pierre-Joseph Proudhon (1809–65) saw in industrialization only exploitation, inequality and oppression. His analysis drew forth a memorable declamation that 'property is theft'.

Not all capitalists applauded the harsh logic of individualism. Self-made English industrialist Robert Owen (1771–1858) thought the workplace could be a socialist community. His New Lanark Mills were run paternalistically, providing workers' families with housing, health care and education. The experiment aroused considerable interest at home and in the USA.

Marx and Marxism

The rural peasantry and the disorganized urban poor of the early nineteenth century could hardly transform society. Hence a key circumstance in the development of socialism was industrialization and the new class structure. This inspired a strand of thought intended to revolutionize the modern world. It came from liberalism's most trenchant critic, the German polymath Karl Marx. Influenced variously – by the Enlightenment, the French Revolution, English liberalism, classical economics, Hegel, Darwin and the earlier socialists, as well as European literature and classical philosophy – Karl Marx (1818–83) identified the most compelling question of the modern era: how can a just community exist in the context of modern industrial society? (Gamble 1981: 114). No modern thinker has a greater claim to have placed his stamp on the intellectual climate of the twentieth century and on the course of world events.

Marx aimed to portray political development rather like natural history: a process obeying scientific laws. His theory was one of **historical materialism**: the key lay in the way work, a necessity imposed by nature, was organized. This 'mode of production' shaped laws, arts, politics, state institutions and the dominant ideology. This simple though little appreciated fact of survival unlocked a

> Capital is reckless of the health or length of life of the labourer, unless under compulsion from society. To the outcry as to the physical and mental degradation, the premature death, the torture of overwork, it answers: Ought these to trouble us since they increase our profits?
>
> Karl Marx, *Capital* (1867: ch. 10)

Pandora's box. In the new industrial society the vital tools, factories and land necessary for survival were not owned by those who did the work, but by relatively few private individuals – the **bourgeoisie** or capitalists.

Although liberalism made citizens legally free, in reality they were bound to the capitalists who purchased their labour, just like any other commodity (the commodification of labour). While labour was purchased in one market, the workers' products were sold in another, so that prices were unrelated to wages. Employers would seek to widen the gap between the two by keeping wages down and retaining a surplus for themselves. Although Locke had asserted that each had a right to the product of their labour, that of the modern worker was being expropriated (stolen). This exploitative relationship was inescapable under **capitalism**, for without it no one would invest in capital.

Moreover, domination went beyond the workplace to penetrate the state itself. Marx disputed the claim that the liberal state had broken free from class domination. Capitalism is not possible unless the state operates in the bourgeois interest, ensuring the conditions for maximizing profit (maintaining order, protecting property, limiting trade union activity, fostering an ideology of inequality). It was but a 'committee for managing the affairs of the bourgeoisie', which was in effect a ruling class.

Marx's socialism   Because the system of government was a function of the mode of production, it was here that the fundamental change had to be made. Marx's socialism followed a broadly Fourierist vision of a workers' state. However, this was but a transitory stage leading to an even greater transformation: a society without a wages system, with no division between manual and intellectual labour, private property or classes. Far from being totalitarian, this was to be a **communist** society in which the state would wither away.

How could such change come about? Here lies the secret of Marx's extraordinary appeal to oppressed peoples the world over. He believed revolution was not only necessary but, owing to the tensions and contradictions within capitalism, inevitable. Such an idea deeply unnerved those living behind the bastions of privilege, making Marx a hated figure within the liberal establishment. The French Revolution had demonstrated what a united people could achieve and Marx saw the new working class as a Frankenstein's monster which would destroy its capitalist creators. He identified a two-stage process: a bourgeois revolution with the liberal overthrow of the aristocratic order and a proletarian revolution with the workers' overthrow of the bourgeoisie. In Britain, the first had already taken place; the second was predestined.

The possibility of this dramatic challenge preoccupied a growing socialist movement and parties formed to prepare for the revolution. However, differing interpretations and circumstances led to tension between those favouring violent action (**voluntarism**) and the moderates prepared to wait for the inevitable collapse of capitalism (**determinism**).

Revolutionary socialism In Russia, the revolutionary leader Lenin (1870–1924) began in a determinist position. However, the backward development of Russian capitalism led him towards voluntarism. He developed a theory of the party as an intellectual vanguard force to spearhead the revolution. The Czarist regime was weakened by its inability to manage the world war, the government was divided and the country in chaos. In the great revolutions of 1917 the Czar was overthrown and in July 1918 the first Soviet Constitution was proclaimed. Whether or not this model was applicable to the special conditions of Russia, its subsequent export led to the inflexible and ruthless imposition of a theory that abandoned Marx's vision. In Russia itself the subsequent reign of Stalinist terror was a mockery of the liberty the revolution had promised.

Reformist socialism In the light of Italian conditions, Antonio Gramsci (1891–1937) advocated more subtle means of reform. He argued that the predicted crisis of capitalism could be averted by the ruling class because they exercised continuing dominance (**hegemony**) by holding influential positions throughout the state and shaping the prevailing common sense of society to legitimize their role. Hence the task of the revolutionary was to infiltrate these establishment bastions, ultimately to unleash the social forces below.

A leading revisionist, the German Eduard Bernstein (1850–1932), believed socialism could be pursued through liberal constitutional structures. This was an attractive idea in those West European nations where such systems were relatively well established. Moreover, the goals were also more moderate – **social democracy** with welfare policies rather than communism. Such an approach was advanced in Britain by the Fabian Society, a group of intellectuals influential at the turn of the century and instrumental in the formation of the Labour Party (see p. 269).

The anarchistic tradition

Although mainstream socialism after Marx took either the radical or parliamentary forms, other strains continued the ideology's more anarchic tendencies, envisaging socialism through workers' associations rather than the state. A movement began in France in the 1890s known as Syndicalism while in England guild socialism in the early twentieth century sought to incorporate into workers' associations the fraternal spirit of the ancient guilds.

Others have argued for market socialism whereby a free market functions with-

> The majestic egalitarianism of the law, which forbids rich and poor alike to sleep under bridges, to beg in the streets, and to steal bread.
>
> Anatole France (1844–1924; French writer), *The Red Lily*

out capitalism. Production is by private cooperatives operating competitively but without profit accumulation. The theory aroused interest in the 1930s though it had many critics. With the collapse of Soviet-style socialism and the failure of nationalization, some form of market socialism could still have a future.

Socialist doctrines make a sectional appeal and were particularly attractive to the rising labour movements. The principal objection from liberals concerned the threat to freedom; they have associated socialism with large bureaucracies, high taxation and totalitarianism. Others saw the ideology as a class-based threat to the natural order of society. These were conservatives, who also opposed liberalism on the same grounds.

Conservatism

If it ain't broke don't fix it.

An Americanism

Conservatism provides a rationale for resisting change; it is a doctrine of reaction. Indeed, the first political use of the term came with English aristocratic resistance to the Enlightenment and French Revolution. Later conservatives have resisted variously republicanism, industrialism, liberalism, utilitarianism and socialism. Although reform may sometimes be necessary, it should not arise from abstract principles which will inevitably distort and oversimplify (Oakeshott 1962). There is also a certain pragmatism: if a thing works it is accepted, with little theory of *why* it works.

Human nature Conservatives aim to see people as they actually are. Hence they reject individualistic theories; real people are always part of society, surrounded by cultural accretions – language, customs, literature and so on. Human reason is limited, wisdom is not the product of rational thought but of feelings, instincts and prejudices evolved over the generations.

The sense of realism leads to a recognition of the Christian idea of original sin; people are not perfect and cannot be made so. Life and politics are about making the best of a bad job.

> Conservatives know there are books to read, pictures to look at, music to listen to – and grouse to shoot.
>
> Harold Macmillan (1894–1986; Conservative leader), quoted by Nigel Nicolson in Thames TV programme *The Day Before Yesterday* (1970)

The form of government Conservatism does not lay down a blueprint; constitutions are not designed, they evolve. Each nation will have its own uniquely fitted system of government and countries should not import alien practices. The particular features British conservatives see as *their* tradition tend to include social hierarchy, the monarchy, the House of Lords, the patriarchal family, property, and a natural ruling class. Inequality is natural and socially necessary, it cannot be eradicated; consequently poverty is nothing to be ashamed of.

I believe it to be of the utmost importance that a territorial aristocracy should be maintained. I believe that in no country is it more important than in this, with its ancient constitution, ancient habits and mixed form of government.

Sir Robert Peel (Conservative prime minister), House of Commons speech (4 May 1846)

The pattern of development

Its anti-rationalism suggests conservativism will produce fewer thinkers than most ideologies. On the other hand, the argument that it is a natural cast of mind allows it to claim a long tradition, exponents not realizing they were talking conservative prose. Thus, 'conservative' thinking can be traced from the Ancient Greeks, including Plato (Auerback 1959: 26), through a range of thinkers who have challenged rationalism in one way or another. However, modern conservatism arose largely as a response to the French Revolution, an event striking fear into English aristocratic hearts.

Classical conservatism Ironically, the father of modern 'Conservatism' was a Whig. An opponent of the Enlightenment, Irish-born writer and politician Edmund Burke (1729–97) outlined the rationale for resisting change in his *Reflections on the Recent Revolution in France* (1790). Generally he argued for a presumption in favour of the status quo; virtue should be assumed in existing institutions. Burke was not against revolution as such, but this should be to reassert the natural order rather than destroy it. Hence he welcomed the outcome of the Glorious Revolution of 1688, which he believed restored the ancient rights of the aristocracy against encroaching royal authority. Similarly he supported the colonists in the American War of Independence, who were demanding traditional English liberties. However, the French affair was a different matter. Here, an ancient order was being challenged, an affront to God, its creator. He saw the enterprise as doomed, predicting the rise of a military dictatorship (he was of course partly right in this). However, Burke's conservatism was augmented with other strains.

Romantic conservatism Industrialization destroyed old patterns of life. For many it created gross ugliness, disfiguring the landscape with factories and urban

squalor and undermining the social fabric by replacing the harmonious feudal
order with exploitative relationships. A romantic reaction in the form of a body
of artistic work expressing nostalgia for the more simple way of life arose in
Germany and England. Numerous figures were involved, including Coleridge,
Carlyle, Wordsworth and Sir Walter Scott. Unlike classical conservatives, the
romantics were not necessarily opposed to rationalism; indeed Wordsworth
wrote enthusiastically of the French Revolution. There was even a romantic
strain within the New Right from those such as Enoch Powell, Roger Scruton
and Maurice Cowling, advocating traditional conservative values from monarchy, hierarchy, patriotism and the uniqueness of national identity, to fox-
hunting (Scruton 1980: 34).

One-nation conservatism With property as the basis of power, the aristocracy
was seen by early conservatives as the only group that could be trusted to govern, its interest being identical with the common good. There is no case for
limiting government; state intervention was recognized as a necessity of the
industrial age well before the reforms of the Liberal and Labour parties. This
paternalism continues the feudal doctrine of *noblesse oblige*. Perhaps the most
important representative of this strain was Benjamin Disraeli (1804–81), astute
Tory Party leader who, in 1854, expressed the sentiment in a novel *Sybil, or:
the Two Nations*. The 'two nations' of rich and poor must be united if the
whole is to be maintained (see chapter 10). However, conservatives have taken
a Janus-like stance over the one-nation principle, some looking more fondly
towards the liberal free market.

Liberal conservatism Opposition to capitalism had, for both principled and
political reasons, certain limitations. Too much social reform would resemble a
rationalist blueprint and paternalism could weaken the nation's moral fabric.
Moreover, state interference could threaten property, the traditional basis of
aristocratic power. As a Whig, Burke had himself favoured free trade because it
weakened monarchy (Hampsher-Monk 1987: 20) and believed that industrialization, as a natural development, should not be hindered. Furthermore, in
the early stages of industrialization the aristocracy had shared some interests
with the bourgeoisie as the railways scored the surface of their land and the
mines burrowed beneath. This liberal strain of conservatism was to come to the
fore in the 1980s (chapter 10).

Fascism Further to the right-wing extreme is **fascism**. Developing in the 1920s,
the term was chosen by Italian leader Mussolini for the movement that carried
him to power. The legend was a bundle of rods, a *fasces*, symbolizing the spirit
of community, beneath an axe-head representing the authority of the state. A
fascist movement began in Britain in the 1930s under Oswald Mosley. The
horrors of the second world war left fascism indelibly tarnished and most
modern-day conservatives would deny any association with it. However, its
values of **nationalism**, inequality, anti-liberalism and anti-socialism are essentially conservative. Other aspects, such as demagoguery, racism and militarism,

may also be seen as logical derivatives from nationalism in its more extreme form. There can be no denying that Enoch Powell's inflammatory speeches in the 1970s evoked racist sentiments while the Falklands war revealed a joy in militarism. Such sentiments were not, however, confined to one party.

The conservative position is seductive; it can be said that we are all conservative at heart (Cecil 1912: 9). Many speak nostalgically of a 'golden age' of this or that; some will agree with Fred Truman that cricketers are not what they were. Moreover, the world is littered with examples of failed rationalist reforms, including the socialist 'utopias' of Eastern Europe. In the arts much is made of wisdom built up over centuries. The great Kirov Ballet, for example, prides itself on a tradition of over two hundred years and the result is unrivalled artistry. Yet there is a fundamental paradox. In arguing for tradition and prejudice over rationalism, conservatism uses reason to attack reason; it is an ideology not to be ideological (Vincent 1992: 82). Moreover, the evidence before us (cannibalism, witch-burning, female circumcision, racism, religious fundamentalism) is that tradition can sometimes be dangerous. In many walks of life we do not slight reason; most would prefer a trained physician to the ministrations of a witch doctor. In practice many conservative thinkers allow some place for rationalism but stress its limitations.

> A democracy of the dead.
>
> G. K. Chesterton (1874–1936; British writer) on conservatism, in *Orthodoxy*

A Changing Climate

Liberalism, socialism and conservatism espouse contrasting views of human nature, society and the good life. Enough ink and blood have been spilled to leave little doubt of these differences. However, they have shared certain things in common; unstated assumptions forming the bedrock of their views of society – a universe of male supremacy, industrialism and economic growth.

Male supremacy Conservatism must necessarily accept male dominance through its veneration of tradition. In contrast, the precepts of liberalism and socialism do not logically imply sexual inequality yet they too are guilty. Even the great rallying cry of the defining event of the modern era, the French Revolution, called not only for *liberté* and *égalité* but also for *fraternité*. There were to be no *sisters* of the revolution. Were they to remain at home to bake the fabled cake? Similarly socialism in Britain, whether through the Labour Party or the trade unions, has been largely a male preserve.

Industrialism and growth Classical liberalism provided the intellectual bedrock for the industrial revolution itself. Even though romantic conservatives and utopian socialists inveighed against industrialism, mainstream thinkers have accepted its material largesse. The landed classes were to benefit from industrialism and British socialists were influenced more by the Fabians than Karl Marx; their goal to secure for workers a fairer share of the economic cake, not to incinerate it.

However, the traditional western ideologies are increasingly revealed as ill equipped to address the most compelling questions of contemporary life. A new uncertainty gives rise to philosophical searching in various directions, some of which are described as postmodern – a vaguely defined concept denoting a stage, or epoch, beyond that ushered in by the Enlightenment (Harvey 1989). This expresses a scepticism towards rationalism, allowing an openness to a wider range of voices in social enquiry, art and political empowerment. From the dissatisfaction emerge two ideologies assuming growing importance. Feminism and environmentalism are not entirely subsumed within **postmodernism** but they resonate with its mood, compelling politicians to modify their agendas. Students of contemporary politics cannot ignore them.

Feminism

> You cannot trust the interests of one class entirely to another class, and you cannot trust the interests of one sex entirely to another sex.
>
> David Lloyd George (1863–1945; Liberal statesman), speech (1911)

People call me a feminist whenever I express sentiments that differentiate me from a doormat or a prostitute.

Attributed to Rebecca West (1892–1983; British novelist)

Political thinkers refer variously to man, his rights, his liberation, his equality, nobility and so on *ad infinitum*. This is no accident; for many the intention is deliberately to exclude women on the grounds that the territory of politics is beyond bounds. Even Rousseau, champion of freedom and equality, made this exclusion. Sometimes the sexist language merely reflects convention but such usage shrouds deeper forces at the level of the subconscious. In the same way that Gramsci saw patterns of class hegemony woven into a 'common sense' of life, so male domination is built into common consciousness through language, family life, personal relationships and work patterns. Hence, many people, including some political scientists (Randall 1982: 1–5), regard it as 'natural' that women are not political. The body of ideological thought termed **feminism** arose as a reaction to this anomaly. Feminism seeks sexual justice. While not presenting an alternative to liberalism or socialism, it meets the requirements of an ideology in its own right, being concerned with human nature and the social arrangements whereby people can live.

Human nature   Here the key issue concerns the idea of gender difference. This is of central importance because difference implies distinct male and female roles. However, we must ask how far differences are natural or the result of conditioning. All strains of feminism agree that the degree of natural difference is far *less* than has been assumed.

The form of government   Feminists broadly attack male dominance in the state territory, calling for more women in government, where their presence will feminize the political agenda.

The pattern of development

It is difficult to plot the development of feminism since history has largely been written by men. A key early figure is Christina de Pizan, who wrote *The City of the Ladies* in 1405. There was also the exotic Aphra Behn (1640–89), who spied for the court of Charles II and was a prolific author of plays and novels ridiculing prevailing patterns of sexual inequality. However, its real birth lies, like other major ideologies, in the Enlightenment. In *A Vindication of the Rights of Man* (1790) Mary Wollstonecraft (1759–97), the greatest of the early feminists, countered Burke's attack on the French Revolution (in which women were active). Two years later she applied the same reasoning to argue for equality for her own sex in *A Vindication of the Rights of Woman*, a major feminist landmark. In America, women were active in another great cause, the fight against slavery. However, after the civil war, when political rights were extended to black men, but not women (black or white), they mobilized as a specifically feminist force. Indeed, the USA has always provided a major spearhead of the movement.

Added impetus came from industrialization, which brought poor women into the new workplaces, while giving their bourgeois sisters issues to ponder and the leisure to do so. The movement saw them active in charitable work, education, propaganda and a sustained fight for the franchise (chapter 9). However, with the franchise secured the movement fell dormant, submerged by economic depression, the second world war and subsequent reconstruction.

The 1960s saw a renaissance as an international civil rights movement sought emancipation for various oppressed groups. Educational advances for girls, changing attitudes towards sex, marriage, divorce and the family, the availability of the contraceptive pill and easier access to abortion altered women's perceptions. In 1961, Simone de Beauvoir's 1949 classic, *The Second Sex*, appeared in paperback, influencing much subsequent literature. In 1970, Germaine Greer's *The Female Eunuch* landed like an Exocet on desks and coffee tables, sending tremors through university campuses and suburbia. The movement has continued to grow exponentially with new journals, books and plays and earlier writers, such as Virginia Woolf, rediscovered. Specialist publishers, such as Virago (1977) and The Women's Press (1978), emerged and universities mounted courses in Women's Studies.

Forms of feminism

As with most ideologies, there is no single version of feminism and approaches range from moderate to extreme. Much present-day analysis is structured around liberal, socialist and radical forms. We also consider the possibility of a conservative variant.

Liberal feminism One could logically expect classical liberalism to be hospitable to feminism. The idea of natural freedoms should surely include women.

The *divine right* of husbands . . . may, it is hoped in this enlightened age, be contested without danger.

Mary Wollstonecraft, *A Vindication of the Rights of Woman* (1792: ch. 3)

Similarly, the utilitarian principle of maximum happiness should endorse sex equality. Moreover, rationalism should be suspicious of ancient patriarchal customs. Yet this has not proved so. The resounding call for emancipation from oppression largely addressed a male world. Indeed, it was a Liberal government that held out against the suffragettes (pp. 234–5). Where women were concerned, liberals fell into the very conservativism they castigated. Mary Wollstonecraft was a lone swallow and J. S. Mill, as a male thinker deeply concerned with women's rights, was a rare bird indeed.

To Wollstonecraft sexual imbalance was a social creation and women's oppression was harmful to society at large. Unique in questioning male presumptions, J. S. Mill noted how the liberal distinction between state and civil society confined women to the latter. In *The Subjection of Women* (1869), he saw their position as a relic of slavery grounded ultimately in force. Such conclusions were deeply disturbing to a male establishment and, compared with Mill's other writings, were to languish in obscurity (Held 1987: 80). However, his prescriptions, including reform of the marriage laws, equal educational opportunities and female enfranchisement, were limited to freeing women to help themselves (Pateman 1983).

Today liberal feminists continue to be distinguished by a moderate agenda framed in terms of equal legal, social and political rights. The goal is *freedom* to pursue their own advancement for the benefit of all society. Although called to share domestic duties, men are not seen as the enemy and the heterosexual family remains the norm.

Socialist feminism The basic premise of early socialist feminism was that women's plight was rooted in class oppression. Some saw sexual equality as integral to a broader socialist vision entailing alternative lifestyles. Fourier borders on eroticism in advocating free love, bisexuality and lesbianism. Owen believed patriarchal marriage sustained the competitive economy lying at the heart of much misery. Marx himself was rather unsympathetic but his collaborator, Friedrich Engels (1820–95), argued in *The Origin of the Family, Private Property and the State* (1884) that women's oppression was rooted in capitalism, their role the maintenance and reproduction of labour without payment.

The demands of socialist feminists today include free and widespread birth control, abortion on demand, state payment for domestic work, state child care and full equality in the workplace (Jaggar 1983: 132). Heterosexual families are not necessarily seen as the norm, though where they exist, they should be restructured to share the domestic burden. Activism takes place largely within established parties of the left.

Radical feminism Partly a breakaway from the socialists, the radical variant sees Marxism as 'sex blind'. The most fundamental basis for discrimination in society is sex; more significant than race or class. The problem lies in the nature of men, with their tendency towards aggression, violence, rape and so on. Yet the natural differences between the sexes are seen as minimal; conditioning is the key. This leads to calls for androgyny, both sexes playing identical roles, not only in rearing children but in work and even (with medical intervention) nurturing foetuses. Where radicals do concede difference they argue for female superiority, women's life-giving qualities making them more peaceable, caring and intuitive.

The movement has attracted overtly sexual lesbians but in addition a form of *political* lesbianism has emerged advocating separatism (living in sisterhood communities), sperm banks (to facilitate birth without direct male participation) and lesbian marriages. It is difficult to discern in radical feminism an underlying theory (Jaggar 1983: 84). Drawing more from postmodernism, it embraces aspects of eastern philosophy and mysticism, seeing rationalism itself as a male characteristic. Action can take direct forms outside mainstream politics and peaked in the 1960s, when passions inflamed brassieres as well as debate. This is the arm of the movement that gains its notoriety and 'women's lib' moniker.

Conservative feminism? It is unusual to speak of conservative feminism; indeed, the term may be an oxymoron. The subjugation of women is historic reality sanctified by ancient custom, the very thing conservatives venerate. Moreover, conservativism often takes religious forms, revering sacred texts and, the world over, these tend to be anti-feminist (Hawley 1984). Muslim fundamentalism confines women to the home (Mahl 1995) while, in the USA, the Christian Right, with 1.6 million active supporters, campaigns for the restoration of 'family values' and pursues strenuous anti-abortion crusades (Dutt 1995). The Anglican Church long opposed women priests, a stance still maintained by the Catholic Church. Moreover, anti-feminism is often a hallmark of the far right. Nazism stressed women's role in rearing children, outlawed birth control and denounced women in politics. Similar calls come from the self-proclaimed Moral Majority in the USA while, in Britain, elements of the New Right, such as the Salisbury Group, pursue an anti-feminist line.

Yet despite all, groups bearing names such as 'conservative pro-family feminism' see traditional roles, such as male-supporting and child-rearing, as valid feminist goals. This can be seen as radicalism in a different guise, according the family role greater value. Such thinking is not entirely foreign to mainstream feminists when they advocate a wage for parenting and housework.

Neo-feminism Another wave can be characterized as neo-feminist. Feminist writer Nikki van der Gaag (1995) notes a younger generation recognizing a need to work with rather than against men. Helen Wilkenson (1995) from the think-tank Demos discerns an historic shift in the relations between the sexes, an 'unravelling of not only 200 years of industrial society, but millennia of traditions and beliefs'. In bringing about a more fully egalitarian society, reform can be seen to be in men's interest as much as that of women. The idea that women are naturally more caring and compassionate makes them eminently suitable for the public sphere, promising a more ethical and compassionate society (Elshtain 1981).

Feminism is weakened by confusing fragmentation. British examples include the National Women's Network, Womankind, Women against Fundamentalism and the Women's Environmental Network. Groups organize around numerous specific issues such as reproductive rights, lesbian rights, welfare, violence, sexist advertising, children and professional career development. Further divisions reflect class, race, nationality and sexuality (Dutt 1995).

Liberal feminists are attacked by radicals as being imbued with patriarchal values. The free market, for example, glorifies competition, seen as an essentially male attribute. Socialist feminists tend to find both radicals and liberals blind to the economic basis of patriarchy. Moderates fear that radicals' tactics will alienate public sympathy and neo-feminists reject the attack on men.

Superficially, feminism could be said to promote an unashamedly sectional interest; feminists are generally women calling for a better deal for women. Criticism comes variously from both sexes, much of it inspired by the broadly conservative notion that sexual roles have evolved naturally. Yet, despite all, feminism has permeated the arts, sciences, humanities, the workplace, the family and the state. In the early 1990s the global nature of the project was underlined in the Fourth World Women's Conference held in Beijing. Today the ideology is woven into the fabric of contemporary politics though it has far to go.

Environmentalism

Today the view is forming that the western ideological tradition is dangerously myopic. Under a broadly liberal banner, the post-war era has seen staggering industrial growth, raising material standards beyond imagination. Yet its costs are becoming increasingly apparent, not only to scientists but to ordinary people in their daily lives. In towns, polluted air causes chronic bronchial conditions, in the countryside rivers and lakes turn brown and lifeless. In supermarkets, shoppers worry about contaminated meat, pesticides and whether the hygienic packaging is wasting limited resources. At the macro level there are problems of overfishing, deforestation, nuclear leakages and the 'greenhouse effect'. There seems no escape; those opting out of the rat race for a place in the sun expose their bodies to ultraviolet radiation seeping through the depleted ozone layer. Modern science and rationalist ideologies may have brought humanity to a 'multifaceted global crisis' (Spretnack and Capra 1986: xv) which prompts new ideological thinking – **environmentalism**. This has a scientific basis in ecology, the study of the relationship of living organisms to their environment, a discipline founded in the late nineteenth century by German zoologist Ernst Haeckel. Its essential view is holistic: a single species cannot be understood without reference to its interactions with other species.

Paradoxically, although many environmentalists betray socialist leanings, the approach follows a conservative logic in questioning progress. Rationalist meddling is arrogant and dangerous; life has a logic beyond our understanding. Environmentalism also reflects the conservative conviction that we inhabit the planet for but a limited time, with a responsibility to future generations.

Human nature Unlike most ideologies, environmentalism downgrades human nature, shifting it from centre stage of the ecosphere much as, in the sixteenth century, Copernicus displaced the earth from the centre of the universe. There are two distinctive perspectives, the **anthropocentric** and the **ecocentric**.

- *The anthropocentric perspective.* Human life remains the principal criterion of value; nature must be respected because it serves us. The depletion of fish stocks, for example, is bad because species may die out and humans will suffer the consequences.
- *The ecocentric perspective.* Value is judged in terms of the ecosystem as a whole; this is the more controversial position (sometimes termed 'deep ecology'). A popular version is the Gaia theory of James Lovelock (1979), which sees the earth as a single organism, worthy of surviving with or without the human species.

The form of government While moderates believe that environmental goals can be met through existing forms of government, radicals see the nation-state as outmoded and call for a return to small communities.

The pattern of development

> The emergence of intelligence, I am convinced, tends to unbalance the ecology . . . It is not until a creature begins to manage its environment that nature is thrown into disorder.
>
> Clifford D. Simak, US journalist, *Shakespeare's Planet*

Environmentalists see in ancient pre-industrial societies a greater ecological awareness than is found in modern society. However, modern environmentalism is tied in with science and industrialization. In 1661, diarist John Evelyn's tract *Fumifugium: the Inconveniencie of the Aer and Smoak of London Dissipated* argued for more trees to purify the city air. In the nineteenth century, the great public health movement, spearheaded by arch-Benthamite Edwin Chadwick, did more to eradicate diseases such as typhoid and cholera than would an army of physicians. The threat of resource depletion was also recognized. Malthus's grim late-eighteenth-century warning that population would outstrip food supply coloured much thinking, as did Darwin's theory of evolution, which underlined the close integration of the human species with nature. Romantic conservativism, with its belief that industrialism despoiled nature, was also influential. For some, including Haeckel himself, nature acquired a spiritual significance, a pantheistic substitute for the God Darwin had eliminated.

Contemporary environmentalism took off in the 1960s. In 1962 Rachael Carson published her influential *Silent Spring*; silent because the birds no longer sang, their reproductive cycles disrupted by pesticides. Other catastrophes followed. In the 1970s the Cuyahoga River became so polluted that it caught fire, while Lake Erie was pronounced dead. In 1968 Paul Ehrlich's *The Population Bomb* heightened the sense of alarm by reviving the Malthusian nightmare of overpopulation. Yet these appeared as local issues, within the scope of national governments to solve (Goodin 1992: 3). The problem moved onto an entirely new plane when the discovery of global warming revealed that actions by single countries (curbing emissions, cleaning up rivers) could not meet the challenge. Traditional ideologies, premised upon a world of competitive nation-states, began to look more like the problem than the solution.

More heterogeneous than most, the movement takes four broad manifestations: individuals pursuing green lifestyles, propagandists working through traditional institutions (political parties, media, churches), green pressure groups and green parties (Parkin 1988: 168). The pressure groups, notably Friends of the Earth and Greenpeace, formed at the end of the 1960s. Many take a high-profile, headline-catching stance. In its daring oceanic encounters, *The Rainbow Warrior*, literally the Greenpeace flagship, features dramatically on

No-fly zone: eco-warriors Matt, Denise and Muppet Pete wait to be evicted from their 'Cakehole' protest camp near Manchester Airport, May 1997

Photo: Times Newspapers Ltd

television screens around the world. Political parties followed, with fully fledged agendas embracing foreign policy, the economy, education, and so on. In 1983 Die Grünen (the Greens) seized the public imagination with a breakthrough into the West German Bundestag, the psychedelic garb of their 27 members contrasting symbolically with the serried ranks of establishment grey. Greens have also penetrated the European Parliament, forming a separate group in their own right. Posing challenges quite beyond the contemplation of traditional politicians, the movement takes two broad forms: one anthropocentric and moderate, the other ecocentric and radical.

Forms of environmentalism

Moderate environmentalism Here action is through the usual political channels. The ecological lifestyle can be achieved by national governments pursuing regulatory policies (Porritt and Winner 1988: 151). This approach accommodates other ideologies.

- *Neoliberal.* Eco-capitalists keep faith with the free market; if green products are demanded, competition will ensure their supply (Elkington and Burke 1989: 239). In this 'New Age Capitalism' firms will, without governmental direction, use alternative energy sources, cleaner technology and biodegradable materials and practise recycling. In Britain, local authorities have developed various policies for recycling waste and protecting the environment as a matter of routine, while shoppers increasingly demand green products. Although the car remains supreme, exhaust standards are growing more stringent. The mainstream parties continue to green their manifestos. For liberals growth is not sacrificed but becomes *sustainable*.
- *Socialist.* Alternatively, eco-socialists continue to see capitalism as a serious problem, calling for state power to take on multinational corporations with regulative regimes and a range of social policies to combat the suffering stemming from environmental abuse (Ryle 1988: 46). In 1992, the government banned the use of two pesticides increasingly found in drinking water and, by 1998, road traffic reduction was a serious policy goal.

The moderate approach has proved the more effective so far. However, for many the idea that the crisis can be ultimately met within existing political frameworks is naive delusion.

Radical environmentalism Traditional politics is about compromise. However, the issue environmentalists address is not about 'who gets what' and there can be no halfway solutions (Goodin 1992: 12). The crisis demands seismic shifts in lifestyles, economies and systems of government.

> Other parties have literally copied parts of our programme. But they don't imple-ment them. They only do it cosmetically.
>
> Petra Kelly (Die Grünen MP, whose sudden death was shrouded in mystery),
> interview in *Living Marxism* (4 Feb. 1989)

- *Lifestyle*. Generally life must be less materialistic, with greater emphasis on spiritual values (often of a Buddhist character). Many contemporary shibboleths (the supremacy of the car, children, foreign holidays) are challenged. People would live more frugally and populations would be stabilized through immigration control, abortion and sterilization.
- *Economics*. A 'New Economics' questions both liberalism and socialism. The talisman of growth is unnatural: the goal is a steady-state economy. Gross national product (GNP) should be replaced with an *adjusted* meas-ure (AGNP), reflecting pollution, waste, health and other quality-of-life indicators. Energy would come mainly from renewable sources (sun, sea, wind), with consumption drastically cut. The global economy must be shut down; the liberal orthodoxy of free trade replaced by autarky (national self-sufficiency).
- *Government*. The centralized nation-state undermines the ecological com-munity and is no longer viable (Goldsmith 1972: 52). Seeking popularity through rising material standards, employment creation and so on, gov-ernments have worked hand in glove with large corporations, legitimat-ing their activities and restricting information on pollution and harmful effects upon food. Radical environmentalists see people living rather like the Ancient Greeks in small communities in sustainable 'bio-regions'. Within deep ecology there are strongly anarchic undertones.

The global challenge

Like feminism, environmentalism has permeated western consciousness. How-ever, environmental problems are global and the real solutions must come at the supranational level, often at the expense of national sovereignty. As Vidal (1996) asserts: 'The changes now taking place in society are, I believe, as pro-found as in the Enlightenment'. In the USA, the Carter administration pub-lished a *Global 2000 Report* and the Club of Rome produced *The Limits to Growth* (Meadows et al. 1972). The role of the European Union (EU) (chapter 5) becomes increasingly significant. Although the Rome Treaty was silent on environmental policy, by 1971 environmentalist lobbying had placed it on the agenda. The Paris Summit adopted an environmental policy and established an Environmental Protection Service. Since then goals have been outlined in En-vironmental Action Programmes (EAPs). The Single European Act (SEA) of 1987 (see p. 116) introduced the Environment as one of its Titles (VII) and 1990 saw the creation of the European Environmental Agency to conduct research and publish reports on environmental issues. The Maastricht Treaty enlarged the environmental provisions, promising financial assistance to states where disproportionate costs were imposed by EU requirements. At the United Nations Rio Earth Summit in 1992, John Major enthused on matters ecological and *Agenda 21* was accepted for implementation at national and local levels. In November 1998 the British government published its first 'quality of life barometer', going beyond economic data to include housing, road transport, waste disposal, life expectancy, pollution and number of wild birds.

A myriad criticisms have been heaped on environmentalism.

- *Self-indulgence.* Although serving no particular interest, environmental activists are sometimes characterized as self-indulgent doom merchants. Lowe and Goyder (1983: 25) note how peaks of environmentalist activity follow expansionary phases of the business cycle (the 1890s, late 1920s, late 1950s and the 1970s), when affluence affords a leisured class the luxury of self-criticism.
- *Scientific fallibility.* Within the science there is a contradiction. When environmentalism attacks the Enlightenment ideals of progress, science is used to attack science. Consequently, some scientists are hostile, doubting the doomsday scenarios.
- *Authoritarianism.* Despite an anarchic tone, the scale of reform required and the potential for conflict would call for a strong central authority. Some critics speak of 'eco-fascism'. Indeed, the Third Reich promoted wind technology, nature reserves, reforestation programmes and organic farming (Vincent 1992: 213–14), while Adolf Hitler was a vegetarian.
- *Inadequacy.* Although a green mantra exhorts us to 'think globally, act locally', this can hardly achieve the response demanded. Environmentalism lacks an adequate theory of overarching authority; a world government to match the scale of the crisis it forewarns of (Goodin 1992: 5).
- *Utopianism.* Some see the proposals, particularly of the deep ecologists, as utopian (or 'ectopian') dreams unrealizable in the real world.

Despite its achievements, environmentalism does not sit easily with western values. While the prescriptions may be in the long-term interest of our species, they appear to be in the short-term interest of very few. Parties will not gain votes offering, say, to outlaw the motor car. Having discovered Benidorm, who will forsake the Mediterranean sun for the Blackpool pleasure beach of their grandparents?

Moreover, the multinational corporations (see chapter 4), masterminding global expansion and sometimes funding political parties, will not sit back while economies are radically recast. At their head is the oil industry, now stronger economically than any country outside the G7. This awesome power was underlined at a major UN Climate Summit at Kyoto in December 1997. While El

Niño was wreaking havoc around the world, progress was held back by US obstructionism following a unanimous Senate resolution to reject any treaty harming its economy. Attending the summit in force was the self-styled Global Climate Coalition representing oil and car interests, including Mobil, Exxon, General Motors, Texaco and Chrysler, and claiming that action on climate change would cause economic crisis. Significantly, the agreed target for reductions in greenhouse gases (from 1990 levels) by 2012 was only 5.2 per cent, falling far short of the EU's proposed figure of 15 per cent and nowhere near the level regarded by scientists as necessary to avert catastrophic climate change.

In Eastern Europe environmentalists initially played a significant role in the overthrow of communism, the movement often becoming a focus for anti-Soviet sentiments. However, as western values gain ascendancy environmentalists become marginalized (Tickle and Welsh 1998). Similarly, by 1998, the UK's neoliberal Labour government was showing signs of backtracking on its traffic reduction promises, while supporting genetically modified foodstuffs.

> Although containing only 4.6% of the world's population the US is responsible for 21.9% of carbon dioxide emissions.
>
> *World Resources* (1996–7)

An End of Ideology?

It is difficult to overestimate the impact of the western ideological tradition. With debate revolving around the central concepts of rationalism, freedom, equality and sovereignty, its power has lain in a capacity to grapple with the unique problems of modernity (Gamble 1981: 17). Some writers envisage an age when ideological debate will cease. To some extent Marx's vision of a communist future in which the state would wither away did this. More recently, Daniel Bell's *End of Ideology* (1960) captured the post-war spirit when western political parties converged around a Keynesian social democratic consensus. With the collapse of East European communism and the neoliberal ascendancy in the West, US academic Francis Fukuyama's *End of History* (1992), proclaimed a final triumph of liberalism.

Yet such theories prove fanciful. States did not wither away under communism and the emergence of the New Right exposed the frailty of the western post-war consensus. The neoliberal triumph itself looked insecure. In Russia and Eastern Europe, people generally used to full employment soon learned that the gods of capitalism demand sacrificial offerings in the form of losers as well as winners and some communist leaders found themselves back in favour.

By the end of the millennium, western world leaders, particularly Clinton and Blair, were again searching for an ideological answer to global economic and political problems in a proclaimed '**third way**' placed somewhere between the social democracy of the early post-war years and the neoliberalism of the Thatcher–Reagan era. With antecedents in the 1920s, this movement was not entirely new (Giddens 1998: 25). Although Tony Blair argued that the third way was to fashion a new consensus, critics saw the project as narrowing debate, with the implication that there was only 'one way' – in other words, yet another attempt to find an end of ideology. Blair's certitude was seen as reminiscent of Thatcher's declaration 'there is no alternative', which earned her the sobriquet TINA. Blair's third way was not attractive to other West European leaders, nor indeed to all in his own party.

Today we inhabit a world of increasing inequality, where the 26 most developed countries, with under 15 per cent of the world's population, enjoy a mean per capita GNP of $18,000 while another 3,000 million people live on a mean per capita GNP of some $330 (Hobsbawm 1992: 57). Moreover, the unending quest for economic growth leads on to ecological disaster. This is hardly a stable world with no room for ideological debate.

Key points

- Ideologies are theories about how people should live together in society.
- Although ideologies are often reflected in political parties, there is no consistent one-to-one identification.
- The western ideological tradition emerged from a dramatic break with the intellectual habits of past ages – the Enlightenment.
- Liberalism cherishes freedom from oppression. It spawned major revolutions which opened the modern era.
- Classical liberalism came from the new discipline of political economy where the justification for limited government lay not in natural freedom but the quest for economic prosperity.
- New Liberalism perceived freedom as liberation from social and economic restrictions.
- Neoliberalism rose in the late 1970s and saw the free market as the *sine qua non* of the free society.
- Socialists reject the view of people as isolated individuals; they are part of a greater whole.
- Karl Marx, the key figure in socialism, believed socialist revolution was necessary to change society.
- Conservatism provides a rationale for resisting rationalist change.
- Feminism seeks sexual justice and an end to male domination.
- Environmentalism judges value in terms of the ecosystem as a whole.
- Despite theories proclaiming an end to ideological politics, the potential for disagreement over the best way to organize life is probably limitless and fuels political action at all levels.

Review your understanding of the following terms and concepts

anarchism
anthropocentric
capitalism
collectivism
communism
conservatism
ecocentric
Enlightenment
environmentalism
fascism
feminism
General Will
hegemony

'hidden hand'
historical materialism
ideology
individualism
Leviathan
liberal democracy
liberalism
Marxism
nationalism
natural rights
neoliberalism
postmodernism
rationalism

Reformation
reformist socialism
Renaissance
revolutionary socialism
social democracy
socialism
state of nature
third way
utilitarianism

Assignment

Study the extract from Ben Elton's *Stark* and answer the following questions.

		Mark (%)
1	Which ideologies are brought to mind by the extract? Are they in harmony or conflict?	15
2	Why does Sly know so little about the company in which he has an interest?	15
3	How do you think the world had changed since the Pastel's honeymoon?	30
4	How can politics successfully address the problem highlighted in the extract.	40

As Sly entered the restaurant in Los Angeles some of his money was floating off the coast of Britain. Of course Sly was aware that a few of his bucks had found a temporary home as a majority holding in a Belgian waste disposal group, his brokers always consulted him before making a share purchase. But what did that tell Sly? nothing about reality. Certainly Sly knew about the company's collateral, its profit and loss curve, its disposable assets, its history on industrial relations and the chances of an injection of public funds should it hit the skids. But that was all he knew. He saw his investment purely and simply as a device by which to make money. What the company actually did was a matter of supreme indifference to him.

He did not know about Captain Robertson; he did not know about the great toilet irony; he did not know about the Pastel family on holiday . . .

Captain Robertson was a sad and bitter man. All his life he had wanted to be a master of a ship. And what sort of ship did he end up being master of? a sludger. Scarcely a dashing or romantic command.

'What do you do for a living mate?'

'I lug shit up the Thames and dump it in the North Sea.' Captain Robertson would occasionally try to cheer himself up. 'It's a rotten job but then people have to do toilet,' he would say to himself as yet another great steaming slick slid out of the bowels of his barge and began its slow journey back to Britain. . . .

The Pastels had had a lovely day wandering around in the freezing rain and the whole family were getting peckish.

'Now then, kids,' said Mr Pastel, 'I'll tell you what we're going to have for our tea . . . Mussels, that's what, just like your mother and I had on our honeymoon.'

So they did, they had mussels and the whole family got the utter and total shits, because the mussels weren't just like on the honeymoon, since then the world had changed and the mussels with it.

Mussels and oysters feed by filtering tiny particles out of the sea water. These days that includes chemical wastes, agricultural poison and heavy metals. Also an awful lot of bacteria and viruses from human excreta, which cooking and cleaning does not always remove (cooking and cleaning the mussels that is, very few people cook and clean their excreta). Poor Mummy Pastel ended up with acute viral gastro-enteritis and died, but we've all got to go sometime.

Sly didn't know Mrs Pastel, she didn't know him, but they were bound together in life and death by money.

Extract from Ben Elton, *Stark*, London, Sphere Books, 1989.

Questions for discussion

1   How important are ideologies to political parties today?
2   Outline the key stages in the evolution of the modern western ideological tradition.
3   Explain the principle of classical liberalism.
4   Contrast the view of freedom implicit in New Liberalism with that of the earlier liberals.
5   Outline Marx's critique of liberalism.
6   Contrast revolutionary socialism and reformist socialism.
7   'Conservatism presents a rationalist case against rationalism.' Discuss.
8   'Feminism does not present an alternative to liberalism or socialism; rather, it draws upon them, noting how they have fallen short of their ideals.' Discuss.
9   How far can a moderate form of environmentalism meet the ecological challenge facing today's world?
10   How valid is the claim that the 'third way' can end ideological debate?

Further reading

Barker, R. (1994) *Politics, Peoples and Government.*
Shows how the main lines of ideological debate have shifted during the twentieth century.

Crick, B. (1987) *Socialism*.
Leading figure of the intellectual left charts growth of various variants of socialism.

Gamble, A. (1981) *An Introduction to Modern Social and Political Thought*.
Places ideas in their historical contexts.

Giddens, A. (1998) *The Third Way: The Renewal of Social Democracy*.
Presented not as an 'end to politics' but as a strategy to renew the left.

Goodin, R. (1992) *Green Political Theory*.
Philosophical discussion of the green political programme, developing the 'green theory of value'.

Gray, J. (1995) *Enlightenment's Wake: Politics and Culture at the Close of the Modern Age*.
Stimulating set of essays examining major ideologies in a contemporary context.

Greer, G. (1970) *The Female Eunuch*.
An important and challenging book which set the tone of much British debate.

Held, D. (1987) *Models of Democracy*.
The nature, application and importance of democracy from classical Athens to modern times.

Hobbes, T. (1985) *Leviathan,* Penguin Classics version, edited by C. B. Macpherson (first published 1651).
One of the greatest works in the English language. Editor's introduction makes the ideas crystal clear.

Jaggar, A. (1983) *Feminist Politics and Human Nature*.
Influence of feminist thinking on political philosophy and political thought.

Oakeshott, M. (1962) *Rationalism in Politics and Other Essays*.
Classic by a modern-day conservative.

Randall, V. (1982) *Women and Politics*.
Contains, amongst much else, a well-aimed feminist critique of traditional political science itself.

Scruton, R. (1980) *The Meaning of Conservatism*.
Essays by controversial contemporary thinker.

For light relief

Bertolt Brecht, *The Good Woman of Seczwan*.
Brilliant Marxist satire. The 'good person' is made bad when she tries to run a shop under the constraints of capitalism.

Deborah Cartmell, I. Q. Hunter, Heidi Kaye and Imelda Whelehan (eds) (1997) *Sisterhoods*.
Examines female relationships as portrayed in the (patriarchal) media, particularly Hollywood.

Charles Dickens, *A Tale of Two Cities*.
Novel on the French Revolution by one of England's greatest writers.

J. B. Priestley, *An Inspector Calls*.
Makes the case for collectivism against individualism with ingenious theatricality.

R. Tressell, *The Ragged Trousered Philanthropists*.
Working-class protagonists ruminate on life. They are 'philanthropists' because it is their willingness to be poor that allows the rich to stay rich.

Virginia Woolf, *A Room of One's Own*.
A classic essay from a feminist viewpoint.

Chapter Three

The Constitution: the Unwritten and the Unknowable

In this chapter we discuss the British constitution as a set of rules and prescriptions establishing the legal framework in which governments operate. This is not a simple matter; what is and is not part of the constitution is not always clear, and the opinions of experts can vary. Moreover, the constitution does not stand above politics; its content, the way it changes, and the criticisms people make of it are themselves manifestations of the political process. The chapter falls into four main sections. The first is concerned with the concept of a constitution, examining the importance of its study, identifying its sources and understanding its evolution. The second and third sections focus on two key constitutional principles – the limitation of government and the protection of individual rights. The final section addresses the important constitutional reform debate.

Seeking the Constitution

Defining the constitution

All kinds of organizations (from sports clubs and hamster societies to trade unions and political parties) have **constitutions**. They usually do two things: define the powers of those holding office and guarantee the rights of ordinary members. At the level of the state the principle remains the same. Hood Phillips describes a constitution as

> the system of laws, customs and conventions which define the composition and powers of organs of the state, and regulate the relations of the various state organs to one another and to the private citizen. (Hood Phillips 1987: 5)

However, another meaning of the term portrays the state constitution as a *description* of everything that takes place on a regularized basis in the process of government. This is a *behavioural* definition; found by discovery rather than laid down by prescription, it was the way in which the political essayist Walter Bagehot (1867) approached the study in his famous work *The English Constitution*.

For the most part, this chapter adopts the first definition – the constitution as a set of rules regularizing behaviour in the process of government. However, this focus does not mean that the distinction between the prescriptive and descriptive aspects of political life is ignored. Indeed, it is particularly important to observe the dissonance between the two, for the belief that they coincide (that the prescriptive rules *describe* actual behaviour) has given the study of constitutions a bad name. Two games of cricket, although played according to the same rules, will be quite different and, although for the English politics might lack the nuances of the revered game, its reality reflects a myriad factors of personality and environment upon which the constitution can only remain silent.

Why study the constitution?

The inevitable discrepancy between prescribed and actual behaviour can render the study of formal constitutions a limited approach. This has led to another tradition of writing on British politics (following the 'behavioural revolution') which ignores the constitution altogether (Bellamy and Castiglione 1996: 413). However, this has as many dangers as an excessive constitutionalism; there are three good reasons for studying the rules of the game.

The constitution bestows authority Chapter 1 showed that politics is about power. In prescribing a framework the constitution bestows legitimacy on certain players. Thus, for example, the prime minister can send people to war and generals can have them shot if they refuse to fight, the police can arrest citizens and judges can send them to prison.

The constitution represents a political prize It is itself *part of* the political process. Many of those engaged in historic struggles have seen constitutional change as their ultimate goal. Thus, for example, after humbling King John, the barons insisted that the new order be enshrined in the Magna Carta at Runnymede in 1215. The Glorious Revolution of 1688 led to the Act of Settlement in 1701, and the rising nineteenth-century bourgeoisie, the working class and the suffragettes all sought the constitutional goal of the right to vote. Many of today's most heated political debates – over Parliament, the monarchy, local government, secrecy, civil liberties, the electoral system, devolution, EU membership, police powers and so on – are essentially constitutional. In fact, the particular features of the British constitution make it more a part of the political process than most (Prosser 1996: 473).

The constitution shapes political consciousness Finally, even if the political analyst wishes to dismiss the constitution as a facade masking the reality of

Magna Charta, and the Charter of the Forests signed by King John.

Source: Mary Evans Picture Library

power, it remains important because of what people believe it to be. Thus, for example, even if people did not really possess effective freedom of speech (perhaps because of libel laws or access to the media), it interests political scientists that they *believed* themselves to have it; their consciousness shapes the political culture (see chapter 8).

Britain's elusive constitution

An American citizen can spend an edifying half-hour perusing the constitution on the bus or as a bedside companion. In contrast, the British constitution – the 'Great Ghost' – is notorious for its mysteriously unwritten manifestation. This is not strictly true because most of it certainly can be found in written form. However, the provisions are *uncodified*; they have not been drawn together in a single document grandly entitled 'The Constitution'. This is just as well, for if all the material was bound together, the British counterpart of the American patriot would be faced with something approaching the seven labours of Hercules.

The constitution takes this form because, unlike many other polities, including great ones such as France, Russia and the USA, Britain has never experienced a popular revolution in which a new class of rulers has wanted to erase all trace of the *ancien régime* and make a fresh start.

Efficient and dignified elements

In looking at constitutions all may not be as it seems. In 1785 Paley noted how in 'the actual exercise of royal authority in England we see these formidable prerogatives dwindled into mere ceremonies', and in the nineteenth century Bentham and the great constitutional authority Dicey both charged the eighteenth-century constitutional chronicler Blackstone with being beguiled by what were no more than *fictions*. The passage of time has much to do with this; Bagehot likened the constitution to an elderly gentleman wearing the fashions of his youth, the outward finery belying the changes taking place beneath.

However, unlike the reforming radicals, Bagehot did not want the outmoded garb consigned to the shelves of the political curiosity shop. He discerned a special significance in empty 'ceremonies', arguing that all well-established constitutions required two elements: the **efficient** and the **dignified**. The former regulated those getting on with the job of ruling, while the latter fulfilled a vital function in generating authority. Bagehot believed that it was useless to expect the masses to understand the arcane mysteries of government but they could be kept happy if they were given pageantry at which to gawp and wonder. Modern political scientists agree with Bagehot that a political system must incorporate some mechanism for securing legitimacy.

> The lower orders, the middle orders, are still, when tried by what is the standard of the educated . . . , narrow-minded, unintelligent, incurious. (Bagehot 1963: 63)

The notion of dignified elements in a constitution means that we cannot ignore things that on the surface seem irrelevant to policy-making; they may be important in shaping mass attitudes. We must also be alert to the possibility that various state institutions may no longer play the part formally assigned to them; indeed we see throughout this book that imperceptible shifts from the efficient to the dignified pages of the constitution leave it in a state of permanent flux.

Sources of the constitution

The constitution has traditionally been seen to flow from five sources: royal prerogative, statutes, common law, convention and authoritative opinion (figure 3.1). However, more recent developments have seen it affected by factors external to the domestic polity: the European Union (EU) and the European Convention on Human Rights (ECHR).

Figure 3.1
The British
constitution flows
from a number of
sources.

Royal
prerogative

Common
law

Conventions

Authoritative
opinion

Statute

Europe

The British constitution

The royal prerogative This is a set of privileges enjoyed exclusively by monarchs since medieval times. *Personal* prerogatives are held by the monarch in person and *political* prerogatives as head of state. The latter are the more important to the efficient constitution and include the rights to declare war or make peace, pardon criminals, dissolve Parliament and appoint ministers. These, like the Crown Jewels, have been carefully preserved. However, with the gradual erosion of the powers of the monarchy, today the **royal prerogative** is in effect exercised by the Cabinet and prime minister.

Statute These are no more than ordinary laws passed by Parliament. It is a rather unnerving fact that a **statute** changing the constitution is not required to undergo any special procedures, as is usually the case under written constitutions. Thus the monumentally important extensions of the franchise were all made by politically motivated governments with little elevated thought of democratic or constitutional principle. Similarly, in 1986 the government was able to erase from the political map part of the local government system (see chapter 19) to do little more than settle a political score. Again, the devolution reforms of 1998 flowed from no more than the normal legislative process, although referendums were held.

Common law This is based on precedent, from an accumulation of court decisions in specific legal cases throughout history (see p. 622). **Common law** is particularly useful for resolving ambiguities in other constitutional sources. The two great virtues claimed for the common-law element are that it reflects past wisdom and is independent of politics. On the other hand, it can be very untidy, leaving judges to wrestle with a bewildering mass of precedents. Recent governments have sought to rationalize much common law into new statutes.

Common law has developed many civil liberties. Examples from hundreds of important cases include the *Case of Proclamations* in 1610 (the king could not create new offences by proclamation), *Anderson* v. *Gorrie* in 1895 (the immunity of judges) and *Bradlaugh* v. *Gossett* in 1884 (the supremacy of Parliament over its internal affairs). As recently as 1999, in *DPP* v. *Jones*, the House of Lords, in reversing a conviction by the Salisbury magistrates under recent public order legislation, decided that a peaceful assembly on the verge of the A344 at Stonehenge did not constitute trespass.

Conventions   These are regularly observed practices, having no legal basis and not enforceable in the courts. All states must evolve **constitutional conventions** to breathe life into their constitutions if they are to be flexible enough to survive. (The conventional elements of the constitution are the most easily changed.) However, in no other country have conventions been as important as in Britain, where they regulate the key processes of government. Democracy itself is based on conventions limiting the prerogative powers of the Crown and enabling them to be exercised by elected leaders. The Cabinet, the epicentre of government, is known only through convention.

In addition, there are many lesser conventions. For example, MPs never tell lies to the House of Commons or, to be more precise, no MP ever accuses another of having done so. In 1987, Labour MP Tam Dalyell broke with this, accusing Margaret Thatcher of lying over the Westland scandal. Consequently, he was 'named' by the Speaker; that is, barred from the chamber. There can be disagreement as to whether or not a convention actually exists. Some have argued that in cutting off relations with the TUC, Thatcher broke a newly minted convention of consultation.

Although conventions are the most obviously 'unwritten' part of the constitution, they are probably the most *written about*. This is necessary because there is more need for guidance in an area where the formal law is silent. This leads to the next source.

Authoritative opinion   It is considered appropriate that learned works of great authority and wisdom be regarded as legitimate constitutional sources, though there may be difficulty in defining precisely what is meant by authority. Great age is taken as important because it may be presumed that ancient texts distilled the wisdom otherwise lost. Examples of such treasures include, among others, Fitzherbert's *Abridgement* of 1516, Hawkins's *Pleas of the Crown* (1716) and Foster's *Crown Cases* (1762). Of course not all authorities agree; indeed it is in their nature to be disputatious. The very belief that one can discover the

Statutes override all other domestic constitutional sources. Some, such as the 1689 Bill of Rights (defining the relationship between Crown and Parliament and ratifying the 1688 Glorious Revolution) and the 1701 Act of Settlement (determining the succession), are extremely venerable. More recently, there have been the Parliament Acts of 1911 and 1949 (determining the relationship between the two Houses of Parliament) and the 1963 Peerage Act (enabling peers to renounce their titles). In addition to statutes, and having much the same character and force, are certain revered historical documents, the most notable of which is the Magna Carta.

constitution from the authorities of the past is itself open to question and was challenged by the Philosophical Radicals. An oft-quoted authority is Walter Bagehot, perhaps the one who first 'discovered' the constitution. Peter Hennessy (1994), one of his modern counterparts, argues that, before Bagehot wrote, there was no constitution that could be recognized or apprehended as a living and working thing.

The European factor The EU is also a source of the modern constitution though this was perhaps not fully recognized when Britain entered the EEC in 1973. It affects the powers of all domestic institutions. If a legal dispute containing a European element reaches the House of Lords, the final court of appeal, there must be an application for a ruling to the European Court of Justice (ECJ, the EU court). Lower courts may also seek ECJ guidance. Moreover, the courts assume that in all UK legislation it was Parliament's intention to be consistent with EU law (unless an expressed statement to the contrary is made). Hence, in *Pickstone* v. *Freemans PLC* (1987), regulations amending the Equal Pay Act were interpreted in a manner different from their literal meaning to comply with EU law. The incorporation into domestic law of the ECHR provides a further constitutional source (see pp. 72–4).

Change and development

All constitutions are political but Britain's is particularly so because it may be changed as part of the normal process of politics. This is potentially threatening because, following the game metaphor, it is impossible to play if the rules are not fixed. On the other hand, a constitution cannot work if it is entirely inflexible and, even in the USA where its veneration rouses religious fervour (there have been only twenty-six formal **constitutional amendments**), small changes occur continually through judicial decisions and the establishment of conventions. However, written constitutions are usually given a propensity to resist change; **entrenched** through deliberately cumbersome processes of amendment. Does this mean the British constitution is unstable and but a flimsy defence of citizens' rights? There is some truth in this, though it contains both conservative and flexible elements.

> **Amending a written constitution**
>
> Amendments to the US constitution must be first proposed and then ratified. Proposals may be made by two-thirds majorities in both houses of Congress voting separately, or by a national convention called by Congress at the request of two-thirds of the state legislatures. Ratification requires a vote of three-quarters of the state legislatures or state conventions in three-quarters of the states. However, written constitutions need not be inflexible. Since 1809 Sweden's has been amended over 200 times – like the workshop hammer, with several new heads and shafts, one wonders whether it is any longer the same thing.

Art or Nature: are constitutions machines or organisms? There are two broad theoretical views on constitutional change: the mechanistic and the organic. The former sees constitutions as machines designed to give people the kind of government they desire. The English philosophers Thomas Hobbes and John Locke belong within this tradition, though it was the Philosophical Radicals who really addressed the issue of *rational* constitutional reform. The essence of their position was that, if a constitution was to serve the needs of a people at any particular time, they should deduce it from first principles. The principle was utilitarianism (see pp. 28–9). For this school of thought statute law is the obvious constitutional source.

> While the mechanical contrivance of political inventors has died away . . . the goodly tree of British freedom selecting from the kindly soil and assimilating its fit nutriment still increases its stately bulk . . . Outliving the storms and vicissitudes of centuries, deeply rooted in the habits and affections of the people, it spreads far and wide its hospitable shade.
>
> W. E. Hearn, *The Government of England* (1868)

In contrast, the **organic** view argues that a constitution grows and develops naturally like a living organism; for thinkers of this school it is a thing of untouchable beauty. Frequent references liken the British constitution to a great tree. Blackstone's view of the constitution, with its veneration of the past, would belong in this category and the cover of Sir Ivor Jennings's *The British Constitution* (1966) is actually adorned with a picture of a spreading oak.

The organic idea has a distinguished pedigree, extending from the Ancient Greeks. Hegel and T. H. Green also conceived the state in organic terms, while

> Poems are made by fools like me,
> But only God can make a tree.
>
> Alfred Joyce Kilmer (1888–1918), 'Trees'

Edmund Burke suggested that the constitution should be treated with awe as a repository of the collective wisdom of the ages. He argued for

> a presumption in favour of any settled scheme of government against any untried project, that a nation has long existed and flourished under it. (Burke 1782: 146)

This distinction is related to the question of the moral justification for constitutions, leading into an important area of philosophical debate centring on a distinction drawn between positive law and natural law.

Positive law is laid down by human agency, say a government or a monarch, or through the accumulation of customs. Prominent amongst the positivists was the Philosophical Radical John Austin (1790–1859), who saw law as nothing more than the commands of the sovereign. Bentham was himself influenced by Austin. Some find this approach (legal positivism) unsatisfactory because it lacks a deeper justification.

Natural law is supposedly derived from something more fundamental than the dictates of any earthly sovereign. This idea can be traced back to the Ancient Greek philosophers, particularly the Stoics, whose ideas were adopted by the Romans when seeking a legal system that could extend over their empire independently of the customary laws of different lands. For some, natural law can be said to derive from an expression of the will of God, though some philosophers, including Hugo Grotius (1583–1645) and Immanuel Kant (1724–1804), argued that this is virtually a special kind of positive law with God as the sovereign. Others argue that it is derived from the idea of certain 'natural rights'. However, this introduces the problem of what these rights actually are. For Locke they included security of life, limb and property, and the US constitution begins by speaking grandiloquently of certain 'inalienable rights'.

Development and change in the British constitution have shown both organic and mechanistic characteristics. Common law and conventions have evolved gradually, while statute law has facilitated some great leaps, such as the extensions of the franchise. The two contrasting views are marked by more than a dispassionate search for the truth; they have been used to support political positions. For Burke's followers (the landowners) the organic and mystical view provided a basis for resisting the forces threatening to erode their privileges, while for the rising industrial bourgeoisie, attempting to shape the constitution in their own interests, the radical mechanistic view was irresistible.

Limiting Government

The essence of **constitutional government** is **limited government**. This is held to be necessary because there can never be any guarantee that rulers will not exercise power in their own self-interest. Most political thinkers have agreed that power corrupts. This limitation can be secured by other institutions, the law, or popular control, and is sought through three fundamental principles: the **sepa-**

ration of powers, the **rule of law** and **parliamentary sovereignty**. The first was regarded by the French jurist Montesquieu, in his *L'Esprit des Lois* (1748), as the key to British liberty. The last two were seen by Dicey as the twin pillars of the constitution (1959: xvii), a view that has continued to colour much constitutional writing (Harden and Lewis 1986: 4).

The separation of powers

The idea of dispersing or separating power between various institutions so that they will curtail each other's actions is based on the theory that there are distinct functions of government, each of which can be entrusted to a different institution. Montesquieu followed Locke in arguing that the best safeguard of freedom was to ensure that those making the laws (the **legislature**) should not also be those with the power of carrying them out (the **executive**). Similarly, those enforcing the laws (the **judiciary**) should be independent. The founding fathers of the American constitution were deeply impressed by the doctrine and today the executive (president), legislature (Congress) and judiciary are not only separate but have extensive power over each other; the constitution imposes 'checks and balances'. It is not unusual for the president to be thwarted in his policy ambitions by both Congress and the courts; indeed at times the system seems in danger of grinding to a complete standstill as vetoes are exercised like power-assisted brakes. Further separation is inherent in the US constitution through its federal structure, apportioning jurisdiction between the federal government and the states.

> The accommodation of all powers ... in the same hands ... may justly be pronounced the very definition of tyranny.
>
> James Madison (1751–1836; one of America's 'founding fathers'), in *The Federalist* (1788)

In February 1989 the Senate Armed Services Committee voted against the newly installed President Bush's nominee, John Tower, as Defence Secretary, a decision subsequently confirmed by the full Senate. Tower had been seen as a hard-drinking womanizer with too cosy a relationship with defence contractors.

In fact Montesquieu was wrong about the British constitution. Bagehot was to stress that its 'efficient secret' was not a separation but a *fusion* of powers (figure 3.2) through the Cabinet, which was head of both the executive and the legislature. Furthermore, the Lord Chancellor is head of the judiciary, a member of the Cabinet (in the happy position of receiving two salaries) and of the legislature, when he sits on the 'Woolsack' as the Speaker of the House of Lords. To increase the fusion, the House of Lords, as well as being part of the legislature, is the final Court of Appeal. The judiciary also makes laws through the doctrine of precedent. Moreover, the growth of a myriad administrative tribunals means that the executive also acts widely in a judicial capacity and, through the practice of *delegated legislation*, is able to make laws (see p. 376).

Consequently there is little scope for applying checks and balances. The executive is virtually unimpeded by Parliament because of party discipline (see pp. 373–5) and the courts have no authority to veto legislation in the manner of

Figure 3.2
A fusion rather than a separation
of powers.

the US Supreme Court. Again, the doctrine of parliamentary sovereignty means that a judicial decision disliked by the government can be reversed by a new statute. However, the courts do have the power to consider the legality of executive action through a process of **judicial review**, a power used increasingly during the 1980s and 1990s (see p. 624) (Klug et al. 1996: 48). Home Secretary Michael Howard was accused of pursuing an agenda set by the tabloid press and the principle of the separation of powers was adduced by Lord Chief Justice Peter Taylor in defence of judicial independence of the executive.

The rule of law

This principle holds that the law is above the whims of any individual ruler. Lying at the heart of the idea of constitutional government, it can be traced back to the Ancient Greeks. It has been brought to bear throughout history wherever people have sought to resist arbitrary rule or despotism; in the Middle Ages the notion that the monarch was subject to God and the law provided a fundamental rationale for challenging royal absolutism. Dicey (1959) expressed the rule of law in terms of three precepts.

- No person can be punished except for a distinct breach of the law.
- No person, of whatever rank, is above the ordinary law.
- The general provisions of the constitution are the result of decisions made by an independent judiciary in deciding particular cases, rather than of declarations by rulers.

However, these break down in practice.

- Innocent people may be detained on the basis of police suspicion that they might commit a crime.
- There are various categories subject to different laws. For example: judges, MPs and diplomats are accorded extra privileges; the police have special powers and members of the armed forces are subject to martial law.
- Because the constitution is formed by statute as well as common law, the government can pass any law it pleases in an essentially despotic manner (see chapter 13).

In Britain, the practical meaning of the rule of law has varied throughout history (Harden and Lewis 1986: 8) but today it largely holds that the government will operate within the law. This is not to say that it, or its agents, such as the secret services, do not sail close to the wind. In July 1993, the House of Lords in its appeal capacity ruled Home Secretary Kenneth Baker in contempt of court over the deportation of an asylum seeker in 1991 in defiance of a court order. The government had claimed that the law had no power by injunction or contempt proceedings against a minister acting in an official capacity but the Court asserted that such a proposition would reverse the result of the Civil War! However, the courts have no power to review the substance of legislation, which leads to the most important criticism of any characterization of the rule of law in the British constitution: it is logically incompatible with the second of Dicey's great 'pillars' – the doctrine of the sovereignty of Parliament.

Parliamentary sovereignty

This doctrine enshrines the outcome of the prolonged constitutional struggle culminating in the Glorious Revolution of 1688, when the Bill of Rights (1689) set out the supremacy that Parliament had gained over the king through a succession of common-law decisions dating from the fourteenth century. However, not until the nineteenth century, following the great Reform Acts which changed the political system out of all recognition, was the principle formally enunciated by Dicey as the one fundamental (or entrenched) element in the British constitution. Parliamentary sovereignty entailed

> . . . the right to make or unmake any law whatever; and . . . that no person or body is recognised by the law of England as having a right to override or set aside the legislation of Parliament. (Dicey 1959: 39–40)

From this follow two principles: that the courts have no power to veto legislation and that no Parliament is bound by existing laws. As Bill Walker MP told the Commons in February 1993: 'If we get something wrong, as we often do, we can rectify it the following year' (quoted in Klug et al. 1996: 537).

At the time Dicey wrote, the generally accepted doctrine of **sovereignty** was that of Austin, that every state must contain some body with ultimate power. This carried no particular moral justification, but Dicey distinguished between two forms of sovereignty – *legal* and *political* – asserting the moral supremacy of the latter. Thus the sovereignty of Parliament was derived not from its inheritance of the absolute powers of the monarch, nor from God, but from the people through the principle of democratic representation.

Today, membership of the EU poses questions for the doctrine. British courts must give effect to laws emanating from Brussels and, in any conflict, these take precedence over those of Westminster. Although such conflict has generally been over technical matters, fundamental questions were raised when the British government passed a 1988 Act to establish a register preventing foreigners from registering ships as British (which was permitted under the 1894 Merchant Shipping Act) in order to use British fishing quotas. In *R. v. Secretary of State for Transport ex parte Factortame* (1990) this was challenged by Spanish fishermen as contrary to Community law. A decision of the European Court of Justice effectively suspended part of a British statute. Incorporation of the ECHR also limits parliamentary sovereignty by enabling the courts to strike down legislation found to violate its provisions. Further restrictions on sovereignty are associated with the establishment of the Scottish Parliament, Welsh Senedd and Northern Irish assembly, giving the UK more of a federal character (see chapter 6). The Westminster and provincial bodies must now accept judicial ruling in any conflict over their respective powers (Thompson 1997: 188).

However, we shall see in chapter 13 that the greatest challenge to parliamentary sovereignty comes not from power-hungry Eurocrats or a dissident Celtic fringe but from the political dominance of the British executive.

Protecting Individual Rights

In addition to regulating government a constitution also guarantees **civil rights** – freedoms and protections for citizens. The two functions are not really distinct; the quantity and quality of personal freedom offered is linked with the nature and degree of the state's authority. Many written constitutions include positive guarantees of fundamental freedoms. In 1787, the framers of the US constitution neglected this and ten amendments were passed subsequently as the Bill of Rights. This guaranteed freedom of worship, speech, assembly, and to petition for redress of grievances; freedom from deprivation of life, liberty or property by unlawful means; freedom from cruel or unusual punishments; and security from unreasonable search of persons or houses and private papers and effects.

The Glorious Revolution

The Bill of Rights following the Glorious Revolution is not like those of France or the USA. Conferring various privileges upon MPs, it is concerned with the rights of Parliament in relation to the monarch, rather than those of citizens in relation to the state.

However, in Britain laws protecting basic freedoms have been nothing more than the ordinary laws of the land; granted only *negatively*, rights are not conferred by the constitution, they are merely not withheld. People can do anything that is not expressly prohibited by law; the freedoms are said to be *residual*. There is nothing to prevent the government enacting harsh laws, which leads many to call for an entrenched US-style Bill of Rights (see p. 72). Of course, under certain circumstances people may be quite happy to relinquish freedom. In his *Essay on Liberty*, J. S. Mill argued that one person's freedom should be permitted only in so far as it did not harm others, and much modern legislation (e.g. libel laws) reflects this principle.

Fundamental rights

Fundamental rights having a direct bearing on politics include freedom of the *person*, of *speech*, of *association* and of *property*.

Freedom of the person The right to go about one's business has long been regarded as a central pillar of the temple of liberty. In the eighteenth-century case of *Leach* v. *Money and Others* (1765) it was held that a general warrant for the arrest of unnamed persons was illegal and void. In *Liversidge* v. *Anderson and Another* (1942) it was held that 'every imprisonment is *prima facie* unlawful, and that it is for a person directing imprisonment to justify his act'. If a person has been wrongfully imprisoned he or she has a range of remedies available in civil and common law, on grounds such as malicious prosecution, false imprisonment, assault and battery. In addition there is the classic guarantee of individual liberty in Britain – the writ of habeas corpus – enabling anyone confined to demand to be brought before the court for a just trial. During its history the writ has served a variety of purposes, including removing apprentices from cruel masters, freeing slaves and establishing that a husband has no right to detain his wife against her will.

However, the executive has the authority to limit freedom of the person by taking on unrestrained powers of arrest on the basis of great national emergency. The Emergency Powers (Defence) Act (1939) gives the Home Secretary the right to detain anyone whom he 'has reasonable cause to believe' may be of 'hostile origin or association', which means, in effect, that anyone may be so detained providing that ministers argue that they acted in good faith. Under emergencies, even habeas corpus can be suspended, as was the case, for example, in the fight against the Chartists (see p. 233). The policy of internment in Northern Ireland, the operation of the 'sus' law against young blacks and the detention of asylum-seekers have all represented further serious infringements of freedom of the person. In a matter of a few days before Easter 1996, the Home Secretary, fearful of IRA activity, was able to give the police new stop-and-search powers under the Prevention of Terrorism Act.

Freedom of speech It is clear that in a democracy the freedom to express political opinion is fundamental; throughout the world the absence of such a right is held to be one of the most visible symptoms of oppression. Yet in Britain the freedom has been restricted in various ways. Individuals are protected from verbal and written assault through the laws of slander and libel. There are also laws on obscenity, though the impossibility of deciding what exactly is obscene often produces ludicrous scenarios, as in the *Lady Chatterley's Lover* trial. The most serious restrictions on freedom of speech tend to come from the agencies of the state. The repressive apparatus, though often lying dormant, carries a formidable potential which is thrown into starkest relief in the reporting of politics by the media and the vexed question of government secrecy (see pp. 454–61).

Freedom of association Politics is essentially about collective behaviour and the voluntary association of individuals. However, the constitution places considerable restrictions on the freedom to associate. There have been, for example, the crimes of conspiracy and public nuisance, and the common-law offences of riot, rout and unlawful assembly, later codified in the Public Order Act (1936). Further restrictions were enacted in the Public Order Act (1986), the Criminal Justice and Public Order Act (1994) and the Crime and Disorder Act (1998). The police hold extensive powers in the event of a breach of the peace, or even the suspicion that such a breach might occur. Under normal circumstances the authorities claim to exercise their discretion in a liberal manner, but within this velvet glove is the clenched fist of state repression (see chapter 21): people can be bound over to keep the peace, road blocks can stop movement (as in the miners' strike of 1984/5) and powers to disperse crowds can curtail rights of assembly. In 1988, workers at the Government Communications Headquarters at Cheltenham lost their right to trade union membership; only nine years later were they to be restored.

Freedom of property This is the key freedom in a capitalist society, which is based on the private ownership of property. The Englishman's home is often said to be his castle, where he may defend himself from his enemies as well as seek repose. This is a view shared by the law; in *Semayne's Case* (1603), it was declared that if thieves enter a man's house to commit robbery or murder, he, or his servants, are entitled to kill them in defence of life and property. In *Stroud* v. *Bradbury* (1952), the rights of 'free-born Englishmen' to protect themselves with 'clothes prop and spade' against the intrusions of a council sanitary inspector were defended. However, when the forces of the state wish to enter private premises they find little practical impediment. It is not difficult for the police to obtain warrants and in cases where they have made illegal entry the courts have taken a surprisingly lenient view if the object has been to suppress left-wing or radical forces. In *Elias* v. *Pasmore* (1934), the illegal seizure by the police of documents belonging to the National Unemployed Workers' Movement was held as excusable on the grounds of state security, while in the bitter miners' strike of 1984/5, the NUM's funds were sequestrated by the courts.

Legitimate violence: policing an NUS demo against student loans, November 1988

Rights in question

> A citizen's person or property may not be interfered with – unless it may. A person is not liable for what he speaks or writes – unless he is. No liability attaches to one who takes part in a public meeting – unless it does.
>
> O. Hood Phillips, *Constitutional and Administrative Law* (1987: 39–40)

When considering individual rights it becomes apparent that in Britain these have been so hedged with qualifications, ambiguities and what has been praised as the 'glorious uncertainty of the law' that it is difficult to know what one may actually do without impediment. In 1995, the UN Human Rights Committee, following its fourth periodic review, concluded that Britain failed to secure basic civil and political rights and provided inadequate remedy where rights were violated (Klug et al. 1996: 537). The government's defence was that the report failed to appreciate the subtle glories of the system (Weir and Boyle 1997).

Britain could have given itself a **Bill of Rights** quite easily by incorporating into domestic law the provisions of the ECHR, which the government had ratified in 1951. Yet despite advocacy by leading lawyers such as Lord Scarman and Lord Lestor, both Labour and Conservative governments resisted. Citizens were able to go to the European Court of Human Rights at Strasbourg on the basis of the Convention once they had exhausted domestic avenues. The outcomes were damning. The Court was to find British governments (both left and right) in violation of the Convention more often than any other signatory state (Klug et al. 1996: 538). Issues included closed shops, prisoners' rights, homosexual rights, immigration, telephone tapping and the operation of the Prevention of Terrorism Act. In addition, businesses have important rights under the Convention and a growing number of companies, shareholders and directors have successfully brought cases involving matters such as arbitration awards, restraints on advertising, trade licences, breach of contract, illegal share trading and competition law. However, the journey to Strasbourg was long and too costly for many. The incorporation of the ECHR directly into domestic law remained the reformers' goal; this was finally achieved in the Human Rights Act (1998), to take effect from January 2000. However, it was in the form of a British version.

Incorporation of the ECHR

Since access to the Convention was available at Strasbourg after the domestic courts had been exhausted, it could of course be said that the Act did not make any new rights available. However, it becomes much easier to claim them and at all levels of the judicial system. Much existing legislation, administrative practice and common law may also be challenged in British courts. The government asked Parliament to establish a Human Rights Committee to scrutinize bills and consider Acts referred to it by the courts. A minister introducing a bill will be required to produce a human rights statement showing whether it complies with the Convention and provisions in breach must be debated. Governments may not always welcome the challenges, which may come in many areas, including the following.

- *Life and personal liberty (Articles 2 & 5).* This opens up questions on police powers of arrest, the use of lethal force and detention at airports under the Prevention of Terrorism (Temporary Provisions) Act (1989). It also questions arbitrary use of stop-and-search powers under such legislation as the Police and Criminal Evidence Act (1984), Emergency Provisions Act (1991) and Criminal Justice and Public Order Act (1994).
- *Fair trial (Article 6).* The use of public interest immunity certificates (as in the Matrix Churchill case) would be outlawed.
- *Privacy (Article 8).* For the first time in UK law people will enjoy a right to privacy. Section 28 of the Local Government Act prohibiting the promotion of homosexuality in schools is a clear violation. However, this could also threaten the freedom of the press.
- *Freedom of expression (Article 10).* The Public Order Act (1986) could well fall foul of the Convention, as could outdated laws on indecency, criminal libel, blasphemy and sedition, which may unnecessarily restrict free speech.
- *Freedom of information (Article 10).* In a political culture renowned for secrecy various issues may emerge. One surprising possibility might be a challenge to the 30-year rule for non-disclosure of public records.
- *Freedom of assembly (Article 11).* This will become a positive right with widespread implications for police and local authority powers to ban marches and demonstrations under the Public Order Acts. It would also question the imposition of bail conditions to prevent people awaiting trial from attending meetings and demonstrations, and police powers to serve exclusion orders on those suspected of aggravated trespass.
- *Judicial review of executive power.* UK courts will adopt Convention standards when determining whether ministers and public bodies have exceeded their powers.

Factors affecting the impact of the ECHR Incorporating the ECHR may have brought Britain to a constitutional watershed. However, in a deferential political culture which has elevated strong government and public order over individual liberties and the rights of minorities (Weir and Boyle 1997: 129), the full impact remains to be seen. Critics could find reason for apprehension over the commitment of New Labour, with its strongly centralized government style and neoliberal agenda.

In government even 'old Labour' had been ambivalent. Although ratifying the ECHR in 1951 and granting citizens the right to petition Strasbourg, it did not incorporate the Convention and resisted calls for a domestic Bill of Rights.

Indeed, it could be argued that it was the influence of John Smith rather than Blair that set the 1998 reforms in train. New Labour's 'tough on crime' mantra saw it supporting many Conservative measures violating the ECHR and in 1996 it was even willing to support the Police Bill which, in allowing state bugging and burgling without prior judicial approval, actually reversed common-law principles respected since the eighteenth century. Moreover, New Labour's espousal of US 'communitarian' thinking emphasized duties of citizenship at the expense of rights and carried strongly authoritarian overtones (Klug 1997); hence Home Secretary Jack Straw's enthusiasm for curfews on the young, Education Secretary David Blunkett's homework rules and Blair's advice to employers during the 1998 World Cup to sack football hooligans.

Hence much debate remains and it centres on the executive–judicial balance. New Labour, buoyed by its massive majority in 1997 and with what critics called a 'control freak' mentality, did not appear keen to bow to a bewigged superior authority.

Towards a rights culture There is also the question of the cultural bedrock of the constitution. Attitude surveys penetrating beyond the drawing rooms of Hampstead reveal greater interest in social rights (education, health care) than civil and political rights. In one poll, fewer than one-third of respondents supported the principle of a defendant's right to silence (Weir and Boyle 1997: 32–3). Moreover, popular xenophobia may produce resistance to 'foreign' notions of rights. This may be stimulated by tabloid jingoism and a revolt against 'meddling judges'.

Reform organizations such as Charter 88 argue that a government wanting real reform must take positive action to promote a rights culture. They call for a Human Rights Commission to promote public understanding, provide advice to Parliament and public authorities and assist individuals. Without this there is a danger that the impact will be largely limited to arcane judicial debate and court cases. However, the government has shown no enthusiasm for such a Commission.

Hence, before the effect of incorporating the ECHR can be known, the dust must settle in that uncertain constitutional territory between what is written and what actually happens. Far from emancipating citizens it may prove an exercise in gesture politics in a political culture remaining set in its elitist past. For reformers only constitutional earth movements will produce the soil for a rights culture. At the heart of this is a written constitution.

A Written Constitution?

Despite the praises sung to the mysterious virtues of the British constitution, its unwritten manifestation is not universally acclaimed. Some argue that the twin guarantees of limited government and protection of individual rights would be far safer if placed beyond the hand of the government of the day through entrenchment. A written constitution would mean the end of parliamentary supremacy because certain laws would be so fundamental that they could no longer be changed by normal legislative means and parliaments would be bound by any constitutional amendments made under their predecessors. Moreover, new laws would be subject to judicial scrutiny to ensure their constitutionality. In addition, the executive could be made subject to effective checks by the House of Commons. It would even be possible to increase the Lords' power (with changed composition – see pp. 351–3) to provide further counterweight.

CHARTER 88

e have been brought up in Britain to believe that we are free: that our Parliament is the mother of democracy; that our liberty is the envy of the world; that our system of justice is always fair; that the guardians of our safety, the police and security services, are subject to democratic, legal control; that our civil service is impartial; that our cities and communities maintain a proud identity; that our press is brave and honest.

Today such beliefs are increasingly implausible. The gap between reality and the received ideas of Britain's "unwritten constitution" has widened to a degree that many find hard to endure. Yet this year we are invited to celebrate the third centenary of the "Glorious Revolution" of 1688, which established what was to become the United Kingdom's sovereign formula. In the name of freedom, our political, human and social rights are being curtailed while the powers of the executive have increased, are increasing and ought to be diminished.

A process is underway which endangers many of the freedoms we have had

The time has come to demand political, civil and human rights in the United Kingdom. The first step is to establish them in constitutional form, so that they are no longer subject to the arbitrary diktat of Westminster and Whitehall.

We call, therefore, for a new constitutional settlement which would:

Enshrine, by means of a Bill of Rights, such civil liberties as the right to peaceful assembly, to freedom of association, to freedom from discrimination, to freedom from detention without trial, to trial by jury, to privacy and to freedom of expression.

Subject executive powers and prerogatives, by whomsoever exercised, to the rule of law.

Establish freedom of information and open government.

Create a fair electoral system of proportional representation.

Reform the upper house to establish a democratic, non-hereditary second chamber.

Place the executive under the power of a democratically renewed parliament and all agencies of the state under the rule of law.

Ensure the independence of a reformed judiciary.

Provide legal remedies for all abuses of power by the state and the officials of central and local government.

Guarantee an equitable distribution of power between local, regional and national government.

Draw up a written constitution, anchored in the idea of universal citizenship, that incorporates these reforms.

Various other provisions could be made. The powers of local government could be fixed to reduce meddling by the centre; the cabinet system could be set out and the lengths of parliaments fixed; a wide-ranging Freedom of Information Act could guarantee people's right to know what their government is doing in their name; the exercise of executive powers of patronage could be limited so that non-elected 'placemen' could not assume positions of power; party financing could be subject to rules; a home-grown Bill of Rights could meet UK needs more fittingly than the incorporation of the ECHR. In addition to protecting citizens in general, such a Bill would, as in most western societies, confer rights upon trade unions rather than permit certain 'privileges' or immunities which governments have easily been able to remove.

Generally a written constitution would release British people from the grip of their monarchical history. No longer subjects claiming privileges from the powerful, they would become citizens legally entitled to demand rights.

The political debate: limited government or social rights?

Constitutional reform is never out of the realm of the political. In December 1988, Charter 88 was established to call for a written constitution and a range of constitutional reforms. Although bringing together figures from many points along the political spectrum, amongst the major parties only the Liberal Democrats give wholehearted support for a written constitution; both Labour and Conservatives have been more vociferous in opposition than in government. Moreover, the motives of left and right can be quite different.

The call from the right: limited government   The right is haunted by the spectre of 'big government', which is seen as directly opposed to the minimal government desired by the capitalist interests and inherent in the nineteenth-century liberal constitution. Extensions to the role of the state are portrayed as the first steps along the dark road to totalitarianism. The rights that the liberal constitution protects are civil and political.

During the 1960s and 1970s, as Labour began to look like a natural party of government, the right became preoccupied with the idea of a written constitution. The cause was given great prominence by the distinguished Conservative lawyer Lord Hailsham (later Lord Chancellor) in 1976, when he delivered the BBC Dimbleby Lecture in which he lamented that the constitution had become an 'elective dictatorship'. The advent of the Thatcher government in 1979 produced the opportunity to put ideas into practice and curb the dangerous threat. However, right-wing fears for the liberty of the 'man in the street' seemed to evaporate. The state was certainly rolled back in some respects, but the arm of the repressive state was extended to suppress any rising social unrest resulting from neoliberal economic policies (Ewing and Gearty 1990). Indeed, a free-market society requires a particularly strong state and this was maintained by the 1997 Labour government.

The call from the left: a positive state The interest in liberties is by no means a prerogative of the right. The restoration of ancient medieval rights has been an historic rallying cry for radicals challenging the established order. The left extends the concept of rights beyond the political and civil to include social rights (education, health, welfare). Here the call is for more, rather than less, state action. In addition, bodies such as Liberty, a pressure group established in 1934 (Peele 1986: 146), are concerned about excessive police powers to arrest or harass people on scant evidence of crime, the militaristic use of the police in industrial disputes, government secrecy and electronic state surveillance of political activists.

Hence, the case from the left for a written constitution is not to limit government but to use the state to create social rights while protecting individuals against its coercive power. In June 1994 Tony Blair told a *Guardian*/Fabian conference: 'A new settlement between citizen and society requires radical reform of our constitution'. Indeed, his 1997 government promptly incorporated the ECHR, adopted the EU Social Chapter, introduced a minimum wage, began the devolution process, established a commission on electoral reform and promised a Freedom of Information Act. However, there were limitations in these, the government pursuing a neoliberal agenda, fiscal austerity and a law-and-order policy no less repressive than that of the Conservatives. Despite some parliamentary reforms the central executive continued to become bloated with power.

Unwritten and Unknowable?

The fact that the constitution is unwritten means that it can never be entirely known and must for ever be subject to interpretation and dispute. In defence, it could be argued that any attempt to codify all the relevant material into a document of manageable size would rob it of its infinite subtlety. Moreover, the great virtue of flexibility would be sacrificed: no longer could changes take place imperceptibly to accommodate social developments. With the loss of parliamentary sovereignty would go the sovereignty of the people; non-elected organs of the state (Lords, monarchy, judiciary) would be able to thwart the wishes of an elected government. Judges and lawyers would become overpowerful, their fingers stained by the acrid alchemy of politics. This might bring problems for the left in that a socialist programme could be thwarted by right-wing judges. Moreover, throughout the world evidence suggests that written constitutions do not work with anything like the precision implied by the legalists; serious abuses of freedom take place in countries with model bills of rights. Finally, it can be argued that the entire exercise would be futile because the reality of politics is shaped by the economic power structure, which would be little affected by any redrawing of the constitutional architecture.

However, the vagueness of the unwritten constitution has meant that in reality the checks and balances adjudged necessary for democratic government have in large measure stemmed from the willingness of political elites to observe informal rules or conventions and practise self-restraint. This was a flimsy bulwark, and from the mid-1970s the two-party system began to disintegrate, giving the Conservatives a seemingly impregnable hold on office (see chapter 10), so that, under Margaret Thatcher, they appeared to ride rough-shod over conventional niceties such as parliamentary control, consultation with interest groups and local democracy (Wass 1986: xi). In 1997 the unbalanced pendulum swung to the other extreme and within a year the government of Tony Blair was generating much the same constitutional alarm over elective dictatorship.

The constitution is only part of the political landscape, the full extent of which we shall explore in the following chapters. This will sometimes take us into parts of the constitution that have passed from the efficient into the dignified realm and sometimes into areas of which the constitution remains formally ignorant. Underlying all is the distribution of power within society, which overrides all else and determines how the polity actually works. Yet the constitution remains central to political life, a crucial element in legitimation and an obscure object of desire for all actors, whether they be reformers or conservatives.

Key points

- The term constitution refers either to all that happens in the process of government, or the set of rules prescribing and limiting the powers of rulers and safeguarding the rights of citizens.
- The British constitution is not codified as a single document. Although unwritten, many documents are involved and much is written about it.
- The constitution is said to flow from five sources: the royal prerogative, statute, common law, convention and authoritative opinion, to which may now be added the EU.
- The role of conventions is far greater in the British constitution than in that of any other country.
- A constitution does not stand above the process of politics; the latter involves interpreting the constitution and seeking to change it.
- Reformers from right, left and centre call for a written constitution, for both political and rational reasons.
- In reality the British constitution can be seen as extremely fragile, requiring government willingness to impose self-restraint if it is to furnish the range of freedoms expected in a true democracy.
- The incorporation of the ECHR gives Britain an important element of a written constitution, a Bill of Rights.

Review your understanding of the following terms and concepts

authoritative opinion
Bill of Rights
civil rights
common law
constitution
constitutional
   amendment
constitutional
   convention
constitutional

government
dignified and efficient
   elements
ECHR
entrenchment
executive
judicial review
judiciary
legislature
limited government

natural law
organic system
parliamentary
   sovereignty
positive law
royal prerogative
rule of law
separation of powers
sovereignty
statute law

Assignment

Study the extract from the *Independent* on p. 80 and answer the following questions.

		Mark (%)
1	Why does Geoffrey Robertson QC regard the Human Rights Bill as the most important piece of legislation in his time?	5
2	Critically evaluate the view that there are situations where the right to privacy should be denied to politicians.	15
3	How far do you accept the distinction Geoffrey Robertson draws between 'toes sucked on a public beach' and 'toes sucked in a private bedroom'?	20
4	What does the extract tell us about the role of lawyers in protecting rights?	30
5	How far is the optimistic view about the way legal reforms may be secured justified?	30

Questions for discussion

1 Identify the sources of the British constitution and evaluate their relative importance.
2 Why does Britain have an unwritten constitution?
3 Discuss the meaning and value of constitutional government.
4 Outline the advantages of a written constitution.
5 'The British constitution is itself more dignified than real.' Discuss.
6 Discuss the principal ways in which you think the introduction of a written constitution would change British politics.
7 Contrast the arguments from the left and the right in British politics for a written constitution.
8 'So-called individual or human rights are no more and no less than political claims made by individuals on those in authority.' Discuss.

The pinstriped revolutionary

The wizard of Oz is a true 90s radical who wants the establishment to have a heart. **Banny Poostchi** reports

He is the man who cut his legal teeth on the infamous *Oz* trial, when, in the summer of 1971, three long haired participants of the permissive society appeared in the Old Bailey facing the threat of life imprisonment. The charge: conspiracy to corrupt public morals. There was the time when he protected *Gay News* from the wrath of Mary Whitehouse.

Today Robertson has not lost any of his zeal for reform. His new mission? Incorporating the European Convention on Human Rights into UK law.

"The Human Rights Bill is the most important piece of legislation in my time."

He believes that the Bill will provide an enormously valuable bedrock set of principles which go all the way back to the Sermon on the Mount and to the life and canons of Christ.

Of all the principles in the Human Rights Bill, it is perhaps the individual's right to privacy for which Robertson has campaigned most vociferously. But does "privacy" mean that the private life of politicians remains private? Was the exposure of Robin Cook's affair in the public interest? "Of course. It was a situation where the private life could not be disentangled from the public."

What if famous people – even Duchesses – were in a semi-private space such as the pool in Fergie's villa in the South of France?

"Hard cases. Toes sucked on a public beach falls on one side. Toes sucked in a private bedroom – a camera secretly put in the wall – invades privacy."

He is the first to concede that the practical application of a privacy law may prove to be extremely complicated: "This is one of the interesting things that you struggle with as a lawyer. You talk in general terms and then when you come to individual cases you see grey areas. Only when these hard cases are taken to trial and tested by the courts can a sensible line gradually emerge."

While legal reform is one way of civilising society, the winds of change can also blow from another quarter. Robertson credits the Sixties flower children, the members of the alternative society for changing the mind-set of the Old Establishment, making legal reforms possible.

Independent, 25 Feb. 1998

---

9   Assess the constitutional implications of Britain's membership of the EU.
10   'Incorporation of the ECHR does not solve Britain's problem of protecting individual rights.' Discuss.

Topic for debate

This house believes that the incorporation of the ECHR gives new and dangerous powers to the judiciary.

Further reading

Bagehot, W. (1963) *The English Constitution*.
First published in 1867, a classic and immensely readable account of politics during the fleeting period of genuine parliamentary government before the 1867 Reform Act.

Bogdanor, V. (1996) *Politics and the Constitution: Essays on British Government*.
Collection of essays aiming to show how the struggle over the constitution is essentially political.

Chrimes, S. B. (1967) *English Constitutional History*.
This slim volume is concise yet erudite on the subject.

Dicey, A. V. (1959) *An Introduction to the Study of the Law and the Constitution* (10th edn).
Classic account (first published in 1885) of the theory of liberal democracy, though author's heart is perhaps more with liberalism than democracy.

Evans, M. (1995) *Charter 88: A Successful Challenge to the British Tradition?*
Examines the rise of the 'New Constitutionalism'. Analyses how the movement influenced the Labour Party.

Ewing, K. D. and Gearty, C. A. (1990) *Freedom under Thatcher: Civil Liberties in Modern Britain*.
Essay by leading authorities on civil liberties. Argues that Thatcher government eroded freedoms by pushing back the frontiers of the common law, the traditional guardian of the people.

Hailsham, Lord (1978) *The Dilemma of Democracy*.
The views of Lord Hailsham, a prominent and rumbustious Conservative politician and lawyer (and Lord Chancellor), must be read with due caution. His 'dilemma' is perhaps felt more acutely when the electorate is misguided enough to elect a Labour government.

Harden, I. and Lewis, N. (1986) *The Noble Lie*.
Adopting a US-style approach (critical legal studies), explores gulf between orthodox constitutional theory (deriving largely from Dicey) and the reality of political power today.

Hennessy, P. (1995) *The Hidden Wiring: Unearthing the British Constitution*.
'Health check' on the British constitution assesses its response to changing circumstances.

Holme, R. and Elliot, M. (eds) (1988) *1688–1988: Time for a New Constitution*.
Critical and reformist essays marking tercentenary of the Glorious Revolution.

Scarman, Lord (1974) *English Law: The New Dimension*.
Arguments for constitutional reform by a distinguished lawyer.

For light relief

William Golding, *Lord of the Flies*.
Allegory exploring mayhem when constitutional rule breaks down and deep-seated savagery takes over.

George Orwell, *Animal Farm*.
Modern fable satirizing Russian revolution and, by extension, all revolutions. New tyranny replaces old.

On the net

http://www.charter88.org.uk
Charter 88's web site contains a wealth of information on constitutional reform and links to other relevant sites.

http://www.parliament.uk
Follow the links from Parliament's home page to locate debate on the Human Rights Act and even the Act itself.

Chapter Four

The Global Context: This Sceptred Isle

The purpose of this chapter is to stress that British politics cannot be seen as a self-contained process. The ship of state is tossed on a stormy sea of world affairs and the idea promoted in much political rhetoric and some traditional textbooks, that the government charts its own course with political compass and sextant, is illusory. Today a process of globalization binds countries together in regional groupings and on a worldwide basis in interdependent relationships which do much to erode traditional state boundaries. These are sometimes symbiotic and sometimes exploitative. The chapter contains three sections. The first examines the factors leading to Britain's particularly intimate relationship with the world economy, the second focuses on world politics and Britain's membership of international associations, and the third addresses one of the most compelling issues relating to Britain's place in the international order – its relative post-war decline.

Much traditional writing on British politics assumes a high degree of state control. If the economy does well it is to our credit and if it fails we look for culprits at home (from trade unions and scroungers to the civil service and management). Explanations looking inwards are termed **endogenous** and are essentially short-sighted. The tendency arises from various factors, including a degree of arrogance, a 'Rule Britannia' conviction that we control world events, the egotistical rhetoric of politicians and intellectual laziness. In reality, few countries have been more closely enmeshed in the economy and politics of the modern world than Britain and any study ignoring this is incomplete. When we do direct our attention at *external* forces we are adopting an **exogenous** perspective.

Many writers have dwelt with pride on the idea of Britain's insularity (physical and metaphorical) and a conviction, implicit or explicit, of political superiority. A much-vaunted factor is the country's geographical setting, shielding it from physical and cultural invasion or other forms of contamination. As it was for Shakespeare's John of Gaunt, it has been

> [a] fortress built by Nature for herself
> Against infection and the hand of war.
> (*Richard II*, Act 2, Scene 1)

The last invasion took place in 1066, and the defeat of the Spanish Armada in 1588 encapsulated in a legendary way this advantage. Yet despite its protective 'moat', Britain's world position has shaped its politics. The modern polity emerged as Britain stepped onto the world stage during the great age of discovery beginning in the fifteenth century and continued to play a leading role through the industrial revolution.

Britain in the Capitalist World Economy

Today much is written on the subject of **globalization,** a phenomenon defining the age in which we live. Essentially it is the intensification of worldwide social relations which link distant localities in such a way that local happenings are shaped by events occurring many miles away and vice versa (Giddens 1990: 64). At the heart of this are changes to the relationship between time and space. Giddens speaks of time–space distanciation to stress how physical space is overcome in modern interaction. Capitalist economies express space in terms of time; distance travelled to conduct business or transport commodities is defined in terms of journey time. From the horse to supersonic travel, from the penny post to email, technology compresses space so that it is possible to speak of a global village.

Part of this process has been the emergence and voracious growth of a capitalist **world economy.** The first steps were taken by the nation-states of Western Europe, which possessed unprecedented military and maritime might, a clear sense of statehood and an ideology to motivate their citizens (Modelski 1972). Nothing has preoccupied Britain's political elite or influenced political affairs as much as this. Indeed Britain played an early part in its formation and has continued as a key player.

The era of colonialism and mercantilism

The great 'age of discovery' opened up a New World and a new world economy developing from the mid-sixteenth century, traversing the Atlantic, to be shared by Portugal, Spain, Holland, France and Britain. This sea-borne trading network was based on **imperialism,** with the emphasis on protecting colonies and trading with them. The **colonial** period was characterized by competitive struggle for territory, raw materials and people. As a sea-going nation, possessing enough farmland to be self-sufficient and safe from land attack,

Britain was uniquely fitted to survive. While rivals warred on land, Britain could develop a strategy of oceanic domination of a world trade in commodities and slaves. In this the state willingly assumed a **mercantilist** role, assisting the commercial endeavours of its traders and settlers; trade wars were fought and Navigation Acts passed granting monopolies. Ultimately, with the gaining of India and Canada and the defeat of France in the Napoleonic wars, Britain emerged as the supreme world power. This dominance was to be increased through the events of the industrial revolution, although the role of the state would change.

> The British Empire is one of the greatest enslavers of human beings in the world.
>
> Paul Robeson (black American singer, victim of colour prejudice), quoted in *News Review* (3 Oct. 1946)

The era of free trade

The **industrial revolution** beginning in the eighteenth century was further good fortune for the English elite. The first country to industrialize, its domination could be increased through superior productivity, feeding on raw materials from the colonies and disgorging manufactured goods to the world. **Free trade**, rather than mercantilism, became the rallying cry of the new bourgeoisie. Following Adam Smith's principle of **comparative advantage** (that each country should specialize in what it was best at), Britain abandoned protection and threw open its doors to all-comers, urging others to do likewise. The country produced a third of the world's manufactured goods and half its iron, steel, coal and cotton goods.

British imperialism: Bombay police fire on rioters

Photo: Mary Evans Picture Library

The cost of this policy was to expose British agriculture (through the relaxing and ultimate repeal of the Corn Laws in 1846) to destructive competition, with an ensuing loss of national self-sufficiency. 'Nowhere did the transformation, the reduction of agriculture to a subordinate role, go further than it did in Britain' (Deane 1963: 188). The industrial bourgeoisie were fully prepared to risk the future of the whole of society in the creation of wealth on an unprecedented scale. The importance of the change cannot be underestimated; it was perhaps the most decisive event in modern British history (Gamble 1990: 52).

The state was brought under the control of the newly enriched bourgeoisie through far-reaching constitutional reforms, and policy acquired an international outlook extending beyond the confines of the empire. Britain pledged itself to a world policing role to secure the vital trade routes. The intention of the Admiralty, stated publicly in a speech introducing the Naval Defence Act of 1889, was to maintain the two-power standard, meaning that the fleet should be at least equal to the combined naval strength of any two rival countries. The pound (sterling), fixed to the gold standard, became the universal currency lubricating an international economic system with a financial, trading and communications network centred on London. Britain's economic empire was to extend even beyond the bounds of its political one. Yet this openness to the world was risky, if not reckless. Although powerful, the country became locked into a state of dependency for food, raw materials and markets. It contained the seeds of decline.

Signs of decline

After so exhilarating a start in the industrial race some initial relative decline was inevitable; markets once opened could be penetrated by rivals. However, Britain's eclipse by Germany and the USA was accomplished not by following the free-trade doctrines of Adam Smith, which were seen as a pseudo-philosophy designed to perpetuate British domination, but by erecting tariff barriers. In response, a tariff reform movement led by Joseph Chamberlain grew up, but in 1905 the election of a Liberal government committed to free trade effectively ended the debate. Britain continued as the world policeman, the international monetary system continued to centre on sterling and British capitalists continued to invest vast sums abroad. The burden was to take its toll; intense European competition culminating in two world wars left Britain gravely disabled and obliged to look to the USA to restore its world status through what was termed a 'special relationship' (pp. 98–101).

> Englishmen know instinctively that what the world needs most is whatever is best for Great Britain.
>
> Ogden Nash (1902–71, US poet); *England Expects*

Reconstructing world capitalism: the Bretton Woods Agreement

A defining moment in post-war reconstruction was the July 1944 conference at Bretton Woods, New Hampshire, where forty-four capitalist nations agreed a grand plan for rebuilding the world economy. A central figure was English economist John Maynard Keynes. The conference sought a new order for international capitalism based on cooperation, cohesion and free trade. However, central to the arrangement was the domination of one nation, which alone emerged from the war in a strengthened state. In this system of hegemonic stability a world capitalist economy would centre on the US dollar – to which other currencies would be tied (and through the dollar to gold) at fixed **exchange rates**. At the heart of the system was to be an International Monetary Fund (IMF), largely administered by the USA, and a World Bank to make loans to weak countries. To critics the arrangements represented 'the American conquest of most of the world' (Pilger 1998: 62). The regime was cemented by a General Agreement on Tariffs and Trade (GATT) drawn up in 1947. Initially intended to be temporary it become central to the system, negotiations to remove tariffs taking place in 'rounds'; the most recent (the eighth) was the Uruguay Round concluded in 1993. In 1995 a World Trade Organization (WTO) was established to enforce the revised GATT agreements.

The post-war boom

Britain played a central role in establishing this system of US hegemony, the outcome of which was an astonishing new era of plenty for the dominant capitalist states. An unprecedented growth of international trade produced a '**long boom**' continuing for some twenty-five years. 'Economic miracles' were wrought in West Germany, Japan and France. The boom was fired by a third 'technological revolution', advanced automation and electronics raising productivity to new pinnacles. In Britain, as in other western states, the boom period meant that political conflict could be replaced by consensus, the two major parties benignly sharing assumptions about the genius of the mixed economy, Keynesian economics and the welfare state (see pp. 275–80).

During this period of **advanced capitalism** new players began to make their presence felt, transforming international relations. These were not countries but private **multinational corporations,** many with their roots in Britain (only the USA producing more). British firms operating six or more foreign subsidiaries expanded from one-fifth (of all firms) in 1950 to one-half in 1970 (Gamble 1990: 110). This was a natural result of the historic outwards-looking orientation of British capital but was often at the expense of the domestic economy, which grew more slowly than those of rivals. Yet it was not to be a boom without end; it was sustained by features that could not be counted upon to last. From the mid-1970s there began what Eric Hobsbawm (1995: 403) has called the crisis decades, 'during which the world lost its bearings and slid into instability and crisis'.

The crisis decades

In the mid-1970s, ominous thunder clouds began to gather over the capitalist horizons as the annual growth in world trade fell from 8.5 to around 5 per cent. Industrial stagnation, high inflation and unemployment stood side by side. The reasons were tied to the very globalizing tendencies that had fuelled the boom. Unconstrained by territorial boundaries or loyalties, the willingness of the multinationals to move to more profitable climes increasingly restricted governments' abilities to regulate their national economies and apply Keynesian-style counter-cyclical policies. Moreover, the increasingly tight integration of the world economy meant that slumps were less likely to be confined to particular states; once a recession set in, all could crash together.

Of particular importance was a serious decline in the US economy. The financial burden of world leadership, the arms race and anti-communist militarism began to tell, the sordid entanglement in Vietnam being particularly devastating. West Germany and Japan had also caught up and no longer needed high levels of imports; indeed, they began to penetrate internal US markets. In 1971 the US balance of trade slid into deficit for the first time in the century. Western economies no longer needed dollars to buy US products and these stockpiled as 'Eurodollars', which banks became unwilling to hold, forcing the dollar's devaluation in 1971 and signalling the end of Bretton Woods stability.

The collapse saw governments vainly trying to sustain home demand by increasing money supply and allowing exchange rates to float downwards. However, this fuelled inflation. Further pressure came from the multinationals, which raised prices to maintain profits. On top of these problems were the oil crises following the Yom Kippur war of 1973. Nothing illustrated the reality of global interdependence more vividly as the quadrupling of oil prices by the Organisation of Petroleum Exporting Countries (OPEC) sent shock waves throughout the developed economies. In the UK, meanwhile, the 1973–4 miners' strike in support of a 47 per cent pay rise began with a new form of crippling mass picketing involving 'flying pickets' travelling to companies using or transporting coal. Attempts to conserve power supplies led to a three-day working week. A new Labour government could do little to improve matters and in 1975 turned humiliatingly to the IMF for a loan. The conditions imposed included renouncing Keynesianism in favour of monetarism (see p. 490).

In 1978 the IMF Articles of Agreement were revised to mark the formal end of the Bretton Woods Agreement and the new competitive climate prevented the re-emergence of a new internationally acceptable currency. Within the European Community (see p. 133) a regional solution had been sought, with agreement in 1971 to fix exchange rates and float together against the dollar. In the new conditions a more flexible European Monetary System (EMS) was introduced in 1979, though Britain typically remained aloof. With Keynesianism discredited and inflation undermining export potential and sucking in imports (a trend that was to continue throughout the 1980s and 1990s; see table 4.1), the Labour government looked exhausted and unable to control events. It was replaced by the Thatcher government, which embraced the new approach with enthusiasm.

Table 4.1 UK trade with the world (£ billion)

	1984	1986	1988	1990	1992	1994	1996
Exports	70.3	72.6	80.3	101.7	107.3	134.6	166.3
Imports	75.6	82.1	101.8	120.5	120.4	145.8	178.9

Source: Data from *United Kingdom Balance of Payments* (1997 edn).

Perpetual crisis

A second oil crisis in 1979, following the Iranian revolution, saw a further doubling of world oil prices, opening a new era for the world economy, one promising perpetual crisis. The forces of the right moved into the ascendant in all westernized economies. Unemployment rose, trade unions were weakened, tax systems became more regressive and welfare states were cut back (Armstrong et al. 1991: 310–11). Privatization and shedding of labour made economies more efficient. Even Sweden, the model social democracy, followed the neoliberal trajectory. Indeed, free-market gurus Friedrich von Hayek and Milton Friedman were honoured with the Nobel Prize for economics in 1974 and 1976 respectively. At home, the Thatcher government was the most zealous of all.

Among the developed states, Germany, Japan and the USA proved best fitted to survive, though the protectionist fight between them was to dominate the world economy, transforming the USA from the world's largest creditor nation to its largest net debtor (Cohen 1995: 521). After the expensive Gulf war, George Bush declared the US economy to be in 'free fall', the recession deeper than that of the 1980s. The only remaining political superpower lacked the resources and will to shoulder the burden of preserving the liberal order and began to look for others to share the costs. At the same time, the newly industrializing countries (NICs) of the East began aggressively entering the global arena, China and much of South-East and East Asia becoming the most dynamic economic region in the world, but adding to the potential for destabilization.

The markets of the weaker capitalist countries (particularly Britain's) were increasingly penetrated by imports of manufactured goods. In the peripheral zone, oil-rich countries sought to industrialize, leaving the others to form a *fourth world* of degrading levels of poverty and deprivation, further impoverished by the ending of Soviet and East European aid. In 1995, severely indebted low-income countries paid $1 billion more into the IMF than they received. Under pressure from non-governmental organizations (NGOs) and the United Nations (UN), the World Bank mellowed somewhat during the 1980s, showing more concern with world poverty and asking that expenditure cuts exclude education and health. At a joint World Bank–IMF meeting in September 1995, for the first time all creditors, commercial banks, multinational institutions and governments agreed to relieve the most heavily indebted poor countries. However, the IMF, the more powerful institution, remained less benign, setting strict monetary rules and worshipping at the altar of the bottom line; stringent conditions placed countries under the western yoke for decades to come (Brazier 1997: 5–7).

A new world order

Despite the problems within capitalism, the collapse of communism, also a consequence of globalization, fuelled right-wing triumphalism as the former Soviet-bloc states began to embrace free-market ideals with fervour. The term 'New World Order' was coined to denote 'capitalism's complete and definitive global sway' (Panitch and Miliband 1992: 1–3), while Francis Fukuyama (1992) argued that the 'end of history' had been reached; free-market liberalism had secured a final triumph. There were important implications for the neoliberal regimes. With no further need to prove capitalism's superiority, the spur driving governments to care for the disadvantaged was blunted. At the same time western socialist parties (although always distanced from those of Eastern Europe) were to have their claims of an alternative to capitalism seriously discredited. Clearly capitalism had not collapsed in the post-1970s period. However, for Hobsbawm (1995: 408) the central fact was that it had become uncontrollable.

This alarming conclusion was demonstrated to Britain in September 1992 when speculation against the pound destroyed the government's economic strategy and forced the country out of the EMS (see p. 133). It was illustrated on a larger scale in a burgeoning crisis originating in June 1997 with speculation against Thailand, one of the minnows amongst the emerging economies in the Asia–Pacific region. Within months the problem had reached Korea and Tokyo, from which it jumped continents to Eastern Europe and on to Latin America and, as oil prices plummeted, the Middle East. As share prices around the world nose-dived, governments found themselves fighting to maintain the value of currencies.

Russia, faced with the huge problems of replacing communism with a free-market economy, plunged into chaos as the rouble crashed and state employees remained unpaid. Clinging desperately to office, President Boris Yeltsin first sacked then reinstated prime minister Viktor Chernomyrdin, only to have him rejected in September 1998 by the lower house of parliament (the Duma), which blamed him for the troubles. The fears sent around the world were not primarily economic; none of the developed capitalist countries had established extensive trading links with Russia and its GDP stood at a mere 0.5 per cent of that of its western neighbour, Germany (*Global Economic and Strategy Weekly*, 26 Aug. 1998). However, the ailing bear remained a formidable nuclear power and any domestic turbulence, with communists confronting free-market reformers, promised horrifying repercussions. In September 1998 President Clinton journeyed to Russia, attempting to pour oil on troubled waters and press the case for continued capitalist 'modernization'. Furthermore, fears that Moscow would default on its debt rather than renegotiate its repayment programme opened the possibility of other troubled countries doing the same and undermining the western banking system. The USA and Western Europe stood precariously on the edge of the whirlpool of shattered confidence, with financial analysts contemplating the possibility of perhaps the most catastrophic capitalist meltdown in the post-war era.

> A soundly functioning American economy is so important to the world that what is good monetary policy for us is good monetary policy for the world.
>
> President of the New York Federal Reserve Bank, quoted in
> *Financial Times* (27 Aug. 1990)

Globalization: an end of sovereignty?

Globalization is no mere academic speculation, it is a constant feature of contemporary experience. The contents of our fridges and kitchen cupboards, the cars we drive, the television programmes and films we watch and the machines on which we play computer games – all provide daily reminders of the astonishing reach of economic production and exchange. The trend is not new, it has been present since the West European states began their colonizing activities in the fifteenth century. However, the exponential rate of technological development, a growing mobility of capital, and cheaper communications and transportation have taken the process to quite new levels (Strange 1992). A key measure is the scale of direct foreign investment made by capitalists in countries other than their own. This tripled during the 1980s to stand at an estimated minimum of US$1.5 trillion in 1990 (Magdoff 1992: 44).

The contemporary globalization process is driven not by states but by private companies of various kinds. Initially multinational in scope, today many are termed **transnational corporations** (TNCs), manifest in multiple locations around the world but owing allegiance to no particular country. With despotic power, they influence thousands of smaller companies which deal with them and, through their ability to pay high wages, they can even seduce trade unions. Enjoying direct political influence with key decision-makers in the capitals of the world, they can fund political parties and influence what people think through their dominance in the production of culture through media conglomerates. The TNCs are owned and controlled by an international capitalist elite class with ambitions beyond the boundaries of any state, acting to maintain the global economic environment outside the regulation of any state in their mission to maximize profits (Brett 1985: 80–102). Indeed, by the late 1990s only twenty-seven countries had turnovers greater than the combined sales of Shell and Exxon (Vidal 1997). A mere 500 corporations control some 70 per cent of all world trade (*Ecologist* 1992) with just ten controlling 'virtually every aspect of the worldwide food chain' (Vidal 1997).

So great is their power that they have transformed international relations. Although lacking social responsibility or democratic accountability, they are virtually units of governance, constituting half the world's hundred largest economies. Indeed, through massive global advertising their logos are more widely

The WTO and
MAI in fact
represent the
birth of a world
government by,
of and for
transnational
companies.

Phil McLeish, in
Red Pepper (April
1998)

recognized than most national flags. Governments must negotiate with them, court them and try to please them much as they would conduct diplomacy with other states. The goal of enticing them to locate is now as important as traditional foreign policy and factors such as union freedoms, wages legislation and welfare policies must often be sacrificed to this end.

The GATT logic moved to a new stage in Paris in February 1998 when representatives from the world's twenty-nine richest countries, the Organisation for Economic Cooperation and Development (OECD), attempted to finalize a little-publicized Multinational Agreement on Investment (MAI) which would give TNCs the power to sue national governments for loss of profits resulting from any policies discriminating against them. This would put at risk workplace and environmental legislation enacted by democratically elected governments, as well as UN treaties on climate change. Renato Ruggerio, Director General of the WTO, stated: 'We are writing the constitution of a single global economy' (Rowan 1998). In the event, growing opposition from pressure groups, the French government and the European Parliament led to the negotiations collapsing later in the year, though concerned interests knew they would have to remain vigilant. While French Prime Minister Lionel Jospin argued against allowing the TNCs 'to bite into the sphere of state sovereignty', the British trade minister reiterated his government's commitment to the worldwide liberalization of investment (*World Development Movement in Action*, Winter 1998).

Matching the global reach of the corporations are the financial and banking

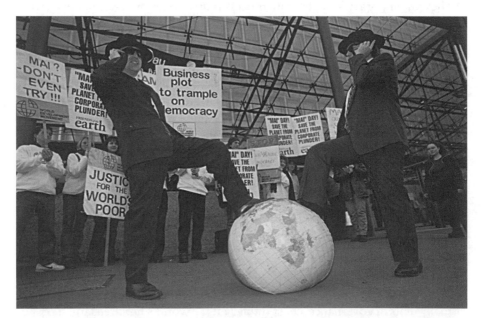

The World
Development
Movement protest
against the
Multilateral
Agreement on
Investment outside
the Department of
Trade and Industry

Photo: David Hoffman/WDM

New Labour, New Friends: traders in the Liffe short sterling futures pit react to Gordon Brown's first budget

Photo: Times Newspapers Ltd

enterprises which can monitor developments in Tokyo, London and New York through advanced computerized networks. In the City of London is the august Bank of England and the futuristic glass and metal stock exchange; currencies, stocks and shares, and 'futures' can speed around the globe at the touch of a button. A few streets away overlooking the Thames is the London International Financial Futures and Options Exchange (LIFFE), opened in 1982. Here the action can be manic as the 'open outcry traders', young men clad in psychedelic blazers (and professing 'balls of steel'), compete for huge bonuses in a frenzy of shouting and waving, gambling on what future prices and exchange rates around the world will be (Baird 1998).

Unsurprisingly, the GATT regime was to favour the interests of international capital. Although the legal and political sovereignty of member states were technically unimpaired, in effect they were seriously weakened. Resident representatives of the World Bank and IMF act rather like colonial governors of old, ordering governments to deflate, reduce taxes and cut public services in order to compete globally. This often means opening up a country to the predatory designs of the TNCs, which are willing to enter low-wage economies with passive workforces and often repressive and sexist regimes, such as South Korea and the Philippines. Dictatorships offer a stable environment for investment. Shell's search for profit led to environmental degradation in Nigeria and world opinion associated it with the execution in November 1995 of author Ken Saro-Wiwa and eight Ogoni environmental activists.

Uneven development Hence the close of the era of political empires was not to mark the end of subjugation or exploitation. Post-war liberal optimism that the Bretton Woods system would spread the fruits of material progress proved ill founded as the economic landscape showed uneven development which many regarded as a form of **neocolonialism**. This produced three readily recognizable zones: a core, a semi-periphery and a periphery (Wallerstein 1979).

> While the poor get poorer, the rich get richer. Here in Britain the richest *ten* people have more wealth than *15 entire countries* in Africa, with over *100 million people*.
>
> Barry Coates (Director, World Development Movement), letter to supporters (Dec. 1998)

- *The core zone* comprised European ex-colonial powers together with the USA, Canada, Germany and Japan, sometimes referred to as the Group of Seven (G7). Here, broadly based economies allowed generally high material standards of living (though not without class differences and inequality). From within these, the levers operating the world economy were controlled and the TNCs encircle the globe with voracious tentacles in the quest for profit.
- *The semi-peripheral zone* was formed by ex-colonial settlements (Latin America, the rest of the white Commonwealth and South Africa), where the development of a bourgeois ruling class through white settlement, some initial wealth and political and military strength facilitated capital accumulation and economic development. The oil-rich countries of the third world began to enter this zone with ambitious development programmes, as did the Asian 'Tiger' economies.
- *The peripheral zone* comprised the third-world countries, with their poorly developed, narrowly based economies, cheap labour, child labour, female exploitation, low levels of consumption and riven with disease, poverty and starvation. Economically dependent on the core states (as markets and the source of vital imports and loans), those at the periphery were rarely in any position to control the price of their exports and found it almost impossible to accumulate sufficient capital for self-sustaining growth. Thus, British teenagers wear trainers costing more than the weekly wage of the workers (including children) making them, whose sight is impaired by the chemicals used. The high research and technology costs meant that even indigenous extractive industries are controlled from outside. The position was worsened by the willingness of the banks in the core states to make huge loans to stave off world recession, thereby creating crippling debts for the poor economies, obliging them to aim for enormous trade surpluses.

Despite the post-1970s crises, economic growth in the core states continued, albeit at a slower pace, as did international trade in industrial products. Moreover, technological advances, in multifarious forms, made it possible for the affluent (G7) states, working closely with the TNCs, to maintain their lead; by

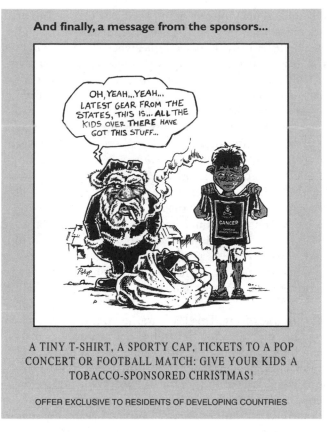

And finally, a message from the sponsors...

A TINY T-SHIRT, A SPORTY CAP, TICKETS TO A POP CONCERT OR FOOTBALL MATCH: GIVE YOUR KIDS A TOBACCO-SPONSORED CHRISTMAS!

OFFER EXCLUSIVE TO RESIDENTS OF DEVELOPING COUNTRIES

Reproduced by permission of the World Development Movement

the end of the millennium they were richer than in the early 1970s and the global economy even more dynamic.

The process also creates uneven distribution of wealth within the core states. An international division of labour drives down workers' wages, weakens trade unions and, by transferring production from old to new countries, leaves

---

- Young women making Barbie and Action Man dolls in Asia receive less per week than the price of one doll.
- Rio Tinto digs up sacred sites in Indonesia in search of gold, despite protests by the indigenous landowners.
- Nestlé harms the health of millions of third-world babies through advertising of its breastmilk substitutes.

World Development Movement (pressure group seeking 'Justice for the World's Poor'), campaign literature (1998) behind rust belts and unemployment in previously prosperous areas. Ironically it also creates pressure to raise salaries and perquisites at the higher managerial levels (Hoogvelt 1997: 146) as, for example, when executives in privatized water authorities in Britain demand parity with their US counterparts. In Western Europe, the 1980s saw increased income inequality, welfare state cutbacks, the abandonment of Keynesianism and a general march of right-wing forces serving the interests of the TNCs, the World Bank and the increasingly mobile finance capitalists. Competitive tax cuts and the power of financial markets appeared to have 'foreclosed the option of single-country "socialism"' (Dunleavy 1993: 144). In Britain, the Major government resisted both a minimum wage and the EU Social Chapter to improve working conditions, while the Labour Party, although establishing a minimum wage in 1998, set it at a lower level than that recommended by the unions.

Hence globalization casts doubt on the reality of national sovereignty and the nation-state as a viable unit of governance (Camilleri and Falk 1992; Horsman and Marshall 1994). For Hobsbawm (1995: 408) 'the crisis decades were the era when the national state lost its economic powers'. More than ever before, governments sat, Canute-like, at the mercy of its global tides.

Globalization in question? This leads to the important question of how politicians respond to globalization. It can be seen as a process rather than an end state and may be less advanced than is sometimes supposed (Hoogvelt 1997: 131). Hirst and Thompson argue that 'globalization, as conceived by the more extreme globalizers, is largely a myth' (1996: 176), noting that many international companies still trade with a restricted number of states and are more accurately described as 'multinational'. Despite threats, the majority maintain a home base and do not strike camp when they are unhappy with state policies. Footloose capital is more a feature of Anglo-American business culture; in Germany or Japan 'there would be a massive political price to pay were a major part of manufacturing to be shipped abroad' (Hirst and Thompson 1996: 198).

Why then does the thesis hold such sway? Part of the answer may lie in domestic politics. The right and the modernizing left both argue that governments can pursue only limited social programmes and cannot protect wage levels. Thus Labour came to power in 1997 promising not to raise income taxes and to keep within its neoliberal predecessor's spending plans. When faced with the closure of the Fujitsu plant in his Sedgefield constituency, Tony Blair was quick to blame global forces, offering no more than sympathy to those losing jobs. On the other hand, the left can also use globalization to stress the weakness of conventional politics against the might of modern capital. Writers doubting the extent of globalization are able to see a continuing role for modern governments in shaping social and economic conditions. However, despite continuing debate on its precise extent, none can deny the heavy constraints globalization places upon politicians.

A global community? Liberal optimism has foreseen globalization as leading to a world society but there is little evidence of this. On the contrary, governments can compete more fiercely in trying to attract capital. Greater mutual awareness between societies can create suspicion and tension as ideological differences emerge (Bull 1977: 208). Moreover, because economic globalization does not distribute its benefits evenly, billions of the world's population live at subsistence level or below, constituting valueless surplus labour with little to lose from violent rebellion. Finally, the globalization of the western rationalist ideological tradition can evoke violent responses within traditional conservative societies, prompting religious fundamentalism and belligerent nationalism.

This tension is fed by another feature of globalization – the international arms trade in which the machinery of torture, destruction and death is shipped from the developed world into the hands of dictators and megalomaniacs. Although New Labour's Foreign Secretary, Robin Cook, had stressed his 'ethical foreign policy', an Oxfam report (1998) revealed business to be very much as usual, with a secret trade worth some £660 million to over a hundred countries, many of them very poor. Oxfam refuted claims that few British companies were involved in the manufacture with a list of 120, all encouraged in their trade with taxpayers' money in the form of export credit guarantees.

Paradoxically, as the power of state governments weakens, so the need for political action to maintain stability increases. It can be argued that the only answer to this is a world polity with a world government (Gray 1998). This requires international coordination and cooperation to create structures of governance and regulation above the nation-state. Such consideration leads us to the political dimension of Britain's world setting.

The Political World Setting

Economic globalization contains enormous potential for political catastrophe. Hence the mixtures of the modern world are marked 'highly inflammable'. Although it is possible to speak of a world economy, there is nothing resembling a world polity; states have jealously sought to protect their **autonomy**. The idea of a world government which could eliminate war has been little more than a philosopher's pipe-dream. Yet ironically, while zealously seeking to retain the concept of national sovereignty, states have been forced to relinquish true independence before the iron laws of world capitalism. If governments cannot control events, who or what can?

The need for political organizations to match the global economic institutions is an accelerating trend. By the mid-1980s there were some 365 **intergovernmental organizations** as well as almost 5,000 international NGOs, the most rapid growth having taken place since the early 1970s (Held 1989: 196). World politics takes place in a network of arenas formed around issue areas, policy sectors and geographical regions, and involves states, intergovernmental associations, bureaucracies, TNCs and international voluntary organizations in a complex process of negotiation, bargaining, brinkmanship and sometimes violence. Full analysis of Britain's position in this is beyond the scope of this book. However, certain key aspects can be isolated for scrutiny, including the

> I am not an Athenian or a Greek, but a citizen of the world.
>
> Socrates (470–399 BC; Greek philosopher), in Plutarch, *Of Banishment*

special relationship with the USA, the extraordinary phenomenon of the **cold war** and its legacy and a range of **international associations** which contain something of the germ of an international polity.

Special relations

One alliance that was to prove central to Britain's relationship with the outside world was not based on treaties or pacts. Different from its relationships with any other country, that with America was termed, at least by the British, 'special'. To the political elite it was at least as important as the relationships with the Commonwealth and the rest of Western Europe. Although America had spurned British rule in 1776 and a festering legacy of hostility towards the British establishment lingered, there remained cultural links between the two states. The language that took root in that polyglot society was English and white Anglo-Saxon protestants (WASPS) formed an elite class. There was also hard necessity. Whether or not the Americans were special relations, they were certainly rich ones. Winston Churchill had worked adroitly to secure US aid and participation in the war and their support was just as necessary in the aftermath.

It was no small irony that in working to defeat one of its principal rivals Britain was obliged to succumb to the hegemony of the other. With its own economy shattered, restoring a free world economy appeared vital. British economic interests and a continued world role for its political class were seen to lie in two conditions: maintaining the international trading network upon which British capital had historically depended, and securing liberal ideology against communism. As the only state with the resources to restore political and economic order to the world, the USA was the key; Britain worked assiduously to construct the Bretton Woods Agreement.

Yet securing US aid was not easy. Initially Americans were loath to lend support to a continuing British empire, which could be seen as a serious trade threat. In addition, with Labour's 1945 election victory they had no desire to finance socialism. The Lend–Lease agreement whereby the Americans had assisted the war effort was abruptly halted and Britain, more like a defeated power than a victor, was obliged to petition cap in hand for further loans for food. These were obtained only on harsh conditions and an agreement not to impede the access of American goods to the imperial markets. However, Foreign Office courtship of the Americans continued ardently until, in a major diplomatic triumph, the British view of the Soviet threat finally prevailed (Gamble 1990: 108). From July 1948 funds to refurbish West European capitalism flowed through the generous Marshall Aid programme, marking 'the *peacetime* assumption of superpower responsibilities by the United States and their *de facto* relinquishment by Britain' (Hennessy 1992: 286).

Britain generally supported the USA in world arenas, accepting its economic and political leadership and supporting its foreign policy and military adventurism as well as shouldering the costly burden of rearming and main-

You see, Mr President, I have nothing to conceal from you.

Winston Churchill to Franklin Roosevelt, when found dictating a letter stark naked in his White House bedroom in 1941, quoted in *The Economist* (7 Feb. 1998)

Give us the tools and we will finish the job.

Winston Churchill, as US Lend–Lease legislation was going through Congress, broadcast (9 Feb. 1941) taining a military presence around the world. In return, the USA enabled Britain to retain some semblance of world leadership, not pressing it to dismantle the empire and preserving an international role for sterling. As the icing on this cake, a highly visible world presence was preserved, with ornate embassies and a glittering diplomatic service proclaiming its world status. The view of Britain's elite was that, while the USA was rich, the British had the know-how and experience for world leadership. To some this was self-delusion. When asked whether Whitehall had ever changed Washington's mind on any issues of substance, Robert Cecil, First Secretary at the British Embassy at Washington during the immediate post-war years, could recall no such occasion (Hennessy 1992: 365). The limits of the special relationship were cruelly exposed in a defining moment of the new era: the Suez crisis.

> Great Britain has lost an Empire and has not yet found a role.
>
> Dean Acheson (US Secretary of State), speech at Military Academy, West Point (5 Dec. 1962)

Waxing and waning during the post-war era (Louis and Bull 1986), the relationship seemed stronger when there was ideological convergence between leaders. Macmillan courted the Americans adroitly after Suez but the relationship weakened again under Wilson (with only half-hearted support for the Vietnam imbroglio). There was some revival under Thatcher, whose foreign policy appeared to amount to supporting whatever the USA felt inclined to do. This included accepting the US invasion of the Commonwealth country of Grenada in 1983 and active support for the air attack on Libya from Britain in 1986. In November 1988, when the USA refused a visa to allow Yasser Arafat of the Palestine Liberation Organisation to address the UN, Britain was the only country (apart from Israel) not to oppose the move. Thatcher and Reagan were simpatico, both personally and in terms of economic philosophy, but relations between Major and Clinton became strained (not least because the British government tried to assist Clinton's opponents in his first presidential campaign by unearthing information on his student days at Oxford).

Increased European integration and US economic crisis weakened the ration-

---

The Suez crisis

In 1954, Churchill reluctantly agreed to withdraw troops from the Canal Zone. This visible loss of prestige was deeply distressing to old-style patriots and a Suez Group formed amongst Conservative MPs, including ever-zealous guardian of the 'English way of life', Enoch Powell. The fears seemed justified when, in July 1956, Colonel Nasser of Egypt, generally suspected of anti-westernism, nationalized the Suez Canal Company. A diplomatic solution was ruled out when the USSR vetoed a UN resolution and an ill-fated military action ensued with the intention of toppling Nasser. Taken in covert collusion with the French and the Israelis, it was based on the bogus pretext of separating the warring factions in the Arab–Israeli conflict, the Israelis advancing upon the canal with RAF cover. The disclosure of the true facts produced world outrage, Prime Minister Eden's position became untenable and he soon resigned on the grounds of ill health. The greatest humiliation was the USA's chilly response. Not only did the 'special relation' openly disapprove, it refused to intervene to halt a run on sterling until an ignominious withdrawal was effected. The adventure appeared to the world as a fantastical journey through a constitutional time warp: the acutely divided British elite was confronted with the harsh reality of its diminished world authority.

ale for a special relationship and, by the late 1990s, the USA was showing more interest in an economically strong Germany. However, Labour's return to office in May 1997 was greeted warmly by Clinton, who, within a month, had crossed the Atlantic on his own initiative for a meeting with Tony Blair. He also played a major part in Blair's peace efforts in Northern Ireland. The similarities between the two were obvious. Both were young, personable and telegenic leaders succeeding older, greyer men. Both were centre-left politicians ending long periods of conservative ascendancy. Both had made themselves electable by stripping away unpopular leftish ideas and repackaging the neoliberal policies of their predecessors in 'third way' rhetoric. Moreover, the New Labour elite had benefited from many Kennedy scholarships and Harvard secondments (Pilger 1998: 95). Indeed, in its 1998 NEC constituency section ballot, the party offered members a prize draw in which the winner would receive a guided tour around the White House. (A tour of the Brussels complex was not on offer, even as second prize!)

The extent of Britain's commitment to the USA was emphasized by its support for the controversial August 1998 bombing of a pharmaceutical plant in Sudan. It was further underlined in December 1998 when, on the eve of Ramadan and despite the condemnation of the other three members of the UN Security Council and most other countries of the world, Clinton, with Blair's support, unleashed a huge missile attack on Iraq following a critical report from UN weapons inspector Richard Butler. In the eyes of many critics the action, in the midst of the impeachment process against Clinton over the Monica Lewinsky

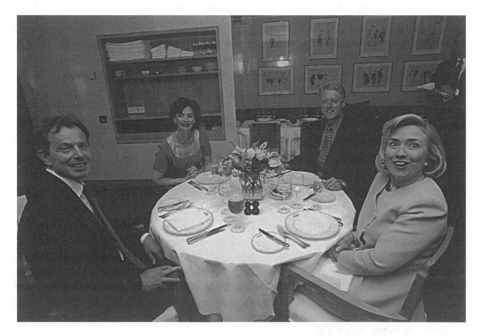

Dinner with friends: the Blairs and Clintons at a restaurant at Butler's Wharf on the Thames, May 1997

Photo: News Group Newspapers

sex-in-the-Oval-Office scandal, was a cynical diversionary tactic and Blair was accused of being the President's poodle.

The cold war

There was one special circumstance without which the special relationship would not have endured: the cold war (Hennessy 1992: 365). Although the term was coined in America and given wide currency by influential journalist Walter Lippmann, it grew from early British warnings of the Soviet threat. A divide based on psychology and ideology, it arose from a consuming and paranoid fear of communism (see p. 34). The essence of the bizarre phenomenon was that the capitalist and communist blocs both acted as if at war (manufacturing weapons, conducting espionage and practising economic and political subversion). Yet, although there were 'proxy wars' such as those in Korea and Vietnam, for much of the time the confrontation avoided actual combat. Nevertheless, its real effect in terms of human suffering among the poor nations of the world was incalculable.

For capitalist interests cold war had the advantage of keeping populations permanently hostile to left-wing policies and politicians (talk of improving working-class conditions could be portrayed as sedition and treachery). 'Reds under the beds' scares were fanned by the media and in the USA the hysteria reached epic proportions in the medieval-style witch-hunts of McCarthyism, when famous figures were pilloried for left-wing sympathies and sometimes hounded from the country. During the second world war, even the goal of defeating Germany had produced some establishment misgivings since it would leave communist Russia supreme in continental Europe – a prospect perhaps more disturbing than the ultra-right German empire which the fighting was all about in the first place.

An entrenched feature in the cold war logic was arms manufacture (Thompson 1980), a vastly profitable industry which could proceed apace without the inconvenience of damage to the economic infrastructure. Yet the arms race had deep implications for world politics, demanding resources more insistently than any real war and preventing their use elsewhere.

The chill of cold war was also felt in the supposedly **non-aligned world**, with the USA bolstering up a motley collection of oppressive anti-socialist regimes in accordance with an intellectually crude 'domino theory'. An anti-communist war was fought in Korea with active British support, the democratically elected socialist government of Chile was illegally brought down by an American-backed insurrection, and the fatal involvement in Vietnam dragged on inconclusively to ignominious withdrawal (mitigated only by a spate of *Rambo* movies in which American hawks could fantasize on how things might have been).

From the initial moves by Churchill, British governments of all shades maintained full commitment to the cold-war spirit. It was a Labour prime minister (Attlee) who agreed to an independent nuclear deterrent despite the US 'nuclear umbrella'. (With imagery appropriate enough for a 'cold' war, Bevan declared that, without the atom bomb, a Foreign Secretary would go 'naked' into the

From Stettin in the Baltic to Trieste in the Adriatic an **Iron Curtain** has descended upon the Continent.

Winston Churchill, public speech, Fulton, Missouri (March 1946)

Our scientific power has outrun our spiritual power. We have guided missiles and misguided men.

Martin Luther King (US civil rights campaigner; assassinated 1968), *Strength to Love* (1963)

world conference chambers.) The cold war enabled the Conservatives to maintain their historic claim to be the party of patriotism, making electoral support no less than a national duty. When Labour finally adopted an anti-nuclear stance, mass opinion had been so shaped as to render the policy electorally suicidal.

Military alliances   The cold war justified various military alliances into which Britain enthusiastically entered. The Western European Union (WEU), a joint defence association of Britain, France and the Benelux states, emerged from the Brussels Treaty of 1948, though before the ink was dry it was largely superseded. In 1949, after the Russian blockade of Berlin, Western Europe allied with the USA to form NATO (the North Atlantic Treaty Organization). In mirror image, the communist bloc allied under the banner of the Warsaw Pact. The USA was to be the biggest contributor to the NATO budget and, with its vast armoury, offered the protection of a 'nuclear umbrella'. However, its strategic dominance entailed a major loss of sovereignty by other members. Thatcher declared any idea of refusing to allow the US Libyan attack to be launched from British soil 'unthinkable'.

Militarism . . . is one of the chief bulwarks of capitalism, and the day that militarism is undermined, capitalism will fail.

Helen Keller (1880–1968; blind and deaf US writer and lecturer),
The Story of My Life (1947)

The thaw   Throughout the period the degree of frost in the cold war fluctuated, with attempts at *détente* interspersed with aggressive imperialism on both sides. However, although good for arms manufacturers and posturing statesmen, a heavy economic toll was felt by both blocs. The decline of the USA and Britain, relative to West Germany and Japan, underlined this. The cost was even greater in the USSR. In the 1980s, the unthinkable began to happen with the accession of Mikhail Gorbachev. His programme of domestic and constitutional reform (*perestroika* and *glasnost*) set off reverberations throughout the eastern bloc and a permanent thaw set in as one by one hard-line regimes in the Stalinist mould were popularly rejected. Meetings between Gorbachev and President Reagan even led to reductions in the nuclear arsenals.

On 9 November 1989, with profound symbolism, the Berlin Wall dividing the city between east and west began to crumble, physically dismantled by the ordinary people who had lived in its shadow. Richard Pearl, former US Assistant Defense Secretary, told Congress it was 'simply no longer possible to imagine a cohesive Warsaw Pact, led by Soviet troops, forcing its way through the centre of Europe' (*Observer*, 20 Jan. 1990) and President Bush began to contemplate major defence cuts. This unexpected end to the cold war appeared to mean victory for the West, though the communist regimes fell before economic forces not marching boots.

From cold war to hot peace

Yet there was a paradox: although few could mourn the end of the cold war, the new world order brought new uncertainties. Disillusion and discontent in the former communist countries saw them respond variously; in some, old leaders found themselves back in favour, while in others communism was replaced not by free-market liberalism but by rampant nationalism, territorial conflict, civil war, religious fundamentalism and the fascist-like horrors of ethnic cleansing. The Russian bear remained a mighty military force, while the dragon of China promised to become a new superpower. Bipolarity gave way to multipolarity, with potential flashpoints which could be ignited by fanatics and unbalanced dictators. Many leaders of developing states were keen to acquire weapons of war (usually supplied by western manufacturers, with Britain to the fore). Moreover, as we have already seen, world economic growth had done little to remove provocative disparities of wealth (figure 4.1).

A defining moment was reached in the Gulf war of 1991. As the first major conflict of the new era it justified the belief that 'mid-intensity conflicts' could flare up at any time, thereby providing a rationale for the continuance of strategic alliances and a large military establishment (Klare 1992). This helped end doubts over the future of NATO and a November 1991 summit agreed to erect a 'business as usual' sign. Some eastern bloc countries even expressed an inter-

Figure 4.1 The increasing gap between the richest and poorest nations in terms of share of global income.

Source: Data from Brazier (1997: 8).

est in joining although fear of antagonizing Russia made the West chary. Closer relations were forged after the failed Soviet coup of August 1991 through the establishment of a North Atlantic Cooperation Council (NACC), offering former Warsaw Pact members and the European states of the former Soviet Union non-military participation in NATO. In May 1997 NATO heads and Russia's Boris Yeltsin signed an historic treaty in Paris, forging closer relations. Two months later, at the Madrid summit, Poland, the Czech Republic and Hungary were invited to join the alliance. In addition, fears of instability in Eastern Europe saw a revival of the WEU, which had been relaunched in Rome in 1984 in response to the US 'Star Wars' programme, set up without European consultation. The Maastricht Treaty of November 1993 made it central to the common foreign and security policy pillar of the EU (see chapter 5).

Uniting the nations

In an atmosphere of military alliances and ideological arm-wrestling, forces for the creation of a world polity (to render war not a glorious expression of national sovereignty but a crime) could make little headway. However, such an idea has long tantalized philosophers and the United Nations Organization (UN) was intended as a step along this road. Its precursor was the League of Nations, established in response to the first world war through the 1919 Treaty of Versailles. Here was a forum where diplomats could upstage the generals. However, the enterprise collapsed into the tragedy of the second world war.

Establishing the UN Formally established in October 1945, the UN was an attempt to pick up the pieces. In 1941, Britain and the USA had signed an Atlantic Charter and the following year twenty-nine other countries signed an agreement (the Declaration of United Nations) to work together to defeat Germany, Japan and Italy. With more members it was agreed to set up a permanent organization for world peace at the Yalta conference in February 1945. Partly through decolonization, UN membership has continued to grow, reaching 185 by the mid-1990s. With headquarters in New York it comprises the following agencies.

- *The Security Council.* This consists of the five permanent founder members (Britain, France, the USA, Russia and China) and ten others serving two-year terms. The permanent members can veto decisions, which has often inhibited decisive action.
- *The General Assembly.* This main forum comprises delegations from all member states. Each has one vote regardless of size, giving a prominence to weak countries not always welcomed by the strong. It meets regularly and may be summoned for emergency meetings in crises (Suez, the Cuban Missile Crisis, the Gulf war, Bosnia, and so on).
- *The UN Secretariat.* The assembly is serviced by a 4,000-strong bureaucracy drawn from all states, headed by a Secretary General, whose role is

to alert the assembly to threats and conduct negotiations between dis-
putants.

- *The International Court of Justice.* International law disputes may come
  before this court, located at The Hague and presided over by judges (serving limited terms) from member countries.
- *Specialized organizations.* The UN fulfils a range of social and cultural
  functions through an extensive network of specialized and largely autonomous agencies such as UNICEF (children), WHO (Health) and
  UNESCO (education).

Yet the UN is not world government; it neither passes laws nor imposes taxes,
member states retain full sovereignty and those dissatisfied can withhold contributions (the USA has been a major offender). During the 1980s the organization came close to bankruptcy. In 1992 Secretary General Boutros Boutros-Ghali
talked of organizational paralysis as the arrears began to mount; by 1995, member states owed $2.6 billion.

Although it can send peacekeeping forces to trouble-spots, the UN's essential
purpose is dialogue, the value of its resolutions lying only in influencing opinion. Generally countries are loath to accept restrictions on their autonomy.
This was illustrated in the Falklands war, when gunboat diplomacy was made
to work again. In early 1982 Argentina invaded the Falklands (or Malvinas),
seeking to repossess the islands, one of the few tiny jewels remaining in the
British imperial crown. As Britain's task force set sail for the South Atlantic, the
UN Secretary General and the US Secretary of State shuttled to and fro between London and Buenos Aires, desperately searching for a civilized solution.
However, the controversial sinking of the Argentinian warship the *General
Belgrano* put paid to any hopes of a peaceful solution. If Argentina wanted a
war, this was their excuse. Troops landed on East Falklands and, after three
and a half weeks' fighting, secured an Argentinian surrender amidst orgasms of
jingoism in the English press. Thatcher claimed 'we have ceased to be a nation
in retreat' (Barnett 1982: 149–53) and a hitherto little-known rock in the South
Atlantic remained, in the face of UN resolutions, forever England. Afterwards,
the British government refused to open talks on the islands' future.

If powerful countries refuse to be bound, then the principle that 'might is
right' must continue to set the tone for international relations. The end of the
cold war did little to enhance UN effectiveness. Left as a monopolistic superpower, the USA used it as a cover for tough military action in the Gulf war.
Moreover, in a strange paradox, increased global interdependence has coincided with a revival of chauvinistic nationalism. Increasingly UN forces have
found themselves involved in dangerous intra-state, ethnic, tribal and religious
conflicts, as in Bosnia and Rwanda, but with confusion over their role leaving
them largely ineffective. With no resources of its own and no power of independent action, perhaps the best that could be said for the UN was that it had
managed to survive throughout the second half of the twentieth century
(Hobsbawm 1995: 430). As it celebrated its fiftieth anniversary, the organization was faced with the challenge of reforming its structure, culture and

decision-making processes to cope with the problems of the post-cold-war world (Rau 1996).

Retreating from empire: the British Commonwealth

> I have not become the King's First Minister in order to preside over the liquidation of the British Empire.
>
> Winston Churchill, speech at Lord Mayor's Banquet (10 Nov. 1942)

Disastrously weakened by the second world war, Britain still retained the high level of imperial responsibilities tolerated by the USA as a reward for the 'special relationship' commitments. Yet imperialism could not be sustained; imposing unrealistic burdens on the 'mother country', it was detested by most of the colonies. A process of retreat was painfully negotiated, virtually completed in 1967 when troops withdrew from east of Suez. The most spectacular of the remaining outposts, Hong Kong, was handed back to China in a sombre ceremony on 30 June 1997. The bitter pill of vanishing splendour was sugared by the evolution of the British Commonwealth, an echo of empire. Initially consisting of the 'white' dominions of Canada, Australia, South Africa and New Zealand, these were joined after 1945 by the 'New Commonwealth' countries in Asia, Africa and the West Indies.

Today the Commonwealth is a loose family of nations with no formal rules, treaty or constitution. Although many are republics, they unite under the Crown rather than the British government. Member states remain sovereign, with the right to leave (as did South Africa, Pakistan and the Republic of Ireland). Indeed, the collapse of many Westminster-style constitutions, bequeathed upon independence, demonstrated that the imposed rule had done little to inculcate English political culture.

However, the legacy of empire inhibits equality of partnership, the UK disdaining Commonwealth support when making important foreign policy decisions (Suez, the Falklands). Strong differences of opinion surfaced during the 1980s over sanctions against the white South African regime, British opposition threatening to shatter the association. Even the Queen was reported to be alarmed by Thatcher's hard line, which appeared contemptuous of the wishes of other members. The issue of Commonwealth relations is tied in with racism and suspicions of racism; suspicions heightened from 1962 with a series of Immigration Acts eroding rights of settlement in Britain (see chapter 7). A change in British attitudes was urged in a report by the House of Commons Foreign Affairs Committee (1996), which called for a more positive approach, emphasizing the advantages for business, particularly in the expanding markets of Asia and the Pacific. Yet although its role is debatable, the Commonwealth embraces a wider cultural, political and economic range than most other group-

It seems that the British Government sees black people as expendable.

Bishop Desmond Tutu (black South African civil rights campaigner), speech (1986) ings, giving it considerable potential as a force for cooperation and understanding (Ramphal 1997). With a membership of around fifty countries, four with advanced economies, economic development and the alleviation of poverty are among its central concerns. Its stand against apartheid finally bore fruit and, in April 1994, South Africa's first democratic elections made Nelson Mandela an heroic president. The following June, amidst celebration, South Africa rejoined the Commonwealth, giving it renewed impetus. The suspension of Nigeria in 1996 again showed the association as a potential force for democracy and human rights.

Britain's Global Future: Still a 'Sceptred Isle'?

Decline and fall

When Britain's position is considered in a world setting the most striking feature since the late nineteenth century is that, while remaining amongst the wealthy core, it has experienced a pattern of economic and political decline relative to comparable states. The post-war chapter has been the most puzzling, becoming from the 1960s a major preoccupation for political debate. The search for an explanation has produced theories and prescriptions from both left and right but, with blame attached variously to most political, social and economic institutions, they tend to look inward. The historical links with the world order are frequently ignored. Yet Britain's particular relationship with the world is itself a factor. The remarkable overseas expansion of the state and its location at the very epicentre of the developing world economy, while serving some of Britain's capitalist interests, were to bequeath attitudes that would become seeds of decline.

A free trade idée fixe The commitment to free trade meant that as world conditions changed during the twentieth century, Britain's markets were penetrated by rivals and many home industries destroyed. At the same time, its global orientation saw capital exploring the world for profitable investments, putting the number of British-based multinationals second only to that of the USA. For the domestic economy this meant persistent under-investment (generally about half that of rivals such as the USA, Japan and West Germany) and restricted productivity (Gamble 1990: 17). This was accelerated by the complete removal of exchange controls by the Conservative government in 1979.

Folie de grandeur Although imperialism and free trade made Britain open to the world, this was a world to be dominated and led rather than joined on equal terms. Consequently it has not been easy for the political class, and indeed ordinary citizens, to come to terms with decline. A rejection of the European embrace in the 1950s (see chapter 5) reflected the belief that the UK could retain great power status in its own right, with heavy overseas defence commitments. The connections cultivated were with the USA and the Commonwealth, from which could be heard the echoes of an imperial past. The strategy was to prove hugely expensive and the level of ambition was delusory. British world authority was put to an acid test in the Suez crisis, a defining moment of the new era.

Yet while imposing heavy burdens on the domestic economy, the apparent *folie de grandeur* can serve a hegemonic function at home, gilding the Establishment with status in the eyes of ordinary people. Thus, though an unmomentous cameo in world history, when the Falklands war allowed the decrepit lion again to yawn its arthritic jaws, the Conservative government, amidst triumphalism and jingoism, was able to surmount previous domestic unpopularity and win an early general election in 1983.

The essential message of this chapter is that the globalization process is a reality that no country can escape or master; territorial boundaries continue to dissolve before a battery of economic, social and technological forces (Held and McGrew 1993: 262). Despite xenophobic characteristics in its culture, the British polity has been conditioned by this world context to a greater extent than most. Another key development in the post-1970s era has been the formation of international regional trading blocs (dominated by the USA and the North American Free Trade Association, and by Japan within the Pacific Rim) which conduct the bulk of their trade internally, placing only small proportions of their GDPs in a truly global marketplace. Perhaps the most significant of these groupings is the European Union. There are strong arguments for seeing this as the key to Britain's future in the global world. It is the subject of the next chapter.

Key points

- British politics cannot be seen as an autonomous activity; today a process of globalization locks states into world economic and political systems which influence internal politics.
- The modern world economy can be conceptualized in terms of three zones: a highly developed and wealthy core, an underdeveloped and impoverished periphery, and a fluid middle section.
- The relationship between zones is seen by some as a form of neocolonialism based on money rather than guns. Others see it as a process of helping poor nations through trade.
- This world system consists not only of states, but of transnational corporations which span the globe, are more wealthy than some states, and can blackmail and destroy regimes. They are generally controlled from the core states.
- Britain, as the first country to industrialize, played a crucial role in developing the world economy, remaining a firm advocate of the concept of free trade.

- There is no such thing as a world polity; although states form associations they are generally loath to subsume their sovereignty under a supranational power.
- Underlying Britain's relative decline in the world has been an obsession with retaining a world leadership role.

Review your understanding of the following terms and concepts

advanced capitalism
autonomy
Bretton Woods system
cold war
colonialism
comparative advantage
détente
exchange rate
exogenous and
   endogenous
   explanations
free trade

imperialism
industrial revolution
intergovernmental
   associations
international
   associations
Iron Curtain
long boom
mercantilism
multinational
   corporations

neocolonialism
New World Order
non-aligned world
special relationship
transnational
   corporations
world policeman role

Assignment

Study the extract from the *Sunday Times* on p. 110 and answer the following questions.

		Mark (%)
1	Why are the basic materials produced in Europe and the stitching done in third-world countries?	20
2	What do you think are the implications for the conditions of British workers from the kind of situation described in the extract?	20
3	Consider whether the fact that Mohammed Shehzad gains satisfaction from his work suggests that talk of exploitation or slavery is alarmist?	30
4	Would you agree with Fawad Usman Khan that the situation can only be changed by action by the multinational companies? Can governments do nothing today?	30

Scandal of football's child slavery

Six-year-olds paid 10p an hour to sew balls that sell for £50

THOUSANDS of footballs used by Britain's highly paid soccer stars, including those for Saturday's FA Cup final at Wembley, are made in Third-World factories employing children as young as six.

The children, often engaged in a modern form of slave labour, spend long hours in workshops around Sialkot, a Punjabi town near the border with India. By a historical quirk, Sialkot is the source of most of the world's hand-stitched footballs, its produce snapped up by household names such as Adidas, Reebok and Mitre.

Many of the children are unable to attend school because their families need the

Caroline Lees, Sialkot and Simon Hinde

10p an hour they earn. The balls, which cost up to £50, feature in football games in which the stars are paid as much as £10,000 a week.

Typical of the illegal workers is Mohammed Shehzad, who spends nine hours daily crouched on the bare concrete floor of his fly-ridden workshop, stitching together panels of synthetic leather footballs. He takes pleasure, however, in knowing that his balls grace stadiums such as Wembley, and will watch Saturday's cup final on the village's ancient television set.

Fawad Usman Khan, a local human rights campaigner, said child labour was an indispensable part of the economy in Pakistan. "This will only change when a manufacturer tells a contractor he won't have children making his products. So far that hasn't happened."

Sub-contractors such as Khan are sent thousands of pieces of footballs to be stitched together each day. The basic materials are imported from Europe, factories cut them up, print on the logos and laminate them before sending them to the villages. One factory made more than 1m balls last year for Mitre, mostly exported to Europe and America.

© Times Newspapers Ltd (14 May 1995)

Questions for discussion

Because this chapter is concerned with the link between the international environment and internal politics, some of these questions may be easier to answer when further chapters have been studied.

1   Discuss the value of taking an exogenous perspective in the study of British politics.
2   What is meant by the term 'globalization'? Examine the proposition that its extent can be overstated.

3 'Britain has been open to the world, yet at the same time politically insular.' Discuss.
4 Explain the meaning of the term 'neocolonialism' in the context of the modern world economy.
5 How far is it true today that Britain has a 'special relationship' with the USA?
6 What were the implications of the mid-1970s oil crisis for internal British politics?
7 'Britain's relative post-war decline was largely attributable to its leaders' delusions of grandeur.' Discuss.
8 What have been the implications of the end of the cold war for British politics?
9 'The unwillingness of the state to sacrifice national sovereignty means that the United Nations is doomed to fail.' Discuss.
10 'The Commonwealth is a mere shadow of the British Empire with no political or economic substance.' Discuss.

Topic for debate

This house believes that the idea of national autonomy in world politics is a complete illusion.

Further reading

Callaghan, J. (1997) *Great Power Complex*.
Ideas of supremacy within Britain's elites led to costly attempts to maintain a world role in the post-war era.

Camilleri, J. A. and Falk, J. (1992) *The End of Sovereignty?*
Examines the theory and practice of state sovereignty against the backdrop of rapid economic, political and technological changes in the modern world.

Chomsky, N. (1997) *World Orders, Old and New*.
Devastating critique of the 'new world order', as ingenious 'historical engineering' whereby old pretexts for cold war have been replaced by new.

Deane, P. (1963) *The First Industrial Revolution*.
Detailed account of the industrial revolution in Britain. Critical of the minimal role played by the government, which is blamed for the later eclipse by rivals.

George, S. (1991) *The Debt Boomerang*.
Critique of World Bank and IMF policies which accelerate deforestation, mass migration, the drugs trade, third-world debt and global instability.

Gray, J. (1998) *False Dawn: The Utopia of the Global Free Market*.
Critique of unregulated global capitalism by leading thinker who discarded earlier free-market advocacy.

Held, D. et al. (1999) *Global Transformations*.
Throws new light on the complex processes that are reshaping the contemporary world. Presented in a clear and accessible way.

Hennessy, P. (1992) *Never Again, Britain 1945–1951*.
Rich account of British politics in a crucial stage of reappraising its world position.

Hirst, P. and Thompson, G. (1996) *Globalization in Question*.
Argues against the more extreme versions of the globalization thesis.

Hobsbawm, E. (1995) *Age of Extremes*.
Marxist perspective on the evolving world economy.

Wallerstein, I. (1979) *The Capitalist World Economy*.
Outlines the zones of the capitalist world economy.

For light relief

Tom Clancy, *Debt of Honour*.
Thriller set within the international economy. Political intrigue and military threat in the context of trade conflict between the USA and Japan.

Ben Elton, *Stark*.
Surreal novel about global capitalist power.

Arthur Miller, *The Crucible*.
A modern classic play about the hysteria surrounding a witch hunt, satirizing McCarthyism.

A. Sampson, *The Seven Sisters*.
Penetrating account of the oil crisis.

On the net

http://www.fco.gov.uk
http://www.dfid.gov.uk
The Foreign Office and the Department for International Development sites include a wide range of information on foreign policy and current international issues, together with links to related organizations.

http://www.oneworld.org.ni
The New Internationalist site deals with issues of world poverty and inequality, and the relationship between the rich and poor nations. It also includes a comprehensive guide to relevant organizations and resources.

http://www.oneworld.org/wdm
The World Development Movement is just one of the many campaigning organizations concerned with justice for the world's poor.

http://www.un.org
For a truly international flavour, try the United Nations site.

Chapter Five

Britain in Western Europe: Awkward Partners?

This chapter considers an aspect of Britain's international setting that is assuming increasing importance and has deepening implications for domestic politics. The first section examines the origins of the European Union and the protracted process that finally brought Britain into what was then the European Community. Next we chart developments through the Single European Act and the Maastricht and Amsterdam treaties to the present. A third section details the anatomy of the EU, explaining the nature and role of the institutions, their internal workings, the relationships between them in the policy-making process and the debates associated with their powers. After this we identify some key domestic debates over British membership and conclude with a consideration of the future.

Despite the empire, the special relationship with the USA and a long history of European rivalry and warfare, Britain remains an offshore island of Western Europe, sharing much of its history and culture. The geographical logic has exerted an inexorable pressure towards integration, which became more compelling during the post-war era. The 1948 Brussels Treaty aimed to promote collective defence and in 1949 a Council of Europe was established to facilitate cooperation, producing the *European Convention on Human Rights* (see p. 72). However, of all Britain's relationships none has generated more internal political heat than that with what is now termed the European Union (EU).

It will be seen throughout this book that membership of the EU sends ripples to all corners of the political system. No other association to which Britain belongs promised to penetrate so deeply into the state and the lives of its citizens. While other associations are intergovernmental, the EU is **supragovernmental**: its legislation distinct from, and constitutionally superior to, that of member states. This has led to profound concern over a feared loss of British sovereignty, dividing the political Establishment and continuing to colour debate on domestic issues.

We are part of the community of Europe and we must do our duty as such.

Lord Salisbury (1830–1903; Conservative leader), speech (11 April 1888)

The Entry Process

The UK has long performed a kind of stately square dance with Europe; advancing, pausing before the promised embrace, only to turn aside to another partner, the USA or the Commonwealth.

The origins of the integrationist movement lie in the need to repair the devastation wrought by the second world war. Yet there was a deeper purpose: to prevent further war in Western Europe. Hence, although the early moves were ostensibly concerned with economic integration, the real agenda was political. During the second world war Winston Churchill had enthused over the idea of a United States of Europe, envisaging the Great Powers accepting government through a joint council backed by a court and an army. However, the moves to establish a Council of Europe revealed a fundamental difference between Britain and its continental neighbours. Again, when in June 1948 sixteen West European countries established the Organisation for European Economic Cooperation (OEEC) to coordinate post-war recovery and administer the US aid programme, hopes that it might develop into a permanent supranational institution were dashed by British and Scandinavian opposition. Yet a **federalist** movement gathered pace under the inspiration of French economist and international administrator Jean Monnet. Even as war raged, he was warning that a post-war reconstruction reflecting nationalistic pride and protectionism would never guarantee peace.

The first major event came in 1951 with the establishment of the European Coal and Steel Community (ECSC). Monnet's reasoning was that if key areas of production were integrated war would be impossible. Yet as Italy, France, West Germany and the Benelux countries joined the dance, the UK again chose to remain a wallflower. Wishing to drive things further, Monnet resigned the ECSC presidency in November 1954 to help found an Action Committee for a United States of Europe, which led to the establishment of a European Atomic Energy Community (Euratom) and the European Economic Community (EEC).

Based on the ECSC model, the EEC was headed by a Council of Ministers in which decisions were based on the votes of ministerial leaders from the member states. It was served by a European Commission, a bureaucracy containing civil servants and headed by commissioners appointed by state governments. In addition there was an assembly with members nominated by governments from national parliaments, leaving each with two jobs (dual mandate). The nature and powers of these institutions and the relationships between them were to generate considerable tension and influence their evolution.

However, there was to be no British signature on the 1957 Treaty of Rome establishing the EEC. This decision to stay out was momentous. Why did a state that had captained a huge empire, pioneered the development of the world economy, been a devoted worshipper at the altar of free trade, taken a prominent role within NATO, with a seat on the UN Security Council and a credible claim to have 'won the war' relinquish all claim to a leadership role in this major arena? The reasons lie in its past success. Despite the ravages of war Britain believed in its world leadership destiny. The political class looked beyond Europe for status on the world stage: to the special relationship with US brawn and to the Commonwealth, with its echoes of empire. Britain flexed its diplomatic biceps by becoming a nuclear power.

In 1959, Britain, with Norway, Denmark, Sweden, Switzerland, Austria and Portugal, formed an alternative grouping – the European Free Trade Association (EFTA), a trading bloc without political overtones. However, this was no rival to the EEC; Britain's relative economic decline during the long boom, and the particular success of West Germany and France, suggested that the decision had been misguided. The cold US response to the Suez crisis revealed that the 'special relationship' did not give Britain political omnipotence and in 1961 Prime Minister Harold Macmillan finally announced that the UK would apply for EC membership.

Although the USA welcomed the decision, Macmillan moved with characteristic languor. His vision was of economic union, with little place for the political dimension cemented into the foundations of the Treaty. Moreover, there was opposition within the EEC, French President General de Gaulle, suspicious that Britain would prove a Trojan horse for US influence, vetoing the application. He did the same with a second overture from the Labour government and only after his resignation in 1969 did the UK receive a sympathetic hearing. Hence, in 1973, Edward Heath, clearer in his European intentions than his predecessors, took the historic step. Yet British scepticism died hard. Labour had opposed the entry terms and, returning to office in 1974, held a promised referendum on continued membership with renegotiated terms. A 'Yes' vote duly came, with a 65 per cent turnout and a two-thirds majority, on 5 June 1975. However, the debate was by no means over. British statesmen had studiously avoided an explicit statement on the loss of national sovereignty (Young 1998) and the gradual realization of this was to fuel the efforts of the **Eurosceptics** and prevent a whole-hearted commitment to the European project.

The Integration Process

The career of the Community has been fitful, with periods of stagnation (*immobilisme*) and dynamism. Although many aspects of the Rome Treaty remained paper promises, the initial decade was dynamic. It was, however, followed by four years of stagnation, beginning with de Gaulle's first veto of UK membership. His retirement permitted further progress; the goal of advancing political union was affirmed at the 1969 Hague Summit and plans were made to coordinate foreign policy. In 1970 the Werner Plan argued for the harmonization of economic, fiscal and budgetary policy and 1979 saw the launch of the European Monetary System (EMS) and democratic elections for the European Parliament.

However, 1979 also heralded a further phase of tension when a new head of government, as nationalistic as de Gaulle, entered the stage and the UK was to underline its role as the 'awkward partner' (George 1990). Britain did not enter the EMS and, echoing her 'No such thing as society' sentiment on the domestic front, Margaret Thatcher was to declare:

> There is no such thing as a separate community interest; the community interest is compounded of the national interests of the ten member states. (Quoted in Urwin 1989: 369)

She began with an acrimonious campaign to reduce the size of the UK contribution to the Community budget. The goal was not unreasonable; Labour also favoured negotiations. However, the tactics entailed denigrating the Common Agricultural Policy (CAP), regarded by the six original members as their greatest achievement, and Thatcher's style of diplomacy did little to enhance the UK's Euro-credentials.

The Single European Act

In 1986 Portugal and Spain joined the Community, preparations for this reinvigorating the integrationist spirit. In June 1985 the European Commission, under the presidency of avowed integrationist Jacques Delors, produced a white paper, *Completing the Internal Market*. The following year saw the Single European Act, with its commitment to cooperation in foreign policy, strengthened social cohesion mechanisms and a programme for a genuine internal market, free of persisting non-tariff trade barriers, by 1992. The target year became a symbol of progress. Although it had signed the treaty, the UK government became alarmed at the idea of a social dimension concerned with workers' rights, social dialogue, collective bargaining and worker participation, and Thatcher was to pour a douche of cold water on the idea in a key speech at Bruges. Yet she did little to dampen the enthusiasm of other member states for a quickened pace of integration; an Intergovernmental Conference in December 1990 on Economic and Monetary and Political Union at Rome foreshadowed a major advance.

A centralised European government would be a nightmare. We have not rolled back the frontiers of the state at home only to see them reimposed at a European level.

Margaret Thatcher, speech in Bruges (Sept. 1988)

The Maastricht Treaty

The previously little-known Dutch town of Maastricht achieved celebrity in February 1992 as the site for the signing of the Treaty on European Union. Its 61,351 words went further than any other Community agreement in promoting integration. The event assumed additional significance because of its momentous historical conjuncture, including the end of the cold war, German reunification and the collapse of the Soviet empire. The term 'Union' signified that the EC became part of a wider framework, which was to include a foreign and security policy and justice and home affairs. (In discussions the UK govern-

EUROPEAN UNION		
EUROPEAN COMMUNITY	**COMMON FOREIGN AND SECURITY POLICY**	**HOME AFFAIRS AND JUSTICE**
– **Treaty of Rome revised by the Single European Act** – **Democratization of the institutions** – **Citizenship** – **New responsibilities** – **Increased responsibilities** – **Economic and monetary union:** • single currency • European Central Bank • single monetary policy • coordination of economic policies	– **Common foreign policy** • systematic cooperation • common positions and joint action – **Common defence policy based on the Western European Union (WEU)**	– **Closer cooperation** • asylum policy • rules on crossing Member State's external borders • immigration policy • combating drug addiction • combating international fraud • customs, police and judicial cooperation

Figure 5.1
The three pillars of the European Union.

Source: European Parliament.

ment initially chose ostentatiously to eschew the term Union.) Yet it did not satisfy all. For true federalists the image would have been of a tree with three branches extending from a common trunk. What emerged was a temple built upon three pillars, combined but essentially separate (figure 5.1).

What's in a name?

Like the association itself the name has evolved. Initially the European Economic Community (often the 'Common Market'), the Single European Act rebaptized it the European Community, signifying concerns wider than trade. After the Maastricht Treaty the term 'European Union' gained wide currency and, although not strictly correct, is widely used in place of EC.

In the common foreign and defence policy the existing joint defence association, the Western European Union (WEU), was to become central, with the international situation monitored by a Political Committee. The justice and home affairs pillar would see cooperation in various areas previously left within national competence. Significantly, the second and third pillars were to remain outside the competence of the EC legislative and judicial institutions; they were based upon cooperation rather than supragovernmentalism. This limitation was one of the proclaimed successes of the UK government in the negotiations. Amongst the treaty's most important features were the following.

- *EC citizenship.* Of both symbolic and practical significance, the concept of EC citizenship had received little publicity. It allowed all nationals certain rights: to reside and move freely throughout the Community, and vote and stand in municipal and European Parliament elections.
- *Policy competence.* The policy remit was extended to cover aspects of education, culture, public health, industry and consumer protection.
- *The institutions.* Decision-making procedures were made more supra-national and the powers of the Parliament and the Court increased (see below).
- *Subsidiarity.* An inelegant neologism became much used and abused in the debate. Essentially it established a principle of devolution: EU insti-tutions should act only if the objectives could not be better met at a lower level. For the UK government **subsidiarity** meant leaving power at Westminster, yet the term could also mean devolving power to regional and local governments, an interpretation largely at variance with trends in Britain since 1979.
- *Social policy.* A set of revised objectives to promote employment and improve working conditions became known as the Social Chapter. It was opposed by the UK, which was allowed by the other members effec-tively to opt out (see p. 135).
- *Economic integration.* The treaty placed considerable emphasis on the open market economy, the convergence of economic indicators and mon-etary union, including the establishment of a single currency (from which the UK, along with the Danes, also negotiated an opt-out; see p. 134). Economic policy would be determined by qualified majority voting so that no single country could veto developments.

Once signed, the treaty required ratifying by national assemblies and, in some cases, the courts. The process was not entirely smooth. The Danes made them-selves unexpected heroes of British Eurosceptics when they narrowly voted 'No', though the decision was reversed in a second referendum in May 1993 after concessions were gained. Subsequently referendums in Ireland and France were supportive, though to the embarrassment of President Mitterrand the French *'Oui'* was equivocal. Despite urging from Baroness Thatcher and others, John Major resisted putting the question in his own country and there were stormy scenes in the Commons during the ratification process. Thatcher was to tell the House of Lords on 8 June 1993 that *she* would not have signed the treaty, and the behav-iour of his Eurosceptics forced Major to announce a confidence motion for 23 July 1993. The gamble paid off with a majority of 40. The UK finally ratified the treaty in August 1993 but Major's problems were not over (see chapter 10).

'Son of Maastricht'   The next major advance also took place in Holland. Some-times billed as 'son of Maastricht', the 1997 Amsterdam Treaty proved a dis-appointingly puny child. It was preceded by an Intergovernmental Conference starting in 1996 but work here was held back by the British Conservative government and made little headway until its fall barely six weeks before the

conference (Duff 1997: xxxiii). The original ambition had been to revise the Maastricht Treaty in line with world developments, including streamlining the institutions to accommodate the growing queue of applicants for EU membership. However, with national interest prevailing over grand vision, the result was a 150-page reflection of defensive pragmatism. For many the overriding priority was to avoid shaking monetary union, the project at the heart of the push for political union. Reforms to voting procedures and the powers of the European Parliament were relatively modest.

An Anatomy of the EU

The institutional architecture of the EU (figure 5.2) is more than a theme park of modernistic buildings and offices in Brussels, Strasbourg and Luxembourg; it is the physical embodiment of the values of supranationalism. Five key institutions dominate the landscape, their powers and relationships providing the mainspring of the system.

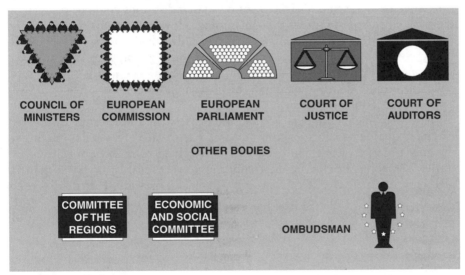

| COUNCIL OF MINISTERS | EUROPEAN COMMISSION | EUROPEAN PARLIAMENT | COURT OF JUSTICE | COURT OF AUDITORS |

OTHER BODIES

COMMITTEE OF THE REGIONS   ECONOMIC AND SOCIAL COMMITTEE   OMBUDSMAN

Figure 5.2 Institutions of the European Union.

Source: European Parliament.

The Council of Ministers

Meeting in Brussels and consisting of national ministers, the Council was created as the political head of the Union; from here come the decisions that increasingly shape the lives of people and organizations in member states. Although a powerful law-making body, Council meetings are shrouded in secrecy. Decisions emerge as:

- *regulations* – having immediate force of law;
- *directives* – binding, but in practice leaving member states with leeway in implementation;
- *recommendations and resolutions* – not compelling.

The Council is led by the country holding the EU presidency, held for six-monthly terms (semesters) in rotation. With extensive coordination responsibilities, the office can be pivotal and states usually try to make their mark during their stewardship. The composition of the Council changes with the policy under consideration. The General Council comprises foreign ministers but a range of other 'councils' bring together ministers for particular policy areas: trade, finance, agriculture and so on. The Council is served by a bureaucracy of some 2,000 headed by a Secretary General. It is also aided by a Committee of Permanent Representatives (COREPER), comprising national ambassadors and their deputies. The system is held together by a dense web of official committees, subcommittees and working parties, some permanent and some ad hoc.

Despite the integrationist purpose of the EU, the Council tends to be a forum where ministers fight their corners. To mitigate this, the Rome Treaty made provision for a system of weighted voting so that decisions could be reached on the basis of a majority rather than unanimity. However, strains resulted in the French boycotting the Community and to resolve this deadlock the 'Luxembourg compromise' was reached in 1966, permitting a state to veto any proposal judged to threaten its vital national interest. Since it was for the state concerned to decide what was vital, the provision, though not often used, was a severe restriction.

Hence the Single European Act and the Maastricht and Amsterdam treaties extended **qualified majority voting** (QMV), particularly over issues relating to the single market. Each minister's vote is weighted to reflect population size (table 5.1), acceptance of a policy requiring 62 votes cast by no fewer than 10 members. Alternatively, 26 votes against will block a measure. The voting process is characterized by complex bargaining with national interests to the fore. Moreover, unanimity is still required in a significant number of areas and on all issues it is generally considered desirable.

Table 5.1 Weighted voting

Votes	Countries
10	France, Germany, Italy, UK
8	Spain
5	Belgium, Greece, Portugal, Netherlands
4	Austria, Sweden
3	Denmark, Finland, Ireland
2	Luxembourg

The Leopold Complex at Brussels

Photo: Airprint

The European Council

In a major development illustrating the evolving nature of the EU, heads of state and foreign ministers have, from the early 1970s, come to play a dominant role through regular 'summit meetings'. Not a creation of the Rome Treaty, the European Council was formalized at the Paris summit of December 1974 and recognized in both the Single European Act and the Maastricht Treaty. It is here that major Community issues are thrashed out; the 1969 Hague summit gave the Community its 'own resources', the 1985 Milan summit will for ever be associated with the Single European Act, the 1989 Madrid summit with the Social Charter and the 1991 Maastricht summit with the Treaty on European Union.

These high-profile meetings, taking place two or three times a year in the country holding the presidency, are ornamented by lavish ceremonial and wining and dining for the political glitterati in the palaces and embassies of Europe's capitals. Two days in Amsterdam in June 1997 reportedly cost £10 million. Providing a major focus for media attention, the run-up usually sees protracted negotiations, febrile rumour-mongering and speculation. The presidency can offer a head of state a chance to shine and Tony Blair was fortunate in coming to it in his first year as prime minister. However, he also had the embarrassment of presiding over the launch of the single currency while his own country remained outside.

Although this development illustrates the increasing importance of the EU, it also testifies to the persistence of nationalism. Thus it was at the Fontainebleau summit of 1984 that Margaret Thatcher fought successfully for a budget rebate, while Major claimed 'game, set and match' for Britain at Maastricht and Blair repeated the 'Britain first' mantra. Indeed, Blair had consulted Thatcher before his first Eurosummit. The five priorities he outlined there ('completing the single market and freeing trade; enlarging the Community; reforming the common agricultural policy; launching a crusade for competitiveness and job flexibility; seeking real cooperation in foreign affairs') showed little of the Delors vision and could have come straight from her handbag.

The European Commission

In the demonology of Eurosceptics, the Brussels-based Commission is redolent of a Kafkaesque superstate. With bureaucrats organized in twenty-three directorates-general it is effectively the EU civil service and the institution most removed from democratic influence. Not only does it implement Council policy, it has sole responsibility for initiating legislation. It also drafts the budget and conducts negotiations with non-member states.

At its head sit twenty commissioners nominated by member states; two from Britain, France, Germany, Italy and Spain and one from each of the smaller countries. Each is responsible for one or more policy portfolios and is expected to develop a supranational perspective, a requirement sometimes putting them at odds with their own governments. However, they can take comfort from their remuneration, receiving salaries over 70 per cent greater than that of the British prime minister, as well as other generous allowances. In the case of Britain, a tradition has been established whereby the commissioners come from each of the two main parties. They are generally prominent ex-politicians (some say failed politicians). Thus Leon Brittan had served as a key member of Thatcher's Cabinet and Neil Kinnock had been leader of the opposition.

The president   The Commission is led by its president, a high-profile figure in world politics. The position has been seen as the motor of integration and Jacques Delors, coming to office in January 1985 and reappointed four years later, was a particularly forceful advocate. Reviled by Eurosceptics, he was often pilloried in the British tabloids. Appointment must be with the common accord of member states and the Maastricht Treaty also made it subject to vote of approval in the European Parliament. At the June 1994 Corfu summit John Major vetoed the appointment of Jean-Luc Dehaene (a federalist and the preferred choice of France and Germany), a nationalistic move to appease his Eurosceptics. The result was the appointment of Jacques Santer of Luxembourg.

A democratic deficit?   The Commission is largely free from the constraints of national interest that bedevil the Council of Ministers and the European Council. It can also take a broader and longer-term world perspective than national politicians. However, its role occasions fierce argument in Britain. It is seen by Eurosceptics as driving the Euro-train at breakneck speed towards federalism with no democratic accountability to the hundreds of millions whose lives are affected, although the nationalistic tendencies of the superior institutions have been a restraining force. Conscious of its vulnerability, the Commission has generally shown itself anxious to gain legitimacy by working in harmony with the European Parliament and welcoming consultation with interest groups at various levels (see chapter 17). Even so, its relationship with the Parliament reached a point of crisis in 1999 (see p. 125).

The European Parliament

Some citizens of continental Europe can expect to be disturbed in the night by fleets of lorries trundling between imposing buildings in Brussels, Luxembourg and Strasbourg. Their cargo consists of many tons of documents, reproduced in all official EU languages on paper of various hues. The reason for this nomadic behaviour is nationalistic wrangling, which has prevented the establishment of a single seat for the EU's assembly. The single-chamber European Parliament (EP) holds plenary sessions one week every month in the splendid Palais de l'Europe at Strasbourg. Although these are the headline-catching occasions, detailed work is done in between, through a committee network

Inside the *Palais de l'Europe* at Strasbourg

Photo: European Parliament

Table 5.2 Representatives at the European Parliament, 1994

Country	MEPs	Country	MEPs	Country	MEPs
Austria	21	Germany	99	Netherlands	31
Belgium	25	Greece	25	Portugal	25
Denmark	16	Ireland	15	Spain	64
Finland	16	Italy	87	Sweden	22
France	87	Luxembourg	6	UK	87

working close to the heart of EU power at Brussels. Servicing these operations is the work of the secretariat located in yet a third venue, at Luxembourg.

Members of the European Parliament (**MEPs**) are elected for five-year terms, the number of representatives from each country reflecting population size (Table 5.2). In the chamber, they do not confront each other as government and opposition but sit in a semicircle. However, they do form political groupings cutting across national boundaries. Figure 5.3 shows the size and political orientation of the groups that emerged after the June 1994 elections. The sixty-two UK Labour MEPs sat with the Socialists and the eighteen Conservatives with the European People's Party (EPP). Two new Liberal Democrats entered the ranks of the Liberal and Democratic Reformists and the two Scottish Nationalists joined the Rainbow group.

Members themselves are torn by conflicting loyalties: to EP group, national interest and national party. The Euroscepticism of British Conservatives creates major problems within the EPP grouping. Although often terming themselves parties, the groupings are not like those of national politics. They do not have mass organizations or fight elections with clear manifestos and, with no executive to support, have little need for continuous party discipline. Indeed, a show

The European Parliament buildings at Strasbourg (left) and Brussels (right)
Photo: European Parliament

of cross-group solidarity can actually be preferred, since this can strengthen the EP hand in negotiating with Council and Commission.

Political complexion Unlike most national parliaments, the EP does not fall under the domination of a single party or coalition. However, it does show an ideological complexion (figure 5.3). The first two elections produced centre-right leanings based around the EPP. In 1989 the balance shifted to the centre-left, with increased Green representation which, although large enough to form a separate group, allied with the Socialists. The 1994 elections saw an almost Europe-wide swing back to the right except in Britain, where two local factors operated: the mid-term unpopularity of the Conservative government and UK insistence on retaining its first-past-the-post voting system (except in Northern Ireland), greatly inflating Labour's representation. This distortion caused frustration and anger to other Christian Democrat and right-wing leaders. Despite some scepticism, the Labour government introduced the use of proportional representation for the 1999 EP elections (see chapter 9).

Power A major debate concerns the EP's powers which, despite increasing involvement in legislative procedures (see below), have remained very limited. Formally, it may reject the budget and dismiss the Commission *en bloc* but these have been seen as draconian measures, too dangerous to use. However, some argued that the 'nuclear button' should indeed be pressed and events reached fever pitch in January 1999 in a tense stand-off amidst parliamentary accusations of Commission fraud and mismanagement. Commission President Jacques Santer urged his team to stand firm and the EP stepped back from the brink, agreeing to an inquiry by a 'Committee of the Wise' – five jurists and auditors. However, their 144-page report (15 March) exposed a devastating

Figure 5.3
Political groupings in the European Parliament after the 1994 election.

PES = Party of European Socialists; EPP = European People's Party; UFE = Union for Europe; ELDR = Liberal, Democratic and Reformist Party; EUL/NGL = European United Left/Nordic Green Left; ERA = European Radical Alliance; I-EdN = Independents for a Europe of Nations; Ind = non-attached.
Source: European Parliament.

catalogue of fraud, mismanagement and nepotism reaching to the highest level. Santer, who had become known as 'Jacques Digestif' because of his liking for the good life, was felt to have little authority. Even his predecessor, Delors, did not escape censure for ignoring allegations of fraud in the Commission's own security service. The outcome was the most dramatic bloodbath in EU history. Outraged MEPs gave the commissioners an ultimatum: 'go with honour or be forced out without honour'. The result was mass resignation, including the President himself.

The Economic and Social Committee (ECOSOC)

Another body with a quasi-democratic function is the Brussels-based ECOSOC, which considers industrial policy. Members are nominated by state governments for renewable four-year terms and are broadly representative of three interests: employers, workers and miscellaneous social and professional groups. ECOSOC gives opinions at the request of the Council and Commission and on its own initiative. As a consultative forum it lacks executive powers, though its presence represents a nod in the direction of corporatism, a style of government more prevalent in continental Europe than in Britain.

The Committee of the Regions (COR)

Some see a vision of the future in terms of a Europe of regions. The Maastricht Treaty made provision for an advisory committee to articulate the regional voice and it held its inaugural meeting at Brussels in March 1995. It is consulted when regional issues are considered and can also issue own-initiative reports. Members are appointed by states and, although they need not be elected local representatives, most have clear party affiliations. The committee shares a common organizational structure and accommodation with ECOSOC, though it remains independent.

The European Court of Justice (ECJ)

The ECJ is the EU's own special court, its existence testifying to its uniqueness amongst international associations. Sitting at Luxembourg, it comprises judges from each member state, one of whom is elected as president. As an international court, a court of appeal, a court of review and a court of referral, it aims to ensure that Community law is applied uniformly across member states. It also plays a creative role by establishing precedents and has ruled on the relative power of institutions and their relationship with member states. It has even clarified Council policy in various substantive areas.

The Court hears actions brought variously by EU institutions, member states and natural or legal persons. The Commission is its best customer, having brought the greatest number of actions and been taken to the Court more than any other body. The procedures would be unrecognizable to anyone versed in the ways of UK courts. Advocates General present the cases before the judges, summarizing the positions of the parties and making observations on the relevant Community law. They also deliver reasoned opinions as to what the verdict might be; these carry considerable weight and are frequently followed. Decisions, which are made by majority, are binding upon member states. The Court also has a responsibility to consider the constitutionality of any laws passed by a domestic legislature, a power not possessed by the British courts. Various criticisms can be made of the ECJ.

- *Membership.* In selecting their nominees, governments have tended to look for a background in public service rather than judicial ability or experience. A safe pair of hands has taken precedence over flair.
- *Slow working.* Not only Hamlet was worried by the law's delay: the gap between a case being lodged and a decision averages over two years.
- *Expense.* While there are no court charges, lawyers can grow rich. Although their fees may not deter giant corporations, states or other EU institutions, they restrict accessibility for citizens and small companies.
- *Fudged decisions.* Although unanimity is not required, the infrequency of dissenting opinions suggests compromises rather than decisive advances in EU law.

A political role? The role of the Court is not only practical, it is deeply symbolic of the EU's supranational character. Some allege that it has a political agenda, generally advancing a federalist vision through its interpretations and precedents (Burley and Mattli 1993). The 1990 *Factortame* case (see p. 68) brought home its ability to limit the legal sovereignty of Parliament.

The legislative process

The formal process of making EU policy is one of the key areas of tension. In this the EP and Council negotiate and bargain, the former generally being the weaker partner. The process entails rounds of formal meetings, much informal discussion, deal making and covert lobbying where interests extend beyond governments to a myriad of pressure groups operating in the Brussels hothouse. Initially the Council reigned supreme but the EP has fought continuously for a greater formal involvement in the evolution of the following procedures.

Consultation From the outset a number of articles in the original EEC treaty have required that draft legislation from the Commission be submitted for an EP opinion before going to the Council of Ministers, but with no compulsion upon the Council to act, the consultation procedure offers little power to the EP.

Cooperation   A significant extension of EP power came in the 1986 Single European Act with a cooperation procedure between EP and Council for particular areas, including measures facilitating the internal market. In essence, a further stage was added to the consultation process, giving the EP another bite at the legislative cherry. Upon receiving the EP opinion the Council must consider it and reach a 'common position', returning it to the EP for a second reading. Although not formally increasing EP power, the procedure compels both Commission and Council to consider its views and encourages inter-institutional bargaining. It also helps to publicize an issue and mobilize political forces, including public opinion. However, the procedure is cumbersome and its use was greatly reduced in the Amsterdam Treaty in favour of co-decision.

Co-decision   The Maastricht Treaty introduced the co-decision procedure (figure 5.4) to increase EP power in a limited number of areas such as research, culture, health and consumer affairs. The Amsterdam Treaty enlarged its scope by transferring to it most items formerly subject to the cooperation procedure, making the EP the 'big winner' of that summit (Duff 1997: 143). Areas covered include the free movement of workers, establishing the internal market, technological research and development, the environment, consumer protection, education, culture and health. If, after two readings, the EP remains unhappy with the Council's common position and rejects it by an overall majority, it can request it to set up a conciliation committee drawn from both institutions and the Commission. Here tough negotiations can take place. Where both parties are able to reach agreement, the legislation is promulgated in their joint names, thereby making the EP a coequal legislator. The procedure was simplified by the Amsterdam Treaty, allowing the EP to reject a proposal if the conciliation process fails. There is evidence that the co-decision procedure has made ministers more willing to compromise. By June 1997, of 103 common positions examined, 56 did not require the intervention of a conciliation committee, either because the EP did not require amendments (33 cases) or the Council had incorporated EP positions into its common position (23 cases). The EP continues to press for more areas of policy to be brought within the procedure.

Assent   Some enhancement of EP rights to genuine joint decision-making came in the Single European Act with a procedure whereby EP assent, by absolute majority, is required for certain Council or Commission decisions. The assent procedure is used where new states are admitted to the EU and in association agreements with other countries. Under this procedure a proposed Association Agreement with Israel failed twice in 1988, succeeding only at the third attempt (Nicoll and Salmon 1990: 80). The Maastricht Treaty extended the scope to include such areas as citizenship, the structural fund, the creation of a uniform electoral system and international agreements. Although the EP wanted the area under this procedure to be increased further, the Amsterdam Treaty failed to deliver.

Legislative initiation   Since Maastricht the EP has been able to set the legisla-

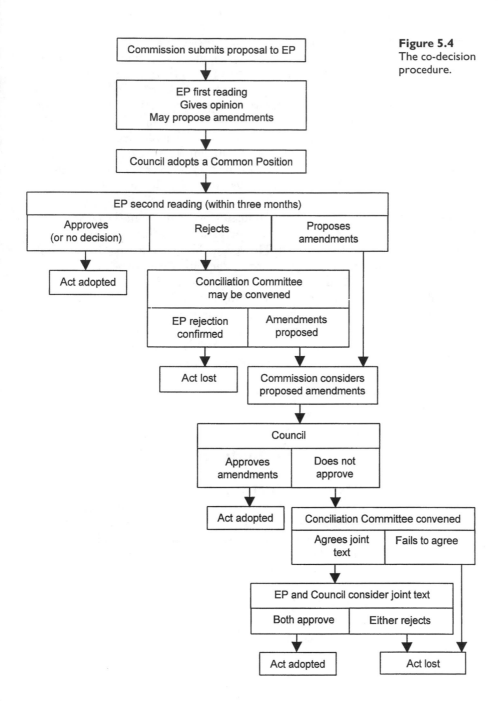

Figure 5.4
The co-decision
procedure.

tive process in motion by submitting an 'own initiative' report to the Commission. This then forms the basis of a proposal to the Council.

Redress of grievance The Maastricht Treaty also gave the EP power to invest-igate citizens' complaints of maladministration in the implementation of Com-munity law and appoint an ombudsman to assist in this.

A democratic deficit? As EU integration and the growth in its power con-tinue, so fears of a European superstate increase. Although the EP is the EU's most democratic institution it made a bad start. Direct elections were not introduced until 1979 owing to the fear, particularly on the part of the French, of an erosion of national sovereignty. During this period the other institutions were able to gain a head start in the power struggle. However, the Commis-sion can often make common cause with the EP since both tend towards a supra-nationalist perspective. The Commission also gains some legitimacy from its association with the elected body and has encouraged the gradual increase in EP power vis-à-vis the Council. However, the fact remains that the only elected EU institution has little power to penetrate a web of secrecy conceal-ing the dealings and settlements between national governments within the Council and the powerful interests lobbying them.

Although the Amsterdam summit moved things forward, a greater role for the EP, together with reforms of the institution itself, are still high on the agenda. The report from the 'Committee of the Wise' (see p. 125) addressed this issue, concluding that it was 'difficult to find anyone who has even the slightest sense of responsibility. The temptation to deprive the concept of responsibility of all substance is a dangerous one. That concept is the ultimate manifestation of democracy.'

The Budget

Like any international association the EU needs money and much can be learned about its dynamics and balance of power from a study of the budget (which finances the EC rather than all three EU pillars). The EC Treaty calls for a balanced budget (Article 199); revenue must equal expenditure. However, the simplicity of this equation does not mean the process is uncontroversial. Major political tensions arise over the redistribution of wealth from richer to poorer areas, the balance of power between institutions and the inextinguishable dis-putation between federalists and internationalists.

Scale

Although the budget has grown steadily with EU enlargement and the acquisi-tion of new functions, it remains small by domestic standards, representing only some 1.2 per cent of the total GNP of member states. However, this can give a misleading impression: further expense is borne by member states, whose national bureaucracies share the task of policy implementation.

Revenue

Unlike national governments, which raise money by taxing citizens, international associations such as NATO or the UN are usually financed by members' contributions. Various consequences follow. The associations can never be entirely confident of funds; some states are too poor to pay, others may withhold payment in protest (even the rich USA has been guilty) and even when the money is forthcoming, the associations can never really regard it as their own.

For such reasons the ECSC founding fathers instigated direct funding from levies imposed on production. However, when the EEC was created, wrangling resulted in finance by government contributions, to be set by the treaty and related to national wealth. This source proved limited and, as crises threatened, the Commission called for the Community to raise its own resources. The loss of national control would be offset by allowing the EP to share the budgetary role with the Council. President de Gaulle objected and not until his resignation in 1969 could the reform materialize (at the Hague summit). The 'own resources' were to be customs duties, agricultural tariffs, sugar levies and, most importantly, a proportion of the VAT collected by member states. This last item was to constitute the lion's share (figure 5.5).

Yet revenue remained inadequate and the Brussels summit of February 1988 finally accepted a Commission proposal that revenue be fixed as a proportion of total Community GNP, thereby linking it to the fortunes of state economies. Once annual Community expenditure was agreed, the total revenue from the existing own resources would be calculated and the difference made up by a payment from each member state in proportion to its GDP. This became increasingly important; starting at 10 per cent of total revenue in 1988, it stood at 40 per cent by 1997. However, with the character of a national contribution, the new resource presents problems for Community autonomy. Moreover, future developments are expected to require yet further sources of revenue and the nature of these will influence the degree of supranationalism the EU can achieve.

Figure 5.5 The EC budget, 1997: income (left); expenditure (right).
Source: European Parliament.

Expenditure

Generally the funds required by international associations are for running costs; they are not burdened with responsibility for substantive policies or redistributing income in the manner of states. However, with the Common Agricultural Policy, overseas aid and regional grants, the EU *does* pursue government-style objectives, making its budget not only far larger than those of other intergovernmental associations but different in character. Expenditure decisions must create winners and losers, thereby producing high-octane fuel for political machination. Rich countries resist redistribution of wealth, poorer regions lobby for social and economic development grants, those with large agricultural constituencies favour price guarantees, and so on.

The budgetary process has provided a key site for trials of strength between the Council and the EP. Generally the Council has appeared uneasy about sharing budgetary power, seeking to limit EP influence. More than an institutional power struggle, it encompasses the federalist/internationalist debate. In this the EP shares the federal aspirations of the Commission, which promoted major budgetary reforms in 1988, increasing its influence.

A budgetary cycle (Article 203 of the EC Treaty) follows a number of stages in the EU financial year (1 January to 31 December). In addition there is an auditing process, a detailed examination of the Commission's accounts made by the Court of Auditors. The EP, with advice from the Council, decides on the basis of the Court's report whether to grant the Commission a 'discharge'. This is no mere technicality; fraud, alleged and uncovered, constitutes a major problem. In early 1998 misgiving over the 1996 budget led to discharge being deferred for a year. In November 1998 the Court revealed alleged fraud and misspending of £3 billion, some 5 per cent of the total EU budget, precipitating a major crisis in the EP's relationship with the Commission (see pp. 125–6).

Europe as a Domestic Issue

It will be seen throughout this book that UK government and politics are increasingly touched by EU membership. As an issue in political debate, it has precipitated considerable political fury, even forcing a break with tradition in the use of a referendum. In the 1980s and 1990s, it contributed to the fall of the UK's most dominant post-war prime minister, blighted the political life of her successor and saw the Conservative Party in disarray in the 1997 general election. At its most fundamental, the question relates to the degree to which the integration project should go: the federalism versus internationalism debate centres on economic and monetary union and social policy. At the outer extremities sceptical voices continue to question membership itself. At heart this debate revolves around the principle of national sovereignty.

Economic and monetary union

Monetary union is the linking of currencies to minimize exchange-rate fluctuations. It is highly conducive to free trade, a key feature of the neoliberal agenda (Grahl and Teague 1990: 97–140). In the days of empire sterling was a world currency and in the post-war years Britain remained enthusiastic about the Bretton Woods Agreement and the preservation of a sterling area. Yet paradoxically, it had been decidedly cool towards European **economic and monetary union** (EMU), dropping out of the system known as the Snake in the Tunnel in 1972 after only one year. Again, when the European Monetary System (EMS) began in 1979, although sterling was included in the basket of currencies used to determine the value of the new European Currency Unit (ECU), Britain spurned the **exchange rate mechanism** (ERM) designed to keep rates within a narrow range of each other, finally entering in October 1990, but on the basis of extra-wide fluctuation bands (±6 per cent). Moreover, the venture was to collapse in the débâcle of 'Black Wednesday' (16 Sept. 1992) when, following currency speculation, Britain was forced to withdraw (see p. 493).

This was to be followed by a major crisis for the ERM itself. The immediate trigger was a decision on 29 July 1993 by the German central bank (Bundesbank) (faced with Herculean currency problems arising from reunification) to resist an expected cut in one of its key interest rates which would have signalled rate cuts in other ERM currencies, thereby easing recessionary pressures. The result was turmoil in the foreign exchange markets, with heavy selling of the Belgian and French francs, the escudo, the peseta and the Danish krone, causing them to slump in value.

The voices of the Eurosceptics were raised in unison to sing the requiem of the ERM. John Major claimed events vindicated the decision to suspend membership: 'The fault lines in the system have been exposed'. Yet emergency meetings resulted in a revival, with the narrow bands (±2.25 per cent) being widened to ±15 per cent. Critics argued that this rendered the system meaningless, but a continuing commitment to EMU was revealed as countries resisted the temptation to exploit the wider bands with beggar-thy-neighbour devaluations. Germany worked strenuously to restore the battered French franc. Indeed, rather than be daunted, ERM enthusiasts argued that events demonstrated the case for a single currency in which destructive speculation was impossible. British Commissioner Sir Leon Brittan was amongst those arguing for fundamental economic convergence so that 'in due course . . . the move to a single currency can be decided and implemented directly, without the artificial prop of years of narrow-band ERM' (Brittan 1993). The implications of this for Britain's control over public expenditure were considerable and lay at the heart of domestic debate (see pp. 498–9).

A single European currency In the Maastricht Treaty leaders had made an historic agreement to take monetary union beyond the ERM with a **single currency** for all EU states. This would centre upon three institutions:

- a European System of Central Banks (ESCB) responsible for implementing domestic monetary and exchange rate policy and managing foreign reserves;
- a European Central Bank (ECB) under a council comprising the governors of the national central banks, with an exclusive right to issue bank notes;
- a European Investment Bank (EIB) to grant loans to underdeveloped regions.

The process would come in three stages though Britain secured an 'opt-out' from the final one: it would only complete this through a separate decision by its national parliament, Major claiming this diplomatic triumph as 'game, set and match'.

Problems for most countries in meeting the convergence criteria, enlargement of the Union and cultural diversity initially placed the future of the project in some doubt. However, the possibility of deferral was denied by Alexandre Lamfalussy, President of the European Monetary Institute and the key player in the project. What emerged was a multi-speed development with some states moving ahead of others. In May 1998, eleven countries formally adopted the single currency based on the new unit: the Euro. From January 1999 it could be used for cheque and credit transactions, the new notes and coinage entering circulation in January 2002 and national issues disappearing the following July. Labour Chancellor Gordon Brown retained Major's 'wait and see' approach, once again sacrificing a 'seat at the top table' and causing one senior mandarin to lament 'we'll be shut outside with our noses pressed to the glass' (*The Economist,* 1 May 1998). With profound implications for the government's role in the economy, the issue reached white-heat level within the nation and within the Conservative Party (see pp. 285–6).

Three stages towards monetary union

1   For completion by the end of 1993. Governments to exercise strict budgetary discipline to get their economies into shape for further progress.
2   Governments enact programmes designed to secure convergence between national economies with respect to certain key variables such as price stability, budgetary deficits, a position within defined fluctuation margins on the ERM and stable long-term interest rates. This period also to see progress towards the independent ECB. Developments overseen by a European Monetary Institute (EMI).
3   Irrevocable fixing of exchange rates, leading to introduction of single currency (the Euro). A meeting of heads of state no later than 31 December 1996 would decide on a qualified majority basis whether a majority of states were ready for the move. If so, the date for the final stage would be fixed. If the date for the third stage had not been set by the end of 1997 it would start regardless on 1 January 1999. Having prescribed the regulatory framework for the ESCB in the third stage, the EMI would be dissolved upon the creation of the ECB.

The social dimension

The single currency is not the only EU issue bearing upon national economies. Another concerns social policy. As presently constituted, the EU cannot have a social policy in the sense that a country does. Not responsible for schools, health care, social services and so on, its role is limited to protecting workers within a largely capitalist system – a role with clearly economic implications. This is not new; the Rome Treaty included provisions for the free movement of workers through equivalence in social security entitlement, educational exchange facilities, working conditions, labour law, vocational training, health and safety at work, rights of association and collective bargaining and equal pay for men and women. It also established a European Social Fund to promote worker mobility and created a framework for a Community vocational training policy. At the same time, the Euratom Treaty established basic standards for the protection of workers and public against radiation.

However, this aspect became more central as economies boomed and social costs, including pollution, health and safety-at-work problems and uneven economic development became apparent. There was also the essentially political problem of maintaining the legitimacy of a predominantly capitalist system which did not distribute the fruits of enterprise evenly. World slump from the mid-1970s heightened awareness by not only precipitating unemployment but stimulating a resurgence of New Right thinking which threatened workers' security and conditions. Hence, the 1980s saw renewed attempts to rekindle the social dimension. A key figure was Jacques Delors. Formerly a socialist finance minister in France, his opening speech to the European Parliament as President of the Commission presented a European vision going beyond a gigantic market-place. His programme for the completion of the single market by 1992 included a range of social objectives to mitigate disruption caused by economic restructuring.

After considerable debate, a Charter of the Fundamental Social Rights of Workers was adopted by the European Council at the Strasbourg summit of December 1989. It was accompanied by a Social Action Programme comprising forty-seven initiatives to be implemented at various levels of government (Gold 1993: 10). There was only one dissenting voice, that of the UK. The mood was to carry through beyond the Thatcher era to Maastricht, where Major negotiated a special protocol whereby the UK opted out of the Social Chapter. Although, to the satisfaction of the unions, the Labour government signed up at the Amsterdam summit, government spin doctors stressed that there was no need for early implementation.

Debating the Social Chapter: the case against The UK position owed much to its domestic neoliberal agenda. Crucial to the vision was a deregulated labour market with lower wages, making British products more competitive and raising profits. There was also an argument based on the subsidiarity principle, social policies falling within that area of administration best left to national governments. Perhaps the darkest fear of the right came from the belief that a social dimension equates with socialism.

Debating the Social Chapter: the case for Opting out may not have proved in the UK's favour at all; the strategy could lose jobs rather than gain them. In an increasingly high-tech world a low-wage economy with an unskilled workforce becomes less attractive to investors, while aggregate demand falls as people have less to spend. Again, deregulated working conditions and weak unions may not be enough to attract investment. International corporations also consider factors such as roads, railways, telecommunications and education in deciding where to locate, yet much UK policy from the 1980s has questioned the state's role in maintaining these. Moreover, the 'we'll have the jobs' argument contravenes the principle of fair competition. This could in turn harm Community spirit and be politically disruptive. There is also the possibility of 'social dumping' whereby the predilection of companies for areas with weakened workers' rights 'exports' these conditions into competitor economies. Finally, the policy conflicts with the idea of equal European citizenship enunciated in the Maastricht Treaty. In fact there was always a fundamental illogicality in the UK position in that many of the Social Chapter principles were already present in earlier treaties, all signed by the UK.

What Next?

The future shape of the EU promises to be one of the most important factors influencing British politics. Will it become more democratic? Will it become more federalist in character? A key issue will concern its size.

Enlargement

The EU has been subject to a continuous process of enlargement (figure 5.6) and there remains a queue of would-be members, including those EFTA states remaining outside, former communist states and a Mediterranean group. They are attracted by the prospect of access to EU markets, grant aid and a chance to participate in decision-making over trade issues. However, this has various implications. The fourth enlargement (in 1995) brought in Austria, Finland and Sweden, increasing membership from twelve to fifteen, extending the periods between which each state holds the presidency from six to seven and a half years and increasing the number of votes in Council from seventy-six to eighty-seven. Norway was invited in but, for a second time, fearful of the Spanish invading their fishing waters, voted 'No' in a referendum.

Enlargement would enhance the political project of reducing tensions and the potential for war. In this respect the collapse of the Soviet empire has created an historic opportunity to end European division. Yet with more members the process of deepening integration becomes more difficult. Generally, UK governments have favoured widening. However, voting procedures designed for a Community of six, particularly the principle of the veto, become increasingly inappropriate as the Community enlarges. A possible trade-off in which

Figure 5.6
The process of EU
enlargement.

Source: European Parliament.

the bigger states give up one of their two commissioners while the smaller countries accept a reduction in their relative voting power reached a stalemate in the Amsterdam summit. In addition, problems of redistributing wealth would pose heavy demands on the richer countries. Finally, human rights controversies emerge as states with dubious reputations knock on the door.

Variable geometry

There are grounds for anticipating that future integration will take place according to a principle of '**variable geometry**', permitting states to proceed at various speeds. Indeed, this is built into the very architecture of the Union. The Maastricht Treaty, in its schedule for achieving a single currency, established that no member would be forced along and no state could hold the others back. Critics worried that this could create a 'hard core' to the detriment of the others.

Democracy

Enthusiasts and sceptics alike agree that the EU cannot progress without further democratization. The events of March 1999 may prove a defining moment. The EP came of age, ending the life of the unelected Commission in the name of democratic accountability. For many MEPs, this was a new dawn presaging expanded powers to regulate and supervise the Commission, though such an ambition could be bitterly contested by the Council of Ministers.

National sovereignty and European integration

It is clear from chapter 4 that national sovereignty in the contemporary world is not as simple as much political rhetoric implies. Despite its dominance in international discourse, the centralized nation-state is by no means the only way in which people can live or have lived. A recent creation of modern Europe, it can be argued that, as traditionally understood, it is becoming an ethical and practical anachronism.

The ethical question Nationalism is a questionable virtue. Patriotism has all too often deteriorated into racism and fascism and it was to avert the latter that the movement for European union arose. Today we witness an alarming paradox noted by Hobsbawm (1990) of increasing global interdependence coinciding with a revival of nationalism. The result is world tension with nationalist extremism in Russia, Germany and France; Islamic fundamentalism in the Middle East; the emergence of the strong Hindu nationalist party in India; the vicious conflict in former Yugoslavia and Britain's own troubles in Ulster. Despite the end of the cold war, the proliferation of sophisticated weaponry means that international relations are conducted on a knife edge. Underlying all remains the bleak threat of nuclear proliferation under the insistent pressure of the world arms salesmen.

The sovereign right of nations to do what they like in their own territories is also questionable. Do governments have a right to violate human rights, persecute minorities or hold political prisoners? Again, there are the major new questions arising from ecology. Can one state legitimately claim a sovereign right to generate acid rain to fall on another? The maldistribution of world resources is in part perpetuated by nationalistic competition, which not only exploits the third world, it depletes finite resources and produces pollution threatening ecological disaster.

The practical question We saw in chapter 4 that the reality of national sovereignty today is questionable under a continuing process of globalization with space–time distanciation compressing the world into a global village. Regardless of whose hands hold the tiller, the idea that the ship of state is free to chart its own course may be illusory. The globalizing economy undermines national systems of control; governments find it increasingly difficult to run welfare states, stimulate employment, control inflation or regulate the money supply. Advanced weaponry decreases rather than increases sovereignty because confrontation promises mutual destruction and gives power to non-state actors, be they terrorists or freedom fighters.

Beyond the state The response to globalization comes in the growth of new political formations to recapture much of the role of nation-states. Security alliances limit the right to wage war. Regional economic groups combat the superpowers and transnationals. The fight against terrorism and crime sees police and security forces amalgamating and systems of international law become increasingly important in the lives of citizens, organizations and states. Associations such as the UN agencies unite governments and also work in partnership with international charities and business associations. The logic of European integration lies within such developments. It can be seen as the retrieval of autonomy rather than its sacrifice (Grahl and Teague 1990: 15). It can facilitate the renewal of legal and administrative regulatory mechanisms to give some control over the social, economic and environmental disruption threatened by global movements of capital. However, democratic problems remain as globalization can render people and politics inconsequential: 'In the international or transnational sites where decisions are taken national electorates have no voice' (Gamble 1993: 328). Hence, a major challenge for the future of the EU is the redress of its own democratic deficit.

Key points

- Of all Britain's relationships none has generated more internal political heat than that with the EU, the key feature being concern over a feared loss of sovereignty.
- The EU's origins lie in the attempt to repair the devastation wrought by the second world war. Yet there was a deeper purpose: to prevent further war in Western Europe.
- The EU differs from all other international associations in that it creates a supranational authority and is partly funded by its own resources rather than member states' contributions.
- The career of the EU has itself been fitful, with periods of stagnation (*immobilisme*) and dynamism.
- Edward Heath took Britain into the Community in 1973.
- Key developments include the June 1985 White Paper, *Completing the Internal Market*, the 1986 Single European Act and the 1992 *Treaty on European Union* (Maastricht).
- The relationships between the various EU institutions and their relative power are important areas of debate; the balance shifting towards the Parliament.
- The future shape of the EU promises to be one of the most important factors influencing British politics into the new millennium. Key areas of development are the single currency, social policy, democracy and enlargement.

Review your understanding of the following terms and concepts

Amsterdam Treaty
assent procedure
Brussels Treaty
co-decision procedure
Committee of the
    Regions
conciliation committee
consultation procedure
cooperation procedure
Council of Europe
Council of Ministers
economic and monetary
    union (EMU)
EEC
EFTA

Euro
European Central Bank
European Commission
European Council
European Court of
    Justice
European Parliament
European Union
Eurosceptic
exchange rate
    mechanism (ERM)
federalism
intergovernmental
    organization
Maastricht Treaty

MEP
qualified majority
    voting
single currency
Single European Act
Social Chapter
sovereignty
subsidiarity
supragovernmental
Treaty on European
    Union
variable geometry

Assignment

Study the extract from *The Economist* and answer the following questions.

		Mark (%)
1	What three reasons are given to argue that Britain is likely to remain on the fringes of the European Union?	10
2	What are the grounds for saying that a Franco-German entente has driven forward the process of European integration?	20
3	What does the extract say are the respective attitudes of diplomats and political advisers towards Britain joining the single currency? On what grounds do you think they assume these?	30
4	What bearing does the 'special relationship' with the USA have on Britain's future role in Europe?	40

Questions for discussion

1   Why did Britain stay out of the early moves towards European integration?
2   Evaluate the importance of the Single European Act and the Maastricht Treaty in the process of integration.
3   How real is the threat of a loss of national sovereignty through EU membership?
4   Is it fair to characterize Britain as the 'awkward partner' in Western Europe?

Britain and Europe

Three's a crowd

The Blair government hopes that the election of Gerhard Schröder in Germany will allow Britain to make a diplomatic breakthrough in Europe. Dream on.

Ever since the foundation of the European Union, the holy grail of British diplomacy has been to disrupt the Franco-German entente which has driven forward the process of European integration. This old ambition has been given a new impetus by the election of Gerhard Schröder as Germany's chancellor. After all, Mr Schröder has said that Britain should join France and Germany in a tripartite alliance to lead the EU. New Labourites sense an historic opportunity.

But there are snags. The euro is the most sensitive political issue in Britain. Diplomats may long for Mr Blair to make a firm statement of intent to join—but their voices are likely to be drowned out by those of political advisers, urging caution.

As some British diplomats acknowledge, no amount of clever new British initiatives is likely to be any match for the sheer density of Franco-German ties. Politicians and civil servants in Germany and France have simply got into the habit of close and regular consultations. By contrast, the number of senior Labour politicians with real knowledge of European politics is small. In trying to understand Europe, the Blairites often still reach for the comfort blanket of familiar categories—witness their habit of classifying German or French politicians as "New" or "Old" Labour. By contrast, the Blairites' understanding of American politics and debates is much closer and more nuanced. For New Labour, as for the Tories, the Atlantic still often seems narrower than the Channel.

The Economist, 10 Oct. 1998

---

5 Outline the various processes whereby the Council, the Commission and the European Parliament work together in policy-making.
6 Assess the importance of the European Council in the working of the EU.
7 Examine the case for a single currency within the EU.
8 In what senses can the EU be said to suffer from a democratic deficit?
9 Why is it considered important that the EU is financed from its own resources?
10 Discuss whether the EU can survive substantial enlargement.

Topic for debate

This house believes that the idea of 'batting for Britain' undermines the EU's fundamental rationale.

Further reading

Butler, M. (1986) *Europe: More than a Continent.*
An inside view by a UK permanent representative.

George, S. (1994) *An Awkward Partner: Britain in the European Community* (2nd edn).
Examines and explains the tortuous nature of British relations with the Community.

Giddings, P. and Drewry, G. (1996) *Westminster and Europe: The Impact of the European Union on the Westminster Parliament.*
Considers the problems experienced by Parliament in exercising influence over EC legislation.

Jones, R. A. (1996) *The Politics and Economics of the European Union.*
Concise, accessible and jargon-free introduction to the EU institutions and associated debates.

Lodge, J. (ed.) (1993) *The European Community and the Challenge of the Future.*
Collection of essays on various aspects by specialists.

Mazey, S. and Richardson, J. (1993) *Lobbying in the European Community.*
Sheds light on the less institutional aspect of Community politics.

Nugent, N. (1994) *The Government and Politics of the European Union* (3rd edn).
Looks at institutions, decision-making processes and policies.

Urwin, D. (1997) *A Political History of Western Europe since 1945.*
Addresses the major political and economic developments, including the consequences of the end of the cold war and progress towards integration post-Maastricht.

Young, H. (1998) *This Blessed Plot: Britain and Europe from Churchill to Blair.*
Excellent guide to the high and low politics in Britain's position in Western Europe.

For light relief

Edwina Currie, *The Ambassador.*
The EU 100 years on is the most powerful state in the free world. Genetic engineering is widespread and the US Ambassador is sent over to investigate.

Jean Monnet, *Memoirs.*
Taste of the cocktail of passion and calculation in early integrationist moves. Also insight on British emotional reservations.

On the net

http://www.fco.gov.uk/europe/index.html
For UK policy on the EU.

http://europa.eu.int/index.htm
The EU home page will lead you to a wealth of information on the EU and its institutions, available in any EU language at the touch of a button.

Chapter Six

A Disunited Kingdom: Territorial Politics

The constitution has for long been seen as unitary, binding England, Wales, Scotland and Northern Ireland into a single state under the Westminster Parliament as the United Kingdom. Yet although formally established in 1800 with the parliamentary union of Great Britain and Ireland, this kingdom has become something of a constitutional curate's egg – united only 'in parts'. By 1997 a centrifugal process of gathering momentum was creating a constitution with clearly federal features. Recognition of these territorial movements is essential to an understanding of the dynamics of contemporary British politics. This chapter begins by examining Scotland and Wales where, after chaffing against the English bit, their peoples voted in 1997 for devolution. Next we turn to the regions of England which, while undeveloped in political terms, have their own identities. Finally we examine the territorial struggle which, with extreme violence and bitter enmities, has placed UK politics in the world headlines: the vexed question of Northern Ireland.

Political scientists once tended to see the British electorate as essentially homogeneous, divided mainly by class but, as chapter 7 will reveal, there are greater complexities in the social fabric. Moreover, the post-war era saw the reopening of another historic schism, reminding politicians in London that the kingdom, though united, comprised four nations. Elections began to reveal a nation dividing, with territories pursuing different agendas, sometimes through different political parties. Paradoxically this mood of **separatism** appeared to heighten under a highly centralizing government from 1979.

Beyond the ballot box was an economic fissure (figure 6.1). The 1980s and 1990s saw massive deindustrialization in the north as heavy industry and textiles declined, while the collapse of mining devastated the communities around the pits. A European Commission report of November 1996 found a growing

Figure 6.1
Regional disparities
in per capita GDP
within the UK,
taking the UK
average as an index
value of 100.

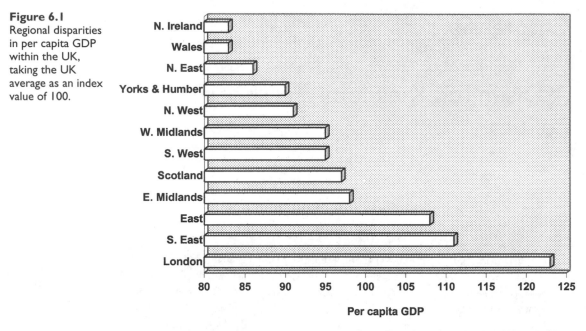

Per capita GDP

Source: Data from *Social Trends* (1998: table 5.31).

regional divide; post-war economic modernization had closed the gaps between Western Europe's richer and poorer states, but wide differences in living standards remained at regional level and these were greatest in the UK. A study of the 459 district councils in England, Wales and Scotland published in 1996 by the economic forecasting organization, the Henley Centre, found per capita income in the south-east to be 20 per cent higher than in the rest of Britain. Those in this favoured garden of England were also likely to be better qualified, to live longer and to do so in larger homes (Wagstyl 1996). The growing divide was compounded by an historical sense of cultural subjugation at the Celtic fringes. These strains on the integrity of the UK were to result in tectonic constitutional shifts in 1998.

Unity and Devolution

Unity was seen by the English political class as essential for security. They needed to capitalize on the insular position provided by nature and remove both the possibility of challenge from within and the establishment of bases for challenge from overseas. The Wars of the Roses and the subsequent Tudor and Stuart dynasties saw the central authority of the Crown established. Scotland and Wales, under English domination, followed a unified pattern of development into the agricultural and industrial revolutions and the age of empire.

Scots, wha hae: Scotland

Unlike the Welsh and Irish, the Scots were never forcibly subdued, unity coming politically with the succession of James I of Scotland to the English throne
in 1603. The 1707 Act of Union established a common parliament but protected certain Scottish institutions, including the legal system, the Presbyterian
Church, the education system and local government (Kellas 1975: 2). In modern times much public administration came under the Scottish Office at Edinburgh and a Secretary of State for Scotland sat in the Cabinet. At Westminster
a Scottish Grand Committee examined Scottish issues, but since its composition was supposed to reflect party balance, Scotland's mainly Labour MPs were
joined by a leavening of English Conservatives.

The so-called
British Empire is
in reality an
English Empire, in
which Ireland,
Scotland and
Wales formed
the original
colonies.

F. A. Ridley, in
Socialist Leader
(Feb. 1948)

A nationalist movement was represented by the Scottish National Party (SNP)
founded in 1928, a Scottish Labour Party founded in 1976, and a Scottish press
(broadsheet and tabloid). The early 1970s saw a resurgence of nationalist feeling with the discovery of North Sea oil. Seen by the government as a UK asset,
many Scots believed the revenues belonged to Scotland. In 1974 the SNP won
eleven seats in Parliament with 30 per cent of the Scottish vote. The Labour
government held a referendum on **devolution** in 1979, but when voters shuffled
to the polls amidst snow and hail, the hurdle of 40 per cent of the eligible
electorate saying 'Yes' proved too high. The general election in the same year
saw the SNP fall back to only two seats. However, the subsequent period of
Westminster rule by a party decisively rejected by the Scottish electorate fuelled
discontent. Under Heath the Conservatives had supported devolution but
Thatcher returned to a hard-line unionism, which Major maintained. Yet ironically, it was Thatcher's poll tax, visited upon Scotland one year earlier than
England, that hardened support for a break from Westminster.

In 1989, a Scottish Constitutional Convention comprising Scottish MPs, MEPs
and representatives of local authorities, churches, trade unions and other interests came out in favour of a Scottish parliament (Levy 1992) and within two
months of taking office in 1997 the Labour government had published white
papers on devolution to a Scottish parliament and a Welsh assembly (Senedd).
Arousing unprecedented interest, *Scotland's Parliament* sold 500 copies within
two hours of going on sale at one Glasgow bookshop (Webster and Bowditch
1997). Largely echoing the Constitutional Convention's proposals, it foreshadowed the biggest change in the link to the rest of Britain for nearly 300
years.

'Yes, Yes' The referendum combined two questions: one on a parliament and
one on tax-varying powers. On 11 September 1997 (the 700th anniversary of
William Wallace's victory over the English at the Battle of Stirling Bridge) the
Scots voted decisively 'Yes, Yes'. Prospects for the Conservatives looked bleak;
holding no Scottish seats after the 1997 general election, they faced the prospect of fighting elections to a parliament that they had consistently opposed
(Mitchell et al. 1998).

The West Lothian question

A devolution conundrum was first raised by MP Tam Dalyell when representing that constituency: should Scottish MPs at Westminster be permitted to debate policy for England, while English MPs are excluded from the Scottish Parliament? Again, should Scotland maintain its existing over-representation at Westminster? This was a sobering question for Labour since without its tartan contingent its Westminster ranks would be depleted. The Scotland Bill promised to end the over-representation at Westminster in the next boundary review (in 2005), reducing the number of MPs from 72 to 57 (and correspondingly reducing the number of constituency members in the Scottish Parliament to produce a 50:50 ratio with additional members; see chapter 9). However, there were no proposals to modify the role of Scottish MPs.

The Parliament The Scotland Bill received the Royal Assent in 1998 with elections planned for May 1999. The Edinburgh Parliament of 129 members elected by the additional member system (see chapter 9) was to become fully operational by 2000, if not sooner. It has primary legislative powers in all areas currently administered by the Scottish Office and a right to vary the basic level of income tax by up to 3p. Matters reserved for Westminster include foreign policy, defence, central economic affairs, social security matters and the constitution (in theory preventing Scotland voting for independence, though a referendum could hardly be prevented if the parliament voted for it). Its Executive (the equivalent of the Cabinet) is headed by a First Minister.

Land of my Fathers: Wales

Wales was yoked to England in 1282 following its conquest by Edward I. The Tudors consolidated this subjugation, banning the Welsh language in administration. Industrialization assisted the colonizing impact with massive English immigration into the South Wales coalfields and steel industries, leaving mid- and north Wales custodians of the remnants of a national culture. The principality was brought under the English legal, health and education systems, the domination underlined when the 1870 Education Act banned the Welsh language for teaching in the newly emerging state schools.

The Plaid Cymru party was founded in 1925 to preserve the Welsh cultural heritage but discontents led to more overtly political ambitions and a call for self-government. Campaigning led the Labour government to hold a referendum in 1979 but, with deep English penetration, many non-Welsh speakers feared second-class citizenship in an independent Wales; devolution was decisively rejected. Some distinctiveness was provided for the principality through a Welsh Secretary in the Cabinet, a Welsh Office (a Whitehall outpost at Cardiff), a Welsh Grand Committee of Welsh MPs and a Select Committee on Welsh Affairs at Westminster. However, Conservative MPs were always heavily outnumbered (disappearing completely in 1997) and a quangocracy (see chapter 18) of Conservative placemen and a succession of (English) Conservative Welsh Secretaries prompted a renewed desire for independence. Other factors added to disenchantment. With 43 per cent of the population working in the public sector, Thatcher's privatization drive hit Wales disproportionately. On the other hand, the Welsh Development Agency, despite serious scandals, was remarkably successful in attracting inward investment from EU countries and the global economy, suggesting possibilities of an independent existence within a wider context (Jones 1997).

Upon returning to office in 1997, Labour's white paper promised *A Voice for Wales*. A referendum on Thursday 18 September 1997 provided one of the most nerve-wracking electoral outcomes of modern politics. In the small hours of Friday morning Wales's 'No' voters might have felt they could retire contentedly to bed with the might of Cardiff, the principality's capital, declaring against the assembly. However, in the final minutes came the voice of Carmarthenshire in south-west Wales, the very last to declare, shifting the mathematical sands to a timid 'Yes'. Yet despite the slender margin, the swing from 1979 of 30 per cent was greater than in Scotland and the government acted as if the result were unequivocal. The Welsh Bill received the Royal Assent in 1998 and the Senedd was to be in place by May 1999.

The Senedd Comprising sixty members elected by the additional member system, the Senedd assumed the responsibilities of the Secretary of State for Wales but with certain areas (foreign affairs, defence, social security and macro-economic policy) reserved for Westminster. There would be no Cabinet; leadership would come from an Executive Committee comprising the leaders of a range of subject committees and chaired by a First Secretary, elected by the Senedd. (Something of the gloss was wiped off the new venture in October 1998 when Labour's candidate for this post, Welsh Secretary Ron Davies, resigned after an 'error of judgement' on Clapham Common.) With no ability to vary tax or pass primary legislation, the Senedd's powers fell well below those of the Scottish Parliament. However, it inherited the decision-making functions of the Welsh Office, together with a large budget (£7 billion in 1997), and was expected to derive some influence through implementing Westminster legislation. In supporting the case for an assembly, ministers even suggested that, had it existed during the Thatcher administration, it might have been able to opt out of the poll tax.

The lack of legislative powers and dependence on a central grant were seen by critics as serious weaknesses. Although the Conservatives, in principle opposing any dilution of the union, came round to a pragmatic acceptance under William Hague, Welsh political elites remained unenthusiastic. Plaid Cymru

---

[Labour] are foolish to tinker with the constitution for short-term political plaudits. Their plan to set up Scottish and Welsh parliaments . . . is a serious error.

John Major, on eve of 1994 Conservative Party conference, quoted in the *Guardian* (11 Oct. 1994)

wanted complete independence in the context of Europe, while the Liberal Democrats argued for tax-varying powers (McAllister 1998: 164–5). The model did not even receive unqualified support amongst Labour backbenchers, who feared that the promised 'bonfire of the quangos' would not occur. Although the absence of legislative powers ruled out a West Lothian question, there was concern about how disagreements between a future Conservative Welsh Secretary and a Labour-dominated Senedd might be resolved.

English regionalism: the forgotten dimension

For the English, the conflict of citizenship within a multinational state goes largely unfelt; indeed 'English' and 'British' are often taken as synonymous. Hence, the regional dimension has hung as a withered limb of the body politic. While Whitehall has practised administrative decentralization and governments have created many ad hoc regional bodies to provide services such as gas, water and health care, calls (for example from the 1969 Redcliffe-Maud Commission on local government and the minority report of the 1973 Kilbrandon Commission on the Constitution) for regional government have long been resisted. Subnational democracy was based on a pattern of local government which, with varying tiers and sizes of authorities, was a patchwork quilt heavily dominated by the centre (chapter 19). Not only have the deprived areas felt neglected, the efforts of their local authorities to improve conditions have been frustrated by Westminster.

Labour had appeared favourably disposed towards reform for some time but, when in government in the 1970s, the ambivalence of its National Executive Committee left English **regionalism** as 'the dog that never barked' (Harvie 1991). Their 1992 manifesto contained a commitment to create Regional Development Agencies (RDAs), which would later form the basis for elected regional assemblies, and a 1995 party document, *A Choice for England*, proposed indirectly elected regional chambers of local authority representatives with two main purposes: strategic coordination and democratic oversight. A precondition for this was a predominantly single-tier system of local government. The chambers would not have tax-raising or legislative powers and three conditions were necessary before they could convert to elected assemblies:

1   approval by the regional chamber itself to ensure majority support from local authorities;
2   parliamentary approval;
3   clear evidence of public agreement, perhaps through a region-wide referendum.

The 1997 manifesto retained this commitment but recognized variations in regional demand for reform: 'Only where clear popular consent is established will arrangements be made for elected regional assemblies'. In their first year of office, a white paper, *Building Partnerships for Prosperity*, and a Regional

Development Agencies Act empowered the Secretary of State for the Environment, Transport and the Regions to create RDAs and designate voluntary regional chambers comprising representatives of local authorities and other interests, to which the RDAs would be accountable.

Yet the Act did not provide for directly elected assemblies or referendums. Richard Caborn, Minister for Regions, Regeneration and Planning, told Parliament's Environment, Transport and Regional Affairs Committee that local people would be given the opportunity to make the chambers directly elected some time after a further general election. Critics, including the Liberal Democrats, accused the government of dragging its feet, while Conservatives feared creeping federalism. Some commentators have seen in regionalism a further erosion of local government (Jones and Stewart 1995).

However, a further dynamic towards regionalism comes from the increasingly important European stage (Elcock 1997). The EU often works at a regional level in its social and economic programmes and the Maastricht Treaty made provision for an advisory Committee of the Regions. The Association of County Councils (1992) argued for regional groupings of local authorities as a means of increasing effectiveness when approaching the EU for grants from the European Social Fund (ESF) and European Regional Development Fund (ERDF). Many authorities have combined in regional or subregional partnerships to prepare EU funding bids, even forging continental partnerships to lobby governments and EU institutions. Some have formed regional consortia with industry and labour organizations, the northern region making the earliest advances (Elcock 1997: 427). Generally the Commission is encouraging, since it needs cooperation and advice in formulating and implementing policy.

Without a genuine regional level of government, England is disadvantaged against Wales and Scotland with their devolved structures. They had already established offices in Brussels for lobbying purposes and the EU had offices in Belfast, Cardiff and Edinburgh. With further EU enlargement the pressure towards English regionalism may be expected to increase (Martin and Pearce 1994). Yet UK governments may not welcome this. The Scotland Bill, for example, made no provision for links between the Scottish Executive and the EU and there is no requirement that the UK government take the views of the Scottish Parliament into account on EU matters.

Ireland: a Terrible Beauty

With its grim chronology of violence, Ireland has mocked claims to unity. The problem of Northern Ireland has seemed an incomprehensible religious conflict, explained in terms of the 'hot-headedness' of the red-headed men, disdainfully contrasted with the secular rationality of the English, who have long avoided religious war. This is wrong; the problem is a cocktail of racism, apartheid, imperialism, class domination, violent resistance and brooding memories of ancestral cruelty and injustice – it is a political issue. Perhaps more than any other, the Irish problem has roots deeply embedded in a long and vicious history.

The seeds of discontent

Although uncomfortably close to England, Ireland remained stubbornly separated by the Irish Sea, hindering English domination. Conquest was finally completed by the Tudors, though the Irish, like the aborigines of the New World, resented subjugation on their own soil. In the English civil wars they saw their chance by favouring the Royalist cause but in the aftermath incurred terrible English wrath in the form of reconquest first by Cromwell and later by the Protestant William of Orange (in the famous Battle of the Boyne in 1690). Relegated to the status of second-class citizens in their own country, Irish Catholics were barred from state office and the professions, denied landownership rights and lived in a squalor unparalleled in Europe. Land in the south was confiscated by the English, who remained comfortably at home as absentee landlords, extracting crippling rents. In the north, where resistance was fiercer, domination required settler colonization. A Scottish Presbyterian landowning class emerged around Belfast, ruling the natives and dependent upon English mainland support. Rebellions were put down with extreme severity, the troops given full licence to torture, maim and kill. The Catholics rose in 1798 only to be cut down in the battle of Vinegar Hill. The Act of Union of 1800, in which the Irish parliament was swallowed up by Westminster, was adorned with manacles rather than wedding rings.

The industrial revolution reinforced the division. In the north the Protestants shared in English prosperity while subjugating the Catholics. In contrast, the south was excluded from the process of industrialization; it was more useful as a granary to feed workers on the mainland, even when the Irish were themselves starving. The suffering was compounded in 1845 and 1846 when a serious potato blight in Ireland removed the means of sustenance for some four million people. England did little to help, around a million people died and over two million crossed the Atlantic, taking with them a cargo of festering resentment.

Thus you have a starving population, an absentee aristocracy, and an alien Church, and in addition the weakest executive in the world. That is the Irish Question.

Benjamin Disraeli (Conservative leader), Commons speech (16 Feb. 1844)

The Home Rule Bills   For most Irish people, the concept of a United Kingdom was farcical, a fact realized in his later years by the great Liberal politician W. E. Gladstone, who determined with some fervour to right the wrong (Bentley 1984: 245). His first Home Rule Bill of 1886 was defeated in the Commons and his second fell in the House of Lords in 1893. Events surrounding a third bill were dramatic, revealing naked class hatred. Although the Liberals had become convinced home-rulers there were other matters to occupy them when they returned to government in 1906, including bitter battles with the suffragettes and the House of Lords. Losing their overall majority in 1910, they became dependent upon support from Irish MPs, and to win this Prime Minister Asquith pledged himself to another Home Rule Bill. Although this passed through the Commons in 1912, the Conservatives regarded Irish MPs as inferior in status and not entitled to vote on constitutional issues (Cross 1963: 123–4). It became apparent that they considered themselves, and the class they represented, to be above the constitution. In 1906 Balfour had declared: 'The great Unionist party should still control, whether in power or whether in opposition, the destinies of this great Empire' (Blake 1985: 190).

In the Lords the Conservatives defeated the bill, thereby delaying it until 1914. This allowed the Protestants of the north to arm as the Ulster Volunteers under the fanatical leadership of Edward Carson, while Conservatives on the mainland contemplated a *coup d'état*. Conservative leader Bonar Law (himself of Ulster descent) told a crowd outside Blenheim Palace:

> There are things stronger than parliamentary majorities . . . I can imagine no length of resistance to which Ulster can go in which I should not be prepared to support them. (Cross 1963: 177)

No left-wing orator would have dared utter such sentiments; the Conservative Party began to resemble a guerrilla band (Bentley 1984: 365).

I have passed with a nod of the head,
Or polite meaningless words.
All changed, changed utterly:
A terrible beauty is born.

W. B. Yeats (1865–1939; Irish poet), 'Easter 1916'

The Easter Rising   However, an impending holocaust was eclipsed in June 1914 by the assassination of Archduke Franz Ferdinand of Austria-Hungary. The bill was passed but placed in cold storage for the duration of the first world war. Yet Irish activists, mistrusting the English, sought German help and, on Easter Sunday 1916, declared a republic. This was put down harshly, the English toasting their triumph with the blood of martyrs through executions and imprisonments. Roger Casement, a British Consul in Germany who had enlisted enemy assistance, was hanged for high treason and his standing undermined by the circulation of diaries revealing his homosexuality.

In the post-war general election Sinn Fein (the republican party) gained an overwhelming victory in Ireland and those elected refused to enter Westminster, establishing an independent Irish parliament at Dublin, the Dáil. Renewing the republic of Easter 1916, they appointed a president, Eamon de Valera, and government. At the same time an Irish Republican Army (IRA) formed under Michael Collins, to which the British responded in 1920 with measures that Asquith said 'would disgrace the blackest annals of the lowest despotism in Europe' (Taylor 1965: 155). The infamous Black and Tans, chosen for their penchant for violence, were recruited to assist the Royal Ulster Constabulary (RUC) in a reign of terror.

Partition After much tortuous negotiation, Prime Minister Lloyd George and the Irish politicians signed a compromise treaty based on **partition** on 6 December 1921, giving birth to the Irish Free State (Eire). The twenty-six counties of the south received dominion status on the Canadian model and six of the nine counties of Ulster remained as a UK province with an elected bicameral assembly (at Stormont) and an executive exercising certain devolved powers. The fact that Ulster had far more autonomy than Wales or Scotland reflected hopes that it would eventually decide to reunite under Dublin. The arrangement was to leave the Ulster Catholics as second-class citizens, living in ghettos in the poorest housing, doing the most unpleasant jobs and receiving the worst education. The constituency boundaries were gerrymandered to ensure Protestant dominance. For the south, the 'solution' had come not as a result of statesmanship but through violence and bloodshed, leaving a fermenting sense of grievance; 1949 saw Eire's departure from the Commonwealth.

Belfast from the 1960s: the killing streets

Although the settlement contained the germs of further violence, the Irish question ceased to be a scourge of British politicians as republicanism gave way to a less confrontational nationalism. However, economic decline was to fan the embers of discontent in the north; heavy dependence on industries in irrevocable decline (shipbuilding and textiles) produced unemployment higher than in the rest of the UK. Prime Minister Terence O'Neil attempted to attract new industries and sought closer involvement with the south. A new generation of Catholics grew into political awareness, inspired by the international civil rights movements of the 1960s. Protestants became alarmed and a reaction set in, partly under the demagogic influence of the Reverend Ian Paisley. The B-Specials, an auxiliary unit of the RUC, attacked civil-rights demonstrators, leading to a retaliatory rejuvenation of the IRA, which had effectively disarmed.

Again the politics of Northern Ireland was to open as a running sore on the British body politic. The divisions were not only reflected in ideological battles, they were overlain with the machinery of violence and death. The participants are religious groupings with constitutional aspirations and sometimes paramilitary connections, rather than conventional parties. With marches and violence their politics have often been of the street rather than the debating chamber.

The two leading Protestant/unionist parties were the Official Unionists and Paisley's more working-class and fundamentalist Democratic Unionist Party (DUP). The Protestants also mobilized through organizations such as the Orange Order and the Apprentice Boys of Derry, engaging in political symbolism through provocative parades and marches. Protestant paramilitary organ-

izations included the Ulster Volunteers, splintering into the Ulster Defence Association and the Ulster Freedom Force. In addition, the RUC was Protestant
dominated and itself used unusual and extremely violent methods. The Cath-
olic/nationalist cause was represented by the Social Democratic and Labour
Party (SDLP), favouring constitutional methods, and Sinn Fein (the political
wing of the IRA). The IRA splintered in the 1970s into the more extreme Irish
National Liberation Army and Provisional IRA.

In this ferment non-sectarian politics had little place and the mainland parties did not seek a serious presence. However, the Ulster Unionists had historic
links with the Conservatives, generally supporting them at Westminster. In 1970
a non-sectarian Alliance Party formed, with links with the Social Democrats,
though its broad position was to maintain the mainland connection. A new
player entered the game in 1969 when, following a request from the RUC,
backed by militant civil rights leader Bernadette Devlin (Hattersley 1996: 77),
the British government took the fateful decision to send in the army to restore
the peace. From initially welcoming the move, Catholics were to develop a
feeling of menacing harassment and the pattern of violence began an unremitting escalation (figure 6.2).

Developments were to see the powers of state repression increase, hardening
Catholic and world sympathy for the IRA. Internment without trial was introduced in August 1971 and on 20 January 1972 British troops fired on civil
rights demonstrators, leaving thirteen dead. Television brought the violence
into living rooms on the mainland, entering the inventory of grim anniversaries
as 'Bloody Sunday'. In March 1972 the Heath government assumed *direct rule*
over the province. The gerrymandered constituencies had meant that Stormont

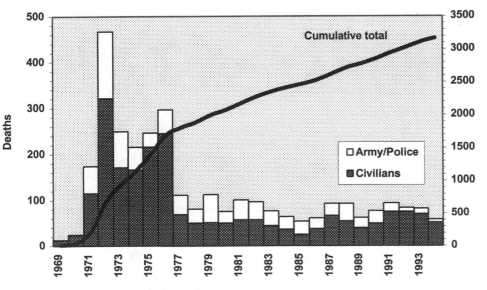

Figure 6.2
Violence in
Northern Ireland:
deaths associated
with the civil
disturbances from
1969 until the
September 1994
ceasefire.

Source: Data from *Guardian* (13 Sept. 1994).

remained under an indelible Protestant majority offering no voice to the Catholics. It was suspended and a Northern Ireland Office created under a Secretary of State, a poisoned chalice for any British politician. In 1974 the Prevention of Terrorism Act was rushed through Parliament (following devastating bombs in pubs in Guildford and Birmingham), outlawing the IRA and further extending police powers. Special (Diplock) courts were created in Ulster which dispensed with juries to avoid their intimidation. Harsh treatment of prisoners was to be condemned by the European Court of Human Rights.

Evidence that the RUC had adopted a 'shoot-to-kill' policy in 1982 occasioned the notorious Stalker affair, in which a British police officer heading an inquiry into the matter was impeded in his investigations, subjected to character assassination and suspended from duty in May 1986, just days before he was to travel to Belfast to interview RUC chief Sir John Hermon. In 1984, an IRA bomb exploded in the Brighton hotel housing Conservative Party leaders (including Margaret Thatcher) attending their annual conference. As the violence escalated, the feared British SAS became involved, shooting eight IRA men and a civilian at Loughall, County Tyrone, in 1987 and, on 6 March 1988, to an echo of excited public celebrity, gunning down three alleged would-be bombers in Gibraltar. No bomb was ever found and the European Court of Human Rights ruled that unreasonable force had been used. The judgement was seen by Downing Street as 'defying common sense' (*The Times*, 28 Sept. 1995).

Seeking a political solution

Paradoxically, although wanting to end the bloodshed British governments refused to talk; Sinn Fein remained a pariah party. Ministers empowered themselves to exclude named individuals from the mainland, including Sinn Fein leader Gerry Adams. In 1988 access to the British media was denied to Sinn Fein (though broadcasters made a mockery of this by using actors to speak their words).

I can only say that it would turn my stomach.

Prime Minister John Major, House of Commons (1 Nov. 1993), in response to suggestion by left-wing MP Dennis Skinner that the government talk with Gerry Adams and the Provisional IRA.

Clearly any return to the Stormont model, with gerrymandered constituencies and no voice for the Catholic minority, could not work. Moreover, the shifting demographic sands had seen, during the 1980s and 1990s, a steady rise in the nationalist vote, reflecting an increase in the Catholic population. UK governments recognized the need to break the stranglehold with some form of **consociationalism** (see O'Leary 1989) and a **power-sharing executive** permitting Catholic involvement.

The Sunningdale Agreement The Heath government tried, through a 1973 agreement, to establish an assembly elected by proportional representation and a Council of Ireland to facilitate discussion between Belfast, London and Dublin. However, these efforts were deeply resented by Protestants and the 1974 general election saw eleven of the twelve seats won by Unionists hostile to the policy. A general strike paralysed the province and the executive collapsed. The next Labour government came no nearer a solution; Unionists would settle for nothing less than the restoration of the majority dominance they had enjoyed at Stormont. The Thatcher government called a conference which the Official Unionists refused to attend and when James Prior was moved to the Northern Ireland Office many saw it as a form of political banishment for a politician regarded as a Heathite. Prior attempted to establish an assembly based on proportional representation but it was boycotted by the nationalists and received negatively in the Republic. It was abandoned in 1985 when the Unionists withdrew in opposition to a new initiative.

The Anglo-Irish Agreement An alternative political solution entails more involvement in Ulster's affairs by the Republic. This was attempted in November 1985 in the Anglo-Irish Agreement, signed by Margaret Thatcher and Irish Premier Dr Garret Fitzgerald, which established a forum in which the republic could comment on Northern Irish affairs. This tacit acceptance that a settlement could not be reached purely within a British framework evoked hostility from a number of Conservative MPs and Thatcher was later to claim that officials had misled her into signing (McKinstry 1998). To Unionists the policy was the thin end of a wedge designed to reunify Ireland as a republic, long the covert goal of British governments according to Enoch Powell. The Unionist MPs resigned their seats, producing an effective referendum through by-elections, but in losing one seat to the SDLP they rather shot themselves in the foot. Paradoxically, Sinn Fein was opposed on the grounds that the Agreement strengthened partition. Although facilitating dialogue, the initiative brought no formula for devolved government and was constantly overshadowed by acts of violence.

The Downing Street Declaration With the departure of Thatcher the Anglo-Irish Agreement was suspended and fresh constitutional talks initiated. These proceeded uneasily but in 1993 John Major and Irish prime minister Albert Reynolds signed an historic Downing Street Declaration asserting the right of the peoples of north and south to unite should they ever so wish, and denying any British government strategic interest in Northern Ireland. Most controversially, it offered a place at the negotiating table to Sinn Fein on the condition that violence be renounced. Throughout the 1990s Gerry Adams had used non-violent tactics, wooing US support with considerable skill, but not always able to control the IRA. Although the Declaration was initially rejected by both sides, the intervention of a US delegation put what became known as the peace process back on track. An IRA ceasefire was declared on 31 August 1994 and Protestant paramilitaries responded with a similar renunciation. It was revealed

> What a God-awful country. Get me a whisky and soda.
>
> Reginald Maudling (Home Secretary, 1970–2) to an official upon his return from a visit to Belfast

> There is doubt whether the Government will ever accept that the IRA ceasefire is permanent and that Sinn Fein has renounced violence.
>
> Northern Ireland Secretary Sir John Mayhew, on eve of 1994 Conservative Party conference (*Guardian*, 11 Oct. 1994)

that secret talks had been taking place between the British government and the IRA.

In February 1995 the two governments produced a Framework Document outlining a consociational democracy (Lijphart 1996). It stressed the need for agreement amongst both parties and ordinary people, the latter to be ascertained through referendum. The proposals included an assembly elected by proportional representation exercising devolved powers and advised by an elected three-member panel to prevent discriminatory legislation. In addition, **cross-border bodies** would consider joint issues such as tourism, and a strengthened set of institutions with representatives from all parties in both north and south, not excluding Sinn Fein, would replace those of the Anglo-Irish Agreement.

Gerry Adams enhanced his peacemaking credentials with visits to the USA and high-profile meetings with President Clinton. Yet Unionists remained suspicious, seeing again the thin end of a republican wedge, and a series of disastrous by-elections left Major's government increasingly dependent upon their support. A warning shot was fired across his bows when they withheld support over the Scott Report, the government surviving by a single vote. Major began holding up progress with a demand that the IRA hand in its weapons, normally seen as a gesture of surrender.

The tense stand-off could not last and, at 7.01 p.m. on 18 February 1996, the seventeen-month IRA ceasefire came to a shattering end when a bomb near South Quay station on the Isle of Dogs rocked east London, injuring more than a hundred. While the British government and Unionists voiced outrage, Adams lamented that an unprecedented peace opportunity had foundered on their refusal to negotiate (*Guardian*, 19 Feb. 1996). A widespread pattern of IRA bombs and bomb scares, causing major disruptions in London and elsewhere in the run-up to the 1997 general election, questioned whether any progress had been made.

Labour's peace process   As prime minister, Tony Blair's first official journey was to Ulster, where he declared that 'the settlement train would leave with or without Sinn Fein', who were invited into renewed peace talks subject to a ceasefire (*Financial Times*, 26 June 1997). Blair pledged to put new proposals to the people in a referendum. There were also to be parallel talks on decommissioning weapons and a Parades Commission was established to regulate marches. In the summer of 1997, plans for a number of particularly controversial parades by Protestant Orangemen through Catholic areas were abandoned

"It's a card from Gerry Adams. While he deeply regrets the shooting of Colonel Mustard in the Library, the responsibility lies with the British Government."

and, in the light of the concessions, Northern Ireland Secretary Mo Mowlam persuaded the IRA to instigate a second ceasefire.

Although Ian Paisley declared it 'total surrender', serious all-party talks began. A foretaste was provided in BBC 'Newsnight's head-to-head debate between Ulster Unionist MP Ken Maginnis and Sinn Fein spokesman Martin McGuinness. While exchanges were heated, the first such encounter on British television suggested a new spirit. Blair himself staked much on the talks but Mo Mowlam, the first woman to play such a central role, proved not only exceptionally tenacious, but also accommodating, even entering the Maze Prison to talk with convicted terrorists.

Another key actor was ex-US senator George Mitchell, who chaired the talks. Although a Catholic with Irish grandparents and an associate of the Kennedys, he trod carefully through the minefield of ancestral enmities. The US involvement dated from Clinton's 1992 presidential campaign when he had courted the Irish-American vote. In office, and backed by the Kennedys and the Irish-American lobby, he roused British fury by allowing a visa to Gerry Adams which helped secure the first IRA truce. From its initial nationalist sympathies, the USA began to see two sides to the problem and Unionist leader David Trimble was accorded equal treatment as the USA began to assume the

---

The violence behind the violence

A Catholic teenager frustrated at not being able to go to a Chinese restaurant at the end of his own street in a Protestant area finally cracked and went for a take-away. He was stabbed in the eye with a screwdriver.

One of thousands of sectarian incidents in Northern Ireland remaining unreported amid the greater atrocities (*Guardian*, 11 April 1998)

role of an honest broker. In November 1995 Clinton visited Belfast and Dublin for talks.

Yet the final negotiations were tense. When Unionist objections seemed to promise collapse, Blair secured eleventh-hour intervention from Clinton. The midnight deadline passed but talks continued into the night until, on 10 April 1998, Good Friday, a potentially ground-breaking sixty-seven-page document was accepted, albeit tentatively, by all sides. The Agreement, which would be put to referendums in Northern Ireland and the Republic, included:

1   a Northern Ireland Assembly of 108 elected by proportional representation with legislative powers and a power-sharing executive;
2   a North–South Ministerial Council to consider issues such as cross-border cooperation;
3   the Irish government to renounce constitutional claims to Northern Ireland and London to replace the Government of Ireland Act;
4   a Council of the Isles comprising members from the north and south of Ireland and the Scottish and Welsh assemblies.

There were also to be releases of prisoners coupled with a decommissioning of arms.

Although there was cross-party agreement in Britain, one discordant voice came from Spain, where Baroness Thatcher was attending a conference. She remembered the bomb at the 1984 Conservative Party conference: 'These people are criminals, not political prisoners' (*Independent*, 23 April 1998). Similar sentiments were expressed by the RUC in June 1998. Indeed, even as the final details of the settlement were being worked out, seventy-five miles to the north, thirty-five-year-old Trevor Deeney, shot dead the previous Tuesday by the INLA, was being buried.

The referendum The sense was of an opportunity that could not be missed. The wording allowed politicians to interpret as they chose; Unionists could claim it strengthened the Union while Sinn Fein could tell their supporters the opposite. Tensions mounted in the days before voting and Ian Paisley gained a new lease of life for his fire-and-brimstone rhetoric. When Mo Mowlam considered inviting Elton John to give a concert at Hillsborough he declared: 'Now she's bringing in the sodomites' (Langdon 1998). Unionists were enraged at the appearance of IRA bombers, released from prison to attend a Sinn Fein rally in Dublin. However, Michael Stone, a Unionist terrorist who had killed three mourners at a cemetery in 1988, was also given home leave to attend a rally. Blair scored highly within the community as the most trusted politician and made the vote a highly personalized affair as he fired off a fusillade of signed newspaper articles, broadcasts and street campaigning to urge a 'Yes' vote. He was reported to have stormed out of a BBC studio when the interviewer spoke of support for the deal 'crumbling' (*Sunday Times*, 24 May 1998). John Major, Paddy Ashdown and William Hague all joined the 'Yes' campaign to signal cross-party support. A pop concert was arranged featuring the Irish band U2 from the south and Ash, a group with Protestant backgrounds, from the north. Here Unionist leader David Trimble and SDLP leader John Hume symbolically shook hands, Trimble bringing his teenage daughter to the concert.

The result of the referendums was a resounding 'Yes' in each case. The 81 per cent turnout in the north exceeded expectations: 677,000 voted 'Yes' and 275,000 said 'No'. In constituency terms, seventeen were for and only one against. A *Sunday Times*/Coopers and Lybrand exit poll found that the 'Yes' vote came from 55 per cent of Protestants and 96 per cent of Catholics. In the Republic, a turnout of 56 per cent showed 94 per cent agreement for relinquishing claims to the north. To the anger of Paisley, the Queen announced her intention to visit Belfast and the Republic as a gesture of support for the agreement.

> My daddy's saying yes. But my mummy's a Christian.
>
> Protestant barmaid, on the eve of the May 1998 referendum, quoted in *Sunday Times* (24 May 1998)

The Assembly Voting for the Northern Ireland Assembly was by single transferable vote (p. 257) in eighteen constituencies with counting completed on 27 June 1998. Fringe parties made some gains, including the Women's Coalition which had campaigned for peace (table 6.1). But the voice of the people in the referendum had not been enough to silence many of those opposing the Agreement, including Ian Paisley's DUP and the UK Unionists. Although contesting the election, their intention was to secure enough seats to wreck the Assembly. In the event, some 75 per cent of voters supported a party favouring the Agreement. David Trimble's Ulster Unionists won the most seats while, with twenty-seven seats between them, the Unionist dissidents lacked the strength to prevent his election as First Minister. His deputy would be the Catholic Seamus Mallon. Trimble was to criticize William Hague and the Conservatives for their behaviour during the campaign, particularly their opposition to the bill releasing prisoners, for what he called 'short term party political gains' (*Observer*, 28 June 1998).

Table 6.1 Seats in the Northern Ireland Assembly, June 1998

Party	Seats
Ulster Unionist	28
SDLP	24
Democratic Unionist	20
Sinn Fein	18
Alliance	6
UK Unionist	5
Women's Coalition	2
Independent Unionist	3
Progressive Unionist	2

A time to forget

Optimists hoped that the time had come to forget the troubled past. Yet there was much to forget: deaths of hunger strikers, 'Bloody Sunday', 3,500 lost lives and 40,000 wounded over the previous thirty years. One in four of those voting in the referendum could claim to have known someone who had been killed. The ancestral voices speak from even greater distance, regularly rekindled by ceremonies and marches to mark bitter anniversaries such as the Battle of the Boyne, the Siege of Londonderry and the Easter Rising.

Indeed, in the week following the elections fears that the whole peace process might unravel arose as the Protestant Orangemen appeared intent upon defying a ban by the Marches Commission on their parade through the Catholic Garvaghy Road. Bowler-hatted, clad in their regalia and waving their banners, their ranks swelled by Scottish Orangemen, they faced the RUC in military-style riot gear across trenches and barbed wire in a tense stand-off lasting several days. They talked of bringing the province to a standstill as they had over the Sunningdale Agreement. The tension was only released by tragedy when three young boys burned to death in a fire-bombed house. Although the Orangemen remained resolute, opinion hardened against them and could not accept that their right to parade along a particular (Catholic) road was worth the life of a child. The pendulum of violence was to swing yet again in August 1998 when twenty-nine people were killed and many more injured in Omagh by a bomb planted by the self-styled Real IRA.

Orange Order
march, July 1998

Photo: Times Newspapers Ltd

However, world recognition of the achievements came when both Trimble and Hume were presented in Oslo with the Nobel Peace Prize, yet astonishingly, on this occasion, the two did not shake hands. Developments remained disappointingly slow as Trimble continued to make decommissioning of IRA weapons a prelude to setting up the Executive. The IRA response was to entirely renounce the idea of decommissioning. Clearly, although the Agreement might deprive the perpetrators of legitimacy, the nightmare of further violence could not be discounted as vicious 'punishment beatings' continued to maim.

> But if the focus remains on the past, the past will become the future, and that is something no one can desire.
>
> *Report of the International Body* (the Mitchell Commission) (22 Jan. 1996: para. 16)

Territorial Politics in the UK

In the days of empire, world dominance forged a British identity that could help unify the state but, as the colonies asserted their rights to self-determination, this cement began to crumble. Hence, an era which has witnessed the end of empire also sees a questioning of the bond between the four nations of the UK and the state is confronted with increasingly demanding problems of **territorial management**. The Labour and Liberal Democrat parties have seen the solution in devolution, which aims to save the union by releasing a safety valve upon a pent-up nationalistic fervour. In contrast, the Conservatives remained resolutely set against any threat to UK integrity, seeing devolution as the thin end of a wedge which would ultimately fracture the union altogether. However, when the 1997 general election left the party entirely bereft of seats in both Wales and Scotland it was difficult to sustain this opposition. In June 1998 William Hague told Scottish and Welsh Conservatives to accept defeat and work to win seats in the new assemblies.

In June 1998 Conservative MP Teresa Gorman introduced a private member's bill calling for a referendum on the establishment of an English Parliament with fiscal powers. Her purpose in this curious enterprise was to highlight a perceived threat to the UK from devolution and an unfairness towards the

Federal leanings

Journalists and others frequently suggest that the UK is acquiring a federalist character. The developments discussed in this chapter reveal grounds for this belief but constitutionally devolution does not of itself mean federalism. The former is, by definition, created by the act of a superior body, devolving some of its own powers and responsibilities to a subordinate one; these could be revoked at any time. In a federal system, the centre and regions stand constitutionally equal, with the distribution of powers and responsibilities set out in a written constitution.

English. However, enthusiasm for the union may even wilt in England. In the 1998 World Cup competition many English supporters rediscovered the red cross of the flag of St George, which was draped across the stadiums of France and flown over English pubs and supermarkets. The historic English quest for unity had produced a highly centralized state which served them well. However, uneven development has seen economic and political power concentrated in the south-east and a deindustrialized northern wasteland generating centrifugal forces within the mother country herself.

Moreover, the unity-through-devolution thesis remains to be tested. EU membership tends to undermine the role and sovereignty of the central state while emphasizing the region. The presence of the smaller EU states, including the Irish Republic, makes a separate Scotland and Wales look viable. Paradoxically, if the new assemblies are successful in holding their own against the central state, the case for autonomy is strengthened. Scottish founder of the Adam Smith Institute, Madsen Pirie, anticipated full independence within a decade of devolution (Groom 1997). In May 1998 an opinion poll (*Independent*, 7 May 1998) in Scotland showed the SNP more popular than Labour, suggesting that its leader, Alex Salmond, would be the First Minister with a 'moral authority' to call for a referendum on full independence. (However, it also held out the possibility of a hung parliament with the Liberal Democrats holding the balance of power.) Moreover, given that in the Anglo-Irish Agreement the British government conceded the right of Belfast citizens to secede from the UK and join the Republic should they wish, there could be no moral grounds for denying the same rights to Wales and Scotland.

Chapter 4 revealed the limitations on nation-state autonomy in a globalized economy. This chapter has exposed the challenge from within. Multinational states in the contemporary environment look increasingly like ill-adapted dinosaurs, vulnerable to legitimacy crises and rising nationalism. In the UK, siren calls from ancestral voices can leave citizens with a sense of cultural and constitutional ambiguity.

Key points

- The UK is a multinational state vulnerable to legitimacy crises and requiring territorial management.
- Historically the English political class saw unity of the British Isles as essential for security. This was accomplished largely by conquest of the Celtic fringe.
- In modern times the distinctiveness of Wales and Scotland was preserved through administrative outposts of Whitehall and Grand Committees at Westminster.
- Increasing disenchantment with the centralized state eventually led to referendums endorsing a Welsh Senedd and a Scottish Parliament and calls for English regional devolution.

- The EU's regional perspective adds momentum to the devolutionary movement.
- English conquest over Ireland was problematic and three attempts to grant home rule proved unsuccessful.
- The compromise of partition established the Irish Free State (Eire) while Ulster remained as a UK province with a parliament exercising devolved power.
- In Ulster the Catholics were treated as second-class citizens.
- The Irish question flared again in the 1960s as Catholic demands for civil rights met Protestant resistance and led to direct rule from Westminster.
- The violence was to continue for three decades.
- A long-drawn-out peace process, culminating in the Good Friday Agreement, led to a new Assembly exercising devolved powers in 1998.

Review your understanding of the following terms and concepts

Anglo-Irish Agreement	nationalism	SDLP
consociationalism	Orange Order	Senedd
cross-border body	partition	separatism
devolution	Plaid Cymru	Sinn Fein
DUP	power-sharing executive	SNP
federalism	regional assemblies	territorial management
home rule	regionalism	Ulster unionism
IRA	RUC	West Lothian question

Assignment

Study the extract from *The Economist* on p. 164 and answer the following questions.

		Mark (%)
1	Why are certain measures in the Good Friday Agreement 'detestable' to Unionists?	20
2	Evaluate David Trimble's grounds for insisting upon a decommissioning of IRA weapons as a precondition of appointing Sinn Fein members to his Cabinet.	40
3	Why do you think the IRA is reluctant to hand in its weaponry?	40

Northern Ireland

Haggling

BELFAST

The two men at the head of Northern Ireland's infant government, the Protestant unionist first minister, David Trimble, and his Catholic nationalist deputy Seamus Mallon, flew to America this week to urge businesses to invest in Ulster. But behind this symbolic togetherness, disagreement lurks. At issue is the familiar and vexed issue of the "decommissioning" of paramilitary weapons.

Mr Trimble wants to defer appointing further ministers to his government—in particular Sinn Fein's entitlement of two—until their military wing, the IRA, begins to get rid of its weapons.

This week Mr Trimble told the Conservative conference that the Good Friday peace agreement contained an "explicit cross-reference between decommissioning and holding office." But Mr Trimble's interpretation—itself phrased more or less precisely at different moments—has been contradicted by Mo Mowlam, Britain's secretary of state for Northern Ireland, Bertie Ahern, the Irish prime minister, and by Mr Trimble's own deputy.

As ever in Northern Ireland, there are several shades of grey in the truth about decommissioning. The issue threatened to destroy the talks, only hours before agreement was reached. Several of Mr Trimble's closest colleagues walked out largely because the proposed text contained no explicit demand for a handover of arms.

Instead it was stipulated that all ministers must commit themselves to non-violence, oppose any use or threat of force, and "use only democratic, non-violent means", or be excluded from office. Mr Trimble sought and received a last-minute written assurance from Tony Blair of adequate legislation on exclusion. But even the language of this text does not warrant Mr Trimble's suggestion of an "explicit cross-reference" between taking office and prior decommissioning.

Unionists will soon have to swallow several measures they detest—such as increased cross-border co-operation, reform of the police, stronger measures on equality between Catholics and Protestants, and the early release of most paramilitary prisoners. Refusing to appoint Sinn Fein ministers before decommissioning is arguably the only strong card Mr Trimble has left. Mr Adams no doubt thinks IRA guns are also crucial to the hand he is playing. But he also knows that decommissioning cannot be ignored.

The Economist, 10 Oct. 1998

Questions for discussion

1   Why did England need to unite the countries of the British Isles?
2   Explain why Wales and Scotland rejected devolution in 1979 but voted 'Yes' in 1997.
3   Why has the Conservative Party opposed devolution?
4   Discuss whether Scottish devolution will lead to further moves towards independence.
5   How important is the historical perspective in understanding the post-war conflict in Northern Ireland?
6   'Without the power to vary tax rates the Welsh Assembly can be no more than a talking shop.' Discuss.
7   Identify the factors inhibiting the establishment of a power-sharing executive in Northern Ireland?
8   Examine the case for political devolution to the English regions.
9   Why do you think referendums were used to decide the devolution issues? Was their use justified?
10   What should be the role and significance of cross-border bodies in the constitutional and political position of Northern Ireland?

Topic for debate

This house believes that the United Kingdom cannot remain intact in the contemporary world.

Further reading

Crick, B. (ed.) (1991) *National Identities: The Constitution of the United Kingdom*.
Essays considering the government of the UK and relations with Ireland in the light of national and regional senses of identity.

Kearney, H. (1990) *The British Isles: A History of Four Nations*.
Emphasizes how an understanding of the present is hindered if we fail to emphasize that a historical perspective must encompass more than just *English* history.

Keating, M. and Loughlin, J. (1997) *The Political Economy of the Regions*.
International examination of regionalism, with chapters on the EU, Wales, Scotland and the English regions.

MacDonald, M. (1986) *Children of Wrath: Political Violence in Northern Ireland*.
Argues that the colonization of Ireland created a problem that could not be resolved.

McGarry, J. and O'Leary, B. (1997) *Explaining Northern Ireland: Broken Images*.
Excellent analysis of the political complexities of the contemporary Irish situation.

Marr, A. (1992) *The Battle for Scotland*.
Explains the 'Scottish question'.

For light relief

The Crying Game.
Award-winning video/film set amidst the contemporary violence over Northern Ireland.

Michael Collins.
Video/film about the Irish civil war.

Braveheart.
Video/film saga of thirteenth-century Scottish revolt against English tyranny.

Michael Shea, *The State of the Nation*.
Set in a Scotland in deep economic crisis after four years of independence. Sinister TNC moves in to take advantage.

On the net

http://www.detr.gov.uk
http://nio.gov.uk
The DETR is a good starting point for material relating to regionalism and the NI Office for Irish issues.

http://www.plaidcymru.org
http://www.snp.org.uk
Visit the Celtic fringe through its web sites.

Chapter Seven

The Social Context: Our Divided Society

In this chapter we examine the social context in which British politics is enacted. A political system does not stand above society as an autonomous machine; it is as much part of society as our weather system is part of the planet's ecosphere. It has long been proclaimed that British society is benignly cohesive but we shall argue that this unity has been a veneer concealing the cracks beneath. The chapter includes four principal focuses. The first examines the political culture, the attitudes of people towards the political system. The following three sections expose great divides arising from class, gender and race.

Political Culture

What is political culture?

Political culture is a rather vague concept referring essentially to the set of attitudes citizens hold towards society and the political system. It reflects a myriad factors including some already encountered in previous chapters: history, geography, the constitution, the institutions and the range of informal practices associated with government. The study of political culture reminds us that maintaining a political regime depends upon thoughts as well as actions. For this reason much political activity at all levels is symbolic, aiming to make people happy with the system – to *legitimate* it. It will become apparent throughout this book that the legitimating function has been performed very well in Britain.

British political culture

A classic investigation of British political culture was carried out in the early 1960s by the American political scientists Almond and Verba (1963), who enthused that in Britain they had found a veritable jewel of a polity; nothing less than the ideal conditions for liberal democracy – a '**civic culture**' entailing respect for government and an unwillingness to resort to disruptive protest. There were three important ingredients in this civic mix: continuity, deference and consensus.

Continuity We saw in chapter 3 that Britain has never made a dramatic revolutionary break with the past. The evolutionary pattern of change has preserved many ancient symbols and ceremonies. A brief republican period was seen as an aberration and was soon ended with the Restoration. However, critics see this conservative strain as holding back the process of social and political change. One symptom of this is the preservation of deferential attitudes belonging to a distant monarchical past.

Deference The best political culture for a capitalist state is a deferential one, where the masses willingly accept inequality and show little desire for change or to participate in government. Indeed, the essence of **deference** is that ordinary people believe that running the state should be left to those who 'know best'. It was noted by Walter Bagehot in 1867, when he argued that the masses were unable to understand the reality of government but were beguiled by a 'theatrical show' of monarchy and other *dignified* elements of the constitution.

Although the virtues of deference are questionable (for Aristotle, not to be involved in politics degraded one to the level of a beast), texts in the orthodox liberal-democratic tradition have generally admired it. This passivity was demonstrated in the depressions of the 1920s and 1930s (the General Strike of 1926 failed to mobilize mass support) and again in the recessions of the 1980s and 1990s, all of which were weathered with considerable patience and stoicism. In the acclaimed 1997 film *The Full Monty*, the men cast aside by the economic system became not revolutionaries but strippers. In 1998, when French students were taking to the streets, their British counterparts were enduring reduced grants, student loans and tuition fees with largely token resistance.

The feeling that things must be accepted has been seen as a very British characteristic and helps to explain why the Labour Party has been at its least electable whenever it has offered a radical programme. Gramsci argued that those wishing to dominate society encourage such a view in order to maintain their hegemony (see p. 35).

A crisis of deference? By the late 1960s orthodox writers began to fear that this 'civic society' was turning sour. Surveys suggested a greater willingness to protest through unofficial strikes and demonstrations (Marsh 1978). When a miners' strike appeared to precipitate the downfall of Heath's government in 1974, the liberal-democratic apologists began a Cassandra-like lament that the country was becoming 'ungovernable'. However, the obituary for deference was greatly exaggerated. In 1980 Almond and Verba 'revisited' the British political culture in a study that confirmed that, although there was cynicism, and even willingness to support unlawful violence against the state, these were confined to a small, unpopular minority (Kavanagh 1980). Labour leaders were actually disowning the actions of their own non-deferential left-wing elements with as much ferocity as the Conservatives. From the early 1980s the rulers sought to persuade the masses that redundancies, cultural impoverishment and increasingly large differences in wealth were necessary for their own good. Thatcher denigrated the welfare state with reference to 'feather-bedding' and 'scrounging', while Major asserted that 'if it isn't hurting it isn't working', his Chancellor Norman Lamont describing unemployment as 'a price worth paying'. There was talk of Britain becoming a more **meritocratic** society in which the talented and thrusting would rise to the top. Yet curiously, such a society is not necessarily non-deferential. On the contrary, the 'success ideology' has been seen as a basis for quiescence by the working class and other disadvantaged groups in the face of social inequalities. Victims have only themselves to blame and revolution is unjustified.

Although newspapers, particularly those of multi-media tycoon Rupert Murdoch, increasingly reported the behaviour of the high and mighty in non-deferential terms, the message remained broadly sympathetic to powerful capitalist interests. The Queen may have been mocked but it was a public-school-educated prime minister that Murdoch helped into Downing Street in 1997. Despite the public's increased resort to direct action over issues such as animal rights, the environment and the road-building programme in the 1990s, the Labour Party itself swung massively to the right. When it finally regained office in 1997, it did so with the voices of its left-wing members muted, a tough law-and-order line and promises of 'no favours' for the unions. Deference was by no means in its coffin.

Consensus It can be argued that British political culture is highly consensual; the majority of the population are happy with the liberal-democratic system. The **consensus** can even extend to policy-making, the major parties tending to aim for the centre ground. Yet the political culture is not as seamless and homogeneous as is sometimes thought. Chapter 6 explained how the UK was united partly by force, with lingering spatial tensions leading to new devolution settlements. In the case of Ireland the maintenance of the union extracted a high price in blood. Beyond this, three other great fissures score the 'One Nation' landscape envisioned by liberal-democratic apologists: class, gender and race.

Classes Apart

The history of all hitherto existing society is the history of class struggles.

Karl Marx, *The Communist Manifesto* (1848)

Defining social class

Generally speaking, **social classes** categorize people on the basis of characteristics such as background, occupation, manners, accent and privilege. **Class** is essentially about hierarchy and inequality, denoting social divisions similar to 'caste', 'rank', 'degree' and 'status'. It is considered to have been of greater political significance in Britain than anywhere else in the English-speaking world

(Butler and Stokes 1969: 90). There are various bases for defining class, including the following.

Relationship to the mode of production More than any other thinker, Karl Marx made class central to his analysis. For him it was determined by the mode of production. Under capitalism there is an essential *dichotomy*: a small upper class (or *bourgeoisie*) owning the capital needed for production, and a large working class (or *proletariat*) with only their labour to sell. The basic relationship between the two is exploitative.

> Misery and poverty are so absolutely degrading, and exercise such a paralysing effect . . . that no class is ever really conscious of its own suffering. They have to be told of it by other people.
>
> Oscar Wilde (1856–1900; Irish author and dramatist),
> *The Soul of Man under Socialism* (1891)

Occupation Another major figure in the theory of class is Max Weber, who, while accepting much of Marx's analysis, argued that other factors were important, particularly the complex structure of the labour market. The capital-owning class contained *rentiers* and entrepreneurs, while the propertyless divided into those privileged with specialist skills and those without. Occupation is certainly a key variable, being generally correlated with a range of other factors – education, accent, social background, leisure activities, lifestyle, housing, and so on.

The categories used in official surveys are based on an occupational classification (table 7.1). In readiness for the 2001 census, this categorization was revised in 1998 to reflect the changing social structure – the growing lower middle class, an enlarging petite bourgeoisie as redundant workers set up their

Social class: Office for National Statistics classes, 1998 (with examples of occupations in each class)

1a *Large employer*: higher manager, company director, senior police officer, newspaper editor, top football manager
1b *Professionals*: doctor, solicitor, engineer, teacher, airline pilot
2   *Associate professional*: journalist, nurse/midwife, actor/musician, junior police officer, lower manager
3   *Intermediate*: secretary, air stewardess, driving instructor, footballer
4   *Smaller employer*: non-professional self-employed, publican, plumber, self-employed sportsperson, small farmer
5   *Lower supervisor*: craft worker, mechanic, train driver, foreman
6   *Semi-routine*: traffic warden, caretaker, gardener, assembly-line worker
7   *Routine*: cleaner, waitress, road-worker, docker
8   *Excluded*: long-term unemployed and sick, never worked

Social class: Institute of Practitioners in Advertising classification

In its efforts to persuade the right people to covet the right things, the advertising industry uses the following classification.

A   Higher managerial, administrative or professional
B   Intermediate managerial, administrative or professional
C1   Supervisory or clerical, and junior managerial, administrative or professional
C2   Skilled manual
D   Semi-skilled and unskilled manual
E   State pensioners or widows (no other earnings), casual or lowest-grade workers and long-term unemployed

---

own businesses, the increased insecurity of employment, more women in work and the emergence of an underclass. A widely used alternative occupational definition is that devised by the advertising industry, aiming to place people in categories reflecting their consumption patterns.

Income This is not necessarily correlated with occupation; there can be impoverished poets and vicars and wealthy scrap-metal merchants. Millionaire Paul McCartney termed himself working class. It generally shows wide variations between the few high and the many low earners. The early post-war period saw some reduction in income inequality, a trend enhanced by the tax system, but since the late 1970s an unprecedented increase has occurred (figure 7.1), widening the gap between the richest and poorest regions and between sections of the population, in a trend that was expected to continue. In 1996, the gap between rich and poor was wider than at any time since 1886 (Goodman et al. 1997), the income of the richest 10 per cent of the population equal to that of the whole of the bottom 50 per cent. The tax rewards to the 'fat cats' are justified by a theory that everyone else, even those in 'Cardboard City', benefit through a 'trickle-down effect'. Research by the House of Commons library for Labour MP Alan Milburn, released in November 1994, revealed that one-

Table 7.1 Class structure of the adult population, 1996/7, according to the definitions used in official statistics (percentages)

Class		Men	Women
I	Professional	8	3
II	Intermediate	29	28
III	Skilled non-manual	12	37
IV	Skilled manual	31	8
V	Partly skilled	15	19
VI	Unskilled manual	5	6

Source: Data from *Social Trends* (1998: table 1.11).

Figure 7.1
Earnings of the top and bottom ten per cent of the working population, 1991–1997.

Source: Data from *Annual Abstract of Statistics* (1998: table 6.16).

third of British people earned below a 'decency threshold' set by the Council of Europe (£5.90 per hour), a 54 per cent increase since 1979. According to the independent Low Pay Unit this placed Britain at the bottom of Western Europe's low pay league (*Guardian*, 22 Nov. 1994), a situation not improved by setting a minimum wage at £3.60 per hour in 1998.

Wealth Beyond the issue of earnings, there remains a basic dichotomy between a wealth-owning minority (table 7.2) and the great mass. Wealth may take various forms, including stocks and shares, property and capital, which is preserved and handed down through the generations. By 1997, the richest fifth of the population were amongst the best-off in Europe (*Independent*, 15 June 1997). Even amongst the richest 500 people, over half is concentrated in the hands of the top 50.

Property is organised robbery.

George Bernard Shaw (1856–1950; Irish dramatist), Preface to *Major Barbara* (1907)

An anatomy of the classes

Britain is often described as a rigidly class-divided society and sometimes contrasted with the USA, which is said to be more open. However, both views are crude stereotypes: the USA is not without a social elite spanning the generations like an aristocracy, while in Britain mobility between classes is certainly possible. Goldthorpe (1987) found that 53 per cent of a sample of 10,000 British men surveyed in 1983 had changed classes. However, Britain remains a particularly class-conscious society. One indication of this comes from attitudes towards the redistribution of income and resources: the rich resist it, and the poor favour it, more strongly than in comparable nations (Evans 1993: 133–4). Moreover, despite considerable social mobility in the mid-twentieth century, research shows that opportunities remain dominated by social origins and, unlike the USA, there is no evidence of a more open society (Devine 1997:

Is he rich, or is he rich!

The Duke of Westminster not only owns a sizeable chunk of London and large slices of Cheshire, North Wales, the Scottish Highlands, Vancouver, Hawaii and Wagga Wagga, he had an income reported to be around £10,800 an hour in 1983 (*Sunday Times*, 20 Feb. 1983). Estimating his assets to be worth around £1,750 million, the *Sunday Times* (19 April 1998) placed him fourth on their 'Rich List' for 1998, just ahead of Labour benefactor Bernie Ecclestone.

---

74). Although the terms are used loosely, much discussion speaks of a broad threefold division into *upper class*, *middle class* and *working class*.

The upper class

The British upper class has evolved through a process of fusion and fission which amalgamated the landowning aristocracy, the lesser gentry, the financiers and the bourgeoisie which emerged with the industrial revolution (Scott 1985: 29–35). In 1923, before the Labour Party and the welfare state had made any inroads into the pattern of distribution (table 7.2), this powerful alliance constituted the richest fifth of the population, owning some 95 per cent of the nation's wealth. By 1972, with the welfare state at its peak, the richest fifth still claimed as much as 85 per cent, leaving 15 per cent to be shared amongst the rest (Urry 1985: 59–60). The holding is cumulative since it generates considerable unearned income.

In addition to the holders of great wealth there are the mega-earners: the Royal Commission on the Distribution of Income and Wealth (1976: 10) estimated that there were some 65,000 very highly paid employees in Britain in the 1970s. However, globalization, deregulation in the City, privatization and the tax revolution of the late 1980s were to swell this category into a new 'Super Class' (Adonis and Pollard 1997). Glimpses of this new breed were seen in the high-profile cases such as Cedric Brown, who took a 75 per cent pay rise to run

Table 7.2 Distribution of wealth in the UK (percentages)

Year	Top 1 per cent	Top 5 per cent	Top 10 per cent
1923[a]	61	82	89
1966[a]	31	56	69
1976	21	38	50
1986	18	36	50
1994	19	38	51

[a] England and Wales only

Source: Data from Atkinson and Harrison (1978: 159); *Social Trends* (1998: table 5.26).

> The stately homes of England,
> How beautiful they stand,
> To prove the upper classes
> Have still the upper hand.
>
> Noel Coward (1899–1973; British actor and playwright)

a monopoly utility for an annual salary of £450,000, 'Superwoman' Nicola Horlick, a City fund manager earning a reputed £1.15 million, and barrister Lord Irvine, who gave up annual earnings estimated at some £500,000 to take up the position of Labour's Lord Chancellor. The main drive in the rise of the super-earners was the financial services industry based in the City but working in an international, US-dominated remuneration regime. In 1996, of some 8,500 people at the top of the private-sector professions, the lowest earners were notching up £190,000 a year, while in the boardrooms the average remuneration for the chief executives of the largest hundred companies was £501,000 in 1995. There are also certain freakishly high, and usually short-lived, salaries of entertainers and sports personalities, the popularity of whom serves to legitimate the culture of inequality. These can even be invited into the places of privilege and they soon subscribe to the accepted values. (Hence Frank Bruno threatened to leave the country if Labour won the 1997 general election.)

Members of this class share much in common in terms of background, lifestyle and profession. Educationally they have remained separate through the public school system, where intense academic study has been complemented by a sense of training for leadership. Upon leaving school they go disproportionately to the elite Oxbridge universities. They also bond together by kinship (and old school) ties: an exemplar family with one son in the army, one in the civil service and another in the church, and a daughter married to someone in the City, might not be entirely apocryphal. Indeed, 'arranged marriages' have ensured that family wealth is augmented rather than dispersed, while accountants and lawyers work assiduously to minimize the effects of inheritance and other taxes.

Professional and social life reinforce commonality. Membership of London clubs, golf clubs and the Freemasons preserves a sense of exclusiveness which is celebrated in ceremonies and great sporting events like the Lord's Test, Ascot, Wimbledon, Cowes, the Boat Race and the Grand National. At all these venues are hallowed places where ordinary folk may not go: the Long Room at Lord's, the Royal Box, the Royal Enclosure.

The presence of the upper class is venerated with archaic symbols: a reigning monarch, a fully fledged aristocracy, a House of Lords, and a host of ancient sinecures such as Lord Lieutenant of the County and High Sheriff. The exclusion process is strengthened by a preoccupation with dress, manners and accent (mocked in Bernard Shaw's *Pygmalion*). These symbols of ancient privilege serve to legitimate the inequality produced by modern capitalism. This explains why the British bourgeoisie sought not to overthrow the bastions of privilege

We are forever being told that we have a rigid class structure. That's a load of codswallop.

Prince Edward, quoted in the *Observer* (21 Sept. 1997)

but to ingratiate itself with the old elite through a process of social climbing. The class has shown a genius for survival, assimilating talented or successful members of the lower orders like a vampire sucking the life-blood of the young. This lack of rigid 'structuration' (Giddens 1979: ch. 6) helps to legitimate the system (in theory anyone can become a millionaire).

In terms of ideology the upper class exhibits a high degree of homogeneity, though there remains a broad division between the paternalistic strain inherited from Tory traditions – a belief that privilege carries duties – and the hard-nosed whiggish tradition of individualism and competition resuscitated in the 1980s as Thatcherism. In addition, much has been made of notions of racial superiority; members of the class saw themselves as shouldering the 'white man's burden' in the great days of empire and of being 'born to rule'. Ideologically their sympathies have generally been towards the right, which has usually meant supporting the Conservative Party, of which many have been members. However, they are equally willing to support Labour if it can deliver the enterprising low-tax regime they desire. Thus David Sainsbury, head of the supermarket dynasty who topped the 1998 *Sunday Times* 'Rich List' (19 April 1998), was an enthusiastic supporter of the New Labour government by which he was ennobled.

The Establishment Students of politics will undoubtedly encounter this vague but expressive term, popularized by journalist Henry Fairlie in the *Spectator* in the 1950s (Thomas 1959). **Establishment** denotes a closed group comprising those in control of the leading institutions (public schools, church, monarchy and aristocracy, mass media, traditional professions, Parliament, armed forces, civil service, the City, and of course the owners and managers of industry) (Sedgemore 1980: 11). Many dislike the term, particularly those alleged to be part of it, and it is clearly related to the idea of the upper class, though some would use the term 'elite'. This is discussed further in chapter 17.

The Establishment talks with its own branded accents; eats different meals at different times; has its privileged system of education; its own religion, even, to a large extent, its own form of football.

A. J. P. Taylor, in *New Statesman* (8 Aug. 1953)

The middle class

Despite his essentially dichotomous view of class structure, Marx did recognize 'middle and intermediate strata' between the two great social formations. However, he believed that the obligation to sell their labour, and hence their inability to accumulate capital, would mean that the middle class would ultimately become part of a massive proletariat. This has not happened in Britain (Mandel 1983: 201–2), a fact with very important implications for the legitimation process. It becomes possible to argue that the growth of a vast intermediate class represents a process of *embourgeoisement* of society which has on the one hand eroded the old upper class, leaving an empty and harmless husk, and on the other, left an insignificant rump of ne'er-do-wells at the bottom, an echo of the working class.

Much media analysis discusses politics and society in these terms, with the intermediate class commonly divided into three – upper, middle and lower – largely distinguished on the basis of occupation. The upper middle class broadly includes the intelligentsia, professional people and managers, which John Goldthorpe (1982) has termed the 'service class' or 'salariat' (see figure 7.2). The middle characteristically contains the petite bourgeoisie, a tenacious class of small business people who resist the drive to large-scale operation. The lower middle comprises white- and blue-collar workers who generally try to espouse middle-class values. The Thatcher era, with its attacks both on the welfare state and trade unions *and* on the old upper-class professions, was seen by many as the final seal on the creation of this middle-class-dominated society, which enthusiasts, including Tony Blair, prefer to call a *classless* society.

There is clearly much in the *embourgeoisement* thesis; capitalism has changed dramatically during the twentieth century. However, objections can be raised (see pp. 533–6). Many of those officially classified as middle class are really performing routine, low-paid, unrewarding jobs, indistinguishable from unskilled manual work (Giddens 1979: 288), and the insecurity of employment for today's blue-collar and routine clerical workers leaves them little different from manual workers (Devine 1997: 219).

It can be argued that the classless society thesis contains an element of mythology obscuring the continued holding and control of great wealth by the few (Scott 1985: 38). Indeed, during a decade of Thatcherism 'old money' prospered as never before in the post-war era. Middle-class vulnerability was demonstrated throughout the 1980s and 1990s as professions such as university lecturers, civil servants and doctors were threatened by a government intent upon reducing the tax burden placed upon capitalism.

Figure 7.2
Britain's class structure according to one version of Goldthorpe's schema.

Source: Data from Devine (1997: 25).

Thatcher's children?

For some acolytes of the New Right, the era of Thatcherism was seen as the period when Britain became a classless society. At the end of the first decade there existed a large group with no adult memories of full employment, trade union involvement in policy-making and plentiful funds for education, the NHS and welfare state. A MORI poll (May 1989) revealed 'Thatcher's children' as tougher than their parents' generation across a wide spectrum, keener to set up businesses and with a different evaluation of social problems. However, by 1997 the British Social Attitudes Survey found little difference between the generations – all believed income inequality to be too great and that big business exploited its workers (Heath and Park 1998).

The working class

> An Englishman's way of speaking absolutely classifies him. The moment he talks he makes some other Englishman despise him.
>
> Professor Higgins, in Alan Jay Lerner's musical *My Fair Lady* (1956)

This essentially Marxist concept does not actually describe what people do. 'Work' can range from stock-brokerage to road-sweeping and, although condemned to idleness, the unemployed are generally regarded as belonging to the working class. The essential feature of this class is that its members lack wealth and power. Yet this great majority of the British people can only be designated as a class in the very loosest of senses and it lacks the homogeneity Marx ascribed to it. There are multifarious distinctions within it in terms of race, colour, spatial distribution, income, gender, occupation and, most importantly, in perceptions of the capitalist system in which they live.

A shrinking class? The decline of mining and heavy industry, new (post-Fordist) industrial practices and the globalization of the production process have eliminated many working-class jobs and decimated traditional communities. Moreover, the steady trend of upward mobility in the post-war era, swelling the ranks of an intermediate stratum, does not accord with the Marxist dichotomy. Lockwood (1966) saw this class splitting into three: traditional proletarians such as miners and shipworkers, who showed great class solidarity; traditional deferential workers, with a sense of hierarchy and respect for their 'betters'; and privatized workers, with an individualistic view of life and work and upwardly mobile aspirations. These were to become electorally significant from the late 1970s.

Is the working class shrinking? Goldthorpe's (1987) class schema identifies a shrunken working class as the upgrading of employment in a range of occupations has created a new enlarged middle class. In contrast, neo-Marxist Erik Olin Wright (1985) argues that the essential class structure has remained unchanged for most of the twentieth century: a large proletariat at the bottom comprising a range of new non-manual but unskilled occupations which stand in the same vulnerable position vis-à-vis capital as the old working class, a small bourgeoisie at the top and an even smaller middle class sandwiched between (figure 7.3).

> The charm of Britain has always been the ease with which one can move into the middle class.
>
> Margaret Thatcher, in the *Observer* (27 Oct. 1974)

Mind the gap: an underclass? It is impossible to argue that British society is characterized by the mass pauperization prophesied by classical Marxism.

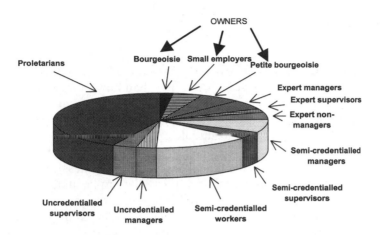

Source: Data from Devine (1997: 21).

Figure 7.3
Britain's class structure according to Wright's schema.

Living conditions for the average person are clearly much better than in the 1840s. However, Marx also saw a class below the working class (the *lumpenproletariat*) and during the 1980s and 1990s J. K. Galbraith (1993) postulated a widening gap between a prosperous majority living securely in a 'culture of contentment' and a depressed minority of many millions of socially vulnerable people with very little chance of fending successfully for themselves. These included the unemployed, low paid, homeless, elderly, handicapped, chronically sick, disabled, ethnic minorities, single-parent families, those with low educational attainments and those dropping out of the 'rat race' of competitive society. In July 1989 a Salvation Army report revealed 75,000 homeless people in London alone. Adonis and Pollard (1997) criticize the term **underclass** as an elite device concealing the true extent of poverty, implying that it is confined to a deviant minority. Indeed, economic journalist Will Hutton argued that government policy from the 1990s, deliberately fostering inequality, had resulted in what he termed a 30/30/40 society (1996: 105–10). Moreover, a UN *Human Development Report* revealed that in 1997 as much as one-fifth of the British population were poorer than their equivalent groups in any other western country for which figures were collected. Nearly a quarter of Britain's elderly (over five times the Italian rate), almost a fifth of children and half of all single parents were classed as poor (*Independent*, 15 June 1997).

The 30/30/40 society

Top 40% privileged: Tenured, secure, full-time jobs or self-employed, a category shrinking by 1 per cent a year.
Middle 30% structurally insecure: Part-time work, little protection.
Bottom 30% disadvantaged: Unemployed, economically inactive, marginalized.

Self-assigned class

There is also a subjective class structure reflecting the way people perceive themselves (figure 7.4). The tendency in the post-war era has been for working-class people to see themselves as going up rather than down in the world. Despite politicians' claims that Britain was becoming a classless society a BBC/ICM poll in September 1998 showed 55 per cent of people describing themselves as working class and 41 per cent as middle class. These proportions broadly accorded with an objective categorization. However, 25 per cent of those in managerial occupations described themselves as working class, while the same proportion of those in manual jobs felt themselves to be middle class. Only 1 per cent claimed to be upper class; well below the objective assessment of 22 per cent. Yet although self-assigned positions can be at variance with objective placings, they are important because they influence people's views on key issues such as the welfare state and trade unions, and their voting behaviour.

Figure 7.4
Self-assigned class: the percentage in each class identifying themselves as working class.

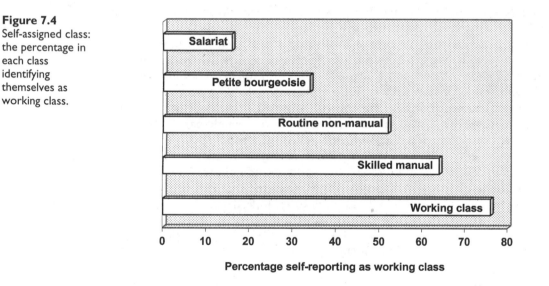

Percentage self-reporting as working class

Source: Data from Evans (1993).

Class and politics

What has class to do with politics? Class is about who has what in society and its political effects resonate throughout the pages of this book. They are felt in voting behaviour, in the media, in the realm of ideas and attitudes, in education, through pressure groups, and even in health. Domination within a wide range of social relationships is often based upon class. Does domination go further than this: can one class collectively dominate the whole of society? In other words, does Britain have a ruling class? This important question is explored further in chapter 17.

The Monstrous Regiment: Sexism in British Society

In turning to the question of gender we are by no means leaving the issue of class because women are predominant in the lower echelons of the class structure (Devine 1997: 44). Moreover, in all classes men tend to dominate women. This remains true despite the fact that from 1979 to 1990 Britain had a woman prime minister. Indeed, other patriarchal societies – India, Israel and Pakistan – have also had women leaders, but they remain lonely swallows showing very little promise of a feminist summer.

> The First Blast of the Trumpet Against the Monstrous Regiment of Women.
>
> Title of pamphlet by John Knox (1505–72; charismatic Scottish preacher)

British patriarchy

British culture is **sexist** and **patriarchal**: a woman's social position is largely fixed by the men in her life, mainly her father and husband. Working-class culture has been particularly male dominated, with the trade unions bastions of patriarchy. The domination is betrayed in our very language with the repetitious use of the male pronoun: not only have committees largely been headed by chairmen, even God is a man. In the human race we are all *Homo sapiens*; where are the *Femina sapiens*?

The modern pattern of domination by gender did not originate with the capitalism that shapes life today. In many African cultures women spend the day in hard physical labour while the men remain largely idle, Asian civilizations retain rigid sexist traditions and in Muslim law the treatment of women is harsh indeed. As long ago as 300 BC, in an idyll by Theocritus, Praxinoa, a fine lady, rushes away from a show at the royal palace telling her friend: 'I must be getting back. It's Diocleidas' dinner time, and that man's all pepper; I wouldn't advise anyone to come near him when he's kept waiting for his food' (Seltman 1956: 134). However, male domination and the concept of the family unit have proved functional for capitalism by providing a means for the reproduction and maintenance of labour.

> Mother is the dead heart of the family, spending father's earnings on consumer goods to enhance the environment in which he eats, sleeps and watches the television.
>
> Germaine Greer (Australian-born feminist), *The Female Eunuch* (1970)

Women and work

The oldest profession?

Even when women have full rights, they still remain factually down-trodden because all house work is left to them. In most cases house work is the most unproductive, the most barbarous and the most arduous work a woman can do.

V. I. Lenin (1870–1924; Russian communist leader), *Collected Works* (vol. XXX: 43)

The multi-faceted subjugation of women is nowhere better illustrated than in paid employment. The growth of capitalism made possible a sharp distinction between two forms of work: the *commodity production* of industry and *domestic production* at home. However, the latter is not usually considered real work at all (Rowbotham 1973: 68) and housewives socialized by the commodity production ethos tend to say: 'I don't have a job'. Figure 7.5 illustrates the extent to which women continue to be classified as 'economically inactive' (a category including housekeeping).

For most women, paid employment must be fitted around the full-time domestic production role, yet this has not significantly altered the basic organization of work practices. The effect is to exclude women from many sections of the labour market (Garnsey 1982: 440). An additional problem is that of the single-parent family. The term is largely a euphemism for families without a man, marital break-up or unintended pregnancy usually leaving the children with the mother. The position can be particularly degrading as the need for an income, coupled with an inability to give a full-time commitment, often oblige women to accept menial, low-prestige occupations. Immigrant women, sometimes from particularly sexist societies, are even more vulnerable, often accept-

Figure 7.5
Working-age population by economic status, 1986 and 1997.

Source: Data from *Social Trends* (1998: table 4.2).

ing sweatshop conditions and denied unionization. Even professional women can expect to be dominated by their male colleagues, denied promotion by a 'glass ceiling', while those returning to work after child-rearing tend to occupy positions far lower than their qualifications warrant.

The propensity to gravitate towards menial jobs means that, unlike men, women tend to work in a limited number of occupations. Over half are in three service sectors – distributive trades, secretarial and miscellaneous services (e.g. catering, cleaning). They are also found predominantly in caring work such as nursing, primary education and social services, thereby reinforcing the cultural definition of their identity as servers rather than creators. Although changes in employment patterns from the early 1980s saw a rapid acceleration in the recruitment of women into the workforce, this was largely in the flexible, vulnerable, poorly unionized and low-paid service industries. Between 1977 and 1988 the number earning below the minimum wage stipulated in the EC Social Charter rose from 8 million to 9.4 million (*Guardian,* 13 Oct. 1993). By the late 1990s there were over 5 million people working part time, over 80 per cent of whom were women (figure 7.5). The increasing casualization of the labour force had seen women taking low-paid, part-time jobs while their husbands suffered redundancy (Hutton 1996: 106).

Political implications of sexism

Male culture does not welcome women in politics, as was amply demonstrated in the suffragettes' battle for the franchise (p. 235). Women's issues have tended to remain off the political agenda and women themselves have rarely become political activists; far less unionized than men, they may even not support their husbands when on strike. They have been poorly represented on the TUC and, although trade union attitudes have become more sympathetic, there remains much deep-seated sexism. Parliament remains predominantly a male club (see chapter 12), seen at its most bizarre when pontificating on abortion, viewing the foetus as male property placed in the womb for safe keeping.

> Women have served all these centuries as looking-glasses possessing the magic and delicious power of reflecting the figure of man at twice its natural size.
>
> Virginia Woolf (1882–1941; English writer), *A Room of One's Own* (1929)

During the 1970s, legislation on sex discrimination and equal pay marked the inauguration of a sex equality strategy. However, the legalistic removal of barriers by governments committed to a minimalist state role did little to change behaviour (Forbes 1996). Indeed, policies from the 1980s were particularly bad for women, with much rhetoric on the theme of family breakdown. Women could be blamed for failings such as low educational standards, drug abuse among the young and juvenile delinquency. Social policies shifted the care of the old, chronically ill and handicapped from the state to the family under a policy termed 'Care in the Community'. The freezing of child benefit payments also specifically targeted women. Labour in power appeared no less harsh in the eyes of critics, with its policy of getting single mothers off state benefits and into work (supported by most of Labour's record new intake of women MPs).

Deeply sexist attitudes vein the state. It will be apparent throughout this book that the world we are examining is one of male dominance. Here there are no female field marshalls, lord chancellors, bishops or heads of privatized industries. The vast majority of cabinet ministers, judges, higher civil servants, MPs, councillors, soldiers and police are still male. John Major's first Cabinet contained no women at all, though he subsequently approved the appointment of women as Director of Public Prosecutions, head of MI5 and head of the Board of Customs and Excise. Blair's first Cabinet began with a record number of five women, but with unintended irony Joan Ruddock's non-cabinet post of Minister for Women was so junior as to carry no salary, and the first cabinet reshuffle saw the axe fall upon Social Security Secretary Harriet Harman. Hence, nearly eighty years after granting women the vote the political system still serves 'to institutionalise and reproduce inequalities between the sexes' (Lovenduski 1996). Even the NHS is run by men, demonstrating their assumed right to control women's bodies as well as their minds. They scrape their cervixes, moralize over the contents of their wombs, and woe betide any female obstetrician attempting to respond to the desire for natural childbirth.

Women on top? However, as we saw in chapter 2, feminism is now a serious ideology and the women's movement is part of politics. A number of concessions have been gained in the areas of equal opportunities and pay. Women have been involved in some major political confrontations, including the 1976–7 strike by Asian women in the Grunwick photographic plant, the Greenham Common encampment against Cruise missiles and the Northern Ireland peace campaign. Mo Mowlam's record here speaks volumes. By the end of the 1990s, girls were outperforming boys in school, women were more able to pursue careers in the professions and a record number were MPs. Women were also becoming more important family earners, sometimes the sole earner.

Race and Politics

Britain is a multiracial society, the 1991 census revealing some 3 million of the population as belonging to an ethnic minority (table 7.3). Of these, more than half lived in the south-east, 44 per cent in the Greater London area. In inner London, ethnic minorities made up over a quarter of the population. Outside London, the largest ethnic minority community was in Leicester, standing at 77,000 (28.5 per cent of the population). One consequence of this is a deep-seated, indelible **racism** within the political culture. Although many white people believe it to be exaggerated for political reasons or unimportant, few with a West Indian or Asian background could feel this way. For them, race and racism lie at the very heart of their social and economic experience.

Table 7.3 Ethnic composition of the British population, 1996/7 (millions)

White	Black	Indian	Pakistani/ Bangladeshi	Chinese	Other/ mixed
52.9	0.9	0.9	0.8	0.1	0.6

Source: Data from *Social Trends* (1998: table 1.10).

What is racism?

The human species may be said to consist of several races distinguished by superficial physical characteristics (size, colour of hair and skin, etc.). These are only broad distinctions: many individuals do not fit the physical type suggested by their racial origins and intermarriage further blurs the picture. Recognition of these differences is not racism. Racism is the practice of discriminating against people on the grounds of race. Some regimes (the European fascists in the 1930s and South Africa in the days of apartheid) have been openly based on the belief that racial differences justify inequality, the implication being that some races are morally or intellectually superior. Apart from being ethically objectional, this is quite impossible to sustain because of differences in cultural environments. It is about as logically defensible as the distinction Gulliver encountered

Source: Mary Evans Picture Library

in Lilliput based upon the method of eating a boiled egg, which resulted in bloody war for 'six and thirty moons' between the 'Big-Endians' and 'Little-Endians'!

Manifestations of racism

Although racism in Britain today does not take the open and violent forms seen in Nazi Germany, the American deep south, or apartheid South Africa, it permeates every nook and cranny of life. It is found in the membership of clubs and societies, sport, housing, newspapers, employment, education and everyday language. The most openly racist white people have a rich lexicon of derogatory terms ranging from 'our coloured cousins', 'nigger' and 'wog', to the more obscene. Such attitudes are also found in state institutions, with the police and army subject to particular criticism (see chapter 21). Although well-meaning liberals deplore racism, they themselves are products of an inescapably racist culture, falling into patronizing attitudes which can sap black morale.

> We shall have to start progressively removing their rights. If bloodshed and racial strife are the result, then all I can say is that that is an acceptable price to pay for clearing out the immigrants.
>
> Anthony Reed-Herbert of the National Front, quoted in *The Times* (24 June 1976)

When Hitler and Mussolini were taking power in the 1930s, Britain had its own fascist movement, led by Sir Oswald Mosley. Although making minimal impact, fascist parties have continued to exist, including the National Socialist Movement, the National Front, the British Movement and the British National Party (which won a council by-election in the Isle of Dogs in East London in September 1993). The establishment of an all-white Britain remains their prime goal.

As racist patterns continue, the threat of further resistance, including violence, increases. One result has been for black people to turn inwards, forming ghettos in the decaying inner cities, where they live a self-contained existence, abandoning the ambition to participate on equal terms in society. It is the young with no experience of a home other than Britain who feel the greatest sense of alienation and despair and who are likely to vent their frustration in riot. By the late 1990s most major cities had experienced clashes between young blacks and the police. The case against white youths accused of murdering black youth Stephen Lawrence was dismissed in 1993 for lack of evidence. This was seen by many as a racist conspiracy of silence and the *Daily Mail* accused certain individuals, challenging them to take legal action for libel. The subsequent inquiry into the affair revealed high levels of police contempt, incompetence and insensitivity (see pp. 643–4).

The roots of racism

The British have long attributed their supremacy to God, who is frequently enjoined to 'make us mightier yet'. Hence it is not surprising that Jews in particular have been vilified. The late-Victorian poet W. N. Ewer mocked: 'How odd of God, to choose, the Jews'. From Shakespeare's *Merchant of Venice* to Dickens's Fagin they have been depicted as miserly and grasping. Similarly, the Irish (notwithstanding Wilde, Shaw, Joyce, Behan, Heaney et al.) have long been considered inferior to the English. Today, along with blacks, they are the butt of offensive jokes told by 'comedians' appearing in clubs and on national television.

The great age of discovery revealed to West European eyes a vast world of 'savages': inferior beings to be tamed, trained, deprived of their land, culture and property, and used as slaves. The seventeenth-century slave trade made the English curiously interested in race. Part of the justification for this abomination was a belief that Africans were so inferior in character and brain that to be enslaved by the white man was actually an improvement in their condition! The development of the empire as an integral part of British capitalism had a particular significance for today's racist attitudes. The status of great imperial power encouraged superiority: the English gained control of the British Isles and defeated European rivals in the pillage of the New World, where they had subjugated the indigenous populations. By the closing decades of the eighteenth century, once the Indian subcontinent had been retrieved from the French, the British Empire was the largest the world had ever experienced. Truly they were a master race. Victorian scientists pictured mankind in terms of a great hierarchy, with the white Englishman invariably at the top and the negro just above the ape at the bottom.

> British thought and British society has never been cleansed of the Augean filth of imperialism.
>
> Salman Rushdie, in *New Society* (9 Dec. 1982)

> Take up the White Man's burden –
> And reap his old reward:
> The blame of those ye better,
> The hate of those ye guard.
>
> Rudyard Kipling (1865–1936; Indian-born British writer), 'The White Man's Burden'

Of course the superiority claimed by the English was attributed to its dominant class, not to the lower orders labouring in conditions scarcely better than those of slaves. However, the extension of the franchise obliged establishment forces to seek their support and this seemingly impossible enterprise was accomplished through the Disraelian concept of 'one nation'. In this great legitimating myth the empire was invoked as a unifying symbol serving to bestow splendour on even the most lowly of the English; they were part of the race that ruled the world. This sentiment was to bequeath a lasting sense of **xenophobia** with peculiarly significant consequences for race relations at home.

The pattern of immigration

All those who are not racially pure are mere chaff.

Adolf Hitler (1889–1945), *Mein Kampf* (1925–6)

Contrary to the Victorian theory, the British 'race' is in no sense pure; it is a mongrel breed including Celts, Romans, Anglo-Saxons, Normans and Danes and could find no class for itself at a *Homo sapiens* Crufts Show. After 1066 the country was host to further immigration waves: the medieval period saw large numbers of Jewish settlers, at the end of the seventeenth century came the Huguenots escaping persecution in France and the eighteenth-century famine in Ireland brought a further major influx. It was never in the British nature to welcome these additions. In 1601 Elizabeth I issued a proclamation to remove the country's few black people and a 1605 Act restricted the rights of aliens. However, time generally soothed irate feelings and the immigrants were well integrated, some to become very successful (amongst the most successful of all were William the Conqueror, William of Orange, the Hanoverians and Prince Albert!). Intermarriage frequently meant that the only sign of foreign origin was an unusual name, and sometimes even these were changed.

A new wave of immigration began in the post-imperial era. The 1948 British Nationality Act gave common British citizenship to all Commonwealth citizens, providing a labour source to compensate for shortages at home (Saggar 1992: 97). Workers from India, Pakistan and the West Indies were encouraged through recruitment drives by public bodies such as the NHS and London Transport. Immigrants' willingness to undertake uncongenial, low-paid work made possible the survival of a number of traditional industries, such as textiles, in an increasingly competitive world economy. Although the first of the immigrants (mainly men) met with resistance, they were buoyed up by the expectation that things could only get better. However, such optimism proved illusory. Despite the efforts of bodies such as the Runnymede Trust, fighting for racial equality and social justice, a second British-born generation remained as black as its parents, excluded from better jobs, confined to poor housing in inner-city areas, with inferior education and health care and subject to racially inspired violence.

Problems intensified as the long boom of western capitalism ran out of steam. Unemployment began an inexorable rise amongst the black population (figure 7.6), which was particularly vulnerable as robots replaced people in manufacturing and textiles. Adding insult to injury, they were seen as one of the *causes* of unemployment.

Institutional racism

Racism was to become **institutionalized** through legislation passed by both major parties designed to restrict coloured immigration. The 1958 Notting Hill race riots marked a grim watershed, leading to the first post-war Immigration Act in 1962. This restricted entry from the black Commonwealth to those able to show they were coming to a specific job, or able to offer a particular skill. Women were subject to strict physical examinations, including a degrading internal virginity test.

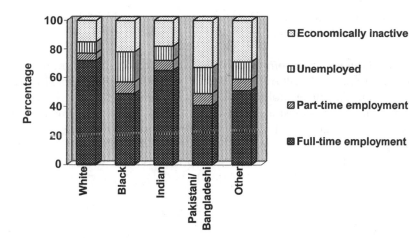

Source: Data from Social Trends (1996: table 4.3).

The hard reality of the Smethwick election result in 1964 (when an openly racist Conservative using the slogan 'If you want a nigger for a neighbour, vote Labour' won a stunning victory) and increasing anti-black hysteria led Labour to introduce even tougher restrictions in 1965, allowing deportation by the Home Secretary (without a court hearing) of any illegal immigrant of less than five years' standing. A new style of rhetoric, speaking of the 'small crowded island', transformed what had been right-wing views into respectable orthodoxy. Home Secretary Roy Jenkins, hitherto a notable advocate of the humane society, stressed the 'social factor' limiting the number that could be absorbed. In 1968 the Commonwealth Immigrants Act (to stem immigration from turbulent Kenya) was rushed through Parliament in only two days.

The Conservatives consolidated the position in 1971 with an Act restricting entry to those with parents or grandparents born in the UK. This permitted Commonwealth citizens only the opportunity available to all foreigners of applying to the Home Secretary and having to prove four years of 'good behaviour'. It also extended state powers of deportation, providing a basis for further official harassment of blacks. The 1981 British Nationality Act effectively closed the door to non-whites while keeping another open for 6 million patrials and the 200 million in the EC. The Conservatives changed the immigration rules again in 1984 in response to anxiety over alleged abuses of the arranged marriage system in India (Bhavnani and Bhavnani 1985: 152). Following the massacre of Chinese students in Tiananmen Square in June 1989, fears arose about the future of Hong Kong's residents after the colony's return to Chinese rule in 1997. After much acrimonious debate, which split both major parties, the British Nationality (Hong Kong) Act of 1990 restricted full British citizenship to certain of the colony's elite (dubbed 'essential workers'), paradoxically to encourage them to stay in Hong Kong. After years of pressure, this was extended in 1997 to around 5,000 non-Chinese Asians who would otherwise have become stateless after the handover.

Brothers in law: race relations legislation Attempts to curb racism have been seen in race relations legislation in 1965, 1968 and 1976 designed to outlaw discrimination, and the establishment of the Commission for Racial Equality (CRE) to enforce its provisions. However, it is debatable how far legislation can change deep-seated prejudices. Liberal critics see the CRE as a toothless watchdog, serving to legitimate the oppressive legislation rather than improving the life-experiences of blacks. Others pour scorn on what they term the 'race relations industry' (Banton 1985: vii).

Racism and politics

> Members of Parliament who represent ethnic minorities – unlike their colleagues who sit for prosperous suburban seats – are always criticised for advancing the claims of their constituents. It is part of the racism which afflicts our society.
>
> Roy Hattersley, *Who Goes Home?* (1996: 284)

The politics of Britain logically gives blacks and working-class whites more reason to unite than divide, yet racism 'appears at its strongest among unskilled working people' (Walvin 1984: 143). Even within the active left there is a strong vein of racism, particularly evident in the trade unions. The employment of immigrants has been seen as depressing wage levels and taking employment from indigenous workers. The TUC has pressed enthusiastically for action against illegal immigrants and there is a lengthy catalogue of disputes involving racist behaviour by members and officials. Hence, although Labour has received more solid support from blacks than from working-class whites, its trade-union roots have inhibited its response. The Scarman Report on the 1981 Brixton riots stressed that black people in the UK 'do not feel politically secure. Their sense of rejection is not eased by the low level of black representation in our elective political institutions' (Scarman 1981: 16). Yet Labour remains strongly opposed to black sections, thereby denying them the distinct political voice allowed to women. Another problem was Labour's rejection of the New Urban Left movement (see p. 585), for it is at the local government level that black political activism has been most evident.

The reality of British political culture means that 'there are votes for the picking in fanning the flames of racial resentment' (Crewe 1983: 263). The racist vote was most effectively garnered for the Conservatives by Enoch Powell, whose lurid speeches lamented the submergence of a halcyon English age under the great alien tidal wave. These sentiments set off resonances throughout society, drawing London dockers out in a strike of clamorous adulation and creating a cultural ecosystem congenial to fascist movements and the National Front,

> The party must learn that holding three or four receptions for Asian millionaires every year does not amount to a race relations policy. Whenever I go to central office the only other black face is the security guard at the door.
>
> John Taylor, defeated Conservative candidate at Cheltenham in 1992 general election (12 Oct. 1993)

which had an estimated membership of 20,000 by 1972 (Taylor 1982). A Gallup poll exposed the hard truth that 75 per cent of the population were broadly sympathetic to Powell's sentiments (Marwick 1982). Fascism had given racism a bad name but Powell helped to rehabilitate it, making it 'respectable amongst those who saw the Tory party as the epitome of conformist respectability' (Bhavnani and Bhavnani 1985: 150). By the late 1970s the National Front had seen its popular support eroded by the Conservative Party which, with its hardline immigration stance, had stolen its central political message (Saggar 1992: 185).

Although party leader Edward Heath promptly ejected him from the Shadow Cabinet, Powell probably helped to propel the Conservatives into office in 1970. He was known to be greatly admired by Margaret Thatcher, who herself had warned of the danger that 'this country might be swamped by people with a different culture' (Sivanandan 1981: 145). Upon becoming Conservative leader she could be seen as 'a poor man's Enoch Powell' (Johnson 1985: 114). While the neoliberalism of the New Right was not itself racist, there was also an authoritarian strand taking a hard line on social issues. From here came a 'new racism' which shrouded its message in a language of social responsibility, stressing Englishness, national identity and common cultural history, and attacking multiculturalism (Gordon and Klug 1986). Norman Tebbit saw support for visiting cricket teams as a 'test'. In May 1993, Winston Churchill MP, grandson of his famous namesake, made a controversial speech calling for tighter controls to protect the 'British way of life' from a 'relentless flow of immigration'. Although convention, or cowardice, normally forbids politicians to speak as openly as Powell on the subject of race, a government may signal its views with such encoded messages.

Hence the claim that there is a gentleman's agreement among politicians not to use race for political advantage may be bogus; racism helps sustain class domination. From the 'one-nation' appeal of Disraeli, Conservatives have vaunted patriotism as more honourable than class loyalty. Yet patriotism is not merely, in the words of Doctor Johnson, 'the last refuge of a scoundrel', it

> As I look ahead I am filled with foreboding. Like the Roman, I seem to see 'the River Tiber foaming with much blood'.
>
> Enoch Powell, MP, on immigration, public speech in Birmingham (4 April 1968)

can also be the first refuge of the racist. Unlike that of gender, the racial division has not cut across class. Despite a growing number of upwardly mobile Asians (Saggar 1992: 207), black people belong largely to the working class, so racism weakens working-class solidarity, particularly at those very times when capitalism is at its most vulnerable – economic recession. The depression of the early 1990s saw a tide of racial assaults in London's East End and in other cities.

> Racism is now beginning to grow in Britain. That was the evidence given to the home affairs select committee by the police, by ethnic groups of all colours and by the government.
>
> Sir Ivan Lawrence (Chairman, Commons Home Affairs Committee),
> in the *Sunday Times* (3 July 1994)

Covering the Cracks

Britain's deferential, united civic culture is rather more complex and tense than that venerated by liberal-democratic apologists. The working of the polity cannot be explained in terms of a large natural consensus. Class, gender and racial cracks in the social fascia are plastered over with political spin and concealed beneath unwritten constitutional wallpaper. It is in exploring how this is accomplished that one gains the key to the true spirit and genius of the system. This long exploration begins in the following chapter.

Key points

- Political culture is a vague term encompassing history, institutions and attitudes towards the political system.
- Characteristics seen in British political culture include continuity, deference and consensus.
- Beneath the apparent tranquillity fester class, gender and racial tension.
- There is little to support the thesis that Britain is a classless society.
- Britain has a patriarchal political system in which women have not been encouraged to take part.
- Racism is found in various forms in Britain and is particularly persistent where skin colour prevents long-term assimilation.

Review your understanding of the following terms and concepts

bourgeoisie	institutional racism	sexism
civic culture	meritocracy	underclass
class	middle class	upper class
consensus	patriarchy	working class
deference	political culture	xenophobia
embourgeoisement	proletariat	
Establishment	racism	

Assignment

Study the extract from the *Independent* on p. 192 and answer the following questions:

		Mark (%)
1	Assess Tony Blair's assertion that the principle of racial equality is shared by all main political parties.	20
2	Assuming the above assertion to be true, how justified is his optimism about the future of race relations?	20
3	How justified is William Hague's claim that Britain has set an example to the world in race relations'?	20
4	If the *Independent* is right in its assertion that 'racism is endemic' in British society, why do the main parties oppose it?	40

Questions for discussion

1 How accurate is it to describe the UK as a cohesive political culture?
2 In what way do you think deference among the British working class contributes to the hegemonic consciousness of the upper middle class?
3 On what grounds can it be argued that the British working class is shrinking?
4 'The rise of the middle classes has rendered redundant the Marxist distinction between the owners of capital and the workers.' Discuss.
5 Identify some of the important manifestations of sexism in British politics.
6 'Politics is for men.' Discuss.
7 Discuss the effects of Enoch Powell's speeches on race relations in Britain.
8 'Racism is largely a social phenomenon. It does not have any significant effect on politics.' Discuss.
9 'You can change your class, but not your colour or gender.' Discuss the political implications of this.
10 In what ways is Britain's political culture changing?

Leaders unite to condemn British racism

By Anthony Bevins
Political Editor

PARTY leaders last night united in an attack on racism after *The Independent* urged them to join forces with Tony Blair to celebrate the multiculturalism of Britain. Their unity is a response to deep-seated concerns over racism and underlines a growing determination to tackle it head on.

Government worries over racism surfaced twice last week: once in Prime Minister's Question Time; and again when Mr Blair went to Southwark, south London, for a community meeting. On both occasions, Mr Blair said the fundamental principle of racial equality was shared by every single mainstream party, which explained "why we can be optimistic about the future of race relations."

But *The Independent* believes racism is endemic, and cannot be answered by silence – it needs to be confronted and taken on, which is why *The Independent* has asked party leaders to speak out.

On the ground, evidence of racism is strong, even in cities believed to be well-integrated, like Liverpool.

In a speech to Asian business leaders in London tonight, the Prime Minister will say much has been done to stamp out racism, but more is needed. Delivering a powerful statement in Southwark last week, he said: "The single most important thing we can do is to make an absolutely clear statement on behalf of the Government, on behalf of all political parties, on behalf of society, that we believe in, and actually welcome a multi-racial and multicultural society: that it's a good thing; that it's not something to be frightened of; that it's a healthy, lifegiving thing; that it's actually the type of society we want to bring our children up in."

William Hague said last night: "I warmly welcome *The Independent's* campaign to promote good race relations. The United Kingdom has set an example to the rest of the world in improving race relations, but we should never be complacent. More needs to be done to bring down the barriers of ignorance and distrust which still exist in parts of our society."

Paddy Ashdown said: "Racism is an evil which undermines the very fabric of society."

Independent, 25 March 1998

Topic for debate

This house believes that women have no place in politics.

Further reading

Adonis, A. and Pollard, S. (1997) *A Class Act: The Myth of Britain's Classless Society*. Argues that, far from diminishing, class barriers are intensifying.

Almond, G. A. and Verba, S. (1963) *The Civic Culture* (reprinted 1989). Remains a classic text despite criticism.

Almond, G. A. and Verba, S. (eds) (1980) *The Civic Culture Revisited*.
Readings re-evaluate the civic culture in the light of events.

Giddens, A. (1997a) *Sociology*, 3rd edn.
Panoramic introduction illustrates how the discipline of sociology addresses many of the questions important to the study of politics.

Giddens, A. (1997b) *Sociology: Introductory Readings*.
Lively readings from a wide variety of sources.

Fryer, P. (1988) *Black People in the British Empire*.
Explores the exploitation of the colonies and presents an alternative view of the place of black people in British history.

Lovenduski, J. and Norris, P. (eds) (1996) *Women in Politics*.
Focusing on Britain, provides up-to-date overview of women's attitudes, behaviour and representation in policy areas affecting them.

Saggar, S. (1992) *Race and Politics in Britain*.
Examines the nature, causes and consequences of racism. Notes link with the political right.

For light relief

Much literature, both from home and abroad, deals with themes that divide societies – class, race and gender.

Martin Amis, *London Fields*.
Surreal vision of London life: four people bound together in a modern urban torment of class, wealth and squalor, destroying themselves within a decaying world.

Jilly Cooper, *Class*.
Light essay by a proud daughter of the upper middle class.

Edwina Currie, *A Woman's Place*.
According to John Julius Norwich, this 'does for Parliament what D. H. Lawrence did for gamekeeping'.

Henrik Ibsen, *The Doll's House*.
Powerful drama about women's oppression.

Kazuo Ishiguro, *Remains of the Day*.
Moving class novel with powerful political overtones. (Also a film/video.)

George Bernard Shaw, *Pygmalion*.
Witty but subversive comedy on upper-class manners and gender relationships by the Irish genius. (Alternatively, see the less subversive musical film/video, *My Fair Lady*.)

On the net

http://www.sunday-times.co.uk
Via this site you can access the *Sunday Times*' annual Rich List, which has extensive information on changing patterns of wealth distribution.

http://www.ons.gov.uk
The Office for National Statistics is a good source for up-to-date socioeconomic information.

Part II

Mobilizing the *Demos*

The Greek *demos* means the people as a whole; when they control the government the polity can lay claim to the title democracy. Few polities today would not at least pay lip-service to the notion of democracy, but few fully realize its demanding ideals. Before there can be even a pretence of democracy there must be mechanisms whereby the *demos* will be mobilized to participate in the processes of politics. In this section we evaluate how this is accomplished in Britain. Above all we are interested in fundamental questions concerning the ability of the state to permit genuine and unimpeded entrance of the masses through its portals. Can all enter with equal ease or are there keep-off signs saying 'Members Only', 'Men Only' or even 'Whites Only'?

We are moving closer to the heart of British politics and encountering some of the very big questions of social life, illuminating not only the nature of the polity we inhabit but the very quality of life. We first look at the way people form the political attitudes discussed earlier. These do not arise spontaneously; they are socially constructed by experience and conditioned through the process we term 'mind politics', a layer of political activity that people encounter before coming anywhere near the ballot box. Chapter 9 examines the most visible mechanism of participation, the electoral system. When everyone has the right to vote the *demos* would indeed appear mighty; or is it? We consider the grudging manner in which the powerful few in Britain extended the franchise to the mass and did so in a way calculated to minimize damage to their own privileges. Chapters 10 and 11 examine the main products of the fully extended franchise, the modern political parties. When these are understood we have some important keys for unlocking the mysteries of the British political system.

Chapter Eight

Mind Politics: What We Think

In this chapter we turn to the processes shaping people's attitudes; that is, the politics of the mind. Mind politics arises from the need for social stability. There are various ways of maintaining this, from the brutal use of force and fear, through attempts by the state to ease the effects of inequality (say by means of a welfare state), to a more subtle psychological process which removes from the disadvantaged the desire to resist. While the British state has not been unwilling to employ force against citizens, it is ultimately necessary that the mass of the people accept their lot with some degree of contentment. In other words, the system must be *legitimated*; the distribution of power in society and the form of government must be accepted as being right and proper. We shall see throughout the chapters of this book that legitimation takes place variously, involving most government institutions. Here we are particularly concerned with those impinging upon ideology and attitudes. The chapter has three broad sections. The first examines influences encountered by the young: the family, religion and school. However, mind politics does not end with adulthood; we are subject to influences until the day we die, through the arts and the business of advertising. The second section concentrates on a profoundly important source of mass persuasion: the press. Finally we consider broadcasting, perhaps the most potent instrument of the mass media in today's society.

Political Socialization

Defining political socialization

The process whereby people acquire their attitudes towards politics is termed **political socialization**. A major flaw in typical studies of political socialization is a preoccupation with voting behaviour, seeking to explain, in the words of W. S. Gilbert:

> How Nature always does contrive
> That every boy and ever gal,
> That's born into this world alive,
> Is either a little Liberal,
> Or else a little Conservative!
> (*Iolanthe,* Act II)

There is much more to the socialization process than explaining the mysteries whereby boys and girls grow up to be Conservatives, Liberal Democrats, Labourites, or even supporters of the British National Party. It is upon the socialization process that the stability of the whole system depends; it determines whether successive generations will vote at all, whether they will be apathetic abstainers, activists, cynics or perhaps revolutionaries.

A central legitimating feature of a deferential political culture is the notion of the neutral state. This may be promoted by venerating basic constitutional principles such as the rule of law and the political impartiality of state institutions (civil service, police force, judiciary). We shall see in later chapters that the institutions themselves play a part in the socialization process in many subtle ways. However, in addition to the state's direct role in reproducing supportive attitudes we find a range of non-state institutions extending into civil society. In addition, there are institutions specially created to talk to (not to communicate with) the masses: the communications media.

The family

> They fuck you up your mum and dad.
> They may not mean to but they do.
> They fill you with the faults they had
> And add some extra, just for you.
>
> Philip Larkin (1922–85; English poet),
> 'This be the Verse'

The family is the first source of attitude formation we encounter. Despite the role played by mothers, it has been an essentially patriarchal organization reproducing sexist attitudes. Girls have been trained for housework and boys may be induced to feel superior. Xenophobia and racism may also be learnt in this private world. The family is also a power structure in which parents exercise authority, although characteristically on the basis of love. Hence we grow up understanding that authority is generally in our own interests. This can help explain why the political right lays great stress on the family: it helps to reinforce a social organization where a dominant class is accepted in the interest of the whole nation. However, the family can also socialize people into non-capitalist values such as mutual care and equality, which is why it cannot in itself provide a sufficient basis for mind-shaping in a capitalist society.

British family life is changing as a result of the growth of non-white communities, feminism and a greater plurality in social norms. South Asian families traditionally honour family loyalty and conformity, including arranged marriages. This clashes with the liberal competitive environment outside, placing conflicting pressures on children. In families of West Indian origin, although fewer mothers aged 20–45 live with a husband than among the comparable white population, these single mothers gain support from the extended kinship networks found amongst this group (Giddens 1997: 146). Through the influence of feminism, patriarchy is less strong among many younger couples and more domestic chores are shared. Greater plurality in lifestyles produces far more unmarried couples living together and rearing children. There is also greater tolerance of gay and lesbian marriages. However, in November 1998 the Labour government's green paper on the family sought to reaffirm traditional values.

The peer group

Friends can also shape our political attitudes. The time spent at school, work and leisure is for most people considerable and psychologists such as Mead and Piaget have stressed the importance of such relationships. Here one finds strong social pressures to conform to **peer group** norms in many respects, including dress, musical taste and attitude towards the opposite sex. Unlike the school or family, peer relationships are usually based on consent and pressures to conform can be more acceptable. Because of their exclusive as well as inclusive nature, peer groups can engender racist and sexist attitudes. They may also encourage crime, particularly amongst young males, and reinforce drug culture.

Religion

Although it is often said that religion and politics should not be mixed, in reality they are rarely far apart. For long most educated people were formally church officials, and leading office-holders such as Thomas Becket, Cardinal Wolsey and Archbishop Cranmer were key political and administrative figures. The English Reformation saw the church formally wedded to the state as the Church of England, headed by the monarch. Today the bishops sit in the House of Lords and the monarch is crowned in Westminster Abbey.

During the industrial revolution capitalism drew its inspiration from the puritan doctrines of nonconformity. Stressing frugality and saving, these justified the great accumulation of wealth necessary to consolidate their position. However, they saw the Church of England as the religion of the upper middle class and social advancement has often required a switch from nonconformity (Thatcher herself crossed this divide).

From the eighteenth century, with the emergence of the great urban masses, social services were pioneered by the churches, including early ventures into mass education in which nonconformist and Anglican organizations competed for the minds of the population. However, capitalism is about selling dear and buying cheap; it could not operate if people did unto their neighbours as they would have them do unto them. Hence British Christianity has been concerned to explain the divine ordination of inequality in this world ('The rich man in his castle, the poor man at his gate'), with the promise of more egalitarian conditions confined to the next, making a particular virtue of the passive acceptance of one's lot. Marx saw this as a vital cog in the machinery of subjugation and exploitation. Not only has religion socialized people into accepting inequality, it has purveyed patriarchal values. The ordination of the first women priests in March 1994 was by no means universally welcomed and within the Roman Catholic Church official doctrine remains implacably opposed.

> Religion is the sigh of the oppressed creature, the heart of a heartless world, just as it is the spirit of an unspiritual situation. It is the *opium* of the people.
>
> Karl Marx, Introduction to *Critique of Hegel's Philosophy of Right* (1844)

Today Britain is a largely secular society with little time for religion (table 8.1); it is said that faith in science has replaced faith in a God and, with Sunday opening of supermarkets, shopping has replaced churchgoing. Although most people claim to believe in God and some 70 per cent profess membership of the Church of England, only around 10 per cent attend church. However, the tensions between Protestant and Catholics in Northern Ireland (see pp. 149–61), the presence of Britain's ethnic minorities, the rise of new religious movements and an increased willingness of church leaders to enter the political domain mean that religion has by no means disappeared from politics.

Britain's non-Christian religions   The presence of significant numbers of Sikhs, Hindus and Muslims, as well as smaller sects such as Mormons and Rastafarians, has presented new issues for the British polity as religious, racial and political issues have become enmeshed. Although not essentially a new problem (Britain's Jewish population has long existed within the predominantly Christian culture), the more fervent (sometimes fundamentalist) views can promote clashes over matters of morality. The *fatwa* passed by the Ayatollah Khomenei on author Salman Rushdie over his *Satanic Verses* followed demonstrations and symbolic burnings of the book by Britain's Muslim community. There are also implications for feminism: Muslim women are expected to follow a restricted lifestyle and some Muslims call for, and establish, separate schools for their girls as a means of limiting their ambitions (Cahanum 1997: 345).

New movements   The postmodernist rejection of Enlightenment thinking and materialism opens the door to thinking with a religious quality, ranging from the pursuit of eastern religions and forms of meditation to informal variants of Christianity, paganism and even mystical practices such as astrology. The trend suggests that social life and politics can never be free of such influences because

Table 8.1 Membership of religious groups in the UK, 1975–1992 (millions)

Religious group	1975	1980	1992
Christians	8.34	7.88	7.18
Muslims	0.20	0.31	0.52
Sikhs	0.12	0.15	0.27
Hindus	0.10	0.12	0.14
Jews	0.11	0.11	0.11
Others	0.04	0.05	0.08

Source: Data from *Social Trends* (1994: table 11.8).

people are by anthropological nature religious animals. The rejection of established religion can be seen to parallel a rejection of established political institutions and be reflected in forms of direct action. Indeed, versions of feminism and environmentalism also embrace spiritual values.

Turbulent priests? Religion can also expose non-capitalist values. The 1980s and 1990s saw some unexpected political interventions from the Anglican Church, for long regarded as the 'Conservative Party at prayer'. Its leaders, including David Jenkins, Bishop of Durham, and David Shepherd, ex-England cricketer and Bishop of Liverpool, began attacking the government's neoliberal policies. In 1985 Archbishop of Canterbury Robert Runcie commissioned a report, *Faith in the City* – a damning indictment of conditions in the older industrial cities. In May 1996 his successor, George Carey, a former prison chaplain, launched a devastating critique of the principles behind Home Secretary Michael Howard's 'prison works' policy, warning that 'if you treat people like animals, they will respond like animals' (Travis 1996). Did such a moral crusade have any political impact? Tony Blair (featured in *Private Eye* as the Vicar of St Albion) proclaimed his own religious convictions, even linking them to his move from a Conservative background to the Labour Party.

> Education is simply the soul of society as it passes from one generation to another.
>
> G. K. Chesterton (1874–1936; British writer), in the *Observer* (6 July 1924)

Education

The British school system is sharply divided, the private sector (public schools) preparing the rulers of the future while the state system has aimed to manufacture the smaller cogs in the wheel. For the most part the latter is shaped by civil servants, many of whom have never darkened the doors of its institutions themselves. In this process of cultural reproduction children learn more than is outlined in the official syllabus; this is the 'hidden curriculum'. Like the family the school is hierarchical in structure, and ideally teachers and headteachers exercise their authority in the interests of pupils, further legitimating the idea of elite dominance. As an obvious source of social control, the state watches over the system with eternal vigilance.

School uniform:
boys at Eton
College

Photo: Times Newspapers Ltd

> A very large part of English middle-class education is devoted to the training of servants . . . In so far as it is, by definition, the training of upper servants, it includes, of course, the instilling of that kind of confidence which will enable the upper servants to supervise and direct the lower servants.
>
> Raymond Williams, *Culture and Society* (1958)

Generations of British children have come to understand their culture through what is alleged to be their country's history. In reality it has largely been the history of the elite: the kings and their conquests. The heroes of school texts are figures like Richard the Lionheart and Henry VIII; of John Wilkes and Thomas Paine children have remained largely ignorant. Although Karl Marx worked in England, and lies buried in Highgate Cemetery, a British child can negotiate the scholastic assault course with little knowledge of perhaps the most influential thinker of the age. Ethnic minorities have challenged the relevance of British history as a basis for understanding their own cultural backgrounds and this has led to some modifications. Yet the obliteration of the history of those from the black Commonwealth is really no stranger than the exclusion of working-class history.

The idea of the state paying for education as a *consumption* good (to be enjoyed in its own right as a gift of citizenship) can be at variance with capitalist values. Some see it as an *investment* good, providing training for the world of work. New Labour, with its 'Education, Education, Education' mantra, made much of the link with jobs and the economy. This kind of philosophy is consistent with an inegalitarian society and a substantial body of research confirms that British education has served to reinforce inequality rather than reduce it (Giddens 1997: 420).

Of course many teachers are unhappy with an ethos in which education is seen in purely utilitarian terms. This accounts for their tense relationship with government; teachers have been poorly paid, placed under increasingly competitive pressures with league tables and associated bureaucracy, and often belittled by politicians. Labour Education Secretary David Blunkett continued the neoliberal rhetoric of rooting out poor teachers and 'failing' schools.

The arts

Ever since Gutenberg set up the first printing press in Mainz in 1440, the power of literature has been both cherished and feared by the mighty. Although offering a means of legitimating their position by directly shaping mass attitudes, it carries dangerous potential for exposing the privilege of the few to the eyes of the many. Even the idea of a Bible that everyone could read was once seen as dangerous, and radical news sheets circulating during the industrial revolution appeared as an insidious virus in the body politic.

The thoughts of geniuses such as Beethoven, Shakespeare, Tolstoy, Dostoevsky, Dickens, Milton and Shelley can be elevating, but a workforce with a soaring spirit has had no place in the logic of capitalism. It was not until the end of the nineteenth century, when it was realized that industry could no longer function without an educated workforce, that mass literacy became state policy. Yet the results were to disappoint. Critics of the 'uses of literacy' perceived only the rise of a demeaning mass culture usurping the real world of art and (possibly subversive) ideas, offering only a 'candy floss world' and 'sex in shiny packets' (Hoggart 1958). The Frankfurt School of neo-Marxist thinkers argued that undemanding homogenized forms of culture removed from the mass of the people the power to look at the world critically. German philosopher Jürgen Habermas saw this as stifling democracy, replacing the 'public space' in which opinion forms through open discussion with manipulation and thought control.

Advertising

The morality of free-market capitalism is based upon the belief that if everyone buys and sells wisely, according to self-interest, all will be well. The consumer is said to be sovereign. This is questionable in practice because people are generally denied enough information or wisdom to know what is in their own interest. It can be argued that modern capitalism is not at all happy to let people

"I like it. It's colourful, eye-catching and deceptive!"

Reproduced by permission of *Punch*

decide for themselves what they want; it is concerned with making them want what is most profitable to produce. Companies devote huge proportions of their budgets not to making products or rendering services but to altering our thoughts. The mega-industry concerned expressedly with getting into our heads and shaping our desires is advertising. Although promoting a particular product, it generally subscribes to the ethos of free-market capitalism and usually favours the political right. However, the political place of advertising in mind politics goes even deeper. We shall see in chapter 9 that it plays a direct part in politics, the parties investing enormous funds to sell themselves to voters.

The Press

The British are great readers (or at least great buyers) of newspapers, circulation figures being the highest in the western world. The eagerness is not matched by enthusiasm for serious weeklies, where more detailed analysis might be found; sales were buoyant in the 1960s but most were finding it hard to survive by the

1980s. However, although these might influence the opinions of the intelligentsia, including newspaper journalists themselves, they are not direct agents of mass socialization. The mass readership preference is for lightweight material, with magazines devoted to television the clear favourites.

In addition, there is a recognized division between the quality press (or **broadsheets**) for the middle classes and the **tabloids** for the working class, the latter well outdistancing the broadsheets in circulation and readership; amongst these the lion's share is split between the *Mirror* and the *Sun* (figure 8.1, note that actual readership exceeds sales by a factor of around three). Broadsheet readers are the best informed about politics, are more interested and feel more confident that they can influence things. Tabloid readers have similar views to nonreaders, suggesting that tabloids do not contribute much to political knowledge. However, even among the better educated the tabloids are more popular than the broadsheets (Newton 1998: 155).

Because the country is small, the major newspapers are national, producing considerable uniformity of view and centring on London. Provincial morning and evening dailies are in decline, being confronted with 'free-sheets' mainly containing advertising and human-interest stories, force-fed through the letterboxes of urban households.

> Freedom of the press in Britain is freedom to print such of the proprietor's prejudices as the advertisers don't object to.
>
> Attributed to Hannen Swaffer (1879–1962; British journalist)

Partisanship

Part of the process of legitimation is an exhortation of the rights of the **free press** and independent broadcasting. These values were fought for in the eighteenth century against a secretive ruling class, when it was even necessary to

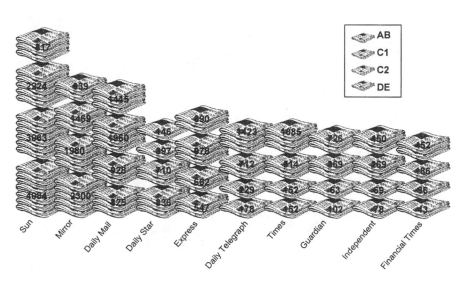

Figure 8.1
National newspaper readership by social class, 1997 (in thousands).

Source: Data from Butler and Kavanagh (1997: table 9.1).

smuggle reports of proceedings out of Parliament. A free press is held to be one of the defining characteristics of the liberal state: a democracy must have freedom of speech for its journalists and free access to information for citizens. However, this freedom must logically suggest a capitalist-controlled media because the newspaper industry is itself part of 'big business'; £3.2 billion is spent on newspaper advertisements each year out of a total advertising 'spend' of £9.2 billion (Leys 1998).

> In the tabloids, virtually every Tory has the stature of Winston Churchill, every Labourite is a lying Leninite.
>
> Glenn Frankel (*Washington Post* journalist), quoted in the *Independent* (15 April 1992)

It is only in times of crisis that the state overtly demands that the press becomes its instrument. In two world wars dishonest reporting was deemed necessary to stiffen people's resolve and the newspaper barons were flatteringly brought into government to ensure their cooperation. However, Britain is unusual amongst democratic countries in having an openly **partisan** press. Although sometimes critical, the newspapers have traditionally spread a generally right-wing message, favouring the right of the Labour Party and the Conservative Party. This has obvious consequences for the political culture. Hence, *The Times* attributed the 1987 general election result to 'the good sense of the majority of voters'. There is an extremely close association between newspaper readership and voting, dwarfing many of the other electoral variables and perhaps as great as class and sectoral cleavages (see p. 241). Not all readers are aware of the bias: the calculatedly yobbish down-market appeal of the *Sun* actually led one-third of its readers to believe it to be a Labour paper (Newton 1986: 324)! Newspaper influence reaches fever pitch as general elections draw near.

By the late 1990s, however, there had been some important changes. 'New Labour' made itself more acceptable to the press as Tony Blair pursued an assiduous courtship of media mogul Rupert Murdoch. At the outset of the 1997

What the papers said in 1992

MAJOR DEFIES LABOUR MOBS, *Daily Mail*, 21 March
THREAT OF RETURN TO PICKET TERROR, *Sun*, 24 March
LABOUR TO RATION MORTGAGES, *Daily Mail*, 23 March
THE KICKBACK: THE SECRET TAX THAT WILL ALLOW LABOUR TO REWARD ITS UNION
   PAYMASTERS, *Daily Mail*, 1 April
NAZI RIOTS IN BRITAIN: PR AIDS FASCISTS CLAIMS BAKER, *Sun*, 7 April
BAKER'S MIGRANT FLOOD WARNINGS: LABOUR SET TO OPEN DOORS, *Daily Express*, 7 April
IF KINNOCK WINS TODAY WILL THE LAST PERSON TO LEAVE BRITAIN PLEASE TURN OUT
   THE LIGHTS, *Sun*, Election morning
IT'S THE SUN WOT WON IT, *Sun*, The morning after

campaign the *Sun* proclaimed: 'THE SUN BACKS BLAIR' (18 March 1997), which it did throughout the campaign. On BBC TV's 'Newsnight' (17 March 1997) Labour's triumphant campaign director Peter Mandelson declared: 'We have earned the *Sun*'s support'. Yet the extent to which newspaper bias affects voting should not be seen as the central issue. Between elections they exert an insidious influence on attitudes, fertilizing the social soil for the roots of the tree of capitalism.

Content: 'All the news that's fit to print' (motto of the New York Times)

News does not come in labelled packages; it must be selected from a great buzzing mass of reality and there are various conventions determining what is

A place in the *Sun*

Photo: *The Socialist*

to be printed. Selling newspapers is business and profit maximization means maximizing circulation. This results in a quest for the lowest common denominator, with the tabloids favouring sensationalism, trivialization and titillation. There is also a deep-seated racism in the sentiments and language, which breaks out into hysterical **jingoism** whenever foreign relations become in any way turbulent. In the Falklands war, in an orgy of bellicose press chauvinism, the Argentinians became the 'Argies' and the infamous *Sun* headline 'Gotcha!' gloried in the agonizing deaths of foreigners. Reporting of the European Cup in 1996 evoked similar sentiments as the German team became 'krauts', while the *Daily Star* headline in March 1998 concerning the French allocation of World Cup tickets read 'FROGS NEED A GOOD KICKING'.

Much day-to-day reporting is preoccupied with the doings of the high and mighty in various walks of life. The activities of the royal family (and other members of the aristocracy) are detailed and the words of certain (acceptable) politicians accorded pride of place on any topic upon which they choose to descant. The reporting of political events concentrates on the immediate, with a marked absence of background analysis. Thus, for example, an IRA bomb is news, portrayed as entirely unrelated to the long-term suppression of the Catholics in Ulster. The tabloid coverage of political news is as scanty as the clothing on the pouting models. Hence, we read as 'news' that which other people feel fit to print and the crucial exercise of journalistic discretion does not treat all sections of society equally. To understand the reasons for this it is necessary to examine press ownership, journalists, and the extent to which the press is subject to regulation.

> Forget all this crap about politicians – who's interested, eh? You only write this bollocks so that you can look good with all your fucking mates in Westminster . . . The readers don't give a fuck about politics.
>
> Kelvin MacKenzie, as *Sun* editor, to his political editor, Walter Terry. Quoted in Peter Chippindale and Chris Horrie, *Stick it up Your Punter!* (1990)

Ownership: the press barons

The proud boast that the British press is not owned or controlled by the state must be countered with the observation that it lies broadly in the hands of a neoliberal Establishment. Never widely dispersed, ownership narrowed down even further during the post-war era. The celebrated *Times*, founded in 1785, was not intended for the masses. Inescapably an organ of the Establishment (a 'parish magazine' for the upper classes, recording their births, marriages and obituaries), it claimed for much of its life to be a newspaper of national record (offering an objective, definitive account of events). The rise of the 'popular' papers followed the extension of adult literacy at the end of the nineteenth century with the creation of the *Daily Mail* (1896), *Daily Express* (1900), *Daily*

Mirror (1903) and *Daily Sketch* (1908). These were the first mass-circulation papers and were to generate vast revenues from advertising, thereby keeping down their prices. They were owned by private individuals who became formidable '**press barons**' wielding awesome power, which was regularly recognized by elevation to the peerage: Alfred Harmsworth of the *Mirror*, *Mail* and *The Times* (regarded as the father of modern journalism) became Lord Northcliffe, his younger brother Harold, who took over the *Mail* on his death, became Lord Rothermere and the Canadian Max Aitken of the *Express* became Lord Beaverbrook. A second generation of press barons included Cecil Harmsworth King, nephew of Lord Northcliffe, who hugely expanded the family empire into the world of magazines and television. A rival empire was the Thomson organization headed by Lord Thomson of Fleet, a Canadian who had expanded his interests from Canada to Scotland, where he had become a millionaire through commercial television. He bought the *Sunday Times* in 1959 and *The Times* in 1966.

What the proprietorship of these papers is aiming at is power, and power without responsibility – the prerogative of the harlot throughout the ages.

Stanley Baldwin (Conservative leader), attacking Lords Rothermere and Beaverbrook in an election speech (18 March 1931)

Modern concentrated ownership, made possible by deregulation from the 1980s, follows the classic advanced capitalist model, with complex transnational conglomerates combining diverse interests in electronic communications, broadcasting, cable TV and the leisure industry. (By 1997 only the Canadian Conrad Black's *Telegraph* titles remained outside a multi-media group.) This renders possible the sustaining of unprofitable titles by cross-subsidization (Thompson 1982). The new-style **media moguls** are typified by the late Robert Maxwell, who purchased the British Printing and Publishing Company (descended from the Harmsworth empire and including the *Daily Mirror*), and Rupert Murdoch of the mammoth News International owning, amongst others, *The Times*, *Sunday Times*, *Financial Times*, *News of the World* and the *Sun*, as well as a number of US papers including the *New York Post*. Another conglomerate was created in 1996 when the *Express* titles were bought by the Labour-supporting Lord Hollick (ennobled by Neil Kinnock), whose group controlled Meridian and Anglia TV. Although having more independence, the *Guardian* and *Independent* are still caught up in this web of multi-media ownership and suffered from the predatory pricing strategy of Murdoch's *Times*. The concentration is even found in the so-called local press, once a basis for radical agitation, about half of which has been progressively bought up by a few large companies.

Owners have always exercised editorial control and both Maxwell and Murdoch continued the tradition. Upon buying the *Mirror* Maxwell declared: 'I have invested £90 million. There can only be one boss, and that is me' (Bower

1988). When Lonrho engaged in the controversial takeover battles which are its life-blood, the *Observer* was to be found, to the surprise of no one, lined up on the side of its paymaster, as in its fight over the ownership of Harrods. Murdoch conducted a continuing crusade in favour of the free-enterprise culture so close to the heart of 1980s conservatism. His power of control was seen in the astonishing about-turn in Labour's relationship with the press in 1995 after Tony Blair's visit to Hayman Island to address a jamboree of Murdoch executives. He praised Thatcher and criticized the Major government's proposals for regulating multi-media ownership (Pilger 1998: 468–9). Doors swung open as Blair gained his place in the *Sun* (and indeed the *News of the World*), articles, often ghosted by **spin doctors**, appearing regularly under his name. As the 1997 general election approached, the *Sun* was backing Labour, its eve-of-poll headline on 30 April reading: WHO BLAIRS WINS. Once in office, Blair's articles continued, as did the meetings. Indeed, in early 1998 Blair conducted a phone conversation with the Italian prime minister in which he was reported to have mentioned a Murdoch bid for Italy's leading commercial TV business, Mediaset. Despite broadsheet outrage, Blair's spokesman, Alastair Campbell, mounted an aggressive defence, describing the report as 'C-R-A-P' (*Guardian*, 30 March 1998).

Journalists

While owners have power it is journalists who wield the pen and mouse. They and their editors usually come from middle- and upper-middle-class backgrounds. A career in journalism, with an inside track to the top, ranks high amongst the glittering prizes the Establishment offers bright young Oxbridge graduates. During their careers they get to know leading figures in the arts, business and politics, and are unlikely to bite the hands that can offer them enticing titbits of useful information. Editors in particular live very close to the heart of the Establishment: Geoffrey Dawson, for twenty-nine years editor of *The Times*, moved comfortably in the country houses of the upper classes; one of his successors, William Rees-Mogg, was a pillar of the Establishment; William Deedes, editor of the *Daily Telegraph*, was a Conservative MP; and his successor, Max Hastings, seemed to personify the hunting and shooting set.

The emergence of the succession of **sleaze** cases in the 1990s saw journalists in more challenging mode. *Sunday Times* journalists posed as businessmen in order to trap MPs taking cash for questions and the *Guardian* pursued minister

---

Nameless men and women whose scandalously low payment is a guarantee of their ignorance and their servility to the financial department.

George Bernard Shaw on journalists, in *Commonsense about the War* (1914)

Neil Hamilton, alleging acceptance of payments for questions on behalf of Harrods owner Mohamed Al Fayed. Hamilton began a high-profile libel action but in September 1996 dropped it minutes before the trial was due to start, agreeing to pay what the paper described as a 'substantial contribution' to its costs. The whole affair was to damage the Conservatives' 1997 election prospects. In its sleaze hunt the *Guardian* also indicted Jonathan Aitken, who responded with a libel action against the paper and Granada TV but again there was to be an eleventh hour withdrawal. In humiliation Aitken was forced to resign from the Privy Council. New Labour were not to be exempt. In July 1998 Labour staffers-turned-lobbyists, Derek Draper and Roger Liddle, were trapped by journalists posing as businessmen in a 'cash for access' scandal.

> He wields far more power than many of the elected politicians at the high table of government.
>
> Andrew Rawnsley on Alastair Campbell, Blair's press secretary, in the *Observer* (1 Nov. 1998)

Yet while attacking personal misbehaviour, these developments do not challenge the Establishment at a radical level. Although causing some ministerial heads to roll, the real interest of the tabloids is sexual peccadillos. If journalists have radical leanings, the structure of the news industry will largely neuter them. Editors can alter stories, career advancement can be blocked by management and, in the final analysis, recalcitrants can be sacked. The process of career development for those of humbler origins from the provincial press will serve to socialize them into the ways of the Establishment or will filter them out before they reach the precincts of Fleet Street or Wapping.

Members of the political elite, particularly ex-government ministers, frequently turn to journalism as a sideline: Winston Churchill distinguished himself in the field, as does Roy Hattersley. In the USA and continental Europe journalists entering politics must give up their day jobs but in Britain they may do both. At the retirement of a leading Fleet Street editor Mrs Thatcher was able to offer public thanks for a key speech he had written for her (Preston 1997). Use of the media was to reach new heights under New Labour, the Prime Minister and his colleagues producing a stream of regular self-justifying articles in both tabloids and broadsheets.

Self-control: avoiding lying in the Sun

The whole point about the concept of a free press is that it is not *regulated*. It is said that in a free society one should have the right to 'publish and be damned'. Those who feel they have a grievance have recourse to the courts and the libel laws. It is argued that rather than **official censorship**, the only acceptable form of regulation is self-regulation. This comes through a Press Complaints Commission (PCC), a body of laypeople and editorial and managerial representatives from within the industry, set up on a voluntary basis to protect their freedom, hear complaints, chastise for misreporting and administer a code of conduct drawn up in 1991. However, critics regard it as a toothless watchdog and it has been made something of a mockery by tabloid reporters plumbing depths of unprofessionalism (fabrication of 'news', malicious character assassination of public figures and the destruction of the lives of ordinary people) that other newspapers could not reach. Rivals have not been slow to follow the coach and horses driven by News International through the PCC gate and, to add insult to injury, some individuals castigated by the PCC, far from being damaged, actually advanced their careers.

Following an enquiry, a statutory framework for the press was recommended in January 1993 by Sir David Calcutt QC and, because the alliance between the media barons and the Conservative Party had come under strain in a post-election recession, some ministers showed interest. The industry was fearful and *Sunday Times* editor Andrew Neil spoke for a largely united profession in asserting that such measures would make the press 'the poodle of the Establishment' (*Guardian*, 11 Jan. 1993). Further defence came from Lord Wakeham, PCC Chairman, who argued that it has become steadily stronger, the number of complaints continuing to rise (figure 8.2).

The royal family were to become particular targets of the press, with transcripts of the 'Squidgygate' and 'Camillagate' tapes (conversations between Princess Diana and Prince Charles and their respective lovers) appearing in the tabloids. Watched and photographed incessantly, sometimes secretly as when exercising in a gym, Princess Diana was literally pursued to her death by the *paparazzi*. Instant hypocrisy reigned as they mourned the 'People's Princess',

JUSTICE and the PRESS

Reproduced by permission of *Punch*

Figure 8.2
Complaints to the Press Complaints Commission, 1991–7.

Source: Data from Press Complaints Commission, *Annual Report,* 1997.

although one US tabloid, *The National Enquirer*, was too late to withdraw its current edition carrying the front page headline 'Di Goes Sex Mad'. This tragic incident concentrated the mind and Lord Wakeham launched an urgent review of the code of practice. This recommended toughening up in five areas: harassment, children, privacy, public interest and intrusion into grief.

Freedom of the press poses conundrums for democracy. Greater protection for ordinary people against harassment and embarrassment may also allow the high and mighty to evade democratic scrutiny. Again, while official censorship spells totalitarianism, press freedom in a class-based society can allow the wealthy to manipulate the ideas and attitudes of the masses, providing a leverage on the polity regardless of which party reigns. This is political power; it is not difficult to see why Thomas Carlyle called the press the 'Fourth Estate'.

Broadcasting

Television is a major factor in British politics, completely transforming the nature of elections, orchestrating political debate, creating a cult of personality politics, helping to elevate the executive, reducing the role of Parliament and projecting the monarchy into a new era of political theatre. Although radio is by no means dead, television has become the organ of a truly mass culture, the principal means of informing perceptions of the political world (Glasgow University Media Group 1976). Although the working class have a greater propensity to view (table 8.2), in all classes the habit is increasing. The 1997 British Social Attitudes Survey revealed that while 10 per cent of the population watch for less than an hour a day, an equal proportion keep vigil for seven hours. On average the British devote twenty-one hours a week to their screens. Avid watchers tend to form a category similar to tabloid readers – older, on lower incomes and with fewer educational qualifications. However, they tend to watch more news than the better educated, often simply 'falling into it' because the 'box' is always on (Newton 1998: 154).

Do the media keep the people well informed?

In the last week of September 1997, researchers from the Gallup polling organization asked respondents whether they knew if the following people were still members of Parliament.

Name	Is	Is not	Don't know/refused
John Major	63	32	5
Michael Portillo[a]	43	48	9
David Mellor[a]	24	64	12
Michael Howard	52	27	21
Kenneth Clarke	78	16	6
Chris Patten[a]	25	60	15
Malcolm Rifkind[a]	37	40	23
Michael Heseltine	64	27	9
Douglas Hurd[b]	31	52	16
Peter Lilley	46	30	24
Stephen Dorrell	36	28	36

[a] No longer MPs
[b] In House of Lords
Source: Gallup Political Index, Oct. 1997. Figures are percentages (rounded to nearest whole number).

The power of TV over minds is potentially Orwellian, a fact testified to in advertisers' willingness to contribute currently some £2.6 billion a year to the coffers of the commercial TV (and radio) companies (Leys 1998). Purveying anything from soap powder to soap opera, it is recognized by politicians as a searing spotlight which can heighten their fretful hour on the political stage or consume them like moths near a candle flame. Margaret Thatcher made mastery of the medium her first priority and Tony Blair's easy TV manner was seen as an essential party asset. In news reporting, the projection of visual images suggests a reality greater than that of the printed word, defying scepticism and compelling belief. A Labour Party rally held in the huge Sheffield Arena on the eve of the 1992 general election greatly inspired many of those present. However, in the hands of the TV producers it was to enter folklore as a grotesque miscalculation by leader Neil Kinnock. Repeated action replays of his triple exultation 'Are we all right!' left the toes of middle England curling with embarrassment.

Evolution

Unlike the press, broadcasters come under two regulatory bodies: the British Broadcasting Corporation (BBC) and the Independent Television Commission

Table 8.2 Socioeconomic characteristics and TV viewing habits

Characteristic	Watch TV for 1 hour or less per weekday	Watch TV for 5 or more hours per weekday
Age (average)	43	51
Annual household income (average)	£21,000	£11,000
Age full-time education completed (average)	17.8	15.5
Socioeconomic group (average)[a]	3.2	4.4
Percentage economically active	71	34
Percentage women	53	60
TV news watched (days per week)	3.7	5.7
Percentage regularly reading tabloid newspaper	27	60
Percentage regularly reading broadsheet newspaper	25	1

[a] Using official classification from 1 (highest) to 6 (lowest); see p. 170
Source: Data from *British Social Attitudes Survey* (1997: 155).

(ITC). The BBC is seen as particularly venerable (affectionately known within Establishment circles as 'Auntie'). Established in 1927 as the successor to a private pioneer, the British Broadcasting Company, it has a Royal Charter to broadcast and is financed independently of the Treasury through viewers' licence fees. In its early years, under its legendary Director General Sir John (later Lord) Reith, it built up a reputation for elitism, pomposity and sycophancy towards the institutions of the state, particularly the monarchy. (It was so much an arm of the Establishment that wireless news readers, though invisible to their audience, wore evening dress, the uniform of the upper class.) The development of television has lessened this, though vestiges remain, as in the reverent tones of commentators at great state or sporting occasions (particularly if attended by royalty), such as the Lord Mayor's parade or Royal Ascot.

The BBC began television broadcasting from Alexandra Palace in 1936 and by 1966 was transmitting to virtually the whole country. It enjoyed a comfortable monopoly until a traumatic challenge came in the form of commercial TV. If the BBC stood for the high Tory element within the Establishment, commercial TV represented its thrusting, free-marketeering spirit. In 1954, after prolonged political infighting among various factions within the Establishment (Wilson 1961), the IBA (later to become the ITC) was created by the Conservative government to grant licences and (renewable) franchises to regional private broadcasting companies financed by advertising. Its patronage was regal and the franchise to operate commercial TV was described by Lord Thomson (who became a millionaire) as a 'licence to print money'. Although the regional structure implies plurality, the biggest companies belong to massive leisure and media conglomerates, most major programmes are intended for national transmission through a networking system and the main news programmes come from London.

With the creation of commercial TV a new kind of media baron appeared (typified in the gigantic personality of Sidney Bernstein of the Granada empire) from the world of capitalism and competition. They recognized that they could only attract the life-blood of advertising by building up mass audiences, which did little to raise cultural standards. The BBC, though free of this restraint, felt obliged to ape the populist strategy to justify the licence fee; *ratings wars* raging continually led critics to fear loss of quality. By the 1990s, the Conservative Party with its deregulatory policies had taken broadcasting to the threshold of a new era of viewer and listener choice. Yet the policy had demonstrated 'little interest in ensuring greater diversity of opinions' (Marsh 1993: 347). Satellite dishes and cable promised choice among some 500 channels, making state control more difficult, as was found over the sex channel Red Hot Dutch. Britain found itself at the heart of this global village with the funeral of Princess Diana in September 1997, which proved the biggest TV event in history, the BBC feeding some forty-five broadcasting companies all over the world.

Yet while channels proliferate and audiences are fragmented, ownership becomes more and more integrated with the media moguls owning TV companies, film studios, publishing houses, film libraries and software companies as well as newspapers. Rupert Murdoch, for example, moved into satellite and cable through his BSkyB TV and controls Hong-Kong-based Star TV, which covers the gigantic markets of India and China. He also acquired a half-stake in Twentieth Century Fox as well as several US TV stations and the US publishers Harper and Row, which became HarperCollins. In this new competitive environment the domestic companies, already losing major sporting events to the wealthy cable and satellite empires with no public service mandate, face an uncertain future. The political potential residing in this multi-media power was demonstrated by Italian mogul Silvio Berlusconi, who used his empire to promote his own political career, becoming prime minister at the head of his own right-wing Forza Italia party in 1994.

The impartiality requirement

Both the BBC and the ITC are formally required in their charters to be impartial in their news reporting. However, broadcasting impartiality means impartiality between political parties and interest groups, not between social classes. Indeed a consistent anti-working-class bias in news programmes has been alleged (documented in an extended systematic study: Glasgow University Media Group 1976, 1980, 1982; Eldridge 1993). In industrial disputes middle-class representatives (management or state) tend to receive deferential treatment and are allowed to define the terms of the debate. In contrast, union leaders or young protesters are more likely to be interviewed in a hostile manner, in a setting detracting from their dignity (a jostling picket line, for example). Critics of the Glasgow University Media Group's conclusions, including some within the TV industry, have questioned their objectivity, arguing that they studied atypical events (Harrison 1985). However, the key point remains that the idea that TV reporting can be impartial and objective is fraught with difficulty (Eldridge 1993).

For much of the time, despite seemingly heated left–right exchanges, all the points of view presented fit within a consensus acceptable to the Establishment. Views outside the narrow central orthodoxy are rendered 'loony' and even 'un-patriotic'. Although it can be argued that this merely reflects a natural con-servatism within British politics, it is equally likely that it contributes to it. In this structuring of political debate the broadcasting media influence not day-to-day decisions between left and right, but the scent in the cultural air we breathe.

Broadcasting journalists Broadcasting journalists are often drawn from the ranks of the press and consequently have similar characteristics and propen-sities. A tendency towards upper-middle-class domination is strengthened by the high kudos associated with TV careers amongst the young; it is a prized niche for Oxbridge graduates. Interestingly, the few black TV journalists usu-ally speak with particularly impeccable upper-class English accents. Although some journalists aim for a robust style of interviewing, they can come under attack. In March 1995, Treasury Secretary Jonathan Aitken accused John Humphrys of Radio 4's *Today* programme of bias and rudeness. Other well-known figures, such as Jeremy Paxman and Anna Ford, have also come under fire.

Political interference

The structure of broadcasting is intended to prevent politicians from meddling. Some evidence of independence was seen in January 1998 in a joint BBC–ITC proposal to scrap party political broadcasts and restrict electioneering broad-casts, on the grounds that they bored the audience. However, whenever it ap-pears that the Establishment cannot count on the kind of *reportage* desired, an underlying conviction that broadcasters should be subservient to the state is forced out into the open.

Patronage The BBC and ITC boards of governors are appointed by govern-ment from the bosom of the Establishment. Requiring no particular expertise or knowledge of broadcasting, they reflect the British tradition of amateurism where, in the old cliché, who you know is rather more important than what you know. Each board delegates day-to-day operations to a Director General whom they appoint. Generally, cautious selection reduces the need for sacking but should an incumbent decide, like Becket or Sir Thomas More, to turn from his patron and serve a higher god, their martyrdom can be speedily effected. The

1980s saw the Thatcher government roused to fury, culminating in January 1987 with the sacking of Director General Alasdair Milne. This move was foreshadowed in the appointment of Thatcherite Marmaduke Hussey as Chairman of the Board of Governors for the purpose of stamping out suspected leftist sympathies; it was he who delivered the *coup de grâce* (Milne 1988). He subsequently made the controversial appointment of John Birt, who was to impose some highly unpopular managerial reforms and criticize his own journalists for being too robust with politicians. The appointment of the right-wing Lord Chalfont as a Deputy Chairman of the IBA in 1989 was also seen as overtly political; it was said to indicate the lengths to which the Establishment was prepared to go in the quest for influence (*Sunday Telegraph*, 19 Feb. 1989).

Direct interference   There are certain formal means whereby governments may influence the media, including D-Notices and the Official Secrets legislation (see chapter 15). However, of far greater importance are the informal workings within the body of the Establishment. Reith laid down the ground rules during the 1926 General Strike, recording in his diary that the government 'know that they can trust us not to be really impartial' (Stuart 1975: 96). He suppressed news that the government did not want broadcast, establishing that 'the vaunted independence of the BBC was secure so long as it was not exercised' (Taylor 1965: 246).

Unwillingness to displease was demonstrated in 1962 when *That Was The Week That Was* introduced a level of popular satire hitherto unseen. Its style was little more than that of an Oxbridge undergraduate revue, part of the middle-class movement that generated *Beyond the Fringe* and the magazine *Private Eye*. However, gamekeepers made effective poachers and the programme startled deferential working-class viewers reared on the unctuous tones of Richard Dimbleby. Amongst other things it stirred up the Profumo scandal, made the Macmillan government uncomfortable and generally disturbed. BBC Director General Hugh Carlton Greene lost his nerve and the programme was taken off on the pretext of an impending general election, which did not actually materialize until 1964.

Pressure became much more intense in the 1980s with the Thatcher government's diagnosis of too many liberals in the establishment kitchen. During the Falklands war, mindful of the effect of Vietnam war reporting on the American public (exposing the falsity of official accounts and effectively ending the war), broadcast news of the task force was restricted and the government would not permit the rapid transmission of TV pictures to British audiences (Select Committee on Defence 1982: xiv).

In 1985, pressure was placed on BBC governors by Home Secretary Leon Brittan, leading to the cancellation of a *Real Lives* programme which included an interview with a convicted IRA member. Even a fictional drama, *The Monocled Mutineer*, offended patriotic taste and was castigated by government. In 1986 Norman Tebbit weighed in with heavily intimidatory tactics against the BBC and Kate Adie for her reporting of the launching of the US attack on Libya from Britain in non-jingoistic terms. His attack sent a shudder down the spines of all journalists; only the stout-hearted would be inclined to risk such wrath, which was no doubt the real purpose of the broadside. In 1988 a radio series examining the security services, *My Country Right or Wrong*, was banned, only to be broadcast later when found to be harmless.

The Broadcasting Standards Authority was established in 1988 under the chairmanship of a pillar of the Establishment, ex-editor of *The Times* Sir William Rees-Mogg. The government insisted it would be concerned only with issues of decency and would not interfere with political content, but opponents feared that once installed it would be but a small matter to extend its remit. By the late 1980s the BBC had become extremely nervous about causing offence. It had even decided to cancel a play criticizing the handling of the Falklands conflict (eventually transmitted some time later), beginning to concentrate on safer targets like battles within the Labour Party and the weakness of Neil Kinnock as its leader. On the eve of the 1992 general election, a *Panorama* programme suggesting that the 'Thatcher Miracle' of the 1980s was a mirage was axed, though the *Sunday Times* (15 March 1992) obtained and published a copy of the script. Another *Panorama* programme, this time on alleged corruption in Westminster Council, was postponed until after the May local government elections after pressure from Conservative Party officials (*The Times*, 25 April 1994).

What changed between January and March 1987 was not the facts or the quality of the programme but the scale to which the [BBC] governors' political and personal views intruded into the corporation's whole management.

Duncan Campbell, referring to the banning of his controversial programme
Cabinet, quoted in the *Independent* (30 April 1988)

A sinister note sounded when the government began to consider allowing advertising on the BBC, which would remove the independence of the licence fee and tie the corporation more closely to the structural constraints of capitalism. Although the report of the Peacock Commission on broadcasting was to reject this option, the possibility remains like a sword of Damocles over the head of the BBC.

Evidence of BBC nervousness came under New Labour when, in November 1998, it was to ban staff and guests from discussing the sexuality of Peter Mandelson in its *Any Questions* radio programme after he had been 'outed' by gay journalist Matthew Parris on TV's *Newsnight*. There was anger amongst journalists and one of the guests, Northern Ireland Secretary Mo Mowlam, described the act as 'a serious error on the part of the BBC' and 'insulting'.

Please will all programmes note that under no circumstances whatsoever should the allegation about the private life of Peter Mandelson be repeated or referred to on any broadcast.

Edict issued to BBC staff, reported in the *Observer* (1 Nov. 1998)

News management   Establishment practices have long allowed the government to propagate the official line through the media. A tidal wave of information is washed up on the beaches of Fleet Street and Broadcasting House each day; many journalists live by the source, faithfully trotting out the platitudes in the press releases. So house-trained are they that officials have organized them into a formal club, the **Lobby**, complete with rules and regulations (Tunstall 1970) and assembling in the Members' Lobby of the Commons, where ministers and spin doctors throw them titbits of information under a cloak of anonymity. Anthony Howard likened them to prostitutes, waiting patiently to provide ministerial gratification (Cockerell et al. 1984: 40).

From the early 1980s the parties began to take control of the media into new waters. Not only did Thatcher and Blair court Rupert Murdoch, their press secretaries became readily recognizable figures in the political firmament, in turns bullying and cajoling journalists and furnishing their political charges with carefully crafted 'soundbites' to encapsulate debate in simplistic generalization. The Labour Party in opposition took **news management** to new levels with an almost obsessional interest in the way their affairs were reported. Blair's press secretary, ex-*Mirror* journalist Alastair Campbell, began to lean on the BBC, complaining, in September 1995, about leading the news with the sensational verdict of the O. J. Simpson trial rather than Tony Blair's conference speech. In government old habits died hard, prompting an exodus of Whitehall press officers (chapter 15).

> We are dealing with a press that basically wants to do us in.
>
> Alastair Campbell, Labour Party media chief, *Guardian* interview (17 Feb. 1997)

However, as Richard Hoggart has pointed out, it cannot be assumed that there are no people in broadcasting for whom the goal of genuine neutrality is real (Glasgow University Media Group 1976: xii). Indeed, the very fact that governments complain and interfere is evidence of this. The establishment of a second commercial channel, Channel Four, a wholly owned subsidiary of the IBA, showed some courage in permitting the airing of non-orthodox points of view, including features with a more than usually left-wing orientation and gay programmes. Courageous reporting, such as that of Paul Foot, John Pilger or Maggie O'Kane does exist but can never be taken for granted.

The internet

From the time that our ancestors inscribed hieroglyphics on cave walls, technology has played a part in communications culture. Marshall McLuhan coined a memorable phrase when he proclaimed that 'the medium is the message'; the way information is conveyed affects what it says. While communications technology has evolved steadily over the centuries, recent advances have generated a breathtaking acceleration, creating a 'global village' with news being transmitted to countless millions the world over. Thus, an English schoolteacher in touch with colleagues in Moscow at the time of the abortive coup in 1991 was able to give them news as reported in Staffordshire which was not available in Moscow itself.

In the cold-war atmosphere of the 1980s the US military developed a means of transmitting scientific information between laboratories. It soon spread to universities and then, with the advent of the cheap PC, exploded into millions of homes all over the world. While the US government spoke of an 'information superhighway', implying some kind of ordered development, the more appropriate image is of a net; uncoordinated and anarchic, where individuals communicate globally in a world of cyberspace – the world wide web – expanding at a rate of 200 per cent each year. There are of course dangers similar to those associated with the press. In September 1997 the Press Complaints Commission agreed to accept complaints about on-line material published by those already subscribing to its code. Yet unlike previous technologies the internet is interactive. Not condemning people to passivity, it can offer some opportunity to reclaim the public space that Habermas believed to have been eroded.

These developments pose a serious threat to those who wish to control minds and ideas. While the Bible could be banned with relative ease, cyberspace is more difficult to patrol. Will technology be harnessed to create the 'Big Brother' society dreaded by Orwell? The spectre of paedophilia is invoked, perhaps to justify attempts at official scrutiny and regulation. In 1998 the US government began a prolonged legal battle with Bill Gates, the man who had created the mighty Microsoft empire, thereby becoming on some accounts 'the richest man in the world'. In creating a monopoly hold over the world of cyberspace he promised to become perhaps the greatest media mogul of all.

Ruling the Waves: State Regulation

The huge media empires tend towards monopoly, justifying state control on competition grounds. The problem is made infinitely more complex by multimedia convergence. In the late 1990s Rupert Murdoch, buoyed by huge profits for his empire, was able to cross-subsidize and use predatory pricing of *The Times* in what was widely seen as an attempt to kill off the *Independent*. Again, in 1998 HarperCollins cancelled its contract for a book by ex-governor of Hong Kong Chris Patten, which was critical of the Chinese government, the Chinese TV market being one Murdoch was keen to enter.

Regulation can come from the Monopolies and Mergers Commission (MMC). However, although there have been some token investigations into the voracious activities of the conglomerate juggernauts, these have failed to halt their march. Murdoch was able to acquire *The Times* and *Sunday Times* without a murmur. The parlous state of some newspapers often means that a takeover is more in the nature of a philanthropic rescue than a predatory act and an investigation is seen as a rather impertinent examination of the teeth of a gift horse. To prevent the takeover would kill the title altogether, reducing plurality and causing job losses.

The 1996 Broadcasting Bill, although seeking to relax regulation on newspapers and commercial terrestrial TV companies buying each other's shares, promised in the longer term a ceiling on the total share of the media market under any one company. Under this regime the holdings of both the Mirror Group and News International would have been outlawed. However, Labour had already come to terms with the might of Murdoch and argued against quotas or limits on cross-media ownership, remaining silent on Murdoch's virtual monopoly of digital TV technology. Although Labour's 1998 Competition Bill was amended in the Lords to outlaw predatory pricing, the government, apparently unwilling to terminate its *rapprochement* with Murdoch, rejected the amendment.

Mind Politics

In shaping our attitudes the agencies of socialization form a rich informational cocktail. Family, education, class background and so on will influence the way we attend to the messages received from advertisers and the media, while what we hear may influence our careers, lifestyle and friendship patterns. This mix forms the ideological bedrock of the political system and its importance cannot be overestimated.

On 1 November 1998 the *Observer* published a list of what it claimed were the 300 most powerful people in Britain, as chosen by a panel of eight worthies (Hutton 1998). Tony Blair headed the list but second and third came two who did not even live in Britain, global multi-media moguls Rupert Murdoch and Bill Gates! Moreover, in fourth place came Peter Mandelson who, prior to his ignominious downfall at the end of the year, had honed the ability to control the media probably more than any British politician before him. Never before had a government entered office with so firm a conviction of the need to monitor and shape public opinion. More than ever the new 'sultans of spin' make modern politics a psychological game – **mind politics**. Yet, while elevating public opinion they downgrade the power of the people's elected representatives in favour of focus groups and advertising gurus.

It is through mind politics that the powerful can make patterns of privilege seem beautiful in the mind of the mass. Although all inegalitarian polities must achieve this if they are to survive, few have done so as smoothly as Britain. On the other hand, Thompson (1995: 42–3) reminds us that passivity can be overstated; the hold of the media does not eliminate the chance for people to form and refine their ideas in the public spaces, be they pubs, clubs or launderettes, or the new spaces created on the internet. The arena of mind politics contains tensions that determine who thinks what, when and how. Our exploration of this psychological dimension of the polity has begun in this chapter but it has not ended; it must continue throughout the book.

Key points

- There is a mental as well as a behavioural dimension to politics. This mental climate shapes the political culture.
- In order for a polity to function there must be some broad consensus on its desirability; it must enjoy legitimacy.
- It is in the interests of those with wealth and power to lead others to share their own views by creating a dominant ideology.

- Attitudes towards politics are developed through a process of political socialization.
- Important agents of political socialization include the family, the school, the peer group, religion, the arts, advertising and the mass media.
- There are many ways in which the powerful can influence the process of political socialization.
- This hegemony is not absolute; ideologies contrary to the one favoured by establishment interests may circulate.
- Politics can thus be seen as a fight for the minds of people as well as for material things.

Review your understanding of the following terms and concepts

broadcasting impartiality	mind politics	regulation
broadsheet	news management	sleaze
free press	official censorship	soundbite
internet	peer group	spin doctor
jingoism	political socialization	tabloid
Lobby	press partisanship	
media mogul	press baron	

Assignment

In a selected future time period (say a week) choose a prominent political news story and collect press cuttings from both broadsheet and tabloid newspapers. Answer the following questions, quoting extracts to illustrate your points.

	Mark (%)
1 Compare the amount of coverage (column inches or words) given to the story by the tabloids and broadsheets.	20
2 Study the degree of sensationalism found in the tabloids and broadsheets respectively.	20
3 Identify any inconsistencies between the tabloid and broadsheet accounts.	20
4 Look for bias (political, nationalistic, gender based, . . .). Is this more overt in one type of paper than the other?	40

Questions for discussion

1   Identify the main agents of political socialization in Britain and discuss their relative importance.

2 'Political socialization removes the will of people to question.' Discuss.
3 'A political culture is more clearly manifest in people's behaviour than in what they say in response to questionnaires.' Discuss.
4 To what extent is the concept of a free press compatible with the freedom of individuals and corporations to own newspapers?
5 'Crusading journalists cannot expect to get very far in a system where newspapers are largely financed by advertising.' Discuss.
6 'The news is not news until it appears in *The Times*.' Examine the political implications of this statement.
7 'The independence of the BBC is secure so long as it is not exercised.' Discuss.
8 How viable is the contention that the British press regulates itself?
9 Discuss whether governments have a right to expect loyalty from the mass media.
10 How do you expect the development of the internet to affect the formation of political attitudes?

Topic for debate

This house believes that the idea of the free press is nothing more than a useful myth.

Further reading

Cockerell, M., Hennessy, P. and Walker, P. (1984) *Sources Close to the Prime Minister: Inside the Hidden World of the News Manipulators*.
Written from an insider perspective, the title says it all.

Glasgow University Media Group (1976) *Bad News*; (1980) *More Bad News*; (1982) *Really Bad News*; and Eldridge, J. (ed.) (1993) *Getting the Message: News, Truth and Power*.
Relentless critique of British TV news reporting, alleging establishment bias.

Hoggart, R. (1958) *The Uses of Literacy*.
Argues compellingly that mass literacy has not been used to edify.

Hollingsworth, M. (1986) *The Press and Discontent: A Question of Censorship*.
Details right-wing bias in the press.

Ingham, B. (1991) *Kill the Messenger*.
Memoir by Thatcher's press secretary lamenting the unhealthy state of current affairs broadcasting in Britain.

Pilger, J. (1998) *Hidden Agendas*.
Crusading journalist reports the voices that consensual news definers filter out. Also trenchant critique of media ownership and management.

Seaton, J. and Pimlott, B. (eds) (1987) *The Media in British Politics*.
Essays discussing most of the important issues in this area.

Thompson, J. B. (1995) *The Media and Modernity: A Social Theory of the Media.*
Analyses the way in which modern societies affect and are affected by the media.

Watts, D. (1997) *Political Communication Today.*
Theoretical perspectives on the role of media in politics as well as interesting anecdotes.
Notes the rise of a 'tyranny of the soundbite'.

Wayne, M. (1998) *Dissident Voices: The Politics of Television and Cultural Change.*
Analyses TV portrayal of events over the past two decades, examining its role as a
subversive medium.

For light relief

Ray Bradbury, *Fahrenheit 451.*
Nightmare future vision where government firemen burn all books. (Also a film/video.)

Peter Chippindale and Chris Horrie (1990) *Stick it up Your Punter!*
Frank story of the *Sun.* Contains nudity and strong language!

Barry Hines, *Kes.*
Goes into the mind of a working-class boy and the narrow world it is permitted to
perceive.

Henrik Ibsen, *An Enemy of the People.*
Mass opinion is mobilized against a man trying to advance the public good against
capitalist interests.

Michael Shea, *Spin Doctor.*
Fiction close to modern reality. Chilling Machiavellian landscape beyond the eyes and
ears of democracy. Author should know; he was the Queen's press secretary.

Orson Welles, *Citizen Kane.*
Classic film/video exploring personality and motives of newspaper baron.

On the net

The availability of all the broadsheet newspapers on the net (both current and retrospec-
tive) enables their treatment of particular political events to be easily studied. The web
addresses are all in a similar form (http://www.telegraph.co.uk) and easily obtainable.

http://www.pcc.org.uk
http://www.itc.org.uk
The Press Complaints Commission and Independent Television Commission sites include annual reports, press releases and statistics.

Chapter Nine

The Electoral System: Parsimonious Democracy

In this chapter we scrutinize the machinery supposed to make Britain a democracy, the means whereby ordinary citizens formally participate in politics. The chapter has five broad sections. The first addresses the underlying concept of representative democracy and outlines the mechanics of the electoral system. Next we examine a crucial chapter in British political history, the evolution of the electoral system. This leads to a discussion on electoral behaviour, asking why and how people vote, noting the impact and relative importance of race, gender, age and class. Section four turns to the behaviour of the politicians and their spin doctors in one of the most visible events in modern politics: the election campaign. We conclude with an evaluation of the electoral system itself and consider the key issue of electoral reform.

Representative Democracy

Democracy and representative government

Over 300 years before the birth of Christ, Ancient Greece consisted of many small self-governing city-states. Adopting a variety of methods and institutional frameworks for conducting public affairs, these presented a unique laboratory for the empirical study of government. As we saw in chapter 1, many of the Greek philosophers, particularly the Athenians, saw democracy as the most desirable form of government, a belief they bequeathed to modern civilization.

In order to be entirely democratic a system of government should permit all citizens to take part in making public policy. There have been examples of such **direct democracy**: the Greek city-states made some provision for it and early parish government in Britain saw the community meeting in the church precincts to make decisions about such issues as roads, bridges and law and order. The government of the small communities formed by the New England settlers in America was also widely participative in character, as are the Swiss cantons today. Although direct democracy in the modern nation-state has generally been seen as impractical, in an age of advanced technology the use of electronic means of consultation makes it more feasible. In July 1997 the Labour government proposed a 5,000-strong 'People's Panel', a focus group to test public opinion on issues, policies and services. This is 'dipstick' rather than direct democracy and reflects a global trend pioneered in the USA. It was a culmination of the market-driven politics associated with Labour's election campaign.

The Greek city-states were very small and intimate, no larger than around thirty square miles. With a considerable number of slaves, citizenship was restricted to fewer than 20,000; abortion, infanticide and a liberal attitude towards homosexual relationships ensured population control. Yet even these polities were too large to govern themselves directly. A mass forum cannot conduct the kind of deliberation necessary for decision-making; this must be entrusted to a smaller group and, if the democratic ideal is to be protected, the selection of this group, and its **accountability** to the people as a whole, are key issues. The Greek city-states made provision for popular voting, office-holding by rotation and various penalties for unsatisfactory officials. In Athens, candidates were elected to a large panel from which office-holders were selected by drawing lots. They believed that those like Macbeth, with 'high-vaulting ambition', who thrust themselves forward for high office, would be the most unsuitable.

In these devices we see the origins of **representative government**. Although a state may be run by a small group of rulers, not unlike a monarchy or an aristocracy, they are not there by virtue of any personal qualities (birth, wealth, religious status, physical strength or even intelligence) but as *representatives* of everyone else. They act in the name of the people and the people retain the right to control and even remove them.

Representative democracy in Britain

Although Britain formally has a system of representative democracy based on elections, it falls far short of the Athenian ideal. Indeed, for long it was believed by the ruling establishment that only a relatively small proportion of the population should vote. Ordinary people were said to enjoy 'virtual representation' – the aristocracy could be assumed to take the views of all classes into consideration when making decisions. However, the franchise was gradually extended as a result of radical leaders fighting for their rights. Those who regarded themselves as the ruling class became fearful of mass rule, seeking new ways to limit democracy.

This they did by keeping MPs unpaid, charging electoral deposits, developing party machines to dominate elections, refusing to adopt working-class candidates and inhibiting the rise of a working-class party (see chapter 10). In addition, they developed a highly elitist theory of representation in which MPs were supposed to act according to their own discretion, with no particular regard for their constituents' opinions. The view received its most authoritative enunciation by Edmund Burke (1729–97) in a famous address to his constituents in Bristol, when he stressed that what they were to expect from him was not servitude but the exercise of 'judgement and conscience'. This view remains deeply ingrained in British political culture, part of the all-important machinery of deference in which the masses forgo their right to influence the high and mighty. An alternative view of representation is that of the **mandate**, whereby election carries an obligation to fulfil promises made in a **manifesto**. In the reality of modern political life we hear both views expressed, politicians choosing the one that best suits their argument.

The Tamworth Manifesto

A set of electoral promises was first made by the Conservative leader Peel on an historic occasion in 1834 to the 586 electors of his Tamworth constituency. The 'Tamworth Manifesto' marked a new style of campaigning based on the electoral mandate.

Referendums Fear of the mass has also been seen in a disinclination to put questions directly to the people. A **referendum** has been used only once for the whole of the UK, to decide on continued membership of the EC in 1975. Unlike the Danes, Irish and French, the British were not invited to register their opinion on the Maastricht Treaty. Although referendums were held in 1979 on Scottish and Welsh devolution, 1997 proved a vintage year, with further referendums on Scottish and Welsh devolution and promises of referendums on the single European currency and the electoral system. The next year saw questions put on the London assembly and mayor and the Northern Ireland peace agreement. However, critics argue that referendums, asking only 'yes' or 'no', oversimplify issues, may be unduly influenced by those controlling information and undermine representative government and parliamentary democracy (Marshall 1997). In October 1998 Lord Neill's Committee on Standards in Public Life recommended that they should be state financed, the rival campaigns sharing £1.2 million. Moreover, the government should remain neutral, not using the state machine to promote its own preference.

Anyone who can claim to understand this issue in simple black and white terms is either a charlatan or a simpleton!

Harold Wilson on Common Market membership, quoted in Anthony Sampson, *The Essential Anatomy of Britain* (1992: 15)

The electoral process today

The British are frequently invited to the polls. Local elections take place somewhere every year (see chapter 19) and elections for the Scottish, Welsh and

Northern Ireland assemblies and the European Parliament occur with regularity. However, it is the process of electing members to the House of Commons that remains the high point in the political calendar. General elections take place around a framework of voters, constituencies and candidates.

Voters Today Britain has a universal **franchise**. With certain exceptions (peers, aliens, bankrupts, imprisoned criminals, people of unsound mind and those guilty of electoral malpractice) all citizens over the age of eighteen are eligible to vote.

Constituencies The basis for representation is spatial; MPs represent areal **constituencies** (659 in 1997, including 17 in Northern Ireland) and a general election is in effect a number of simultaneous contests, each electing one member. Constituency populations tend towards equality (at around 69,000) and population movements are monitored by Boundary Commissions, independent bodies chaired by the Speaker of the House of Commons, which recommend changes every ten to fifteen years. These can have important consequences. Post-war readjustments to reflect declining inner-city populations tended to favour the Conservatives; Labour opposed the 1979 proposals, even taking the matter to court. However, the Conservative government's insistence that the timetable for the 1994–5 review be speeded up for the 1997 contest may have been one factor contributing to their defeat (Johnston et al. 1998). A number of their MPs were victims of the revision, their constituencies disappearing or becoming more marginal. On the other hand, some used the opportunity to move in a 'chicken run' to safer seats.

Candidates Almost any resident British citizen over twenty-one (not eighteen) may stand; the excluded are the police and armed forces, certain civil servants, judges and Anglican and Roman Catholic clergymen and those ineligible to vote. There are few independents, virtually all clothing themselves in a party garb. Each candidate must formally appoint an agent, who ensures compliance with electoral law and will probably also be the campaign manager (organizing canvassing, press conferences and so on). Most agents are well versed in the arts of political intrigue and some are highly professionalized.

By-elections

Elections are called in particular constituencies following the death or retirement of a sitting member. These are interesting for various reasons, providing a measure of government popularity and allowing minority parties to shine. The Conservatives suffered a series of defeats throughout the 1979–97 period, frequently with swings against them in the 20–30 per cent range. Yet although stimulating political debate and media hype, these contests provide a poor guide to long-term trends. The party in power is often victim of a 'protest vote' from those wishing to administer a 'kick in the pants' without dislodging it and the successful minority parties are usually banished to the wilderness at the next general election. However, when Labour transformed an 8,000 Conservative majority into an 8,000 majority for themselves in the Wirral by-election in February 1997 the writing was on the wall at Conservative headquarters.

General elections A general election follows a number of stages.

1 *Naming the day.* The date is not fixed by law; a government's term of office is merely subject to a five-year maximum. This gives the prime minister the undemocratic advantage of firing the starting pistol at the most politically convenient time. Attlee called the 1951 contest after only one year and Wilson waited only two before consolidating his narrow 1964 victory. Thatcher finely judged the 1983 contest to capitalize on the 'Oh what a lovely Falklands war' factor but John Major delayed the 1997 contest, waiting in vain for a 'feelgood' factor.

2 *Mobilizing the electorate.* In the four-week run-up to the election, candidates and parties conduct publicity campaigns designed to woo voters. These take an increasingly sophisticated form (pp. 247–51).

3 *Determining the result.* Voting in Britain has been the essence of simplicity, an 'X' being placed alongside the name of a single candidate. The one with the largest number of votes – the 'first past the post' (FPTP) – is the winner. In this simple plurality system the absolute number of votes is immaterial, MPs regularly being elected with well below 50 per cent.

4 *Forming the government.* A general election results in the emergence of a government, usually formed from the party with an **absolute majority** in the House of Commons. In a two-party system a simple majority will necessarily be absolute but with more parties complications set in; the emergence of a *hung Parliament* becomes possible and politicians have to retire to rooms (smoke-filled in less health-conscious times) to consider **coalitions** or party agreements. In 1974 the narrowly defeated

Edward Heath (with 297 seats) conducted a tentative flirtation with the Liberals (14 seats) before conceding defeat to Labour (301 seats). By the time he called the 1997 election John Major headed a minority government dependent on Ulster Unionist support.

Economizing with Democracy: Evolution of the Electoral System

The history of Britain's electoral system is no account of legalistic reform, nor a psephological nightmare of figures, swings and majorities, but a story of violence and political struggle in which the prize was control over the state. Reforms were not born of rational thought or an enlightened desire for democracy on the part of the powerful; they came after a slow and painful political labour. The belief (perhaps misguided) of those calling for reform since the seventeenth century was that entry into the House of Commons would advance their political ambitions. This conviction averted revolutionary challenge to rock the constitutional boat, making British history more tranquil than it might otherwise have been.

A democratic travesty

At the beginning of the nineteenth century the system was a democratic travesty. Of a total population of 16 million, a mere 400,000 were eligible to vote in parliamentary elections. Of the two chambers, the House of Lords was reserved for those of noble birth while the Commons was largely peopled on the basis of patronage and corruption. MPs came from two types of constituency. *Counties* showed no consistency in size or population and the franchise was tied to landownership; each returned two MPs. *Boroughs* were towns that had at some time been granted royal charters. Here franchise rights varied widely and, although some allowed almost universal male suffrage, the scope for malpractice was considerable. In the so-called 'rotten boroughs', the population had shrunk since their days of medieval splendour, leaving a mere handful of citizens with an absurd right to an MP (Dunwich had fallen into the sea and Old Sarum had a population of zero). In 'pocket boroughs', rich landowners controlled elections through threats and bribery, while the new thriving and populous industrial towns, many with highly efficient local government institutions, remained starved of representation. Voting was not secret and, since MPs were obliged to be entirely self-financing, candidature was restricted to the wealthy. Parliament was thus held securely in the grip of a landed establishment.

Forces for change

In common with most other institutions, the electoral system was transformed to suit the purposes of the new industrial bourgeoisie. For the emergent class, archaic practices of law, administration and government were not the cherished legacies praised by Burke but barriers to enterprise, trade and social advancement. The clash was typified in the 1815 Corn Law which, by denying free trade, blatantly favoured landed interests over commerce. The bourgeoisie realized that the parliamentary compost required some more earthy additives for the bloom of private enterprise.

Justifying claims for a stronger voice in Parliament through the utilitarian philosophy of the Philosophic Radicals, they called for representative government through rational and fair elections. Although self-interested the bourgeoisie required allies, whom they found in the bottom half of the curious social sandwich in which they were squeezed. Here was a class that they themselves had, in Marx's view, 'called into existence', whose potential for insurrection was made more ominous by the chilling excesses of the French Revolution. It offered a force that, if harnessed, could drive the piston of reform as effectively as steam power drove their industry.

Wellington's victory at Waterloo in 1815 had produced little relief from the misfortunes that war had heaped upon the poor. Economic slump, the return of soldiers and Irish immigration produced unemployment, destitution and rising costs. The workers were willing to accept the leadership of middle-class radicals working for a reform promising them a voice in Parliament. Agitation operated on a number of fronts, with Hampden Clubs (named after a great seventeenth-century parliamentarian), radical city newspapers, strikes, marches, mass meetings and political discussion classes to prepare ordinary people for rule.

The 1832 Reform Act

Although working-class agitation was easily suppressed by state violence (as in the 1819 Peterloo Massacre), voters felt that the Whigs were better able to reduce the tension in the long term. In 1830 they were returned to government after almost fifty years of continuous Tory rule. The scene appeared set for a democratic revolution but once in office they revealed no less a respect for property than the Tories. The difference lay only in their view that factories, machines, raw materials and even the urban labour force could represent property as well as rolling acres in the countryside. In the 1832 Reform Act many small boroughs lost their MPs as seats were redistributed to the more populous counties and new urban kingdoms where the bourgeoisie reigned.

The working class gained nothing. The franchise was parsimoniously extended (from around 500,000 to just over 700,000) to middle-class property-owners (valued at £10 or more a year). MPs remained unpaid, potential candidates faced a prohibitive property qualification, electoral corruption was not eliminated and wealthy individuals could still exert undue control. Of course, the Whigs had never wanted popular democracy; they had dreamed only of a prudent middle-class control over Parliament from which they could command their empire of trade at home and around the world.

Chartism

The radicals' disappointment led to bitterness, violence and renewed calls for electoral reform. In 1836 William Lovett formed the London Working Men's Association, which drew up a *Charter* incorporating the following demands:

1 universal manhood suffrage;
2 annual election of parliaments (to render bribery prohibitively expensive and increase accountability);
3 abolition of the property qualification for candidates;
4 payment for MPs (to enable the poor to serve);
5 equal-sized constituencies (to make all votes of equal weight);
6 secret ballot (to end intimidation).

The working class was now more receptive and working men's clubs developed under the name of **Chartism**. However, Parliament rejected their demands and those favouring violence rather than argument took the initiative. The government's reaction revealed it to be as willing as its Tory predecessors to use draconian methods involving imprisonment, vigilantes (special constables and spies) and the army. By the late 1840s Chartism was a spent force, battered by the power of the very state in whose government it wished to participate.

The Representation of the People Act 1867

In the 1860s, partly as a result of unease over the American civil war, popular attention again focused upon electoral reform as a means of containing unrest. In 1866 a Liberal reform bill was defeated by a combination of government rebels and Conservatives. The government resigned, to be replaced by a Conservative minority government led by Disraeli who, to the surprise of many, promptly introduced the 1867 reform bill. Dropping the restrictive property qualifications, this enfranchised all male urban householders. In 1868, with around two and a quarter million eligible voters, it was possible to speak of a *mass electorate*. This had far-reaching consequences: to attract mass support and keep out working-class parties, politicians were forced to take serious interest in social conditions, education and trade union rights.

> The politician who once had to learn how to flatter kings has now to learn how to fascinate, amuse, coax, humbug, frighten or otherwise strike the fancy of the electorate.
>
> George Bernard Shaw, *Man and Superman* (1905)

The 1867 Act further underscored the supremacy of the Commons over the Lords and marked the end of the ascendancy of Parliament over the executive. The so-called 'Golden Age', which began in 1832, was closed by the rise of disciplined parliamentary party cadres (see p. 268) affording ministers a grip over the legislature that the Tudors would have envied. From this time the voters, not the Commons, would choose governments.

The full impact of the reforms could not take effect without certain other measures. The 1872 Ballot Act made voting secret; workers no longer had to risk their livelihoods by opposing their employers' interests. The Corrupt and Illegal Practices Act (1883) reduced bribery and the following year the electorate was almost doubled by the Franchise Act, which introduced virtual universal male suffrage by extending the 1867 provisions to rural constituencies. The Redistribution of Seats Act (1885) had the profound effect of making the working class a majority of the electorate (McKenzie and Silver 1968: 9). However, the franchise was still withheld from certain categories of men, and all women were excluded. MPs were still not paid as such and voters were obliged to select from two competing factions of the elite rather than choose genuine working-class representatives.

Votes for women

Throughout the reform era, the phrase 'one man, one vote' meant exactly that; women continued to be regarded by middle and working class alike as political ciphers. Hence, their struggle for political equality was even greater. Moreover, the number of new voters would be considerably larger than any previous increase, a fact contemplated with consternation by the male establishment and intensifying its resistance.

The achievement of near universal male franchise was a potent catalyst. The idea of a middle-class male monopoly might have irked some of their wives but extending the right to all men, regardless of social status, was even more intolerable. Various associations formed, such as the Nottingham Female Political Union (1838), the Sheffield Association for Female Suffrage (1851) and a Woman's Franchise League (1889). In 1897 Millicent Fawcett sought to unify the movement in the National Union of Women's Suffrage Societies but the approach was too timid for some and in 1903 Emmeline Pankhurst and her two daughters established the Women's Social and Political Union, which became the most famous instrument of the **suffragettes**.

The movement began with education and propaganda but the pipe-smoking, leather-armchaired Establishment and Asquith's Liberal government were uncompromising and prepared to employ the same state force that had resisted the Chartists. Suffragettes were subject to ridicule, physical attack, forcible ejection from meetings, imprisonment and hard labour. Victorian judicial attitudes were constrained by the mysteries of child-bearing; menstruation was a common explanation for female deviancy and suffragettes were said to be suffering with their ovaries or from spinsterhood (Kennedy 1992). Hunger-strikers were sadistically force-fed through the nose, an ordeal leaving some permanently injured. To avoid creating martyrs, the government passed the notorious 'Cat and Mouse' Act in 1913, enabling it to release weakened hunger-strikers only to reimprison them upon recovery. Yet they could not prevent Emily Wilding Davison's dramatic martyrdom when, in the same year, she hurled herself under the galloping hooves of the King's horse in the Derby.

War and the franchise Where Asquith would not help the women the Kaiser could. The arrival of an enemy at the gate produced domestic truce and the Pankhursts rallied their supporters behind the flag. On 15 July 1914 they staged their final demonstration, marching down Whitehall to demand not the vote but the 'right to serve'. Their reward was the 1918 Representation of the People Act, which A. J. P. Taylor (1965: 94) describes, with apparently unintended irony, as the victory 'of the radical principle of "one man one vote"'. This gave women the vote and completed the male franchise but it still stopped short of full equality: men could vote at twenty-one but fear that young women might prove radical, engendered by socialist revolutions in Europe, confined their participation to the mature over-thirties (an anomaly not remedied until the 1928 Equal Franchise Act, which was followed by the 1929 Labour victory, perhaps justifying establishment fears). Yet the move added more new voters than all previous franchise acts together. It also gave women the right to stand for Parliament and later that year seventeen did so. Although Lady Astor, amidst some ceremony, made history as the first woman MP, the occasion did not mark the opening of any floodgates.

> The most important thing women have to do is to stir up the zeal of women themselves.
>
> J. S. Mill, letter to Alexander Bain (14 July 1869)

> Women had always fought for men and for their children. Now they were ready to fight for their own human rights.
>
> Emmeline Pankhurst (1858–1928), *My Own Story* (1914)

War also led some to muse on the anomaly that, while young people of eighteen could be required to fight and die for the country, they were not entitled to vote for its government. But it was not until the 1960s, with improvements in education at all levels, many more adolescents going up to universities and a prevailing cult of youth, that Harold Wilson, in tune with the *zeitgeist* (to establishment shock the Beatles received MBEs), lowered the voting age to eighteen in the 1969 Reform Act. However, his reward was rebuff in the next general election, though perhaps by a smaller majority than would otherwise have been the case, and in 1974 the young vote helped him back to power (Butler 1995: 69).

The extension of the franchise had been gradual and grudging. The effect of the 1832 Act was to give the vote to a mere 20 per cent of the men in England and Wales. After 1867 this became 33 per cent, reaching 67 per cent in 1884. Full adult franchise was withheld until 1928. No major concession was secured without the threat of violence. How has the universal franchise been used? To answer this we must turn to the study of electoral behaviour.

Electoral Behaviour

People voting

The Philosophical Radicals argued that if everyone voted, governments would be forced to rule for the good of all. Yet universal franchise has not resulted in anything resembling popular rule. Traditional elites have maintained their ascendancy and capitalism has continued its dominance. This conundrum partly reflects the Burkean notion of representation. It may also be explained by the way people have used the vote, the study of which is known as **psephology**.

Why do people vote? Since any single vote, even in a marginal constituency, has a negligible impact, it can be argued that a rational being would be better occupied tending pigeons or reading Shakespeare than entering the polling booth. Some countries (such as Australia) attempt to combat such disinclination by making voting compulsory but the right to **abstain**, to say 'a plague on both your houses', is itself a democratic freedom. However, voluntary abstainers tend to belong to the most deprived sections of society, a marginalized category seeing politics as largely irrelevant (Johnston and Pattie 1997). There is also a significant category of involuntary abstainers, those experiencing particular difficulties (illness or absence for example) which they will only overcome if the local situation promises a close contest.

The returns from voting are usually so low that even small costs [time, energy, etc.] may cause voters to abstain.

A. Downs, *An Economic Theory of Democracy* (1957: 274)

The decision not to abstain may reflect various sentiments: class solidarity, a herd instinct, a sense of civic duty, or (particularly among women) a tribute to those who fought for the franchise. Voting is an endorsement of the political system itself; mass abstention would constitute a legitimacy crisis. However, the proportion of the population staying at home on election day has been

Figure 9.1
Overall turnout
(adjusted) in post-
war general
elections.

Source: Data from Denver (1997: table 1). Adjusted turnout reflects the length of time since the electoral register was compiled, to reflect deaths, etc.

rising steadily, turnout reaching a post-war low in 1997 (figure 9.1). A comparative measure comes from the European Parliament elections, the British tending to be among the least enthusiastic (figure 9.2).

What do people vote for? Conflicting interpretations of what exactly one is supporting when placing an 'X' on the ballot paper reflect different views on the function of elections. Ostensibly voters are supporting a *candidate* but even charismatic figures attract a limited personal vote. Most feel they actually vote for *parties*, a view reinforced by the theory of the mandate. Alternatively, many see a general election as a presidential-type contest in which they are choosing a prime minister (p. 421).

Stability and volatility

Studies have shown that most people are stable voters, always supporting the same party (Butler and Stokes 1969), while a more volatile minority are described as 'floating voters'. Since the 1970s, however, an increase in net volatility has resulted in greater support for centrist and nationalist parties (figure

---

Volatility in the electorate

Gross volatility refers to the total amount of vote-switching, as revealed by large-scale national sample surveys, while *net volatility* represents the final effect. If 10 per cent of Labour voters switch to the Conservatives, while 10 per cent of Conservative supporters move in the opposite direction, the gross volatility would be 20 per cent but the net figure would be zero.

Figure 9.2
National variations in turnout in the
1994 European Parliament elections.

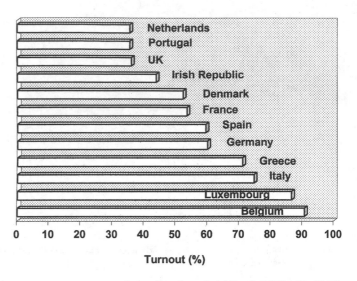

Source: Data from *Social Trends* (1997: table 13.28).

9.3). The explanations for **electoral volatility** and stability are key elements in the study of electoral behaviour and are considered in the following sections.

Stable party identification

There are various hypotheses as to why people repeatedly support the same party.

Loyalty Loyalty is fundamental to human existence, producing the cohesion needed to withstand hostile environments. It was not only Dumas's legendary trio who recognized this; unity lies at the very heart of politics, facilitating the formation of associations – basic units of political action. Loyalty towards a political party inspires the **party identification** voting model. Around 80 per cent of voters have identified with a party in much the same way as they take sides in other great contests – the Cup Final, the Grand National or the Boat Race. This model does not postulate that voters act with self-interested calculation; they vote unthinkingly, responding only to vague mental *images* of the parties. In the 1950s and 1960s, when politics reached 'the end of ideology', with little partisan differentiation, there were high turnouts (over 80 per cent) with 90 per cent of voters sticking to their party. According to Butler (1995: 66), 'most citizens vote as they always voted – and usually as their parents voted before them'.

Ideology Within the ideological terrain parties move as much by pragmatism as principle (see figure 2.1 on p. 22). The Conservatives under Macmillan were

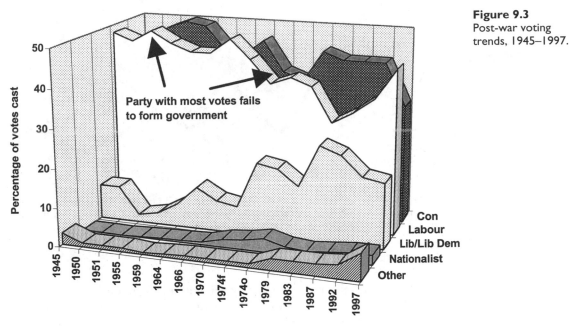

Figure 9.3
Post-war voting trends, 1945–1997.

Source: Data from Butler and Butler (1994: 216–19) and national newspapers.

social democrats but under Thatcher were neoliberals, while Blair's Labour Party effectively dropped the word 'socialist' from its vocabulary. Generally the middle classes are more ideologically polarized than the working class and all three main parties tend to be closer to their middle-class supporters (Crewe 1993: 104). Thatcher's revival of ideological distance between the parties may have accounted for some partisan dealignment (see p. 244) and there were sightings of Essex Man pursuing a rugged individualist lifestyle in the terrain of the south-east. However, despite Thatcher's crusade, voters' ideological positions changed very little and tended towards the left rather than the right (Crewe 1988).

Gender Despite male establishment fears of radicalism, working-class women have traditionally shown a greater propensity than their husbands to vote Conservative. Various explanations have been offered for this. In the first place, they were less exposed to the forces heightening class consciousness associated with employment in large industrial undertakings – camaraderie, unionization and clubs, pubs and sport. An alternative explanation was that greater longevity gave them more chance to lose the radical fervour of youth (Hills 1981). Hence Norris (1993) argues that rather than a gender gap one should consider a gender–generation gap. Both explanations suggest no causal link between voting and gender as such. Indeed, there are so many differences between the social experience of men and women that any suggestion that they vote differently for some biological reason must be highly suspect. Moreover, the dis-

Figure 9.4
Post-war trends in
the Conservative/
Labour gender gap.

Gender gap

Source: Data from Norris (1996b: table 1) and BBC/NOP exit poll, 1 May 1997. This shows the difference in the Conservative/Labour lead between women and men, higher figures indicating that women are more Conservative than men.

tinction between male and female voting behaviour has diminished (figure 9.4). The 1979 general election was the first in which more men voted Conservative than Labour. Margaret Thatcher may have actually antagonized women. Following her departure, the 1992 general election saw the gender gap re-open, with Conservative support some 5 percentage points higher amongst women than men and Labour support 3 points lower (Sanders 1992: 188). However, in 1997 the BBC/NOP exit poll showed virtually no difference between the sexes.

Figure 9.5
Voting by age, 1997
(percentage in each
age group voting
for each party).

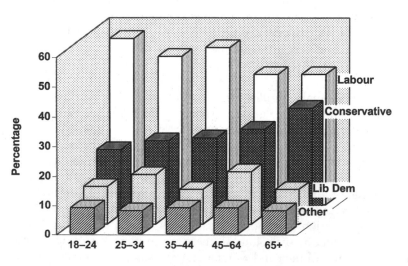

Source: Data from Curtice (1997: table 3) and BBC/NOP exit poll, 1 May 1997.

Age The universal franchise was at first limited to those over twenty-one, in the belief that the young are more likely to question established values and favour radical policies. Voting tends to confirm this view (figure 9.5) though the differentials give no cause for establishment alarm and do little to substantiate Shakespeare's claim. However, in 1992 the youngest cohort was more Conservative than Labour, suggesting the effect of a generation socialized by unbroken Conservative rule. The increasing potential of older people's votes was shown in 1997 as Age Concern mounted roadshows and produced glossy brochures to mobilize the elderly (politically speaking), pointing out that as 24 per cent of the electorate they had considerable voter power. However, the greatest rise in the Labour vote in 1997 was amongst the young.

Crabbed age and youth cannot live together: Youth is full of pleasure, age is full of care.

Shakespeare, *The Passionate Pilgrim*, xii

Race Generally black people have been less inclined to register to vote than whites (Todd and Butcher 1982: 13). However, those of Asian descent are more likely to vote than their white neighbours, while Afro-Caribbeans are less so. In both cases the strong preference has been for Labour. In 1992 some 90 per cent of Afro-Caribbean and 72 per cent of Asian voters supported Labour (Crewe 1993: 102). Although there are grounds for thinking that non-manually-employed Asians, a growing category, will gradually defect (Studlar 1983), such predictions may be premature (Saggar 1992: 169). Increasingly the parties have courted the ethnic minority vote, though without explicitly focusing on race relations or immigration issues. In fact, the 1997 general election proved a largely non-racial one, suggesting that either the parties feared stirring up issues or that there is no distinctive black agenda (Saggar 1997: 706–7).

Newspaper readership   Unlike broadcasters, newspapers can take sides during an election. Although it is debatable whether readers choose the papers sharing their views or are influenced by their reading (Curtice and Semetko 1994), the correlation between voting and newspaper choice is strong. One much feared by politicians is the *Sun*, the tabloid with the least politically interested but most volatile readership (Miller 1991: 192). Its 1992 post-election boast, 'IT'S THE SUN WOT WON IT', was not merely self-aggrandizement (Harrop and Scammell 1992) and in 1997 it again backed the winner, paraphrasing its previous claim with 'IT'S THE SUN WOT SWUNG IT'. However, so did most of the other papers. We saw in chapter 8 that the press tends to favour the political right and in the 1980s tabloid support for the Conservatives reached fever pitch. However, in a surprising turnabout, which can be dated to Black Wednesday, the British press became more agents of dealignment than stability as they lined up behind New Labour, only the *Daily Express* remaining loyal to Major (Seymour-Ure 1997). Of course it is a moot point as to whether the press had moved to Labour or Labour towards the position preferred by the media barons. Blair's courtship of Rupert Murdoch was one of the most compelling symbols of New Labourism. If the party were to disappoint, its new friendships could soon evaporate.

Social class   The most durable explanation for party identification has been class. In four successive general elections in the 1960s and 1970s some 80 per cent of the middle class consistently voted Conservative, while about 70 per cent of the working class supported Labour (Gallup 1976). Yet **cross-class voting** – the presence of working-class Conservatives and middle-class Labour voters – shows that class identification has never provided a complete explanation.

The phenomenon of the working-class Conservative is crucial to the pattern of hegemony in British society; without it an upper-middle-class elite could not maintain its supremacy. Although this obvious mathematical truth haunted the nineteenth-century Establishment they need not have lost any sleep, for around one-third of working-class voters were consistently to support a party with its origins in the aristocracy and dedicated to preserving traditional privileges and inequalities. This apparent puzzle has excited various hypotheses.

- *Political deference.* A deferential political culture sees the working class voting for their 'betters', whom they believe to be 'born to rule'. Norton and Aughey (1981: 175) perceive working-class Conservatives as individuals who 'prefer, despite not having . . . privileges, what is known and predictable in the system and who believe that this is how things should be'.
- *Social aspiration.* For many members of the working class the desire for self-betterment is seen in ruggedly individualist terms rather than col-

lectivism. D. H. Lawrence (1950: 119) speaks of his own working-class community in which 'it was a mother's business to see that her sons "got on"'. The individualism in Conservatism can appeal to this sense of aspiration and to 'be Conservative' in a working-class community can, in a snobbish way, represent social improvement in itself.

- *Neighbourhood.* Working-class voters in predominantly middle-class areas show a greater propensity than others to be Conservative. It may be, of course, that people move here because they already hold such values.
- *False consciousness.* Marxists, notably Gramsci (1971), have argued that the working class are led to the mistaken belief that their lowly role in life is in their self-interest, perhaps divinely ordained. This **false consciousness** is fostered through ruling-class hegemony which has forestalled revolution.

However, underlying this debate should be a realization that the British working class has not been driven by strongly left-wing attitudes or egalitarian instincts. There is considerable genuine support for many right-wing positions, ranging from attitudes to race and immigration and the monarchy to council house sales, law and order, trade union reform and social security 'scroungers'. The popularity of Enoch Powell between the 1960s and 1980s testifies to many of these sentiments and the TV character Alf Garnett, a grotesque caricature of the working-class Conservative, evoked ready recognition to become a loved national symbol. New Labour showed a keen awareness of this across a wide policy range.

In contrast, a not insignificant 20 per cent of the middle class have supported Labour. Possible explanations for this include the following.

- *Intellectual socialism.* Members of the intelligentsia are, by definition, likely to take a reasoned rather than an entirely self-interested view of politics. Much Labour support and leadership has been drawn from the intelligentsia, with the elitist Fabian movement a significant force in the party from the outset. In 1987, the Conservatives fared markedly worse in those Conservative city constituencies (including Oxford and Cambridge) with high concentrations of professional middle classes, university dons and students (Curtice and Steed 1987: 332).
- *Residual class loyalty.* Not all upwardly mobiles pull up the ladder; some retain a sense of fidelity to the values of their parents.
- *Public-sector employment.* Public-sector employees are predominantly middle class and, by the 1970s, comprised around 30 per cent of the workforce. They have a career interest in welfare-orientated policies and a natural antipathy to the right-wing preference for a small state. (An exception is the police force, which traditionally supports the right.)
- *Mistrust of the 'New Right'.* Some 'one-nation' Conservatives were uncomfortable with the neoliberal policies of the post-1979 Conservative Party. By branding them 'wets' Thatcher showed little inclination to keep their support, though Major and Hague tried to win them back.

Volatile voting patterns

By no means all voters are stable. Non-stable voters are particularly important because, although they may constitute only a small proportion of the electorate, they precipitate the **electoral swings** that can sweep governments from office. A movement of only 3.6 per cent in 1964, for example, served to erase a seemingly impregnable Conservative majority. Increased volatility became a striking feature of the politics of the 1980s and 1990s. A study based on data from the British Household Panel Survey (10,000 adults) even suggested that 'the majority of British voters no longer readily identify with a political party' (Johnston and Pattie 1996: 299). The 1997 Labour landslide indicated that many lifelong Conservative voters had for the first time changed allegiance.

Partisan dealignment From 1945 the overall level of class-based voting for both major parties began to fall until over half the electorate was rejecting the class imperative (Crewe 1986: 620). **Partisan dealignment** (figure 9.6) was confirmed using a sophisticated multidimensional definition of class as well as one based simply on occupation (Rose and McAllister 1986). The collapse was particularly injurious to Labour. Between 1945 and 1970 its share of the vote had stood, like that of the Conservatives, at around 45 per cent, but it subsequently plummeted, reaching a nadir of 28 per cent in 1983 and only increasing slightly in 1987 to 31 per cent. Although 1997 saw a dramatic recovery, it clearly demonstrated the features of dealignment (Denver 1998: 210). The swing of 10.3 per cent was almost double that of the previous record swing in 1979, indicating high volatility. Moreover, of those voting in 1992, almost a quarter had changed allegiance. Class-based voting reached an historic low with non-manual workers dividing evenly between Labour and Conservative. Hypotheses explaining partisan dealignment include the following.

   (1)   *The third force.* During the 1970s the bipartisan model of British politics was threatened as a rejuvenated Liberal Party offered electors a third choice. Its share of the vote rose dramatically from 7.5 per cent in 1970 to 19.3 in 1974 (see figure 9.3). The SDP further muddied the partisan water when it entered the fray in March 1981. After forming the Alliance their support remained buoyant (25.4 per cent in 1983 and 22.6 per cent in 1987) and as the Liberal Democrats they claimed around 17 per cent of the vote in 1992 and 1997. Owing to the electoral system, however, seats were not delivered in proportion.
   (2)   *Tactical voting.* The entry of a third horse in the electoral race opened the door to **tactical voting**: supporting a party, or candidate, which is not the first choice in order to *prevent* the election of the least-liked. There was some evidence of this during the 1980s, a trend encouraged by the centre parties. Studies of the 1987 and 1992 results show that opposition parties that had finished in second place in the previous election generally improved more than those that had finished lower (Curtice and Steed 1987, 1992). In the final days of the 1997 contest, newspapers launched an unprecedented campaign to en-

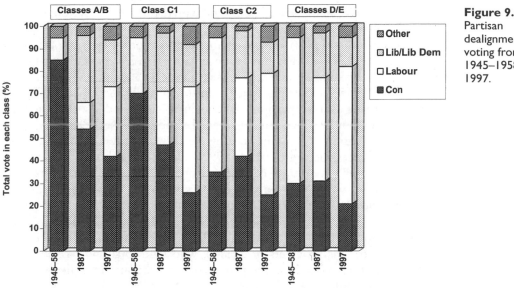

Figure 9.6
Partisan
dealignment: class
voting from
1945–1958 to
1997.

Source: Data from Abrahams (1958), ITN/Harris poll in the *Independent* (13 June 1987) and Curtice
(1997: table 3).

courage tactical voting, with lists of vulnerable seats and advice on how to get
this or that candidate out. A 'Get Rid Of the Tories' (GROT) campaign was
encouraged by Democratic Left. With forty-six seats, the Liberal Democrats
were the principal beneficiaries. Electors were demonstrating greater sophistication, though their behaviour could also be taken as frustration with the first-
past-the-post system.

(3)   *Shrinking working class.* The tendency of the working class to acquire
middle-class values and lifestyles (*embourgeoisement*) has been accelerated by
the ethos of aggressive individualism promoted by the Conservatives. Although
working-class loyalty to Labour may have remained solid, long-term electoral
movement away from the party may be explained by the class itself shrinking
(Heath et al. 1987). Since the early 1970s the percentage of manual workers in
Britain has declined from around 47 to 34, while the proportion of people
belonging to the salaried managerial class has risen from around 18 per cent to
some 27 per cent.

(4)   *A new working class.* Crewe has identified a 'new working class' which
may be contrasted along a number of dimensions with the 'traditional working
class', swelling the ranks of the working-class Conservatives. Among the new
working class Labour's share of the vote fell from 45 per cent in 1979 to around
34 per cent in 1987.

(5)   *Geographical cleavage.* From the 1970s, in a major new shift in the
sands of electoral geography, Britain became 'a nation dividing'. It was once
possible to speak of a national swing at election time which would sweep the

country uniformly, enabling psephologists to predict the composition of Parliament from relatively few results. However, the country became riven by a deep fissure between the north (voting predominantly Labour) and the south (Conservative). (There is a lesser Labour–Conservative divide between the west and the east.) This was not new; it was present in the 1930s but had largely been erased in the 1945 Labour landslide (Johnston et al. 1988: 9). Intimations of the division came as nationalist movements in Scotland and Wales gained momentum, though in 1979 Scotland moved to Labour, against the national trend. Regional differentiation continued during the 1980s, reinforced in 1992 by the geography of recession (Pattie et al. 1993). However, although the electoral map of May 1997 left no trace of blue in Scotland, Wales or large areas of the north and south-west, New Labour had begun to shade the south-east red, making the **North–South** divide less marked.

(6) *Public–private **sectoral cleavage**.* Since 1945 there has been a fundamental dichotomy between those whose lives are predominantly locked into the public sector (as providers or clients), who tend to support Labour, and those operating largely within the private sector, who are more likely to vote Conservative (Dunleavy and Husbands 1985). After 1979, however, Conservative policies such as selling council houses and privatization reduced the number of people dependent on the public sector.

(7) *The leaders.* A process of 'presidentialization' has tended to reduce elections to a contest between party leaders (Brown 1993; Mugham 1993; Clarke and Stewart 1995). In 1983 Michael Foot cut a poor figure and in 1987 and 1992 there was some evidence of a Kinnock factor blighting Labour. By contrast, for much of her reign Margaret Thatcher excited personal admiration amongst Conservatives and within three months of taking over as Labour leader John Smith's popularity rating had overtaken Major's. From July 1994 Blair consistently dominated, with an average rating of 39 per cent to Major's 19 and Ashdown's 14. Yet the importance of this factor remains debated by scholars (see Crewe and King 1994).

(8) *Consumer voting.* The **consumer voting model** sees voters as shoppers in a political market-place (Downs 1957; Himmelweit et al. 1985: 70; Rose and McAllister 1986), choosing policies as they choose a powder that 'washes whiter' or a lager to reach inaccessible parts. This model became popular in the era of partisan dealignment, for when blind loyalty weakens, issues and policies are more likely to be examined. For example, Saunders (1995: 136) found that Labour's promise to renationalize the water and electricity industries frightened off 'a substantial proportion' of its potential supporters who had bought shares. Generally Labour has fared better in areas such as health, employment and education, the Conservatives traditionally inspiring more confidence in law and order, defence, taxation (notwithstanding the poll tax débâcle), inflation and the economy. In fact, given the Conservative record on the economy, the electorate's faith in them is one of the puzzles of British politics (Newton 1993). In 1992, in conditions of recession, enough voters (particularly in the south-east) believed the Conservatives to be the best party to solve the problems they may have helped to create (Sanders 1993; Pattie et al. 1995). However, by

1997, this confidence had been undermined, Labour outscoring the Conservatives on almost all policy fronts. Only on defence did the Conservatives retain a slender (2 per cent) lead (Denver 1998: 212).

(9) *Slings and arrows*. Outrageous fortune between elections can send short-term shock waves through the electorate. Examples include the Profumo affair, the winter of discontent and the Falkands war (curiously Suez did not precipitate a Conservative fall). 'Black Wednesday' in September 1992 finally sank the Conservatives' reputation for economic competence and defeat began to stare them in the face. The sleaze farrago also coloured perceptions in 1997, highlighted by the agreement of BBC journalist Martin Bell, famed for his white suits, to stand as a whiter-than-white anti-corruption candidate against Neil Hamilton, under investigation in the cash-for-questions affair.

(10) *Feeling good*. The objective state of the economy, always a key reading on the political barometer, may not accord with voters' psychological experience. The notion of the 'feelgood factor' entered journalistic parlance as a measure of the latter. Despite improvements in certain economic indicators, it remained elusive in 1997, confirming Will Hutton's 30/30/40 society thesis (see p. 177) that under rampant capitalism even those in employment may feel insecure. In fact the BBC/NOP exit poll showed the electorate split evenly on the state of the economy, 35 per cent believing it to have improved since 1992, 31 per cent thinking it weaker and 34 per cent observing no change. Thus John Major had the curious distinction of winning in a recession (1992) and losing in an upturn. However, this did not mean that the economy had ceased to matter to electors. Peter Kellner's (1997) analysis of BBC exit-poll data argued that the economic recovery did help the Conservatives; without it their fate would have been even worse.

> It's the economy stupid.
>
> Aide memoire in the Clinton office during 1992 presidential election.

Finally it must be remembered that, despite the considerable body of academic and commercial research since the 1950s, the reasons why people vote as they do remain obscure. Human motives and emotions are seated in the subconscious and not easily unlocked by the researcher with the clipboard. People are not entirely self-interested consumers of policies; 'some form of conditional altruism may be at work' (Gavin 1996: 322). Moreover, views can be manipulated through the processes of mind politics. At election times this layer of politics comes to the fore in the campaigns the parties wage.

Influencing Voters: the Election Campaign

Packaging the parties

Despite its limitations, the consumer voting model is important in a way its proponents may not intend; while it may not account for much of *voters'* behaviour, it does explain that of the leading actors (politicians, pundits, parties and the parasitic psephological media), all of whom operate as if it were true. Politicians like to think that the country is enraptured by their comings and goings and make punishing efforts to inform, analyse and persuade. Such activities reach their climax in the grand celebration of the **election campaign,** one of the most compelling symbols of modern politics. Increasingly the real campaign is preceded by a phoney one during which the prime minister teases the pundits and opposition over the election date. In both 1992 and 1997 the parties were effectively campaigning well before the starting pistol was formally fired.

Traditionally campaigns involved an unveiling of manifestos, followed by hustings and public meetings, door-to-door canvassing, flattering constituents and kissing sticky babies, with candidates fighting individual constituency battles. Indeed research reveals that local campaigning and the role of party activists on the nation's doorsteps can still be crucial (Seyd and Whiteley 1992: ch. 8; Whiteley et al. 1994: 213–18). The Liberal Democrats' 1997 successes were achieved by targeting expenditure and campaigning on key seats, often moving reinforcements in from neighbouring constituencies.

However, more than ever campaigns are conducted by the central party machines, with a sophistication undreamed of a few decades ago. It is a battle of media spin doctors and large-scale advertising, with enormous sums being spent. From 1979 the Conservatives, backed by mighty capitalist enterprises, called the tune. However, learning much from Clinton in the USA, Labour raised the art to new levels in 1997, operating from its high-tech media centre at Millbank. Although the official campaign was itself of record length, Labour's own offensive can be said to have started from the moment Blair took over. During this time technology, discipline, focus groups, grooming of leaders and news management were honed to a fine degree (Kavanagh 1997a).

Today politicians have become products to be packaged and sold. Their actions (speeches, interviews and photo opportunities) are planned in detail. What they say, how they dress, their hair-styles, where they go, whom they meet, which politicians or party they attack, which section of the electorate they target, by whom they will be interviewed on television – all is decided for them after careful analysis. Even the manifestos may be written by media men (the 1987 Conservative manifesto was drafted by John O'Sullivan of *The Times*). Shadowy figures like Tim Bell, Gordon Reece (Thatcher media gurus) and Alastair Campbell, Peter Mandelson, Charlie Whelan and David Hill (for Labour) emerge to become as familiar to *aficionados* as the politicians themselves. Criticized as 'control freaks', the spin doctors can stifle any real debate, emphasizing personalities rather than policies (Scammell 1995).

Campaigns are physically and psychologically gruelling. Politicians rise early, travel daily to and from London, attend frequent strategy meetings, make and remake speeches, give daily press conferences, sweat before television cameras and snatch only a few hours' sleep in each 24-hour cycle. In 1997 all the main parties ensured that their leaders visited each marginal constituency at least once (McAllister 1997: 654). All takes place under the scrutinizing eyes of the

"Oh no — canvassers — pretend we're not in... "

media, eager for a gaffe or an encounter with a banana skin. For Labour, the position has traditionally been made worse by general press hostility, though Conservatives carried the strain of knowing that the capitalist interests were counting on them to deliver.

The Conservative press has usually come galloping to the aid of the party but in the spring of 1997 John Major was to hear the sound of retreating hooves. Undermined by print (Rogaly 1997), he turned to television for salvation, accepting a challenge to a US-style head-to-head debate with Tony Blair (who promptly backed down). Campaigning took an increasingly aggressive and negative direction in 1997; rather than promoting themselves the parties attacked opponents. Tony Blair gazed from Conservative hoardings across the country with sinister 'red devil' eyes. Broadcasters, bound by their particular perception of 'balance' as required in the Representation of the People Act, aided and abetted by reporting the campaigns themselves rather than the fundamental issues at stake (Semetko et al. 1997).

Television has become ever more dominant. Although political commercials are not allowed in Britain, slick party election broadcasts use skills developed in advertising. In 1987, a highly acclaimed production presenting Neil Kinnock, written by Colin Welland and directed by Hugh Hudson (director of the film *Chariots of Fire*), was said to have lifted the Labour leader's rating by 16 percentage points (Harrison 1987: 154). These campaigns create tensions at party headquarters as the advertising consultants and party officials vie for control.

The 1987 campaign saw conflicts between Thatcher, for whom Tim Bell (having fallen out with the brothers Saatchi) was working in secret and party chairman Tebbit, working with Saatchi and Saatchi as the official agency (Hollingsworth 1997).

Throughout all, the public are reduced to passivity. People cannot confront and heckle, as they could at the traditional hustings (a foot projected through the screen will do nothing to register opposition to the relentless talking head) and questioning can only take place vicariously through the medium of the professional interviewer (whose line may be governed by career considerations). The development of 'phone-ins', permitting the public to address politicians directly while others listen, does little to capture the robust spirit of true debate. Questions can be carefully monitored beforehand and the programme controllers can reduce an awkward or abusive caller to mute impotence at the press of a button. The spin doctors seek to manipulate and bully the media, so that what appears on the screen is 'politics on the politicians' terms', with little real information dispensed by the 18-second 'soundbite' (Harrison 1992: 170).

Monitoring the campaign

The analogy with selling is extended by the ever-increasing use of market-survey organizations (such as Mori, NOP, Marplan and Gallup), commissioned by the media and the parties to conduct **opinion polls** on voting intentions and related matters (figure 9.7). There are grave dangers in such saturation and some countries ban polling during the campaign. Sometimes the polls themselves displace real news. Believing with Oscar Wilde's Lady Bracknell that statistics 'are laid down for our guidance', the 'bandwagon effect' may lead people to be swept along like sheep to be on the winning side. Alternatively, supporters may stay away if they see their party is well ahead, while lukewarm voters may be galvanized to assist one falling behind. Moreover, the pollsters may get their predictions wrong. In 1992 they emerged with much egg on their clipboards as the Conservatives secured a victory against all expectations (Butler and Kavanagh 1992: 146). This occasioned much heart-searching. Interviewees may have been expressing their disapproval of individualistic government policies while still intending to support it in the secrecy of the ballot box (Denver 1994: 163–4). In addition, a late swing to the Conservatives, differential refusal rates, a higher propensity to vote among Conservative supporters and sample bias may all have contributed to the errors (Crewe 1992; Curtice 1996).

Hence, the pollsters revised their methods and 1997 was seen as a critical test. When Labour romped home, they claimed to have redeemed themselves. Yet with such a landslide how could they have failed? Ivor Crewe pointed out the need for some modesty. Had the result been narrower (as they usually are), and allowing for the margin of error, some polls would almost certainly have been wrong. Moreover, the forecast of a Labour majority of 170–220 was made

Source: Data from Butler and Kavanagh (1997: table 7.2).

Figure 9.7
An exact science? Labour's lead over the Conservatives according to the last published poll during each week of the 1997 election campaign.

by assuming a uniform national swing based on a lead of 17–22 points. In the event the actual lead was only 13 points and the Labour majority of 179 was achieved because the swing was *not* uniform (Crewe 1997).

'Sound and fury, signifying nothing'?

Whether the new trends in campaigning are desirable or effective is debatable. Voters' familiarity with modern advertising tactics may induce scepticism. Short, easy-to-remember messages exorcize all subtlety from discussion and the sheer quantity of coverage may induce torpor and apathy. This is a genuine threat to democracy; it may not be insignificant that the excessively long 1997 campaign coincided with a turnout of 71.4 per cent, a post-war low. Finally, the great expense and energy consumed in this intense heat may well be wasted. Although the Conservatives' 1987 campaign was often in disarray they found themselves drinking the champagne with a handsome parliamentary majority. In 1992, John Major stepped back from the spin doctors' wizardry to take a soap-box into the shopping precincts and gained the last laugh. However, in 1997 his constituency visits appeared to do little for the Conservatives whereas a visit by Paddy Ashdown raised the Liberal Democrats' vote by 18 per cent (McAllister 1997: 654–5). Although Labour spent over £7 million on press and poster advertising in 1997, many commentators regard this election as one the Conservatives lost by their own disarray. One study of the campaign concluded that nothing could have altered the result (Whiteley 1997). Indeed, in the view of some psephologists, elections are won and lost before the campaigns ever begin (Clifford and Heath 1994: 21).

The British Electoral System: Disproportional Representation?

The first-past-the-post (FPTP) system is said by its supporters to be quintessentially British, having evolved to be uniquely fitted to the political culture. It is conducive to bipartisan politics, offering electors a clear choice and producing stable majorities, moderate policies and an ethos of strong government. Extremist parties are excluded: despite its 30,000 membership in the 1930s, the British Union of Fascists did not gain a single seat in Parliament. Single-party governments can count on a full term, enabling them to follow their mandate without compromises through coalition-building or fear of a *coup*. It also produces a coherent opposition – a 'government in waiting' – and allows a regular alternation of governments. Small, single-member constituencies permit close links between MPs and people and ensure that the interests of far-flung regions are not forgotten in Parliament. Moreover, its simplicity makes it easily understood, voters are used to it and a fairly high turnout is said to demonstrate their satisfaction. However, these virtues are open to question.

- *Mandated government.* A victorious party cannot always be expected to execute all its promises as, for example, when the Conservatives jettisoned their 1992 pledge not to increase VAT and Labour reneged on its 1996 vow not to privatize Air Traffic Control.
- *Clear choice.* This idea is belied by the tendency of the two main parties to converge on the centre ground. A consensus developed in the post-war period, broken only by Thatcher, and it was not long before Labour was moving rightwards across a wide policy range. Even over Europe, the differences were largely *within* the parties rather than between them. On the key question of the single currency, both favoured a wait-and-see strategy.

> The kind of economy that we are faced with is going to be a market economy, and we have got to make it work better than the Tories make it work.
>
> Neil Kinnock, Labour Party conference speech (1988)

- *Strong single-party government.* During the twentieth century Britain has experienced some twenty-one years of government by a combination of parties, through a coalition or National government. There have also been periods when a single party in office has lacked an absolute majority, sustained only by a third-party agreement. Moreover, even with a majority, strong government is only possible with disciplined troops; Major was brought to his knees by his Eurosceptics.
- *Regular alternation in office.* Even in the post-war era, when this thesis appeared most plausible, by 1997 the Conservatives had reigned for thirty-

five of the post-war years (figure 9.8). Once in office, the 1997 Blair government was making no secret of its ambition to build for a second term.

- *Moderate government.* Thatcher demonstrated, to both admirers and critics, that the system did not necessarily prevent a degree of extremism.
- *Single-party opposition.* For much of the early twentieth century the Liberals coexisted with Labour in opposition. In the 1983 general election, the first-past-the-post system was kind to Labour, masking the reality of the centre-party vote. However, in 1997 the Liberal Democrats, with 46 seats to the Conservatives' 165, could lay some claim to be an alternative opposition.
- *Popularity.* The record low turnout in 1997, representing a decline of 12 per cent since 1950, and increasingly sophisticated tactical voting, did little to support claims that the system was popular or that people wanted simplicity.

Figure 9.8 Party dispositions in the House of Commons after general elections, 1945–1997.

The case against

Hence, first-past-the-post has many critics. In the 1970s, an orchestrated re-form campaign of academics and politicians gained considerable momentum but came to nothing (Finer 1975), partly through lack of strong public feeling. The problem for reformers is that the system has for long served the two dominant parties well. However, as conditions change, with a stronger third party and the growing significance of the EU, it is increasingly necessary to re-evaluate it.

- *Disenfranchisement.* In a single-member constituency only one set of opinions can ever be represented, leaving many votes 'wasted'. Even votes cast for successful candidates are superfluous where majorities are large, as in many northern Labour seats. Such constituencies remain impervi-ous to national swings and thousands of voters are without influence. Local party oligarchs become the effective electorate through their right to select the candidate (the 'selectorate'). This subversion of democracy could be reduced by some form of **primary election**, passing the choice to the party rank and file (closed primary) or the public at large (open primary).
- *Apathy.* These factors reduce inducements to vote; in Hackney North, for example, the 1997 turnout was as low as 51 per cent. Analysis shows turnout in proportional systems to be some 9 per cent higher than non-proportional systems (Lijphart 1994).
- *The third-party effect.* Despite widespread national support, third par-ties may not be in a position to win in many constituencies. Liberal Demo-crats have been particularly vulnerable. By 1997, thanks to targeting and tactical voting, their support became less uniform but, attracting a total of 5,242,894 votes, over half that of the Conservatives, their 46 seats fell disproportionately below the Conservative tally of 165. Conversely, mi-nority parties with spatially concentrated support can achieve a parlia-mentary presence quite out of proportion to their *national* strength. In 1997 Scottish and Welsh nationalists secured 10 seats with only 782,570 votes.
- *Over-amplification of opinion change.* It has been estimated that a shift in support from one party to the other of only about 1 per cent will result in a change in Parliament of about 13 seats. In 1992, for complex rea-sons of electoral bias, this did not happen (Curtice and Steed 1992: 348), but in 1997 a 10.3 per cent swing gave Labour a 147-seat gain.
- *Policy discontinuity.* The fact that government change entails a complete clean-out may threaten continuity of policy. This can partly explain the 'stop–go' policies impairing Britain's economic performance in compar-ison with Western Europe, where continuity is secured through centrally dominated coalitions.
- *Issue submergence.* The pressure towards bipartism means that voters are offered only two very broad policy *tables d'hôtes* from which to choose.

The system is incapable of accommodating debate on certain crucial issues, such as Europe or the environment, where the fissures run largely within the two main parties rather than between them.

- *Lack of legitimacy*. Once there are more than two horses in the race, winners may actually be rejected by well over half the electorate. Anomalies at constituency level are transposed to Parliament; since 1935 no governing party has polled over half the votes cast although almost all have enjoyed substantial *parliamentary* majorities. In 1987 the Conservatives, with 42.3 per cent of the votes, were able to push through the poll tax because the system gave them 57.8 per cent of the seats. Ten years later Labour's 419 'landslide' was a product of only 44.5 per cent of the votes and Scottish and Welsh Conservatives were left entirely bereft of parliamentary representation. Indeed, in Scotland they had gained 17.5 per cent of the vote while the Liberal Democrats, with only 13 per cent, won 10 seats. It is even possible for the party with the parliamentary majority to poll fewer votes than the opposition, as was demonstrated in 1951 and February 1974.

A final anomaly has nothing to do with first-past-the-post but, in the absence of fixed parliamentary terms, there is an *incumbency advantage* whereby the prime minister fires the starting pistol, despite also running in the race.

The alternatives

The FPTP system is largely reserved to systems that developed under English influence: the USA, India, Canada and many states in Africa and Asia. Most polities seek an assembly that reflects the pattern of voting on the principle of **proportional representation** (PR). In referendums in 1992 and 1993, the people of New Zealand rejected FPTP in favour of this. There are various forms of PR, of which the following are the principal basic models.

Alternative vote (AV) This well-known system is used for the Australian House of Representatives. It does not produce genuine PR because it operates on the basis of single-member constituencies. However, it does ensure that members have an absolute majority by considering the alternative preferences (**preferential voting**) of those voting for minority candidates (figure 9.9).

Supplementary vote This system was advocated by Labour MP Dale Campbell-Savours as a way of avoiding the problem with the AV system of overvaluing third and subsequent preferences in the redistribution process. It came into prominence by being recommended by the Labour Party's Plant Report. The ballot paper is the same as in FPTP but voters may choose a second preference. If any candidate wins over 50 per cent of the vote the matter ends there. If not, all but the first two candidates are eliminated and their votes redistributed on the basis of second choices.

Figure 9.9
The alternative
vote system.

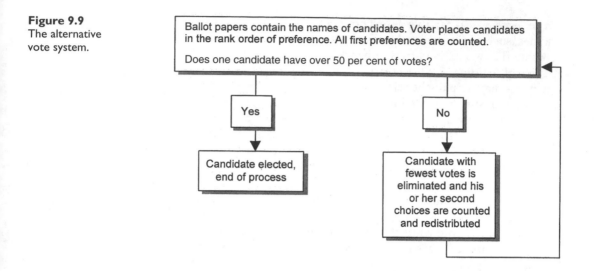

Ballot papers contain the names of candidates. Voter places candidates
in the rank order of preference. All first preferences are counted.

Does one candidate have over 50 per cent of votes?

Yes

No

Candidate elected,
end of process

Candidate with
fewest votes is
eliminated and his
or her second
choices are counted
and redistributed

Second ballot Instead of expressing a second preference, if no candidate secures an absolute majority the voters return for a second chance to vote. A
crucial period comes between the two ballots when weak parties may withdraw, others indulge in horse-trading over policies, voters can think again and
abstainers may decide to turn out. The system is used in France.

Regional list Widely used in Western Europe, including Denmark, Finland
and Belgium, this system is based upon **multi-member constituencies**. Parties
prepare lists of candidates, which may be 'open', where voters can indicate
their favoured candidates, or 'closed', where they merely indicate the *party* of
their choice and candidates are returned in the list order. The latter increases
the power of the party machine and is less democratic (a point emphasized by
the House of Lords in rejecting the European Parliamentary Elections Bill in
1998, though it apparently worried them less when considering election to
the Scottish and Welsh assemblies). Some systems allow voters to split the
ticket between parties. The percentage vote obtained by each party is calculated and seats are awarded on a pro rata basis starting from the top of the
list.

The multi-member constituency

This is fundamental to the PR principle. If in a given constituency party X polls 60
per cent of the votes, party Y 30 and party Z 10, a minimum of ten candidates must
be returned if strict proportionality is to be observed. This implies that constituencies cannot be small; indeed a 'constituency' may be a large region, or even a
whole country.

Additional member (AMS) This system combines single-member constituencies with proportionality. The voter has one vote for the constituency MP and an additional one for a regional list. The balance between the two can vary (it is often around 50–50); the more 'additional' or top-up members, the greater the proportionality. Various versions are employed in Germany, Italy and Mexico and it is now used in New Zealand as the 'mixed member proportional' system.

Alternative vote plus (AV-plus) Recommended by the Jenkins Commission (see p. 259), this combines AV and AMS. Voting takes place as in AMS except that constituency members are chosen by AV rather than FPTP.

Single transferable vote (STV) With certain resemblances to the AV system this is probably the best-known PR system. A version was used in Britain between 1918 and 1948, when multi-member university seats existed. It was also recommended by the Kilbrandon Commission on the Constitution for the separate assemblies it advocated for Wales and Scotland. Although requiring multi-member constituencies (usually three to five MPs), these may be relatively small. Parties may put up as many candidates as there are seats and voters are thus given considerable choice. The procedure has three main stages.

1 Voters record on the ballot paper their order of preference for candidates.
2 An **electoral quota** (EQ) is calculated using the following formula:

$$EQ = \frac{Votes}{Seats + 1} + 1$$

3 First preferences are counted and those obtaining the EQ are elected. If seats remain vacant, surplus votes for successful candidates are redistributed on the basis of second choices, so that further candidates reach the EQ and no votes are wasted. If all seats cannot be filled in this way, the last candidate's ballot papers are redistributed on the basis of second choices.

Although counting is complicated, in principle the system is simplicity itself, voters merely having to number the candidates in order of preference. However, research by Democratic Audit (Dunleavy et al. 1997b) found that ballot papers were difficult to understand in comparison with systems such as AMS. The system is used in Ireland, Malta and Australia, but was rejected by the Jenkins Commission as being too great a change from FPTP and outside its remit of maintaining the constituency link.

Time for a change?

Britain's adherence to FPTP proved particularly anomalous in the case of the European Parliament (excepting Northern Ireland). Here the purpose is not to

Figure 9.10
The discrepancy between votes and seats in the 1994 European Parliament elections (excluding Northern Ireland).

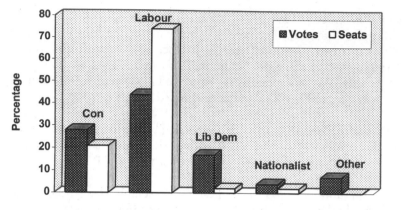

Source: Data from Butler and Butler (1994: 221).

form a government (a key argument for FPTP) and all other member states used PR. The 1994 elections produced angry complaints from frustrated centre-right leaders. While Europe generally swung to the right, the Socialist group (PES) boosted its representation from 198 to 221, thanks to the disproportionate increase in the number of Labour MEPs (a 4 per cent rise in the vote giving them 17 more seats, whereas PR would have produced around 6) (figure 9.10). There was talk of insisting that Britain introduce PR. The proposed regional list system outlined in the abortive 1998 European Parliamentary Elections Bill entailed nine English regions electing 71 MEPs, with Wales and Scotland constituting single regions returning 8 and 5 MEPs respectively. Northern Ireland continued to elect 3 MEPs by STV.

Devolution is also introducing more PR into the UK. Members of both the Scottish Parliament and Welsh Senedd are elected for four-year terms by AMS. Initially, there are 73 constituency members and 56 from **party lists** in Scotland, while in Wales the numbers are 40 and 20. The Northern Ireland assembly, arising from the Good Friday Agreement, uses STV to elect its 108 members in order to ensure that all voices are heard (see p. 160). Moreover, discussions on the modernization of local government have raised the possibility of PR here. However, the government's preference for closed-list systems for the Euro elections and the Scottish and Welsh assemblies may still consolidate patronage in the hands of central party machines. Candidates on the Labour lists were ranked by caucuses of regional delegates and officials, while Conservatives and Liberal Democrats ordered their lists on the principle of one member, one vote.

With respect to the UK Parliament, the two major parties had long resisted reform but a third consecutive defeat in 1987 concentrated the collective Labour mind. Within the party a vigorous Campaign for Electoral Reform formed, with over 60 MPs, including front-bencher Robin Cook and under the presidency of Professor (later Lord) Raymond Plant, who had chaired a Labour-sponsored working party on electoral reform. Reporting in April 1993 it recommended a regional-list system for the European Parliament and a supplementary vote system for the House of Commons (and a reformed second chamber). Party leader John Smith promised a referendum if Labour took power. Although Tony Blair was more equivocal, in March 1997, on the eve of the general election, he struck an historic deal with the Liberal Democrats. Once in office Labour established an independent commission to recommend one proportional system to be pitted against FPTP in a referendum before the next election. Chaired by Liberal Democrat Lord Jenkins of Hillhead, one of the 'Gang of Four' who had dreamed of breaking the mould of British politics, its terms of reference required that the recommendation fulfil a number of criteria:

- broad proportionality;
- stable government;
- extended voter choice;
- maintaining the MP–constituency link.

The inquiry included open meetings across the country where individuals and interest groups were able to put their views. The report, published in October 1998, recommended AV-plus, with redrawn boundaries to reduce the number of constituencies from 659 to between 530 and 560. With the majority of MPs (80–85 per cent) as constituency MPs and the remaining 15–20 per cent selected from regional lists, the system would be much more proportional than FPTP and was broadly welcomed by those campaigning for electoral reform.

A uniquely British system

Charter 88 believes that the strength of AV-plus is that it has been specifically designed to fit in with Britain's political culture . . . if adopted [it] will foster a more productive and efficient style of politics.

Extract from Charter 88 press release (Nov. 1998)

Effects of PR in Britain

The introduction of PR would in all probability revolutionize British politics, though different systems would yield differing results. One sophisticated simulation is shown in figure 9.11, using a mock election with 1,800 electors and allowing for factors such as regional variations, advantages to incumbent parties and targeting by smaller parties. The possible effects of PR include the following.

- Campaigning styles would probably become even more centralized. In New Zealand, the reform saw the parties fundamentally changing their strategies, moving from constituency targeting as they sought to maximize votes everywhere (Denemark 1996).

- Parliamentary representation of minority parties such as the Liberal Democrats and the Greens would increase at the expense of the old duopoly.
- Depending on the system chosen, hung Parliaments and coalition government could become more common.
- The centre parties, despite minority status, would gain authority and could expect to remain part of successive coalitions. After the first New Zealand election under the new system, it was two months before a fragile coalition was finally in place, the seventeen MPs of the Maori-based New Zealand First finding themselves in a pivotal position.
- In the longer term, smaller parties might lose their minority status, becoming more attractive once people felt that votes would no longer be wasted.
- Alternatively, electors might decide that they preferred a two-party system and reduce their propensity to support minority forces.
- The 'broad churches' of the major parties might fragment into their different factions.
- Turnouts might rise if voters felt their votes would not be 'wasted'.

What the Tories need, did they but know it, is electoral reform. They could then divide into the two parties – European Social Democrat and English Nationalist – that they are.

Andrew Rawnsley (journalist), *Observer* (6 July 1997)

A Crisis of Legitimacy?

At the end of the twentieth century Britain found itself with a problematic electoral system. By 1997, the eighteen-year Conservative reign had been the longest since the great Reform Act of 1832. An equally long period of Labour rule would hardly redress the balance. If some people come (as did the Northern Ireland Catholics) to feel the system gives them no constitutional means of influence, a crisis of legitimacy looms. As the new millennium approached, many thought that it was indeed 'Time for a change'.

Key points

- British democracy is based on the principle of representative government, in which a few govern on behalf of the many.
- Representative government may have various interpretations, ranging from the Burkean view to the doctrine of the mandate.
- The evolution of the British system has been slow. Extensions to the franchise were given unwillingly.

- The FPTP principle is not proportional but can produce strong, single-party government. It has favoured the continued dominance of the two main parties; this helps explain its persistence.
- The study of voting behaviour has concentrated on seeking reasons why people vote one way or another. Class has been regarded as one of the principal determinants but significant dealignment has occurred since the 1970s.
- Many other factors influence voting, some long term and others reflecting particular circumstances.
- The alternative to FPTP is some form of PR which, by the late 1990s, was being introduced for the Scottish and Welsh assemblies.
- In November 1998 the Jenkins Report recommended AV-plus for British general elections.

Review your understanding of the following terms and concepts

absolute majority
abstention
additional member
alternative vote
Chartism
constituency
consumer voting model
cross-class voting
direct democracy
electoral quota
electoral stability
electoral swing
electoral volatility
embourgeoisement

false consciousness
first-past-the-post
floating voter
mandate
manifesto
multi-member
    constituency
opinion poll
partisan dealignment
party identification
preferential voting
primary election
proportional
    representation

psephology
referendum
regional list
representative
    government
sectoral cleavage
simple plurality
single transferable vote
spin doctor
suffragette
tactical voting
universal franchise

Assignment

Study figure 9.11 on p. 262 and answer the following questions.

		Mark (%)
1	Which system gives the closest approximation to pure proportionality?	10
2	Which systems would produce coalition governments? Explain why.	10
3	Which systems give the best geographical representation? Explain why.	10
4	Which systems are kindest to small parties? Explain why.	10

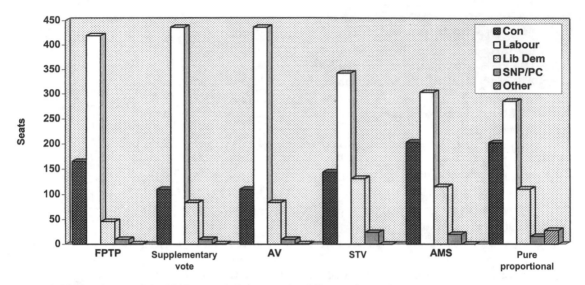

Figure 9.11 Simulation of the 1997 general election under different electoral systems.
Source: Data from Dunleavy et al. (1997b).

5 Is FPTP the least proportional system shown? Explain
   your reasoning.   10
6 Does this analysis support the view that PR gives undue
   weight to fringe parties?   20
7 Can it be assumed that people would have voted in the
   ways shown had one of these systems been in place?   30

Questions for discussion

1 What reasons can explain why a substantial proportion of the working
   class have always voted Conservative?
2 'For all its defects, the British electoral system ensures strong government.' Discuss.
3 Why has the extension of the franchise to the working class been so
   grudging?
4 How important is the concept of the mandate in British politics?
5 What might be the effects of the introduction of primary elections into
   British politics?
6 How important are class, age and gender in explaining voting behaviour in Britain today?
7 Which system of PR would you consider most suitable for Britain?
8 Why did Labour win the 1997 general election?
9 Why might PR be considered more appropriate for the European Parliament than for Westminster?

10 In the 1997 general election, turnout fell dramatically and was lowest, and fell most, in Labour constituencies. However, the Conservative vote collapsed while Labour enjoyed a landslide victory with a substantial increase in its vote share. How would you explain this paradox? (Seek assistance from Denver 1997.)

Topic for debate

This house believes that proportional representation will revitalize politics in Britain.

Further reading

Butler, D. (1995) *British General Elections since 1945.*
Concise and accessible account of elections and electioneering.

Butler, D. and Kavanagh, D. (1997) *The British General Election of 1997.*
Latest in long line of Nuffield election studies dating from 1945. Lively, accessible and conscious of the politics behind the numbers.

Dunleavy, P. and Husbands, C. (1985) *British Democracy at the Crossroads: Voting and Party Competition in the 1980s.*
Presents the sectoral cleavage model.

Farrell, D. (1997) *Comparing Electoral Systems.*
Gives details and histories of various electoral systems, capturing the flavour, with example ballot papers, of what it is like to vote.

Himmelweit, H., Humphreys, P. and Jaeger, M. (1985) *How Voters Decide.*
Explains the consumer voting model. The authors try to show that attitudinal variables are more relevant than class in explaining voting.

Kavanagh, D. (1995) *Election Campaigning: The New Marketing of Politics.*
Thorough analysis of post-war campaigning strategies tracing the link with media developments and a process of Americanization.

Norris, P. (1996) *Electoral Change since 1945.*
Accessible overview looking at change and the causes of change.

For light relief

Melvyn Bragg, *Autumn Manoeuvres.*
Cumbrians work out their personal and public salvation with passion and deceit during 1970s election campaign.

Douglas Hurd, *The Truth Game.*
A stylish novel by a once-leading politician.

H. G. Nicholas (ed.), *To the Hustings.*
Entertaining election stories.

H. G. Wells, *Ann Veronica*.
Controversial when first published. Relationships between men and women against suffragette background.

Virginia Woolf, *Night and Day*.
A suffragette novel.

On the net

The internet is full of electoral information. During (and after) general elections the broadsheets and the BBC, for example, maintain special sections devoted to the topic. Using any good search engine you will also be able to track down statistics about particular elections. On electoral reform and electoral systems, look at the sites of the campaigning organizations, such as the Electoral Reform Society (http://www.gn.apc.org/ers) or Charter 88 (http://www.charter88.org.uk).

Chapter Ten

The Politics of Power: a Life History of the Party System

This chapter is the first of two on political parties. Although unknown to the constitution, parties dominate the real world of politics; they are symbols of the modern age. The first section examines the concept of the modern mass party. Parties in a democracy should not be seen in isolation; it is in their essential nature to be linked through competition and cooperation and the following sections identify a series of key periods in the evolution of the party system. The conclusion evaluates British two-party politics.

Defining parties

Any political movement can so describe itself but in a democracy **political parties** are essentially associations with a common set of beliefs and goals, desiring to take office by constitutional means. Some commentators see the quest for office overriding all else, portraying parties as vote-maximizing machines (analogous to profit-maximizing firms) prepared to pursue any policy commanding support (Downs 1957: ch. 7). While much behaviour lends credence to this characterization, parties usually reflect ideologies to some extent, though over time they may pick and choose from the ideological cafeteria in the quest for support (see pp. 21–3).

The modern mass party The major British parties are large associations comprising essentially three elements: a parliamentary cadre of elected MPs, a bureaucracy and a large extra-parliamentary army in constituency associations. These **mass parties** evolved as a direct result of extensions to the franchise.

Functions of parties Parties play multifarious roles in political life. Elections are their great celebrations; they energize campaigns, feed the media and mobilize voters. In addition, they organize the life of Parliament; without them the Palace of Westminster would be an empty shell of anachronistic ritual. They

No Government can be long secure without a formidable Opposition.

Benjamin Disraeli, *Coningsby* (1844: book II, ch. 1)

also shape popular opinion, set the political agenda, stimulate public debate and provide political education for citizens. Recruiting people into politics and training them in the Machiavellian arts is another party function; historically Labour has been important in enabling working-class participation. Mass parties also aggregate diverse interests, constructing the compromises that help maintain social stability. When out of government they continue to play a crucial role, providing political opposition: without this, democracy is in peril. In the 1983 election campaign Conservative minister Francis Pym expressed fear of too weak a Labour opposition, sentiments repeated by some commentators after Labour's 1997 triumph.

The party system

Parties in a democracy do not exist in isolation. As they have evolved, the British parties have been inextricably entwined, cross-fertilizing each other with philosophy, policy, strategy and organizational form. They have even made physical contact, to fight or to hold together in the warm embrace of coalition, sometimes even exchanging vital fluids as factions have surged from one to impregnate the other. Hence any party can only be understood as part of a wider whole. It is usual to classify **party systems** in terms of *number* of parties and their relative dominance, thus distinguishing four types.

- **Multi-party**: more than two parties; governments usually coalitions.
- **Two-party**: two parties share dominance, each capable of forming an entire government. In the real world, minor parties always exist and a more realistic term is *two-party dominant*.
- **Single-party-dominant**: several parties compete but one stands like Gulliver among the Lilliputians, able to command either an overall majority or remain the dominant partner in successive coalitions.
- **Single-party**: Such 'systems' are unlikely to arise naturally and occur mainly under totalitarian regimes (Nazi Germany, communist Eastern Europe or certain ex-colonial states), usually after the opposition has been eliminated.

Although it is common to characterize Britain as having a two-party system this must be subject to qualification. The system is best understood through its evolution.

Genesis

From the settling dust of seventeenth-century constitutional struggles emerged two parliamentary groupings – the Tories, a landowning cadre avowing fidelity to the King, and the Whigs devoted to trade and the parliamentary cause. These dominated into the nineteenth century. As **cadre parties** they existed only in

Parliament and had little ideology save the protection of self-interests. These primitive organisms were forced under the radical sun, to crawl from the mud of eighteenth- and early nineteenth-century court and parliamentary intrigue onto the hard ground of democracy. The nineteenth-century extensions of the franchise opened the age of the modern mass party.

The Conservatives: the era of Peel and Disraeli

By the 1820s, under the leadership of the Duke of Wellington, the Tories appeared to be collapsing before the radical pressures unleashed by the industrial revolution, fatally vulnerable before any extension of the franchise. However, following the 1832 Reform Act, they experienced an unexpected revival under resourceful leader Sir Robert Peel (1788–1850), who gave them a *raison d'être* beyond self-interest by identifying with Burke's view of conservatism (see p. 37). Asserting tradition over radicalism, it was exceedingly attractive to those whose interests lay in the status quo – the landed gentry. Thus the Conservative Party rose phoenix-like from the ashes of the old Tory Party.

> The right honourable gentleman [Sir Robert Peel] caught the Whigs bathing and walked away with their clothes.
>
> Benjamin Disraeli, Commons speech (28 Feb. 1845)

However, another crisis occurred in 1846, the party splitting over the repeal of the Corn Laws, which ended tariff protection of agriculture, favouring commerce and industry at the expense of land. Two groups emerged, the more radical one (containing many who had entered Parliament as a result of the 1832 Reform Act) favouring free trade, moved towards the Whigs with whom they finally merged (forming the Liberal Party). The future of the landed interests again seemed vulnerable but the party was to find a second visionary to lead it from the wilderness. Benjamin Disraeli (1804–81) not only parted the difficult waters of further franchise extensions, he also created an image to carry the party into the era of mass politics.

Disraeli's inspiration was to perceive how the interests of privilege could be allied to those of the ordinary folk whose votes were needed. With a rallying cry of 'One Nation', he stressed the Conservative claim to be the natural guardians of *all* sections of society, evoking the empire as a symbol to unite them as members of a dominant race. The life-saving bond entailed a paternalistic commitment to social reform through Acts regulating the sale of food and drugs, public health, artisans' dwellings, river pollution, factory conditions and trade unions. So effective was the strategy that it was a Conservative government that felt confident enough to extend the franchise further in 1867. In gaining working-class support Disraeli had laid the foundations for the modern Conservative Party.

However, after his death the future looked bleak as the traditionalists reasserted their influence. They were saved by the tormented obsession of Gladstone, the Liberal leader, with the Irish question. This split the Liberals in 1886, propelling a group of unionist defectors, led by a radical Joseph Chamberlain, into the Conservative ranks. Subsequently the party acknowledged its commitment to Ireland's link with the mainland by adopting the title 'Conservative and Unionist Party'. The influx returned to the party some Whiggish blood, enabling it to accommodate the rising bourgeoisie increasingly dominating the social order. The Tory and Whig strands offered a formidable electoral potential which was to become fundamental to the party's remarkable width of appeal.

The Liberals: the era of Gladstone

The Liberal Party was a major force for only around half a century. In its heyday it experienced some great periods of office, its social and constitutional reforms standing as its monument. Yet like a figure in classical tragedy, the party (and its leaders) seemed to contain from the first the seeds of self-destruction. The modern party was established in 1859 through the fusion of the old Whigs with the new Radicals and the free-trade faction haemorrhaging from the Tories. This latter infusion provided one of its greatest figures: William Ewart Gladstone (1809–98), whose austere presence, the very antithesis of the polished Disraeli, dominated in the nineteenth century. The rationale of liberalism lay in radicalism and reform (pp. 24–32); impatient with traditional institutions it supported business and commerce through *laissez-faire* and free trade. Beyond the economy there was Irish home rule, nonconformity, parliamentarianism and social reform.

> You cannot fight against the future. Time is on our side.
>
> W. E. Gladstone, speech on the Reform Bill (1866)

The emergence of mass parties

The two great Reform Acts hardened the fluid parliamentary alliances with a new sense of party discipline, greatly enhancing the leaders' authority. Gladstone and Disraeli forged the characteristic two-party system with its **adversarial** style of parliamentary thrust and parry. It was no longer possible to gain election through corruption and the parties fostered organizations in the constituencies (registration societies) to ensure that all sympathizers would vote. The local associations were also given the crucial responsibility of choosing candidates.

To oversee the local activists two London clubs – the Carlton for the Conservatives and the Reform for the Liberals – became party headquarters and federations of local organizations were established to forge a sense of national unity. The Liberal Registration Association, founded in 1861, was followed in 1867 by the National Union of Conservative and Unionist Associations. The mass membership suggested problems of control: the Conservative Union seemed content to serve the leaders but the Liberal Federation claimed rights over party policy which Gladstone resisted. Both associations also held annual conferences in which the toilers in the constituency fields could voice their opinions. By the end of the century the mould for the modern system had been cast: parties were ideologically based mass organizations, led by elites, seeking office by courting the electorate.

Challenge to the Established Order: the Rise of the Labour Party

One of the remarkable aspects of franchise reform was the failure of a working-class party to capitalize on the potential in the mass vote – a manifestation of the power of the dominant classes to keep mass participation as a choice between two elites. Conservatives set out their 'one-nation' stall while the Liberals embraced the new liberalism and promoted major social reforms in the early twentieth century (national insurance, pensions, unemployment benefits and employment exchanges). However, a revolutionary ideology was taking shape; Marx's trenchant critique of liberalism meant that things could not remain as they were. Socialist movements were forming and some working-class activists sought to enter the parliamentary stage themselves.

Labour pre-history

The Labour Party was born of a long and painful confinement. Although opposed by establishment forces, the Chartists had argued from the 1830s for a working-class parliamentary voice. In 1869 the trade unions created a Labour Representation League but, although two of its thirteen candidates were returned in 1874, it showed little promise. Some working-class candidates also managed to enter Parliament under the Liberal banner; by 1885 there were eleven Trade Union Liberal MPs. However, the Liberals remained reluctant to cooperate. Keir Hardie, Ramsay MacDonald and Arthur Henderson were all spurned as candidates – had they not been, there might never have been a Labour Party.

During the 1880s and 1890s a socialist dynamic came from three associations. At the extreme left was the London-based Marxist group, the Social Democratic Federation (SDF), led by H. M. Hyndman. Of different character was the Fabian Society, founded in 1884 by George Bernard Shaw and the indefatigable social researchers Sidney and Beatrice Webb. It took its name from Quintus Fabius Maximus ('the Delayer'), a Roman general who achieved success by small, cautious moves and delaying tactics rather than reckless bravado – such was the avowed strategy of **Fabianism**. Most important was the Independent Labour Party (ILP), founded in 1893 to pursue moderate socialism and numbering amongst its members Philip Snowden, MacDonald and Hardie. Yet in the 1880s there were only some 2,000 active socialists in the entire country. Despite meagre social improvements, the working class remained content to vote for the elite duopoly and the ILP gained little support. However, a more aggressively socialist New Unionism introduced a new dynamic. In the late 1890s, damaging defeats in large strikes made the case for direct parliamentary representation more compelling.

Emerging from the womb

In 1900, the Trades Union Congress (TUC) made the momentous decision to seek a parliamentary presence. The might of sixty-five trade unions, with their hundreds of thousands of members, combined with the intellectual vigour of the three small organizations to establish the Labour Representation Committee (LRC). Significantly, its strategy was to be in the Fabian tradition; revisionist ('Labourism') rather than revolutionary socialism. At a very early stage the SDF disengaged from the inhibiting embrace.

The Conservative government reacted with intense hostility, portraying the movement as a threat to the constitution and requiring harsh treatment. A series of judicial decisions, culminating in the infamous Taff Vale Judgement of 1901 (holding that unions could be cripplingly sued for tortious acts of members), convinced more unions of the need to combine under the new banner and one of the movement's key figures, Ramsay MacDonald (LRC secretary), worked to develop a national mass organization.

> MacDonald owes his pre-eminence largely to the fact that he is the only artist, the only aristocrat by temperament and talent in a party of plebeians and plain men.
>
> Beatrice Webb (1858–1943; founder member of Fabian Society), *Diary* (May 1905)

Labour and the Liberals Although a fundamental principle of the new party was to oppose established elites, an early pragmatic advantage was gained by a secret agreement with the Liberals. Each would withhold candidates from selected constituencies to unify the anti-Conservative vote. Through this stratagem the new party signalled its entrance onto the parliamentary stage in 1906 with twenty-nine MPs, who together took the title Parliamentary Labour Party (PLP). The election also saw the return of twenty-four Lib–Labs. For the first time there was a formidable working-class phalanx in Parliament. An early success was the 1906 Trades Disputes Act, reversing the Taff Vale Judgement. However, their prime object was to ingratiate themselves with the Establishment by demonstrating *responsible* behaviour (Miliband 1961: 28). At this stage the Liberals felt no threat and formed a highly distinguished government, laying the foundations of the British welfare state.

Yet these were turbulent times. The Liberal programme led to a dramatic confrontation with the House of Lords, resulting in the 1911 Parliament Act (see chapter 12) and near civil war over Ireland (see p. 151). Labour became more closely wedded to the Liberals, a development derided by its left wing, which argued for a distinct identity. The first world war provided an opportunity for this.

ELEVATION.

Wife (of newly-elected Working-Man M.P. to her Visitors). "'OW D'E DO, MRS. FUZBUSH? PRAY TAKE A CHERE, M'UM. THOUGH I HAM A LADY NOW, IT WON'T MAKE NO DIFFERENCE IN MY MANNERS!"

Source: Mary Evans Picture Library

War and the Inter-war Era

The year 1914 marks the beginning of the Liberals' decline (Wilson 1966). It was the party's misfortune to be in office at the outbreak of war. As prime minister, Asquith became the leader of a coalition in 1915 but soon proved unequal to the task. 'His initiative, if he ever had any, was sapped by years of good living in high society' (Taylor 1965: 14) and, following a series of military defeats, he was ousted in 1916 by fellow Liberal Lloyd George, who formed a new coalition with a Conservative majority.

For Labour, war provided a taste of office and a chance to demonstrate patriotic qualities. It shed its pacifist garb and MacDonald (supported by the pacifist ILP) resigned the leadership to be replaced by Arthur Henderson, who gained influence and was even included in the War Cabinet. However, dealings with international socialism led to his ejection in 1917, leaving him free to prepare for the greater role that Liberal disarray seemed to promise. With MacDonald and intellectuals such as Sidney Webb, Henderson drew up a new socialist constitution, including the famous *Clause Four*, with its commitment to public ownership of the means of production, distribution and exchange. It also recognized the importance of widening party membership, making provision for individuals to join constituency associations in their own right rather than as trade unionists. The 1918 conference formally approved a wide programme, *Labour and the New Social Order*, which was to be the mainspring for policy for the next thirty years (Pelling 1968: 44).

The birth of the 1922 Committee

The immediate aftermath of war proved disastrous for the Liberals. Lloyd George rushed into an opportunistic general election in 1918 by offering further coalition government. Coalition candidates were endorsed with a letter signed jointly by Lloyd George and Conservative leader Bonar Law, dubbed the 'coupon' by Asquith, leader of the independent Liberals, in sarcastic evocation of wartime rationing. Asquith lost his seat and only twenty-eight of his supporters were returned, but Lloyd George had played into the hands of the Conservatives, delivering his own party into a political netherworld.

Though faring badly against what was an anti-socialist alliance, Labour demonstrated its muscle by fielding 361 candidates, a considerable increase on its previous best of seventy-eight in 1910, and the freak circumstances gave little indication of real trends. The coalition proved unpopular and, after a string of by-election failures (mainly gains for Labour), Bonar Law agreed, at a momentous meeting at the Carlton Club in 1922, that it was time to bid farewell to Lloyd George before he destroyed the Conservatives as he had the Liberals. As a by-product, a new institution had been created: the Conservative 1922 Committee.

Labour: a viable government

The Liberals were left in disarray, candidates fighting the ensuing general election as either 'Lloyd George' or 'Asquith' Liberals. Labour's parliamentary strength rose to 142, giving it second-party status. The number of ILP-sponsored candidates reached 32, with an influx of intellectuals giving a wider appeal and more rhetorical virtuosity. It began to attract ambitious young Liberals despairing of the schism within their own party. With increased parliamentary strength, the heady possibility of taking over the reins of government could be contemplated. Ambitions were realized in late 1923 when Baldwin dissolved Parliament over tariff reform. Although the Liberals revived with 158 seats, Labour increased its presence to 191 (39 ILP). The single-issue nature of the election meant that, despite its 258 seats, the government had been rejected. The Liberals felt justified in supporting Labour, which momentously ruled for ten months as a **minority government**. Not surprisingly, so tenuous a period of office produced little reform and was attacked by socialist purists; a hard judgement on the leaders, who had been faced with a task hitherto the preserve of those with wealth, position and a solid tradition of parliamentary organization. Labour providing a government was, like the proverbial dog walking on its hind legs, remarkable for being done at all.

Labour versus the Establishment Yet the experience offered a stark illustration of establishment power. The government was undermined with alarmist propaganda and deceit, Anglo-Soviet relations being a particularly sensitive area. The final straw came in the Campbell case. The decision of the Attorney General to drop sedition proceedings in a minor case against the editor of a small communist journal was fanned up as evidence of corruption. The Liberals grew nervous, withdrawing their support and forcing MacDonald to dissolve Parliament. The ensuing election campaign saw one of the shabbiest scandals of British politics – the Zinoviev letter (see p. 665). Chilling press warnings that a vote for Labour was a vote for a Soviet system saw the Establishment regain its hold on the tiller.

Yet the value of Parliament to working-class aspirations was underlined in the abysmal failure of the 1926 general strike, which renewed commitment to the Labour Party. With 288 seats it emerged from the 1929 election as the largest single party; a turning point in British politics. The Liberals had crossed the electoral Rubicon, the bias of the electoral system beginning to weigh against them. Their future seemed to lie only in some form of union with Labour and a second minority government was formed, though for the Liberals the embrace was to be that of the praying mantis.

MacDonald's disgrace However, Labour was also to encounter troubled waters. From the outset the government was severely hamstrung by the Liberals in the Commons and the Conservatives in the Lords. Problems were exacerbated by economic depression, the Cabinet split over expenditure cuts (particularly

---

The Liberals: decline and fall

The collapse of the Liberal Party remains one of the cautionary tales of British politics. Despite a landslide victory in 1906 and a period of great reform, a decade after the outbreak of the war it had a parliamentary presence of only forty-two. There is no simple explanation. One historian likened the demise to that of a frail old gent, troubled by a variety of serious ailments (Labour, suffragettes, Ireland), with misfortunes compounded by a meeting with a rampaging bus (the war); his state of health is easy to diagnose but not the actual cause of death (Wilson 1966: 20–1). In this political whodunit a number of suspects may be assembled along with the butler in the drawing room:

● a congenital tendency to fragment;
● strong personalities whose ambitions overrode party interest;
● the prolonged fight with the suffragettes;
● the misfortune to be in office at the outbreak of the war;
● an inability to adapt to a harsher twentieth-century climate (Dangerfield 1936);
● the loss of radical reformers like Chamberlain, Dilke, Churchill and Lloyd George;
● a healing of the old social cleavage between landowners and capitalists, who began to unite as Conservatives (Taylor 1965: 172);
● failure to embrace leading Labour figures;
● a willingness to allow Labour to gather strength through electoral pacts (Wilson 1966: 19);
● defections to Labour in the inter-war years;
● the British electoral system.

> There are no professions he ever made, no pledges he ever gave to the country, and no humiliation to which he would not submit if they would allow him still to be called Prime Minister.
>
> Viscount Snowden on MacDonald, House of Lords speech (3 July 1934)

unemployment benefit) as a condition of international loans and on 23 August 1931 MacDonald resigned as prime minister. However, the following day he stunned colleagues by accepting the King's invitation to form a Conservative-dominated *National Government*. Together with some followers he was disowned by his party and in the coalition became a prisoner of his Cabinet. In leaving the gold standard, he agreed to the very thing that Labour had been warned off in office, and none of the dire predictions followed. He was obliged to fight the next election in the grip of the coalition; 'National candidates' sought a 'doctor's mandate' to heal the country's maladies. Labour fared disastrously with only 46 seats and Conservatives dominated the new coalition. For Labour, these events marked the end of an era, fortunes remaining at a low ebb until 1935. Ex-barrister Clement Attlee (1883–1967) became leader, the first to lack genuine working-class credentials, and although not recovering its 1929 position, the party revived with 154 seats, while the Liberals wandered further into the wilderness.

The close of an era: the second world war The next war led to Labour's further entrenchment. The party at first refused to join a coalition but later agreed, providing it would not be led by Neville Chamberlain, discredited for his appeasement policy. Thus it could claim to have brought Churchill to power and did well in the apportionment of offices, with Attlee and Greenwood both in Churchill's first War Cabinet of five. In 1940, Bevin was also brought in, along with left-winger Cripps. Attlee became generally recognized as deputy prime minister, taking control of home affairs and gaining a reputation for incisive decision-making. Internally the party became more stable and harmonious. The political climate improved with the publication in 1942 of the Beveridge Report, the blueprint for the welfare state. Ironically, it used the language of new liberalism rather than socialism, justifying state social programmes in terms of *freedom* from the five giants of squalor, idleness, ignorance, disease and poverty.

At the fringe During the inter-war years a number of small fringe parties emerged. The Communist Party was founded in 1920 though its attempts to affiliate to Labour were rebuffed. Plaid Cymru was established in 1925, more to preserve Welsh cultural traditions than seek independence. The nationalist movement was stronger in Scotland, coalescing into a party in 1928. The period also saw Oswald Mosley leaving the Conservatives in 1932 to found the British Union of Fascists, which grew to over 30,000 members.

The Era of Consensus: the End of Ideology?

The masters now

We are the masters at the moment – and not only for the moment but for a very long time to come.

Lord Shawcross (member of 1945 Labour government),
Commons speech (2 April 1946)

After the war Churchill agreed to an early general election and 'business as usual'. The 1945 result gave every indication of a revolution in British politics, a Labour landslide producing its first overall majority. The swing in the marginal seats introduced a new kind of Labour MP, drawn from the professions and giving the PLP a broader character. Despite a regime of severe post-war austerity, the government embarked upon an agenda intended to shake the foundations of economic and social life. Within the party, the aura of office increased the leader's authority, which was further enhanced by trade union loyalty. Attlee was even able to make the momentous decision to manufacture atom and hydrogen bombs without consulting colleagues. He remained anxious for establishment respect, supporting capitalism, reining in socialistic expectations and even expelling extreme left-wingers.

Yet the popular verdict prompted alarmist talk in middle-class drawing rooms and concentrated Conservative minds, enabling them again to demonstrate the protean qualities that preserved them throughout the era of modern politics. Under party chairman Lord Woolton, the architect of recovery was R. A. Butler, who recognized that the ideological heartland had shifted. Liberal democracy had given way to social democracy. His strategy was to challenge Labour at its own game, the Conservatives embracing the new welfare state and Keynesian economics.

By the end of its first hectic term the government was showing fatigue strains; many stalwarts were well past their prime, some stricken with illness and some dead. Furthermore, people were weary of austerity. In 1950 Labour narrowly clung to office but, lacking confidence, Attlee returned to the country the following year. This time, although Labour polled the most votes ever cast for a British party the idiosyncrasies of the electoral system produced a Conservative majority. Butler had fashioned a bipartisan consensus opening a peace spoken of by the Archbishop of York in Shakespeare's *Henry IV* when 'both parties nobly are subdued, and neither party loser'. Yet the tranquil consensus interpretation can be misleading; within Labour a minority, led by Aneurin Bevan, were never comfortable pitching the manifesto tent in the middle of the ideological field and prompted enervating infighting. The dissidents were mainly the newer members, highly articulate and able to propagate their views through their journal – *Tribune*. After tenacious resistance, Attlee finally departed in 1955. His replacement, the sternly moderate Gaitskell (1906–63), inherited worsening disciplinary problems. Moreover, the supportive trade union old guard was passing on and the largest union, the TGWU, had fallen under the leadership of left-wing Frank Cousins.

The Suez crisis There were also Conservatives unhappy with consensus. When Churchill finally stepped down, party and government seemed healthy and the succession passed to the smoothly aristocratic Anthony Eden. Yet despite an early election success in 1955, domestic problems mounted, and by spring 1956 his popularity rating had nose-dived from 70 to 40 per cent (Butler and Rose 1960: 36). He was certainly in no state to handle the Suez Crisis in 1956 (see p. 99), which traumatized the Establishment. A right-wing Suez Group was incensed by the ignominious withdrawal, while another faction of around forty MPs abhorred the initial action. Despite jingoistic support from the constituencies (Nicolson 1958: 133), Eden retired in humiliation, leaving the party in morbid contemplation of loss of office and possibly two decades in the wilderness.

Winds of change: the Macmillan era

By far the most radical man I've known in politics wasn't on the Labour side at all – Harold Macmillan. If it hadn't been for the war he'd have joined the Labour Party . . . Macmillan would have been Labour Prime Minister, and not me.

Clement Attlee, quoted in James Margach, *The Abuse of Power* (1981)

Eden's departure exposed the arcane process whereby the Conservatives chose (or more accurately, did not choose) their leader. Party elders conducted soundings and Harold Macmillan was preferred over the diligent Butler. Yet the choice was to prove inspired. With an Edwardian dilettantism concealing shrewd recognition of the consensus era, he was able not only to rebuild the party substructure but modernize its facade. He also restored self-confidence at home and repaired the damage to Anglo-American relations, earning the cartoonists' moniker 'Supermac'. Yet despite his success the right mistrusted him. In 1960 the Monday Club formed to commemorate 'Black Monday', when he made a celebrated speech on reform in racist South Africa.

The wind of change is blowing through the continent. Whether we like it or not, this growth of national consciousness is a political fact.

Harold Macmillan, speech in South African Parliament (3 Feb. 1960)

Labour in the wilderness The Suez crisis did not help Labour as expected. Although shocking the intelligentsia, a popular jingoism was shared by many Labour supporters (Pelling 1968: 118). In 1959 the Conservative majority reached 100, a third successive defeat leaving Labour reeling. The post-war inheritance seemed to have been squandered and younger members began to talk of policy revision. In *The Future of Socialism* (1956), Anthony Crosland argued that in an age of affluence public ownership was an anachronism. The theme was taken up by Gaitskell, who confronted the left in a momentous 1960 party conference, where he suffered an heroic failure to remove Clause Four from the party constitution. He also fought against unilateral nuclear disarmament, which he finally won the following year, having gained the support of four of the largest unions.

Do you think that we can become overnight the pacifists, unilateralists and fellow travellers that other people are? . . . There are some of us, Mr Chairman, who will fight, fight and fight again to save the party we love.

Hugh Gaitskell, speech to Labour Party conference (5 Oct. 1960)

The Night of the Long Knives The government had its own troubles. On 13 July 1962, beset by economic problems and falling popularity, a desperate Macmillan reversed the action of *Julius Caesar*, removing one-third of his Cabinet in the greatest bloodbath in the party's history: 'The Night of the Long Knives'. There was also the resignation in 1962 of Thomas Galbraith, an Under Secretary at the Foreign Office in the Vassall affair, a Le Carré-like plot of spying and homosexuality. However, it was the more exotically heterosexual Profumo affair that brought the leader's failing touch to a wider, tabloid-devouring public. The party's image was also not helped by the early 1960s penchant for cynicism and lightweight satire. Oxbridge undergraduates began poking fun at the Establishment in the theatre (*Beyond the Fringe*), in the press (*Private Eye*) and on television (*That Was The Week That Was*). The last was so feared that it was taken off the air (see p. 218).

Constitutional change in the Conservative Party

Macmillan's retirement through ill health in 1963 produced controversy. The patient Butler was again the natural heir, but the aristocratic Sir Alec Douglas-

---

Scandal

The Profumo scandal arose from an intriguing *ménage à trois* involving a government minister, John Profumo, who resigned in 1963, a high-society prostitute (Christine Keeler), a Russian naval attaché and a host of exotic bit players including Mandy Rice-Davies (a prostitute), Stephen Ward (an alleged procurer of ladies for the gentry) and a mysterious man (believed to be a respected pillar of the Establishment) featured in photographs wearing a black mask (and little else). It is doubtful if the public were concerned with the security aspects of the affair. The massive newspaper coverage showed the main interest to lie in the intoxicating contemplation of hanky-panky in high places.

> He is used to dealing with estate workers. I cannot see how anyone can say he is out of touch.
>
> Lady Caroline Douglas-Home, speaking of her father's suitability as prime minister, quoted in the *Daily Herald* (21 Oct. 1963)

As far as the 14th Earl is concerned, I suppose Mr Wilson, when you come to think of it, is the 14th Mr Wilson.

Sir Alec Douglas-Home, BBC TV interview (21 Oct. 1963)

Home was raised from entombment in the House of Lords by renouncing his title (as did rival Lord Hailsham). Macmillan influenced events from his sickbed and the succession process became a topic for serious debate (see chapter 11). Home continued the party's Tory rather than its Whig strain but he seemed out of touch with the *zeitgeist*. The 1964 election campaign saw him ravaged by Labour's adroit new leader, Harold Wilson, who mocked the aristocratic antecedents of his opponent. Labour won a narrow majority of four; with a different leader the Conservatives might have secured a fourth term. It was agreed that a ballot of the parliamentary party should become the basis for leadership selection and Home resigned to allow the new system to come into operation.

The white heat of technology: the Wilson era

> The Labour Party is like a stage coach. If you rattle along at great speed everybody inside is too exhilarated or too seasick to cause any trouble. But if you stop everybody gets out and argues about where to go next.
>
> Harold Wilson, quoted in Leslie Smith, *Harold Wilson: The Authentic Portrait* (1964)

Acceding to the Labour leadership in 1963 as a result of Gaitskell's unexpected death, Wilson brought a more conciliatory tone, which was crowned with election victory. His style was said to have been modelled on the charismatic and youthful President Kennedy. Although there were dissidents on questions of immigration, incomes policy and defence, they could only mutter in dark corners, while party conferences applauded their witty young leader. By early 1966 he felt confident enough to ask for a stronger mandate, increasing the overall majority to ninety-six. The influx was predominantly from the middle classes, producing a professional image to back up Wilson's 'white heat of technology' rhetoric. Although the left were dissatisfied, the party began to look more like a 'natural' party of government and Wilson was attacked by the establishment press. Even so, there was some surprise when the government was ejected in 1970 and a glittering decade, the 'swinging sixties', closed.

TARGET PRACTICE

Reproduced by permission of *Punch*

On the fringe

The Liberal Party During the consensus era the Liberal Party had been no more than a bit player; to some a buffoon, to others a figure of tragedy. In the bipartisan scenario it had no place, being neither regionally based nor radical. Its desperate condition was symbolized in the fate of its leader, Jeremy Thorpe, who in the 1970s became embroiled in the Norman Scott affair, a sordid scandal involving homosexuality, blackmail, threatened murder and even caninicide.

Northern Ireland parties In 1955 Sinn Fein had reappeared as a political force, contesting all twelve Northern Ireland seats, though their three successful candidates were disqualified as felons. The 1960s saw rising unrest and in 1970 the

Social Democratic Labour Party (SDLP) was founded as the main vehicle of the Roman Catholic minority. At the same time cracks began to appear in the Ulster Unionist Party, which had dominated Northern Ireland's Westminster representation: Ian Paisley, standing as a Protestant Unionist, captured the North Antrim seat (see chapter 6).

The Consensus Cracked: the 1970s

Heath: the rise and fall of Selsdon Man

Conscious of Wilson's appeal, the Conservatives applied Newton's Law of Motion to politics by attempting to counter with an equal and opposite force. Edward Heath, the first leader to be elected, was also the first hailing from the party's *petit bourgeois* strain. Yet this failed to yield immediate results: in 1966 the party polled fewer votes than under Home. However, Heath worked to manufacture a technocratic image to match Labour's. A conference of businessmen and politicians at the Selsdon Park Hotel, Croydon, led to sightings of a new species of *Homo Conservatus* – 'Selsdon Man' – able to survive as well in the rugged terrain of private industry boardrooms as in the more temperate climes of Whitehall and Horse Guards' Parade. In 1970 Heath pulled off an unexpected *coup*, gaining an overall majority of thirty seats and surprising his own party as much as his opponents.

A long-standing Europhile, he led the nation into the EEC in 1973 and promoted a neoliberal economic agenda at home. However, inflation and rising unemployment led to policy reversals, branded 'U-turns' and taken as evidence of weakness. To compound his agony Heath experienced unrelenting union hostility, Arthur Scargill of the NUM proving a particular *bête noir*. In February 1974, Heath called an ill-timed general election to ask 'Who governs?'. Although a majority supported him, the idiosyncrasy of the electoral system again thwarted voters. Yet Labour lacked an absolute majority and Heath flirted with the Liberals over a possible pact before conceding defeat. The indeterminate situation forced Wilson to return to the country in October, but an overall majority of only three did little to clarify the confusion. The efficacy of two-party politics was beginning to look doubtful.

In April 1976 Wilson shocked his party with his unexpected retirement. 'Making way for an older man', he bequeathed to James Callaghan bad union relations, economic crisis, IMF-imposed monetarism (see p. 490) and public-sector strikes. The media and some academics proclaimed a crisis of governability. By-election defeats rendered the government increasingly fragile until it could be sustained only with the life-support machine of the 1977–8 Lib–Lab pact, a development bringing joy to Liberal hearts as they contemplated a new era in which a centre party might hold the balance of power. All was to culminate in some cold and gloomy months of 1978–9, entering the political record as the 'winter of discontent'. The government finally lost a no-confidence vote in March 1979 and the Conservatives returned rejuvenated. Again they had used their time in the reformatory of opposition gainfully, emerging ready to take British party politics into a new era.

No such thing as society: the coming of Thatcherism

Heath's humiliation in 1974 had led to further ordeal by election. On 10 February 1975, to the amazement of many, a dark horse emerged on a second ballot. Margaret Thatcher was to seize radical initiatives on all policy fronts, the objective no less than a frontal assault on post-war social democratic orthodoxy. Her mentor was Sir Keith Joseph, who had experienced a Pauline conversion to free-market philosophy. He had created the Centre for Policy Studies under guru Alfred Sherman and, in this laboratory, outside the formal party machinery, the alchemy of neoliberalism was brewed which was to alter the course of British politics. Joseph became chairman of the Advisory Committee on Policy which prepared for the 1979 general election, presiding over sixty policy groups of MPs and advisers (Riddell 1985: 31).

> Any woman who understands the problems of running a home will be nearer to understanding the problems of running a country.
>
> Margaret Thatcher, quoted in the *Observer* (8 May 1979)

The general election was critical. The new leader avowed that (as a woman) she would be permitted just one chance, and the spoils of victory promised riches in the form of a gushing supply of North Sea oil available for generous tax cuts or increased welfare, according to political fancy. By the time of the campaign the party, its coffers now brimming, was in good shape for battle. Thatcher recognized the increasing importance of the mass media and, more than any previous leader, was assiduous in her courtship of the cameras. Saatchi and Saatchi were engaged to harness the skills of Madison Avenue. Tim Bell, who handled the account, revealed himself as the very apotheosis of New Right man. The relationship was to prove symbiotic. For the brothers Saatchi, company stock soared and the general election gave the Conservatives 339 seats, a majority over Labour of 60 and Britain's first woman prime minister.

Enterprise man

I always dreamt of owning a Ferrari. I work very long hours, and I like to drive to and from work in a lovely luxurious car. I enjoy being stared at and seeing the car being admired.

Tim Bell, quoted in the *Observer* (22 April 1979)

The Thatcher Era: Fractured Consensus or New Centre?

By the end of the 1980s it was possible to speak of a Thatcher era. Commentators varied in the extent to which they ascribed all developments to the domineering personality of the Conservative leader but few would deny that momentous changes had been wrought.

The party begins to swing

Initially the new programme faltered; the Cabinet contained a large contingent inherited from Heath which impeded radical progress. Unemployment rose and Thatcher's popularity sunk to an all-time low for a prime minister. However, she was a lucky politician in several respects and a lifeline came not from domestic politics but from the South Atlantic. The Falklands crisis gave Thatcher the boost she needed. In an upsurge of popular chauvinism the party was once again able to assume its mantle as protector of Queen and empire and the 1983 election was eagerly anticipated. Within the party Thatcher's ascendancy became virtually absolute; those who came to scoff very quickly began to pray. The years between 1983 and 1987 saw an ideological flowering, though people spoke not of conservatism but of 'Thatcherism'. The 1987 general election gave the Conservatives a third term with a majority of 102. However, the pattern of support was becoming increasingly concentrated in the prosperous southeast. Thatcher's assertion that 'there is no such thing as society' renounced the party's 'one-nation' appeal.

Labour in the 1980s

As if on a see-saw, the fortunes of Labour sank as Conservative stock rose. Michael Foot, once a doyen of the left, replaced Callaghan as leader in 1980. Like the New Right apostles, the hard left abhorred consensus; the years from Attlee to Callaghan were depicted as a betrayal and Tony Benn berated himself for his past involvement in government.

Although the trade unions had shifted leftwards, it was the constituency associations that became key centres for agitation. In 1973 the party had opened its doors to the far left and Militant Tendency had taken control of many local branches. Two principal demands of the left were accepted in 1980: the election of the leader by a franchise wider than the parliamentary party and the compulsory reselection of all MPs between elections. In 1981, Tony Benn narrowly failed to dislodge Denis Healey in a deputy leadership challenge. For some the pressures had become too great: choosing flight rather than fight, they founded the Social Democratic Party (SDP) in March 1981 to re-establish the centre ground.

Labour's 1983 manifesto offered unilateral nuclear disarmament, withdrawal from the EC, an end to council-house sales, renationalization and increased taxation. It was described from the right as 'the longest suicide note in history'. In the final stages of the campaign Labour support began to wilt before the new centrist force and only the quirks of the electoral system ensured its survival (figure 10.1). Foot resigned and Neil Kinnock, who had moved to the centre, was elected leader with the moderate Roy Hattersley as deputy. Though fighting a much better campaign in 1987, the result was again failure when the Conservatives gained a dominating 147-seat majority. The new third force in British politics had created a major new difficulty for the centre left.

The rise of the third force

The birth of the SDP appeared as one of the most dramatic developments in the party system during the 1980s. Growing from a rib plucked from Labour's breast, its leading figures were seasoned parliamentarians. Dubbed 'the Gang of Four', William Rodgers and David Owen were sitting MPs, while Shirley Williams and Roy Jenkins had served in government. The rhetoric spoke of 'breaking the mould' of adversarial politics and re introducing consensus through European-style coalitions (supported by electoral reform). By late 1981, twenty-seven Labour MPs, and even one Conservative, sailed under the new flag and in the country a mass membership of some 70,000 had mushroomed. The fledgling party signalled its presence with some notable by-election victories, two returning Gang of Four members – Shirley Williams (Crosby) and Roy Jenkins (Glasgow, Hillhead).

These developments gave new heart to the Liberals and in 1983 they fought under a common Alliance banner with the SDP, gaining 26 per cent of the vote, only 2 per cent below Labour. PR would have bestowed around 160 seats, but they received a meagre 23. They fared no better in 1987, with 22.6 per cent of the votes and 22 seats. After this, Liberal leader David Steel opened discussions on complete merger, which took place in March 1988. SDP leader David Owen sulked in his tent, to be left with a rump party in terminal decline. Paddy Ashdown was elected leader and the following year an all-member ballot adopted the name Liberal Democrat.

At the fringe In 1985 the Ecology Party relaunched itself as the Green Party and achieved some success in local elections. National Front (NF) support fell away, partly won over by Thatcher's brand of Conservatism, and subsequent internal splits saw the formation of the British National Party (BNP).

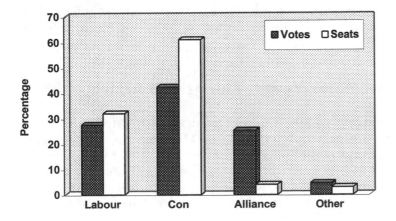

Figure 10.1
General election results, 1983: votes and seats compared.

The end of an era

New times, new realism It became apparent to Labour leaders that the party was no longer tuned to the march of history. The New Right agenda was recognized throughout Europe by socialist parties in or out of government. Even the USSR had fallen under the *perestroika* of Mikhail Gorbachev, who established a surprising rapport with Thatcher. A 'Labour Listens' initiative was launched to rediscover the popular mood and repackage the party. For the hard left, this attempt to don Thatcher's clothes was a perverse form of transvestism but a policy of expulsion removed some 200 of them from the party during the 1980s. By 1989 opinion polls were consistently placing Labour above the Conservatives, a popularity confirmed in the European Parliament elections.

> The Great Parliamentary Sausage Machine which sucked in public opinion at one end and spewed out popular politics at the other.
>
> Roy Hattersley, retrospectively, on the Labour Listens initiative, in *Who Goes Home?* (1996: 284)

The fall of Thatcher Events in late 1990 were to rock the Conservatives. Dramatic resignations by Chancellor Nigel Lawson and Geoffrey Howe (Leader of the House and deputy prime minister, respectively) intimated that all was not well in Cabinet, the main source of dissatisfaction being Thatcher's lukewarm European vision and domineering style. Moreover, fierce hostility towards the poll tax had seen her popularity plummet to around 29 per cent. A leadership challenge by Michael Heseltine forced a humiliating second ballot (p. 314). Thatcher consulted her Cabinet individually and the consensus was that she should go, John Major emerging as the new Conservative leader. Heseltine's reward was a seat in the new Cabinet. Thus, the longest premiership since 1827, marked by three electoral triumphs and a series of dramatic policy advances, was terminated not by the electorate nor the party rank and file, but by the Conservative establishment in perhaps the most brutal political knifing in modern political history. However, the wound was to fester on into the next era.

The Major Years: Things Fall Apart

Major's succession continued the trend away from the party's aristocratic roots. In contrast to his two main rivals (Heseltine, the Oxbridge-educated, self-made millionaire, and the patrician Douglas Hurd with his landed background), he had left school at sixteen, experienced unemployment and advanced through local politics. A beneficiary of the changing face of the parliamentary party, he was the candidate Thatcher favoured. Most of her votes flowed his way on the second ballot.

> But there was one more duty I had to perform, and that was to ensure that John Major was my successor. I wanted – perhaps I needed – to believe that he was the man to secure and safeguard my legacy.
>
> Margaret Thatcher, *The Downing Street Years* (1993: 860)

The Major years were extraordinary ones for what had long been regarded as Britain's natural party of government. Without Thatcher's confrontational style or zeal, Major seemed a more traditional Conservative. When Thatcher asserted that there was no such thing as 'Majorism' he did not dissent (Norton 1993a: 60). On the home front, he removed the poll tax and seemed more willing to listen to interest groups but at the same time he adhered to the neoliberal agenda. Although sceptical about further integration, he spoke of being 'at the heart of Europe'. Yet he had accepted a poisoned chalice; his task to please both those who yearned for Thatcherism by other means and those wanting change. He began in her shadow; her conference appearances attracting unnervingly rapturous adulation. The 1992 general election victory was particularly important; like Heath in 1970, he could take considerable personal credit. Yet pragmatism led to vacillation, often described as dithering, and a flimsy majority left him vulnerable to rebel factions. The most troublesome were the Eurosceptics (some even in his Cabinet), whom he described in an unguarded moment as 'bastards'. (It is doubtful that he ever changed the assessment.)

Eurobastards Unlike Thatcher's 'wets', Major's enemies were emboldened with a sense of mission and armed by right-wing think-tanks. The fires were fanned by newspaper editors who did little to conceal personal dislike of Major (Rogaly 1997). Ratification of the Maastricht Treaty was tense (chapter 5) and problems did not end there. The humiliation of 'Black Wednesday' (p. 493) was seen as a defining moment of a blighted premiership and a portent of electoral doom. The 1994 European Parliament elections saw the Conservatives lose half their seats, leaving them with just eighteen out of eighty-four. Major's June 1994 vetoing of the appointment of Jean-Luc Dehaene as President of the Commission suggested abject appeasement of the Eurosceptics. Europhiles were enraged and Chancellor Kenneth Clarke fought to limit the damage at Brussels.

'Put up or shut up' Tensions reached a crescendo in June 1995 when, in an astonishing resignation of the party leadership, Major threw down the gauntlet. While heavyweights shrank from the first ballot, Welsh Secretary John Redwood came forward. The pretender, whose demeanour had earned him the moniker of 'Vulcan' (of *Star Trek*), was held off and, with Heseltine and Portillo waiting in the wings with campaign machines assembled, the party was saved a bloody contest. Yet with 111 MPs withholding support, Major's endorsement was only lukewarm. The vacuum left at the Welsh Office was quietly filled by a figure known mainly for his schoolboy speech at a party conference; unlike his predecessor, William Hague began to learn Welsh. Yet although the rebels had

I'm still here.

Satirist and impressionist Rory Bremner as John Major proclaiming his greatest achievement.

put up, they did not shut up. The EU ban on the export of British beef during the BSE crisis made their voices shriller. In the 1997 election campaign many insisted on Eurosceptic statements in their personal addresses and John Redwood actually brought out a book attacking the single currency.

'Back to Basics': low behaviour in high places

There was another zone of embarrassment. In 1993 Major had launched a 'Back to Basics' initiative, extolling traditional morality and social discipline. It could hardly have come at a worse time. Accusations of sexual and constitutional impropriety saw a lengthening roll of shame, including a motley collection for whom back to basics meant back to the backbenches. By 1997 some 10 per cent of the parliamentary party had been involved in some kind of scandal (*Observer*, 30 March 1997). Other *causes célèbres* haunted the government. In March 1994 the Public Accounts Committee castigated the 'entanglement' of aid for the Malaysian Pergau Dam project with defence contracts, and the Arms-for-Iraq affair was subject to the 39-month Scott inquiry, which reported unfavourably on ministerial conduct in February 1996.

The incredible shrinking majority In addition to by-election losses came defections. In October 1995 Alan Howarth crossed to the Labour benches, while Emma Nicholson did little for Major's Christmas cheer that December by accepting the Liberal Democrat embrace, reporting 'an increasing venom in the internal faction-fighting within the party' (*Observer*, 31 Dec. 1995). In October 1996, she was joined by Peter Thurnham, leaving Major's majority at two. The nine Ulster Unionist MPs found themselves in a pivotal position, reducing Major's room for manoeuvre in an area where he had moved adroitly – the Downing Street Declaration (see p. 155).

A natural party of government? The polls showed the Conservatives entering the 1997 campaign further behind their rival than any party since 1832. With Labour and the Liberal Democrats giving a clear run to white-suited journalist Martin Bell in Neil Hamilton's Tatton constituency, it was impossible for the party to put sleaze behind it. In its Euro-angst it appeared to have sacrificed its historic strength: unity. Perhaps this was part of the Thatcher legacy. The Eurosceptics were mainly Thatcherites, their mission to preserve her neoliberal trajectory. Indeed, as Baroness Thatcher in the Lords, the lady was still amongst them.

New Labour, New Consensus

Another of Major's problems was the opposition. The Liberal Democrats enjoyed a string of by-election successes and during the 1992 campaign Ashdown consistently outscored the other leaders. The party itself rose from 15 per cent in the opening opinion polls to as high as 22–23 per cent, polling 17.8 per cent of all votes in the election. With twenty MPs it emerged stronger than in 1987 and, with rising membership and a more secure financial position, was poised for progress.

Labour reached a nadir in 1992. A fourth successive defeat led many to ponder whether Britain had become a one-party state. Some declared Kinnock's triumphalist behaviour at an eve-of-poll rally in Sheffield to have snatched defeat from the jaws of victory (Heffernan and Marqusee 1992) but he had moved the party a long way since the 1983 débâcle. He resigned and his successor, John Smith, slid into place in something of a 'stitch up' with no serious competition (Dunleavy 1993: 142–3). In September 1992 two of his biggest critics, Bryan Gould and Dennis Skinner, were thrown off the NEC in favour of two fresh-faced modernizers, Tony Blair and Gordon Brown. Clearly a figure of the right, Smith lacked Kinnock's vision and a question mark hung over his health.

The decline in union membership and the shrinkage of the traditional working class argued for a broader appeal. The spectre of the winter of discontent could be exorcized only by 'modernizing' the relationship with the unions. This was faced at the 1993 conference (see chapter 11). Although some unions opposed, others welcomed an opportunity to extend membership into the white-collar sector and establish links with other political organizations. TUC General Secretary John Monks argued that unions could no longer lay all their hopes on a Labour victory (Monks 1993: 4). Smith gained agreement for the one member, one vote (OMOV) principle for candidate selection. The party extended its commitment to Scottish and Welsh devolution, a Bill of Rights, reform of the Lords, proportional representation for Scotland and European elections, and a referendum on PR for Westminster.

However, in May 1994 a body blow came in Smith's sudden death. A leadership battle promised damage and the contest was delayed until after the European elections. Three contenders emerged: deputy leader Margaret Beckett, Tony Blair and John Prescott. Most importantly, Shadow Chancellor Gordon Brown agreed to curb his own ambition to avoid splitting the modernizing vote. Robin Cook, to some the most incisive debater, was apparently persuaded not to press his case because of a poor media image (an alleged likeness to a garden gnome). The result came as no surprise, Blair being supported by all sections of the electoral college. The contest had not been divisive and the scale of the victory endorsed modernization. Harmony was further promoted by the election of Prescott, trusted by traditionalists, as deputy leader.

Trust me, I'm a spin doctor

Unlike Kinnock, or even Major, Blair sported no working-class credentials. Educated at Fettes College, Edinburgh, one of Scotland's foremost schools, he progressed via St John's College, Oxford, to become a barrister, entering Parliament as MP for Sedgefield in 1983. Like all his generation he was starved of office but had shadowed some key areas, including Treasury and Economic Affairs (1984–

Labour Party leaders

1906	K. Hardie		1921	J. Clynes		1963	H. Wilson
1908	A. Henderson		1922	R. MacDonald		1976	J. Callaghan
1910	G. Barnes		1931	A. Henderson		1980	M. Foot
1911	R. MacDonald		1932	G. Lansbury		1983	N. Kinnock
1914	A. Henderson		1935	C. Attlee		1992	J. Smith
1917	W. Adamson		1955	H. Gaitskell		1994	T. Blair

7), Trade and Industry (1987–8), Energy (1988–9), Employment (1989–92) and Home Affairs (1992–4). Just forty, and with a barrister's verbosity, a beautiful careerist wife (Cherie), two sons and a daughter, he was a spin doctor's dream.

The modernizers had actually been impatient with Smith (Kavanagh 1997), and if Blair had a model it was that of Labour's arch enemy, Margaret Thatcher. Master of the soundbite, he spoke of 'fairness not favours' for the unions, no more 'tax and spend' on the economy and, on Labour's other Achilles' heel he would be 'tough on crime and tough on the causes of crime'. In industrial disputes he studiously withheld support from strikers while seeking the confidence of business leaders, even wooing media baron Rupert Murdoch. The mission was to reassure 'middle England'. Blair was even willing to sound a Eurosceptical note, assuring the CBI conference in November 1995 that European social legislation would not automatically be adopted by a Labour government.

Perhaps the most symbolic item of Blair's agenda was the rewriting of the venerated Clause Four. After widespread privatization this looked even more dated than in Gaitskell's time. Yet at the 1994 conference the motion was nar-

Figure 10.2
Labour Party members' opinions on five statements used as indicators of modernization.

Source: Derived from data in Seyd and Whiteley (1992: table 7.9) and excluding members with no strong feelings either way on each issue.

rowly rejected and, the following January, thirty-two of the party's MEPs placed a critical advert in the *Guardian*. Calling them 'infantile', Blair embarked upon a programme of regional consultations to convince the faithful. On 29 April 1995, at a special conference at Methodist Central Hall, Westminster, where seventy-five years earlier the original clause had been adopted, the party voted two-to-one to back the reforms. Although the replacement clause called for 'power, wealth and opportunity to be in the hands of the many not the few', it also extolled the 'enterprise of the market'. The unions, holding the majority of the conference votes, were only narrowly in favour but constituency parties gave overwhelming support. Arthur Scargill was slow handclapped when he objected and the leaders of UNISON and the Transport and General Workers' Union were forced to accept defeat philosophically.

By 1995, party membership had risen by 40,000 since Blair's election (figure 10.3) and his own popularity dwarfed that of both Major and Ashdown (Dorey 1995: 258). He took a tough line with dissidents. Those seen as loose cannons such as Clare Short were quickly tied to the deck and little was heard of Ken Livingstone, Tony Benn et al. A watchful eye was also kept on local government; in November 1995 the NEC suspended the leader and deputy leader of Walsall council, calling them a 'party within a party'. In March 1997 the modernization strategy went a stage further with an historic pre-election deal with the Liberal Democrats promising a referendum on electoral reform.

For critics 'New Labour' showed more froth than substance. The Machiavellian spin doctors dispensed with ideology to follow the beacon of the opinion polls. At their head was Peter Mandelson, grandson of earlier Labour moderate Herbert (later Lord) Morrison. The acid test came in May 1997 but the size of the landslide victory, though suggested by the polls, came as a shock. The

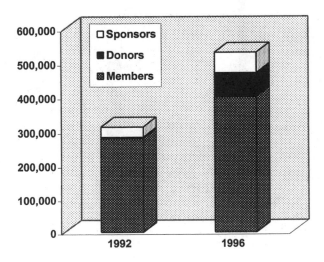

Figure 10.3
Labour Party
membership and
supporters, 1992
and 1996.

Source: Data from Labour Party NEC reports.

Conservatives were entirely banished from the Celtic fringes (figure 10.4). Critics argued that their lemming-like behaviour had guaranteed a Labour victory, but to the modernizers it was an overwhelming endorsement. If symbols were needed they were aplenty. At the 1998 Labour conference, avowedly the last at Blackpool, with its old Labour odour of fish and chips, delegates wore name badges sponsored by a supermarket chain (though some refused) while journalists from the radical magazine *Red Pepper* were banned.

Meltdown

The Conservatives' worst defeat since 1832 meant the end for Major; within hours hats were in the ring. However, a record seven cabinet ministers had fallen, including four who might have aspired to the leadership, the most surprising being Michael Portillo. After the first ballot came the arm-twisting; Kenneth Clarke was less willing to strike deals than William Hague, so when Michael Howard and Peter Lilley stepped down, their weight went behind the young pretender. John Redwood stayed in for the second round, after which he caused astonishment by endorsing the Europhile Clarke. However, his supporters did not follow, Euroscepticism taking precedence over all else in a bitter contest (Alderman 1998). As with the Thatcher and Major elections, it was the least-feared candidate that won (p. 314).

Unlike Labour, the Conservatives did not consider the photogenic qualities

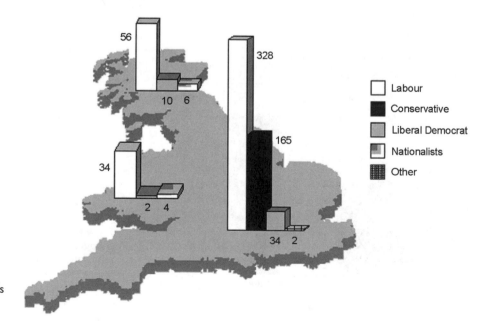

Figure 10.4
Conservative meltdown: the national distribution of MPs after the 1997 election.

Labour
Conservative
Liberal Democrat
Nationalists
Other

Table 10.1 The party's over? Attitudes towards the Conservative Party, 1997

Statement	Percentage of respondents agreeing
A party that does not have a bright future	74
A party with very few new ideas	84
A party without a clear sense of direction	75
A party that lacks strong leaders	81
An out-of-date party	77
A party that does not look after the interests of ordinary people	74

Source: Gallup Political Index, October 1997.

of their leader. If Blair was a spin doctor's dream, William Hague, with a flat Yorkshire intonation and looking preternaturally aged, was perhaps a nightmare. At thirty-six he became the youngest leader since Pitt the Younger, his experience confined to junior positions in social security before becoming Welsh Secretary. Educated at a South Yorkshire comprehensive he had arrived at Oxford University preceded by a *wunderkind* reputation following his schoolboy party conference speech. Effectively a career politician, he had worked as a political adviser and consultant before winning a 1989 by-election in Richmond, North Yorkshire (adjacent to Sedgefield, constituency of another ambitious politician – Tony Blair).

Hague inherited a broken-backed misalliance with a poor showing in opinion polls (table 10.1), its traditional bases of support eroded at least partly as a legacy of Thatcherism (Gamble and Wright 1998: 109). With some of his backbenchers showing barely disguised derision (*Sunday Times*, 21 Sept. 1997) and party-wide dissatisfaction with the selection process, his chalice contained more hemlock than had Major's. One of the party's key thinkers, David Willetts (1998), argued that they should learn from their previous major defeats in 1906 and 1945, refurbishing the organization and reaching out to those alienated. At Central Office a sweep-out began under the impetus of Archie Norman of the supermarket chain Asda, who gave every impression of aiming to play Mandelson to Hague's Blair. The party needed to regain touch with public opinion (Garnett and Gilmour 1998: 131). After a six-month consultation

---

Conservative Party leaders since 1900

1900	Marquis of Salisbury	1923	S. Baldwin	1963	A. Douglas-Home
1902	A. Balfour	1937	N. Chamberlain	1965	E. Heath
1911	A. Bonar Law	1940	W. Churchill	1975	M. Thatcher
1921	A. Chamberlain	1955	A. Eden	1990	J. Major
1922	A. Bonar Law	1956	H. Macmillan	1997	W. Hague

period a special conference at Harrogate in March 1998 endorsed Hague's proposals. However, some two-thirds of those eligible had not bothered to vote.

Liberal Democrats: no room in the centre

At the 1992 general election the Liberal Democrats had nursed hopes of a hung parliament in which they would hold the ring. In the event, they had to share Labour's cup of disappointment though, with 17.8 per cent of the vote, they had captured the 'normal' level of third-party support and remained a serious force, particularly in marginal constituencies (Stevenson 1993: 141). Beginning with Newbury in May 1993, a string of by-election successes provided cause for optimism. In addition, they made a breakthrough onto the European stage, securing two seats in the 1994 elections with 3.2 per cent of the vote. (The Greens, with the same percentage gained none.)

However, Labour's shift eliminated the vacuum at the centre. Indeed, on many issues they appeared to be left of Blair. Abandoning its policy of 'equidistance', the party agonized as to how far it should 'snuggle up' to New Labour as advocated by Shirley Williams and Roy Jenkins, the very people who had wanted to break the two-party mould. Moreover, Labour was raiding their wardrobe as well as that of the Conservatives. Perhaps the party had served its purpose, with little future except as a home for the disenchanted – 'an unheroic but useful role' (Kavanagh 1996: 44). However, the 1997 result produced the biggest third-party breakthrough of the post-war period, the forty-six seats promising to become significant should Labour cohesion melt in the heat of internal friction.

Life at the fringe

The 1992 general election saw nationalist support remaining stable; Plaid Cymru's four seats was one up on 1987 and the Scottish Nationalists (SNP) maintained their three. With a 19 per cent swing in the Monklands East by-election, the SNP almost stole John Smith's old seat. In 1997 Plaid Cymru held their four seats and the SNP gained another three. However, devolution was to mean a changed climate for the nationalists.

As the Major term progressed the significance of the Ulster Unionists increased until, just before the 1997 election, they held the balance of power. They were courted not only by Major, but also Blair, who even altered the composition of backbench committees to allay Unionist fears (*The Times*, 17 Feb. 1997).

Although single-issue parties are rare in Britain, a curious phenomenon arose when wealthy Eurosceptic businessman Sir James Goldsmith formed his Referendum Party for the 1997 contest. Money (£20 million) tried very hard to talk as citizens were deluged with material, including video tapes, warning of a European super-state. The party's first conference in October 1996 was adorned by famous figures including ex-Speaker Lord Tonypandy and ex-Conservative treasurer Lord McAlpine. Perhaps it was no coincidence that one speaker, actor Edward Fox, had played an early Eurosceptic, the would-be assassin of General de Gaulle in *The Day of the Jackal*. Yet despite polling over 800,000 votes, the party's lack of regional concentration meant a trail of lost deposits.

Life was bleak for the far left. Britain's Communist Party had declined since the 1950s, relaunching itself in 1991 as the Democratic Left with some 6,000 members – more a pressure group than a party. Militant Tendency and the Socialist Workers' Party also found little resonance in the New Labour mood. In January 1996, Arthur Scargill severed his Labour connections to form a Socialist Labour Party but gained no seats in 1997. At the other extreme, the BNP caused ripples by winning a council seat in Tower Hamlets, east London, in 1993. The Greens had also declined during the 1990s although they made their presence felt as pressure groups, greening the agendas of the main parties.

From Butskillism to Blatcherism?

Finally back in power Labour hit the ground running. The Queen's Speech in May 1997 detailed twenty-two bills covering a wide range of policy areas including the NHS, education, devolution, Northern Ireland, a strategic government for Greater London, independence for the Bank of England, minimum wage legislation and incorporation of the European Convention on Human Rights. Its publicity machine spun added gloss around the package and within a year much legislation had been passed and battalions of task forces were examining numerous other policy options.

However, in economic terms the government had chosen a procrustean bed in its promise to preserve Conservative spending limits. It was unusual to say the least for a party to promise to do the same as its opponents! It would be impossible to find a better indication of a return to consensus politics; Thatcherism by other means. Indeed, Blair expressed admiration for the ex-Conservative leader and his domination over his party resembled hers. The economy would be led by the market, shaped and refined by the state rather than regulated (Gamble and Wright 1997).

The policies were justified variously by reference to Christian values, communitarianism, stakeholding and talk of a 'third way' which, while seeking a society that did not tolerate social exclusion, could accept inequality (Giddens 1998). Yet New Labour could also be charged with having pursued a Downsian strategy (p. 265) of vote maximization with little regard for principle. The party's old guard, and some left-leaning intellectuals, appeared uneasy with a project that mirrored past 'betrayals' of socialist ideals. Neo-Keynesians such as Will Hutton were also to become disenchanted (see chapter 16).

However, it could also be argued that New Labour had come to terms with the modern world and would not repeat the mistake of promising much in opposition only to disappoint in office. Much of Labour's frustration in government had been related to the effects of the globalizing economy which lay beyond its control. In recognizing this, Blair could argue that debates about the state versus the market were no longer appropriate platforms for economic thinking (Kenny and Smith 1997: 227–8).

Spinning out of control   Yet in the midst of his ascendancy Blair was to be reminded of his mortality. While the July 1998 cash-for-access embarrassment could be swept aside (see p. 211), it would be difficult to have imagined a more shocking disaster than that of December 1998, when the arch-priest of New Labour was brought down. Sometimes called the 'Prince of Darkness', Peter Mandelson had many enemies inside the party as well as without.

> Dear Tony, I can scarcely believe I am writing this letter to you.
>
> Opening of Peter Mandelson's resignation letter (Dec. 1998)

Revelations that he had failed to disclose a £373,000 loan from fellow minister, millionaire Geoffrey Robinson, towards the purchase of his London house left him in acute embarrassment. Both ministers resigned, depriving Blair not only of two key advisers but two icons of the New Labour project; some said that one had invented it and the other had paid for it. To compound the discomfort, rumours began to circulate within the Westminster hothouse that the architects of the fall were not the opposition but colleagues of Chancellor Gordon Brown. While this was denied, Brown's close confidant and spin doctor Charlie Whelan opened the new year by announcing his own resignation.

More than any other cabinet member, Mandelson had been associated with the grand design of recasting the centre-left of British politics. This entailed working with the Liberal Democrats, a development evoking scepticism amongst traditionalists within both parties. With Mandelson's departure Prescott was soon voicing tribal warnings against cooperation, a sentiment echoed by leading Liberal Democratic figures. Amidst this growing tension Paddy Ashdown had been working diligently at 'constructive opposition' with the goal of a place at the high table of power. However, in January 1999 he stunned his party by announcing his forthcoming retirement. Some commentators believed his departure to reflect frustration with a loss of momentum on electoral reform and a feeling that alliance with Labour was in terminal decline. The future direction of the party looked in serious doubt with two of the heirs apparent, Charles Kennedy and Simon Hughes, firmly set against close links with Labour.

Time to call it a day?   With Blair having so successfully plundered the centre-right wardrobe, the Conservatives could find little to wear. In July 1998 Hague

---

Liberal/Liberal Democrat Party leaders since 1900

1900	H. Campbell-Bannerman	1931	H. Samuel	1967	J. Thorpe
1908	H. Asquith	1935	A. Sinclair	1976	D. Steel
1926	D. Lloyd George	1945	C. Davies	1988	P. Ashdown (resigned 1999)
		1956	J. Grimond		

launched a 'listening' roadshow to tour the country, seeking out rank-and-file views in much the same way that Kinnock's 'Labour Listens' campaign had launched his modernization process. Yet could the party rebuild its membership base without clearly defined and appealing policies (Peele 1998: 145)? It had been a party of empire but this was gone. It had been a party of the Union but had no MPs in either Wales or Scotland and devolution was now a bitter pill which could only be swallowed. It had been a party of constitutional stability but Labour was instigating change on many fronts. In its whiggism and neoliberalism it had been a party of world trade but was now set in opposition to the single currency. Indeed, this was the one area where Hague had positioned the party decisively with a referendum in September 1998 on ruling out the single currency for two parliaments. Although 84 per cent of those voting supported him, a large proportion did not bother to return their pre-paid envelopes and the big Euro-guns such as Heath, Heseltine and Clarke refused to be silenced. The policy also lacked CBI support, was not an obvious vote winner and lost Hague two of his front-bench team in resignations. If the single currency were to succeed and a referendum were held, the party could split asunder. The last time this had happened was over the Corn Laws in 1846 and it had been followed by twenty-seven wilderness years. A change to proportional representation could increase the effect. Had the shifting sands of politics moved for ever?

Evaluating British Two-party Democracy

Under the influence of the first-past-the-post electoral system, a broadly **bipartisan** politics has evolved in Britain, held by apologists to have features peculiarly favourable to democracy and contrasted with the multi-partism in Western Europe. Much writing has extolled virtues such as strong single-party government and alternation of governments in office. Yet these virtuous features can be subject to sceptical review.

The party system in Parliament

The fact that two parties dominate Parliament does not mean that single-party government has invariably been the case. During the twentieth century Britain has experienced some twenty-one years of rule by a combination of parties, either in simple coalition, or as members of a National government. Moreover, there have been periods when a governing party has lacked an absolute majority, being sustained only by an agreement with another party. As recently as 1997 Major needed the support of the Ulster Unionists. The notion that two-partyism produces alternation in office is also unconvincing. Even in the post-war era the Conservatives sustained the claim to be the natural party of government with the lion's share of office (see figure 9.8).

The parties in the country

Looking beyond Westminster, there is even less evidence of a two-party culture. Since the 1970s, the memberships of the centre parties have been by no means inconsequential. They also contain some of the most enthusiastic workers, the Liberal Democrats bringing local activism back into fashion. In terms of electoral support, ever since the emergence of Labour, there has been a greater party diversity in the country than at Westminster. Not until the immediate post-war decades did Labour and Conservatives begin to carve up the popular vote, and the period was ended with a groundswell of support for the nationalists and centre parties. In 1983 and 1987 the Alliance polled around a quarter of the total votes, little less than Labour (28 and 30 per cent, respectively) and over half the number polled by the victorious Conservatives. Another measure of party support is local government, where during the 1980s and 1990s the 'third party' became second to Labour.

The bipartisan nature of Parliament has been in large measure a distortion produced by the electoral system. Labour's pledge for a referendum on electoral reform leaves Britain, at the end of the millennium, at an evolutionary crossroads, the most significant constitutional issue since 1832. Parties waiting in the wings would hear their cue, soliloquies and dialogues perhaps giving way to turbulent crowd scenes and a rather more colourful *dramatis personae*.

Key points

- A political party is an association formed for the purpose of taking power by constitutional means.
- Although parties often claim to reflect ideologies, the quest for electoral support weakens this link.
- The early British parties were parliamentary cadres.
- Modern parties are *mass* organizations, with thousands of members.
- The first mass parties emerged as a result of franchise extensions.
- The Labour Party was established in 1900 by a merging of the trade unions and certain socialist groups. It was not intended to be a revolutionary party.
- The post-war party system has seen an era of consensus; the cracking of the consensus; the rise of a new centre party and the emergence of a new consensus in many policy areas in the 1990s.
- The view that Britain has a two-party system is simplistic. The two main parties have not shared office equally, and in the country, voting patterns do not mirror the polarization found in Parliament.
- The electoral system is a key factor in creating the two-party system, and a change to PR could be expected to make a difference.

Review your understanding of the following terms and concepts

1922 Committee
adversary politics
bipartisan politics
Black Wednesday
cadre party
consensus
Eurosceptic
Fabianism
fringe party

Gang of Four
mass party
Militant Tendency
minority government
multi-party system
Night of the Long
 Knives
party system
Profumo scandal

registration society
single-issue party
single-party system
sleaze
Tory
two-party system
Whig
'winter of discontent'

Assignment

Blair's snake-oil democracy

WHAT DO MPs do all day? It's an unfair question, of course, because most of them work very hard – albeit on tasks which would make a strange definition of "work" for most of their constituents: sympathising, speechifying, looking serious, politicking.

But is it unfair for the Labour Party to dictate to its 417 MPs the terms and conditions of their employment? As we report today, the party is working on "contracts" which would set out what MPs are expected to do in terms of talking to and visiting their voters in return for support from party HQ. Above all, it would seem Labour MPs are to be required to engage in a programme of "voter contact" which should see them on the doorsteps of their constituency for two hours every weekend and every day for two weeks when Parliament is not sitting in the summer. On the knocker or the phone, Labour MPs are expected to contact 100 new households on their patch every week. The maths of the petty dictators of Millbank Tower are impeccable: over the five-year maximum period between elections, that would amount to 26,000 households. Their politics, though, are faulty. MPs are, after all, employed by the people themselves, not by the people's party.

This is a strange notion of leadership, and points to a fundamental flaw at the heart of the New Labour idea of democracy. Mr Blair and Mr Mandelson are right that the old mechanisms are worn out, but there is an alarming tendency on their part to confuse democracy with marketing. We have seen it in the slow hollowing-out of Mr Blair's rhetoric, circa 1993–94, about a vibrant Labour Party, a democratic part of its local communities. Contrast that with the disappointing centralism of the system of closed party lists which has become Labour's default form of proportional representation – for the European Parliament, Scotland, Wales and London.

In this light, it seems as if Labour MPs are being recruited to a vast exercise in the selling of Mr Blair's snake-oil (not to mention being kept busy to be better kept out of mischief). "Voter contact" does not sound like a genuine exercise in participatory democracy, more like highly structured and efficient soft soap.

We have too many MPs and they cannot all declaim majestically, with electric flashes of Wildean wit, of course, on the Great Issues of the Day all day and every day. Their pastoral role is important, but it must be a two-way contract between the people and their representatives.

Independent, 22 April 1998

Study the extract from the *Independent* and answer the following questions.

		Mark (%)
1	Who are 'the petty dictators of Millbank'?	10
2	'MPs are employed by the people themselves, not by the people's party.' Discuss with reference to the extract.	20

3   How does the role of the Labour MPs, as implied in the
    proposed contracts, square with the role of Parliament as
    a watchdog over the executive?   20
4   How far is the accusation that New Labour confuses democracy
    with marketing justified?   50

Questions for discussion

1   Explain the concept of 'party system'. How would you characterize that
    of Britain?
2   What did Disraeli mean when he spoke of Peel stealing the clothes of
    the Whigs?
3   Identify the factors that led to Labour supplanting the Liberals as the
    main challenger to the Conservatives.
4   'The first-past-the-post electoral system will defeat any attempt to
    establish multi-party politics in Britain.' Examine this statement in the
    light of developments during the 1980s and 1990s.
5   Examine the effects of the two world wars on the evolution of the
    Labour Party.
6   Explain the reasons for the era of party consensus following the second
    world war.
7   Account for the breakdown in the post-war consensus.
8   How radical was Blair's modernization of the Labour Party?
9   Does the Labour victory of 1997 mark a new age of consensus politics?
10 'What if?' Give an account of British politics up to May 1997 on the
    assumption that John Smith had not died.

Topic for debate

This house believes history shows that a socialist party can never expect power
in Britain.

Further reading

Blake, R. (1985) *The Conservative Party from Peel to Thatcher*.
Classic text.

Crewe, I. and King, A. (1997) *SDP: The Birth, Life and Death of the Social Democratic
Party*.
The life and times of the 'Gang of Four'. Explores the role of personalities, rivalries and
non-rational factors in the destiny of parties. A large book about a small party!

Heffernan, R. and Marqusee, M. (1992) *Defeat from the Jaws of Victory: Inside Kinnock's
Labour Party*.
Hitherto untold stories, revealing anecdotes and concise analysis of the Labour hier-

archy in action – rigging votes, stage-managing meetings, dispensing patronage and settling scores with enemies.

Kavanagh, D. (1997) *The Reordering of British Politics: Politics after Thatcher.*
A clear mapping of the shifting sands of post-Thatcher politics.

MacIver, D. (ed.) (1996) *The Liberal Democrats.*
With contributions from academics and party members, this helps fill a gap in analysis of British parties.

Norton, P. (ed.) (1996) *The Conservative Party.*
Essays by academics and a Conservative MP. Editor's opening chapter probes deeper philosophical grounding.

Pelling, H. and Reid, A. J. (1997) *A Short History of the Labour Party*, 11th edn.
Economical account of the rise of the party with clear narrative.

Shaw, E. (1996) *The Labour Party since 1945: Old Labour, New Labour.*
Balanced assessment of post-war Labour governments and their commitment to social democracy. Objectively critical of New Labour.

Wilson, T. (1966) *The Downfall of the Liberal Party 1914–1935.*
Probes a key event in modern history.

For light relief

Julian Critchley, *A Bag of Boiled Sweets.*
This autobiography from a perennial backbencher is also a social history of the Conservative Party.

George Dangerfield, *The Strange Death of Liberal England.*
Reveals apparent calm of Edwardian England as a facade concealing seething forces leading towards civil war.

Benjamin Disraeli, *Sybil, or: the Two Nations.*
Celebrates the ideas of Disraeli's Toryism; a romance with a Chartist background.

David Hare, *Absence of War.*
Play showing the trials and frustrations of a Labour leader. Said to be based on Kinnock experience.

Scandal.
Video/film of the Profumo affair.

On the net

http://www.conservative-party.org.uk
http://www.libdem.org.uk
http://www.labour.org.uk
In addition to current organization and policies, these sites include considerable historical information. Use a search engine or some of the academic political resources sites to track down information on numerous smaller parties.

Chapter Eleven

Inside the Parties: Masses, Leaders and Powers behind Thrones

Having examined the development of the parties and the system in broad terms we turn inward to the organization and character of the parties themselves. The chapter falls into three sections. The first focuses on the anatomy of the mass party organization. The second examines internal party dynamics: cohesion, power relationships, control mechanisms and the basic relationship between mass membership and leaders. The final section analyses the location of the parties within the structure of power in society at large, addressing the sensitive issue of funding: who pays the piper and do they call the tune?

Anatomy of the Mass Party

In essence the main British parties comprise three elements: a parliamentary cadre of MPs, a central bureaucracy and a large mass membership of voluntary workers in the country (figure 11.1). Chapter 10 showed that in the Conservative and Liberal parties the parliamentary cadres came first, while the Parliamentary Labour Party (PLP) was created by the mass movement. The emergence of the Social Democratic Party (SDP) in the 1980s was, like that of the older parties, the result of Westminster-based initiative, but it quickly worked to build a mass membership. The parties have organizational similarities because they all exist in the same environment and must fulfil certain necessary functions to survive. They often show a tendency to copy each other, a phenomenon termed contagion.

The constituency associations

These have been crucial in fighting elections – organizing local campaigns, distributing propaganda, holding meetings, liaising with the local media and canvassing. In addition, they raise funds and recruit people into politics. Each has an organizational structure with a chairperson and executive committee of some

Figure 11.1
The mass party
organization.

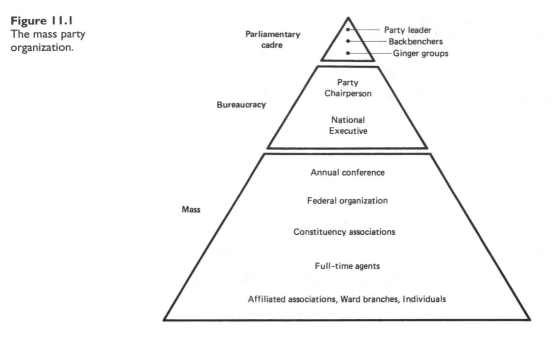

kind, and many employ a full-time agent. New Labour took particular care to strengthen its professional core. Probably the most politically significant act undertaken by local associations is the selection of parliamentary candidates (see pp. 316–19).

> I find most of them boring, petty, malign, clumsily conspiratorial and parochial to a degree that cannot be surpassed in any part of the United Kingdom.
>
> Alan Clark on his local constituency organization, *Diaries* (26 Nov. 1985)

Ward associations The grassroots structure may be further fragmented into ward committees, reflecting the community substructure. These are often active in the politics of local government and in the 'community politics' approach favoured by the Liberal Democrats.

Individual membership In principle anyone can join a political party. Workers are volunteers devoting their spare time to political activity as a hobby or even an obsession; indeed, it is at this level that some of the fiercest zealotry is encountered, from the 'wild-eyed' hard left to the 'goose-stepping tendency'. Of course, by no means all local activists are extremists, though most feel more strongly on issues than other people (Seyd and Whiteley 1992: 216–17). Membership is also a social activity, involving parties, fundraising dinners and

> There are a fair number of constituency parties in the commuter belt which are run by people who, frankly, might quite properly be labelled neo-fascists.
>
> Unnamed Conservative MP, quoted in S. Ingle, *The British Party System* (1987: 83)

auctions, concerts and so on; the Young Conservatives were traditionally admired as a dating agency and marriage bureau. At one time Conservative associations were controlled by local aristocrats, but are now largely in the hands of small businessmen and professionals.

Party records are often haphazard and it is difficult to ascertain membership size, which waxes and wanes with the political climate. Throughout the 1970s and 1980s falling numbers tended to leave the zealots in command and party leaders in the 1990s worked to widen membership, Labour being particularly successful (table 11.1), swelling its army of footsoldiers to some 400,000. In contrast, by the end of the 1990s the Conservative membership was quite literally dying; sacks of voting slips sent out in September 1997 to endorse Hague's leadership were returned marked 'Deceased'. Despite success at the polls, party membership had plummeted from a high point of three million in the mid-1950s to only a few hundred thousand. The decline was particularly rapid during the eventide of the Major government, membership falling by 40 per cent between 1994 and 1997 (Pinto-Duschinsky 1997). Unlike that of Labour, its membership base was not being renewed; one estimate suggested that over 95 per cent of members were thirty-five or older (Whiteley et al. 1994: 42), the youth membership (Young Conservatives plus students) having fallen from around 34,000 in 1979 to only 10,000 in 1997 (Conservative Party 1997: 2).

Affiliated associations In addition to individual membership the Labour Party has offered a form of indirect membership whereby associations such as

Table 11.1 Membership of the main British parties, 1997

Party	Membership
Conservative Party	400,000 (est.)
Labour Party	400,000
Liberal Democrat Party	103,000
Scottish National Party	15,000 (est.)
Plaid Cymru	10,000
Green Party	4,000

Conservative membership figures are difficult to estimate. The party itself estimated 750,000 in 1996, but Pinto-Duschinsky's survey (1997) suggested 350,000–400,000. It is SNP policy not to release membership figures, but estimates range from 10,000 to 20,000.

Source: Data from *British Elections and Parties Yearbook 1997*, p. 263; Pinto-Duschinsky (1997).

socialist societies and trade unions affiliate, producing an inflated paper membership. The result was often union domination and part of Labour's recruitment strategy was to curb this.

Intermediate-level associations Neighbouring associations may combine for purposes of coordination at area, regional or provincial levels. This was most significant in the SDP, where the Area became the primary unit of association, enabling the party to rapidly establish itself as a viable national force. The Liberal Democrats are similarly divided into twelve English regional parties, plus Scottish and Welsh parties. European elections, with their larger constituencies, also bring adjacent party organizations together.

The federal organizations The constituencies are united through federal associations. The Conservatives form their National Union (see p. 268) while the constituency Labour parties (CLPs) constitute the Labour Party as such.

Red flag and blue rinse: the annual conference

Each party holds an annual conference which, in an age of mass communications, is its most important shop window. Although bringing all sections together, it is really a mass membership celebration, a jamboree in which all who have laboured in the fields on behalf of their leaders may draw near to pay homage. **Party conferences** last for several days in the pleasant environs of the seaside at the end of the season but before the weather is too cold to enjoy a publicity-seeking dip. With something of the air of a great sporting event, all takes place before the unblinking eyes of the television cameras, supplemented with a ball-by-ball commentary by the pundits.

The order of play entails a succession of debates on resolutions submitted by members, with speakers drawn from all sections of the party. Formally the Labour and Liberal Democrat conferences have a policy-making role (see below). Voting in the Labour conference has involved a particularly controversial feature – the **block vote**, whereby delegates enjoyed overwhelming influence by casting votes weighted to reflect the size of the membership represented. This acute embarrassment became a key target of the modernization process after the 1992 election defeat (Alderman and Carter 1994).

The appropriate parliamentary leader (minister or shadow minister) will usually conclude a debate and individual popularity is gauged by the length and intensity of the applause. The audiences have their favourites: Michael Heseltine, with his handsome profile and golden mane, was often accorded the adulation of a matinée idol, as was Michael Portillo. It is often the more extreme views that gain the plaudits. Mrs Thatcher's legendary 'resolution' produced frenzied hero worship. A Conservative home secretary often has the most difficult time since, however tough the rhetoric, it may not satisfy the demands of the hanging-and-flogging school of penal reform. Michael Howard, however, came close to doing so in the 1990s with his tabloid 'prison works' message. Likewise, Labour conferences have often exposed a sharp duality between the parliamentary leaders preaching the doctrine of moderation and trying on capitalist clothes, and the fundamentalist prophets who see sackcloth and ashes as the only garb suitable for those who have repeatedly betrayed the faith. However, under New Labour this was dramatically changed with a degree of stage management surpassing that of the Conservatives. In 1998 controversial debates were even held behind closed doors with the press excluded.

Conferences tend to spill out, both socially and politically, into the surrounding environs. The foyers of conference halls are festooned like bazaars with stands set up by sympathetic pressure groups and stalls selling trinkets and memoirs of party giants or even scandalmongers. Parties of the non-political kind proliferate and there is a brisk business in fringe meetings where leading figures challenging party orthodoxy and 'managed' out of the main event, such as John Redwood (after his challenge to Major) or Ken Livingstone (under New Labour), can expound their views in an atmosphere often more lively and stimulating than in the official forum. Increasingly the media direct attention here; Michael Heseltine claimed that his fringe appearance in 1988 received 'more serious coverage than for any speech I ever made at a Conservative conference' (Pienaar 1988).

> No member of the conference wants to let down the party in front of the national [TV] audience. Everybody is on his best behaviour, naturally a great aid to the leadership.
>
> Ian Gilmour (Conservative MP), *The Body Politic* (1969: 80–1)

Conference organizers make strenuous efforts to ensure that the boat is not rocked. Conservative leaders for long demonstrated a clear superiority in the art of stage management, employing public relations experts to orchestrate their entrances and exits. In the Labour Party, speakers often emerged believing that, like justice, the washing of disgusting linen should be seen to be done, preferably on the launderette of television. However, the party learned its lesson and by the 1990s had acquired consummate public relations skills, debates on issues such as gay rights being carefully scheduled to take place when the cameras switch off for children's television. Conversely, under Major, Conservative conferences began to lose their sense of decorum. Receptions for Baroness Thatcher were themselves unnerving, the rapturous acclamation reminding leaders that many lamented her departure. All end on an emotional note with a rousing speech from the leader, the content and style of which are regarded as a key test of political virility. The Labour Party places the final seal on its business with the fraternal rendition of 'The Red Flag', sung with varying degrees of enthusiasm by the modernizers. Yet although some conferences are momentous, most are soon forgotten (Kavanagh 1996).

The central machinery

The executives As large organizations parties need executives to direct their business. The Conservative Executive Committee consists of around 150, including party officials, representatives of the constituencies and of business interests, MPs and Central Office. Its Labour counterpart is the National Executive Committee (NEC). Although constitutionally the servant of the mass party, the NEC's practical role has been leadership. Meeting regularly, it has a key position in policy formation, various subcommittees submitting conference resolutions. Moreover, in conjunction with the parliamentary leadership, it determines which elements of the programme to include in the manifesto. The NEC also handled disciplinary matters but, under the Blair reforms, these were referred to a new National Constitutional Committee.

Acting on behalf of the conference, the NEC has exerted a greater dominance than any extra-parliamentary body in the other parties. Its membership is determined by elections from various sections of the party and it elects its own chair and vice-chair. However, it could embarrass the leadership; the trade unions were for long able to control a majority and the method of election (figure 11.2) meant that it could be captured by the left. Under Blair, however, its composition was changed. Powerful left-wing party figures are ruled out because the six members elected by the constituencies must not be MPs and the combined ranks of the PLP and the European Parliamentary Party (EPLP) are allowed only three representatives. The Cabinet also nominates three members while the party leader and deputy leader are *ex officio* members. However, the leadership was unable to avert the election of some non-parliamentary left-wingers to the constituency division in 1998, including Liz Davies, who had been preventing from standing as parliamentary candidate in Leeds North East (see p. 319). In November 1998, the NEC adopted guidelines proscribing the leaking of discussions and obliging members to notify the party's press office before making public statements about NEC business. Critics bemoaned the leadership's 'control freak' tendencies.

The Liberal Democrat Federal Executive, under the leadership of the party president, is responsible for directing, coordinating and implementing party activities. Responsibility for conference organization lies with a Conference Committee, while policy proposals are initiated and developed by the Policy Committee, which draws up election manifestos in conjunction with the parliamentary party.

The bureaucracies These are the professional backbone of the parties. The Conservatives have their Central Office in Smith Square and Liberal Democrat headquarters are nearby in Cowley Street, both within a stone's throw of Westminster. Labour's Head Office was for long popularly known as 'Transport House' because of its location in the headquarters of the Transport and General Workers' Union. In 1980 it moved, not without a certain symbolism, south of the Thames to Walworth Road (John Smith House) but by 1997 was achieving greater visibility from its state-of-the-art media centre at Millbank Tower on the banks of the Thames.

Ex Officio Party Leader Deputy Leader General Secretary EPLP leader							
Unions	Socialist Societies	Constituency Parties	Local Government	PLP EPLP	Cabinet	Treasurer	Youth Rep
Elected at Annual Conference. At least six must be women	Elected at Annual Conference (Unopposed)	Elected by all members. Cannot be MPs. At least three must be women	Elected from Association of Labour Councillors. At least one must be a woman	Elected at Annual Conference. At least one must be a woman	Nominated by Cabinet	Elected at Annual Conference (Unopposed)	Elected at Youth Conference

Figure 11.2 Composition of the Labour NEC, 1997.

The bureaucracies have a wide range of management and control functions over the voluntary arms, coordinating local activities, providing a link with the leader and giving advice and information. At Westminster level they conduct public relations (liaising with the media and advertising and producing party literature), manage the annual conference, organize research and service backbench committees. They also oversee candidate selection policy (such as number of women) and maintain the central list of hopefuls. Finally, they control party finances and fundraising.

Conservative Central Office was established in 1870 largely as a personal machine to serve the leader (Pinto-Duschinsky 1972). Significant developments took place between 1906 and 1911 during opposition, when the key position of party chairman (responsible for running the Office) was created, to be held by a cabinet-ranking MP. The appointment was to become one of the leader's most significant patronage gifts, though the relationship can be tense. Thatcher had some trouble with her chairmen; with Norman Tebbit in post, she seemed to rely more on advertising experts such as Tim Bell. William Hague appointed erstwhile Thatcher loyalist Cecil Parkinson to signal his political leanings.

In contrast, Labour Head Office was created by the NEC and is not formally responsible to the leader. However, in practice its role is similar to that of Central Office. At times it has suffered from the parlous state of the party's finances but was replenished with an army of temporary staff for the 1997 election campaign as it made a huge fundraising push. The smaller parties maintain more modest bureaucratic support, reflecting the lesser demands of their parliamentary cadres.

The parliamentary cadres

At the apex of the party structure sits the parliamentary cadre of MPs, including the leader, the front bench and the backbench organizations (see p. 372). The political mainsprings of Parliament, the extent of their independence from the rest of the party is a key question in political analysis. There are also the European parliamentary cadres, though the Westminster MPs have not been entirely warm in embracing their MEP cousins, reflecting a fear that Parliament's much-cherished sovereignty will be eroded. For their part, most MEPs will, *ipso facto*, espouse the integrationist ideal, a tendency increased by pressures to go native in the *communitaire* climate of Strasbourg. Indeed, the Euroscepticism of Margaret Thatcher left Conservative MEPs rather in the cold. Labour has shown a more friendly face, making the leader of the European Labour Party an *ex officio* member of the NEC, permitting MEPs to attend Westminster backbench meetings and including them in the electoral college choosing the leader. However, they showed some willingness to bite the hand that fed them by criticizing Blair's reform of Clause Four and his social policies.

The life and soul of the parties: satellite groups

Within and around the main parties is a constellation of smaller organizations or ginger groups comprising various combinations of MPs and ordinary members. Although having separate identities, they owe their *raisons d'être* to the parent party, which they often feel an ideological compunction to influence. They can give a party much of its character, claiming variously to be its soul, its conscience, or its ideas bank, though often seen by leaders as unwanted carbuncles or diabolical incarnations requiring surgery or exorcism. In September 1998 Blair accused the Grass Roots Alliance of posing as 'critical supporters' while really being 'outright opponents' (*Independent*, 26 Sept. 1998).

Conservative In 1883, the Primrose League was formed in an attempt to keep alive the 'one-nation' spirit of Disraeli (being a reference to his favourite flower). The Bow Group was founded by Conservative intellectuals in 1951 as a counterpoise to Labour's Fabian Society. It professes moderation, disseminating its message through a journal, *Crossbow*. When the right-wing Monday Club formed in 1960 to oppose Macmillan on South Africa it was mainly concerned with defence, but it went on to espouse a broader right-wing position and was accused of dealings with the National Front. The spirit of neoliberalism kindled by Heath led to the establishment in 1973 of the Selsdon Group. Such views have been propagated subsequently by a rich vein of right-wing think-tanks, including the Centre for Policy Studies, the Adam Smith Institute, the Institute for Economic Affairs, and the Salisbury Group (publishing the *Salisbury Review*). Anti-Thatcherite forces included the Tory Reform Group (founded 1975) and Care, formed after the 1983 election by over 100 Conservative MPs to call for more compassion. In 1985 the deposed Francis Pym established Centre

Forward to oppose the extreme right. John Major suffered from troublesome associations. These who stung him into his 1995 resignation termed themselves the Fresh Start group (though he used a different term). In August 1995 John Redwood announced the establishment of a right-wing think-tank, Conservative 2000 Foundation, while in March 1996 the Macleod Group was relaunched to promote leftish, pro-European values. Away from the centre are the Young Conservatives and the Women's National Advisory Committee, both with national structures.

Labour There has been no shortage of Labour ginger groups, the most well known being Tribune (propagating its views through the journal of that name). Founded in 1964, it has often been troublesome, but highly respected, and has included some prominent figures. Thorns in the moderate side have been persistent. The Bevanites were well known, but even the moderate Harold Wilson headed Keep Left and in 1958 Victory for Socialism formed to oppose Gaitskell's revisionism. The 1970s saw the Campaign for Labour Party Democracy and the Labour Coordinating Committee, which sought successfully to gain control of the NEC and instigate reforms in the party constitution.

Militant Tendency believed in a mission to oppose the Fabian tradition, using the Trotskyite tactic of entryism into the party. It was criticized in an internal party report prepared by Lord Underhill in 1975 and by the early 1980s moderates felt its tactics to be seriously damaging. There was talk of witch-hunts and, in a largely symbolic gesture, Michael Foot expelled the five-member editorial board of its journal, *Militant*. In Parliament, the Campaign Group was founded in 1982 as a more radical alternative to Tribune, to oppose witch-hunts. During the cold war, CND penetrated deeply into the Labour ranks.

On Labour's right was the Manifesto Group, established in 1974, though its first two chairpersons went on to form the SDP. From the first the Fabian Society has exerted a profound influence on the party, providing illustrious figures as well as ideas. Although appearing moribund during the Thatcher era, under Blair it was rejuvenated in a more rightist mode, becoming closely aligned with the Institute for Public Policy Research, set up with union backing in 1989 to pioneer the left's intellectual fightback. A third new force was Demos, a rightish think-tank launched in 1993 by Martin Jacques, formerly editor of *Marxism Today*. Several single-issue groups are also close to Labour, notably the 'Eurorealist' Centre for European Reform and the Constitution Unit. Others, such as Charter 88, contributed to the New Labour mood but, with a more radical agenda, remain more distanced from the party.

The Young Socialists organize nationally and tend towards more extreme policies. Some of the party's women also maintain a separate identity as local women's sections, coordinated through a National Labour Women's Conference. However, a major shift began in the late 1970s as feminism began to lose direction and a number of activists focused on the party itself. The modernization drive, with its weakening of the unions and constituency activists, gave women a key opportunity (Perrigo 1996), a dramatic breakthrough coming in the all-women shortlists (p. 318). Although Labour remains deaf to calls for special black sections, these began to arise spontaneously in some thirty constituencies during the 1980s.

Of course, the most towering external presence for Labour has been the trade union movement, historically its *raison d'être* though greatly reduced under the modernization programme, a matter to which we return later.

Inside the Parties: Tweedledum and Tweedledee?

Textbooks have often painted party politics as a great battle between two equally matched Titans, part of a legitimating myth of British liberal democracy. Historically the internal processes and power structures of each party reveal significant differences. Yet it is true that the pressures of modern politics increasingly force them to resemble each other in the quest for power.

Internal cohesion

In a multi-party system each stands for a narrow interest or ideology, thereby promising internal solidarity. However, one of the *raisons d'être* of parties in a two-party system is **interest aggregation** – they have been termed 'catch-all' parties (Kirchheimer 1966). Yet to attract votes they must present a united front and this generates tension between ideological forces and political expediency. All British parties carry a deep-seated basis for schism; the Conservatives with their traditional Whig and Tory strains (the wet/dry dichotomy under Thatcher), Labour bedevilled by a revolutionary/Fabian divide, and even the centrist Liberal Democrats harbouring Liberal and Social Democrat wings. The way inner tensions are handled constitutes a key focus for analysis; history shows the Conservatives to have been by far the most successful, Labour continually searching for an antidote to the virulent factionalism coursing through its veins. However, from the early 1990s things began to change dramatically as Labour learned from the Conservatives, who themselves appeared to lose their magic touch.

Social composition Although the Conservatives have always been able to command a wide range of electoral support, their traditional membership came from a narrow and homogeneous social base within the upper-middle class and *petite bourgeoisie*. However, the Thatcher era saw a new breed of Conservative MP with self-made, meritocratic backgrounds. In April 1988, Major John Stokes, Conservative member for Halesowen and Stourbridge, enquired during Prime Minister's Questions whether 'there is still room in the party for the nobility, the gentry, and the middle class'. Even so, it remains overwhelmingly a middle-class party (86 per cent of membership according to Whiteley et al. 1994: 45–6). By contrast, Labour has been more a microcosm of society, class tensions being reproduced within its own ranks. However, the New Labour intake of MPs in 1997 showed increased homogeneity around a meritocratic norm with 75 per cent university educated (see p. 359).

Experience of office A party forming a government is constitutionally and politically pushed towards coherence. The doctrine of collective responsibility, official secrecy, the need for Commons' support and the duty to represent the whole community all conspire to unite. A long history of office has given the Conservatives considerable exposure to these forces. As Labour sought a second term after its 1997 victory, party spin doctors worked strenuously to keep backbenchers 'on message'.

Ideology Labour has traditionally espoused socialism but this can have a variety of meanings, implying contrasting strategies. Hence, the leadership has regularly sought to reduce the 'red in tooth and Clause Four' commitment to socialism, Gaitskell's attempts to disembarrass the party of this talisman being particularly disruptive. In contrast, the Conservatives' traditional goal has been office rather than ideological purity. Thatcher, however, with her espousal of neoliberalism, reversed this. MPs who had cut their teeth during her reign learned that politics was the art of confrontation and Major found himself at the wheel of an unruly ship. Conversely, Labour under Blair jettisoned much ideological baggage (including rewriting Clause Four) in the bid for power.

Hegemonic consciousness Probably of greatest importance is the fact that the Conservatives have regarded themselves (and are regarded by others) as the 'natural' party of government. Even in opposition they have tended to remain united, believing office is never far away. By contrast, some figures within Labour have seen its role primarily in terms of protest. This was very evident during the early years of the Thatcher government; the essential project of Kinnock, Smith and Blair was the Sisyphean one of convincing the party it could govern.

The imperatives of capitalism Under capitalism an important government role is unifying the competitive and potentially disruptive forces of private enterprise. As the party of private capital the Conservatives accept a key responsibility in this respect, forcing members to place a high premium on unity within the party ranks. Recognition of this in the form of 'new realism' also made Labour more capital-friendly during the 1990s (see p. 288).

Tendencies and factions A distinction has been made between the concepts of faction and tendency (Rose 1964). A **faction** is a group united across a wide front. Labour has been said to contain two factions broadly differentiated in left–right terms, confronting each other on a broad range of issues and producing a fundamental fault line. In contrast, Conservative disagreements tend not to precipitate the same formations every time. *A* and *B* may oppose *C* on one issue, but on another *A* and *C* may unite against *B*, these fluid **tendencies** never destroying overall coherence.

> What a genius the Labour Party has for cutting itself in half and letting the two parts writhe in public.
>
> Cassandra (William Neil Connor; 1910–67; Irish journalist), in the *Daily Mirror*

However, this analysis can be questioned. Disagreements over Europe cut deeply into the Conservative flesh in the 1990s, illustrating an historic problem with foreign relations and reflecting the divide between the old Tory strain emphasizing nationhood and the whiggish element of thrusting commerce. This had produced divisions over the Corn Laws in the 1840s, imperial protection in the early twentieth century, Indian government in 1935, South Africa under Macmillan and Rhodesia in 1965 (Norton 1978). Moreover, with the Bruges Group, No Turning Back and Conservative Way Forward, the 1980s saw greater factionalism than ever (Kavanagh 1998: 41). Although William Hague talked of reuniting his party, at the October 1997 conference he gave notice of his intention to fight the next general election opposing the single European currency, thereby placing his Europhiles in confrontational mode (*The Times*, 10 Oct. 1997). While the Conservatives fought internally, New Labour grew flesh over its old scars and claimed the 'one nation' mantle of Disraeli.

Choosing the leader

The selection of leaders and their security of tenure have important implications for a party's culture.

Labour From the beginning, the Labour leadership was elective, with voting the exclusive right of the PLP. In theory leaders were subject to annual re-election but, although Wilson unsuccessfully threw down the gauntlet before Gaitskell in 1960 and Tony Benn vainly challenged Kinnock in 1988, this has largely been avoided and evidence shows Labour leaders to be more secure than their Conservative counterparts. Attlee was able to cling to office far longer than his younger colleagues wished; Gaitskell, although his reign was turbulent, died with his leadership boots firmly laced and Harold Wilson was sufficiently secure after fourteen years that his resignation came as a shock to colleagues and pundits alike. Even James Callaghan, after stormy battles with the left, was able to depart with dignity. The demise of Michael Foot probably came closest to a Conservative-style hounding from office. He had proved an electoral liability, nicknamed Worzel Gummidge (a scruffy but well-meaning scarecrow featuring in a current TV series) by *Private Eye*.

Left-wing criticism in the 1980s blamed the leadership for shortcomings and at a special conference at Wembley it was agreed that the electoral college choosing the leader and deputy should be widened to embrace the trade unions (40 per cent), the constituency associations and the PLP (30 per cent each). (The left fought unsuccessfully for the whole of the Shadow Cabinet to be so chosen.) However, the new system disappointed reformers by choosing the right's 'dream ticket' of Kinnock and Hattersley in 1983. Paradoxically, the reform actually increased the leader's security in three ways: it gave authority over all sections of the party; the PLP lost any moral right to a vote of no-confidence; and the cumbersome procedure could inhibit challenges.

The 1993 conference agreed further changes, strengthening ordinary members against local oligarchs. Union influence was further reduced by making the proportions in the electoral college equal thirds and both unions and constituency parties were obliged to ballot members individually on the principle of 'one member, one vote' (OMOV), producing a leadership electorate of millions.

Conservative The process whereby Conservative leaders emerged was for long shrouded in a mystique that would puzzle even England cricket selectors. The party elders, including the outgoing leader, would practise secret rites, take soundings within the party and a new heir would emerge. This was not necessarily corrupt or even irrational; it permitted sensitivity to candidates' qualities and reflected *intensity* of feeling in a way that a simple vote would not. However, the Douglas-Home experience discredited the method and election by MPs was introduced in 1965 (table 11.2). The reform proved highly significant in that it shifted the leadership class basis. First came Heath, son of an artisan, to be followed by grocer's daughter Thatcher, who was a particular beneficiary of the system (Blake 1985: 320) and would probably not have been the choice of the Lords, party elders, Shadow Cabinet or the constituencies. Major and Hague continued the new pattern of class background.

The reform also affected the leader's security of tenure. Conservatives have a tradition of staunch loyalty to a leader when in office coupled with a reputation for the elimination of old warriors that would be envied by the Mafia (Bruce-Gardyne 1984: 22). With the exception of Bonar Law, every incumbent appointed during the twentieth century was either forcibly removed or placed under heavy pressure to go. Like the manager of a league football team, leaders appear safe as long as they deliver victory. Thus, all deposed leaders are tainted with a fatal electoral flaw: for Chamberlain it was Munich, for Eden Suez, for Macmillan the Profumo scandal, for Douglas-Home an unfashionable aristocratic style. Election made removal even easier, opening up the possibility of annual challenges. Heath, whose fatal flaw was the 'U-turn', added to the distinction of being the first elected leader that of being the first to be 'unelected'.

Conservative leadership elections, 1965–1997

Although only MPs voted, the officers of the 1922 Committee took soundings amongst peers and MEPs. MPs were also required to canvass their constituency associations.

1st ballot: to win, candidate requires overall majority, plus a 15 per cent lead over nearest rival – a difficult hurdle.

2nd ballot: candidates re-enter, along with any new entrants. Allows cabinet colleagues to enter without seeming disloyal to sitting prime minister. Any candidate with overall majority of all entitled to vote wins and contest settled.

3rd ballot: a shoot-out between the two highest candidates.

4th ballot: only to be used in the event of a tie in which the candidates were unable to resolve the matter between them.

Winner attends meeting of MPs, peers, MEPs and the Executive Committee of the National Union to be approved by acclamation.

Table 11.2 Conservative leadership elections, 1965–1997

Candidates	1st ballot	2nd ballot	3rd ballot
1965			
Heath	150	–	–
Maudling	133	–	–
Powell	15	–	–
1975			
Fraser	16	–	–
Heath	119	–	–
Howe	–	19	–
Peyton	–	11	–
Prior	–	19	–
Thatcher	130	110	–
Whitelaw	–	79	–
1989			
Meyer	33	–	–
Thatcher	314	–	–
1990			
Heseltine	152	131	–
Thatcher	204	–	–
Major	–	185	–
Hurd	–	56	–
1995			
Major	219	–	–
Redwood	89	–	–
Spoiled papers and abstentions	22	–	–
1997			
Clarke	49	64	70
Hague	41	62	92
Howard	23	–	–
Lilley	24	–	–
Redwood	27	38	–

The poll tax was Thatcher's *pons asinorum* and she experienced the crueller side of the electoral coin in November 1990 when Heseltine challenged from the backbenches. Major was called a ditherer and his undoing was Europe. After 1 May 1997 he did not need the fabled men in grey suits to tell him it was time to go.

> 'I must congratulate you on the combination of loyalty and restraint that you have shown in going on television to announce your intention to vote against the prime minister in the Leadership Election.'
> 'Alan, I'm perfectly prepared to argue this through with you if you'll listen.'
> 'Piss off.'
>
> Alan Clark on his encounter with Edwina Currie behind the Speaker's chair during the tense moments surrounding the fall of Thatcher, *Diaries* (21 Nov. 1990)

In September 1997 new leader William Hague sought to insulate himself from challenges with a rule change but received a quick rebuff from the 1922 Committee (*The Times*, 21 Sept. 1997). However, his election had promoted considerable unease in the constituencies (Alderman 1998). The realization that the rump of 164 MPs would choose the next leader produced calls for an OMOV system. When the 1922 Committee resisted, disgruntled party officials polled thousands of members through meetings and telephone banks organized by the Electoral Reform Society. Although these opted decisively for Kenneth Clarke, MPs remained deaf to their voices (and to the consultation requirement).

Conscious of this, in October 1997 Hague offered members a 'back me or sack me' challenge by postal ballot. The result was 143,299 votes in favour, 34,092 against and 2,622 spoiled papers. However, the endorsement was diluted in that it was tied to approval of a reform package that few could gainsay. Finally, a special constitutional conference in March 1998 decided upon an electoral college for leadership contests that would include all party members, choosing from a shortlist of candidates supported by more than 25 per cent of MPs (a system that would probably have rejected Hague himself).

Liberal Democrats Until 1976 the Liberals had followed their traditional practice of allowing the parliamentary cohort, such as it was, to choose the leader. However, following Jeremy Thorpe's resignation over the Norman Scott scandal, party-wide election was instigated. Generally, post-war Liberal leaders appeared secure in office: Jo Grimond left with dignity, continuing as a respected party elder; and although Thorpe's position became untenable, he survived for an astonishingly long time. David Steel, though subject to some rough treatment, remained secure until he voluntarily stood down in 1988 for the SDP merger, at which point Paddy Ashdown was elected as the new party's first leader by a postal ballot of all members. His own resignation was both voluntary and extremely surprising; he had enjoyed eleven years of unchallenged supremacy. The Liberal Democrat constitution stipulates that a leadership election should normally be held at least once each parliament, or when a majority of members or seventy-five local associations so demand.

A hollow crown? The fact that Labour offers its leaders a more secure tenure does not necessarily mean they are the more powerful. It may be in the interests of party members to preserve a weak leader in order to enjoy greater freedom to rule from behind the throne. Caesar was slain not because he was weak but because he was powerful. The uncertainty of the tenure makes the party leadership a lonely position, many incumbents becoming brooding and paranoic, and fearing amongst their retinue those who, like the lean and hungry Cassius in Shakespeare's *Julius Caesar*, lie awake at night and 'be never at heart's ease whiles they behold a greater than themselves'.

Party patronage

Leaders can counter the advantage others have to make or break them by using their own **patronage** powers. Those of Conservative leaders are almost unbounded: whether in office or opposition they appoint the front-bench team and the significant officers of Central Office. The position of party chair has become particularly significant. Thatcher stamped her authority on the party with a thorough shake-up at Central Office. In contrast, the Labour leader is more tightly circumscribed. In opposition, the front-bench team is elected by the PLP and must be taken into government in the event of a general election victory. However, in October 1993 John Smith broke with tradition by keeping Harriet Harman as shadow chief secretary to the Treasury despite her failure to be re-elected by the PLP. The powerful NEC makes appointments to the bureaucracy and is itself elected by the party. Leaders can also appoint advisers and spin doctors to key positions, a power used increasingly by Blair. The Liberal Democrats stress their democratic procedures: the party president is elected biennially by all members and a majority of the members of all three executive bodies are elected by the conference.

Candidate selection

To be a genuinely national force a party must field over 600 candidates, their selection representing a widely based patronage exercise. Theoretically this gives the constituency associations a key 'gatekeeper' role.

Conservative In theory anyone can apply to be a Conservative candidate; selection committees may be faced with the mammoth task of reducing a list of a hundred or so to a shortlist of around six. These are subjected to scrutiny: interviewed, invited to deliver an address and their profession and lifestyle noted. Those with spouses are preferred and these may be vetted for acceptability on platform and in drawing-room. Throughout the process Central Office presence is felt. Yet although guidelines are issued on candidate policy and a Standing Committee maintains a list of possibles upon which the local associations may draw, local associations have traditionally resisted pressure from above. Thus, when senior figures called for the head of Piers Merchant in 1997, following tabloid stories of an affair with a seventeen-year-old hostess, the Beckenham party defied with an overwhelming vote of confidence. In like vein, the Tatton Conservatives stood by Neil Hamilton before the 1997 election. Many local parties resented the manner of Thatcher's departure and Major was obliged to appeal to activists not to act against MPs who had supported Heseltine's challenge. Big names are not necessarily favoured; ex-Chancellor Norman Lamont was spurned by eight associations without even an interview before being selected by Harrogate and Knaresborough for the 1997 election. Sir Nicholas Scott argued that his deselection was a result of his pro-European views, though trouble with drink and being found face downwards on the pavement at the 1996 party conference did not help. However, in selecting Alan Clark as his replacement, his Kensington and Chelsea party could not be accused of choosing a less colourful candidate.

Until the post-war Maxwell-Fyfe reforms it was possible for wealthy aspirants effectively to purchase nomination by agreeing to contribute to party funds. A preference for breeding and education remains, with a predilection for company executives (141 stood in 1997, along with 88 lawyers). However, from the 1980s, a new kind of professional politician emerged, working as ministerial advisers and lobby consultants with no outside experience. Dame Angela Rumbold, who took charge of candidate policy in 1993, reacted against these 'clones', arguing for a return to traditional candidates, but despite her efforts many of the forty-one first-timers entering the Commons in 1997 were party apparatchiks (Criddle 1997a: 196). She had no more success in getting more women selected as 'the blue rinse mafia' dug their block heels in but Hague promised a campaign to increase the number of Conservative women candidates to at least 25 per cent. Black candidates are even rarer (see p. 363). The typical Conservative candidate remains resolutely middle class, middle aged, white, married and male.

Labour Here the selection process is significantly different. The original lists are considerably shorter because applications are restricted to those nominated by affiliated associations. The NEC maintains a list of approved candidates and has taken increasing interest in candidate selection. This list once distinguished between sponsored and non-sponsored candidates. **Sponsorship** meant that nominating associations met a substantial proportion of election expenses and made a contribution to funds; a powerful inducement to a local association, and the advice of Oscar Wilde to the tempted is often followed. In the post-war era about half the Labour MPs could be described as politically kept men.

Sponsorship did not entail the use of *personal* wealth to gain office, it assisted working-class participation and was in line with Labour's original *raison d'être* of union representation in Parliament. However, it meant that selection was often controlled by union-dominated general management committees and, because the sponsors chose the safer seats, younger and more radical candidates were left with unwinnable ones. It also showed a male bias (Lovenduski and Norris 1994). Hence the system was discontinued in 1996 with contributions going to the constituency parties rather than to candidates. This opened up the possibility of directing resources away from the safe seats to the marginals.

The requirement from 1983 that all Labour MPs undergo reselection each

Trade-union sponsorship of the Labour Shadow Cabinet, 1992

GMB	TGWU	RMT
John Smith	Margaret Beckett	Robin Cook
Ann Taylor	Gordon Brown	Frank Dobson
Jack Cunningham	Tony Blair	John Prescott
Jack Straw	Harriet Harman	Donald Dewar
Tom Clarke	Ann Clwyd	
Cohse	**MSF**	**Nupe**
Mo Mowlam	Chris Smith	David Blunkett
Michael Meacher		David Clark

Source: Guardian (13 Aug. 1992)

parliament was intended to increase the power of local parties over the PLP. However, Kinnock countered this by introducing local electoral colleges with unions limited to 40 per cent of the vote. This proved cumbersome and was replaced in 1993 by OMOV. To placate the unions a 'levy plus' system entitled political-levy payers to participate in voting by 'joining' the party at a reduced rate. At the same time, MPs' security of tenure was strengthened by instigating unopposed reselection if they received at least two-thirds of all nominations.

To increase the representation of women, a 'W' (women-only) list was established in 1989, but perhaps the most dramatic innovation was the agreement in 1993 to establish all-women shortlists for 50 per cent of all winnable seats. Hotly resented in many constituencies, in 1996 a tribunal declared it illegal under the Sex Discrimination Act. However, the thirty-eight candidates already selected were unaffected and a further fifteen went on to be chosen for winnable seats from open shortlists, suggesting seismic movements in the party's cultural bedrock. In elections for the Scottish Parliament and Welsh Assembly, Labour paired constituencies, with the intention of having one male and one female candidate.

Although black candidates are nominated by Labour, they usually fight unwinnable seats. Prior to the 1997 election a number of acrimonious selection disputes arose in inner cities with sizeable ethnic populations where incumbent white MPs were loath to step aside. In some cases OMOV led to mass signings of new Asian members to influence selection. However, NEC inquiries revealed irregularities, with some names not on the electoral register, some not wishing to be members and some entirely fictional. A number of court cases ensued and candidates were imposed through NEC intervention. A serious case concerned Mohammad Sarwar in Glasgow Govan who, after being elected, faced bribery charges (Criddle 1997a: 191–3). However, the 1997 result gave Labour a record number (nine) of non-white MPs

Despite OMOV the NEC has generally sought a greater influence than Central Office over selection, showing itself quite willing to veto local choices and 'parachute' in favourites, as in the Vauxhall by-election of June 1989 when

Kate Hoey was imposed on the CLP, despite members' desire for a black candidate. Central dominance increased in the run-up to the 1997 election. There was particular determination to find a seat for Tory-defector Alan Howarth, despite two failures to make local shortlists. Conversely, in Leeds North East the NEC refused to endorse the socialist Liz Davies, despite her coming from an all-women shortlist.

Further intimations of the tight central rein came with the proposed closed lists for the European elections. Rather than OMOV, Labour MEPs were to be required to go before selection committees in the eleven regions. There was a feeling amongst sitting MEPs that this would be used to root out those on the left, including the group who had openly opposed the Clause Four reforms.

Liberal Democrats Local associations are responsible for selecting candidates, who are drawn from a national approved list. Generally the party vaunts its federal structure and an emphasis on community politics has permitted considerable local autonomy. One woman (if available) must be on any shortlist of three. For the 1999 Euro-elections the party adopted 'zipped lists', consisting of alternating men and women.

Party policy-making: mass rule or iron law of oligarchy?

The ability to shape policy is probably the most significant index of power within a party. There are two extreme models: *top-down*, in which the mass obediently plays follow-my-leader; and *bottom-up*, where they see leaders as parliamentary delegates. The emergence of the local associations in the nineteenth century created fears of mass control. Ostrogorski's famous (1902) study sounded a dire warning that the parliamentary parties had created monsters that would soon undermine representative democracy. Others feared the reverse – that the masses would be denied influence. In the early twentieth century the German/Italian sociologist Roberto Michels enunciated his well-known **iron law of oligarchy**, postulating that within any mass party ineluctable sociological and psychological processes would result in domination by a small elite (Michels 1962). Various related factors influence internal power relationships, including the party's genesis, its constitution, its experience of government, its attitudes towards office and its leader's personality.

Lenin's method leads to this: the party organisation at first substitutes itself for the party as a whole. Then the central committee substitutes itself for the party organisation, and finally a single dictator substitutes himself for the central committee.

Leon Trotsky (1879–1940; Russian revolutionary), quoted in N. McInnes, *The Communist Parties of Western Europe* (1975: ch. 3)

Genesis Because the Conservative and Liberal parties originated as parliamentary groupings, the extra-parliamentary organizations were from the first seen as their handmaidens. There was never any reason to address the question of control; it remained within the provenance of the elite. Attempts by Joseph Chamberlain and Randolph Churchill to establish some degree of democratic control within their respective parties came to nothing. However, the conception, birth and growth of the Labour Party implied a quite different relationship. As the offspring of the trade union mammoth, the Labour Representation Committee was essentially subservient. Even the title 'leader' was denied in favour of 'chairman', who was co-equal with the NEC chair.

Party constitutions These formally *prescribe* the internal power structure. Like the country over which it has so long presided, the Conservative Party had no formal constitution but party literature has generally paid homage to the leader's supremacy. However, during the 1980s the party conference began to show some signs of greater assertiveness. Hague secured the endorsement of a formal constitution at a special March 1998 conference which established a governing board formed from the party's three sections. With an ethics committee and powers to expel MPs, it seemed largely designed to remove the taint of sleaze rather than limit the leader's power.

The Labour constitution imposes an ostensibly democratic pattern of authority, with three centres of policy formation: the PLP, the NEC and the annual conference. Policy, as contained in the *programme*, was to be determined by the annual conference on the basis of a two-thirds majority. In 1945, NEC chairman Harold Laski argued that if Attlee, as prime minister, attended the three-power peace conference at Potsdam his position should be approved by the NEC (an interpretation Attlee rejected; see McKenzie 1967: 330).

The authority of the conference declined from the 1950s (Minkin 1980). The six largest unions wielding their massive block votes generally supported the party line. However, as the union leadership moved to the left from the 1970s, fundamental tensions emerged. Beyond practical difficulties for the leadership, the block vote symbolized the union domination alleged by critics and thus became a key target of the modernizers. Reforms in September 1993 gave individual delegates each a share of the affiliated vote, the CLPs having delegates in proportion to their membership. An electoral college allocated 30 per cent of the conference vote to the CLPs and 70 per cent to the unions. This moved to parity in July 1995 when total CLP membership reached 300,000. Other constitutional reforms under Blair (such as Clause Four and NEC composition) have further strengthened the leadership.

The Liberal Party constitution was decentralized in 1983, giving a predominantly 'bottom-up' procedure (despised by Alliance partner David Owen as anarchy). The reality of party democracy was shown in 1986 when a defence resolution of the executive was defeated, leaving leader David Steel in some embarrassment. The Liberal Democrats preserved the 'bottom-up' constitution, making the federal conference sovereign. However, most conference resolutions are drawn up by the party's central Policy Committee.

The experience of government When a party assumes office its leader inherits the supreme powers of the Crown, and when ejected these clouds of glory may be trailed into opposition. This has given an advantage to Conservative leaders but, whenever they have experienced power, Labour leaders have also worn a halo of authority. However, such periods have been tantalizingly short-lived, punctuated by lengthy spells in the wilderness, when the steel discipline of office is softened in the heat of internal friction. However, the Conservative meltdown of 1997 suggests that a point can be reached when prolonged power breeds complacency.

Attitudes towards office Political parties mainly exist to gain office and leaders must frame their manifestos accordingly. If the followers share the hunger for office there will be little basis for disharmony. The traditional Conservative conviction that they are the chosen ensured that when displaced by Labour, the mass has loyally followed the inspiration of the leadership in radical policy revision. By contrast, the idea of some on the left that it is better to lose than compromise on principle often curbed Labour leaders' rights over policy. By 1997 the party hungered more for office than for pure socialism, enabling Blair to push through a radical modernization project. The party became voter-responsive rather than activist-orientated (Kavanagh 1998: 38). At the same time, under Major the Conservatives seemed to be losing the hunger for office, voicing their convictions over European integration regardless of electoral cost.

> Winning is the *sine qua non* and a lot of leeway must be allowed to a leader who is successful at winning.
>
> Ben Pimlott (historian and former Fabian chairman), quoted in the *Observer* (12 Jan. 1997)

The charisma factor Personalities matter in real-world politics. Labour's contentious policy revisionism in the 1950s and early 1960s in part reflected the combative character of Gaitskell, while the relative calm under Wilson can be largely attributed to his ability to pour liberal quantities of oil on the party's sea of troubles. The importance of personality was underlined by Thatcher, with her strident insistence that there was no alternative to her radical policies, while Major gave the appearance of dithering and weakness. Thatcher may have been the model for Blair, who stamped his personality on the party in despatching a number of sacred cows, including Clause Four, to the abattoir. The Social Democratic Party was dominated by the demonic presence of David Owen. Liberal Democrat leader Paddy Ashdown seemed to personify the new party. He personally jettisoned the policy of 'equidistance' between the two main parties, despite much distaste amongst some for 'snuggling up' to Labour.

A climate of oligarchy   Policy determination by the mass party, whether through conference resolutions or in some other way such as postal ballot, has been considered undemocratic because the views of activists may be at variance with those of the leader and 'still further removed from the mass of those who actually provide the vote' (Butler 1960: 3). McKenzie (1967: 635) argued that such fears were unnecessary, the imperatives of political life (electioneering and governing) providing a procrustean bed forcing parties to become oligarchic. Hence, although Labour's reforms in the early 1980s posed a threat to leaders, the modernization process diluted the mass voice by widening it beyond the local oligarchs (Seyd and Whiteley 1992: 218) and the 'highly pluralistic party with an institutional dispersal of power' was transformed in line with the Michels thesis (Shaw 1996: 219). *The Times* (21 Sept. 1997) was able to conclude that 'Mr Blair's New Labour has become the natural party of deference in which power flows from the top and only the reckless ask awkward questions'. In this model the leaders aim to bypass their own mass members to fashion their appeal to the wider electorate. We saw in chapter 9 how elections are increasingly conducted from the centre with mailshots and telephone canvassing. The paradoxical result of this is a concentration on the soft vote, those only weakly attached to parties and least interested in politics, parties becoming increasingly concerned with image rather than substance.

However, in discussing power relationships within the parties we have not addressed an all-important question. There is power behind the throne held by those who never draw up manifestos, fight elections or hold high office. This leads us deeper into the labyrinthine world of power.

Who Pays the Piper?

Money can try very hard to talk in politics. In 1997 wealthy businessman Sir James Goldsmith showed this by single-handedly forming the Referendum Party to fight the general election. At the same time northern millionaire Paul Sykes promised Conservative candidates up to £3,000 towards election expenses if they were prepared to repudiate their leader's 'wait and see' policy over the single currency; 237 took the wealthy man's shilling (*Guardian*, 30 April 1997). Fighting elections and maintaining an organization are increasingly expensive undertakings. Although parties are required to stick to constituency spending limits, these are routinely flouted by the increasingly centralized campaign techniques because there have been no national limits. More was spent during the 1997 campaign than any before. In the twelve months preceding the election, Conservatives and Labour accounted for £47 million while the Liberal Democrats weighed in with £3 million. Hence, today's parties cannot operate without vast funds, a hard reality raising some compelling questions about power and democracy. The classic distinction between parties and interest groups becomes blurred; the two are bound together by chains of gold.

Conservative Party

The funding of the Conservative Party is one of the mysteries of British politics. Until 1968 no accounts were published and when they did appear they were economical with ink. Although becoming more detailed in 1993 they continued to conceal the size of private donations. While the 1985 Companies Act obliged companies to declare political donations of over £200, it could take two years before such information surfaced. Ex-Party Treasurer Lord McAlpine admitted in the House of Lords to 'tons' of offshore accounts into which donations were paid (Harrison 1993) and the magazine *Business Age* reported some £200 million salted away in a 'slush fund' in three overseas tax havens (Fisher 1994). The party finally published accounts in November 1998 (see below).

Although much constituency work is directed towards fundraising, at critical points like general elections the broadly capitalist interests of Britain have reached for their wallets to achieve what has generally been regarded as a key requirement of successful capitalism – a Conservative government. The party chair and treasurer have the task of rattling the begging bowl before industry, but this was for long as difficult as fishing in a trout farm.

We need funds and I look to the City of London to give a lead in providing that support which as businessmen they should be prepared to give, in view of our efforts to make their business safe.

Appeal by Conservative leader Stanley Baldwin, in the *Daily Telegraph* (2 Feb. 1926)

The intermediaries In addition, various associations have existed for fundraising purposes.

- *The Economic League* was formed after the first world war by the ex-head of naval intelligence to raise party funds and propagate a 'Free enterprise' message. In addition, it compiled lists of 'subversives' and 'communists' to be blacked by employers and has been linked with the intelligence services in the fight against left-wing movements.
- *British United Industries* was formed after the second world war, again for the purpose of fundraising and propaganda.
- *Aims* (formerly Aims of Industry) is the best known of the fundraisers. It was established in 1942 by a group of businessmen and remained active. A celebrated Mr Cube campaign in 1949–50 featured a talking sugar lump who successfully saved Tate & Lyle from being dissolved in the thick collectivist tea of post-war nationalization.

> The CBI's character, and perhaps its main *raison d'être*, is geared to a dialogue with government . . . But it must be emphasised that the CBI is politically neutral.
>
> John Davies (CBI Director General), quoted in I. Gilmour, *The Body Politic* (1969: 351)

Party financing became central to the sleaze scandals of the 1990s. Ian Greer, a lobbyist involved in the cash-for-questions affair, claimed in October 1996 to have raised £750,000 for the party by encouraging donations from businessmen and clients over the previous ten years. He even alleged that ministers had approached him for help with their own election expenses (*The Times*, 7 Oct. 1996). However, there had also been some help, albeit small, for Labour, though shadow health secretary Chris Smith suggested that Greer was 'covering his back' in case of unfavourable publicity (Hamilton and Rufford 1996).

Party givers Not all donors use intermediaries in bestowing largesse; large companies can inject main line into the veins of the party. The merchant banks are especially important, their directors often being active within the party or its fundraising intermediaries. Almost half the corporate donations have come from banking, insurance, food, tobacco, drink and construction (Scott 1991: 147). Thus munchers of KP nuts, Hula Hoops, McCoy's Crisps, Penguins, McVitie's and Crawford's biscuits were themselves unwitting Conservative benefactors; between 1979 and 1993, United Biscuits, makers of these, headed the list of party givers with a total of £1,004,500. In addition, the party has encouraged personal donations with fundraising activities including dinners with ministers and dining clubs such as the Millennium and Premier (see p. 514). Membership fees need not be classed as political donations and range from £10,000 to £100,000. By 1996 a new generation of entrepreneurs who had thrived during the 1980s were coming to the aid of the party with a 25 per cent increase in donations, reducing its overdraft by £2 million to £12 million (*Sunday Times*, 21 May 1997).

Friends abroad A particularly sensitive issue for the Conservatives is the extent to which they have sought and received overseas donations, raising fears that British home and foreign policy may be compromised. A bruising encounter between party chairman Sir Norman Fowler and the Commons Home Affairs Committee in June 1993 revealed millions of pounds secretly donated by governments, or individuals close to them, and foreign businessmen. Some of these lived under a cloud of suspicion, one (Asil Nadir) fleeing the country to avoid prosecution for fraud. Although knowledge of this foreign largesse was confined to a select group at the top of the party hierarchy, Major General Sir Brian Wylde-Smith, for twelve years the party's fundraising director, disclosed that they had received £7 million from foreign backers before the 1992 general election (Harrison 1993). In his memoirs Lord McAlpine (1997) was to report how, a year after retiring as party treasurer, he was asked by John Major to solicit funds from a wealthy foreign businessman known for his past generosity. The result was a cheque for £500,000, the benefactor being identified as Greek shipping tycoon John Latsis (*The Times*, 3 March 1997). Donations from Hong Kong ranged from £100,000 to £200,000 and there were even donations from individuals involved in the Yugoslavian civil war, including an associate of human rights violator Radovan Karadžić (Fisher 1997). Mounting fears of foreign influence over policy led to reforms agreed at the March 1998 constitutional conference. The sources of donations over £5,000 were to be revealed and foreign donations rejected. However, in April 1998 party chairman Cecil Parkinson told the Neill inquiry into party funding that the threat of disclosure had caused overseas funding to dry up anyway (*Independent*, 23 April 1998).

Feathers and favours Donations arouse suspicion of policy rewards and even personal favours. Indeed, when unhappy with government policy, BA openly threatened to cut donations. Some were not surprised when United Biscuits chairman Sir Hector Lang, often described as Mrs Thatcher's favourite businessman, became Lord Lang upon retirement in 1990. The Honours (Prevention of Abuse) Act (1925) makes it a criminal offence to make party donations as an inducement to receiving an honour (following Lloyd George's 'selling' of honours) but in practice it is almost impossible to prove a connection. Lord Shackleton, former member of the Privy Council's Political Honours Scrutiny Committee, told the House of Lords that he believed honours were effectively being bought. From 1979, around 6 per cent of companies were making donations and they received about half of all knighthoods and peerages – statistically unlikely to be an accidental correlation (Bogdanor 1997a). The Labour Party alleged that between 1979 and 1992, eighteen life peerages and eighty-two knighthoods were shared between seventy-six companies donating over £17 million to Conservative coffers, often using 'front organizations'.

> Nobody gives money to a political party for nothing. They all want their feathers stroked from time to time . . . some . . . more often and more lovingly than others.
>
> Senior Conservative, quoted in the *Observer* (20 June 1993)

The privatization programme excited further allegations of rewards. It was claimed that eight merchant banks and stockbrokers, contributing a total of £1.4 million in party donations, gained the lion's share of the £1 billion fees paid to the City for advising on the flotations (*Sunday Times*, 17 Nov. 1991). Another source of rewards can be positions on prestigious quangos, offering political power to the unelected (see chapter 18).

Hard times Yet despite the rich veins of finance it is able to tap, the party complains of financial difficulties. When Margaret Thatcher appointed Lord McAlpine as party treasurer in August 1975 (he served until July 1990) the party was £500,000 in debt. By the early 1990s finances looked even more unhealthy (Whiteley et al. 1994). The 1992 campaign was the first for which it had to borrow from the banks, incurring a deficit of £19 million, much due to the exorbitant fees of the advertising agencies. It finished the 1997 campaign slightly better – only £10 million in the red.

The constituency source, which until the 1980s had provided 20–25 per cent of total funds, was also declining, a trend most marked in Conservative-held seats through a combination of alienation and atrophy (Pattie and Johnston 1996). Of even greater significance, the party began to lose its corporate donors. In November 1998 the list of benefactors giving donations over £5,000 duly appeared (though confined to funds received during the first eight months of Hague's leadership). With only thirty-three individual and corporate givers, it was modest compared with past levels of generosity, revealing a party forced to call upon personal loans and gifts from its own senior officers (*The Times*, 21 Nov. 1998). The change in the party's fortunes was, for Hague, a depressing straw in the political wind, the significance of which remained to be seen. It was largely explained by the loss of the party's own reputation as well as the increased confidence felt in New Labour's economic competence.

Labour Party

Traditionally Labour's funds came from the poorest section of society, the unions (since the Trade Union Act, 1913) collecting a political levy from individual members to form a political fund. In 1984 Conservative legislation requiring members to opt in, rather than out, of the levy made it more difficult to collect. This source was for long a political Achilles' heel, ever open to allegations of sinister union paymasters. As recently as 1996, William Hague, as Welsh Secretary, was alleging that the unions bought positions on Labour's NEC. Although the British Election Study revealed that voters' perception of unions as 'too powerful' had declined significantly from 77 per cent in 1979 to 30 per cent in 1992, Labour's modernizers were stung by the taunts. Repeating the new mantra of 'fairness not favours', they sought to loosen if not cut the embarrassing umbilicus. However, in turning from the devil they knew well they were obliged to court new ones: individual members, private corporations and wealthy benefactors.

The first produced a recruitment drive launched from the centre. The other entailed a search for new friends in the unfamiliar territory of the business world. Little could better symbolize the New Labour style. The Labour Business Plan was launched with high-profile dinners with party leaders. Donations came from companies including Pearson, Tate & Lyle, the Caparo Group and from wealthy individuals including (the late) Matthew Harding and David Sainsbury. There were also contributions from showbiz personalities such as Melvyn Bragg, Mick Hucknell, Lisa Stansfield, Eddie Izzard, Ben Elton and Jeremy Irons. By late 1996 the new sources were accounting for some 25 per cent of income, the party amassing assets of nearly £3 million (Fisher 1997). However, it could not escape the same kind of charges as were made against the

Conservatives; both Sainsbury and Bragg were ennobled within Labour's first year in office. Moreover, a great furore arose in November 1997 when the government reneged on a pre-election promise to ban tobacco advertising connected with sport by exempting Formula One motor racing. It emerged that motor racing mogul Bernie Ecclestone had donated £1 million to the party just prior to the election. Moreover, Labour had apparently requested a further £1 million from him just at the time the government was engaged in EU negotiations over the same issue. On the advice of Lord Nolan the donation was returned and an embarrassed premier 'apologized' on Sunday television.

Labour also began to operate a system of blind trusts whereby ministers were supposed to be unaware of who was donating to their private offices. These were denounced as evil by fundraiser Henry Drucker, alleging: 'I don't believe these people would have given a bean unless there were enough nods and winks that Tony was, of course, very grateful' (*Independent*, 30 April 1998). The potential for embarrassment reached bizarre heights when the *Observer* (20 Sept. 1998) revealed police recordings of a notorious London gang family dealing in drugs and murder boasting of large donations made to Labour to make things 'all right' for themselves.

However, although union donations were becoming less important (figure 11.3), they still formed the largest proportion of party income (54 per cent in 1995). Although Blair claimed that they accounted for less than 40 per cent, this was denied from the union side, which put the total figure at around 84 per cent, including the underwriting of the Business Plan (*Sunday Times*, 6 Oct. 1996). In 1997 the Amalgamated Engineering and Electrical Union showed that it still had muscle by withholding £250,000 from the election fund as a protest against the parachuting of candidates into union seats, and in February 1998 the party's

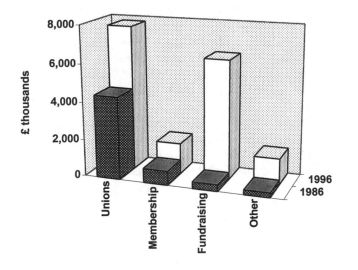

Figure 11.3
Labour Party funding sources, 1986 and 1996.

Source: Data from Labour Party NEC reports.

largest benefactors (UNISON, the Transport and General and the GMB general union) announced cuts of £400,000 in donations because of disquiet over the government's policy direction (*Independent*, 23 Feb. 1998). With debts of £3.5 million by 1998, plus an overdraft of £4.75 million for a £23-million election campaign, Labour could hardly ignore the implications of these moves.

Liberal Democrats

The gargantuan financial appetites of the two major parties leave a centre party with little potential sustenance. Liberal Democrats rely heavily on members' donations and fundraising activities. They fight lean campaigns and favour state funding of political parties.

Regulating the paymasters

In 1994, in response to scandals and misgivings, the Commons Conservative-dominated Home Affairs Committee recommended regulating donations but Major refused Lord Nolan's request to inquire into this area (*Guardian*, 12 May 1995). However, Labour promised reform. This was begun in April 1998 by Lord Neill's Committee on Standards in Public Life. Its report in October 1998, with 100 recommendations, called for an end to the culture of secrecy, with tough penalties, including imprisonment. Foreign donations should be banned, while national donations above £5,000, and local donations over £1,000, should be declared on an open register. Although no restriction was proposed on the size of individual donations, national general election spending should be limited to £20 million per party, with fines for transgressors. Restrictions would also apply on election spending for the new provincial assemblies. In addition, the report recommended that campaigning by pressure groups on behalf of parties should be limited to £1 million, 'benefits in kind' (such as loan of offices) should be declared, blind trusts should be abolished and a special scrutiny process should guard against the selling of honours. An independent electoral commission should police the system.

However, reforms such as these cannot completely eliminate the problems that arise when finance and politics meet. Wealthy givers will still be sought by parties and rules can be bent or evaded. For many reformists, such as Charter 88, and the Houghton Committee in 1976, only state funding (as in continental democracies and Canada) will end questionable practices and reduce the impression that influence can be bought.

State funding

State funding would end this link between wealth and political power. It would also allow the state to place social obligations on political parties. Indeed there is already some public funding, including free delivery of one election leaflet per candidate and free party political broadcasts. State funding also enables opposition parties to function at Westminster (£3,254 for every seat won plus £7.04 for every 200 votes). In addition, indirect state aid during the 1992–7 parliament amounted to some £17 million through postage and research costs alone.

Yet state funding is no panacea and raises new questions. What of the smaller parties: what would be the formula for determining the level of funding? Would frivolous parties be eligible? Should the state finance dark forces wishing to undermine democracy or persecute minorities? Moreover, as the climate of sleaze and obfuscation showed, it would be difficult to monitor the system. There is also a fundamental question of the freedom to use one's money according to personal choice. And should state funding exceed the amount raised by the party itself?

The Neill committee ruled out large-scale public funding (though recommending that money paid to opposition parties should be increased to £4.8 million). However, one exception was made for referendum campaigns, which should receive public funding, with both sides sharing £1.2 million, to prevent the government from using public funds to push its own case.

Masses, Leaders and Powers behind Thrones

As developments conspire to reduce the role and importance of the mass membership in the British parties, the iron law of oligarchy retains a compelling significance. However, it is clear that the debate over power does not end with the consideration of internal organization. The imperatives of finance mean that there are crucial sources of influence outside the formal party structure. Although for much of the post-war period these were stable, the unions financing Labour and capital financing the Conservatives, the rise of New Labour introduced a new fluidity into the balance of power in today's society. In the next section we move further into the heart of political power by focusing on the central institutions of the state.

Key points

- Modern political parties consist of three elements: a parliamentary cadre, a bureaucracy and a mass membership.
- The question of where the power lies is an important subject for analysis. Michels's 'iron law of oligarchy' asserts that the mass will always fall under a small elite.
- Historically the Conservatives have been less internally democratic than Labour or the Liberal Democrats, allowing greater authority to the leader in patronage, organization and policy-making.
- However, the 1980s and 1990s saw Labour leaders tightening their grip over the mass.

- The Conservative Party has traditionally shown greater internal cohesion than any other. This appeared to have broken down by the 1990s.
- The increasing need for funds makes parties dependent on economic interests and raises profound questions about the public interest and modern democracy.

Review your understanding of the following terms and concepts

affiliated association
all-women shortlist
block vote
candidate selection
Conservative Central
   Office
constituency association

faction
ginger group
interest aggregation
iron law of oligarchy
NEC
party bureaucracy
party conference

party executive
patronage
sponsorship
tendency
ward association

Assignment

Study the extract from *The Economist* on p. 331 and answer the following questions.

		Mark (%)
1	How realistic is William Hague's ambition to end party wrangling over the single European currency with a party referendum?	20
2	Assess the significance of fringe meetings at party conferences.	20
3	Does the extract support the view that the Conservative Party had recovered from its May 1997 disaster?	20
4	What if Kenneth Clarke had become leader of the Conservative Party after Major? Describe your imaginary picture of the 1998 party conference.	40

Questions for discussion

1 Explain how and why parties have varied their methods of appointing leaders.
2 Discuss whether internal party democracy is a necessary condition of a democratic state.
3 What factors have given the Conservative Party its longevity?
4 Compare and contrast the security of tenure of Labour and Conservative party leaders.

The Tories

Incontinent

BOURNEMOUTH

As the Tories gathered in Bournemouth this week, opinion polls showed them sinking to a new low.

William Hague is training for a judo black belt. He may need it. This week's party conference highlighted the continuing divisions within his party, and saw the Tories fall to a record low in the opinion polls. Just 23% of the public now say they would vote Tory at the next election—down from 31% at the last election.

The cause of the row was—as ever—the single European currency. Mr Hague's strategy is to tie the party to a firm policy and so close off debate. After a ballot of members, the party is pledged to oppose abolishing the pound for another parliament—up to nine years. But will a clear policy end the squabbling? It had little effect this week. On the fringes of the conference, prominent Europhiles such as Michael Heseltine and Kenneth Clarke continued to cause trouble.

And Theresa Villiers, a candidate in the European elections, was applauded for attacking "yesterday's men talking yesterday's politics"—code for Messrs Clarke and Heseltine.

The ballot has changed the rules. The Tory policy on the euro, for better or for worse, is now fixed, so there is no longer a policy prize to fight for. And a clear policy on the euro will also make clear who is deviating from the party line.

Europhiles are obviously less comfortable with the new policy. Yet even as they complained about the ballot, some were beginning to shift the fight away from the euro and on to broader European issues. At Mr Clarke's main fringe meeting, he argued for a Britain at the heart of Europe, not for British membership of the single currency. His theme was echoed by Mr Heseltine.

The Economist, 10 Oct. 1998

---

5 'Too much power for constituency associations in candidate selection undermines party government.' Discuss.

6 How realistic is it to imagine that party policies can be made by means of a 'bottom-up' process?

7 'The financing of the British parties undermines the democratic process.' Discuss.

8 Examine the pros and cons of all-women shortlists in candidate selection.

9 Assess the value of the annual party conference.

10 'Groupings within parties create dysfunctional tensions.' Discuss.

Topic for debate

This house believes that the Conservative Party is no longer the 'natural party of government'.

Further reading

See also reading for chapter 10.

Bogdanor, V. (1981) *The People and the Party System*.
Critical view of party politics.

McKenzie, R. (1967) *British Political Parties* (first published 1955).
Presents thesis that political constraints force parties to resemble each other.

Michels, R. (1962) *Political Parties* (first published 1911).
Classic statement of 'iron law of oligarchy'.

Muller, W. D. (1977) *The Kept Men*.
Examines trade union sponsorship of parliamentary candidates.

Peele, G. (1991) *British Party Politics: Competing for Power in the 1990s*.
Focuses on the problems of party management and leadership, techniques for marketing parties and party organization.

Riddell, P. (1993) *Honest Opportunism: The Rise of the Career Politician*.
Charts the changing character of the parliamentary parties.

Seyd, P. and Whiteley, P. (1992) *Labour's Grass Roots*; and Whiteley, P., Richardson, J. and Seyd, P. (1994) *True Blues: The Politics of Conservative Party Membership*.
Fascinating empirical analyses of mass memberships.

Willetts, D. (1996) *Blair's Gurus*.
Lively right-wing challenge to a battery of New Labour thinkers (Hutton, Marquand, Kay et al.).

For light relief

Geoffrey Archer, *First Among Equals*.
Ambitious politician attempts to climb the greasy party pole.

Wilfred Fienburgh, *No Love for Johnnie*.
Love, romance and committee meetings in the Labour Party (also a film).

Chris Mullin, *A Very British Coup*.
Labour MP explores (old) Labour's problems in dealing with the Establishment.

Jim Wilson, *The Labour Man*.
Comic novel. Labour has a majority of one, and all depends on Harry Beamish, who, tortured by his socialist ideals and the contradiction between power and honour, disappears.

On the net

See chapter 10.

Part III

Government at the Centre

Significantly we do not arrive at the formal centre of British government until the middle of the book. This underlines the fact that the comings and goings of the high and the mighty by no means represent the whole of the political story. Here we address the most central and exhilarating concepts in politics – official power; who holds it, who uses it, and who is able to influence its exercise. Our search takes us through the most ornate institutions of government (the monarchy and Parliament) to the heart of the Westminster/Whitehall complex, the Cabinet, the prime minister and the higher civil service. Finally, we delve even deeper into the mysteries of power by seeking sources of influence lying below the surface of ministerial pomp in the more shadowy recesses of political life. We shall find that although all may not be as it seems, nothing is without significance; every cam and cog in the machinery of state has a function and our task is to try to discover what that is.

Chapter Twelve

Pomp and Circumstance: the Living Dead of the Constitution

In this chapter we meet the more ornate parts of the constitution, the parts visitors come to see and which are shown on the postcards they send home. These include the monarchy with its robes, jewels and golden coaches, and the Palace of Westminster housing the two chambers of Parliament – the House of Lords and the House of Commons. Here we see much flummery lovingly preserved from bygone ages, a celebration of the much-vaunted continuity of the British constitution. However, although as lifeless as the waxworks at Madame Tussaud's, like the mystic ritual of high church and courts, the ceremonial is by no means without significance. It induces respect and reverence for authority; it is the living dead of the constitution.

The physical setting

Parliament formally comprises the monarchy, House of Lords and House of Commons, with a very tangible presence as the picturesque Palace of Westminster. One of the major landmarks of London, situated grandly on the bank of the Thames at the end of Whitehall, it is a popular tourist destination, around a million visitors a year queuing to be conducted on guided tours and purchase trinkets marked with the prestigious portcullis logo (also found on its official notepaper). The Commons and the Lords have a cathedral-like aura, intimidating all but the initiated. Around them a labyrinth of corridors, quadrangles and staircases leads to offices, committee rooms, smoking-rooms, tea-rooms and of course bars. MPs can be seen variously talking in intimate clusters, meeting groups of eager constituents, playing host to interest-group representatives or lobbyists, or lying low in places of refreshment trying to avoid such encounters.

The chambers are surprisingly small and could not seat all members if they were to descend simultaneously. This is quite deliberate; the opportunity to rebuild was presented by the German Luftwaffe in 1941 but the decision was taken to retain the sense of intimacy conducive to debate. Unlike most chambers, the benches are arrayed in a confrontational manner (figure 12.1) and, in the Commons, the front ranks are two sword's lengths apart, commemorating an age when the thrust and parry of debate could be more than figurative.

The evolution of Parliament

The three elements of Parliament represent the great estates of the realm which have fought over the centuries for control of the state: the Crown, the aristocracy and the common people. Its origins lie in the assembly of Anglo-Saxon kings which met as the *Witangemot*. In Norman times kings governed assisted only by their officials, although the country was divided into territorial units

Figure 12.1
Chamber of the House of Commons.

ruled by barons whom the kings would summon as the *Magnum Concilium* for discussion, advice and to raise money. The barons demanded more control, securing this through the Magna Carta signed at Runnymede in 1215. Herein lies the origin of the House of Lords.

The House of Commons was conceived in the kingly practice, from the thirteenth century, of calling additional meetings of the less-important local representatives, the commoners (knights from the shires and burgesses from the incorporated towns), as a further source of revenue. They would assemble humbly before the monarch, who would tell them how much was required and dispatch them to find it, leaving the aristocracy to discuss important matters of state. However, the Commons, recognizing its potential power, began making demands. When expensive wars forced Edward III (1327–77) to summon frequent parliaments, they took the opportunity to attach a list of reforms when accepting the tax demands. At the beginning of the fifteenth century Henry IV agreed that grants of money would only be initiated in the Commons, recognizing the lower house as part of Parliament.

This hold over the purse-strings saw the gradual erosion of the monarch's position. Coming soon after the profligate Henry VIII (1509–47), Elizabeth I (1558–1603) recognized the reality and was careful to court Parliament. However, the Stuarts lacked the Tudors' realism and Charles I sought to govern without parliamentary consent by raising taxes directly from towns ('ship money'). By this time the Commons had become powerful enough to oppose him and events led to the Civil War (1642–6) between the Royalists (Cavaliers) and the parliamentarians (Roundheads). It resulted in Charles losing not just the Crown but a head upon which to rest it. Britain entered upon a brief period as a **republic** (1649–60) with the Puritan Oliver Cromwell supreme as 'Lord Protector'.

The Restoration in 1660 saw Charles II return in glory from exile but things were to be different. He was a *constitutional monarch*, constrained by Parliament. The anniversary of his father's execution was marked by a grizzly ceremony in which Cromwell's disinterred corpse was hung on the infamous gallows at Tyburn. Yet James II could not accept the limitations and further skirmishes culminated in the Glorious Revolution of 1688, which placed William (of Orange) and Mary (daughter of James II) on the English throne, their powers clearly restricted in the 1689 Bill of Rights. It was not until the 1701 Act of Settlement that the subordinate position of the monarchy was satisfactorily established, made easier by the fact that the Hanoverian line (established in 1714) had little interest in British affairs.

> I would rather hew wood than be a king under the condition of the king of England.
>
> Charles X of France (1757–1836)

The upper house had also been abolished during the republic and was reinstated at the Restoration. In the 1689 settlement the Commons concerned itself with commerce while the Lords attended to affairs of state, including foreign policy, subject to the convention that money supply was in the sole gift of the Commons. However, the Commons remained under the control of aristocratic and royal factions, both exercising a corrupt influence on elections and nominations. It was the great nineteenth-century Reform Acts that delivered the *coup de grâce*, through the moral authority given to the Commons by the popular vote.

Yet the message was not immediately clear to their lordships. In 1883 they rejected the second Irish Home Rule Bill and the reforming Liberal government of 1905 found eighteen of its bills rejected. Matters came to a head when Chancellor Lloyd George, needing £16 million in extra revenue to finance the planned social programme as well as build *Dreadnought* battleships, determined that the money should come principally from taxing the landed interests, against whom he had been conducting a campaign. His 1909 'People's Budget' was rejected by the Lords, precipitating a constitutional crisis in which a reluctant monarch, weakened by 'four gargantuan meals a day together with endless wine, brandy, whisky and cigars' (Cross 1963: 106), was told he might be forced to create sufficient new government-supporting peers to swamp their lordships' opposition. The outcome was the 1911 Parliament Act, which not only legalized the convention regarding financial legislation but reduced the Lords' veto over other legislation to a power to delay for two years (shortened to a year in 1949 by the Labour government, nearing the end of its life and fearful of the fate of its steel nationalization bill).

The Monarchy

Constitutional monarchy means that although the Queen may be said to *reign*, she does not *rule*. Perhaps the monarchy's last dying gasps were heard under Victoria. Initially influenced by her consort Albert (who took his authority seriously) and later encouraged by the flattering Disraeli, she made several efforts to exert the royal prerogative. It was the lot of the austere Gladstone to school the Queen in her role and cut the modern pattern of British democratic kingship (Magnus 1963: 42–7). Today the monarch formally continues to hold hundreds of prerogative powers, the extent and scope of which are largely determined by convention. They range widely, covering appointments, legislation, emergency powers, and summoning and proroguing Parliament, but are generally exercised on advice (usually prime ministerial) and conflict has been rare during the twentieth century.

Why study the monarchy? Some commentaries on British politics and sociology omit the monarchy. This may be intended to betoken a jettisoning of meaningless symbolism in order to focus on the world of reality but it is a mistake, betraying a short-sighted and superficial vision. The monarchy affects modern politics by being a significant element in political culture.

The use of the Queen, in a dignified capacity, is incalculable. Without her in England, the present English government would fail and pass away.

Walter Bagehot, *The English Constitution* (1867: ch. 2)

Characteristics of the monarchy today

Today Buckingham Palace, the main royal residence, stands at the end of the Mall in some 40 acres of gardens. Together with Horse Guards' Parade, Westminster Abbey and the Palace of Westminster, all within a cannon's shot of each other, it is part of a baroque Disneyland of the past, gradually becoming overgrown by a towering office-block jungle. Inside the palace, courtiers and flunkeys, with titles and sometimes costumes of a bygone age, perform the tasks of running the monarchy industry. Many are themselves nobly born and treasure their families' links with the sovereign, passing the positions down through the generations. Today's monarchy is distinguished by certain characteristics.

Hereditary No one votes for the British Head of State. Although faltering from time to time, the succession is based on inheritance, Elizabeth II being the fortieth monarch since the Norman Conquest.

Ceremony While Britain is not alone as a constitutional monarchy (Luxembourg, the Netherlands, Belgium, Spain, Sweden, Denmark and Norway are the same), it is unique in the degree to which the pomp and **ceremonial** have been preserved. (The Scandinavian royals have been slightingly dubbed 'bicycling monarchies' because of their exorcism of ostentation.) The British monarchy, although never able to match the French in its extravagant prime, can on great occasions in the royal life-cycle (births, weddings and funerals) reach a scale only matched in Hollywood epics.

Political neutrality Although informed on a weekly basis by the prime minister, the Queen remains above the political fray. Like all members of the aristocracy, she does not vote, neither is she expected to express partisan opinions.

Familial Like the Ewings of Dallas or the Archers of Ambridge, the Windsors of London present to the public an extended family supported by a galaxy of bit players. Indeed, the Queen was faced with a similar challenge to that of Snow White's mother, her personal popularity (measured as 'the member of the royal family you would most like to meet') falling from 34 per cent in 1981 to 19 per cent in 1987, while that of the Princess of Wales soared.

Expense The monarchy does not come cheap. In 1761 George III agreed to surrender the income from the Crown Estate (worth some £95 million a year today) in exchange for a regular grant from Parliament – the Civil List – to cover expenditure relating to the monarch's official duties. Although remaining constant for a considerable time, it was revised under Elizabeth II to keep pace with inflation (set at £7.9 million in 1990 for a period of up to ten years). Other expenses include the upkeep of five palaces and the travel costs of up to 2,500 official engagements annually, which are met by Grants-in-Aid from Parliament. One of the most ostentatious sources of expenditure was the royal yacht

Britannia, which, in addition to normal annual running costs of some £2 million, required a £5-million refit every three years. It was not replaced under the 1997 Labour government. In addition there is the Privy Purse, primarily used to meet official expenditure not met from the Civil List.

The Queen's private expenditure is met from her own considerable personal fortune, its precise size subject to much speculation. Estimates of £100 million and upwards in 1993 were said by the Lord Chamberlain to be 'grossly overstated'. Although her property includes two royal residences, Sandringham and Balmoral, certain 'inalienable' items are held not as private property but on behalf of the nation (though most of the nation will never see them). These include the internationally renowned art collection, heirlooms in the Queen's jewellery collection and the Crown Jewels.

For long the Queen's income was exempt from tax and death duties, giving her a touch similar to that of King Midas and enabling her to outdistance all aristocratic rivals (some of whom, even after the second world war, were actually richer than the king). While they were collecting the tickets for the roller-coasters and zoos in their estates, the wealth in the royal coffers continued to swell. In November 1992, however, part of Windsor Castle (which was not insured) was destroyed by fire and the Conservative government's immediate response was to shoulder the £50-million repair burden. Such uncharacteristic generosity with taxpayers' money provoked controversy and it was announced that from 1993 the Queen would join her subjects as clients of her tax inspectors. The money for the restoration would be raised by opening Buckingham Palace to a fee-paying public. In addition, the Civil List would be cut to the bone (table 12.1), leaving only the Queen herself, the Duke of Edinburgh and the Queen Mother. A city accountant replaced the aristocratic appointee as guardian of the royal finances.

Table 12.1 The Civil List: parliamentary annuities paid to the royal family (1997)

Name	Amount
Not repaid by the Queen	
HM Queen Elizabeth the Queen Mother	643,000
HRH The Duke of Edinburgh	359,000
Repaid by the Queen	
HRH The Duke of York	249,000
HRH The Prince Edward	96,000
HRH The Princess Royal	228,000
HRH The Princess Margaret	219,000
HRH Princess Alice, Duchess of Gloucester	87,000
TRH The Duke and Duchess of Gloucester	
TRH The Duke and Duchess of Kent ⎫	
HRH Princess Alexandra ⎬	636,000
Hon Lady Ogilvy ⎭	

Popularity Before the second world war, shaken by the abdication crisis, the future of the monarchy was uncertain but the post-war era, with the coronation, weddings, many royal offspring and even dramatic marital disasters, saw the public appetite for its dignified constitution grow to gargantuan dimensions. In addition to the tabloid reporting, quality newspapers carried the 'Court Circular'. Despite the travails of the 'Royals', a raucously vulgar television debate in January 1997 found around 2.5 million telephone callers voicing their support.

> If Her Majesty stood for Parliament – if the Tory Party had any sense and made her its leader instead of that grammar school twit Heath – us Tories, mate, would win every election we went in for.
>
> Alf Garnett in Johnny Speight's TV series *Till Death us do Part*

The functions of the monarchy

The monarch's functions are both practical and symbolic, including the following.

Ceremonial The expectations of British kingcraft were virtually defined by Walter Bagehot in 1867. He argued that 'the masses of Englishmen are not fit for an elective government; if they knew how near they were to it, they would be surprised and almost tremble' (1963: 97). The monarchy was the keystone in the dignified facade concealing real processes of government from the uncomprehending masses (particularly women).

Symbol of national unity As a tangible object of veneration the monarch can symbolize the unity of society in a way that a party leader cannot. Patriotism can become xenophobia and it may be prudent if it can be channelled off in support of a constitutional icon.

Head of the armed forces Members of the royal family frequently hold ceremonial military ranks and the armed forces and police are constitutionally servants of the Crown, supposedly symbolizing their independence from politics.

Head of the Commonwealth This is an area where the Queen's authority is not controlled by the prime minister. Indeed, it was widely reported in 1987 that she was displeased by Thatcher's opposition to sanctions against apartheid South Africa.

Formal head of state Monarchy or not, any system of government requires a large element of formality, from entertaining foreign leaders to opening hospitals and presenting awards. Without a sovereign the role falls on elected leaders, perhaps fattening their egos or removing them from real politics.

Fidei defensor In Britain the Reformation established the Anglican Church with the monarch at its head as defender of the faith. Many royal ceremonies have a religious nature, including the coronation itself. However, with increasing multiculturalism Prince Charles has spoken of being the defender of the *faiths*.

Virtual regality It can be argued that the royal family can add colour to the lives of people with otherwise drab existences, thereby helping to maintain social stability.

Moral leadership The presentation of the monarchy in this way has been seen as a basis for giving the public a moral example for family life. The role was to become an absurdity as the Queen's children entered into a succession of failed marriages and courted other scandals (see below).

The throne behind the power Experience can make a monarch a source of wisdom. Although believing a republic had insinuated itself beneath the folds of a monarchy, Bagehot asserted a famous trio of royal rights: to be consulted, to encourage and to warn. In 1884 even Gladstone formally thanked Queen Victoria for her 'wise, gracious and steady exercise of influence' (Magnus 1963). By 1998, Elizabeth II had reigned for forty-five years with ten different prime ministers, giving her more experience of public life than any other political figure. This influence is likely to be greatest over issues not fundamental to party ideology (Bogdanor 1996a), particularly the Commonwealth, a point borne out by James Callaghan:

> the Queen's initiative on Rhodesia [when she openly disapproved of Ian Smith's declaration of UDI] was a perfect illustration of how and when the Monarch could effectively intervene to advise and encourage her Ministers from her own wide experience and with complete constitutional propriety. (Callaghan 1987: 382)

Moreover, in conditions of constitutional crisis powers may go beyond Bagehot's modest assessment. Few would deny that the monarch would be justified in intervening if events 'subverted the democratic basis of the Constitution' (Jennings 1959: 412). However, even in less dramatic circumstances the powers to dissolve Parliament and appoint the prime minister could become real. Although no prime ministerial dissolution request has been refused since before the 1832 Reform Act, this could happen if, in the words of Sir Alan Lascelles (former private secretary to George VI and Elizabeth II), 'the existing Parliament was still vital, viable and capable of doing its job' or if the monarch 'could rely on finding another prime minister who could [govern] for a reasonable period, with a working majority in the House of Commons' (Hennessy 1994). Although outgoing prime ministers will advise, this is informal advice that may be rejected rather than formal advice that must be followed. A judgement might be made of the national interest against the political interest of the parties. Peter Hennessy (1994) suggests that since 1949 the possibility of such powers being used has loomed on at least five occasions: in the spring of 1950 when the general election cut Attlee's majority from 146 to 6; in July 1953 when Churchill and Eden were seriously ill; in January 1957 following Eden's post-Suez resignation; in October 1963 following Macmillan's resignation, and in March 1974 when the defeated Heath attempted to do a deal with the Liberals.

The hollow crown

While supporters of monarchy extol its virtues and agnostics dismiss it as harmless sideshow, republicans point to more disturbing aspects.

Out of touch The life experience of the Queen, despite her known enthusiasm for *Coronation Street*, can hardly be said to have brought her into contact with the feelings of ordinary people. Her personal circle has remained largely within the aristocracy. According to a BBC report (25 Feb. 1998) Prince Charles apparently managed to complete a nine-day trip round Central Asia in 1996 without once saying hello to the small press party with him.

> Kings are not born, they are made by artificial hallucination.
>
> George Bernard Shaw, *Man and Superman* (1905)

Vulgarization If Bagehot were to return he would have cause to rue the day he praised the virtues of royal ceremonial. Today the masses gape through the vulgarizing lens of the tabloid press, spurred by the money-making ethic of the media barons. These were to become obsessed with royalty, seeking to report with astonishingly poor taste and monotony their most intimate comings and goings, reducing them through cloying, over-familiar diminutives ('Andy' and 'Fergie', with *Private Eye* long referring to the Queen unregally as 'Brenda'). The 'Royals' have been elevated to the status of show-biz celebrities and hounded all over the world by the *paparazzi*, aptly named the 'rat-pack'. The intense scrutiny led the Queen to label 1992 in her Christmas message her *annus horribilis*.

Falling popularity According to one opinion poll, less than half the population support the monarchy; the proportion thinking the country would be worse off without the Royals fell from 70 per cent in 1994 to 48 per cent in 1997 (*Guardian*, 12 Aug. 1997). This issue was soon to be raised to white heat with the shocking death of Diana, Princess of Wales.

A dysfunctional family The idea that the royal family could exert an uplifting moral force became almost risible. In an earlier era Princess Margaret had denied herself marriage to Group Captain Peter Townsend because he was divorced, yet by 1996 she and three of the Queen's children were themselves divorced. Moreover, the romance that had enchanted millions disintegrated in a moral morass in 1992 when first the 'Camillagate' and then the 'Squidgygate' tapes allowed the world to hear the fairytale couple murmuring sweet nothings to other than each other into their mobile phones. The public who had cheered along the wedding route were to discover that the royal establishment had allowed the heir apparent to make a cynical marriage for the purpose of royal procreation. Even former Archbishop of Canterbury Robert Runcie was to disclose that he too had known of Charles's relationship with his mistress, Camilla Parker-Bowles, sitting in row three as he conducted the glittering ceremony in Westminster Abbey (Holden 1997).

Because we do not have the guts to sweep the monarchy away, we shall do the only thing we dare. We shall mock them until they wish they had never been born.

David Hare, playwright and polemicist, in the *Guardian* (24 May 1993)

Democracy as deception: **panem et circenses** Bagehot's views reflected a widespread elite fear of the extending franchise but, where J. S. Mill argued for more political education, he preferred constitutional sleight of hand. Like the emperors of imperial Rome, the elite would provide bread and circuses to divert popular attention from affairs of state. However, a political culture that values deception is one that can tolerate secrecy and even lies.

Legitimates inequality Unlike other constitutional monarchies, Britain's does not stand alone; it is the tip of an aristocratic iceberg of inherited wealth and titles, the survival of which is one of the political wonders of the world. This legitimates elitism and maldistribution of wealth, helping to keep the social soil fertile for capitalism.

Well, what are you socialists going to do about me?

George V to Ramsay MacDonald, when he first presented himself at Buckingham Palace (1924)

A neutrality myth? Finally, the convention of political neutrality is open to question. It is partly a consequence of the two-party system: rarely has the sovereign actually had to exercise discretion in the choice of prime minister or the dissolution of Parliament. However, royal leanings can be discerned. Disraeli's 'one nation' brand of Conservatism made the Crown one of its symbols. To be a patriotic member of society entailed support for the Crown, loyalty which could be expressed by voting Conservative. Indeed, the Queen is head of the Anglican Church, long described as the Conservative Party at prayer.

Things seemed to change with the New Right agenda. Legend has it that, as a student at Cambridge, Prince Charles asked the Master of Trinity if he could join the university Labour club and in 1988 he criticized Conservative social policy, earning a rebuke from Norman Tebbit, who alleged that his sympathy for the unemployed stemmed from his lack of a job. He also set up a Trust to help the young urban unemployed and, when Labour came to power in 1997, wrote to Blair noting their shared agenda. Moreover, the *Sun* reported the Queen inviting the 'Blair kids' to join princes William and Harry at Balmoral. Former Australian prime minister Bob Hawke disclosed that the Queen had difficult relations with Margaret Thatcher on matters of domestic policy and Ben Pimlott's

1996 biography prompted tabloid headlines: 'The Queen's a Lefty'. Princess Diana was reported by a Paris journalist to have described the government's landmines' policy as 'hopeless'.

> Peter Mandelson: You're a secret Blairite.
> Prince Charles: I gather Mr Blair is a secret me.
>
> *Sunday Times* (15 June 1997)

Whither the monarchy?

Death of a princess The monarchy debate was thrust to the front pages with the death of Princess Diana. She had spoken of being the queen of people's hearts and her funeral became her tragic coronation, provoking an unprecedented mass outpouring of grief. Yet this was no demonstration of love of royalty. Many were offended by what was seen as the family's slow response to the public mood. As the tide of flowers engulfed the railings around Buckingham Palace, protocol forbade the flying of the flag at half-mast and the royal family remained at Balmoral. Only after government intervention was a public rather than a private funeral agreed and, even here, resting the coffin on a gun carriage seemed inappropriate.

A people's princess: flowers left by mourners at the gates of Buckingham Palace after the death of Princess Diana

Photo: Times Newspapers Ltd

While the royal family tried to reclaim Princess Diana in death, repeats of her astonishingly frank 1995 *Panorama* interview reminded people of her unhappiness. She had confronted the monarchy with the values of the late twentieth century while, at the same time, exposing a degree of hypocrisy. Rejected and effectively banished on her divorce, stripped of her royal rank, she became 'a totem of protest against that ringfenced elite that has quietly run Britain from gentlemen's clubs and secret societies' (Holden 1997). Whether the monarchy should be abolished or reformed, few could imagine it remaining unchanged.

Abolition While abolition, and even execution, has been the principal basis for constitutional evolution in some countries (until the first world war monarchy was prevalent throughout Europe), Britain's relatively smooth transition to democracy has never produced a sustained call for republicanism. Although the 1997 Labour government's wide-ranging constitutional reform programme implied republicanism, the events surrounding the death of Princess Diana changed the climate. Indeed, during the week of crisis, Blair, sensitive to the public mood, moved adroitly and effectively to rescue the institution. There was even talk of Labour spin doctors advising the Queen how to save the day and fears that she would be booed at the funeral were allayed.

Attitudes to the monarchy after the death of Princess Diana

Which of these options for the monarchy would you prefer?
Continue in its present form: 12%
Continue but be modernized: 74%
Be replaced with a republic when Queen dies: 5%
Be replaced with a republic immediately: 7%

Observer/ICM poll in the *Guardian* (17 Sept. 1997)

Reform: New Labour, New Monarchy? Princess Diana was no republican; she herself had a hereditary title and wanted her son to be king. However, she had begun to forge a new and popular style suggesting that the institution could be modernized. What are the alternatives?

> She was always trying to get across to people like us.
>
> East London girl, on Princess Diana, quoted by Simon Jenkins in *The Times* (3 Sept. 1997)

- *A bicycling monarchy*. A scaling down to Dutch or Scandinavian proportions would entail less ostentation and less attention to 'minor Royals'. Jack Straw, as Labour's home affairs spokesman, had affirmed such a vision. Yet for many this would destroy the magic.
- *A hands-on monarchy*. Princess Diana's style was to pay more attention to meeting ordinary people while retaining the glitter. The personal frailty and humanity she displayed revealed a public longing for a more humane and caring monarchy. Although this approach did not meet with Palace approval, the Queen's eve-of-funeral broadcast declared that 'lessons would be learned'. However, such a transformation might prove difficult for a family schooled in the art of the stiff upper lip rather than the gentle touch.

- *A fresh-start monarchy.* With Prince Charles's rehabilitation by no means certain, some have seen Prince William as the great hope. Robbed of his mother and with her looks, he carried her imprimatur. There was considerable popular approval for such a move, 53 per cent of those polled in September 1997 feeling that the crown should pass to Prince William (only 38 per cent preferring Prince Charles; *Guardian,* 17 Sept. 1997). While this could set the republican cause back a generation, it would require a self-denying ordinance from Charles. This appeared unlikely as the royal family sought, with the aid of spin doctors, to rehabilitate itself throughout 1998. Indeed, when Prince Charles held his fiftieth birthday party, Camilla Parker-Bowles was able to act as hostess.

In defence of monarchy

It does not necessarily follow that there is no place for constitutional monarchy in the modern world. In a democracy, it is generally good for politicians to be kept down to size. They are supposed to represent the interests of others and should be restrained from self-aggrandizement. Thatcher's style in the late 1980s was criticized by some as inappropriately imperious and usurping the role of the real queen. Without a monarchy some other institution would be required as head of state. Certain functions could perhaps be handed to the Speaker of the House of Commons, but the Speaker, though supposed to act impartially, is a politician. For most abolitionists the solution lies in some form of presidency, elected either by the people or Parliament. However, this would engender a new set of controversial issues over self-aggrandizement and politicization.

The monarchy's uncertain future is tied in with a host of other variables, including the demise of press deference, the demand for a written constitution, the possibility of PR, the future role of the Commonwealth and Britain's place in an increasingly integrated Europe. Some reforms have already been made and the institution has shown considerable flexibility in surviving over the centuries. There is perhaps more to the institution than constitutional logic. As Bogdanor states:

> If the conjunction of monarchy and democracy may seem a contradiction, it would be well to bear in mind Freud's aphorism that it is only in logic that contradictions can not exist. (Bogdanor 1996a: 421)

We have become a grandmother.
Margaret Thatcher

On the whole it is wise in human affairs and in the government of men, to separate pomp from power.
Winston Churchill, speech in Ottawa (1952)

The House of Lords

Beneath the monarchical tip of the iceberg has long floated an edifice of ancient privilege – a fully fledged aristocratic class of titled lords and ladies, sighted on special occasions and in special places such as the royal enclosure at Ascot, Cowes and, most visibly of all, in the House of Lords. It remained one of the most curious of the anomalies in British public life, defying any rule book of democratic and secular politics. The general atmosphere of the upper house has been seen as somnambulant; it has been likened to a mausoleum or adduced as evidence of life after death.

If, like me, you are over 90, frail, on two sticks, half deaf and half blind, you stick out like a sore thumb in most places, but not in the House of Lords.

Harold Macmillan (Lord Stockton), quoted in the *Observer* (19 May 1985)

Composition

In 1998 the House comprised around 760 hereditary **peers** and nearly 500 life peers. In addition, there were 26 bishops and 28 Law Lords. Lords outnumber ladies by around 13:1. Membership was based on hereditary right; certain people are 'born to rule', a distinction acquired by emerging from a particular womb following an aristocratic impregnation. To this principle was added, through the Life Peerages Act (1958), another equally undemocratic one: life peers (who could not hand down their titles) appointed by the prime minister, thus reviving the House with a transfusion of fresh (though not always young) blood.

For long, peers could not stand for the House of Commons. In 1960, after ten years as MP for Bristol South-east, Tony Benn had to leave upon inheriting the title Viscount Stansgate. He was refused re-entry even after winning the ensuing by-election in 1961. His case against 'feudal nonsense' was rejected by an election court which regarded a ruling of 1626 as a suitable authority for the 1960s (Benn 1980: 15). Yet continued pressure and public feeling finally led to legislation permitting peers to renounce their titles; Lord Stansgate became a commoner again and prompt acts of renunciation by Lords Hailsham and Douglas-Home enabled them to throw their hats into the ring to succeed Macmillan as Conservative leader.

Politics in the House of Lords

Though cryptically referred to in the Commons as 'the other place', the Lords is linked to the Commons by a short corridor. Despite the leisurely atmosphere, the Lords has come to work harder over the past fifty years (Shell 1994: 734). Sittings take place from Mondays to Thursdays for about thirty weeks a year, usually between 2.30 and 7.00 p.m. Only towards the end of the session do they meet on Fridays. Debate is chaired by the Lord Chancellor, sitting on the traditional 'Woolsack', which symbolizes national prosperity through trade. In November 1998 the Lords agreed to some minor reductions to the pomp surrounding the office, allowing the Lord Chancellor to dispense with breeches and tights in favour of trousers at certain less ceremonial times, though traditionalists feared the office was losing its dignity.

This is a rotten argument, but it should be good enough for their lordships on a hot summer afternoon.

Civil servant's note on a ministerial brief, read out by mistake in Lords debate; quoted in Lord Home, *The Way the Wind Blows* (1976)

Debates are rarely acrimonious and the Lord Chancellor does not pretend to be independent, often leaving the Woolsack to join the cut and thrust. The party machines have been less dominant than in the Commons, around a fifth of members sitting as independent **cross-benchers,** often having renounced former allegiances (figure 12.2). Of the regular attenders, Conservatives did not have an outrageous majority but if all were to descend they would have swamped the House. These were the 400 or so 'backwoodsmen' and, when the trumpet sounded, they forsook their estates to answer the call; as in 1968 to vote against a trade ban on Rhodesia and in 1998 to defeat New Labour's proposed closed-list system for EU elections. Peers who had never voted before, and who did not even know their own leaders, were to be found wandering in bewilderment around the precincts of Westminster.

The House of Lords is not the watchdog of the constitution; it is Mr Balfour's poodle. It fetches and carries for him. It barks for him. It bites anyone that he sets it on to.

David Lloyd George, House of Commons speech (21 Dec. 1908)

Figure 12.2
Political allegiance in the House of Lords, November 1998, excluding peers without writs of summons (68) and bishops (26).

Source: Data from parliamentary web site (http://www.parliament.uk).

The functions of the House of Lords

> The House of Peers, throughout the war,
> Did nothing in particular,
> And did it very well.
>
> The Peers in Gilbert and Sullivan's *Iolanthe*

The essence of the argument of those wishing to retain the upper house lies in its claim to a number of important functions.

Legislation Usually originating in the Commons, bills pass through both Houses; the Lords can propose amendments and have the power to delay non-financial legislation (see p. 378). They can also be useful for tidying up legislation passed in haste in the lower house. With its packed programme, the 1997 Labour government used the reverse route much more intensely, some major pieces of legislation (including the Crime and Disorder Bill, the Higher Education Bill and the Human Rights Bill) starting life in the Lords.

Criticism The Lords can demonstrate a freedom of expression not found in the Commons, speaking out where elected mortals favour discretion. Unlike MPs, they are less dependent upon patronage and often beyond the age of ambition, at least in this life. Since the early 1970s the House has made greater use of select committees, the most significant being those on the European Communities and Science and Technology.

Informed debate The presence of certain life peers, appointed because of some particular expertise (from the professions, industry or academia), can at times sustain a high level of debate, while the bishops can inject a moral dimension.

Restraint The Lords can preserve Parliament's historic role of checking the executive. With less party discipline, there can be more sense of a separation of powers and a full veto remains in the case of any government seeking to extend its life beyond five years. The threat of delay can mean a bill will be lost and governments may accept unpalatable amendments. After 1979 something of a resurrection was witnessed, the upper house inflicting regular body blows on Conservative bills, beginning with a notable defeat in March 1980 over the imposition of school transport charges. Over a hundred defeats caused Thatcher, according to one senior peer, 'to scream and kick her legs in the air' (Gunn 1988). Yet ironically, as Baroness Thatcher she herself was to prove a thorn in the government's side over EU policy.

Major's Home Secretary, Michael Howard, was particularly accident prone. Shifting alliances of former home secretaries, judges, police officers, bishops and opposition peers ravaged his police reforms and tough penal programme. February 1997 saw the defeat of the Crime Bill, laying down minimum sentences, and a triple defeat was inflicted upon the Firearms Bill. The trend was to continue under Labour, the Lords inflicting some thirty defeats during its first year of office. One prominent example was its rejection of the Commons' amendment to the Crime and Disorder Bill on lowering the homosexual age of consent to sixteen. However, in November 1998, the fiercest confrontation of all saw the Lords defying convention and sending the European Parliamentary Elections Bill back an astonishing five times (p. 378).

Judicial decision-making One function remaining central to the living constitution is that of final court of appeal. This is not performed by the House as such but by the *Law Lords* headed by the Lord Chancellor (see p. 609).

Peer pressure: reform attempts

Lloyd George regarded the Lords with contempt and the 1911 Parliament Act was intended only as a stop-gap, a prelude to a revolution. However, despite much huffing and puffing, for long no wolf emerged with the constitutional lung power to blow the House down. Although people looked to Labour for action, they did so in vain, the party barking in opposition but unwilling to bite in office. A 1968 white paper announced some half-hearted reforms but the subsequent Parliament (No. 2) Bill was dashed on the rocks of an unholy alliance between two unlikely bedfellows – Enoch Powell (favouring the status quo) and Michael Foot (favouring the constitutional bulldozers). Dennis Skinner's 1976 private member's bill for abolition was only narrowly defeated and, although the following year's Labour conference supported him, the 1979 party manifesto fought shy of such a commitment.

In May 1988 Lord Scarman called for a strengthened upper house to resist encroaching prime ministerial dictatorship and Labour's 1989 policy review proposed an elected second chamber. This was also advocated by the Liberal Democrats and Charter 88, which envisaged much stronger powers to initiate, revise, delay and even veto legislation. Labour's 1997 manifesto promised reform and once in office Blair began to redress the Lords' inbuilt Tory domination, his first Honours list containing thirty-one 'working' Labour peers. Expected to attend regularly, they included a glittering array of leading industrialists, writers and showbiz figures. The Liberal Democrats gained eleven new working peers and the Conservatives five.

In October 1998 the government announced a two-stage timetable for reform. First the voting and sitting rights of the hereditary peers would be removed and then wholesale reform considered. There were some fears that stage two might never materialize, leaving the country with a highly undemocratic second chamber and enhanced scope for political patronage. Moreover, it transpired that Labour would not even purge the house of its aristocratic element in stage one. Leader of the Conservative peers, the aristocratic Viscount Cranborne, had brokered a deal with the government in which ninety-one hereditary peers would remain. Negotiations had proceeded without the knowledge of the Con-

> If all the Government is going to do is to abolish the right of hereditary peers to sit and vote and then kick the second stage into touch, it will be a great missed opportunity.
>
> Lord Richard, interviewed shortly after being sacked as Leader of the Lords in Blair's first cabinet reshuffle, in *The Times* (30 July 1998)

servative leader and an incensed William Hague promptly sacked the noble lord while at the same time welcoming the deal.

In January 1999 a three-page bill was introduced to end the sitting and voting rights of hereditary peers. To curb criticisms of cronyism, the prime minister's sole right to nominate life peers during the interim period would be reduced, with an independent appointments commission recommending non-political appointments. In a populist move emblematic of New Labour, the public would have the chance to nominate a number of 'people's peers'. The bill was accompanied by a white paper announcing the stage-two operation with a Royal Commission to consider the powers and composition of a reformed House. Its report (to be produced by the end of the year) would be considered by a joint committee of both Houses. To some surprise its chairman was Conservative peer Lord Wakeham, once a close associate of Margaret Thatcher (and chief whip, 1983–7). The white paper outlined four options for the reformed chamber:

1 fixed levels of representation for interest groups and professional associations;
2 direct election with all people able to vote;
3 indirect election with members seconded from the devolved institutions, including the Scottish, Welsh and Irish Assemblies, local authorities and the European Parliament;
4 a mixed chamber comprising elected and nominated members.

The government's preference was for the last alternative. The position of the Law Lords was to be considered by the Royal Commission but the government recommended retaining the bishops, though supplemented with leaders from other faiths. However, purged of the hereditary element and perhaps with elected members, the new House would possess greater legitimacy than before. To counter the problem of a clash with the Commons the Royal Commission was also asked to consider some reduction in its powers.

More rigour or rigor mortis?

It is difficult to deny that the Lords has been a blot on any democratic landscape. How did it avoid constitutional clearance orders for so long? Although there is a case for retention based on the Burkean grounds that what is must have sublime virtues, beyond this is the fact that governments can find the life peerage system very useful. Its value is undiminished by the removal of the hereditary element. The life peerage system extends the patronage state, enabling prime ministers to bribe and reward colleagues and those who have helped the cause financially or (as media barons and advertising executives) practically. Indeed, when Norman Lamont became the first recent former Chancellor *not* to be immediately honoured, some suggested a revenge motive, denied by 'sources close to John Major' (*The Times*, 2 Aug. 1997). Sitting MPs can be moved 'upstairs' to make way for a favourite, as was suspected when Labour's Roy Hughes (ennobled in August 1997) relinquished his Newport seat to Conservative defector Alan Howarth. Again, people can be brought into government without the inconvenience of confronting the electorate. In this way Thatcher made David Young Secretary of State for Employment and Blair brought in media executive Gus Macdonald as Scottish minister, to the considerable anger of Scottish Labour MPs. Blair's appointees were mockingly dubbed 'Tony's cronies'. Lord Falconer, quickly ennobled and made Solicitor General, had been a long-time friend and soon found himself on fourteen cabinet committees, more than all but one of his elected ministerial brethren.

Ministers can even overcome rejection at the ballot box; thus Lynda Chalker, transmogrified into Baroness Chalker, remained at Overseas Development despite the adverse judgement of her constituents in 1992. It can even be an elixir of everlasting life to ageing politicians. In June 1992, Thatcher entered the chamber, along with many of her former Cabinet, though her Commons opponent, Michael Foot, true to his principles, became the first Labour leader since 1935 to spurn the honour.

Of course there is no guarantee that life peers will fulfil their promise. The voting record after Blair's first year revealed only about three-quarters of the new working peers to be regular voters. In consequence the government lost many votes, some on flagship measures. However, critics look to Canada, where the second chamber consists entirely of appointees and is seen as no more than a government poodle.

The alternative to patronage is democratic election, the basis for populating most upper houses. However, this legitimacy would promise more power (the US Senate is the senior house) and competition would develop with the Commons. Yet to reject election on these grounds would be tantamount to a call for unicameralism (Shell 1994: 736). Moreover, such a Guy Fawkes solution would throw an intolerable burden on the Commons, necessitating further reforms there.

Are there any virtues in an hereditary element? Compared with their appointed colleagues hereditary peers had less reason to succumb to sycophantic behaviour and their road to Westminster did not involve the compromising, deal-making and backroom skulduggery required of the party apparatchiks. Indeed, critics found a certain irony in the fact that Labour life peer Baroness Jay, who as leader of the Lords introduced the reforms to their lordships and castigated the anomaly of the hereditary system, was, as daughter of Labour ex-prime minister Lord Callaghan, hardly best placed to decry political position through 'accident of birth'!

There are perhaps deeper reasons why the preservation order has remained operative. Establishment interests can find great symbolic value in the House: one of the remaining bastions that only the select (or the selected) may enter. A key element in British political culture, Britain's upper house reflects hierarchy and exclusion, reminding the mass where they belong – on the outside.

The House of Commons

The third element in the parliamentary triumvirate is the only one that may be called democratic. Seating 659 members chosen by popular election, the House of Commons is also the chamber of the prime minister, the leading ministers and opposition front bench. However, although the site where Britain's political Titans confront each other on a daily basis, it is by no means free of flummery and ceremony.

Parliamentary mumbo-jumbo

The Commons embraces Westminster ritual from the very beginning with the annual opening of Parliament. Black Rod, the officer responsible for maintaining order in the House of Lords, carrying an ebony cane for the purpose, summons the Commoners to hear the Queen's Speech. All is conducted in Norman French. When he approaches the lower house the doors are slammed in his face (because in 1642, the last time the Commons allowed the monarch in, he arrested five members). Undeterred, he gives three solemn knocks, the doors are opened and the MPs, led by prime minister and opposition leader, advance in pairs like a *corps de ballet* towards the other place. The flummery of the State Opening engages ladies of the bedchamber in long evening dresses and officials with Ruritanian titles such as 'silver stick in waiting'.

MPs are required to swear an Oath of Allegiance to the Crown. This is a problem for anyone professing republican principles and some Labour MPs do so with tongue in cheek. Two Sinn Fein MPs, elected in 1997, were denied office space at Westminster for their refusal. In understanding Commons discourse there are various arcane terms requiring translation. The 'usual channels' means consultation between party whips; in the chamber MPs should refer to each other as honourable friends or honourable members for this or that constituency, and when they vote they troop through division lobbies. Members raising a point of order in a division do so wearing an opera hat. Privy Councillors (cabinet and ex-cabinet members and leading members of the opposition parties) enjoy certain privileges: 'right honourable', rather than 'honourable', they receive precedence in debate. New Labour came to power promising to end such flummery, but past experience has seen many Young Turks seduced by the ritual of the club.

I think . . . that it is the best club in London.

Mr Tremlow on the House of Commons, in Charles Dickens's novel *Our Mutual Friend* (1864–5)

The Speaker

At the centre of Commons life is the Speaker, who chairs debate. Yet there is more to the role than this: adorned with wig and black robes, the Speaker presides over a variety of solemn ceremonies often held in his or her official baroque residence situated within the Palace of Westminster. Although now considered an honour, the position was once unenviable, entailing facing the monarch on behalf of MPs; a newly elected Speaker thus makes a show of resistance before being forced into the chair by colleagues.

I have neither eye to see, nor tongue to speak here, but as the House is pleased to direct me.

> William Lenthall, in the House of Commons on 4 January 1642, in reply to Charles I asking if he had seen five MPs whom he wished to arrest. A classic statement of the Speaker's role.

The Speaker is chosen by MPs, usually from the ranks of well-respected uncontroversial figures. The position of George Thomas's successor was rendered unusually difficult when Mrs Thatcher, in an unprecedented move, tried to treat the office as one within her patronage. Although she did not get her way, when Bernard Weatherill was elected in 1983 his authority was weakened (Heffer 1988). The appointment of his successor, Betty Boothroyd, the first woman Speaker, was a landmark.

The Speaker is attended by the Sergeant at Arms, equipped with sword and mace. Responsible for maintaining order, he will eject the unruly, including MPs banned by the Speaker, and could imprison enemies in the clock tower of Big Ben. Each day the Speaker leads a dignified procession into the House following the Sergeant, and during debate the mace rests on the table at the centre of the chamber. Michael Heseltine etched his name in parliamentary folklore by brandishing it in the face of the Labour enemy; only by prostrating himself before the House the following day did he gain forgiveness. When Labour's Ron Brown made a similar gesture he refused to apologize and the whip was withdrawn for three months, the sternest punishment imposed for twenty-five years.

In debate, the Speaker is supposed to call members fairly, and with due weight to their expertise, interest and status. She or he also gives rulings on points of procedure, emergency debates, money bills and **parliamentary privilege**. The latter are rights and immunities from court action granted to MPs to ensure free debate. Thus, for example, in 1987 Ken Livingstone could accuse Conservative Airey Neave (later killed by an IRA bomb in the Commons car park) of nursing knowledge of treasonable activities practised by Britain's security officers in Northern Ireland (Pienaar 1987). The Speaker also keeps discipline. Although there were raucous scenes during the 1980s, turbulence is nothing new. Conservative opposition to Lloyd George's 'People's Budget' produced uproar,

Yesterday as today: the arrival of the Speaker, 1884

Source: Mary Evans Picture Library

giving the reaction of Labour backbenchers in 1988 to Chancellor Lawson's 'rich people's budget' the air of the proverbial vicarage tea party. Where MPs persist in bad behaviour the Speaker will 'name' them, whereupon they are banned for a prescribed period. Thus in July 1992 Dennis Skinner was ordered from the House for refusing to withdraw the unparliamentary term 'wart' as a description of Agricultural Secretary John Gummer. The Speaker is generally accorded great respect. In December 1995 Betty Boothroyd summoned the Conservative Chief Whip for a serious dressing down after a whispering campaign against her by his MPs.

The timetable

The life of a *parliament* is the period between two general elections, which must not, except in exceptional circumstances, exceed five years. This divides into annual *sessions* commencing each autumn, punctuated by *recesses* (holidays) over Christmas, Easter, Whitsun and summer. An Order Paper outlines each day's events and is the responsibility of the Leader of the House, liaising with the Opposition. This was often criticized as difficult to understand and in July 1997 the new Modernization Committee recommended its replacement with a 'Daily Agenda' clearly setting out the day's business and timetable (see p. 384) and also available on the internet.

Sometimes a debate will continue as an *all-night sitting* but on Fridays sittings adjourn by mid-afternoon, enabling MPs to return to their constituencies. In 1994 certain reforms were introduced, including Wednesday morning sittings (for backbencher-initiated debates), no sittings on ten constituency Fridays and rearrangements of business to cut all-night sittings.

An MP's job

The House has for long retained the characteristics of a Victorian establishment club, with bars, smoking rooms and leather armchairs. A useful quality for an MP is to be 'clubbable', to be able to mix easily and enjoy a good joke. While parties separate them, MPs can form cross-party friendships and clubs for activities ranging from skiing and football to chess and jazz. However, the club ethos was subject to a seismic shudder in May 1997 with the entry of a veritable regiment of women. The organization of the parliamentary day is highly inconvenient for those with children and many changes were called for, ranging from fewer all-night sittings to more creche facilities and women's toilets.

The times they are a-changin'

New, younger MPs of both sexes have, probably, brought more sex into Parliament.

Liberal Democrat MP Dr Evan Harris, leading calls for condom machines
in the Commons, in the *Guardian* (13 March 1998)

There is no job description for an MP, each must make of it what they will. Some do much, some little. Those yearning to ascend the 'greasy pole' must define their role in conformity with a culture of obedience (see chapter 13). There is little glamour in this. If they seek the limelight with a controversial article or challenging speech they run the risk of incurring displeasure. Hence, with no demands for their appearance on television or in newspaper columns, they must cast envious eyes on the opportunities enjoyed by their seniors. Some (particularly those with professional backgrounds) may experience a sense of *ennui*. They spend their time in the many tearooms and bars, sometimes appearing 'tired and emotional' (MPs are never drunk) and sometimes even falling into casual adultery. Broadly MPs have two stages upon which to act, one in Westminster and one in their constituencies.

Parliamentary matters Wednesdays excepted, 'full-time' MPs spend their mornings dealing with correspondence, sitting on committees, meeting constituents and receiving lobby groups. Although belatedly improved by taking over premises round about (the Norman Shaw Building, Abbey Yard, Parliament Street and Millbank), the facilities for such activities have been notoriously bad and MPs may still hold meetings in corridors and bars. In the afternoons and evenings they may attend debates in the main chamber, meet fellow MPs, feed information to the press, gossip and plot; Parliament is a hot-house of rumour, character assassinations, secret agreements and broken confidences. MPs maintaining outside jobs, often in the professions, will be less in evidence.

Constituency matters　MPs represent geographical areas, by which titles they courteously address each other, and can find much employment in dealing with their constituents. Today a daily postbag may contain over 100 letters. This is an area largely free from the straightjacket of party discipline and it has increased significantly (Norton 1994). Various factors account for this, including the growth of the welfare state, MPs' role in the ombudsman system, greater sophistication amongst constituents, more voter volatility and the need to secure readoption by local parties. More recently there has been the rise of the Liberal Democrats with their community politics approach, the creation of the civil service agencies, the neoliberal view of citizens as state customers and the Citizen's Charter initiative. The influx of women MPs could also be expected to accelerate the trend, women expressing greater concern about social policy issues and giving a higher priority to constituency work (Norris 1996c). MPs themselves have encouraged developments, advertising regular surgeries, developing web sites and holding public meetings. While 'to be a good constituency MP is still . . . downgraded by the ambitious' (Mitchell 1994: 703), the careerist may find in the constituency dimension a means to attract attention and gain fuel for parliamentary questions and adjournment motions. Yet there are costs. MPs are not trained counsellors, social workers or civil rights lawyers. Moreover, the deflection from the Westminster role may be welcomed by an executive eager to swell its power. Critics impugned such a motive when, in 1998, Labour leaders began working on contracts laying down the amount of constituency work expected of MPs (see p. 298).

Being a backbencher is really a very good job; . . . and if they've got intelligence and guts and a good relationship with their constituents then it's a better job than in most parliaments of the western world.

Michael Foot, interviewed by Bill Jones in *Talking Politics* (vol. 9, no. 3)

Honourable members

Who are these people who purport to represent their fellow citizens? Placing them under the microscope we find they can differ from the general population in various ways.

Age　The Commons tends to mirror the mature population, the 40–60 age group being best represented. Labour tended to be the older party with some 20 per cent over sixty. One reason for ripe age is the need to demonstrate ability (in

A Parliament elected by the universal suffrage of voters grouped according to geographical areas is about as truly representative as a bottle of Bovril is a true representative of an ox.

Eleanor Rathbone, in the *Observer* (29 March 1931)

business, the professions, academia, trade unions or local government) in order to impress a selection committee. The longest-serving member enjoys the title 'Father of the House' (Sir Edward Heath, born 1916, the current holder) and, with no compulsory retirement age, there is competition for the honour. In 1970, the local Labour oligarchs of Merthyr Tydfil decided that at eighty-three their candidate, S. O. Davies, was beyond his best. Although resisting their slight by winning handsomely as an independent, his death shortly afterwards gave them what would in other circumstances have been the last laugh. With an average age of forty-five, the class of '97 have lowered the age profile (figure 12.3), with Christopher Leslie, at twenty-four, the baby of the House.

Education Increasingly MPs tend to be among the better educated, some 67 per cent of the 1997 intake being graduates (Criddle 1997a: 203). Labour's graduate count has risen from 32 per cent in 1945 to 66 per cent. For much of the post-war period the majority of graduates were from Oxbridge and this proportion remains high, despite an increase in those from other institutions (figure 12.4). Traditionally the public schools provided the pre-university

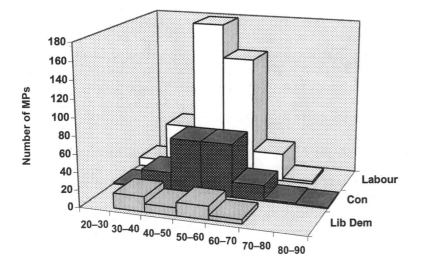

Figure 12.3
Age profile of MPs, 1997.

Source: Data from Criddle (1997a: 203).

Figure 12.4
Educational
background of MPs,
1997.

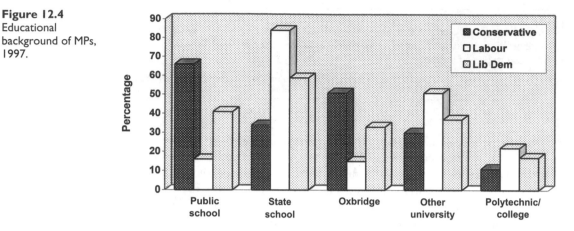

Source: Data from Criddle (1997a: 203).

education for the great majority of Conservatives (mainly Eton, Harrow and Winchester), but during the 1980s this began to change, with more from the meritocratic state grammar school assault course. Ex-public schoolboys have also not been absent from Labour's ranks.

Occupation Occupational backgrounds stretch Conservative and Labour MPs further apart (table 12.2). During the post-war era, both parties have included a high proportion (around 45 per cent) classed as professional, though in the case of Labour these have mainly been teachers and academics – usually first-generation entrants to the middle class. Generally under 10 per cent of Labour MPs have had business backgrounds compared with around a third of Conservatives. Indeed Conservatives are not merely businessmen, they are *big* businessmen. Of the 273 company directors elected to Parliament in the three decades following the second world war, no fewer than 245 were Conservatives. The working class is virtually unrepresented on the Conservative benches and is declining sharply in Labour's ranks (from over 40 per cent in 1945 to 13 per cent in 1997). A particular feature of Labour's 1997 intake was a predominance of ex-public-sector employees (40 per cent), a category barely represented amongst the Conservatives (Criddle 1997a).

Political experience Many MPs cut their political teeth in local government; of the new intake in 1997, 70 per cent of Liberal Democrats, 64 per cent of Labour and 25 per cent of Conservatives had been councillors. Another indication of increasing professionalization is early work for political parties as 'staffers' (researchers or consultants). Of the 1997 new intake, 40 per cent of Conservatives and 20 per cent of Labour had such experience (Criddle 1997b). Labour has always relied on a considerable body of trade union grounding and was also becoming a home for student union ex-presidents.

Table 12.2 MPs' occupational background, 1997 (percentages)

Occupation	Conservative	Labour	Liberal Democrat
Professions			
Law	18	7	13
Education	5	26	15
Publishing and journalism	8	7	9
Civil service and local government	3	7	4
Armed services	5	–	2
Other	5	2	13
Business and management			
Company directors/senior executives	32	4	20
Other	7	5	4
Miscellaneous white collar[a]	1	16	2
Political staffers	9	10	11
Manual	1	13	2
Other	4	<1	2

[a] Includes occupations such as trade union officials, social workers and voluntary-sector employees.
Source: Data from Criddle (1997b: 205).

Sexual orientation If the House is representative of the wider population in this respect, then a number of gays and lesbians must choose life in the parliamentary closet. However, Westminster is a place of a thousand rumours. Indeed, when Conservative David Ashby lost his libel case against the *Sunday Times* over allegations of homosexuality, he was removed by his constituency, complaining 'they are behaving like Smithfield meat-porters – love the Queen Mum and bash the queers' (Criddle 1997a: 197). When Edwina Currie's 1994 amendment to lower the age of consent to sixteen for homosexuals failed, the pressure group Outrage threatened to 'Out' any unsupportive MPs they thought were homosexuals. Homophobia is of course as inappropriate in a democratic parliament as is racism or sexism; Labour's Ben Bradshaw and Chris Smith are openly gay. A homophobic campaign was waged against Bradshaw by his Conservative opponent in the 1997 general election. In 1998, following the Ron Davies Clapham Common farrago, gay journalist Matthew Parris 'outed' Peter Mandelson. Shortly afterwards Nick Brown came out under threat of exposure by the *Sun*, which also ran the headline 'TELL US THE TRUTH TONY – ARE WE BEING RUN BY A GAY MAFIA?' A *Guardian* poll (10 Nov. 1998) revealed public attitudes becoming more relaxed about gay MPs and ministers.

Of course, heterosexuals can also deviate from sexual norms, as the press, ever zealous in their democratic responsibilities, will inform us.

> The House of Commons is not so much a gentleman's club as a boy's boarding school.
>
> Shirley Williams (SDP politician), on Granada TV (30 July 1985)

Gender Since an ostensible purpose of Parliament is to represent society in microcosm it is anomalous that only a small proportion of MPs have been women (figure 12.5). Only becoming eligible in 1918, the first three all represented seats formerly held by their husbands. This poor record leaves Britain out of step with many other western democracies. In Sweden, for example, around 40 per cent of MPs are women. In 1928, when the franchise was extended to all women, suffragette Millicent Garrett Fawcett declared: 'Our cause is a long way from full success'; today the Fawcett Society continues her mission. The 300 Club has that number as its goal for women MPs, while the Labour Women's Network was set up in 1988 in response to the poor showing in the 1987 contest. Emily's List (Early Money Is Like Yeast) was launched by Barbara Follett in 1993 (who herself won Stevenage in 1997) to give women candidates independent financial resources. She was also credited with getting Labour women out of jeans and donkey jackets and into smart suits. However, the shortage of women MPs is not essentially a fault of the House itself. Parliament is a barometer reflecting women's status in society (Perrigo 1985: 126). Although women actually join political parties in similar numbers to men, they have not tended to seek nomination and have not been favoured by selection committees.

The 1997 breakthrough, with 120 women elected, doubled the previous number. However, any applause belongs largely to Labour, the Conservatives

Figure 12.5
Women MPs, 1945–1997.

Source: Data from *The Times Guide to the House of Commons* (1992: 282) and Criddle (1997a: 199).

returning only 13, the Liberal Democrats 3 and the SNP 2. This reflected Labour's short-lived policy of all-women shortlists (see p. 318). In Parliament, Labour women soon began forming networks to work together (Lovenduski 1997: 719). However, immaculately turned out, the new women promised little that was radical and the media were soon joking of 'Blair's Babes' and the 'Stepford Wives'. The future was by no means certain; all parties had shown little faith in their women in their election campaigns (Lovenduski 1997). Eleven of Labour's new women had been swept in from 'unwinnable' seats on an unexpected tidal wave and were vulnerable to being washed out with the receding tide of waning popularity.

Race Racism has held back the representation of ethnic minorities; parties do not field black candidates for fear of losing votes. In 1979 the Conservatives broke an all-white tradition with two Asian candidates and the 1987 election produced four black Labour MPs. The number increased to six in 1992 (five Labour, one Conservative) and to an all-time high of nine (all Labour) in 1997. John Taylor's nomination for Cheltenham in 1992 caused much controversy in the local Conservative association and he subsequently lost the election. In 1997 the Conservatives fielded ten black or Asian candidates, but only one was in a winnable seat and even he lost heavily. The Liberal Democrats fielded the largest number of ethnic minority candidates, though all nineteen fought unwinnable seats.

Monstrous regiment or Blair's Babes? Tony Blair with some of the 101 Labour women MPs, May 1997

Photo: Times Newspapers Ltd

Table 12.3 Parliamentary salaries (as recommended by the independent review body, 1996)

Position	Salary (£)	Position	Salary (£)
Prime Minister	143,000	Cabinet ministers (Lords)	77,963
Cabinet ministers	103,000	Ministers of state	74,125
Speaker	103,000	Junior ministers	66,623
Leader of the Opposition	98,000	Backbench MPs	43,000

Source: Data from the *Guardian* (4 July 1996).

Amateurs or professionals This issue goes to the heart of democracy, being concerned with what kind of people become MPs. Before 1911 they were expected to give their services freely, unsullied by pecuniary motivation. Reflecting an historic establishment fondness for amateurism this meant that, as on the county cricket and rugby union field, only the wealthy were welcome. Until as recently as 1964 MPs received only the equivalent of part-time salaries, working- and lower-middle-class members often being unable to eat in the Westminster dining-rooms. In July 1996, amidst considerable criticism, MPs voted themselves substantial rises of up to 30 per cent, following review body recommendations (table 12.3). Despite this, the salary only equals that of a relatively junior professional and is below those of the Clerks serving the House. Yet effective representation requires the participation of all classes. When rich MPs oppose higher salaries they threaten democracy (Batty and George 1985: 171). Moreover, low salaries can leave weaker MPs open to temptations.

Dishonourable members: private interests and public confidence

Some MPs have not seen the work as a full-time job. Conservatives have characteristically held company directorships, worked in the professions (often law), or been large-scale landowners. When James Prior was ejected from the Thatcher Cabinet he soon re-emerged in public view as chairman of GEC, while Cecil Parkinson joined the boards of no fewer than nine companies when he resigned in 1983. Some, often Labour, supplement their incomes by journalism. It is argued that these activities keep MPs in touch with the real world, though it is debatable how many ordinary people inhabit the boardrooms of industry, the Inns of Court, or even the inns of Fleet Street and Wapping.

In addition, MPs have long been associated with interest groups, Conservatives particularly with business interests and Labour MPs with promotional groups and trade unions. So overt is the practice that the Speaker will often choose MPs to speak not on the basis of constituencies, but because of the interests they are known to represent (Roth 1981: xxvi). However, from the late 1970s developments took a dangerous turn.

Registering interest There are two levels of concern over MPs' outside interests. First, there is the possibility that they will lack time for the job. Indeed, multiple interests appeared to be associated with safe seats, where members need spend less time courting their constituents (Norris 1996b). Secondly, there is a fear that they may favour sectional interests over the public interest. The Poulson affair, involving prominent Conservative Reginald Maudling, led to the establishment of a Register of Members' Interests in 1975. This revealed a growing profession termed 'parliamentary consultant'. Initially there were only twenty-eight, working for a total of thirty-three organizations, but by 1995 the Nolan Committee (see below) numbered 168 MPs (30 per cent of those eligible for consultancy work) holding between them 356 consultancies. Although most lead to financial gain, Tony Banks received twelve jars of honey from the London Beekeepers Association!

The 1980s saw a new growth industry: commercial lobbying firms existing expressedly for the purpose of approaching MPs on behalf of clients, some, such as Ian Greer Associates, even advertising in *Dod's Parliamentary Companion*. By mid-1994 fifty such firms were plying their trade on the terraces, and in the corridors, bars and tearooms of the Palace of Westminster (Chittenden and Grice 1995). These actually began to employ MPs, so that instead of being lobbied they would do the job themselves. Despite journalistic concern, the Commons Select Committee on Members' Interests showed no haste to adjust its rules of disclosure; MPs were not required to record payments received, give details of their own shareholdings or name the interests represented by their lobbying forms. Although the rules were tightened following the John Browne affair, during the 1990s allegations of widespread corruption and venality at the heart of government began to circulate (Wintour and Pallister 1995). The final straw came when two Conservative MPs, Graham Riddick and David Tredinnick, were trapped by *Sunday Times* journalists posing as businessmen offering £1,000 for a question in Parliament. They were duly suspended but some suspected this was only the tip of an iceberg of sleaze. Further disclosures resulted in the resignation of one junior minister, Tim Smith, and the sacking of another, Neil Hamilton. Rising public concern led to the establishment in October 1994 of a Committee on Standards in Public Life, a standing body, chaired first by Lord Justice Nolan and then Lord Neill.

Reporting in May 1995, Nolan concluded that the Register was inadequate. To combat seven of the deadly sins available to MPs he set out seven Principles of Public Life and a draft code of conduct. While permitting outside interests, their financial value was to be declared and paid parliamentary work for lobbyists should cease. An independent Parliamentary Commissioner should police the system, though with final judgements remaining with Parliament.

Major immediately accepted the report's broad thrust though senior colleagues warned that many Conservatives would oppose it and some bitter debates ensued. In November 1995, with votes split 322 to 271, MPs grudgingly agreed to reveal outside earnings. In addition, all paid advocacy would be banned and a Select Committee on Standards and Privileges established. Sir Gordon Downey (ex-Comptroller and Auditor General) took up the position of Parliamentary

Nolan's seven Principles of Public Life
Selflessness
Integrity
Objectivity
Accountability
Openness
Honesty
Leadership

Commissioner for Standards, to advise the committee and individual MPs and investigate complaints from MPs and the public.

However, the commissioner has fewer powers than the Ombudsman or Comptroller and Auditor General with respect to sending for persons and papers, taking oral evidence, publishing findings and imposing sanctions; these powers lie with the Standards and Privileges Committee. Hence, the commissioner operates within the framework of the 'Westminster club' and a government can control the committee through its majority (Woodhouse 1998). An example of how the system could be subverted came when John Major prorogued Parliament in time to prevent publication of the 'cash-for-questions' report before the 1997 election. Some said stronger controls were needed and in June 1997 Labour Home Secretary Jack Straw unveiled proposals for a Corruption Bill to close a legal loophole dating from the 1689 Bill of Rights that gave MPs immunity from public prosecution. This could lead to jail for corrupt MPs. However, sceptics were not holding their breath.

In this chapter we have introduced the three great estates of the realm. To different degrees they are all parts of the dignified constitution, serving to legitimate the exercise of power. The extent to which they do this is under question; each has reached a state of crisis marked by profound public dissatisfaction and calls for reform abound. However, there is more to the life of Parliament than representing the three estates. The reality today can only be understood by reference to its processes and internal power structure. We turn to these in the following chapter.

Key points

- All polities contain ceremonial elements, though Britain is particularly rich in this respect.
- Bagehot took an exceedingly elitist view of such ceremony, believing its purpose to be that of keeping ordinary people in the dark about the real process of government.
- Britain has a constitutional monarchy but the idea that the monarchy is above politics can be questioned.
- The death of Diana, Princess of Wales created a crisis for the monarchy.
- The House of Lords, with its composition based on breeding and prime ministerial favour, is a relic of an undemocratic age.
- Any reform of the Lords runs the risk of constitutional turbulence.
- Any idea that the Commons is a microcosm of society is questionable. The working class, women and racial minorities have been long under-represented.
- The 1990s saw the prestige of the Commons plunge, with widespread perceptions of venality.

Review your understanding of the following terms and concepts

backbencher
Black Rod
ceremonial
Civil List
constitutional monarchy
cross-bencher
division lobby
hereditary peer
honourable member
Leader of the House
life peer

Lord Chancellor
mace
Magnum Concilium
mumbo-jumbo
Order Paper
other place
parliamentary privilege
Parliamentary Commissioner for Standards
patronage
Privy Councillor

Register of Members' Interests
republicanism
Restoration
right honourable member
Select Committee on Standards and Privileges
Speaker
usual channels

Assignment

Study the extract from the *Independent* on p. 368 and answer the following questions.

		Mark (%)
1	What inference do you draw from the publication date of this article?	5
2	What advantages might there be from a chamber selected on the same principle as a jury?	15
3	What alternative methods for selecting members of the upper house can you suggest?	20
4	Why does an elected, or partly elected, upper house threaten the Commons?	30
5	What are the dangers of appointing members to the upper house on the basis of patronage?	30

Questions for discussion

1 Consider the consequences for British politics if the monarchy were to be abolished?
2 In what sense was the death of the Princess of Wales a crisis for the monarchy?
3 'Without the attentions of the media the British monarchy would die.' Discuss.
4 Why do you think the process of government is surrounded by ceremony and display?
5 What changes in Parliament and policy can be expected from the 1997 influx of women MPs?
6 'Parliament cannot be described as a representative assembly if its composition is not a microcosm of British society.' Discuss.

'People's Lords' to replace hereditary peers

Exclusive

By Charles Suter,
Constitutional Affairs
Correspondent

A CABINET committee drawing up plans for the abolition of hereditary peerages has proposed their replacement with temporary "People's Lords", according to documents leaked to *The Independent*.

Under the changes, existing hereditary Lords will stay in place until they die. Their seats will then be taken by "ordinary citizens" chosen at random in a system similar to jury service.

The new "People's Lords" will serve for fixed terms of one, five or fifteen years. It is expected that the first citizens to be elevated in this way will take their seats in time for the Millennium celebrations at the end of next year. There will be no change to the system of life peerages.

The committee, chaired by the Prime Minister and including Peter Mandelson, Lord Irvine and constitutional experts – was established soon after last May's Labour landslide.

Confidential minutes seen by *The Independent* reveal the committee examined the possibility of replacing the House of Lords with an elected second chamber, similar to the US Senate.

The idea was rejected because the committee was worried that "even a partly elected Upper House would challenge the democratic legitimacy" of the Labour-dominated Commons.

There were also fears that outright abolition of the Lords would bring renewed and direct pressure on the Monarchy itself – something which new Labour is keen to avoid.

The document details discussion of the "middle way" which Labour hopes will "preserve the stability and continuity" provided by the inherited peerage.

By allocating seats in the second chamber by lottery, appointments to the Lords will "remain beyond the political fashions of the day".

At the same time, the removal of the hereditary element will get rid of an "out-of-date principle which is an affront to the sensibilities of a modern inclusive and increasingly classless democracy".

According to the plan, the "Lottery Lords" will be chosen by computers using the electoral roll. Citizens selected to serve in the Lords will be paid a salary "commensurate with their current earnings with an additional element of compensation" for their period of office. Attendance will be mandatory, though as with jury service it will be possible to seek exemption.

Systems will be introduced to ensure that equal numbers of men and women are elevated to the peerage. The young, together with members of ethnic minorities "and the just plain average" would have an equal chance of gaining a seat in the second chamber and thus an opportunity to scrutinise legislation, suggest changes and draft new clauses and amendments.

Opponents of the plan were quick to register their protest. Professor Pamella Benlott of London University, an influential new Labour intellectual, said: "The British constitution is fragile. Hereditary peers have centuries of in-breeding in their blood. The fact that many Lords are congenital idiots is a subtle and unique part of the constitutional settlement with which Tony will tinker at his peril."

Henry Masingbird-DeMonforte, who as 27th Earl of Thanet can trace his ancestors back to Harold Haffacanute, warned of a "mass uprising along the lines of the Countryside March . . . but more violent" if new Labour took his seat away.

Independent, 1 April 1998

7 Examine the pros and cons of MPs having outside jobs.
8 Has Parliament adequately protected itself against sleaze?
9 'The development of the MP's constituency role detracts from the constitutional role of the Commons.' Discuss.
10 Evaluate reform proposals for the House of Lords.

Topic for debate

This house believes that the abolition of the House of Lords is a prerequisite for social reform.

Further reading

Bagehot, W. (1963) *The English Constitution* (first published 1867).
Highly elitist and disdainful of the masses, but contains enduring truths about the relationship between the rulers and the ruled, and the place of symbolism in politics.

Bogdanor, V. (1997) *The Monarchy and the Constitution.*
Accessible academic analysis on the monarchy in politics. Ultimately a defence of the institution.

Cannadine, D. (1992) *The Decline and Fall of the British Aristocracy.*
Title tells all.

Judge, D. (ed.) (1983) *The Politics of Parliamentary Reform.*
A varied collection. Opening chapter takes a neo-Marxist view, noting that reforms that succeed are those legitimating the rule of the economically powerful.

Norris, J. and Lovenduski, J. (1994) *Political Recruitment: Gender, Race and Class in the British Parliament.*
Examines relative dearth of women, black and working-class MPs and discusses whether the social bias in the political elite matters.

Pimlott, B. (1996) *The Queen: A Biography of Elizabeth II.*
Divides long reign into key periods: from fairytale to nightmare.

Shell, D. (1992) *The House of Lords.*
Perceptive overview.

For light relief

Julian Critchley, *Palace of Varieties.*
An entertaining insight into an MP's role by one of its mavericks.

Edwina Currie, *A Parliamentary Affair.*
Obsessive ambition, eroticism and political intrigue.

Frances Edmonds, *Members Only.*
A sharp and witty analysis of the Commons as seen by a feminist.

Anthony Holden, *The Tarnished Crown*.
Express columnist and keen monarchy watcher with paradoxically republican sympathies.

Andrew Morton, *Diana: Her True Story*.
Book which put the cat among the corgis on the break-up of the fairytale marriage.

Sue Townsend, *The Queen and I*.
Life for the royal family on a council estate.

On the net

http:/www.royal.gov.uk
The monarchy's web site.

http://www.parliament.uk
Parliament's home page has links to the Commons and Lords and an enormous amount of information on parliamentary history, customs and procedure.

Chapter Thirteen

Parliament: Not to Reason Why

In this chapter we turn from the overtly ceremonial and structural aspects of Parliament to its more active functions, focusing mainly on the House of Commons. We begin by noting the overwhelming dominance of political parties before turning to three central parliamentary functions: legislation, debate and scrutiny of the executive. After this we consider how parliamentary proceedings are brought to the attention of the mass population in whose name it operates. We conclude by trying to look behind the formal trappings to clarify Parliament's essential role today.

Parliament's procedures are scrupulously regulated by its Standing Orders. However, these make no mention of the most pervasive source of influence within the chambers, committee rooms and even the bars and terraces: the political parties. Journalist Martin Bell, entering as an independent on an anti-sleaze ticket in 1997 was, in his white suit, a lone figure. The idea that Parliament has a distinct identity of its own is really part of the dignified constitution; such life that it has is breathed into it by the political parties through their front-bench teams and their massed backbench ranks. What is the *raison d'être* of such dominance? For the majority party it is nothing less than producing and sustaining a government, for the others it is the less heroic role of opposing and waiting.

The Parliamentary Parties: Sustaining Government

Today party leaders are invariably from the Commons; in earlier times they came from the Lords, but Salisbury, who retired in 1902, was the last of this breed. In 1906, after a landslide victory, the leading Liberals in the Commons – Asquith, Grey and Haldane – plotted (unsuccessfully) to dispatch their leader, Campbell-Bannerman, to the Lords, knowing that this would neuter him and allow Asquith in the Commons to become *de facto* prime minister (Cross 1963: 14–15). In 1963 Douglas-Home had to renounce his peerage and enter the Commons before he could become prime minister.

Backbench organizations

Backbench organizations meet regularly once or twice a week. The Conservatives form the 1922 Committee (see p. 272). Its chairperson, who is elected annually, retains direct access to the leader and is always a commanding party figure; the position is cherished. In 1994 and 1995 Sir Marcus Fox was obliged to fight off challenges by critics of his style and advanced age. Proceedings are conducted informally with few rules, day-to-day affairs being organized by an executive committee of around fifteen, also elected annually. When in government the party leader and ministers are not members, the former attending only rarely, the event usually something of an occasion. In 1965, the Committee assumed the key function of electing the party leader, though in 1998 this was reduced to selecting a shortlist to be placed before the mass membership.

The Labour Party formed its near-equivalent in 1923 as the Parliamentary Labour Party (PLP). This is not exclusively a backbencher group; the leaders are also members, as are the party's MEPs. When in office it elects a chair but in opposition the party leader takes control. The front-bench team is elected annually as the 'Shadow Cabinet' and the leader and deputy were themselves elected in this way until 1980. When in office, a parliamentary committee with one-half government representatives and one-half elected by the PLP acts as a channel of communication.

The vicissitudes of the electoral system have left third parties at their weakest on the parliamentary stage and their organization is more informal. At one time it was unkindly said that the Liberals could hold their meetings in a telephone kiosk, but with forty-six members after the 1997 general election the Liberal Democrats can laugh at the joke.

In the upper house things are more relaxed but all three parties have a leader and chief whip. The near-equivalent of the 1922 Committee is the Association of Conservative Peers. Labour peers may attend PLP meetings but also meet separately.

There remains an element of mystery about the workings of the backbench organizations. Although in the 1970s the PLP agreed to press reporting of its meetings, there is no constitutional requirement that they conduct their affairs before the public gaze. The 1922 Committee practises its rites behind closed doors and sinister stories have circulated, some of the earlier ones started, not surprisingly, by Lloyd George. On balance, the evidence is that the 1922 Committee, although having less formal authority, receives a more studious ear from its leaders than does the PLP. Even Thatcher observed the tradition. Loss of confidence can see ministerial heads roll, as may have been the case in the resignations of Mellor, Mates and Lamont in the 1990s. The removal of Thatcher in 1990 demonstrated just how brutal the backbenchers can be.

Policy-making

Backbenchers form party committees specializing in particular policy areas, regions of the country and items of legislation. When in opposition there is some feeling in the PLP that votes should be binding on the front bench. This possible conflict is avoided by the Conservatives since shadow ministers often chair the committees themselves. Committee influence is always weaker when a party is in government since the leaders become more remote. Not wishing to antagonize their troops, however, party leaders generally take soundings on the general mood through the whips. Heath's reputation for aloofness contributed to his downfall. The all-male club atmosphere of the House placed Mrs Thatcher at a disadvantage, though she encouraged cabinet colleagues to act as her eyes and ears in the bars and corridors.

The culture of obedience

> I always voted at my party's call,
> And never thought of thinking for myself at all.
> I thought so little they rewarded me,
> By making me the leader of the Queen's navy.
>
> Sir Joseph Porter in Gilbert and Sullivan's *HMS Pinafore*

The role of MPs today is largely one of humility, their lot being to follow rather than lead. The reason for such obedience is ambition; a career is advanced through the patronage of those above. The first advancement a backbencher can expect will be as a parliamentary secretary or a junior minister (or shadow minister) at one of the lesser departments, and continued obedience is required to reach further rungs on the ladder. Discipline is even stronger for government members. Indeed, in free votes prime ministers may still expect loyalty from this 'payroll vote', as John Major did over abolition of corporal punishment in state schools in November 1996. Those entering the House later in life and not expecting to ascend far up the greasy pole may lack the incentives to grovel, yet such members rarely exhibit radical tendencies.

> The principle of Parliament is obedience to leaders. Change your leader if you will, take another if you will, but obey No. 1 while you serve No. 1, and obey No. 2 when you serve No. 2. The penalty of not doing so, is the penalty of impotence.
>
> Walter Bagehot, *The English Constitution* (1867)

The mavericks A small category of MPs, scorning the party leaders and placemen, will speak their minds and can be more influential than their docile colleagues. Enoch Powell, for example, caused both major parties to harden their lines on immigration and the Eurosceptics influenced attitudes towards European integration. Sometimes these mavericks spend their earlier years as orthodox careerists. Powell was Minister of Health in 1962, and Michael Heseltine, who was poised at the crossroads between orthodoxy and Mavericksville in the late 1980s, was to return as a veritable pillar of the Establishment. Fiery Welsh radical Aneurin Bevan accepted the warm embrace of orthodoxy for a time as the lure of office beckoned. Tony Benn strayed progressively from the Labour centre throughout a long career. Of two ex-local-government mavericks, Ken Livingstone remained at the fringe while Tony Banks entered the Labour government in 1997. Indeed, mavericks are not always without ambition, a rebellious stand on a populist issue, say capital punishment, can promote popularity (Pattie et al. 1994). Harold Wilson resigned from the government in 1951 over NHS charges but by 1964 was prime minister.

The mechanics of discipline A key figure in **party discipline** is the chief whip, aided by assistants. In the Conservative Party the leader makes the appointments but Labour's **whips** are elected by MPs. In both cases, however, their loyalty is to the leadership, ensuring that members will be in the House to vote as required (the title comes appropriately enough from the world of the hunt where the 'whipper in' is charged with the management of the hounds). The whips circulate weekly memorandums outlining the pattern of business and showing the relative importance of the votes by underscoring the request to attend with one, two or three lines. A 'three-line whip' indicates top priority with grave consequences for backsliding, ranging from a dressing-down in the chief whip's office to a 'withdrawal of the whip' (a form of excommunication, to be restored only when the offender has purged his political soul). Labour has proved far more likely to use stern measures, even resorting to the expulsion of rebels. In 1954 the whip was withdrawn from Bevan and seven of his supporters on the left.

Stern measures do not always work. In November 1994, eight Conservatives abstained over the European Communities (Finance) Bill, which the government was treating as a vote of confidence. Major scraped home and the whip was withdrawn from the rebels. However, far from becoming pariahs, as 'the whipless Tories' they were to enjoy a collective notoriety, gaining much media attention; the whip was restored the following April with little sign of atonement.

Dead certainties

As chief whip in the Wilson government, Edward Short had sick and unconscious members wheeled through the division lobby while hooked up to oxygen tubes.

Reported in the *Observer* (26 Feb. 1989)

> While we were in opposition Humphrey Atkins had been a most objectionable Chief Whip, and had marked my card. . . . he gave me a spastic 'dressing down' for smashing one of the House telephones. . . . 'We don't do that sort of thing.'
>
> Alan Clark, *Diaries* (1 Jan. 1990)

The constituency associations can be part of the machinery of obedience, recalcitrant MPs finding themselves ground between the upper and nether mill-stones. In the 1960s, Wilson employed canine imagery to warn Labour rebels that although every dog might be permitted one bite, he should not forget that his constituency 'licence' would need renewing. Of the seven left-wing rebel MPs voting against Eden over Suez, four failed to secure readoption as parliamentary candidates. Sir Anthony Meyer, who had the temerity to challenge Thatcher for the party leadership in 1989, suffered deselection soon afterwards. In January 1997, the Reigate association deselected sitting MP Sir George Gardiner, a Eurosceptic who had described Major as a ventriloquist's dummy for the chancellor. He subsequently alleged Central Office influence, the constituency chairman 'taking orders daily' (BBC Radio 4, 'World at One', 28 March 1997). When Francis Pym founded the anti-Thatcher group Centre Forward, his local association sought reassurance that he was not plotting a *coup*. However, during the 1990s, some Conservative associations appeared less supportive of the leadership: the 'whipless Tories' were buoyed by local support, minister Tim Yeo was forced (against Major's wishes) to resign in 1994 for fathering a love child, while Neil Hamilton, under investigation for sleaze, was retained by his Tatton party, despite the embarrassment to leaders in the 1997 general election.

Disciplining the Lords Party discipline is more relaxed in the upper house and *cross-voting* can be acceptable. Despite dignified titles (the chief government whip is the Captain of the Gentlemen at Arms and his deputy, the Captain of the Yeomen of the Guard) there are few sticks with which to fright the souls of old warriors and few carrots to dangle before the eyes of peers who already own much of the country.

> Three-line whips are very rare, and if I get 150 peers in to vote, using a really strong two-line whip, I am doing jolly well.
>
> Lord ('Bertie') Denham (Conservative chief whip in the Lords), in the *Independent* (27 April 1988)

Yet in the final analysis backbenchers are colleagues of the leaders; discipline and cohesion are in their own interests. The fratricide under Major contributed to the Conservatives' disastrous result in 1997, many finding themselves expelled from the 'best club in London'.

Making Laws

Parliament is the British legislature; free to make any law it chooses and subject to no legal restraint from any other constitutional body. It is in this that its constitutional sovereignty is manifest. Although this supremacy is constrained by EU membership, it is always free to secede. However, we shall find that in practice this supremacy is not all it seems.

Bills All Acts of Parliament begin life as **bills** which, broadly speaking, are of two kinds.

- *Private bills* are introduced by some body (a local authority or public corporation) wanting some special power in the form of a *by-law*. These were common in the nineteenth century as the local bourgeoisie (as councils or ad hoc authorities) sought new powers to develop the industrial cities.
- *Public bills* constitute the lion's share of all legislation, becoming the normal laws of the land. Most are government bills but some are introduced by private members.

Delegated (or secondary) legislation Much legislative power is delegated to civil servants, who frame detailed clauses through statutory orders and regulations. Although freeing Parliament from 'technical details', as long ago as 1929 the Lord Chief Justice Lord Hewart (1929: v) feared the dangerous 'pretensions and encroachments of Bureaucracy', in which he discerned a 'new despotism'. Most Acts conferring such powers contain provisions for Parliament to consider **delegated legislation** and pass affirmative or negative resolutions.

The legislative process

All bills travel a lengthy **legislative process** (figure 13.1). If this is not completed within a single session, they are 'lost' and cannot be resumed in the following session, a restriction that reformers wish to remove. If necessary the process can be accelerated (the 1911 Official Secrets Act passed through the Commons in one day, as did the Landmines Bill in July 1998). Usually beginning in the Commons, bills travel through both Houses, via a number of stages.

(1) *Pre-legislative scrutiny*. Consultation documents and white papers often precede major legislation to permit widespread discussion. Increasingly governments release draft bills for pre-legislative scrutiny by select committee. Once the policy is decided bills are prepared by parliamentary draughtsmen with the exactitude of lawyers.

(2) *First reading*. This is a formality when the bill is introduced by its sponsor who, in the case of government bills, is a minister.

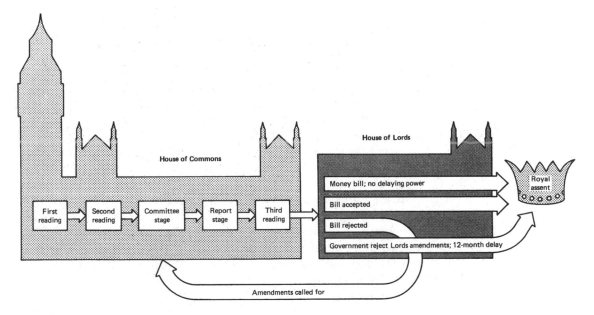

Figure 13.1 The legislative process.

(3) *Second reading.* The broad principle of the proposed legislation is debated, but modifications are not permitted.

(4) *Committee stage.* The bill is considered clause by clause, sometimes leading to small amendments. Meetings take place 'upstairs' in a **standing committee**. The term is a misnomer since, when a bill has been considered, the committee disbands, allowing no opportunity for MPs to build up specialist expertise. Membership (around 16–50) reflects party balance in the Commons, giving the government the last say. For matters of major constitutional importance, as with the Scottish and Welsh devolution legislation, this stage can take place before a Committee of the Whole House, when different rules apply and unrestricted discussion may be permitted.

(5) *Report stage.* The committee reports back to the full House which debates the clauses in detail. Amendments may be made but most are introduced by the government as a tidying-up function. Voting usually follows party lines though if the government's own supporters stand up the boat may begin to rock. Thus, in April 1988 the Conservative majority was slashed to a humiliating twenty-five in the report stage of the 'poll tax' bill.

(6) *Third reading.* This final Commons stage is nowadays largely a formality. There is no debate unless a matter of particular political importance arises, in which case six members must table a motion. No amendments are permissible.

(7)   *House of Lords*. From the Commons the bill proceeds to the Lords, where it follows a similar route for much of the time. No real challenge is expected, though during the 1980s and 1990s there were significant attempts at self-assertion (see pp. 350–1). Lords opposition to the Local Government (Interim Provisions) Bill (paving the way for GLC abolition) gave condemned GLC leader Ken Livingstone an eve-of-execution conversion to bicameralism. If amendments are made the bill is returned to the Commons for reconsideration and, if the amendments are not accepted, the Lords, having made their point, are expected to comply gracefully. If they demur they have the power to delay non-money bills for twelve months, which towards the end of a session can amount to a government defeat.

Generally the Lords have had little substantive effect. This was clearly demonstrated in the progress of the 1993 Criminal Justice and Public Order Bill. Despite receiving an eloquent and informed mauling by Lord Lestor QC and the Law Lords, all amendments were reversed by the Commons (Klug et al. 1996: 547–8). However, astonishing events in 1998 suggested that Conservative leader William Hague, using tactics reminiscent of those seen during the 1909–11 crisis (see p. 338), did not understand, or was prepared to ignore, constitutional conventions. According to the Salisbury Convention (named after one of Viscount Cranborne's ancestors), the Lords will not frustrate the Commons when the latter is expressing the will of the majority. By convention, the Lords' demand that the Commons think again is used only once (or *in extremis*, twice). Only if a government was clearly acting unconstitutionally (for example, attempting to extend its life beyond five years) could further opposition be justified. Yet in July 1998 the Higher Education Bill (which had begun in the Lords) was so batted back and forth that it was termed 'Wimbledon in Ermine'. Next, the European Parliamentary Elections Bill, at the very end of the 1997/8 session, was defeated in the Lords no less than five times and eventually lost by the government. The introduction of closed lists for European elections, while a constitutional matter, could not really be seen as a case worthy of such action by the Conservative peers. Radical reformers believed Hague to be playing neatly into their hands.

La Royne le veult.

Norman French formula for the Royal Assent

(8)   *Royal Assent*. The Queen formally approves the bill, whereupon it becomes an **Act of Parliament**. This stage has been entirely ceremonial since Britain became a constitutional monarchy; the royal assent was last withheld in 1707.

Control of legislative debate

The essence of the parliamentary process is debate ('parliament' derives from the French *parler*), yet governments have become adept at preventing such activity (and hence the amount of publicity and inconvenience) during the passage of a bill. In 1902, standing orders were introduced enabling the government to decide what subjects could be raised and for how long they would be discussed (dubbed 'Balfour's railway timetable'). Both front benches accept this curtailment, the opposition recognizing that they too may enjoy the advantages when in government, and negotiations between them are conducted by the whips through 'the usual channels'. Devices curtailing debate include the following.

- *Committees.* The committee stage excludes the majority of MPs from detailed discussion.
- *Closure motions.* These permit the House to agree that the vote be put without further discussion, thereby ending the particular stage in the process.
- *The guillotine.* While tedious speakers are not decapitated, the debate itself is put under the blade at a government-determined time. This frequently arouses opposition accusations of steamrollering, as in the case of the bill for the devolution referendums in June 1997.
- *The kangaroo.* Only a limited number of the proposed amendments are discussed, 'hopping' over the others in the manner of the antipodean marsupial. Committee members are at the mercy of the chair's selection.

Promises of modernization Labour had eighteen years of opposition in which to suffer the restrictions and in July 1997 a new Modernization Committee produced an early first report on reforming the legislative process. Key recommendations included:

- a more open and formal programming of legislation (as an alternative to the guillotine) determined by the standing committees;
- increased opportunity for pre- and post-legislative scrutiny;
- improvements in the explanatory material published with bills;
- more effective use of the committee stage, with debate on the principle of a clause before amendments are considered, chairs able to limit the length of speeches and committees able to reconvene during later legislative stages;
- constraints on times of sitting to be removed and standing committees to be allowed to sit during Recess;
- in certain circumstances bills to carry over from one session to the next.

Private members' legislation

It is here that Parliament comes nearest to a policy-initiating role, yet nothing better betokens the humility of MPs than the provision made for them to introduce bills of their own. In each session a mere ten Fridays are reserved for **private members' bills**, during which time they must attempt to negotiate the legislative hurdles. Demand outstrips the niggardly supply of opportunity and a ballot (drawing lots) selects the first twenty. Moreover, of these lucky ones, fewer than half will ever see their bills discussed, let alone complete the obstacle course to become an Act of Parliament. The reefs upon which their bills can founder are various.

Procedural problems Friday is the day when many return to their constituencies and there is a danger that the House will not be quorate. Malevolent opponents may 'talk' the bill out, preventing debate from closing, as happened to Labour backbencher Mike Foster's attempt to ban foxhunting in March 1998, despite a 250 majority in favour on first reading. Between 1967, when David Steel steered his abortion bill through, and 1988, when David Ashton introduced another on the same subject, no fewer than fifteen private members' bills on abortion law fell foul of procedural devices.

Government attitude If a government wishes, it can put various spanners in the legislative works. It can mobilize its majority to strangle a bill at birth, or it may be more devious. In May 1994 a bill on rights for the disabled was derailed by feeding selected MPs a large number of amendments prepared by civil servants, forcing it to run out of time. Lady Olga Maitland earned a stern rebuke from the Speaker for her part in the ploy. Alternatively, if it welcomes the measure, government can make time available. This is a convenient means of passing legislation with which, for reasons of discretion or cowardice, a government may not wish to be associated – say, homosexual law reform or abortion. Don Foster's 1997 Road Traffic Reduction Bill received significant cross-party support, successfully negotiating the parliamentary speed humps before dissolution for the general election. Sometimes a government will make known a number of topics upon which it would welcome legislation.

Government takeover A government may induce a member to drop a bill in order to bring in a similar one of its own, as in the case of the 1965 Health Services Complaints Act. In 1996 Labour MP Janet Anderson drafted a bill with police support to make stalking punishable by up to five years in jail. Believing its scope too wide, the government withheld support, promising to produce its own proposals 'at the earliest opportunity' (*Guardian*, 10 May 1996). This tactic may be used to water down a proposal, as with the 1988 reform of the Official Secrets Act.

Despite the restrictions, some MPs use the opportunity to demonstrate parliamentary flair and make their mark, as did Roy Jenkins (obscene publication), David Steel (abortion law reform) and Margaret Thatcher (admission to public meetings). Even if a bill meets an ignominious end, MPs have had an opportunity to publicize their views and stimulate debate, as with Foster's failed foxhunting bill.

Legislation from Europe

EU membership produces an alternative source of law affecting British subjects. Critics see this as a dramatic affront to parliamentary sovereignty and MPs have sought some element of control. In May 1974 a sixteen-member Committee on European Secondary Legislation was established to examine draft proposals submitted to the Council by the Commission. However, unable to question proposals it can only recommend their submission to a standing committee or the House. Even here no amendments can be made; the House debates it as a 'take note' motion in the hope that ministers will reflect its views in the Brussels. Matters are additionally complicated because the Westminster and Brussels timetables are not synchronized and proposals may surface during a recess. The Lords also has a European scrutiny committee, working through seven specialist subcommittees. Unlike its Commons counterpart it may discuss the merits of a proposal and call upon expert witnesses. However, debates are again confined to 'take note' motions. Some improvement was promised in November 1998, a white paper recommending greater powers for Parliament to scrutinize and delay EU legislative proposals and so prevent ministers from agreeing to any measure until both Houses have finished considering it. In practice the Commons committee has proved unpopular with MPs but, rather than testifying to the dominance of Brussels, this is a symptom of the might of the British executive. In Denmark, for example, the Folketing has secured far greater powers to influence its own government's position in Brussels.

The value of the legislative process today

The legislative process bestows the official seal of approval. Ordinary people can rest in their beds secure in the knowledge that the laws affecting their lives have satisfied their elected representatives, rather in the manner that a car might go through its MOT test. Or can they? If vehicles were examined in the way MPs examine legislation, the roads would be littered with wrecks. Scrutiny of this order produces only a false sense of security. The constitutional brakes may be failing and the wheels about to come off, yet Parliament is as rigorous as the mechanic in the back-street garage with pockets full of greasy folding pictures of the Queen.

Although outwardly the process remains essentially that of the nineteenth-century 'Golden Age', it has become in large measure part of the dignified constitution. Like all such ceremonial its value lies in its ability to beguile and deceive. Although the legislative process may not have *policy-making* significance, it remains of considerable *political* significance as a means of legitimation. It would, however, be mistaken to conclude that all stages of the process are as empty as the Royal Assent. Parliament fulfils two useful roles in the legislative process: *publicity* and *criticism*. Although imperfect, and capable of being subverted, these are not to be entirely dismissed as contributions to democracy.

Debates in Parliament

A second major parliamentary function is debating issues of the day. MPs such as Enoch Powell, Tony Benn and Michael Foot (all virtuoso performers), who have been particularly identified with the parliamentary cause, always stressed

Gladstone defends
his Home Rule Bill,
1893

Source: Mary Evans Picture Library

the profound importance of this. Various opportunities are provided, including
the following.

- *The **Queen's Speech**. Delivered in the House of Lords at the beginning of
  each session, this catalogue of proposed legislation (written by the prime
  minister) is debated over the following five days.

- *General government debates.* The government will normally devote around fifteen days each session for debate on topics of its choice. In this way it can test ideas, hear views on green or white papers, and outline its position.
- *Opposition Days.* Originally called Supply Days, these are twenty occasions when the choice of topic is determined by the opposition parties (seventeen to the largest and three to the second largest). The aim is to attack the government.
- *Estimates Days.* Since 1981, three days have been set aside each session for debating the Estimates, the topics chosen by the Liaison Committee.
- *Adjournment debates.* On four days a week, a half-hour debate at the end of the sitting traditionally allows the House to consider grievances. The motion is chosen by a backbencher, often raising some constituency matter, and is answered by a relevant minister. They are popular with MPs, who must ballot for the opportunity. The final adjournment debate before a recess is a larger affair, the motion selected by party leaders.
- *Wednesday morning debates.* Three Wednesday mornings are now devoted to select committee reports, the remainder being used to debate issues raised by backbenchers (see p. 384).
- *Emergency adjournment debates.* In an emergency a government may propose the adjournment of business at the beginning of the day to debate a major event, such as the Gulf war of 1991. The House may even sit on a Saturday to debate an emergency, as with the Suez crisis in 1956 and the Argentinian 'invasion' of the Falklands in 1982.
- *Emergency debates under Standing Order No. 9.* Here an MP can ask for an adjournment to debate a 'specific and important matter that should have urgent consideration'. The Speaker only agrees if convinced of the urgency and such debates are infrequent. Their value lies in forcing discussion of issues that the government might wish to keep from the public eye. One such debate was held on the GLC Fares Fair case.
- *Private members' motions.* In each session a number of Fridays are reserved for motions put by private members. Although constituency matters may be raised, debates often centre on government policy.

Early Day Motions

Citizens may read that their MP has put down, or signed, an Early Day Motion, though may never see any record of the debate. This puzzle arises because 'Early Day Motion' is today a colloquial term for a notice of a motion for debate with no expectation that it will ever take place. A number of such motions are tabled each day, enabling MPs to record their feelings on a subject and gauge support. One signed by sixty-nine of his backbenchers in June 1992 gave John Major a forbidding warning of his Eurotroubles to come. Sometimes much can be achieved. In November 1994 an Early Day Motion forced Michael Heseltine to drop Post Office privatization plans.

An extract from the Daily Agenda for Wednesday 20 January 1999

9.30	Prayers
Afterwards	Adjournment Debates:
	Mr Tony Worthington: Cairo conference on population and development – five years on
11.00	Mr Tim Boswell: Horticultural industry
12.30	Mr Stephen Twigg: Sentencing policy in road death cases
1.00	Mrs Jacqui Lait: Disposal of Health Services Accreditation
1.30	Mr Gareth R. Thomas (Harrow West): Developing social enterprise (until 2.00 p.m.)
2.30	Oral Questions to the Secretary of State for Northern Ireland
3.00	Oral Questions to the Prime Minister
3.30	Private Notice Questions, Ministerial Statements (if any)
Afterwards	Greater London Authority Bill (Clauses 1 to 4 and Schedules 1 and 2): Committee [2nd allotted day] (may continue until 10.00 p.m.)
At the end of the sitting	Adjournment Debate: Education funding for South Gloucestershire (Steve Webb) (until 10.30 p.m. or for half an hour, whichever is later)

Empty debate

Despite the opportunities, commentators make several criticisms of the way Parliament uses its debating powers.

Blind loyalty Debate is rather a misnomer. There is little real cut and thrust and speakers tend to read from prepared briefs, rarely responding to previous points and not even remaining in the chamber to hear how others respond. Final votes reflect not the qualities of wit or wisdom but party loyalty.

Backbench frustration At all times front-benchers are preferred. In calling members the Speaker is supposed to look to those with particular expertise or interest, but frequently MPs are left seething at not having been called. The inexperienced spend fruitless hours preparing speeches never delivered. In 1988 backbenchers openly attacked Speaker Bernard Weatherill for being over-conscious of the rights of Privy Councillors (Heffer 1988).

Superficiality Debate can emphasize meretricious rhetorical skills. Members performing stylishly may triumph over less articulate, but more sound, colleagues. When John Davies, Director General of the Confederation of British Industry, became a cabinet minister, his serious, non-histrionic style left members cold, drawing from party colleague Enoch Powell the mocking jeer: 'They've got a right 'un there' (Wyatt 1973). The parliamentary style, with the confident accent spiced with the Shakespearean quotation, can seem particularly ill suited to working-class politicians.

Ill mannered The televising of Parliament brought into shocked viewers' homes scenes of booing, fist-waving and shouting down, often likened to a bear garden. Indeed, the Speaker's cry of 'Order, Order' became the 'signature tune' of the broadcasts.

Weak in substance Debates tend to be of a low quality (the Lords may sometimes give a more informed treatment of a subject). Ministers rely blindly on a crutch of bureaucracy (providing statistics, arguments and information), while the opposition struggles to build its case on the basis of outside advice, intuition and invective.

The empty chamber Backbenchers do not always support each other very well; once opening speeches have been made they drift from the chamber, sometimes to their offices, sometimes to places of refreshment, only to re-emerge for the front-bench winding up and to cast their all-important votes.

In March 1998 the Modernization Committee's report on conduct in the chamber recognized many of these points. Questions and answers were to be brief and members were called upon to respond to comments of previous speakers and, having spoken, to remain in the chamber. It was also suggested that the Speaker cease to give Privy Councillors precedence. Yet even with some reform, debates in Parliament are likely to take the form of a party clash rather than a dialogue between executive and legislature. In the effort to hold the executive more effectively to account Parliament has sought other mechanisms. It is to these that we now turn.

Scrutiny of the Executive

It is said that the price of freedom is eternal vigilance and the idea that Parliament should scrutinize the executive remains a key aspect of its rationale. MPs probe through **parliamentary questions** and through an ancient instrument, the select committee.

Questions in the House: a fretful hour

The first hour of the day (except Wednesdays and Fridays) following Prayers is **Question Time**. Here government members are questioned on their areas of responsibility in one of the few opportunities MPs have to shine. A relatively modern innovation, it began in the nineteenth century as a means of strengthening Parliament against an enlarging executive. The occasion can prove testing to ministers. Although answers are prepared by civil servants (work in the upper echelons of a department can come to a virtual standstill while this is done), the hour receives keen media attention and those who falter may be earmarked as political liabilities; for junior ministers it can be make-or-break time.

Oral and written answers   Questions may, at the choice of the member, receive an oral answer in the chamber or a written one (indicated by an asterisk on the order paper). With almost 50,000 questions tabled each session, about three-quarters receive written answers. The distinction has considerable importance. Written answers can be prepared by civil servants in the name of the minister and arouse little media attention. When giving oral answers, ministers are forced to become personally involved, which gains publicity, and the member will have further opportunity through supplementary questions.

Supplementary questions   Ministers cannot get away with a mere recital of a civil servant's brief, they must also be prepared to deal with follow-up questions. Skilful MPs will lure the minister to the dispatch box with an innocuous question, only to unsheathe a rhetorical stiletto. Supplementaries have steadily increased, reducing the number of questions answered each day from around sixty in the 1920s to around twenty. This leaves some forty questions unanswered, though they will be printed in the following day's *Hansard* (the report of parliamentary proceedings) as if they had been (and with a written answer). Successive Speakers have urged members to cut supplementaries, but this reduces MPs' power and is resisted.

Prime Minister's Questions   The highlight occurs on Wednesdays at 3.00 p.m. (previously Tuesdays and Thursdays), when for half an hour the prime minister stands at the dispatch box. Parliamentary broadcasts frequently place this at the top of the bill. There are more oral questions for the prime minister than any colleague, ranging widely over issues of the day. Sometimes these can be deflected to the responsible minister but, to prevent this, members began to adopt the strategy of asking very specific personal questions; enquiring into the prime minister's immediate plans and engagements, and following this up with their real concern. Nowadays most MPs merely table their questions as 'engagements'. A ballot determines which members will be able to ask their real questions as supplementaries. The 'engagement' question is not even answered once a reply has been given to the first one. In recent times, Wilson, Thatcher and Blair have appeared to revel in the opportunity to enthuse supporters and ridicule opponents during Question Time.

Question Time in question   The present system owes much to Balfour's reforms at the beginning of the century, which were intended to restrict rather than encourage debate. Amongst other things, he wanted Question Time at the end of public business when MPs were becoming weary and, although this was resisted, he instigated the *written answer* and limited the time for oral questions. Tony Blair's replacement of two quarter-hour sessions with one of half

Andrew Mackinlay: Does the Prime Minister recall that, when we were in opposition, we used to groan at the fawning, obsequious, softball, well-rehearsed and planted questions asked by Conservative members of the right honourable Member for Huntingdon [Mr. Major]? Will my right honourable friend distinguish his period in office by discouraging such practices – which diminish Prime Minister's Question Time – during this Parliament? Furthermore, in view of the rather depleted official Opposition, will he encourage rather than discourage – without fear or favour, and without showing partiality or affection – loyal Labour backbenchers who wish to seek and provide scrutiny and accountability in this place? The Prime Minister: I fully respect my honourable friend's independence of mind, and shall do my very best to ensure that he retains it.

Exchange between Labour backbencher and Tony Blair during Prime Minister's Questions (3 June 1998)

an hour was seen by critics as further weakening the system. Various other problems remain.

- *The rota.* Particular ministers come to the dispatch box on certain days only. The result is delays in answering, with issues becoming 'stale' and a backlog developing.
- *Written answers.* These are used increasingly (a daily average of over 100). However, although providing much detailed information with which to evaluate the government, they cannot be subject to spontaneous debate.
- *Time.* Despite various suggestions for improvement (an extended question hour, Friday sessions), Question Time remains a very inadequate fifty-five minutes.
- *Evasion.* Ministers have an increasing capacity to evade by claiming that a matter lies outside their control (local government, civil service agencies and the NHS, for example). They may also refuse on matters of security, including policing, or on 'public interest' grounds. With a long-term decline in oral answers prime ministers are by no means exempt (Dunleavy and Jones 1993; Burnham et al. 1995).
- *Party domination.* Despite MPs' alleged freedom at Question Time, the parties insinuate their tentacles. Governments can 'plant' questions, detailing tame backbenchers to ask what they want asked, or crowd out opposition questions. Alternatively, the opposition can use backbenchers for an attack masterminded by the leaders (Gould 1978: 87). Both Labour and Conservative MPs are 'invited' to briefings on Wednesday mornings, given their questions and coached in them. This reached a new low under Blair, forcing the Speaker to intervene and complain of 'sycophantic questions'.

Scrutiny by committee

Much of the work of Parliament is done by committees. Many of these are **select committees** drawn from all parties to fulfil some function on behalf of the

House. Thus the Procedure Committee regulated its internal working, the Committee on Standards and Privileges (established November 1995 to replace the Privileges and Members' Interests committees) guards ethical standards and oversees the work of the new Parliamentary Commissioner for Standards (see p. 366) and the Committee on the Modernization of the House of Commons (established June 1997) considers reform. Select committees are also involved in policy issues (in the nineteenth century they functioned rather like royal commissions) or are used to gather information.

One of the most successful has been the Public Accounts Committee (PAC), created in 1861 to examine the departmental accounts. This provided a model for a pattern of reform that began in the 1960s. It was felt that MPs lacked information and expertise, debates continually seeing backbenchers and even the opposition front bench woefully out-gunned by the government. The cause was taken up in 1966 by Leader of the House Richard Crossman. Committees were established with the power to 'send for persons, papers and records', and hold public hearings. However, for the government the experiment seemed little more than an exercise in self-flagellation and it was allowed to languish.

Returning to power in 1970 the Conservatives were more encouraging and the Estimates Committee was replaced by an Expenditure Committee working through six specialist subcommittees. The beleaguered 1974 Labour government had little enthusiasm for reform but the next Conservative administration brought the reformist Norman St John Stevas as Leader of the House. Twelve committees were created to cover the major spending departments. Although these were to become a lasting feature their road was not always to be smooth.

A mandarin's charter If the bureaucracy conceded with one hand it took with the other. A hitherto unknown assistant secretary in the Civil Service Department secured modest immortality in May 1980 by codifying some earlier guidelines. These became known as the Osmotherly Rules: a hitchhiker's guide to the committee galaxy designed to keep officials out of trouble on hazardous voyages through Westminster. The black holes of questioning into which civil servants should not allow themselves to be lured included:

- advice to ministers;
- interdepartmental policy exchanges;
- matters of political controversy;
- confidential information supplied by firms or individuals;
- delicate information concerning foreign powers.

Furthermore, in no circumstances were MPs to receive extracts from cabinet papers or be told anything about cabinet discussions. Decision-making details were also to be clasped to the bureaucratic bosom. These guidelines could be seen as a mandarin's charter and gave an excellent indication of the official view of Parliament's place in government.

Although less powerful than envisaged in the Procedure Committee's report, the committees were superior to anything seen before. They could choose the

---

House of Commons: Select Committees, July 1997

Agriculture	Liaison
Culture, Media and Sport	Modernization
Defence	Northern Ireland Affairs
Deregulation	Public Accounts
Education and Employment	Public Administration
Environment, Transport and	Science and Technology
Regional Affairs	Scottish Affairs
European Legislation	Social Security
Foreign Affairs	Standards and Privileges
Health	Trade and Industry
Home Affairs	Treasury and Civil Service
Information	Welsh Affairs
International Development	

---

topic for investigation, call for persons and papers and were served by a staff. They were also able to receive written and oral evidence from ministers, civil servants, local government officials and other interested parties, including pressure groups, and could appoint advisers to prevent witnesses pulling the wool over their eyes. Established for the complete duration of a parliament, they could not be disbanded by government. Membership, reflecting party strength, would be kept small (around eleven), with chairs shared between parties and the system overseen by the Liaison Committee, comprising the committee chairs.

Some were to produce stinging reports. The Treasury and Civil Service Committee was particularly scathing of economic policy in the 1980s. In January 1994, the PAC published a highly critical report on standards of probity, integrity and financial control in many parts of the public service. Some commentators saw in the committees a new dawn for Parliament. However, the threat to restrict them was always present, surfacing dramatically in the enquiry into aspects of the Westland affair.

The Westland affair This issue concerned the leak by the Department of Trade of a letter from the Solicitor General criticizing Michael Heseltine, who was at odds with the Prime Minister over how to save the Westland helicopter company. Sensing an opportunity for real scrutiny the Defence Committee launched an investigation. However, in January 1986 the government prevented key civil servants (Colette Bowe, John Mogg, Bernard Ingham and John Mitchell) from testifying, Thatcher claiming 'major implications for the conduct of the government and for relations between ministers and their private offices' (*The Times*, 31 Jan. 1986). In their place Permanent Secretary at the Department of Trade, Sir Brian Hayes, was sent in to play a straight bat. When reminded of the committee's unqualified power to investigate he unabashedly referred to a memorandum of guidance to civil servants produced by Cabinet Secretary Sir (later Lord) Robert Armstrong, saying in effect that although a committee may get a horse to the water, the minister can still forbid him to open his mouth. Leon Brittan, whose behaviour was to lead to his resignation, refused nine questions in succession, finding the committee's observations 'unworthy and unfair'.

Subsequently, Sir Robert Armstrong was asked by the Prime Minister to conduct his own enquiry (bordering on a farce since he must have known who was responsible before starting; see Hennessy 1990: 305) and after this he too went before the committee to obfuscate. Thus Parliament was never to know the extent of Downing Street's involvement in what Armstrong admitted to be the 'discourtesy, impropriety, and unwisdom' of the leaked letter (Evans 1986b). The committee's report was a damning indictment of those involved in the cover-up. Yet the sabotage did not end there; the Conservative majority on the committee delayed publication until the eve of the summer recess, thereby muzzling debate. No US executive could have got away with such evasion; Thatcher avoided a British Watergate.

> For a Prime Minister to sit there for half an hour and allow the Secretary of State [Leon Brittan] to mislead the House was a most extraordinary procedure.
>
> Roy Jenkins, at the time of the Westland affair, in House of Commons (13 Jan. 1986)

Life after Westland? Major's administration also showed little affection for the select committees, infuriating its own backbenchers by removing a raft of independently minded members by 'inventing' a rule that no MP could serve on a committee for over twelve years. Nicholas Winterton, struck off the Health Committee, which he had chaired, accused the whips of 'saying free speech and an independent mind can have no role in Parliament' (*Observer*, 12 July 1992). Another scandal arose over the Pergau Dam project in Malaysia, where government aid was tied to arms contracts. Although the Public Accounts Committee produced a critical report in March 1994, Baroness Thatcher refused to give evidence to the Foreign Affairs Committee in May 1994.

Further evidence of disrespect for the committees came when David Willetts, as a government whip, attempted to influence the Members' Interests Committee investigating the cash-for-questions scandal. Called before the Standards and Privileges Committee, his tortuous explanation was regarded as 'dissembling', precipitating his resignation as Paymaster General in December 1996. New Labour proved no less willing to ride roughshod over Parliament. In May 1998, Labour's Diane Abbott accused Denis MacShane, PPS at the Foreign Office, of trying to intimidate the Foreign Affairs Committee in its arms-to-Sierra-Leone investigation; her own questioning was regarded as disloyalty (*Sunday Times*, 24 May 1998). The committee found its access to documents blocked by Foreign Secretary Robin Cook and when the final critical report surfaced it was dismissed by the Prime Minister as 'disproportionate and unfair'. It later transpired that a draft had been leaked to Cook by Labour committee member Ernie Ross, who was forced to resign. Even more disturbing, it emerged that Labour MPs on other committees were doing the same.

Everyone thought it was very harsh on David Willetts. All he was doing was his job.

Former Conservative whip, in the *Independent* (14 July 1997)

Scrutiny and the constitution Given a paucity of resources (staff, advisers, expenses for witnesses, time and formal powers) the committees can be said to have achieved much. They have produced hundreds of reports, publicized some important issues and sometimes influenced government policy. However, they work under a major constitutional handicap. Across the Atlantic congressional committees exert considerable sway, their chairpersons nationally recognized figures able, as British television viewers witnessed in the Watergate and 'Irangate' hearings, to put the US executive on the spot. However, British committees could never operate with the same authority. Congress is set within a constitutional separation of powers; in Britain the Cabinet and prime minister dominate the House from which the committees come. All the formidable powers the government has to control Parliament can be used to limit its committees.

Moreover some (such as Enoch Powell and Michael Foot) have argued that the whole development is misguided. Parliamentary debate is traditionally wide ranging, concerned with points of broad principle. The micro-level scrutiny of the committees may lose sight of the ideological wood for the trees. In this view, the argument that MPs require more information in order to be better at their jobs may be fallacious.

Reporting Parliament

> Burke said that there were Three Estates in Parliament; but, in the Reporter's Gallery yonder, there sat a *Fourth Estate* more important far than they all.
>
> Thomas Carlyle (1795–1881; Scottish essayist and historian),
> *Heroes and Hero Worship* (1841)

Whatever its faults, Parliament remains the nation's central democratic forum. Even though debate rarely leads to direct policy change, it can have a longer-term influence by shaping public opinion. The mechanism for reporting Parliament is therefore crucially important.

Problems of reporting Parliament

Although all debates and discussion are faithfully reproduced in *Hansard*, the vast majority of people wishing to follow the proceedings of Parliament do so through the mass media. There are certain problems with this.

- *Selectivity.* It is impossible to cover everything said in this palace of a million words. Journalists must be selective, seeking the essence of a speech or debate.
- *Simplification and trivialization.* In the tabloids single-syllable words are *de rigueur*, while the broadsheets have a tradition of amusing reporting

'Parliamentary Sketch' columns, often highlighting the antics of the more bizarre and exotic parliamentary creatures.

- *Sensationalism*. In the quest for circulation, any suggestion of scandal will take precedence over serious news. In October 1998, Welsh Secretary Ron Davies's strange encounter on Clapham Common took precedence over debates on devastation caused by hurricane Mitch. Able ministers, such as David Mellor, can even be forced from office. Broadsheets and broadcasters are not immune from this criticism.
- *Bias*. Right-wing bias has seen editorial selection generally favouring the Conservatives or centrist Labour case. 'Rowdyism' on the left has been reported in lurid detail.
- *Tame reporting*. Much reporting merely relays information disseminated by ministers, press secretaries and spin doctors through the lobby system (see p. 220) and press releases.

The media can reduce the status of the House by encouraging statements outside its precincts under the eyes of the cameras. This can catch opponents unprepared and evade critical debate. Even Enoch Powell, a fervent parliamentarian, was guilty. In March 1998 the Speaker admonished Labour *'apparatchiks'* for playing a public relations role for ministers; this was appropriate in opposition but not in government. In June 1997 Blair began a monthly series of question-and-answer sessions, not in Parliament but on television with selected members of the public. Sir Archie Hamilton, Chairman of the 1922 Committee, lambasted this bypassing of Parliament (*Guardian*, 9 June 1997).

The *Times* has made many ministries. When, as of late, there has been a long continuance of divided Parliaments, of governments which were without 'brute voting power', and which depended upon intellectual strength, the most influential organ of English opinion has been of critical moment.

Walter Bagehot, *The English Constitution* (1867: ch. 1)

Live from the Commons: broadcasting Parliament

No technological innovation has had a greater impact on the political life of the nation than the unblinking eye. Campaigning is now mainly a television art and between elections politicians feature regularly in news stories, as chat-show guests and hosts, and on phone-ins and 'question time' programmes. On Christmas Day viewers are even taken into their homes to share their festivities and hear them singing carols with their families. Yet the cameras for long remained out of the House.

In March 1976 the Commons agreed in principle to sound broadcasting, though this was not to be the thin end of the television wedge. Not until 1986 did the Lords agree to submit to the cameras and the historic first live television broadcast from the Commons took place on Tuesday 21 November 1989 with the debate on the Queen's Speech. Although officially an experiment the cameras had come to stay, both in the House and in the committee rooms. Today, those with cable TV can watch debates in their entirety.

The debate When the British Parliament finally agreed to experiment, Australia, Austria, Belgium, Canada, France, Greece, Holland, Italy, Japan, West Germany and the USA had all accepted the principle (*Sunday Times*, 14 Feb. 1988). What was the reason for the reticence? Those against argue that it highlights the 'worst' aspects of debate, encouraging members to play to the gallery. Moreover, as with sports coverage, editing concentrates on 'highlights' in the quest for ratings. In 1998 'Yesterday in Parliament' was removed from Radio 4's FM frequency for fear of losing listeners (part of a process termed 'dumbing down' by its critics). The counter-argument is that, having been courted for their votes, people should be allowed to witness the results of their choices. Moreover, in a televisual age, if the cameras did not enter the House, coverage would be confined to studio confrontations between academics, journalists and a chosen few media politicians or ex-politicians: not public debates but private debates upon public matters.

Official reticence is hardly surprising in the most closed and secretive political culture in the western world, where democracy, unlike justice, has been deemed better for not actually being seen. In Westminster, the public gallery is small and usually full of sightseeing tourists. This was very convenient for those who wished to emasculate the people's representatives. Today the public gallery contains some 54 million at home and even a worldwide audience. However, with jeering MPs and an expanse of empty green leather benches, people do not always like what they see (Norton 1997: 364–5).

From Golden Age to Golden Sunset?

An incessant theme of post-war debate has been the reform of Parliament, the underlying critique centring on its inability to bridle, or even effectively scrutinize, the executive. While formally regarded as sovereign, it is rather like the aged parent of an arrogant son, grown beyond discipline.

The Golden Age of Parliament

It is sometimes contended that, from its origins, Parliament has never been strong vis-à-vis the executive, and that it is not in the nature of the British constitution that it should be. However, there was a **'Golden Age'**, extending from the first great Reform Act of 1832 to that of 1867, when MPs really mattered. This was before the parties began to dominate, when governments were genuinely vulnerable to being turned out of office without a general election (as in 1852, 1855, 1858 and 1866) and ministers could be individually censured and forced to resign. MPs controlled the organization of the House and could shape policy through

debates. Information could be demanded from government and select committees would conduct authoritative investigations and even draft legislation. During this period the legislative process began with a formal request for leave to
introduce the bill, justification being required before a first reading. Second and
third readings, and the committee stage, were genuinely critical scrutinies in which
MPs set their own time and secured amendments. Gladstone's financial reforms
subjected public expenditure to real control.

Today MPs are members of their parties first and of the House second. The
unity of Parliament is like that of a gigantic pantomime horse in which two ill-
matched thespians wrestle with each other about who should be the head. What
was vividly revealed during the Major government was that the greatest check
on the executive comes not from Parliament as such, but from the government
backbenches.

Friendly fire: backbench opposition

A new MP entering the chamber with Winston Churchill remarked that it was time to face the enemy. 'No', came the reply; the facing benches contained the 'opposition', the 'enemy' sat behind!

If a party has consolidated the executive hold over Parliament it can also im-
peril it. It is within the parties that the real executive/legislature tension can be
seen (Brand 1992). A government's own backbenchers can become an effective
opposition. This important facet in appreciating the role of Parliament has been
a key theme in a continuing analysis by Philip Norton. From the 1970s MPs
appeared to be becoming less disciplined, resulting in a greater incidence of
government defeats. Heath (1970–4) experienced six such setbacks, three on
three-line whips. The 1974 Labour government suffered no fewer than fifty-
nine defeats, although there were special circumstances, including fragile
majorities, minority government and the uneasy Lib–Lab pact.

The Conservatives' success in broadening their social base brought in young
meritocrats displaying less instinctive loyalty. Hence government vulnerability
became more apparent under Major. Not only were there serious defeats, often
at the hands of the Eurosceptics, there was a vote of confidence and even
Major's exasperated resignation as party leader. Following his sacking in the
face of hostile backbench rumblings, Norman Lamont spoke in June 1993 of a
government 'in office but not in power'. As his majority dwindled, Major's
hands became tied over his Northern Ireland initiative and even individual MPs
could take advantage; Sir John Gorst warned in December 1996 that his vote
was conditional on the removal of a hospital closure threat in his constituency.

Bloody good news for democracy.

Speaker Bernard Weatherill, on government defeat on a three-line whip over its Shops Bill to bring in Sunday trading; quoted in the *Independent* (24 Dec. 1987)

A secure majority does not guarantee peace since backbenchers may feel free
to air their consciences without real damage. In 1964, when Labour had the
barest of majorities, Wilson could enjoy loyal support, but after the 1966 victory the left began to make demands, particularly on defence issues. Similarly,
the seemingly impregnable Thatcher governments experienced many challenges
(over matters as varied as rate-capping and charges for dental and optical tests)
and some backbench victories were gained (the 1986 Shops Bill and the 1982
amendment to the immigration rules). Dramatic revolts in April 1988 over the
poll tax and housing benefits also forced government concessions.

However, after Major's uncertain reign, Blair's government was to reassert the position of the executive through unprecedented attention to party discipline. MPs were allegedly being kept 'on message' by spin doctors; in March 1998 Tony Benn reported in *Tribune* that Labour backbenchers regularly received faxed personalized press releases ready to be sent unchanged to their local newspapers.

> One MP told me that four of his colleagues had refused to take part in a charity swim because it would mean removing their vibrating bleepers for an hour.
>
> Labour MP reported in *Index on Censorship* (1998, no. 5: 57)

Hence, the power to check the executive, while real, is contingent; it depends on a government's majority, the willingness of MPs to toe the line and the effectiveness of internal party discipline. This is not the constitutional check of a genuine separation of powers. Indeed, its fragility was demonstrated over the damning findings of the Scott Report when 'a majority of MPs voted, in effect, to be repeatedly misled by civil servants', demanding no ministerial heads although the House had been subjected to lies and deception (Norton-Taylor et al. 1996: 197).

Reform and talk of reform

The scale of the problems facing the Commons can be measured in the length of the catalogue of possible reforms (see, for example, Norton 1997). In the first year of the Blair government, the Modernization Committee produced four reports covering issues such as the legislative process, select committees, scrutiny of European legislation, voting procedures, the parliamentary calendar and the conduct of debate. However, while promising to streamline procedures, these offered no greater controls on the executive. Indeed, Blair's prompt 'modernization' of Prime Minister's Questions, strengthening rather than weakening his position, was done without consulting the House.

Inhibitions to reform   All hope of reform must come up against the 'great ghost' of the constitution. Bagehot saw virtue in the Commons' *fusion* with the executive; the constitution's 'efficient secret'. Yet it was this, together with party discipline, that was to render parliamentary sovereignty so palpable a fiction. The very disease renders the House unable to administer the medicine. Only the executive has the power to effect change, but why should it connive to reduce its omnipotence? Governments may be enthusiastic about rearranging the deckchairs but will they alter the course of the Titanic? In the USA, where there is genuine separation of powers, Congressional leaders are not members of the executive, neither do they depend on executive patronage for advancement; these are the conditions required for a genuine check on the executive. Clinton, for example, was subjected to unremitting hostility and lost some of his most cherished legislative ambitions.

Moreover, one can doubt MPs' commitment to a stronger role. Some are happy enough to engage in constituency work or pursue their business interests, leaving their leaders to govern, while the new breed of young professional politicians see their future not on select committees but as front-benchers and must court the patronage of their leaders. In the constituencies most associations do not expect their representatives to rock the boat and, for the general public, executive domination is entirely compatible with a political culture that admires strong government. Many would be disturbed to find their representatives continually frustrating the actions of government. Thatcher enjoyed much adulation and Tony Blair swept to victory as a dominant leader, even professing admiration for the lady and wearing much of her finery. Finally, the establishment of the Nolan Committee, the appointment of a Parliamentary Commissioner for Standards, and Jack Straw's 1998 Corruption Bill cast doubt on the ability of this 'mother of Parliaments' to guarantee its *own* integrity, let alone that of the executive.

Denouement: a deeper function exposed

If Parliament is flawed with respect to its key roles, what then is its function in modern politics? Perhaps the answer lies in Bagehot's analysis of the value of monarchy: outward display serving to beguile the masses, leaving the real process of government in the hands of a political elite. Perhaps this reading can help explain the Commons. Politicians of all hues, representatives of powerful interests, the media and civil servants all pay unctuous tribute to the idea of parliamentary sovereignty.

It is crucially necessary for the economically and politically powerful that the House of Commons *should* have this apparent centrality in British political life, because it stands alone in the constitution as the embodiment of democracy. Without it there would be little to justify the exercise of state power. More than any other institution, it can foster a popular belief that ordinary folk control their rulers. In other words, it is one of the most powerful legitimating devices in the political system. In the following chapter we shall look deeper into the modern executive which so dominates the people's elected representatives.

Key points

- Parliament is largely energized by political parties, with little real identity of its own as the collective voice of the people.
- Party discipline, the absence of a separation of powers and the tendency of the electoral system to bestow absolute majorities mean that parliamentary sovereignty is effectively hijacked by the executive.

- The principal functions of Parliament may be said to be legislation, debate and scrutiny of the executive. In all these the executive holds the whip hand.
- EU membership produces an alternative source of legislation limiting parliamentary sovereignty.
- Because it is the forum of popular debate, the reporting of Parliament is constitutionally significant.
- There are latent powers in Parliament which under certain circumstances a government's backbenchers can use.
- To an extent Parliament serves to conceal the reality of power in Britain.

Review your understanding of the following terms and concepts

Act of Parliament
adjournment debate
backbench organization
bills, private and public
delegated legislation
Early Day Motion
emergency debate
'Golden Age' of
   Parliament

Hansard
legislative process
legislature
Opposition Day
parliamentary question
party discipline
private member's bill
Queen's Speech
Question Time

scrutiny committee
select committee
standing committee
supplementary question
whip
written answer

Assignment

For this assignment you must refer to *Hansard*, the record of parliamentary debate. Do this in your library or on the internet (http://www.parliament.uk). Look up the debate on 'Parliament and Politics (BBC Coverage)' which took place on Wednesday 21 October 1998 beginning at 11.00 a.m. (column 1215). Answer the following questions.

		Mark (%)
1	What kind of debate is taking place?	5
2	What parliamentary device had been used by Nigel Evans to show his concern over BBC policy?	5
3	Summarize in around 500 words the case against the BBC made by Paul Tyler.	20
4	Which MP lends support to the BBC? Assess the validity of his argument?	10
5	Why do backbenchers place a particular value on regional broadcasting?	20

6	Upon what grounds does David Winnick assert that 'the BBC is treating Parliament with utter contempt' (column 1218)?	10
7	What does Richard Allan mean by a 'reality lag' (column 1228)?	10
8	Consider the validity of the BBC's argument that parliamentary broadcasting should be reduced if it is found boring by the mass audience.	20

Questions for discussion

1 Explain the way in which the Labour and Conservative backbenchers organize in Parliament.
2 What factors account for the high level of party discipline in the Commons?
3 'The legislative process was designed for the mid-nineteenth-century Parliament and is nothing more than an anachronism today.' Discuss.
4 Evaluate Parliament's role with respect to EU law-making?
5 What is the value of the parliamentary question today?
6 Evaluate the opportunity for, and value of, private members' legislation.
7 How important today is Parliament as a forum for debating current issues?
8 To what extent can select committees enable MPs to control the executive?
9 Consider the pros and cons of televising Parliament.
10 What Commons reforms do you consider necessary?

Topic for debate

This house believes that the modern House of Commons is little more than a part of the dignified constitution.

Further reading

See also reading for chapter 12.

Adonis, A. (1993) *Parliament Today*.
Stresses Parliament's role as a focus of national attention.

Brand, J. (1992) *British Parliamentary Parties: Policy and Power*.
Illustrates how intra-party tension constitutes the real executive–legislative tension.

Hansard.
Official reports of proceedings (available in libraries and on internet).

Hansard Society (1993) *Making the Law: Report of the Commission on the Legislative Process.*
Examines question of reform of the Commons.

Norton, P. (1993) *Does Parliament Matter?*
'Yes', says one of Britain's leading authorities.

Richards, P. G. (1970) *Parliament and Conscience.*
Illustrates the backbencher's role in legislating on sensitive issues of morality.

For light relief

Tony Banks, *Out of Order.*
Parliamentary anecdotes from a colourful MP.

Hilaire Belloc, *Mr Clutterbuck's Election.*
Satire on early-century political life.

Michael Dobbs, *House of Cards.*
Follows the progress of evil chief whip, Frances Urquhart, who will stop at nothing for power. Fictional of course. Available on video.

Greg Knight, *Right Honourable Insults.*
Tory MP of Tony Blair: 'He's so vain he'd take his own hand in marriage', and so on. Hundreds of wicked insults from the experts.

Matthew Parris, *Great Parliamentary Scandals.*
Entertaining mapping of the moral swampland of British politics over four centuries.

Howard Spring, *Fame is the Spur.*
Labour politician's rise to power and subsequent disillusionment.

On the net

http://www.parliament.uk
Parliament's home page includes links to *Hansard*, select committee reports and the progress of bills through the legislative process. Some MPs now also maintain web sites of their own.

Chapter Fourteen

The Heart of Government: of Cabinets and Kings

In this chapter attention turns from the elected assembly to the relatively small group of MPs who head the executive arm of government, and to the environment in which they work. However, the complex territory around the cabinet system comprises individual actors (officials, spin doctors and advisers, junior ministers), committees of politicians and officials, and institutional structures. Together this network constitutes Britain's core executive. The chapter comprises two broad sections. The first begins by examining the nature of cabinet government and its evolution in Britain. Next we begin to map the anatomy of the core executive, identifying a range of associated political debates. In the second section we turn to one of the most compelling questions of modern government: the role of the prime minister. Is it, or is it not, becoming more presidential in character? Alternatively, does Britain have cabinet government: collective rather than singular, the principle of rule by the *one* having been repudiated in the long series of constitutional struggles against monarchy? Or is the modern core executive so complex that neither answer can be appropriate? This chapter tells us much about the living constitution, revealing a dense network of relationships and dependencies in which power is diffuse and found in many guises.

Defining the executive head

Every state has a centre of political authority. Decisions made here determine how we live, how we are educated, our health, our employment and perhaps, where war is concerned, how we may die. Formally the head of the British system of government comprises the prime minister and around twenty other senior ministers, most heading ministries. This is the **Cabinet,** which works through weekly meetings in the Cabinet Room at the prime minister's residence, 10 Downing Street, a familiar backdrop for the comings and goings of the important and self-important. The Cabinet has also become integrated into the EU and can be expected to become more so. Ministers operate at the very heart of the decision-making process in the Council of Ministers, while the prime minister sits on the European Council, sometimes assuming its presidency.

The Cabinet and the government Journalists often write as if the terms 'Cabinet' and 'government' are synonymous. In the eighteenth century this was largely true but today the Cabinet is but a small part of a complex web comprising

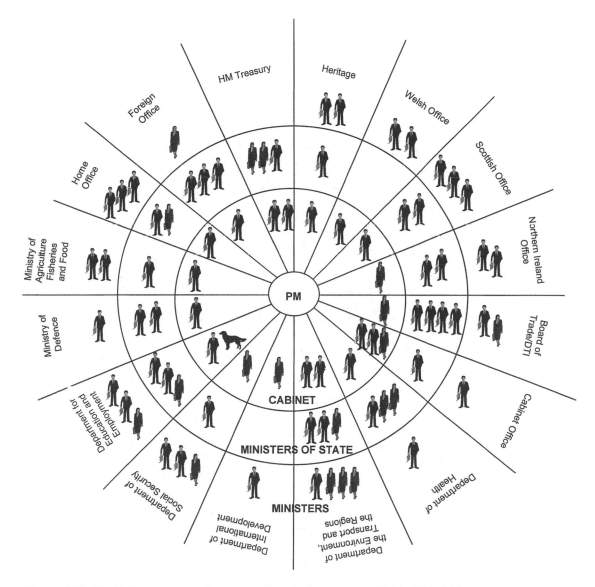

Figure 14.1 The Cabinet stands at the centre of a web of government: Blair's 1997 Cabinet.

over two hundred politicians, forming a hierarchy ranging from secretaries of state to junior parliamentary private secretaries assisting ministers (figures 14.1 and 14.3). This web of power extends even further to embrace the senior public servants at the heads of the departments of state and executive agencies to form the '**core executive**' (Dunleavy and Rhodes 1990).

An Anatomy of Cabinet Government

What is cabinet government?

The Ancient Greek philosopher Plato believed that rule by a divine 'philosopher king' would be the most perfect form of government. However, this could only exist in an ideal world; in reality it would deteriorate into the *worst* form – tyranny. Regimes that have terrorized populations have characteristically been dominated by single rulers – tyrants, dictators and demagogues, their very names synonyms for oppression. Constitutions are designed to prevent tyranny; this is what the English sought to do in 1215 and 1689 and the Americans in 1787. After Stalin the Russians vowed they would never again permit one person so much power. Yet the British executive, inheriting the powers of the monarch and able to dominate Parliament, knows no constitutional constraints. Hence, faith in **cabinet government** is crucial.

Cabinet government entails the sharing of authority, with decision-making based upon discussion and compromise. However, this self-moderating form of government is only protected by conventions and these are among the most fragile in the constitution. If there is a document to be consulted, it is *Questions of Procedure for Ministers,* finally released in 1992 after some fifty years of official secrecy. However, the dry passages of dos and don'ts of this ministerial highway code say little about the politics of power. For this reason, one of the most crucial questions in modern British politics is whether cabinet government is real or just one more myth in our slippery and elusive constitution?

Evolution of the Cabinet

The history of the Cabinet cannot be traced as a continuous line linking a distant past indissolubly to the present. The modern Cabinet owes much to political forces generated by the rise of capitalism and is linked with the nineteenth-century constitutional reforms. It is certainly true, however, that monarchs have always surrounded themselves with small bands of loyal advisers and confidants and this helps explain the structure of the modern executive and the culture of power within it.

The Privy Council By the sixteenth century the practice of monarchical consultation had become institutionalized in the Privy Council, a body that had itself evolved from a council of royal advisers in Norman times (the *Curia Regis*).

The following century saw the Civil War and the republican period with government through *executive committees*. This proved unworkable, but after the Restoration, when Charles II sought to re-establish what he believed to be his divine right to rule alone, he found the Privy Council difficult and resorted to a smaller group, a committee of the council. This was called the 'cabinet' as a term of abuse, a synonym for 'cabal' – a devious, inner group. The modern Cabinet remains constitutionally a committee of the Privy Council, members retaining the title 'right honourable' for life. Consigned to the dignified part of the constitution, the full Council nowadays meets only rarely, to mark great state occasions such as the sovereign's marriage or death.

The Glorious Revolution In 1681 Charles II dissolved Parliament, establishing an alternative 'Oxford Parliament'. The ensuing struggle led to the 'Glorious Revolution' of 1688, resulting in the flight of James II (who had acceded in 1685), and his ultimate replacement by William (of Orange) and Mary. Matters of state were transacted in the full Privy Council and, to prevent royal influence, ministers were excluded from Parliament. However, this principle was soon abandoned because Parliament wanted ministers in its midst for questioning. Had it been retained, Britain would have developed a separation of powers and a significantly different constitution. As it was, membership of Parliament, rather than being forbidden, became an essential requirement of office, thereby clearing the way for a *fusion* of powers – Bagehot's 'efficient secret' of the constitution.

The Act of Settlement Later anxiety about the succession, resulting from the death of Queen Anne's son, was allayed in the Act of Settlement (1701) establishing the Hanoverian succession. It has been said that between 1714 and 1760, George I and George II showed little interest in British politics, thereby allowing the Cabinet to play an increasingly dominant role. This may contain an element of truth but there were also more fundamental forces at work. Ministers had in fact met in the absence of the monarch during Anne's reign (1702–14) and when George III attempted to reassert a degree of royal authority in 1784 he was castigated as unconstitutional; the roots of the modern Cabinet had taken hold. The monarch reigned but the Cabinet had effectively hijacked the royal prerogative. It did not, however, possess all the essentials of its modern counterpart.

- Responsibility was to the Crown rather than to Parliament, so that it was possible to govern without a majority.
- Parliamentary groupings (Whigs and Tories) were only loose coalitions, making it possible for a Cabinet to contain representatives of both and enjoy cross-party support in the House.
- Cabinet members were responsible only for their own ministries and quite prepared to attack each other's policies.
- The resignation of the First Lord of the Treasury (the prime minister) did not mean that other ministers also had to depart.
- A significant number of MPs owed allegiance to neither 'party' and could be courted through patronage and bribery.

The Cabinet Room in Downing Street, 1870

Source: Mary Evans Picture Library

The industrial revolution The rise of the industrial bourgeoisie in the nineteenth century challenged the *ancien régime*; the new men entered Parliament through the extended franchise and dominated it through party discipline. This added a second dimension to the power of the Cabinet.

- Cabinets became more tightly knit with members drawn from one party only.
- Members accepted collective responsibility for policy.
- So long as their backbenchers remained loyal, governments enjoyed a degree of supremacy unknown since the Tudors.

Here was the modern Cabinet: relatively autonomous and drawing authority from various constitutional and political sources, including its lineage to the Privy Council, its inheritance of the prerogative powers of the Crown, and its domination of the constitutionally sovereign Parliament.

Collective responsibility

The constitutional basis of cabinet government is sometimes said to lie in the doctrine of **collective responsibility**, which implies a form of collective decision-making. Interpreted variously by participants and commentators, it generally implies the following features.

- All (or several) members play a part in formulating policy.
- All members support each other in public (even if privately disagreeing).

- Any member unable to lend support should resign.
- Cabinet proceedings are regarded as confidential (though resignees earn the right to a resignation speech revealing their reasons).

The convention probably originated in the eighteenth century when ministers sought to strengthen their hand vis-à-vis the monarch by sticking together. Today its prescriptive force lies in the ideal of collective decision-making as a curb on power. However, in reality it is honoured more in the breach than the observance.

Now, is it to lower the price of corn, or isn't it? It is not much matter what we say, but mind, we must all say *the same*.

Attributed to Lord Melbourne (1779–1848; Whig prime minister), quoted in Walter Bagehot, *The English Constitution* (1867: ch. 1)

Collective responsibility or collective expediency? An important reason for the doctrine's persistence is political expediency (which is why we even find it applied to the Shadow Cabinet). A united front has proved a valuable asset. Indeed, the collective cloak can be thrown over all members of the government, usually encompassing around one-third of the parliamentary party. In 1983 Nicholas Budgen, a mere assistant whip, resigned over the provisions of the Northern Ireland Bill, while in April 1994 Jonathan Evans resigned as a PPS over a disagreement on local government reform in Wales. The doctrine can thus be a basis for party discipline, giving the government a 'payroll vote' that can be relied upon by the whips.

However, submerging differences can be stressful. Once in opposition, former Home Office minister Ann Widdicombe, in a passionate forty-minute Commons speech, revealed the tension between her and the Home Secretary over the dismissal of prison service chief Derek Lewis. Again, Geoffrey Howe's momentous resignation, marking the beginning of the end for Thatcher, revealed anguished feelings submerged beneath a famously ovine exterior when he lamented the futility of

> trying to stretch the meaning of words beyond what was credible, of trying to pretend there was a common policy . . . That conflict of loyalty has become all too great. (House of Commons speech, 13 Nov. 1990)

In practice journalists can reveal much cabinet dissent. A number of Major's ministers in the 1990s gave indications of variance over the EU while remaining in the Cabinet. Indeed, when arch-Eurosceptic John Redwood resigned in 1995, it was to challenge for the leadership rather than express dissent.

"*Our minutes are going to make pretty boring reading in 30 years' time with no one ever dissenting.*"

Reproduced by permission of *Punch*

Cabinet structure

Within the cabinet hierarchy, the most senior members hold titles such as Home Secretary, Chancellor of the Exchequer, Foreign Secretary, or Secretary of State for this or that. Generally ministers are not expected to have specialist knowledge; indeed regular reshuffles positively discourage this. They are *generalists* rather than *specialists*. The status of a position can vary with circumstances and personalities. When Howe was made deputy prime minister it was seen as an insult, but when Heseltine took the position after supporting Major in the leadership challenge some even saw him as the *de facto* prime minister. This new locus of power was retained by Blair, with John Prescott in the post while also presiding over a large empire of the Department of the Environment, Transport and the Regions. Northern Ireland secretary was regarded as something of an incubus but in 1998 Mo Mowlam became a veritable heroine. A Cabinet can also contain ministers without portfolio with responsibilities reflecting a prime minister's priorities. This appointment was used by Tony Blair to include Peter Mandelson in 1997, seen as a Svengali-like spin doctor, with a responsibility for coordinating and presenting policy.

Composition Cabinets were traditionally drawn largely from the social elite, a large proportion having aristocratic backgrounds and very few with working-class credentials. However, in both major parties there has been, throughout the twentieth century, a steady increase in the *petit bourgeois* element, reaching a high point in the Thatcher Cabinets of the late 1980s (figure 14.2). In terms of education, ministers have been by no means typical of those they govern, a high proportion having attended public school (particularly Eton) and Oxbridge (Guttsman 1963). However, Blair's first Cabinet contained only four Oxbridge alumni (including the Prime Minister himself). A further four came from Durham, three from Edinburgh and ten other provincial universities were also represented. Ron Davies enjoyed the distinction of being the first cabinet member from a polytechnic (Portsmouth).

Like Parliament, the Cabinet has been largely a male preserve, women often having had only a token presence. Ironically Thatcher showed no desire for female colleagues and Major's first Cabinet contained none at all, though Blair began with no fewer than five. However, he failed to deliver on a promise of a cabinet-level minister for women, making this an unpaid junior post for Joan Ruddock.

We still thought in terms of appointing a statutory woman. 'Who should she be?' asked Ted [Heath]. 'Margaret Thatcher', was my immediate reply.

James Prior (Conservative cabinet member), *A Balance of Power* (1986)

Cabinet size

Aug 1945 Lab. 20
Oct 1951 Con. 16
Oct 1964 Lab. 23
Jun 1970 Con. 18
Mar 1974 Lab. 21
May 1979 Con. 22
Nov 1990 Con. 22
May 1997 Lab. 22

Aristocrats (with hereditary titles amongst grandparents)

Middle class

Working class (fathers with manual occupations)

Figure 14.2
Social composition of incoming Cabinets, 1945–1997.

Source: Data from Butler and Butler (1994: 66), *Dod's Parliamentary Companion* (1998), Waller and Criddle (1997) and various on-line information sources.

By the time a minister reaches cabinet rank he or she will normally be experienced in government. However, Blair's first team began at a considerable disadvantage as a result both of an unusually prolonged period in the wilderness and a convention that limits opposition access to Whitehall. There had, however, been some relaxation of the rules to allow some contact with permanent secretaries and agency heads from January 1996, enabling prospective working partners to size each other up. Other preparations included seminars at Oxford University to receive the collective wisdom of retired mandarins and ex-Labour ministers.

Size The size of the Cabinet is no mere technicality; it has implications for the way it works. Eighteenth-century Cabinets contained around five to nine members, which grew to twelve to fifteen in the following century and by Asquith's time had reached twenty-three, whereupon the figure remained constant (figure 14.3). Today the law allows for twenty-two salaried members. Although this might not seem very large, it is so by international standards. The mighty US president, for example, surrounds himself with only around ten colleagues. Critics generally believe British Cabinets to be too large for effective collective decision-taking but various pressures tend to increase size.

- *Growth in the public domain.* Since the nineteenth century, government has taken on many more areas of responsibility. Wilson defended his Cabinet of twenty-three on the grounds that it was 'inconceivable that important sectors of our national life should be excluded' (Walker 1972: 35).
- *Bureaucratic pressure.* Representation in Cabinet remains politically important to departments as they compete for resources.
- *Interest group pressure.* Outside Westminster, groups see in cabinet composition indications of a government's priorities. Doctors, farmers, trade unionists, and so on, all look for visible confirmation that they are recognized.

Figure 14.3
The increasing size of peacetime governments.

Source: Data from Butler and Butler (1994: 66).

- *Parliamentary pressure.* Leading party figures such as, say, John Prescott, usually have bands of supporters in the House pressing for their inclusion.
- *Party faction.* A prime minister will try to appease factions of party opinion; hence Major's inclusion of the troublesome Eurosceptics.

Critics allege that large Cabinets can be slow and cumbersome; vulnerable to factionalism (Thatcher Cabinets were characterized in terms of 'wets' and 'drys'); liable to leak – 'The more you have,' said Harold Wilson, 'the more people can be got at' (Hennessy 1986: 149); and lacking a strategic vision as ministers develop departmental tunnel vision. Reformers, including journalists, academics and politicians, advocate a slimmed Cabinet as a way of improving government.

- *Policy Cabinet.* One of the most discussed models is the **Policy Cabinet** advocated by Leo Amery, who served under Bonar Law and Baldwin. He argued for around six members, each free of departmental ties, to consider collectively the full range of policy from an overarching strategic perspective (Amery 1947). Ex-Chancellor Nigel Lawson put forward a similar proposal.
- *War Cabinets.* The exigencies of war have produced some enforced experiments. In 1916 Lloyd George's War Cabinet contained five members, forming a nucleus within a larger system encompassing departmental ministers and service chiefs, attending as required. At the beginning of the second world war Chamberlain formed a Cabinet of nine, reduced to five by Churchill in 1940. Even the skirmish with Argentina in the 1980s saw the fleeting emergence of a War Cabinet.
- *Policy Cabinets in peacetime.* The nearest peacetime version of the model was an experiment by Churchill upon his return to office in 1951. In a Cabinet of sixteen he appointed three non-departmental ministers, described as 'Overlords'. This is generally regarded as a failure, with a return to 'normal methods' two years later (Daalder 1964: 110–18). There was speculation in early 1997 that a 'super minister' system might be reintroduced by Blair to oversee large programmes such as welfare reform and transport (Grice 1997). John Prescott was duly made Secretary of State for the Environment, Transport and the Regions and the Lord Chancellor, Derry Irvine, also had something of an overlord role in masterminding constitutional reform across a wide front.
- *Inner cabinets.* While outward forms remain, informal evolution takes place beneath the surface. One such has been the rise of what has been termed the **inner cabinet**. Very much a political creation, even more unknown to the formal constitution than the Cabinet itself, the term 'inner circle' is perhaps the more appropriate for most post-war groupings (James 1994: 628). This is a group of about four ministers closest to the prime minister meeting independently and informally. Burch and Holliday (1996) found key decisions regularly being made in this way in the mid-1990s.

This can threaten genuine cabinet government, carrying connotations of devious secrecy like those evoked by the term 'cabal'. However, it has proved irresistible to most prime ministers and could be said to constitute an informal Policy Cabinet.

Yet the policy cabinet principle assumes that strategic thinking can be separated from day-to-day matters. Douglas Wass, ex-joint head of the civil service, questioned this proposition in his Reith Lectures: 'In my experience of administration I have found it almost impossible to think constructively about general policy issues if I have not been involved in particular practical cases' (1984: 29).

Cabinet committees

Modern cabinet government in Britain is enmeshed in a dense network of committees and subcommittees (table 14.1), the growth of which is one of the most significant post-war constitutional developments. Yet it long remained cloaked in secrecy, with accounts pieced together from memoirs, leaks, press guesswork, and occasional parliamentary statements. In 1972 Patrick Gordon Walker gave some clear indications in his book *The Cabinet*, Mrs Thatcher acknowledged them in the House in 1983 and the following year *The Times* published a detailed list. Finally, in 1992, the Whitehall ribcage, if not the flesh, was detailed in X-ray, with the official release of all cabinet standing committee details, including terms of reference and membership. These are now readily available on the internet.

Keeping the people informed

He agreed that no Prime Minister has ever explained why the numbers and membership of Cabinet Committees were kept secret. Why were they? I asked.

There was a long pause. 'Erm,' said the former Secretary to the Cabinet. 'Well. Erm. Are we on the record or off the record?'

'On the record.'

'Then I think I'd rather not go into that.'

Lord Hunt (ex-Cabinet Secretary), interviewed by Michael Davie
in the *Observer* (11 Oct. 1987)

In principle, committees are created to assist the Cabinet, which remains the 'parent' body. There are two broad categories – ad hoc and standing committees.

Ad hoc committees Created for specific problems these have only ephemeral lives. The first was established in 1855 to handle the Crimean war, to be followed by others concerned with aspects of foreign policy. Towards the end of the nineteenth century, with a massive tide of legislation, others emerged to formulate policy and draft bills. They remain very important. In 1984 an

Table 14.1 Cabinet committees and subcommittees, 1997 Labour government

Code name	Chair	Terms of reference
Economic and finance		
PX	Chancellor of Exchequer	Public expenditure allocation
EA	Chancellor of Exchequer	Economic policy
EA(WW)	Chancellor of Exchequer	Welfare-to-work policies
MISC 3	Board of Trade President	Utility regulation
Home and social		
HS	Deputy PM	Home and social policy
MISC 2	Home Secretary	Youth justice reform
HS(H)	Leader of Commons	Health strategy
HS(D)	Leader of Commons	Drug misuse
HS(W)	Social Security Secretary	Women's issues
MISC 1	Chancellor of Duchy of Lancaster	Food safety
ENV	Deputy PM	Environmental policy
GL	Deputy PM	Local government
GL(L)	Deputy PM	London policies
Overseas, defence and security		
DOP	Prime Minister	Defence and overseas policy
E(DOP)	Foreign Secretary	EU membership
IN	Prime Minister	Northern Ireland
CSI	Prime Minister	Security and intelligence services
Legislation and constitutional reform		
QFL	Lord Chancellor	Legislative programme and Queen's speeches
LEG	Leader of Commons	Parliamentary procedure and examination of draft legislation
CRP	Prime Minister	Constitutional reform
CRP(EC)	Lord Chancellor	Incorporation of ECHR
CRP(FOI)	Lord Chancellor	Freedom of information issues
CRP(HL)	Lord Chancellor	House of Lords reform
JCC	Prime Minister	Joint committee with Lib Dems
DSWR	Lord Chancellor	Devolution

ad hoc committee addressed the abolition of the GLC and the metropolitan counties, while Thatcher controlled strategy towards the 1985–6 miners' strike in this way. In June 1997, a powerful committee, chaired by Labour Social Security Secretary Harriet Harman and consisting mainly (but not exclusively) of female ministers, was established to promote women-friendly policies across

Whitehall. Labour's raft of new policy initiatives required a range of committees such as those on constitutional reform and welfare-to-work. Thatcher had shown a preference for highly informal groupings, Major reverted to a more formal structure characteristic of the Wilson, Callaghan and Heath years, while Blair returned to the informal style of Thatcher.

Standing committees Dating from a later period, the first of these was the highly successful Committee of Imperial Defence (CID) with its network of subcommittees. Its creation in 1903 marked a watershed in cabinet government. Concerned with particular areas of policy (education, defence, the economy, and so on; see table 14.1), standing committees have continuing existence. Ministers most involved in European matters sit on a special committee chaired by the foreign secretary. Code names, initials and acronyms (E for Economic and MISC for Miscellaneous) add to the mystique.

Composition and functions The committees characteristically include a core of cabinet ministers with a central interest, some junior ministers and civil servants attending as the secretariat or in their own right. Sometimes outsiders are included. Tony Blair caused some consternation in July 1997 by announcing a new cabinet committee chaired by himself and including five Liberal Democrat MPs, amongst them leader Paddy Ashdown. Meeting monthly, it was to focus on issues of mutual interest, including the constitution. To veteran MP Tony Benn this was 'the beginning of the end' of party government. In November 1998 its remit was broadened to include areas such as welfare, education, health and the single currency.

Government by committee? Although the role of the committees is recognized in *Questions of Procedure for Ministers*, there remains an underlying fear that they reduce the Cabinet to a rubber stamp, leaving no room for ministers to discuss each other's policies or take an overall strategic perspective. Some committees have exceedingly high status, often chaired by the prime minister or another senior minister. The great 1944 Education Act was largely the product of a committee led by R. A. Butler. In 1967 Wilson formally enhanced their status, decreeing that matters should only be reconsidered by the Cabinet with the agreement of the chairs. Mrs Thatcher herself chaired committees on the economy and other key areas, including ad hoc committees on replacing the Polaris defence system and on the future of the Falklands. Blair's reforming constitutional committees were chaired by Lord Chancellor Derry Irvine, who enjoyed an exceptionally close rapport with the Prime Minister. Although the committees formally operate on a *nem. con.* basis, with determined opposition and competing options only being resolved in Cabinet, in the view of Whitehall-watcher Peter Riddell (1997), under Blair 'the full Cabinet has lost even its residual role as a court of appeal or as a forum for discussing big issues'.

Official committees The system of cabinet committees is paralleled by one of official committees meeting to prepare the ground. There is a danger that deci-

> Most of my work when I was Minister of Education was done outside the Cabinet, and hardly referred to the Cabinet at all.
>
> Lord Butler, interviewed by Norman Hunt (later Lord Crowther-Hunt)
> in the *Listener* (16 Sept. 1965)

sions may really be made before the politicians actually meet, with ministers being given briefs that foreclose their options.

The Cabinet Office

Over the past twenty years power has seeped from cabinet committees in a process of informalization and centralization around the Number Ten complex. Central to this is the Cabinet Office. The cabinet territory is by no means the exclusive preserve of politicians. Civil servants, and some outsiders, exert a dominant presence through this key department of some 2,000 lying at the epicentre of power. It is organized into sections and units responsible for various aspects of government business, such as the machinery of government, senior public appointments and top management. Its role has increased during the past two decades as various new specialist units have been added, enlarging it by some 300 per cent (Burch and Holliday 1996).

The Cabinet Secretariat

The most politically sensitive part of the Cabinet Office is the **Cabinet Secretariat**. With the exception of its head, the **Cabinet Secretary**, the 200 or so civil servants comprising the secretariat are seconded from other departments and there is much competition for these prestigious positions within the super-elite of the service. Its ostensible functions are similar to those of any other secretariat: circulating information to the Cabinet and its committees, preparing and distributing papers and agendas for meetings, advising on procedure and

---

Agenda for the Cabinet meeting of 1 August 1963

1 Future pensions increases	6 Policy towards South Africa
2 Incomes policy	7 Butter imports
Construction industry	8 Commercial policy
3 Foreign affairs	Barley imports
United Nations	9 Commercial policy
4 Commonwealth and Colonial	Jute imports
Affairs	10 Welfare services
5 Finance for the United Nations	School meals
in the Congo	

taking minutes (conclusions). The cabinet secretary conveys decisions to departments and monitors their implementation. These functions give the secretariat great political significance. Its role in establishing compromise solutions that enable ministers to present a unified front, both domestically and to the EU Council of Ministers, affords considerable influence (figure 14.4).

Evolution   Until the early twentieth century it was traditional for the Cabinet to work informally with no agendas or minutes and no officials present. The only records were notes and personal letters from prime minister to monarch or diary entries (Gladstone's diaries are a particularly rich source of information). Sometimes ministers were unclear about outcomes, their civil servants being obliged to deduce what might have been decided. This seeming madness had some method: meetings were regarded as highly secret and the involvement of non-elected outsiders as unconstitutional. However, the first world war was to undermine such constitutional niceties. When Lloyd George took over he commandeered the much admired secretariat of the CID, including its head, Maurice Hankey, for the War Cabinet. Housed in huts in the garden of 10 Downing Street it became known as the 'garden suburb'. After the war the innovation was reappraised; opponents associated it with Lloyd George's overbearing style and the Treasury saw it as a rival in Whitehall. However, the 1918 Haldane Report on the machinery of government recommended its retention.

As the main architect of the secretariat Hankey deserves an honoured place in the bureaucratic hall of fame. Remaining to serve five very different prime ministers (Lloyd George, Bonar Law, Baldwin, Ramsay MacDonald and Chamberlain) in a variety of circumstances (war, reconstruction, coalition and both Labour and Conservative administrations), he demonstrated the value of the new machinery. Today the cabinet secretary is frequently described as the

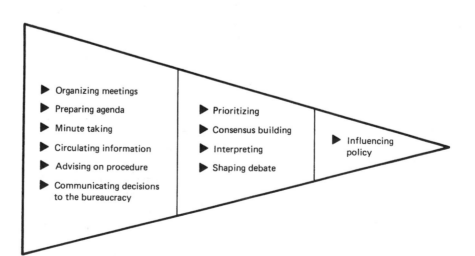

Figure 14.4
Administrative functions have political implications.

most powerful civil servant in the country. Since 1983 he has been formally designated Head of the Home Civil Service. In addition to Herculean formal responsibilities, cabinet secretaries can find themselves in politically sensitive trouble-shooting roles, as was Sir Robert Armstrong over the 'Spycatcher' and Westland affairs and Sir Robin Butler over the Scott enquiry and alleged breaches of the rules on MPs' outside interests.

The minutes: how they run Initially Hankey kept near-verbatim accounts, attributing opinions and attitudes to individuals. Criticized as unconstitutional, this was modified to include only a general view of the debate, making it possible to use the 'conclusions' as the directions for civil service action. This practice places the secretariat in a pivotal position, with disturbing possibilities. In a break during a meeting, Richard Crossman examined the notes of Cabinet Secretary Sir Burke Trend and was shocked to see that the report of the Prime

---

139

THIS DOCUMENT IS THE PROPERTY OF HIS BRITANNIC MAJESTY'S GOVERNMENT

Printed for the War Cabinet. November 1942.

SECRET.   Copy No. 48

W.M. (42)
159th Conclusions.

TO BE KEPT UNDER LOCK AND KEY

It is requested that special care may be taken to
ensure the secrecy of this document

WAR CABINET 159 (42).

*CONCLUSIONS of a Meeting of the War Cabinet held in the Prime Minister's
Room, House of Commons, S.W.1, on Thursday, November 26, 1942, at
12·30 P.M.*

Present :

The Right Hon. WINSTON S. CHURCHILL, M.P., Prime Minister (*in the Chair*).

The Right Hon. C. R. ATTLEE, M.P., Secretary of State for Dominion Affairs.	The Right Hon. ANTHONY EDEN, M.P., Secretary of State for Foreign Affairs.
The Right Hon. Sir JOHN ANDERSON, M.P., Lord President of the Council.	The Right Hon. ERNEST BEVIN, M.P., Minister of Labour and National Service.

The Right Hon. HERBERT MORRISON, M.P., Secretary of State for the Home Department and Minister of Home Security.

The following were also present :

The Right Hon. Sir KINGSLEY WOOD, M.P., Chancellor of the Exchequer.	The Right Hon. VISCOUNT CRANBORNE, Lord Privy Seal.
The Right Hon. Sir ARCHIBALD SINCLAIR, Bt., M.P., Secretary of State for Air.	The Right Hon. Sir STAFFORD CRIPPS, K.C., M.P., Minister of Aircraft Production.
The Right Hon. ERNEST BROWN, M.P., Minister of Health.	The Right Hon. BRENDAN BRACKEN, M.P., Minister of Information.
The Right Hon. Sir WILLIAM JOWITT, K.C., M.P., Paymaster-General.	The Right Hon. JAMES STUART, M.P., Joint Parliamentary Secretary, Treasury.

Mr. W. WHITELEY, M.P., Joint Parliamentary Secretary, Treasury.

Secretariat.
Sir EDWARD BRIDGES.
Mr. NORMAN BROOK.

CONTENTS.

Subject.	Page
Social Services	176
The Beveridge Report. Question of Publication.	

[24681—1]

176

Social Services.	THE War Cabinet had before them a Summary of the Report by Sir William Beveridge on Social Insurance and Allied Services (W.P. (42) 547). and considered the date of publication of the Report and what statement the Government should make as to their attitude in regard to it.
The Beveridge Report.	
Question of Publication.	
(Previous Reference: W.M. (42) 153rd Conclusions, Minute 5.)	The War Cabinet's conclusions were as follows :—

(1) The Report should be made available to Members of Parliament at 3 P.M. on Tuesday, the 1st December, and released to the Press for publication in the morning newspapers of Wednesday, the 2nd December. (Arrangements should be made by the Minister of Information to allow Editors to have copies, in confidence, in advance of publication, so as to enable them to study the Report.)

(2) No objection should be raised to Sir William Beveridge broadcasting on the Report after publication.

(3) The Paymaster General, in the Debate on reconstruction matters, should make a statement on the following lines :—

The questions dealt with in the Report were of great interest. and the Report itself was a notable contribution to their study. Time, however, would be required for detailed examination of the recommendations by all those concerned, including the Government and their advisers.

An undertaking should be given that the Government would be prepared to make some general statement on the position after Parliament had reassembled in the New Year.

A reminder should be added that, not only must the practicability of the recommendations contained in the Report be examined. but also that the Report must be considered in relation to the main measures which would have to be taken over the field of reconstruction as a whole. not forgetting what was necessary to maintain international security.

(4) The Chancellor of the Exchequer and the Paymaster-General were asked to prepare a statement on these lines and to submit it to the Prime Minister.

*Offices of the War Cabinet, S.W.1,
November 26, 1942.*

Minutes ('Conclusions') of the Cabinet meeting of 26 November 1942, which discussed the Beveridge Report (PRO document reference CAB 65/28)

> Now that the Cabinet's gone to its dinner,
> The Secretary stays and gets thinner and thinner,
> Racking his brains to record and report,
> What he thinks what they think they ought to have thought.
>
> Anon., quoted in S. S. Wilson, *The Cabinet Office to 1945* (1975)

Minister's position was 'not the substance of what he had said, and if it had been the substance he would have divided the Cabinet' (Crossman 1975: 103–4). Michael Heseltine complained that the Prime Minister prevented discussion on certain matters and 'insisted that the Cabinet Secretary should record my protest in the Cabinet minutes', yet when circulated 'no record of my protest' was to be found (Heseltine 1986: 2). Under Blair the quality of the minutes changed, with much important business transacted elsewhere and a more informal flow of discussion. The secretariat were left to write things up as best they could so that some non-cabinet ministers (and no doubt future historians) found them among 'the least important part of their weekly reading' (Hennessy 1998: 11).

The Shadow Cabinet

Even less known to the constitution than the Cabinet is its shadow on the opposing front bench at Westminster. Often ignored in studies of government, the **Shadow Cabinet** constitutes a ready-made governmental cast waiting in the wings; its members are shadow ministers with shadow portfolios and the leader is the shadow prime minister. It is a particular feature of a two-party system, where a foetal government will lie curled in the womb before the general election.

Evolution In the eighteenth century parliamentary factions would organize into groups to oppose those in office (Turner 1969). If a government seemed likely to fall, lists of possible ministerial teams would begin to circulate. The relatively frequent fall of governments meant that there were always ex-ministers in Parliament able to provide well-informed criticism; thus the 'ex-Cabinet' is the natural forebear of the Shadow Cabinet. Once a general election meant the removal of a government *en bloc*, it followed that a new one must be ready to emerge overnight (Punnett 1975: 144).

The Shadow Cabinet today Although the difference between shadow and substance is that the former has no executive responsibility, in many respects members conduct themselves in the same manner as the Cabinet: holding meetings, appointing specialist committees and practising collective responsibility and secrecy (and suffering leaks). In September 1992 Bryan Gould resigned to voice his support for a referendum on the Maastricht Treaty, complaining that the Shadow Cabinet was a 'gag and a straightjacket', and in 1998 Hague was to sacrifice two senior Shadow Cabinet members when he articulated an anti-single-currency position.

Shadow Cabinets are valuable to democracy. Americans see little of any alternative president until the campaign period and do not see the Cabinet until well after. In Britain, the alternative government is displayed on the shelves of the Westminster supermarket. The role is officially recognized with salaries for the opposition Leader and chief whip. Yet its value is reduced by lack of information; ex-mandarin Sir Douglas Wass (1984) has argued that it should be power-assisted with a special civil service department.

The Central Policy Review Staff 1970–1983: RIP

No student of cabinet government can ignore Edward Heath's experiment in 1970. The Central Policy Review Staff (CPRS) was baptized with this dry title by Cabinet Secretary Burke Trend, who, belying his own name, found the US term '**Think-Tank**', preferred by Heath, rather too racy for bureaucratic sensibilities. However, the media preferred Heath's choice, giving it the wider currency feared by the mandarin. The CPRS was to be a small unit in the Cabinet Office, its role to:

- provide ministers with wide-ranging information to prevent departmental 'tunnel vision';
- offer advice on policy alternatives;
- promote interdepartmental cooperation;
- help determine relative priorities;
- provide continuing performance review in the light of overall strategy.

Heath briefed the infant CPRS on the lawn of 10 Downing Street, recalling how he had seen 'Cabinets which all the time seemed to be dealing with the day-to-day problems' with 'never a real opportunity to deal with strategy' (Heath 1972: 5). Its first head was Lord Rothschild, an academic and scientist personally chosen by Heath, and its multidisciplinary composition drew representatives from academia, industry and the civil service. The impression was of a smart set of young intellectuals from society's privileged enclaves which Rothschild (aged sixty-two when appointed) described with affectionate tolerance as 'a bunch of 15 anarchists' (Fox 1975: 285).

The career of the CPRS However, after the honeymoon years, the CPRS experienced an erratic rake's progress, its function varying according to the government in office. Retained by Wilson, it encountered its *pons asinorum* under Thatcher (Fry 1986: 98). Its leaked report on the future of the NHS under private insurance forced the Prime Minister to her impassioned 1982 conference declaration that the service was 'safe with us'. She did not promise the same to the think-tank and after her re-election the axe fell. Its demise was little mourned; resented by bureaucrats and seen as essentially lightweight, it was often ignored by ministers. Yet with ministers burdened by departmental duties and little time for strategic thought, Wass (1984) regards something like the CPRS as essential to genuine cabinet government.

Cabinet government: dead or sleeping?

Clearly the idea that Britain is governed by a tightly knit team is grossly simplistic. The Cabinet today is but one body in a labyrinthine network at the core of the state. It is now time to replace the wide-angle lens with a microscope and peer more deeply into the heart of state power. Most particularly, we must address the key debate over the position of the prime minister.

The Prime Minister: Elective Dictatorship?

Who is the prime minister?

No one elects the prime minister as such; he or she is the one asked by the monarch to form a government on the basis of being able to command a majority in the Commons. Normally this means the leader of the majority party yet this has been less common than is usually realized. Although Britain has had only three fully fledged coalition governments in the twentieth century, all in times of national emergency, governments with a single-party majority had, by 1997, held office for a total of only fifty-three years. Under a coalition or party pact the prime minister is most likely to be the leader of the largest party, although the minority partners might influence the choice. Thus Labour refused to serve under Chamberlain in 1940 and in 1987 David Steel of the Alliance declared that serving in a Thatcher-led coalition would be 'inconceivable'.

The circumstances of political life mean that prime ministers will usually be of mature years, with substantial political experience (table 14.2). In 1964, however, Labour's thirteen years in the wilderness meant that Wilson had only been Secretary for Overseas Trade and President of the Board of Trade and Mrs Thatcher's experience amounted to but four years as Secretary of State for Education and Science. In 1997 Tony Blair came to the office, like MacDonald in 1929, with no ministerial experience whatsoever. Lack of experience can be compensated for by youthful vigour: Mrs Thatcher took the reins at the relatively young age of fifty-four but, at forty-three, Blair was a veritable infant prodigy. On the other hand, when Callaghan moved from 10 to 11 Downing Street in 1976, he had at sixty-four reached the age where most people stop working and turn their attention to growing vegetables.

Evolution of the office   It was the Hanoverians, through lack of kingly interest in things British, who allowed Sir Robert Walpole (1676–1745), the First Lord

Table 14.2 Age and experience of prime ministers since 1895

Name (and party)	Date of first coming to office	Age	Years in Commons before becoming PM
Salisbury (Conservative)	1895	55	15 (+ 19 in Lords)
Balfour (Conservative)	1902	53	28
Campbell-Bannerman (Liberal)	1905	69	37
Asquith (Liberal)	1908	55	22
Lloyd George (coalition)	1916	53	26
Bonar Law (Conservative)	1922	63	22
Baldwin (Conservative)	1923	56	15
MacDonald (Labour)	1924	58	14
Chamberlain (Conservative)	1937	68	19
Churchill (coalition)	1940	65	38
Attlee (Labour)	1945	62	23
Eden (Conservative)	1955	57	32
Macmillan (Conservative)	1957	62	29
Home (Conservative)	1963	60	15 (+ 13 in Lords)
Wilson (Labour)	1964	48	19
Heath (Conservative)	1970	53	20
Callaghan (Labour)	1976	64	31
Thatcher (Conservative)	1979	54	20
Major (Conservative)	1990	47	11
Blair (Labour)	1997	43	14

of the Treasury, to fill the power vacuum. He is usually cited as the first prime minister, though the term was used abusively, to deplore his dominance over his colleagues. After his fall in 1742, his immediate successors were denied the same authority. However, by the time of William Pitt the Younger, the position had become firmly established by constitutional convention.

Yet to accept a cabinet leader was not to confer supremacy. The purpose of the historic constitutional struggles had been to curb monarchy, not replace one with another. Early prime ministers were regarded as only *primus inter pares* (first among equals). Indeed, when highlighting the significance of the nineteenth-century Cabinet, Bagehot placed little stress on the role of the prime minister. Subsequent developments saw a shift in the balance of power, so that in 1963 Richard Crossman argued in the introduction to a reprint of Bagehot's great work that

> . . . the post-war epoch has seen the final transformation of Cabinet Government into Prime Ministerial Government. (Crossman 1963: 51)

The prime minister as president

This question is central to an understanding of modern British government. Real-world **presidential government** takes various forms; some presidents share power with a prime minister, as in France, while others, as in Germany, are mainly symbolic, rather like the British monarch. However, exponents of the 'presidential prime-ministerial' thesis think in terms of a powerful model such as that of the USA, where incumbents stand in a particular relationship with the other political structures.

- *The state.* The president is head of state, holding some key powers. The title itself confers status and legitimacy.
- *The people.* Presidents are directly elected in a country-wide constituency, enjoying a popular legitimacy greater than that of any other person or institution. Moreover, they remain in direct contact through the media, regularly addressing the nation over the heads of other institutions.
- *The Cabinet.* The Cabinet is not elected but appointed by the president on the basis of personal choice.
- *The bureaucracy.* The upper echelons of the bureaucracy are appointed by the president, again on the basis of patronage.
- *A personal department.* Presidents are served by a formidable White House staff, providing powerful intellectual and political support.
- *The legislature.* Presidents are not members of Congress and their position is independent of its support.

Yet despite their personal ascendancy, presidents face certain *restrictions*. The separation of powers allows the judiciary to examine the constitutionality of executive actions and Congress can block presidential legislation and veto certain appointments.

The position of prime ministers appears quite different; they are not heads of state, not directly elected, their Cabinet choice is restricted to Parliament, they are not independent of the legislature, they depend upon their position as party leaders to hold office, the bureaucracy is permanent rather than politically appointed and they do not have personal departments like the White House staff. However, our examination cannot end with the formal constitutional position; on the contrary, this is where it begins.

Head of state

Although this position is formally held by the monarch, in many respects the prime minister functions as a head of state. The important prerogative powers of the Crown are only exercised on the advice of the prime minister. Moreover, meetings with other heads of state allow some of the presidential gloss to rub off, Thatcher characterizing her encounters with President Reagan as meetings of 'two heads of state'. Regular European Council summits enhance this impression. Early in his premiership Blair came to the presidency of the European Council and journalists began to speak of 'President Blair' with some irony. A hagiography on *Blair's 100 Days* by a Labour staffer even employed the term as a chapter title (Draper 1997). At the death of Princess Diana it was Tony Blair rather than the Queen who expressed the nation's sorrow.

The populist connection

Although prime ministers are elected only as ordinary MPs, political practice provides an increasingly **populist** link with the nation (figure 14.5).

General elections   It can be argued that modern general elections are effectively contests between party leaders. Before the 1987 election Mrs Thatcher proclaimed '*I* can handle a big majority' and in the 1997 campaign, Blair challenged Major to a US-style face-to-face televised debate (only backing down when the latter accepted). The result is that prime ministers can claim a personal mandate.

The media   Throughout the world, the media have transformed politics, making demagogy more feasible; at the touch of a button presidents can address nations. Prime ministers' press offices have become increasingly dominant in politics, feeding journalists with a 'carefully filtered version' after cabinet meetings (Hennessy 1986: 5). Blair had of course courted media mogul Rupert Murdoch and regular press articles appeared under his name, though these were often ghosted by journalists appointed to his new Strategic Communications Unit. As the term 'spin doctor' gained currency, the arch-operators stressed government as the art of communication and prime minister's press secretaries have risen to become their closest confidants (see p. 427).

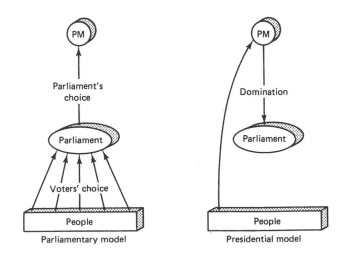

Figure 14.5
Choosing the prime minister.

Opinion polls The increasing application of market-research techniques to politics tends towards personalization, dwelling on the ratings of party leaders. Despite his upper-middle-class background, Blair played the common touch. In managing the aftermath of Princess Diana's death his sureness of touch caught the popular mood and after a year in office his popularity rating had actually risen since the landslide victory.

Image-politics Further presidentialization comes from the politics of image, ex-film actor President Reagan representing the apotheosis of this trend. Wilson modelled himself on the youthful President Kennedy but Mrs Thatcher carried image-making well beyond anything practised by her predecessors: following the advice of publicity experts she altered her hairstyle, expression, clothes and even the pitch of her voice. Blair, known to have been an amateur thespian in his youth, appeared to mirror much of the style of Clinton. The Labour government began to promote a 'Cool Britannia' image with parties at Number Ten for showbiz personalities.

Quite suddenly, he who had been looked upon as something of a bore became both a formidable debater and a funny speaker . . . He once told me that he set out deliberately to make himself amusing, writing out his jokes in longhand, late at night.

Alan Watkins on Harold Wilson, in the *Observer* (19 Oct. 1986)

Political culture Finally, it can be argued that the British actually prefer strong figures at the helm. 'Churchillian' is a term of approbation and, while Thatcher and Blair were applauded, Major's willingness to consult was often seen as weakness. British history is replete with examples of great individuals – from kings and generals to explorers and social reformers; there are no 'great' committees or working parties to stir the imagination. Even the Knights of the Round Table and the Merry Men of Sherwood Forest had leaders who were by no means *primus inter pares*. At the time of the 1997 general election, 79 per cent thought Blair to be a 'strong leader' (Denver 1998: 212).

The cabinet connection

This relationship lies at the heart of the debate and contains various facets.

Creating the Cabinet Unlike the president, the prime minister cannot make wide-ranging choices from social, commercial, industrial and academic life, ensuring a team of trusted allies. However, the restrictions are not inhibiting. The appointment of the Cabinet from amongst parliamentary colleagues is a powerful source of patronage, giving an iron grip over all those wishing to attain, or keep, high office. Moreover, the life peerage system frees prime

> Weak and hopeless.
>
> Norman Lamont on John Major, quoted in *The Times* (29 Jan. 1994). He claimed to have been misquoted but was absent from Major's honours list in July 1997.

ministers to appoint non-MPs to the government (see p. 353). Thus Blair brought in Derry Irvine, his ex-head of chambers, as Lord Chancellor. With the right to hire comes the even more devastating power to fire. Her Majesty's ministers hold office at her first minister's pleasure and those incurring displeasure can have their careers abruptly terminated; by the late 1980s the benches behind Thatcher were littered with the white bones of ex-ministers. Blair's July 1998 reshuffle was believed to be designed to curb the advance of his ambitious Chancellor Gordon Brown by removing some of his allies and bringing in his bête noir, Peter Mandelson.

Cabinet meetings Although colleagues are often leading figures, the conduct of the meetings remains securely under the prime ministerial thumb. Control of the *agenda* gives the power to decide what is discussed. Wilson was able to prevent debate on devaluation and Mrs Thatcher avoided consideration of economic strategy and the decision to purchase the Trident missile system from the USA. Indeed, Blair dispensed with formal agendas 'in the sense of an item by item discussion', preferring to choose the order in which topics were discussed during the meeting (Hennessy 1998: 11). In April 1998 it emerged that he had approved a secret deal with Clinton to reprocess a shipment of enriched uranium from the former Soviet republic of Georgia without a cabinet meeting.

Furthermore, as chairperson the prime minister decides who shall speak, when and at what length; dissident voices can be limited or studiously ignored. Even seating can be manipulated: Heath placed the *ingénue* Margaret Thatcher at an inconvenient position at the table, from which she found it difficult to interject, and Lord Home (1976: 192) tells how Macmillan took measures to avoid having the 'steely and accusing eye' of Enoch Powell facing him across the table. The prime minister can also decide the frequency and length of meetings; under Blair they were reported to be cursory affairs, taking place once a week on Thursdays, often for little more than forty minutes. Finally, prime ministers can define precisely what was concluded at meetings through their prerogative to sum up and shape the content of the all-important cabinet minutes (or conclusions).

> This is not a collective government. We have to accept that the old model of Cabinet government is as dead as a doornail.
>
> Whitehall insider to Peter Hennessy (1998: 12)

Cabinet committees Cabinet committees might seem to offer ministers key positions of influence. However, it is the prime minister who manages the network – appointing members, designating chairs and chairing those critical to major initiatives. In 1979 Thatcher took control of the 'E' committee on the economy, packing it with sympathizers. The committee handling the poll tax under her chairmanship kept opponents in the dark as it 'acquired a jargon-laden life of its own' (Howe 1994: 602–3). The main Thatcher strategy was to reduce the role of the *standing committees* and work more through *ad hoc* groupings which she could dominate. The gestation of the Next Steps programme, NHS reform and the poll tax all took place beyond the Cabinet and its formal committees. Ministers lose any right to attend informal meetings and, when no minutes are taken, outsiders cannot be privy to discussions. This style was reproduced under Blair. He also ensured that Minister without Portfolio Peter Mandelson, although not initially a cabinet member, was on most of the important groups.

Collective responsibility When ministers feel they are inadequately consulted they have constitutional grounds for complaint. Yet today the doctrine decrees little more than that all support the prime minister or resign. Blair's first Cabinet was tightly bound and Harriet Harman and Frank Dobson were rapped over the knuckles by Alastair Campbell, his press secretary, for stepping out of line.

> If the basis of trust between Prime Minister and her Defence Secretary no longer exists, there is no place for me with honour in such a Cabinet.
>
> Michael Heseltine, after his resignation over the Westland affair,
> quoted in *The Times* (10 Jan. 1986)

The inner cabinet Here is one of the most significant sources of the modern prime minister's power. Government has become both more centralized and more informal and inner cabinets more dominant. By this means prime ministers encircle themselves with cronies. Thus the large number of 'wets' in the first Thatcher Cabinet was soon countered by a loyal band of insiders. Major's inner group varied with the matter under consideration (what Gordon Walker called partial cabinets), with Kenneth Clarke, Michael Heseltine and Douglas Hurd reserved for the big decisions. Thus the policy of non-cooperation with the EU over its ban on British beef exports was hatched up by such a group in May 1996 with no reference to the Cabinet or its committees. Under Blair a 'big four' emerged – John Prescott (Deputy Prime Minister), Robin Cook (Foreign Secretary) and Gordon Brown (Chancellor). From this gathering came the momentous decision to cede power over interest rates to the Bank of England.

The official connection

When US presidents take office they sweep like new brooms through every nook and cranny of the White House. While their wives have traditionally changed furniture and wallpaper, they have changed the people, some three or four thousand of them. This is the **spoils system**, giving awesome power to reward, bribe and command. In contrast, incoming prime ministers are faced with a marble face of public bureaucracy, constitutionally as permanent as the Sphinx. Or are they? The idea that the public service is beyond the reach of political manoeuvring is but one more myth of British public life.

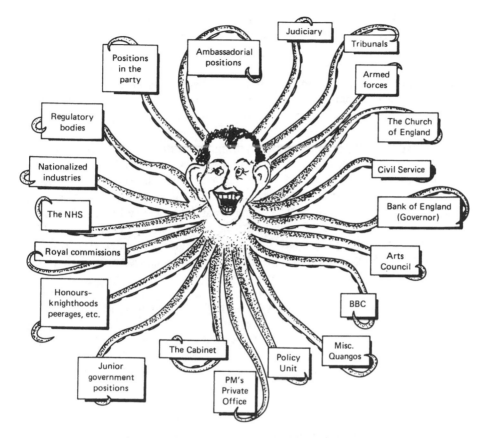

Figure 14.6 In an age of patronage to make Walpole blush, the tentacles of prime ministerial patronage reach deeply into the state machinery.

'One of us' Though less dramatic and sudden than the presidential shake-out, prime ministers are able to control key positions and distribute considerable prestige and power. These powers were originally inherited from the monarch and since Walpole's day have been used to enhance prime ministerial standing (figure 14.6). Positions within the prime minister's gift include:

- honours (peerages and knighthoods);
- state offices (armed forces, church and judiciary);
- government posts (from senior ministers to parliamentary private secretaries);
- ministerial advisory posts;
- top jobs beyond Whitehall (in water authorities, the NHS, nationalized industries, tribunals, royal commissions and committees of enquiry, the BBC, a diversity of quangos, and so on);
- party offices (mainly Conservative Party);
- Whitehall (although seen as conventionally immune from the web of

patronage, from the 1980s even this came under threat (see p. 466) as Thatcher sought to promote civil servants sympathetic to her views (Richards 1996)).

Unlike a president, the prime minister is not accountable for these appointments; there are no parliamentary or judicial vetoes. Early beneficiaries of the Blair regime were quickly dubbed 'Tony's cronies'.

Shaping the machine In addition to making appointments, the prime minister shapes the very architecture of government, thereby determining what it is capable, or not capable, of doing. The administrative skyline can be transformed overnight. Wilson created a Department of Economic Affairs (DEA) and the Civil Service Department (CSD) to usurp Treasury power, while the CPRS was Heath's brainchild. The CSD and CPRS both perished under Thatcher. Civil service agencification proceeded apace under Major. Michael Heseltine and John Prescott were both given new administrative empires to symbolize their enhanced status as deputy prime ministers.

In 1997 Tony Blair quickly began to take a firm grip on the government machine, much as he had done with his party. The number of ministerial advisers increased, cabinet committees were reduced and interdepartmental taskforces, headed by ministers and staffed by civil servants and outsiders, were to be created on an ad hoc basis to handle major policy initiatives such as the welfare-to-work package and constitutional reform (Timmins and Kampfner 1997).

A prime-ministerial department?

Unlike the US president, prime ministers do not have their own departments. They appear to stand alone against cabinet colleagues powered by high-octane information and advice from their bureaucratic forces. Yet this is a misleading picture; today's prime ministers are buoyed up by various agencies.

Personal offices Prime ministers have developed personal offices containing staffs of around 100, comprising sections such as the following.

(1) *Private Office.* Housekeeping functions, managing day-to-day affairs.

(2) *Political Office.* Responsibility for party and constituency matters.

(3) *Policy Unit.* Introduced by Wilson in 1974 and concerned with policy-making. Thatcher may be said to have needed such a unit more than her predecessors and the succession of eminent figures she brought to head it became well known. Under Sarah Hogg the Policy Unit produced Major's 'big idea' – the Citizen's Charter. The unit was made even stronger under Blair. Key strategists had observed well in the thinking-house of opposition, laying plans for a

government with a steel centre, a more proactive Cabinet Office, and power assisted by an enhanced Policy Unit (Mandelson and Liddle 1996). Efforts were made to lure a captain of industry as its head to consolidate the capital-friendly image. However, many on the shortlist fought shy of the job, which finally went to intellectual Labour 'staffer' David Miliband. In July 1998 there was much press speculation that the Policy Unit was assuming supreme importance in Whitehall, vetting all green and white papers and watering down proposals that might prove unpopular with Blair's new constituency of Middle England. Experienced civil servants were obliged to see their advice overturned by 'policy wonks' only a few years out of Oxbridge.

(4)   *Press Office*. Recent decades have brought into prominence a new and dominant political presence, the prime minister's press secretary. Described as 'communications', the function was more frequently called 'news management'. Thatcher's Bernard Ingham became better known than many politicians and his belligerent style was replicated by Blair's Alastair Campbell, who was soon being accused of news management on an even greater scale (sometimes by Ingham). Both were reported to have briefed against their respective prime ministers' colleagues (for example, Geoffrey Howe was described as a 'semi-detached member of the Cabinet' and Gordon Brown as 'psychologically flawed'). In July 1997 Blair revised *Questions of Procedure for Ministers*, already a severe straightjacket, to insist that all ministerial speeches, press releases, interviews and media appearances be cleared with his press office.

> They have got to know I'm running the show.
>
> Tony Blair defending the right of his press secretary to call ministers to account, quoted in the *Sunday Times* (26 April 1998)

The Cabinet Office   The Cabinet Office is a bureaucratic shell within which units to achieve new purposes can easily be housed. These have played an increasingly important role in policy, undermining both the Cabinet and its committees. Thatcher's Efficiency Unit under businessman Sir Derek Rayner was of enormous significance. From this unelected acorn grew such initiatives as the Next Steps programme which 'reinvented' much of the state machine (see chapter 15). Major's Office of Public Service and Science pushed through civil service reforms. Labour established its own units, including the Orwellian-sounding Social Exclusion Unit with representatives from five Whitehall departments as well as from business, local government and the police. In addition, Blair ensured that members of his Policy Unit and Efficiency Unit sat 'on all the comprehensive expenditure review teams' (Hennessy 1998: 15).

The Cabinet Secretariat   Although supposed to serve the Cabinet, the cabinet secretary can become close to a prime minister; the relationship has been likened to that between a minister and permanent secretary (Walker 1972: 54). From the beginning Lloyd George relied heavily on Maurice Hankey. Sir Burke Trend, who served from 1963 to 1973, denied that he was 'the Prime Minister's exclusive servant' (Hennessy 1985) but he worked closely with Wilson, accompanying him, for example, to Washington as an equal and opposite force to Nixon's Henry Kissinger (Wilson 1974: 947).

Thatcher established an exceptional rapport with Sir Robert Armstrong –

her 'oracle' (Hennessy 1986). Indeed, critics questioned whether his loyalty exceeded that of a neutral public servant, the select committee on the Westland affair worrying that so close a confidant should simultaneously be the head of the civil service. Blair envisaged the secretariat as a 'Whitehall whip', driving the state machine as never before. There was talk that it might finally transmogrify into a prime minister's department (Grice 1997).

Think-tanks and advisers   Prime ministers can also look outside for advice and support. Some saw the CPRS as Heath's instrument and Thatcher maintained contact with a number of right-wing intellectual groups, including the Centre for Policy Studies, the Institute of Economic Affairs and the Adam Smith Institute. The weight she gave to the views of economic adviser Sir Alan Walters led Chancellor Nigel Lawson to resign. Blair turned to bodies such as the Fabian Society, the Policy Studies Institute and Demos, often placing New Labour wrapping around Thatcherite policies (Pilger 1998: 83).

> I resigned on a matter of fundamental principle, because it seemed to me that the Prime Minister [Wilson] was not only introducing a 'presidential' system into the running of the government . . . far too often outsiders in his entourage seemed to be almost the only effective 'Cabinet'.
>
> Lord George Brown, *In My Way* (1972)

What's in a name?   If the British prime minister were to have a department it would, perhaps more than any other development, 'symbolise the shift from cabinet to prime ministerial government' (Jones 1983: 84). The ability of prime

Figure 14.7
A prime minister's department?

ministers to establish think-tanks and policy units at the drop of a hat or hand-bag leaves them with abundant support. This may explain why, despite repeated speculation as new leaders take office, the temptation to establish a formal department is resisted. The existing arrangements (figure 14.7) offer a *de facto* department, while formalization would invite accusations of presidential self-aggrandizement. This moved a step further in July 1998 when Blair's cabinet reshuffle merged the Cabinet Office with the Office of Public Service, creating, in the view of at least one Whitehall-watcher, a prime minister's department in all but name (Kellner 1998).

The Westminster connection

Finally there is a relationship in which the prime minister is constitutionally stronger than the president. We saw in chapter 13 how, with a fusion rather than a separation of powers, the British executive dominates the legislature and the prime minister gains from this.

Leader of the House The parliamentary timetable, the committee network, the process of reform and so on are the responsibility of the Leader of the House. However, until 1915 the prime minister held this position and today makes the appointment from the party faithful; the two work hand in glove. Ann Taylor's 1997 modernization strategy clearly reflected the Blair agenda and the changed format of Prime Minister's Questions came without parliamentary debate.

Debates Prime ministers can appear to be adroit parliamentary performers but the odds are heavily stacked in their favour. With extensive civil service back-up, most dominate the House. Alternatively, they can make institutional changes to reduce debate, which helps explain a long-term decline in their accountability to the Commons (Dunleavy and Jones 1993).

Power of dissolution Like Samson, the prime minister can bring down the temple on all heads, sending members off to the country, perhaps to lose their seats. Wilson made a dissolution threat after a near-mutiny by George Brown and others over the supply of British arms to South Africa, as did Major during the passage of the Maastricht Bill.

The party connection As we saw in chapter 11, the British parties fall inexorably under Michels's iron law of oligarchy. Thatcher's dominance was legendary and Blair soon established an iron grip on all sections of his party, the few dissidents being chastised by the whips, as in the case of the opposition to student fees in May 1998. In November 1998 a leaked document showed the Labour leadership seeking to prohibit the members of its NEC (which included some of an 'old Labour' disposition) from expressing disagreement in public.

Sharks and banana skins

> There are no true friends in politics. We are all sharks circling and waiting for traces of blood to appear in the water.
>
> Conservative ex-minister Alan Clark after the fall of Thatcher, *Diaries* (30 Nov. 1990

There can be no doubt that Britain's ancient, ambiguous and elusive constitution leaves a formidable armoury in the hands of the prime minister. However, in the real world of politics, where personalities and interests clash, the weapons can be double-edged. Although popularity can confer authority, public opinion can be fickle; a poor showing in the polls can weaken, as Thatcher discovered in November 1990. Neither is the Cabinet always compliant. Unlike presidential appointees, its members are career politicians who, like Macbeth, entertain vaulting ambitions of their own. Within the Cabinet sits the likely heir apparent and plots and rumours of plots against the prime minister are regular features of political *reportage*. Major's colleagues, such as Michael Heseltine, Kenneth Clarke and Michael Howard, were serious rivals, as was a lean and hungry Cassius in the form of John Redwood, who picked up the gauntlet in 1995. Even the seemingly impregnable Blair had reason to lie awake at night when a biography of Chancellor Gordon Brown revealed that, although standing aside in the leadership battle to unify the modernizing vote, a residue of bitterness remained and ambition continued to gnaw.

> Prime Minister, you will not bother yourself about the New Hebrides.
>
> Reported reply from Thatcher's Foreign Secretary Lord Carrington when asked for details, quoted in the *Guardian* (1 March 1989)

Cabinet membership is subject to political constraints and there will be a core of senior MPs with strong followings who cannot be omitted. Moderate Labour leaders have been obliged to endure some unwelcome company from the left. After the 1990 leadership election Major could hardly exclude rivals Hurd and Heseltine. Again, the fear of prime ministerial displeasure does not afflict all. Thatcher's wealthy Foreign Secretary, Lord Carrington, could afford an outspoken line.

The opportunity to butcher can also be questioned. Macmillan was weaker after his 'Night of the Long Knives' and the weight of Thatcher casualties built up a brooding discontent only waiting for the demoted Howe to produce one of the most bitter denunciations in modern history and precipitate her downfall. Overall, Major feared sacking colleagues; many went reluctantly following scandals. Even so, the removal of Chancellor Norman Lamont in 1993 and John Patten in 1994 produced political enemies, the former proving particularly bitter. In his victory reshuffle, following the unwanted leadership contest of July 1995, Major might have been justified in some radical surgery but still did not feel up to removing the carbuncle of Euroscepticism.

Neither is collective responsibility always the gag it might seem. Most prime

Cooling Britannia:
John Prescott
doused by Danbert
Nobacon with the
contents of an ice
bucket at the Brit
Awards, February
1998

Photo: Times Newspapers Ltd

ministers feel plagued by leaks and Thatcher was to lament in her memoirs the lack of some 'good men and true'. Even access to the media can provide rope for a noose; only the telegenic can prosper. Sir Alec Douglas-Home's cadaverous features were no asset before the cameras and Major's grey persona and monotone defied the image-makers while proving irresistible to satirists. Even Blair's 'Cool Britannia' initiative became too cool for comfort in February 1998 when Danbert Nobacon, of the band Chumbawamba, emptied an ice bucket over Deputy Prime Minister John Prescott at the Brit Awards. Moreover, Samson did not come out of Gaza well and the power of dissolution may still lie more in the threat than the use. An election precipitated by a cabinet crisis would suggest unfitness to rule. When Major brandished the weapon he appeared more desperate than strong.

What of Michels's iron law ensuring support from the ranks? The Achilles' heel of the prime minister is the need to retain party support. Having been elected by the people, a president's security of tenure is absolute. Only upon some gross misdemeanour (such as Watergate) should the process of impeachment roll into action (Clinton's impeachment over the Monica Lewinsky affair was an exception). Prime ministers occupy their positions only as long as the party is prepared to back them. The unreliability of this was exposed when the inconceivable happened and Margaret Thatcher was driven out by her backbench troops in November 1990. Perhaps as a consequence Major lived amidst constant rumblings of discontent and rumours of challenge.

Destiny and disposition

Hence, the prime minister's powers are potential, their reality depending upon two factors: *prevailing contingencies* and the *personality* or character of the incumbent.

The contingency factor Like sportsmen and businessmen, politicians need a helping hand from Lady Luck; the circumstances surrounding prime ministerial tenure are largely a matter of fortune. Attlee was obliged to reign during the years of post-war austerity while Macmillan inherited the years of plenty. Gaitskell's untimely death gave Wilson his big chance (although in office he suffered extensive economic restrictions), Heath was forced into humiliating U-turns amidst world economic crisis and Callaghan was squeezed by the IMF and undermined by those upon whom he most relied – the trade unions. Major reaped the bitter harvest of a fractious party and an overheated economy caused by the Lawson–Thatcher credit boom. However, for 'Black Wednesday' he could not entirely blame his stars; as Chancellor it was he who had persuaded a reluctant Thatcher to enter the ERM at a fatally high rate. Victory in the World Cup and the Beatles may have helped Wilson, contributing to the feelgood factor, and he distributed honours appropriately. Tony Blair surfed on the crest of a wave of fortune. Coming to the party leadership through the untimely death of John Smith, he led a party united by weariness of opposition and faced a flagging Conservative Party. Upon victory in May 1997 he inherited a relatively healthy economy and a popular mood for a change of cast.

Particular circumstances will call for different leadership styles and an individual can seem right for one situation but wrong for another. Wars have been of particular significance. Asquith and Chamberlain were unequal to the challenge while Lloyd George and Churchill thrived, though in the aftermath they were less sure-footed. Suez proved to be Eden's downfall and the overbearing manner of Heath occasioned hostility. In contrast, the Falklands war saved the unpopular Thatcher, her inflexible style reinvented as 'resolution'. Blair was quick to align himself with Clinton's sabre-rattling in the Middle East.

Another aspect of the hand of fate is the parliamentary arithmetic. While Thatcher sailed on buoyant majorities and Blair sealed his good fortune with a record majority on 1 May 1997, Major's slim twenty-one-seat margin in 1992 soon haemorrhaged with a succession of disastrous by-elections, leaving little scope for manoeuvre.

The personality factor Weber noted charisma as a significant source of power and Asquith etched his name in the textbooks by declaring that the office of prime minister is what the holder makes of it. All prime ministers will share a fondness for power; as individuals who have risen up the greasy pole they are likely to possess political skill, ambition and a desire to dominate. However, each is unique and the informal nature of the office permits infinite scope for interpretation. This helps to explain why the debate remains unresolved and of unquenchable interest to journalists and academics.

For the most part, incumbents have interpreted their role cautiously, content to preserve the constitutional status quo. Macmillan is credited with having been surprisingly radical but Labour leaders were repeatedly accused of wilting in the face of the Establishment. However, things were to change under Thatcher. Even before coming to office, the effect might have been anticipated.

> No political leader that I have ever known has been less dependent upon the advantages and trappings that attend high office for the impact she made; and none more dependent on the force of her own character and mind. (Cosgrave 1978: xx)

Interviewed in the *Observer* (25 Feb. 1979), she appeared to reject the very principle of cabinet government: 'As prime minister I could not waste time having any internal arguments'. In this era, personalized politics in Britain came of age. The state relentlessly asserted its authority under a philosophy so personalized that it bore the name 'Thatcherism'. A child reared during these years would be unable to understand why William Pitt (the Elder) was compelled to resign in 1761 because the majority of his Cabinet refused to support his policy towards Spain.

Major brought a quite different personality, having 'all the charisma of a provincial bank clerk' (Charmley 1998: 124). Without Thatcher's confrontational style or zeal, he was to be plagued by accusations of weakness. Eurosceptic MP Sir George Gardiner referred to him as a 'ventriloquist's dummy' of chancellor Kenneth Clarke while others believed his deputy Michael Heseltine to be the real prime minister.

In opposition Blair had certainly not looked *primus inter pares* as he stamped his modernizing imprint on his party, even rewriting the totemic Clause Four. *Sunday Times* columnist Andrew Grice (1997) was not alone amongst Westminster-watchers in prophesying that 'the overwhelming influence on Blair in power will be Labour's arch-enemy, Margaret Thatcher', whose style he professed to admire. Indeed, on the eve of his first meeting with European leaders in May 1997, he sought her counsel in a Downing Street *tête-à-tête*.

He has real star quality. There were few enough Tories on *EastEnders* – there is one less now.

Barbara Windsor on seeing Tony Blair at Labour's election gala,
quoted in the *Observer* (26 April 1998)

A Monarchical Culture?

The last twenty years of the millennium saw a testing of the ambiguities, myths and conventions that had long misted any clear vision of the British constitution, and upon which apologist textbooks have preferred to turn a benevolently blind eye. It became clear that Britain's ancient monarchical lineage was no mere curio; it held deep implications for contemporary politics. Cabinet powers are derived from the royal prerogative and a hijacking of the supremacy of Parliament bestows an authority surpassing that of monarchs of old. Yet within the Cabinet sits the prime minister in a potentially despotic position.

Recent decades have shown that the much-vaunted freedom from an overweening executive depended not upon checks and balances but upon conventions of moderation. A driver blind to the political road signs and speed limits could career on a dangerous course. Thatcher took the constitution at its face value, extending 'the repertory of available styles' at the disposal of the office (King 1985: 137). Did her unceremonious fall vindicate this unwritten highway code? Hugo Young declared: 'finally the system, which says that this is cabinet and not prime ministerial government, reacted. There was a point beyond which it declined to be flouted' (*Independent*, 23 Nov. 1990). Yet she had enjoyed an astonishing eleven years of supremacy and when the fall came it was precipitated not by constitutional checks but by a nervous party cadre suspecting that its leader had passed her electoral sell-by date. To protect this one Achilles' heel the Blair regime established an astonishing level of party discipline in Parliament.

The tercentenary of the Glorious Revolution was celebrated in 1988 in a most muted manner (privatization of the steel industry receiving far more publicity). In marked contrast to the French celebration of 1789 the following year, the British appeared to see little to applaud in the notion of freedom from tyranny. With the monarchical character of the British constitution laid bare Charter 88 declared:

> No country can be considered free in which the government is above the law. No democracy can be considered safe whose freedoms are not encoded in a basic constitution.

However, as this chapter has made clear, although rich in the resources of constitutional and political power, prime ministers are also crucially dependent upon others: cabinet committees, the Cabinet Office and its specialized units, the cabinet secretary, spin doctors, think-tanks, advisers, press secretaries, ministerial colleagues, an inner cabinet and so on. The complex web of interrelating structures and processes extends out to encompass the departments of state and even the security and intelligence services (Dunleavy and Rhodes 1990). From outside the executive terrain figures such as journalists, media moguls, business magnets and trade union leaders also penetrate the shell of the core executive. Dispersed throughout this network, power becomes elusive and fluid and the answer to the question 'where does it lie?' can never settle simply upon either Cabinet or prime minister (see Smith 1999). Hence, issues concerning the working of the cabinet system do not tell us all we need to know about policy and power. The next chapter takes us further into this labyrinthine world.

Unlimited power is apt to corrupt the minds of those who possess it.

William Pitt the Elder (1708–78), House of Lords speech (9 Jan. 1770)

Key points

- Formally speaking, Britain has cabinet, as opposed to monarchical or presidential, government. This means government based on discussion, compromise and moderation.
- This system is recognized constitutionally in the convention of collective responsibility.
- The modern Cabinet works through a system of committees.
- Cabinet government in Britain cannot be appraised without considering the office of the prime minister, who is formally constrained by a *primus inter pares* convention.
- The prime minister is able to control the composition of the Cabinet and its method of working.
- Control over the machinery of government allows a prime minister to have much of the administrative back-up and advice that a personal department would offer.
- In important respects the prime minister is potentially more powerful than a typical president in a democracy because there is neither separation of powers nor a written constitution to restrain the executive.
- The last two decades of the millennium have seen British government become more centralized and more informal; both developments enhance the prime minister's authority.
- However, there are still constraints and prime ministers vary in their capacity to exploit the position.

Review your understanding of the following terms and concepts

cabinet committees
cabinet government
Cabinet Office
Cabinet Secretariat
Cabinet Secretary
Central Policy Review Staff
collective responsibility

core executive
Efficiency Unit
elective dictatorship
executive arm of government
inner cabinet
patronage
Policy Cabinet

Policy Unit
populism
presidential government
Privy Council
Shadow Cabinet
spoils system
War Cabinet

Tony's cronies: the A-list

AFTER he waves off the Gallaghers at the end of the next glittering Downing Street bash, the Prime Minister might do worse than to pick up *Alan Clark's Diaries* for his bedtime reading.

There are few signs of blood yet, of course, but who can Tony Blair really trust? Who are in the charmed circle that he can draw around him with confidence, knowing that they have no one's best interests at heart but his own?

Labour's first year has brought just one big surprise in this department: one name notably absent from the list is Gordon Brown. Of course the Chancellor is still a close political contact of the Prime Minister, and the two men still meet very regularly. But the publication of a biography revealing Brown's bitterness over the 1994 deal which, he feels, deprived him of the leadership, has left its scars. Recent networking by the Chancellor with constituencies and the unions has been interpreted as an attempt to garner support.

In other areas, though, there have been no such surprises. The few men regarded as closest to Mr Blair know well that if and when the blood begins to seep, it will probably be mixed with their own.

Alastair Campbell, the Prime Minister's press secretary, has been a constant and loyal aide, pulling together speeches and – most memorably – helping to craft the killer soundbites with which Mr Blair is apt to carry off the headlines. The "people's princess" line which struck a chord after Diana's death almost certainly had some of his magic worked into it.

Other loyalists who owe their senior positions to the Prime Minister include Peter Mandelson, the Minister without Portfolio, and Lord Irvine, the Lord Chancellor. Both still enjoy close and regular contact with Mr Blair.

Other former Labour staffers who have made the transition include David Miliband, Peter Hyman and Liz Lloyd, all of whom now reside in the Number 10 policy unit. While Mr Miliband is in overall charge, Mr Hyman has a significant input into Mr Blair's speeches and Ms Lloyd briefs him each week for Prime Minister's Questions.

Geoff Mulgan, centre-left guru and founder of the Demos think tank, has been brought into Downing Street to oversee the Social Exclusion Unit, expected to be a major driving force in terms of policy direction over the next few years. Other recent acquisitions include two journalists, David Bradshaw from the *Daily Mirror* and Philip Bassett from the *Times*, who have been appointed to the new Strategic Communications Unit and who are often the true authors of the Prime Minister's newspaper articles.

Fran Abrams

Independent, 30 April 1998

Assignment

Study the extract from the *Independent* and answer the following questions.

		Mark (%)
1	Why is it said that Tony Blair can have few trusted friends?	25
2	What do you think is Gordon Brown's purpose in 'networking' within the constituencies and trade unions?	25
3	Discuss the pros and cons of newspaper articles carrying Tony Blair's name being ghosted by journalists.	25
4	Consider the possible dangers of Blair surrounding himself with non-elected 'cronies'.	25

Questions for discussion

1 Outline the essential features of cabinet government.
2 Critically evaluate the role of the Cabinet Secretariat in British government.
3 Discuss the function of the Shadow Cabinet in British politics.
4 How important is personality to the authority of the prime minister?
5 By what means is the British prime minister able to establish a direct link with the public? How significant is such a link?
6 How far is 'news management' a legitimate role for the prime minister's press secretary?
7 Compare and contrast the leadership styles of John Major and Tony Blair.
8 In what ways would the establishment of a prime-ministerial department alter the process of government in Britain?
9 How might the British cabinet system be reformed?
10 'The real question is not whether or not the powers of the British prime minister are presidential, but how far they are monarchical.' Discuss.

Topic for debate

This house believes that the British love a strong leader.

Further reading

Benn, T. (1979) *Arguments for Socialism.*
A stimulating essay expressing extreme distaste for presidential-style premiership.

Burch, M. and Holliday, I. (1996) *The British Cabinet System*.
Well-crafted case studies showing the increasing centralization of power.

Hennessy, P. (1986) *Cabinet*.
Lively account by academic and master journalist with an intimate knowledge of the geography of the corridors of power.

Lawson, Nigel (1993) *The View from Number 11: Memoirs of a Tory Radical*.
Challenging account of some of the Thatcher years by notable resignee, with some thoughts on the nature and reform of cabinet government.

Mandelson, P. and Liddle, R. (1996) *The Blair Phenomenon: Can New Labour Deliver?*
New Labour, New Cabinet. The blueprint for executive power straight from the arch-spin doctor's pen.

Pimlott, B. (1992) *Harold Wilson*.
Rehabilitation without hagiography of a key post-war prime minister.

Rhodes, R. A. W. and Dunleavy, P. (1995) *Prime Minister, Cabinet and Core Executive*.
New and previously published pieces examining the centre of the web of power in Britain.

Smith, M. (1999) *The Core Executive in Britain*.
Emphasizes the fluid network of relationships around Britain's cabinet system.

Young, H. (1989) *One of Us*.
Excellent account of Thatcher in government. Clever punning title sets the tone.

For light relief

Peter Bradshaw, *Not Alan Clark's Diaries*.
Entertaining parody from *Evening Standard* feature, but read the real thing first (see below).

Alan Clark (1993) *Diaries*.
An irreverent account of Whitehall and Westminster life and beyond.

Michael Dobbs, *To Play the King*.
Sequel to *House of Cards*. Evil chief whip Frances Urquhart becomes prime minister. You may like this, I couldn't possibly comment. Available on video.

Michael Dobbs, *Final Cut*.
Frances Urquhart's eventful career reaches a dramatic conclusion.

Douglas Hurd, *The Shape of Ice*.
Novel from a once-leading politician about political life in a Cabinet with a dominant woman and a weak dithering prime minister. Any resemblance to real people is entirely coincidental of course.

On the net

http://www.number-10.gov.uk
http://www.cabinet-office.gov.uk
Two web sites at the heart of government. You can even have a virtual tour of Number Ten.

Chapter Fifteen

The Village of Whitehall: of Ministers and Mandarins

In this chapter we move to the engine room of the modern state – the central government bureaucracy, constitutionally part of the executive arm of government. We first detail the anatomy of the modern civil service and its evolution. Next we examine the bureaucrats who rub pin-striped shoulders with ministers in the process of government. What kind of people are they? Do their life experiences resemble those of the people they serve? From this we turn to a contentious issue that has characterized this world of power: official secrecy. This leads to the key debate on the influence of the bureaucrats: are they really the 'obedient servants' they claim at the end of their polite letters? We conclude by assessing the impact of the reforming gales gusting through the corridors of power during the 1980s and 1990s.

An Anatomy of a Bureaucracy

The British **civil service** is the central government **bureaucracy**, its function in the great liberal-democratic scheme of things to serve faithfully the people's elected representatives. Writers in the apologist tradition have had no difficulty in believing this to be the case, depicting the bureaucrats in the way seventeenth-century painters portrayed the nobility, in romantically idealized poses without warts or wrinkles. Thus E. N. Gladden (1967: 199) notes: 'On its record of public service it stands unchallenged, setting an example that the lesser breeds of official strive, almost hopelessly, to emulate'. This tradition of approval is partly explained by the fact that many writers (like Gladden) are themselves ex-members. Sir John Hoskyns, an outsider brought in by Mrs Thatcher to shake up this comfortable world, observed:

> No one is qualified to criticise . . . unless he has first hand experience of working in it. But if he *has* worked in it, then there is a convention that he should never speak about it thereafter except in terms of respectful admiration. (Hoskyns 1984: 4)

The constitutional position of the civil service is said to entail three related characteristics.

> Empires fall, ministries pass away but bureaux remain.
>
> Duc d'Audiffret-Pasquier (1823–1905; French statesman)

- *Permanence*. Political storms may rage and politicians be swept in and out of office but the bureaucrats cling like pin-striped limpets to the solid grey rocks of Whitehall. They are career civil servants, not political appointees.
- *Neutrality*. Taking no sides, and favouring no class, civil servants are above the sordid world of politics, the very embodiment of the liberal-democratic ideal of the *neutral state*.
- *Anonymity*. Ministers alone are *responsible* to the outside world (through Parliament) for departmental actions. Civil servants remain in the shadows, neither named nor blamed when issues are debated.

However, the myths and ambiguities clouding the British constitution are nowhere more evident than in the role of the civil service. In this chapter, we must try to substitute a microscope for rose-tinted lenses, first setting the scene by identifying our specimens and the environment in which they civilly serve.

The civil servants

Not all state employees are civil servants. They may broadly be defined as servants of the Crown working in a civil (non-military) capacity and not holding political or judicial office. Said unkindly in caricature to be rarely civil and

The ornate facade of Whitehall: the New Home and Colonial Office, 1875

Source: Mary Evans Picture Library

never servile, they are popularly thought of as grey, passionless beings who sometimes exercise discretionary power over our lives. They, and the study of them, are often characterized as rather boring, which may well be precisely what the Establishment likes the masses to think; people do not look too closely at boring subjects. However, despite evident efforts by some writers to avoid over-exciting their readers, the role of the civil service in our lives is certainly not a boring subject; it is about nothing less than running the state we inhabit. When examining the balance of power in society, its role must be central to analysis.

Civil servants may be broadly dichotomized as industrial and non-industrial. Thus, although the civil servant of popular imagination wears a suit and carries a rolled umbrella, many are obliged to roll up their shirt sleeves, others have stripped to the waist in government dockyards and the exotic Quentin Crisp entitled his autobiography *The Naked Civil Servant* because, when posing for students in state art colleges, he wore nothing at all. Today the industrial civil service (primarily employed by the Ministry of Defence) has shrunk to minute proportions (figure 15.1). The non-industrial service broadly comprises three main elements: the *Administrative Group*, a category of *specialist groups* containing experts such as scientists, doctors and lawyers, and a set of departmental classes employing *specialists* in areas such as taxation.

From the mass of workers at its base to its tiny elite pinnacle (figure 15.2), the service is a social microcosm. However, our principal focus is on the 1 per cent at the top, those whose daily lives bring them into intimate contact with the highest and most mighty in the confident world of the Establishment. These comprise the **mandarin** class. Named after the officials in imperial China, they sit at the top of what, from April 1996, has formed the Senior Civil Service, comprising some 3,000 members from what used to be known as grade 5, or

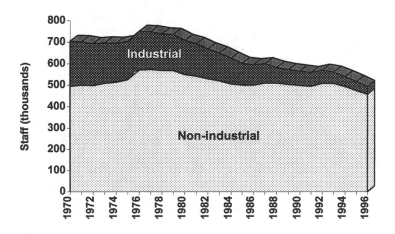

Figure 15.1
The industrial and non-industrial civil service, 1970–1996.

Source: Data from *Civil Service Statistics* (1997).

Assistant Secretary and above. Although there is now some limited open competition for Permanent Secretary vacancies, members form a closed caste networking across departmental boundaries (Mountfield 1997: 309). At the apex sit the departmental permanent secretaries, the apotheosis of the mandarinate.

> From *mander*, to command, mandarin is not a Chinese word; it was used to describe the officials (*Khiouping*) by the Portuguese colonists at Maca'o. Mandarins were appointed on the basis of imperial birth, long service, illustrious deeds, knowledge, ability, zeal and nobility.

The structure of the civil service

Following nineteenth-century reforms, the civil service grew steadily. In 1900 membership stood at around 50,000 but growth was promoted by two world wars and the emergence of a complex welfare state to reach a peak of 751,000 in 1976. With a changing political climate the number had fallen to 476,000 by 1997 (see figure 15.1).

The great historic departments at the centre of government (Treasury, Foreign Office and Home Office) stand in the environs of Whitehall, the dignified corridor surveyed by Nelson from his vantage point in Trafalgar Square and leading to the Palace of Westminster. Their origins lie in the royal household.

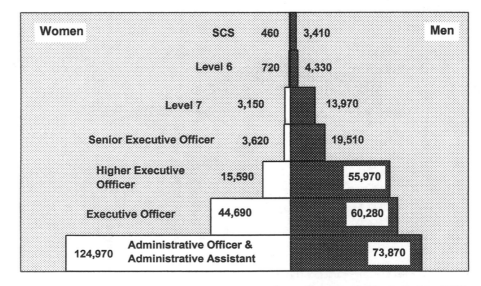

Figure 15.2
The civil service hierarchy: staff in post by grade in the non-industrial civil service, April 1997.

Source: Data from *Civil Service Statistics* (1997).

The newer departments, such as the Department of Social Security (DSS) and the Department for Education and Employment (DfEE), reflect the changing role of government and inhabit less grand areas of the metropolis.

Outside London is a national network of semi-autonomous **executive agencies** (figure 15.3) Formerly offices of the central departments, these were **hived off** from 1988 onwards under the 'Next Steps' initiative; by April 1997, over a hundred of them employed 77 per cent of all permanent civil servants (figure 15.4). This left a central core around Whitehall of some 50,000, the size of the service in 1900. Another change, not unrelated to agencification, was an increasing casualization of staff, numbers rising from 11,100 in 1976 to 19,600 by 1997. In the same period the number of part-timers rose from 31,100 to 56,100 to cope with the shrinkage of permanent staff.

The EU impact Membership of the EU makes increasing demands on Whitehall. Although no special department of European affairs has been created, those departments closely involved (Treasury; Agriculture, Fisheries and Food; Education and Employment; Trade and Industry) have established dedicated

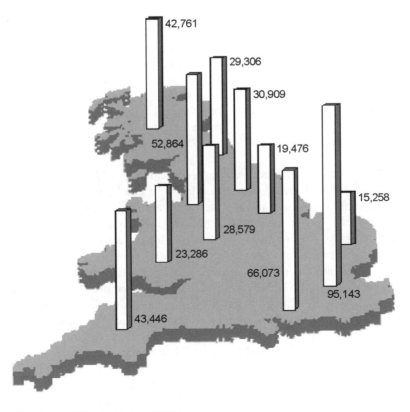

Figure 15.3 The national distribution of civil servants, April 1996.

Source: Data from *Civil Service Statistics* (1996).

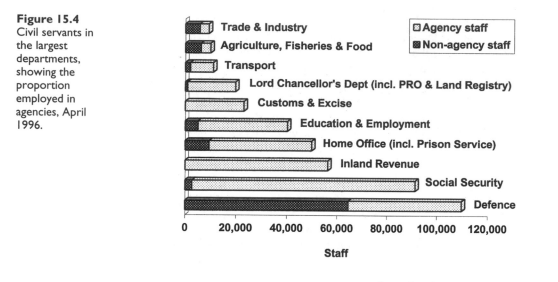

Figure 15.4
Civil servants in
the largest
departments,
showing the
proportion
employed in
agencies, April
1996.

Source: Data from *Civil Service Statistics* (1996).

EU sections. While the Treasury and Cabinet Office are the traditional leaders, in an internal power struggle the Foreign and Commonwealth Office (FCO) has found a lifeline to arrest its declining importance. Mandarins meet in committees to take a strategic perspective and over all sits a special EU Committee to coordinate policy. Some leave to serve on the UK Permanent Representation at Brussels and once breathing its heady air they can be accused of 'going native', becoming disdainful of the Whitehall world as they act on the larger stage of European summitry (Sampson 1992: 40–1).

The politics of structure Structure is no technical matter lying outside politics. The beauty of the unwritten constitution is that it can be forever reinvented at prime ministerial whim and usually serves some political purpose. Indeed, as we see below, the very creation of the modern civil service was itself a political project. During the 1960s and 1970s a fashion for departmental fusion created new giant departments such as Health and Social Security (figure 15.5). This enabled governments to remove certain controversies from the public eye by resolving them within Whitehall and created empires for prominent politicians. By the mid-1970s the climate began to change and the giants were dismembered. However, within days of Labour taking office in May 1997, John Prescott's Department of Environment, Transport and the Regions (DETR) was born, giving the Deputy Prime Minister a new empire. Again the merging of education and employment in 1995 made a statement of educational philosophy, suggesting that education was a service providing workers for the capitalist economy. Proposals to create a Food Standards Agency following the BSE crisis and other food scares looked like an attack on food producers, and these mighty interests were soon pressuring the government to water down the initiative.

The Civil Service Department created in response to the Fulton Report to control management and effectiveness was abolished by Thatcher in 1981, its functions drawn into the Cabinet Office and therefore under the prime minister (Hogwood 1997: 704). In 1994 these functions went to an Office of Public Service, within the Cabinet Office, which became responsible for agencification, itself a reform with political implications (see p. 469).

The genesis of the modern civil service

Like many institutions the civil service owes much to its evolution. Orthodox accounts stress the nineteenth-century reforms, which are said to have replaced the corruption of an old aristocratic order with rational administrative principles. Less readily acknowledged is the fact that these reforms made this powerful state institution the property of the bourgeoisie.

Its ancestral roots lie in the courts of Anglo-Saxon kings who required clerks to accompany them around the realm (Stenton 1941: 349). As officers of the royal household, their functions persisted through episodes of constitutional turbulence, some offices, such as the Chamber and the Wardrobe, gradually

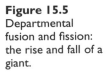

Figure 15.5
Departmental fusion and fission: the rise and fall of a giant.

I was asked to copy some lines from *The Times* newspaper with an old quill pen, and at once made a series of blots and false spellings. 'That won't do, you know,' said Henry Freeling to his brother Clayton. Clayton, who was my friend, urged that I was nervous and asked that I might be allowed to do a bit of writing at home and bring it as a sample on the next day . . . With a faltering heart I took this on the next day to the office . . . But when I got to 'The Grand', as we used to call our office in those days, from its site, St Martin's le Grand, I was seated at a desk without any further reference to my competency. No one condescended even to look at my beautiful penmanship.

Anthony Trollope (1815–82; English novelist), *Autobiography* (1883)

giving way to newer ones. However, there was no single service and many positions were little more than sinecures, with appointments made through nepotism and bribery. Civil servants were often the sons of the aristocracy too dull to survive in any other walk of life such as church, law or army. Trollope's autobiography recounts his own selection process. Salaries were supplemented by bribes and gifts, a practice well documented by Samuel Pepys, who served in the Admiralty in the mid-seventeenth century.

Going out of Whitehall, I met Capt. Grove who did give me a letter directed to myself from himself; I discerned money to be in it and took it, knowing, as I found it to be, the proceed of the place I have got him . . . But I did not open it till I came home to my office; and there broke it open, not looking into it till all the money was out, that I may say I saw no money in the paper if ever I should be Questioned about it. There was a piece of gold and 4/- in silver. So home to dinner with my father and wife.

Samuel Pepys (1633–1703; diarist and naval administrator), *Diary* (1 April 1663)

The rise of the industrial bourgeoisie Eighteenth-century radicals lamented the failings of the service and a campaign for reform emerged under Burke and Fox. However, it was the new industrial bourgeoisie that fashioned the modern service. A critical element was the experience of empire, where the model for reform was found: the Indian Civil Service (ICS), which had evolved from the East India Company to become a complex instrument of British colonial rule. It was manned by the brightest sons of the bourgeoisie, who would take the passage to India, reigning there as the epitome of the over-dressed, over-confident Englishman (depicted by writers such as E. M. Forster). It is clear from the fading sepia photographs that the adventure was luxuriantly pleasurable and exceedingly good for the ego.

The young bureaucratic conquistadors prepared themselves to rule a race about which they knew little, in a climate for which they were singularly ill suited, by means of the newly revived public school system with its umbilical link to the universities of Oxford and Cambridge. Under the stimulus of men like Thomas Arnold of Rugby, these schools became forcing houses for transforming the sons of rough-talking businessmen into scholars and (more importantly) gentlemen. They sought to place a stamp of superiority on their alumni through the study of the classics, team games and a hierarchical prefect system which, while appearing sado-masochistic, simultaneously stressed a natural right to rule and passive obedience. The ICS used examinations in selecting candidates, and the classics, the intellectual diet of the universities, were seen as the best indication of excellence. As **generalists**, with no practical skills, successful candidates confidently sailed away to command a vast subcontinent. The ICS seemed to the bourgeoisie to offer the very best model upon which to reform the home administration.

> What we must look for here is, first, religious and moral principles; secondly, gentlemanly conduct; thirdly, intellectual ability.
>
> Dr Thomas Arnold (1795–1842; headmaster), address to his scholars at Rugby School

The Northcote–Trevelyan Report (1854) This report, the result of an enquiry established by Gladstone, set out the blueprint for radical reform. Its driving spirit was Sir Charles Trevelyan, a zealous member of the ICS. The report recommended that the separate departments be amalgamated to form a single *home civil service*. The work was characterized hierarchically, from clerical drudgery, through a range of executive tasks, to the intellectualism of policy-making. Recruitment was to reflect these distinctions in appropriately Platonic terms: men of iron would labour at the lower levels, while the upper echelons were reserved for the men of gold forged on the public school–Oxbridge anvil.

Merit would replace patronage and nepotism. Yet in this praiseworthy ideal lay the key to a bourgeois capture of the service. The examinations would be geared to the Oxbridge syllabus and neither aristocrats nor the working classes could match the sons of the bourgeoisie on such territory. The report was warmly welcomed by Gladstone: the class he represented would have 'command over all the higher part of the civil service, which up to this time they have never enjoyed' (Morley 1903: 649). The old guard were not blind to the writing appearing on their decaying walls, Queen Victoria worrying where 'the application of the principle of public competition is to stop' (Magnus 1963: 118).

The twentieth century The fact that the civil service took this shape is by no means remarkable: it was fashioned to serve a new political order. What *is* remarkable is that, as society changed during the twentieth century, the model persisted. Even an era of reform instigated by Thatcher, including the Next Steps initiative (which undermined the Northcote–Trevelyan principle of a single service), could not penetrate the bastions of the mandarinate (see p. 471).

The Culture of Whitehall

Following the nineteenth-century reforms the civil service evolved its own particular culture which preserved its elitist character. It has been likened to an Oxbridge college, with much attention to status, ritual displays of courtesy, esoteric speech codes involving Latin phrases and much cricketing jargon, and a general air of superiority.

Social make-up: unrepresentative bureaucracy?

Post-war mandarins have been asked to run a complex welfare state. Do they know what it is like to sit at nights with a loved one in pain on an NHS waiting list? Have they known unemployment, discrimination or harassment by the forces of law and order? How far has the service reflected the society it serves in terms of gender, race and social class? Has the selection process aimed for a representative bureaucracy?

Gender The civil service has not welcomed women into its ranks. The Victorian era was marked by overwhelming male hegemony, shown in all-male London clubs, limited education for girls and a male House of Commons elected by a male electorate. While their opportunities in the service have improved (no longer forced to retire if they marry), women remain grossly under-represented at the upper levels (see figure 15.2). Although the Crossman diaries conferred a modest fame upon Dame Evelyn Sharp, the first woman Permanent Secretary, she remained a rare bird; in 1998 there were no women flying at this altitude.

Diary of Jim Hacker: Oct. 27th

'How many Permanent Secretaries', I asked Sir Humphrey, 'are there at the moment?'
'Forty-one I believe.'
A precise answer.
'Forty-one,' I agreed pleasantly. 'And how many are women?'
Suddenly Sir Humphrey's memory seemed to fail him. 'Well broadly speaking, not having the exact figures to hand, I'm not exactly sure.'
'Well, approximately?' I encouraged him to reply.
'Well,' he said cautiously, '*approximately* none.'

J. Lynn and A. Jay, *The Complete Yes Minister* (based on TV series) (1981: 355)

In 1994 the government made its fourth five-yearly report to the UN Human Rights Committee, claiming 'significant progress for women at all levels of the Civil Service since 1984'. However, while 29 per cent of those in the glittering diplomatic service were women, only 3 per cent had reached ambassadorial level. At the upper reaches of the mandarinate (grades 1–4) women held only 9 per cent of the 652 jobs and only 2 of 34 permanent secretaryships. Six departments remained skirt-free zones, while the Ministry of Defence numbered only 2 women among 60 senior staff. The government was strongly criticized by Elizabeth Symons, leader of the First Division Association (the senior mandarins' 'union'), for failing in its 1991 Opportunity 2000 commitment to fill 15 per cent of senior posts with women (*Independent*, 17 Oct. 1994). Women's value is seen to lie in performing routine tasks at the level of administrative assistant and as insecure casual employees. Of the part-time staff, 95 per cent are women.

Race   The prospects for ethnic minorities in the upper echelons remain bleak. Even at the lower levels they are poorly represented (figure 15.6). In October 1997 Labour MP Keith Vaz, in a report based on replies to parliamentary questions tabled between May and July 1997, described a failure to recruit Asians as a 'national shame'. The Foreign Office and the Ministry of Defence were singled out for particularly poor records.

Social class   Nowhere has the Northcote–Trevelyan legacy been more evident than in the class make-up of the mandarinate. Moulded from the same establishment clay as the heads of industry, commerce, the City, the army, the church and ancient professions, they attended the same schools and universities (Kellner and Crowther Hunt 1980: 193; Theakston and Fry 1989: 132), join the same London clubs (the Athenaeum and the Oxford and Cambridge being particular favourites) and meet at the same house parties. Harrovian Cabinet Secretary Robert Armstrong was succeeded by Etonian Robin Butler, who was in turn followed by Sir Richard Wilson, educated at Radley College. Class bias has

Figure 15.6
Ethnic minorities in the civil service and the general population, April 1996.

Source: Data from *Civil Service Statistics* (1996).

been reinforced by working-class graduates' disinclination to apply, reflecting the deferential British culture and low expectations of success (see below). It is sometimes pointed out that there has been an increased tendency for civil servants to come from 'minor' public schools – hardly a social revolution!

Socialization   There has also been some increase in the number of state school entrants. However, coming from the diligent middle classes, these are likely to be pursuing personal ambition rather than social reform. Moreover, despite meritocratic procedures, career advancement requires informal patronage from above and the ambitious will need to catch the eye of their superiors (Richards 1996: 665). Consciously or unconsciously they will assume the colours of their environment, joining the right clubs, attending the right parties and adopting the right speech codes.

'Yes Permanent Secretary'

There are those who are always on the side of authority and quite exceptionally adept at formulating the answer that will be most acceptable to those at the top. It is no secret that they get on better than those who are outspoken and speak their minds.

E. N. Gladden (retired civil servant), *Civil Services of the United Kingdom* (1967: 199)

Skimming the milk: selecting mandarins

The selection process is the key to understanding mandarin culture. Northcote–Trevelyan established that potential mandarins would enter directly into a closed upper elite – the Administrative Class. This at once removed the inconvenience of working through the ranks and precluded aspirants rising from the lower strata. Subsequent reforms maintained this principle; today a Policy Management Programme (formerly the Fast Stream) provides a gilded staircase to the top. From the start entrants inhale the oxygen of power, meeting and even advising ministers. Competition is intense: 7,000 applied for just 115 vacancies in 1994 (*Financial Times*, 25 Oct. 1995). After a filter of written tests a small number proceed to several days of interviews and work simulations where subjective assessment searches for ill-defined 'right qualities'. Elite cloning has enabled the service to reproduce in its own image.

Between 1965 and 1986, Oxbridge entry swelled to 75 per cent (Theakston and Fry 1989: 132). When in 1993 Cabinet Secretary Robin Butler told the Treasury and Civil Service Committee that public school entry had fallen to 51 per cent he was, like his predecessor Robert Armstrong, being 'economical with the truth'; casting his net over a far wider area of the service than is usual in defining the mandarinate. An *Economist* analysis (19 March 1994) of the 'true mandarinate' found that, of twenty permanent secretaries, sixteen (80 per cent) had been so educated and fourteen (70 per cent) were from Ox-

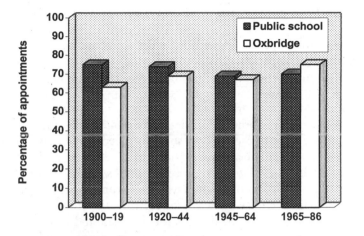

Figure 15.7
The public school/
Oxbridge background
of permanent
secretaries recruited
during four time
periods, 1900–1986.

Source: Data from Theakston and Fry (1989: 132).

bridge. These proportions have remained remarkably stable throughout the twentieth century (figure 15.7). Although the mandarins frequently talk of revamping their image, scepticism amongst redbrick graduates must die hard. In June 1996 the government revealed that of Leeds University's 349 applicants in 1995, just 2 per cent entered the fast stream – compared to 10.6 per cent of Oxford applicants. Meanwhile, universities with strong science backgrounds (such as Aston and Brunel) had no successful candidates at all (*Financial Times*, 13 June 1996).

Vetting An additional safeguard against social infiltration has been through security vetting. Although officially a means of excluding communists and fascists, interest has focused rather more on those with leanings towards the former. 'Neither the vetting procedures nor the ideological climate in the upper reaches of the civil service required a man or woman to abjure strongly held conservative views; but there was a problem for anyone with more than mildly reform-oriented leaning' (Miliband 1984: 103).

Promotion Progression to the highest levels, while subject to various 'objective' meritocratic processes, including the work of the Senior Appointments Selection Committee, is really controlled through a secretive, club-like process at the highest level of the mandarinate. At an early career stage individuals likely for advancement will be identified and apparently meritocratic procedures will be but a facade to legitimate their rise (Richards 1996). Some challenge came to this cosy process in the 1980s (see p. 466).

The expertise of the mandarins: gentlemen versus players?

The social bias in the upper echelons is defended with the argument that the criterion is brains, the apparent class domination arising because the best and brightest issue from the loins of intelligent and successful parents. Yet severe doubts have been expressed about the mandarins' expertise. While doctors attend medical schools and lawyers study law, Britain's mandarins, in sharp contrast to the practice in many other countries, have remained almost untouched by the disciplines relevant to their work (sociology, economics, civil engineering, and even social and public administration).

It is argued that high-level work requires *generalist* rather than *specialist* abilities, a preference redolent of the nineteenth-century reforms. Yet in truth the reformers had little choice; it was classics that the public schools and universities taught, so it had to be classics for the examinations. Had it been in practical subjects the 'barbarians' from the urban technical colleges might have entered the establishment gates. This approach could work during the nineteenth century, with the state's minimalist 'night-watchman' role, but the post-war era brought government into new areas of economic and social life. Britain slipped behind its main competitors as civil servants wrestled with problems they did not understand, their cultivated air of superiority concealing shallow dilettantism (Balogh 1968). The retention of the generalists' hegemony was justified variously. Only they knew their way around the Whitehall system, only they could understand the (equally generalist) minister's mind; that is, the best people to lead the blind would be the blind. Legitimation came in a doctrine which condescendingly declared that experts must be 'on tap not on top'.

The Fulton Report: anything but action The arrival of a Labour government in 1964 promised an attack on both social exclusiveness and amateurism and a committee was soon established under Lord Fulton, with Norman Hunt, a reformist academic and the Prime Minister's nominee, a key member. The 1968 Fulton Report castigated the 'cult of the amateur' yet, of over a hundred recommendations, one was politely declined – that entrants should possess *relevant* degrees. This seemingly small reservation effectively sabotaged the enterprise. Hunt was later to confess that he had been made a dupe 'in an unequal struggle with arch-mandarin, Sir William Armstrong' (Kellner and Crowther-Hunt 1980: 63). Ten years later the Commons Expenditure Committee saw little evidence of change and disenchanted high-flier Clive Ponting (1986: 85) reported how in 1983 four of the senior officials responsible for the entire defence budget of £18 billion 'were all classicists who had read Greats at Oxford'. By the 1990s, the generalists' promotion prospects were still considerably brighter than those of the specialist (Richards 1996). Although a 1996 white paper (Cabinet Office 1996) contained a resolution to increase the proportion of fast-stream recruits with science backgrounds from 20 to 33 per cent, David Willetts, as junior minister in the Cabinet Office, insisted the drive was not intended to reduce the chances of Oxbridge generalists.

Mandarins in the hereafter: life after Whitehall

Mandarins have not feared retirement; indeed some greet their professional demise with the relish of Christians in Foxe's *Book of Martyrs*, so certain are they of paradise to come. The close of a career brings rather more than a pocket watch; titles have been dispensed twice a year in the honours lists. These awards reflect status reached rather than any particular contribution; the most senior can expect peerages. Although the practice was curbed by Major and Blair, the rewards do not end with ennoblement. Though gone, the mandarins are not forgotten, their names are entered upon the revered list of the great and the good from which are chosen the heads of university colleges, quangos and government commissions. Their value lies in assiduously cultivated conformity; they can be relied upon not to rock the establishment boat. Thus was Sir Thomas Legg (a long-serving 'Sir Humphrey' and Garrick Club member) brought in to investigate the arms-to-Sierra-Leone affair in May 1998.

There is also a tendency, once the winter of retirement threatens, for some to migrate like starlings to the warm climes of the private sector in merchant banks and industry (Balogh 1968: 21). In the 1980s, public service could increasingly be seen as a prelude to private gain (Doig 1984) and senior mandarins could feel considerable anguish if they had not ensured that when the Whitehall door closed another was ready to open. Sir Leslie Rowan left the Treasury to head Vickers, Sir Edward Playfair went from Defence to International Computers and, amidst much controversy, the ex-head of the civil service, Sir William Armstrong, became chairman of Midland Bank. The move can even come mid-career on the 'revolving door' principle.

The real concern here is not that these favoured beings are able to continue to draw upon their capital of privilege while others draw their meagre pensions but that many civil servants in key positions will be 'inclined to take a general view of things not awkward to large private interests' (Balogh 1968: 23). In 1994, amidst controversy, Sir Duncan Nichol, NHS chief executive, joined the board of BUPA, Britain's largest private health care organization. In the same year Richard Thomas went from the Office of Fair Trading to Clifford Chance, an influential lawyer-lobbyist firm. It is not difficult to see why those with an unrivalled knowledge of the workings of Whitehall and its denizens should be prized by private interests, including multinational companies.

Although some restrictions have ben introduced, these remain light. For two years after leaving the service mandarins' appointments are subject to an independent vetting body, but its declarations are only advisory. In June 1994 the Public Accounts Committee disclosed that a senior Home Office official responsible for privatizing the Wolds prison had joined Group Four less than twelve months after it had won the five-year contract to run the prison with a remarkably uncompetitive bid.

Secrets of Success

Whitehall may be characterized as an incestuous 'village'. The inhabitants of Whitehall-on-Thames have their own private world of shared experiences 'united by coherent patterns of praxis' (Heclo and Wildavsky 1974: 2). This image is particularly apposite with respect to sharing information with outsiders: the locals like to keep themselves very much to themselves. Yet the mandarins are supposed to serve the world outside and if they are miserly with information they threaten democracy. The issue is thus central to the analysis of British government.

Information and power

Endemic throughout British society, secrecy, rather than flagellation, is perhaps the real *vice anglaise*. It is a necessary instrument of a dominant elite; ignorance among the masses helps maintain deference. It is no small irony that Privy Council, the cherished name of a respected constitutional building block to which key political figures belong, actually means *secret council*. Official information has long been seen as the property of the high and mighty, who have been as likely to distribute it as they have their land, money and capital. The civil service, as keeper of the keys to the informational vaults, has been able to make British government one of the most closed in the world.

Not only is secrecy bad for democracy, it can be bad for the health. We have been denied information about the air we breathe, the food we eat and the harmful effects of medicinal drugs. There are countless examples. Relatives of soldiers meeting accidental death, mistreated hospital patients, victims of Gulf war syndrome and pursuers of justice on various fronts have all met the wall of official silence. Richard Lacey (1997), a scientist who worked strenuously to highlight the BSE threat (and whose own career was undermined in the process), was to dub MAFF 'The Ministry of Truth' in evocation of Orwell's visionary nightmare of official deception: *Nineteen Eighty-Four*.

Beyond the state lie powerful forces with their own interests in a government that can keep a secret (see chapter 17). When junior health minister Edwina Currie warned in December 1988 of the danger of salmonella in egg production, she angered the National Farmers' Union and was forced to resign. In 1993 it emerged that the government was holding back the names of five brands of soft drink known to have levels of patulin, a carcinogenic toxin, above the World Health Organization's safety level. To Maurice Frankel, director of the Campaign for Freedom of Information, this was another example of government succumbing to 'the unbearable temptation to work problems out in secret with industry' (*Guardian*, 11 Feb. 1993).

There is no shortage of some kinds of information, bland material likely to mislead, confuse and obscure. The civil service is a giant information processing plant, producing each week thousands of memos, answers to parliamentary questions, **white** and **green papers**, and streams of data on the state of society, the economy and the international situation *ad infinitum*. The creaking shelves of 'Government Publications' in any university library present precipitous mountain faces which only the most intrepid (or foolhardy) attempt to scale. Yet all this can be seen as part of a legitimation process: much turgid material disgorged from the Whitehall intestinal tract has served to mask the true level of **official secrecy**.

Official Secrets Acts

Having enacted them in 1889, 1911, 1920, 1939 and 1989, Britain is extremely good at passing Official Secrets Acts. The most restrictive element in this corpus was for long the infamous Section 2 of the 1911 Act, which made it a criminal offence for *any* Crown servant to disclose without authorization *any* information learned at work. It was also an offence to receive such information and the claim that disclosure was in the **public interest** was no defence. Ironically, the 'public interest' is the basis upon which government itself justifies withholding information. Moreover, in the Ponting case the judge, following an earlier House of Lords judgement in *Chandler* v. *DPP* (1962), ruled that the public interest could only be defined by the government, thereby opening the door to political interpretation. The jury was not impressed and surprised many by acquitting Ponting.

Section 2 was a 'catch-all' provision or a blunderbuss: a civil servant could be imprisoned for disclosing the colour of Whitehall toilet paper. Originally

It is an official secret if it's in an official file.

Sir Martin Furnival Jones (one-time head of MI5), quoted in C. Aubrey, *Who's Watching You?* (1981: 19)

intended as a form of press censorship, it was rushed through a Parliament fearing war with Germany. In 1971 it was reviewed by the Franks Committee which declared it 'a mess' (Franks 1972: para. 88). Yet for those wishing to keep things under wraps the 'mess' was extremely useful. Thus Sarah Tisdall, a Foreign Office clerk, was sentenced to six months' imprisonment in March 1984 for leaking to the *Guardian* information on the arrival of US Cruise missiles in Britain. As in the Ponting case, the prosecution appeared merely to be revenge for political embarrassment.

The 1989 Official Secrets Act finally laid to rest the infamous Section 2 but did little to open Whitehall's doors. No past or present employee of the security services could disclose anything about their work; there was no defence on the grounds of public interest or that the information was already in the public domain. Those charged under the old system would still have been prosecuted. In November 1998 a Paris court refused a request for the extradition of David Shayler, a former MI5 officer who had reported incompetence in the service. Again the charges were brought under the Official Secrets Act and, not to be denied, the government promised to pursue him in the civil courts.

Beyond Official Secrets Acts

The wall of secrecy contains more than official secrets acts. The Franks Committee reported sixty-one statutes criminalizing the disclosure of information but none punishing unnecessary secrecy. In addition, the thirty-year rule laid down in the Public Records Act consigns forty categories of government papers to the state vaults; the period during which they gather dust may be extended at the discretion of the Lord Chancellor. Another restrictive tool reached the front pages in the arms-to-Iraq affair, when Public Interest Immunity Certificates

"What rankles is that, after years as a civil servant, one has never been trusted enough to be put in a position from where, if one wished, one could have passed on state secrets."

(PIICs) were issued to prevent the release of documents embarrassing to the government, even though they were vital to the defendants in the Matrix Church-ill trial.

It might be expected that MPs would enjoy special rights to information. Indeed, a House of Commons Public Service Committee report (1996: para. 32) called upon the executive 'to provide full information about and explain its actions to Parliament'. However, armed with their Osmotherly rules (see p. 388), mandarins have kept their lips as well locked as their briefcases and filing cabinets in the face of parliamentary questions and scrutiny committees. In its section on ministerial accountability the Scott Report on the arms-to-Iraq affair cited seven examples of ministers failing to give information, while an archaic practice was used to impede the Commons Foreign Affairs Committee's invest-igation of the shipment of arms to Sierra Leone in 1998. It could be argued that Parliament could compel disclosure through its power to punish for contempt, but this is impeded by party discipline.

Anthony Wright: Did ministers behave in ways that ministers ought constitution-ally not to have behaved?
Sir Richard Scott: I have said so, yes.
Anthony Wright: Was Parliament denied information that Parliament constitu-tionally ought to have been provided with?
Sir Richard Scott: I think so, yes.

Sir Richard Scott answering Labour MP Anthony Wright before the House of Commons
Public Service Committee (HC 313-III, 1995/6, paras 378–80)

Official secrecy and the media

Official secrecy legislation must be of central concern to the media. There is an additional means of government control over reporting matters pertaining to defence. Introduced in 1906, it was an alternative to formal censorship though its admirers call it 'responsible journalism'. **D-notices** are issued by a Defence Press and Broadcasting Committee, comprising representatives of the media and senior civil servants, with a full-time Whitehall secretary who is constantly available for day-to-day advice. As a non-statutory body it relies on media bosses playing the game but has been used to hide establishment embarrassment.

A further government control over journalists is the lobby system (p. 220). Journalists stepping out of line and citing sources can have their membership cards removed. Blair's press secretary, Alastair Campbell, abolished the un-attributed briefing to speak on the record, though this did not prevent leaks from other ministers. Moreover, the increasingly practised art of 'news man-agement', through judicious leaks (even of budgetary information; see p. 485), avoids the inconvenience of parliamentary criticism. Of course not all journal-ists are lobby hacks and Whitehall poodles. Some crusade in the cause of the unauthorized version and papers can rebel; the *Guardian* and *Independent* both withdrew from the lobby during the Thatcher years. Sometimes a more accurate account of events may be gleaned from maverick publications such as *Private Eye*, *Punch* and *Red Pepper*.

A la recherche du temps perdu: *political memoirs*

Political memoirs rarely threaten security yet the attempts to suppress them have been reminiscent of Savoy operas, the goal usually being to avoid embarrassment in high places. Probably the most important of these were the diaries of Richard Crossman (1975–7), published posthumously from his taped account of the Wilson government. Whitehall tried in vain to prevent publication and during the debate a further secret was revealed – the existence of unwritten 'guidelines' on memoirs, ruling out various subjects such as cabinet discussions and civil service advice. This gentleman's agreement entailed the inspection of proposed memoirs by the cabinet secretary. Despite objections, the Crossman diaries emerged and for the first time a full-blooded account of Whitehall life surfaced (Barberis 1996: 264). The *Spycatcher* case represents the apogee of memoirs furores, the government literally pursuing its prey to the antipodes. Here it was possible to argue that national security was involved because author Peter Wright had worked for MI5. However, the absurdity arose from the book's free circulation throughout the capitals of the western world while the po-faced servants of the Establishment were trying to conceal it from the eyes of their own people.

> What I wanted to do was to show Wilson that we'd got him and that we wanted him to resign.
>
> Peter Wright, referring to a secret MI5 file on Harold Wilson in TV interview reported in the *Guardian* (14 Oct. 1988)

Memoirs or diaries were to become almost commonplace from Labour politicians, the chroniclers including Harold Wilson, George Brown, Barbara Castle, Tony Benn, Roy Jenkins, Denis Healey and Roy Hattersley. Conservatives also took up their pens, Alan Clark's uninhibited revelations in 1993 raising many eyebrows. Nigel Lawson's *View from No. 11*, detailing souring relations with his next-door neighbour, was to be answered with several autobiographical tomes from the ex-Prime Minister herself. By the 1990s, memoirs, often conveniently packaged for the party conference season and newspaper serialization, had become big business and critics lamented the sight of ex-ministers 'on the make'. With a few notable exceptions, the accounts were largely self-congratulatory and rather turgid, shedding little new light on the inner workings of government.

A right to know: towards a Freedom of Information Act

If we look to other countries we find an emphasis not on the state's right to conceal but on a people's right to know. After the second world war, the UN declared this 'a fundamental human right'. Denmark, Sweden, Norway, France, Holland, Australia, Canada, Finland, New Zealand and the USA all passed laws giving a presumptive right of access to government-held information. Those wishing to withhold must make their case in the courts (Birkinshaw 1991). Calls for a British **Freedom of Information** Act have come from libertarian groups such as the Campaign for Freedom of Information (established in 1984) and Charter 88. However, governments fought shy and private members' bills introduced in 1978, 1981, 1984 and 1992 met with little encouragement.

As an alternative came a feeble compromise, the 1977 *Croham Directive*, an attempt to encourage departments to publish the background information for major policy studies. With delicate irony it was itself a 'confidential' document and had to be leaked (Ponting 1986: 205)! One of its effects was an increase in official smoke-screening with uninteresting information. The Citizen's Charter initiatives of 1991 also made available some limited information on public services. In 1992, details of cabinet committees were finally released, followed by the publication of *Questions of Procedure for Ministers* (ironically revealing another basis for cabinet secrecy). Indeed, they were updated by Blair in July 1997 to strengthen prime ministerial control over the dissemination of information by ministers (Hennessy 1998: 17). In July 1993, prompted by judicial criticism over the Kirk Sancto case (a soldier's accidental death) and a private member's bill with wide all-party support, the government unveiled its 'Open Government' initiative (Cabinet Office 1993), which included a code of practice to be policed by the ombudsman. Taking effect the following year, this offered more details on policy-making but contained a draconian list of exemptions. People were offered information as consumers of services rather than as citizens (Raab 1994).

In opposition, Labour had criticized secrecy, Blair asserting that freedom of information legislation was 'absolutely fundamental'. The incorporation of the ECHR promised new rights to citizens and a white paper on Freedom of Information duly emerged in December 1997. Proposals included an independent Information Commissioner with powers to compel official release and a new criminal offence of evading disclosure or destroying records. However, a list of exemptions remained and all departments were to retain a right to withhold in the public interest (figure 15.8). It remains to be seen how far the reform will change an age-old culture and campaigners were concerned that the date for the draft bill was repeatedly postponed.

A right to tell

When public servants feel a government is compromising the public's right to know, what are they to do? In the USA a code of ethics enjoins officials to put

Figure 15.8
Processing an
application under
the Freedom of
Information Act.

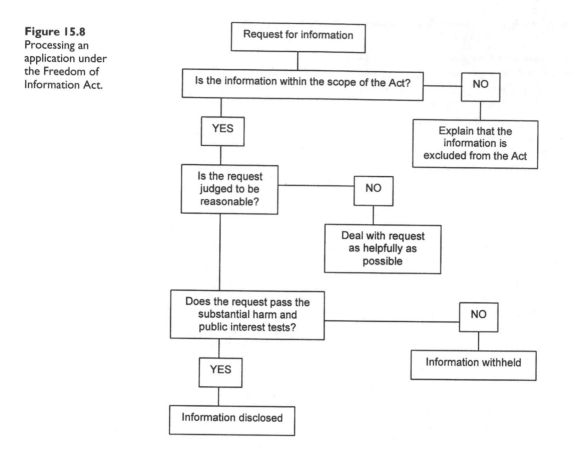

Request for information

Is the information within the scope of the Act? — NO

YES

Explain that the
information is
excluded from the Act

Is the request
judged to be
reasonable? — NO

Deal with request
as helpfully as
possible

Does the request pass the
substantial harm and
public interest tests? — NO

Information withheld

YES

Information disclosed

Source: Based on proposals outlined in the Freedom of Information white paper.

loyalty to country above that to persons, party or government. However, the British 'good chap' theory of government denied any need for such checks. Yet from the 1980s confidence began to wilt as affairs such as Ponting, Tisdall, Westland, the Pergau Dam and Matrix Churchill highlighted the ethical dilemmas facing civil servants. The First Division Association (FDA) pressed for a US-style code and a reluctant government finally complied in January 1995, allowing any official faced with a crisis of conscience to appeal to a Civil Service Commissioner. Sir Michael Bett was appointed to the position and by June 1996 the FDA was pursuing several 'serious incidents' of allegedly improper ministerial conduct (*Financial Times*, 26 June 1996). Yet critics remain unsatisfied, arguing for a statutory whistle-blowers' charter (Birkinshaw 1997). The issue also interested Lord Nolan, who argued in his first report on standards in public life that public servants should have a right to complain anonymously without going through the management structure.

> **Political public information**
>
> Government spending on advertising was planned to increase by twice the rate of inflation from £109 million in 1988/9 to over £120 million in 1989/90. Civil servants complained that they were encouraged to 'expound half-truths, produce dodgy material and leak in the Government's interest' (*Sunday Telegraph*, 2 April 1989).

A monarchical inheritance

The key to the informational constipation that seizes up the bowels of government is not restrictive legislation but the culture that has engendered it. State information belongs to the Crown not the people, the thirteenth-century Privy Councillor's Oath, lovingly preserved, making secrecy a constitutional rule. Such monarchical disdain permitted Cabinet Secretary Sir Robert (later Lord) Armstrong to boast in the Australian courts of his 'economy with the truth' and allowed minister William Waldegrave, in March 1994, to defend his position in the arms-for-Iraq affair by claiming it was at times proper to lie to Parliament.

Power in Whitehall: Disobedient Servants?

The liberal constitution portrays politicians as being in charge in Whitehall; otherwise the whole edifice of democracy becomes a sham. Around the turn of the century German sociologist Max Weber, a liberal troubled by the decline of liberal culture, noted an inexorable trend in developed states:

> It is obvious that technically the large modern state is absolutely dependent upon a bureaucratic basis. The larger the state . . . the more unconditionally this is the case. (Weber 1978: 971)

Fearing a body politic trussed in red-tape he outlined a theoretical *ideal-type* bureaucracy recruited on merit, bound by impersonal rules and playing defined roles which resulted in a politically neutral, disciplined hierarchy under the control of the elected government. Apologists for the British system see in the civil service much of this model and Weber himself was one of its admirers.

The assumption behind the idea of an obedient bureaucracy is that there is a clear distinction between politics (**policy-making**) and administration (**policy implementation**). The **politics–administration dichotomy** underlies much writing on public bureaucracy and was enunciated in 1887 by Woodrow Wilson who, concerned about corruption in American public life, argued that administration should be divorced from political skulduggery. Yet the distinction is untenable in practice. In the first place, policy can only be made in the knowledge of how it will be implemented. Secondly, no public servant implements policy like a robot; all instructions must be interpreted in the light of particular circumstances. In other words, the policy is being modified. Finally, in their advisory relationships with ministers, the mandarins exert considerable influence at the epicentre of the policy-making process.

Individual ministerial responsibility

Lying at the very heart of liberal democratic theory, the doctrine of **ministerial responsibility** articulates the relationship between minister and department. Because they are elected, it is ministers alone who are *responsible* to the outside world (through Parliament) for departmental actions. Various corollaries follow: civil servants should not themselves speak publicly, they must remain anonymous and, when praise or blame is apportioned, it must fall on the minister who should, in cases of serious error, resign like an officer and gentleman. In the words of the House of Commons Treasury and Civil Service Committee: 'Ministerial preparedness to resign when ministerial responsibility for failure has been established lies at the very heart of an effective system of parliamentary accountability' (1994: para. 133). A shining example of this was the resignation in 1954 of Sir Thomas Dugdale in the Crichel Down affair (see p. 627) in which officials had behaved improperly.

My husband has saved your service from being torn to pieces.

Lady Dugdale, to Head of the Civil Service Sir Edward Bridges after her husband's resignation. Quoted in letter from G. L. Wilde, Dugdale's principal private secretary, to the *Daily Telegraph* (20 May 1998)

However, despite its detailed exposition, the convention is largely illusory. Mandarins are increasingly to be found addressing the media, their roles overtly politicized, even their names becoming well known to the public. Cabinet Secretary Sir Robert Armstrong found his a household word through his trials and tribulations in the *Spycatcher* affair, while his successor, Sir Robin Butler, hit the headlines variously: approving a £4,700 payment towards Chancellor Norman Lamont's legal costs for evicting a sex therapist from his London home, appearing before the Scott enquiry and even featuring on BBC Radio 4's pantheon, *Desert Island Discs*. Not only named, they can be blamed, as in the Vehicle and General case in 1971 and the Courtline crash in 1975. In the latter case, an official enquiry produced a hierarchy of bureaucratic shame, indicting humble officials and entirely absolving ministers. In the Westland affair, Collette Bowe enjoyed an unsought hour of notoriety as an instrument in the devious political stratagem, her anonymity broken by Leon Brittan in attempting to protect himself (Birkinshaw 1988: ch. 4). In 1972, the governor of Holloway Prison was publicly rebuked by the Home Secretary for an 'error of judgement' in taking Myra Hindley for a walk. In 1996 minister Nicholas Soames blamed civil servants for not making him aware of research on Gulf war syndrome and in September 1998 the BSE inquiry blamed senior civil servant Elizabeth Acridge for advising minister John Gummer to reject scientific advice to establish a computer base for tracking cows.

Moreover, ministers are loath to atone by accepting the loaded pistol. In the Maze Prison breakout case, Northern Ireland Secretary James Prior sweated it out, securing the resignation of the prison governor instead. Although Leon Brittan departed (belatedly) over Westland, it was widely felt that Mrs Thatcher's office was implicated yet she remained. When Lord Carrington took the honourable way out after the Foreign Office failed to foresee the Falklands crisis he appeared a relic of another age. Indeed, he would be an exception in any age; Finer's (1956) classic study of cases dating from the mid-nineteenth century shows how rarely the convention is honoured.

Moreover, by the 1990s it appeared that ministers did not resign, even if *they themselves* were culpable. A key event was 'Black Wednesday' in September 1992. After the humiliating collapse of his economic strategy and the loss of some £4 billion, Chancellor Norman Lamont continued his economic stewardship. In November 1994, the High Court condemned the giving of aid (£234 million) towards the Malaysian Pergau Dam project, which had been tied to arms deals, arms that might well be deployed against the very people supposedly being helped. Select committee investigation revealed that Foreign Secretary Douglas Hurd had ignored civil service advice that this was 'a very bad buy'. A politician of the old school, Hurd considered his position but in the end did not go. Even more surprisingly, no heads rolled after the Scott inquiry into the Matrix Churchill affair despite direct criticism of Attorney General Sir Nicholas Lyell, whose actions could have sent innocent men to jail.

Centralizing power – decentralizing blame The agencification of the civil service had profound consequences for ministerial responsibility. The Northcote–Trevelyan structure – unified, hierarchical and rule-based – had been held to stand for integrity and probity against corruption. Critics found numerous problems in the new structure, including poor coordination, duplication, waste, institutional complexity, barriers to communication, information concealment, loss of experience, reduced public participation, impaired central coordination and ultimately loss of accountability (Rhodes 1994). In September 1997, with retirement looming, Robin Butler, Cabinet Secretary and head of the civil service, voiced his own concern at an Economic and Social Research Council conference that agencification 'obscures and blunts the democratic accountability of ministers' (*Financial Times*, 25 Sept. 1997). As in the case of the old public corporations, MPs found themselves frustrated by ministers refusing to answer questions on the grounds that they were no longer responsible. There is, however, an element of discretion in this; thus in May 1998 Home Secretary Jack Straw announced his willingness to answer prison questions.

In 1993–4 widespread criticism of the Child Support Agency resulted in the resignation not of a minister but of its chief executive. Even greater controversy arose over the Prison Service Agency (PSA) as riots, breakouts and problems over IRA prisoners led to buck-passing. The 1995 Learmont Report on the

Parkhurst Prison breakout chronicled 'mind-numbing bureaucratic incompetence' (*The Times*, 18 Oct. 1995). Home Secretary Michael Howard, claiming the matter to be 'operational' and therefore not within his responsibility, promptly sacked PSA head Derek Lewis. Lewis protested that he was being scapegoated and that his operational independence had been undermined by detailed 'breakfast, lunch and tea' interference, including an insistence that the Parkhurst governor be sacked (*Guardian*, 18 Oct. 1995). (Home Office Minister Ann Widdicombe was later to substantiate Lewis's account.)

Ministerial responsibility appears to be in a state of crisis. For politicians, the question of resignation is determined by political expediency, not constitutional imperative. Generally those who go, do so not for accountability issues but for sexual peccadillos or personal impropriety, often destroyed by tabloid reporting. Where policy or administrative failings are exposed, an ability to 'tough it out', sometimes at the expense of civil servants, becomes a mark of government virility. Thatcher, Major and Blair all stood by colleagues against calls for resignation. At the same time, ministerial frankness before Parliament has come seriously into question. After analysing the Scott Report, Bogdanor (1997: 83) concluded that the deepest lesson in its 1,800 pages 'is that we have no constitution and that it is time we had one'.

Mandarins and ministers: 'Yes Minister'?

What of the relationship between mandarins and their political masters? Are they the compliant instruments of Her Majesty's Government? Some agree that they are. Attlee is a widely quoted apologist, always finding them 'perfectly loyal . . . That's the civil service tradition, a great tradition. They carry out the policy of any given government' (Williams 1969: 79). In evidence to the House of Commons Expenditure Committee (1977: para. 1877), Edward Heath avowed that in his experience civil servants were definitely all 'under ministerial control', while Harold Wilson declared that any minister unable to master his civil servants 'ought to go' (para. 1924). On gaining office, Richard Crossman confided to his diary:

> Now at last I was a Minister in charge of an important Department and I could take decisions [and] lay down the law. (Crossman 1976: 293)

'*Yes Minister, but . . .*' Yet there is reason to doubt the passive civil servant thesis since they have numerous advantages over ministers:

- highly educated, long experienced and street (or corridor) wise to the ways of Whitehall;
- with access to information and the ability to control its flow to the ministerial desk;
- well connected with powerful outside interests impinging on the departmental portfolio;

- armed with detailed historical knowledge of departmental policy;
- more numerous than the ministers and able to collude informally and in committees (of which there are hundreds) within and across departmental boundaries;
- with security of tenure;
- from the confident classes who assume a right to rule.

Moreover, even if blessed with the wisdom of Solomon and the strength of Hercules, the width of a departmental ambit means that no minister (or ministerial team) can possibly be aware of everything going on. Civil servants are thus indispensable: they answer parliamentary questions, write speeches, arrange meetings, draft memos and reports and generally organize ministers' lives.

It is not surprising, therefore, that an alternative body of evidence comes not from government publications or officially sanctioned memoirs but from exposés. Crossman's *Diaries* reveal how, from an initial state of euphoria, he was to feel he had, as if in a horror movie, sought refuge in the very room where the vampire was hiding; the accounts of his enervating battles with Permanent Secretary Dame Evelyn Sharp should not be read by those of a nervous disposition. Other chroniclers (Benn, Castle, Hattersley) give equally frank insights into bureaucratic power.

Victor, if you go on arguing with me I'm going to crawl under the table and chew your balls off.

Denis Healey (Defence Secretary) to General Sir Victor Fitz-George Balfour (Vice Chief of the General Staff) in discussions on Northern Ireland; reported in Roy Hattersley, *Who Goes Home?* (1996: 80)

There are also civil servants who have come out of the bureaucratic closet. Brian Sedgemore, first a mandarin and then an MP, was uniquely qualified to illuminate the private world of public policy. From him we learn of the

> . . . arrogant and subtle way in which they dealt with ministers . . . developing departmental policies which weak ministers could call their own, using delaying tactics, skilfully suborning powers of patronage that belonged to ministers. (Sedgemore 1980: 26)

For Kellner and Crowther-Hunt (1980) the mandarins were nothing less than 'Britain's ruling class'. Through these sources we enter a world making that of Sir Humphrey Appleby and Jim Hacker seem tame. A House of Commons Expenditure Committee report (1977: para. 137) confirmed that 'some departments have firmly held policy views . . . When they are changed, the department will often try and reinstate its own policies through . . . the erosion of the minister's political will'.

One of us? However, Thatcher was to send tremors through Whitehall. Her radical agenda needed to break the legendary capacity to resist and she began to take an unprecedented interest in senior appointments, asking whether, ideologically speaking, those looking for advancement were 'one of us'. In this she was assisted by Cabinet Secretary Sir Robert Armstrong, with his additional role as head of the civil service. Prudent careerists recognized that 'if you can't beat 'em', there remained only one sensible thing to do. A salutary case was that of William Ryrie, a Treasury official who had the misfortune to cross swords with Thatcher as leader of the opposition. Once tipped as a future cabinet secretary, his career was forever blighted (Richards 1996: 666). Ex-mandarin Lord Bancroft noted the rise in the Whitehall 'grovel count' (*Guardian*, 12 Nov. 1985) as monetarists and managerialists began to emerge from the closets. By the end of the decade over two-thirds of the mandarinate had been newly appointed and critics argued that the service was becoming **politicized**. Government defector Emma Nicholson (1996: 196), veteran of three ministries, noted in her memoirs how 'permanent secretaries can now lose their jobs so that a ministerial favourite can be brought in'.

Civil servants were even found doctoring figures by 'redefining' unemployment and directly falsifying returns (*Guardian*, 29 March 1997). In the Scott inquiry they confessed to drafting inaccurate, misleading and 'clearly wrong' ministerial replies. In the run-up to the 1992 election, officials were asked to help cost Labour's manifesto and NHS chief executive Sir Duncan Nichol publicly defended government health policy while attacking Labour. In 1994 the *Observer* (24 April) reported the Cabinet Secretary advising departments to avoid anything controversial until after the local and European elections. Emma Nicholson (1996: 196) saw the civil service as being 'so close to party politics that lines were constantly being crossed over, even redrawn'.

The Civil Service is slowly being destroyed. Unless the Government changes course, we'll go right back to the 19th-century days of nepotism, corruption and incompetence.

John Sheldon (General Secretary of the National Union of Civil and Public Servants), quoted in the *Independent* (7 Nov. 1994)

Advising ministers

The use of **ministerial advisers** is another way of countering civil service influence. However, the steps of Whitehall have become littered with their sun-baked bones as they encounter a wall of impeccably polite intransigence. Only during the heat of two world wars did such 'outsiders' make any impression and they were quickly demobbed once normal service resumed. Economist Thomas (later Lord) Balogh, brought in by Wilson in 1964, found himself effectively frozen out through a series of 'Yes Minister' ploys. Heath's team of businessmen encountered similarly cold pin-striped shoulders. The 1974 Labour government

> To give spurious intellectual justification to the Secretary of State's political prejudices.
>
> Maurice Preston's mock job description as adviser to Roy Hattersley, Secretary of State for Prices and Consumer Protection, in Roy Hattersley, *Who Goes Home?* (1996: 169)

permitted cabinet ministers two advisers each but their experiences were also frustrating.

However, from the 1980s the climate changed. Advisers and think-tanks became as well known to the public as the politicians they served, hard-line monetarist Alan Walters a familiar face on television screens. The new factor was determined Downing Street backing and the advisers began to turn the tables. The FDA made an official protest that even junior ministers were rejecting official advice, sometimes with contempt and adding emphasis with the 'F word' (McKie 1994). To vie with the advisers civil servants began to feel pressure to say what ministers wanted to hear (Plowden 1994). The privatization programme saw government turning outside the civil service to commercial consultants such as Price Waterhouse, their work seeing the light of day in the form of government white papers (Ward 1993). This could be seen as the privatization of policy formation.

When governments change

The left had long doubted civil service neutrality, Harold Laski arguing that it was only so because the political system never threw up radical governments. He predicted that any challenge would signal a point of crisis, expecting it to come from the left. In the event it came from the right, and throughout the Thatcher and Major years questions were asked as to how far a radically recast civil service would be able to work with Labour. Would a set of hard-nosed free marketeers have to be pensioned off?

Some claimed that the Rolls Royce neutrality was still intact. Robin Butler had declared: 'If my position wasn't acceptable to an incoming government that would weaken the tradition of impartiality' (Williamson 1995). In the Major government's eventide one ex-mandarin observed:

> No one at the moment . . . is going to waste time putting up a paper on trade union rights . . . But all a Labour minister will have to do is ask for a full range of options and they'll get them. (Timmins and Kampfner 1997)

The Labour government also welcomed much of the remodelled Whitehall architecture, including the use of advisers. Blair even planned to appoint political adviser Jonathan Powell as his principal private secretary (a job traditionally held by a career civil servant), reportedly leaving Cabinet Secretary Butler 'seriously un-relaxed' (i.e. 'apoplectic with rage'). While Robin Cook was prevented from appointing his mistress, by June 1997 Labour had appointed fifty-three advisers paid from public funds, an increase on the thirty-eight employed under the Conservatives. With eighteen members, the Downing Street advisory staff became the largest ever.

The new mastery of the art of public relations acquired by Labour in opposition left the official information service particularly exposed. Early complainants included Health Secretary Frank Dobson, Northern Ireland Secretary Mo Mowlam and Social Security Secretary Harriet Harman, all unhappy about the presentation of their policies. Civil servants complained to the Cabinet Secretary about ministers politicizing press releases and eight press officers resigned. In October 1997 Jonathan Haslam, formerly Major's press secretary, joined the exodus after a contretemps with education minister Stephen Byers. Permanent Secretary Michael Bichard was reported (*The Times*, 17 Oct. 1997) to have upbraided the minister, reminding him of the official guidance on press releases, which should be: 'objective and explanatory, not tendentious or polemical' and certainly not 'party political'.

This further increase in the number of appeals by parents shows how hollow the claim of the previous Government that they were extending parental choice really was.

Offending paragraph from Stephen Byers's draft press release, quoted in *The Times* (17 Oct. 1997)

However, the coming of New Labour posed few serious problems of ideological clash since, in line with Laski's argument, the system had once again thrown up a government with much in common with its Conservative predecessor.

Managing the Mandarins: Reinventing Government?

Despite their backgrounds it does not follow that mandarins lean to the political right; the newer departments associated with the welfare state have a vested interest in its maintenance. A body of rightish thought (**public choice theory**) depicts bureaucrats as profligate users of public money, intent on enlarging their empires and 'over-supplying' their services (Niskanen 1973). The 1980s and 1990s saw attempts to curb this through a 'new public management' movement. The process was portrayed by ministers as 'reinventing government', following the title of a book by US authors Osborne and Gaebler (1992). Reform proposals began to strike at the foundations of Whitehall like Exocet missiles, the momentum maintained by the creation of the Office of Public Service in the Cabinet Office.

Private lessons A major theme in civil service reform has been the belief that it can learn from the private sector. Such calls came from the 1961 Plowden Report and the 1968 Fulton Report, and were exemplified by Heath's 'Selsdon Man' approach in 1970, but all initiatives were skilfully neutralized by the mandarins, who preferred the intrigue of managing their ministers to the more prosaic task of managing their departments.

However, Thatcher moved with greater zeal on the **managerialism** front than any predecessor. Sir Derek Rayner of Marks and Spencer's became head of an Efficiency Unit in 1979. He had already served as one of Heath's disillusioned businessmen and knew the wily ways of Whitehall. A system of 'scrutinies', with teams of young civil servants probing established practices, achieved more than any previous initiative (Hennessy 1990: 619). In the changing climate, the environment became inhospitable to traditional bureaucratic life-forms; at jolly parties at Number Ten, permanent secretaries learned to hold their views, like their vols-au-vents, close to their chests. In addition, management consultants were brought in at various levels. They did not come cheap. A report by the Efficiency Unit in August 1994 revealed Whitehall spending on consultants to have quadrupled between 1985 and 1990 to over £500 million. Critics were sceptical of the quest for efficiency, which seemed to threaten the traditional ethos of public service (Chapman and O'Toole 1995).

> Now, can you tell these bozos about the real world?
>
> Reported remark of Conservative minister to group of businessmen with reference to his civil servants, quoted in the *Independent* (17 July 1994)

Agencification: accountability or accountancy? A feeling that the Rayner reforms had not gone far enough led to a further report by the Efficiency Unit (1988). Popularly known as the 'Next Steps' report, this presaged the full-scale agencification of the service (p. 443). Although suggested in the Fulton Report, the principle had made only a limited impact. This time, however, the ideas were backed by strong political will and the bureaucratic terrain was relandscaped, part of a process of 'hollowing out' the state (Rhodes 1994). Although a structural change, its essential purpose was managerial (Elcock 1991: 236–42). The new chief executives, on fixed-term contracts, were given considerable managerial freedom; able to introduce performance-related pay and short-term contracts. Civil servants were to be 'deprivileged'.

Yet critics argued that democratic government imposed restrictions on the extent to which public-service managers could be granted autonomy (Elcock 1991: 188). A House of Commons Public Service Committee's report (1996: ch. V) stressed the need for more precise definitions of the roles of ministers and agency heads.

Culture shock The Northcote–Trevelyan reforms had centralized recruitment through an independent Civil Service Commission. However, in 1991, in a seismic challenge to Whitehall culture, the government abolished this for some 95 per cent of appointments. Recruitment was to be conducted by the departments and agencies themselves. They could, if they chose, engage the services of a newly created Recruitment and Assessment Service which, amidst heated controversy, went on in 1991 to be privatized. The result was a variety of terms and conditions of employment with private-sector-style contracts, the Civil

Service commissioners remaining merely to oversee the process. Only the top echelons successfully resisted the change (see below).

Market-testing: reinventing or abandoning? A further Efficiency Unit report led to a white paper (Treasury 1991) introducing '**market-testing**' to the service; civil servants had to compete with private firms for the work they had already been doing. Earlier Thatcher had argued that agencification was an alternative to privatization, not a halfway house towards it, and those just settling into agency life felt demoralized. Moreover, the Treasury and Civil Service Select Committee noted that in 1992/3, £768 million worth of activities out of the £1.119 billion subjected to market-testing was contracted out without any in-house bid having been allowed (*Independent*, 25 Nov. 1994). By 1996 the process had eliminated some 34,800 posts (*Civil Service Statistics* 1996: 8). One American computer company, Electronic Data Systems, reached the point of controlling more than half the government's IT services (*Guardian*, 10 April 1997). The minister responsible for market-testing argued that 'the government's job is to steer not to row' (Hencke 1992). One bizarre manifestation was a proposal by the Ministry of Defence in January 1996 to sell off Admiralty Arch.

Critics feared constitutional landmines in the path ahead: private contractors, anxious to win or keep contracts, would lack motivation to confront government with criticism. The privatization of the Recruitment and Assessment Services Agency caused particular concern. Describing it as 'the sale of an ethos' (*Guardian*, 20 Dec. 1995), ex-mandarin Lord Bancroft mobilized 124 peers to defeat the plan in the Lords, while Richard Chapman (1996) saw both 'tragedy and farce' in a profound government disregard for civil service ethical values. It was suggested that it was not reinventing government but abandoning it (Painter 1994).

Plus ça Change: Room at the Top

Britain's civil service appears to be at a crossroads, its neutrality, permanence and anonymity in question. The traditional boast that Whitehall provided a 'model for the world' has become less credible for various reasons. The increased use of advisers invites comparison with the French *ministerial cabinet* system, political appointments and career advancements suggest some leaning towards the US spoils system, while agencification is redolent of the Swedish bureaucratic structure.

However, in a constitution moulded through evolution rather than revolution, the idea that the architecture of the central state can be 'reinvented' in less than two decades invites caution. Did the reforming hurricanes whistling along the corridors of power penetrate the closed offices of the mandarinate at the very heart of the state? Radical ministers such as Michael Heseltine had certainly wanted to shake up this elite world with short-term contracts, market-testing and large-scale appointments from outside on the 'revolving door' principle.

However, after much fevered consultation the Efficiency Unit (1993) produced the Oughton Report on recruitment to the top three grades. This was to prove a 'classic civil service holding operation' (Theakston 1995: 154) in which the mandarinate would survive as a 'Senior Civil Service' of around 3,500, encompassing posts at grade 5 and above. There would be no market-testing or privatization and, although accepting some opening of top appointments to national competition (Michael Bichard came from local government to head the Benefits Agency, moving in 1995 to become permanent secretary at the Department of Employment), the service would continue to 'grow its own timber'. Little change was heralded in the white paper *The Civil Service: Continuity and Change* (Cabinet Office 1994a), which showed more enthusiasm for the former than the latter, and a review of fast-stream recruitment (Cabinet Office 1994b) declared that this gilded staircase, renamed the Policy Management Programme, should remain.

Employing the reasoning of public choice theory, Dunleavy (1991; see also Dowding 1995) accounted for the outcome with a 'bureau-shaping model'. In conditions of financial restraint, rather than maximize their empires, senior officials will try to shape their own bureaux as small agencies, removed from the actual delivery of policy and insulated from the chill winds of cuts. The paradoxical implication of this was, as Andrew Marr noted (*Independent*, 14 July 1994), that the mandarins' interests came to coincide with those of anti-statist politicians. The mandarins had dug their heels in as they had over all previous reforming initiatives and avoided the fate they had visited upon hundreds of thousands of their more lowly colleagues. The nineteenth-century model of the mandarinate has survived two world wars and the Keynesian revolution. It remains a limb of a formidable Establishment and, despite bold words from reformers, it is not time to write its obituary.

Key points

- The civil service is a key part of the executive, headed by the elected government through a system of ministerial posts.
- The modern service was born in the mid-nineteenth century, when the bourgeoisie used their new political and economic power to gain control of the state.
- Civil servants are said in liberal-democratic theory to be permanent, politically neutral and anonymous. All these features can be critically questioned.
- The mandarin class has traditionally enjoyed a significant role in shaping policy.
- Studies have demonstrated that the bias in favour of the public school and Oxbridge candidates deliberately sought in the nineteenth-century reforms has been broadly maintained.
- Whitehall has for long been characterized by secrecy. Reforms are slow.

- Despite their social backgrounds civil servants are not necessarily right wing and have a considerable stake in the welfare state.
- The 1980s and 1990s saw some major assaults on the traditional Northcote–Trevelyan model with agencification and managerialism. However, at the elite pinnacle the mandarinate emerged largely un-scathed.
- The Labour government of 1997 did not have a radical agenda and, as before, found little problem in working with the service as it found it.

Review your understanding of the following terms and concepts

agencification
bureau-shaping model
bureaucracy
bureaucratic power
Citizen's Charter
civil servant
D-notice
Freedom of
   Information Act

managerialism
mandarin
market-testing
meritocracy
ministerial adviser
ministerial
   responsibility
official secrecy
policy implementation

politics–administration
   dichotomy
public choice theory
public interest
Senior Civil Service
specialist and generalist

Assignment

If you are able to do so, visit the Public Record Office at Kew (a short walk from Kew Gardens underground station). Locate the Cabinet Minutes (Conclusions) section and look up reference CC(63)39 relating to the meeting held on 20 June 1963. Locate agenda item number 3 on the Resignation of the Secretary of State for War. Answer the following questions.

		Mark (%)
1	What is the affair under discussion?	5
2	Why can this assignment not refer to the minutes pertaining to a recent event such as, say, the imposition of the poll tax?	5
3	Why are the cabinet minutes referred to as 'Conclusions'?	20
4	How far do you feel that this account captures the true flavour of the stormy events under discussion? Seek out some contemporary press reports to assist you.	40
5	What objections to a select committee inquiry does the Cabinet raise? To what extent do you think these are justified?	30

Questions for discussion

1 How useful is it to characterize the world of Whitehall as a village?
2 What factors lead to the view that civil servants will tend to dominate ministers in their professional relationship?
3 'Individual ministerial responsibility is a convention honoured more in the breach than in the observance.' Discuss.
4 How did the Northcote–Trevelyan reforms reflect the power structure of nineteenth-century British society?
5 Examine the constitutional and administrative implications of civil service agencification.
6 What might be the long-term effects of introducing a 'spoils system' for appointing top civil servants in Britain?
7 Examine how the Thatcher government challenged the role and structure of the higher civil service.
8 Discuss whether the composition of the civil service should reflect the demographic profile of the country at large.
9 Explain the nature and causes of secrecy in British government.
10 What developments lead to the assertion that the British civil service has become politicized?

Topic for debate

This house believes that the model of the British civil service is no longer able to meet the needs of the modern state.

Further reading

Barberis, P. (ed.) (1996) *The Whitehall Reader*.
Short readings from academics, politicians and officials giving various angles on debates, both current and perennial.

Castle, B. (1980) *The Castle Diaries 1974–6*.
Barbara Castle was one of the most energetic politicians of her era and her account is lively and perceptive.

Crossman, R. H. S. (1975–7) *Diaries of a Cabinet Minister*.
Published posthumously, this frank account forced the Establishment door a little further open.

Drewry, G. and Butcher, T. (1991) *The Civil Service Today*, 2nd edn.
A highly readable and authoritative account.

Elcock, H. (1991) *Change and Decay: Public Administration in the 1990s*.
Sustained critique of the quest for efficiency, effectiveness and economy in the public domain. Latter half contains extracts from key sources.

Fry, G. K. (1995) *Policy and Management in the British Civil Service*.
Lively approach to the civil service, giving a scholarly summary of basic information, and with a critical edge.

Hennessy, P. (1990) *Whitehall*.
A *tour de force*. The Whitehall ecosystem clinically dissected.

Mallalieu, J. P. W. (1941) *Passed to You Please*.
A short early polemic against overweening officialdom from an earlier age, with a penetrating introduction by Harold Laski.

Osborne, D. and Gaebler, T. (1992) *Reinventing Government*.
Work by US authors inspiring (or justifying) much British civil service reform.

Rogers, A. (1997) *Secrecy and Power in the British State*.
Argues that state secrecy perpetuates elite rule.

Theakston, K. (1995) *The Civil Service since 1945*.
Concise account of the period, demonstrating the ability of the mandarins to thwart the reformers most of the time.

For light relief

E. M. Forster, *A Passage to India*.
A study of English manners, arrogance and racism in the Indian Civil Service.

J. Lynn and A. Jay (1981) *The Complete Yes Minister*.
Edited version of the television series. Perhaps not as astonishing as the real thing in the form of the Crossman *Diaries*, but shorter. Also available on video.

Giacomo Puccini, *Tosca*.
More corrupt officialdom, set to music.

William Shakespeare, *Measure for Measure*.
Corrupting effects of high office as a state official uses power to seek sexual favours.

C. P. Snow, *Corridors of Power*.
While some find passion in action and sex, Snow finds it in the ambitions and memos of the men in pin-striped trousers. Title added a term to the English language.

On the net

http://www.open.gov.uk
The starting point for an incredible amount of government information, with links to all departments and agencies.

Chapter Sixteen

Getting and Spending: the Politics of Public Expenditure

It is impossible to understand politics without appreciating the financial dimension. Much of the controversy around who gets what, when and how in society comes down to questions of money. The Chancellor of the Exchequer, the keeper of the nation's purse, is the second most powerful cabinet figure and the prime minister is formally titled First Lord of the Treasury. This chapter has three main sections. First we examine the nature of public expenditure and the associated processes, including the fixing of public spending levels, the raising of money and the public accounting process. Next we note how public expenditure has been used as an instrument of economic management within the capitalist economy. The final section assesses the extent to which the approach to public expenditure can be seen as a factor contributing to Britain's post-war pattern of economic decline.

The Nature of Public Expenditure

At its simplest, **public expenditure** is the money used by the agencies of the state in its multifarious operations from waging war to emptying the nation's dustbins. Its absolute level is beyond intuitive grasp – total government spending for 1996/7 was in the region of £300 billion; around 41 per cent of gross domestic product (GDP – the total annual output of the economy). The lion's share of this is raised through taxation, supplemented with borrowing and trading enterprises. Since November 1994 the government has also sponsored a national lottery to raise money for sport, the arts and charities, though this is run by Camelot, a private, profit-taking company rather than the state (making it unique within Europe). Thus the state draws money from society, passes it from one agency to another, and returns it to society in the form of services and grants in a complex network of financial flows (figure 16.1).

Figure 16.1
The flow of public
expenditure.

Public expenditure can also be conceived in more philosophical terms as an expression of community – one of the most important factors in our survival on earth. A polity is cemented by public expenditure; ensuring national security, preserving its culture and guaranteeing social rights through welfare policies. The collective nature of our psyche is denied by *individualists*, who object if the richer are taxed to assist the poorer. Margaret Thatcher asserted that 'there is no such thing as society' (Kingdom 1992). From this stems much heated political debate concerning relative priorities (figure 16.2). Although centring on technical, dry-sounding processes, this leads to decisions which affect the quality of all our lives.

Trends in public expenditure

Public expenditure has grown inexorably throughout the twentieth century, a ratchet effect ensuring that gains during emergencies are never fully relinquished afterwards. Until the first world war it had stood at around 15 per cent of national income, but had climbed to over 50 per cent by 1918, stabilizing at around 25 per cent through the 1920s and 1930s. The second world war exerted further pressure, driving it up to 75 per cent, and it subsequently settled at around 35 per cent from 1950 until the mid-1960s. At this point further

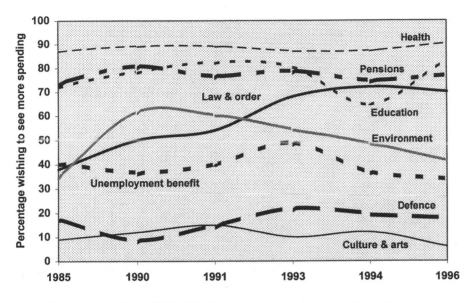

Figure 16.2
Public support for
government
expenditure in
various policy
areas, 1985–1996.

Source: Data from *Social Trends* (1998: 121), showing the percentage of respondents thinking that
there should be more spending in each particular area.

dramatic growth occurred, both in real terms and as a percentage of the GDP,
peaking in 1975, a time of economic crisis when the IMF demanded cuts (see
p. 490). Real spending has more than doubled over the past two decades, only
falling in a handful of years.

The purposes of public expenditure

Intuition suggests that the purpose of state expenditure is, like that of a household, to finance its activities. Figures 16.4 and 16.6 show how this can take two
forms: providing services and redistributing income through transfer payments
(table 16.1) to individuals (say pensions or student grants). Another purpose is
less self-evident and has no analogue with family budgeting. The colossal scale
of state finance means that government is able to use its taxation and spending
muscle to influence the economy in what is termed **fiscal policy**. When post-war
governments have made their getting and spending decisions, economic objectives have been as much in their mind as the services the money is to fund. The
following sections consider these two purposes in more detail.

Paying for the State

In figure 16.1 a number of taps interrupt the financial flows, and a key question
considers whose hands are on these. The issue has been at the heart of British
constitutional history and remains at the epicentre of modern political debate.

Table 16.1 Income redistribution through taxation and benefits

Item	Poorest 20% of households	Richest 20% of households
Original income	£2,430	£41,260
Benefits	+ £4,910	+ £1,200
Income tax, national insurance and council tax	− £1,130	− £10,480
Indirect taxes	− £1,930	− £5,090
Value of benefits in kind (NHS, education, etc.)	+ £3,950	+ £2,310
Final 'income'	£8,230	£29,200

Source: Data from *Social Trends* (1998: table 5.20). Figures are averages per household in each category.

Controlling public expenditure: developing the machinery

We saw in chapter 12 how public expenditure was the key to increased parliamentary control over the executive. The sovereign's crown was hollow without funds, and as Parliament became the effective payer of the piper it sought to call the royal tune. By the time of Elizabeth I it had acquired a control over taxation that was to be consolidated in the Glorious Revolution of 1688. Since then, Parliament has remained nominally in control of public finance, although as we are about to discover, today this is seen as largely a fiction.

Further important reforms came in the 1780s under the stimulus of Pitt and were intended to simplify public accounting and strengthen parliamentary control. Of particular significance was the creation of the Consolidated Fund in 1787, amalgamating a complex muddle of accounts into one into which all state revenue would flow and from which all expenditure would be drawn. This is in effect the government's bank account and is lodged with the Bank of England. The modern system of public finance was largely a nineteenth-century invention, fashioned by the industrial bourgeoisie as part of its greater creation – the liberal-democratic state set in the capitalist economy.

Britain's capitalist economy

In a capitalist economy such as Britain's, the means of production (land, raw materials, factories, machines, and so on), which provide the basic essentials needed by all citizens to sustain their lives, are owned by a relatively small proportion of the population, rather than by the public at large. These broadly represent the capitalist interests, which can extend beyond the state to the global economy (chapter 4). Although it may be argued that since the second world war we have had a **mixed economy**, with certain key industries owned and managed by the state (the public sector), this mix was always designed to maintain the dominance of private capital (Miliband 1984: 95); privatization (chapter 18) has reduced the mixed economy further.

Capitalism has proved itself a particularly effective mode of production, with an incomparable ability to apply technology and expand voraciously to find new materials and markets. Although releasing people's dynamic entrepreneurial spirit, and enhancing the material living standards of countless millions, the achievement is not without its costs, which have important political consequences.

> [The capitalist bourgeoisie] has accomplished wonders far surpassing Egyptian pyramids, Roman aqueducts, and Gothic cathedrals . . . It draws all nations into civilisation . . . has created enormous cities . . . rescued a considerable part of the population from the idiocy of rural life . . . and . . . has created more massive and more colossal productive forces than have all previous generations together.
>
> Karl Marx, *The Communist Manifesto* (1848: ch. 1)

" Oh, Mabel, is it not dreadful ? What a miserable place to bring up such a lovely dog !"

Source: Mary Evans Picture Library

The development of capitalism The capitalist mode of production first emerged in agriculture by replacing feudalism. Peasants were deprived of their historic rights to use land to produce crops for themselves in the notorious eighteenth-century enclosure movement, landowners forcing them to work over larger areas, using new machinery, for a wage. The industrial revolution saw the rise of industrial capitalism with large-scale mass production in the factories, which spawned new urban centres. The capitalist order even brought with it a new ideology – liberal individualism, promoted by the classical economists and the utilitarians (see chapter 2).

> The public be damned. I am working for my shareholders.
>
> William Henry Vanderbilt (1821–85; US millionaire railway owner), refusing to answer a reporter asking questions on behalf of the public

The Protestant work ethic and the ethos of parsimony Another important part of capitalism is the concept of accumulation. When the early capitalists acquired wealth, they did not use it extravagantly like the merchants and landowners of old but, like Dickens's Ebenezer Scrooge, tended towards frugality. In this way they could invest in yet more capital and amass wealth quite beyond their needs for personal survival. The cumulative effect was to consolidate the position of the capitalists and their families, who formed an increasingly dominant class. The importance of this was stressed by sociologist Max Weber, who attributed it in large measure to religion – to Protestantism and Calvinistic puritanism. The Protestant work ethic, in Weber's view, explained the ascendancy of capitalism in Western Europe by adding religious zeal to the lure of profit. This parsimony was to inform the approach to public expenditure. The prime goal was to become that of Victorian prudence – a *balanced budget* as advocated by Mr Micawber.

> Annual income twenty pounds, annual expenditure nineteen nineteen six, result happiness. Annual income twenty pounds, annual expenditure twenty pounds ought and six, result misery.
>
> Mr Micawber in Charles Dickens's novel *David Copperfield* (1849–50)

Against this background, the key figure in a series of rigorous reforms was Gladstone who, as Chancellor, determined that government finance should be as tightly controlled by the bourgeois paymasters as were their own prudently managed businesses. Money was spent, money was earned, and the main objective was to ensure that expenditure was as low as possible and did not exceed receipts. The aim was to evolve a system that would tax capitalists' profits as little as possible, taking just enough to keep open the trade routes and contain the potentially unruly masses at home. The system was conceived in terms of an annual cycle which would balance expenditure and taxation.

The Gladstonian cycle

> It is the mark of a chicken-hearted Chancellor when he shrinks from upholding economy in detail . . . He is not worth his salt if he is not ready to save what are meant by candle-ends and cheese-parings in the cause of the country.
>
> W. E. Gladstone, quoted in F. W. Hirst, *Gladstone as Financier and Economist* (1931)

Through Gladstone's reforms Parliament was (nominally) given the kind of control over the economy that a Victorian husband would want over his family, overseeing three basic housekeeping functions:

1   granting of prior approval to planned expenditure (the estimates process);
2   considering the ways and means of raising the sum required (the budgetary process);
3   checking that all past expenditure had been conducted in a proper manner (the accounting process).

Prior approval: who gets what, when, how in Whitehall?

Supply procedure of the House of Commons   The supply of funds to the Crown was a key factor in the evolution of the House of Commons. In constitutional theory the Crown asks for Supply and the House considers whether to grant the amount requested or allow only a reduced level; it would never gratuitously offer to increase it. Today of course the Crown means the government ministers. The position suited the parsimonious founders of the liberal state and eighteenth- and nineteenth-century reforms saw the examination of the Estimates (of the year's expenditure) consuming much House time, with each departmental vote being moved separately and amendments to reduce even small items. Between 1858 and 1872 the Estimates were reduced seventeen times. Yet despite talk of a golden age this period was tantalizingly brief, the process soon becoming little more than ritual. Government majorities could generally override all opposition and debates were used not to scrutinize the Estimates but to criticize policy. Governments ceased to care which Estimates were debated and allowed the choice of topic to pass to the official opposition.

> In prehistoric times there might have been some [parliamentary] control over the expenditure but there certainly has not been in my parliamentary experience.
>
> Arthur Balfour (Conservative prime minister) in 1905, quoted in Heclo and Wildavsky, *The Private Government of Public Money* (1974: 242)

Some reformers were unhappy and attempts to strengthen the House's role in expenditure matters included the creation of an Estimates Committee in 1912 (replaced with a Select Committee on Expenditure in 1970). In addition, a Treasury-inspired Public Expenditure Survey (PES) process aiming to consider expenditure and the anticipated level of resources was instigated, following the 1961 Plowden Report. This was intended to produce major debates on expenditure white papers looking five years ahead. However, from the first the debates fell flat, the process not inaccurately described in the House as 'flogging a dead mouse' (Heclo and Wildavsky 1974: 199–251). Try as they might the reformers could do little to revive parliamentary control over Supply. The Procedure Committee decided that evolved practice represented the wishes of the Commons and in the early 1980s Supply Days became Opposition Days, with three days reserved for discussion of the Estimates with topics selected by the Liaison Committee.

Does this mean that departmental spending decisions escape the ears, eyes and teeth of any constitutional watchdog? The answer is 'No'. A key instrument in the eighteenth- and nineteenth-century reforms was Her Majesty's Treasury, the centrepiece of Whitehall, which became accountable to the Commons for all departmental expenditure. At first its authority increased hand in hand with that of Parliament but, as the latter waned, the Treasury star rose; by the mid-nineteenth century it was no longer the junior partner.

Whitehall: private government and public money Beneath the charm and courtesy of the Whitehall 'village' there is, as in Agatha Christie's St Mary Mead, an undercurrent of gossip, competition, mistrust and sublimated violence. 'Who gets what' in the interdepartmental battle is the prize in the Whitehall wars. Allocating funds to the departments is 'the most pervasive and informative operation of government' (Heclo and Wildavsky 1974: xii). From the early 1960s the Treasury remit was to extend beyond the confines of Whitehall to encompass the full range of public expenditure, including the nationalized industries and local government, as part of the PES process.

A process of negotiation entails a protracted series of 'bilaterals' between each department and the Treasury, having more in common with a north African *souk* than a rational decision-making process; yet the outcome is nothing less than the policy of Her Majesty's Government. The bilateral nature of the encounter is very significant, enabling the Treasury to 'divide and rule', and there is often blood on the carpet as senior mandarins and ministers fight for their share of funds. In the 1980s arbitration came from an ad hoc 'star chamber' of senior ministers, replaced in 1992 by a powerful cabinet committee (EDX) containing one-third of the Cabinet itself. Labour Chancellor Gordon Brown hoped to put an end to this annual process of negotiation by announcing in July 1998 the government's overall spending plans for the next three years. However, this could not be expected to reduce the level of interdepartmental competition for the limited pool of resources and he was reported to be incensed by Foreign Secretary Robin Cook's unwillingness to make departmental savings to divert money to education and welfare (*Sunday Times*, 24

The Treasury directorates

Macroeconomic Policy and Prospects: Prepares economic forecasts (two a year), works with the Bank of England, coordinates work relating to EU monetary policy, particularly with reference to EMU.

Budget and Public Finances: Coordinates Budget and Public Expenditure Survey.

Spending: Bilateral negotiations with spending departments (and local government via DETR), nine teams each focusing on one or more department.

International Finance: EU finance, export credits and international debt, relations with international financial institutions.

Financial Management, Reporting and Audit: Relations with the National Audit Office and Public Accounts Committee, internal audit in the public sector.

Finance, Regulation and Industry: Promoting private finance and privatization, maintaining the financial regulatory regime, relations with Securities and Investments Board, international regulatory cooperation and EC directives.

Personnel and Support: Management of the Treasury itself.

May 1998). Much of the bargaining is done by the Chancellor's second in command, the Chief Secretary to the Treasury. The way in which this process is conducted was indicated by the publication of extracts from a leaked letter from Chief Secretary Michael Portillo to President of the Board of Trade, Michael Heseltine, strongly attacking his spending (*Guardian* 30 July 1994).

The Treasury   The Treasury employs the best and brightest of the mandarinate, who specialize in the spending of particular government departments. Organized hierarchically, they have since January 1995 worked in seven directorates with various specialist *supply sections*.

The budgetary process: who pays, when, how much?

The second operation in the control cycle entails raising the money – the **budgetary process** – through a variety of forms of taxation (see figure 16.4). Constitutionally the government's right to tax must be renewed by Parliament annually; this is why the Chancellor presents the Budget. Taxation may be direct or indirect.

Direct taxation falls upon individuals or organizations. This includes inheritance tax (on assets left after death), capital gains tax (on profit made in selling certain assets) and corporation tax (on company profits). Most important is income tax. Introduced in 1799 as a temporary measure to fund war against France, it has become a keystone of the system, a rise of 1p in the rate netting some £1.6 billion a year. Direct taxation can be used to redistribute income in the manner of Robin Hood; when a greater proportion is taken from the rich than the poor the system is termed progressive. National Insurance contributions are also effectively a direct tax, which means the true income tax rate is higher (and less progressive) than it appears.

Indirect taxation is tied to goods and services and includes excise duties levied on items such as alcohol, tobacco and petrol. VAT falls across a wide range and is the best known (part of the take goes to the EU). Although rates on commodities can vary (some are zero rated), they fall equally on all regardless of means and are therefore regressive. Thus a move from direct to indirect taxation favours the rich. Although the bulk of taxation is levied by Westminster, the Scottish Assembly has limited powers, as do local authorities (chapter 19). In the latter case there has been much central interference through capping and reform. The poll tax, though direct, was non-progressive but its replacement, the council tax, being tied to property values, has a more progressive character.

Although the national lottery (figure 16.3) is not a tax, the heavy odds against winning have led some to declare it a tax on stupidity! The proceeds going to 'good causes' count as general government revenue, available to reduce public borrowing (see below) and finance capital projects. In 1997 the Labour government began using some of this for certain items of NHS expenditure. With an estimated 90 per cent of adults having played and around £65 million spent weekly, totalling almost £5 billion in 1995, it has been acclaimed a success.

Figure 16.3
Where each pound spent on a lottery ticket goes.

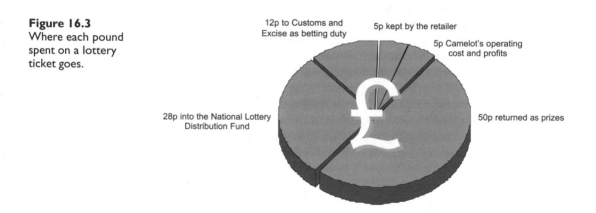

12p to Customs and Excise as betting duty

5p kept by the retailer

5p Camelot's operating cost and profits

28p into the National Lottery Distribution Fund

50p returned as prizes

The budget The budget is prepared over the course of the financial year deep in the bowels of the Treasury by high-powered committees. Although working below the level of the public eye, the door is opened to thousands of interest groups. The proposals are embodied in the Finance Bill and the Chancellor, with the aid of a private secretary and various experts, drafts the Budget Speech – the focal point of Budget Day. Parliament gives automatic approval to the proposals though days of debate follow and the Finance Bill proceeds upon a ritualistic voyage through Parliament.

> Convention permits Chancellors alcoholic refreshment during their speech, a privilege not extended to other MPs. Denis Healey drank brandy, Sir Geoffrey Howe took a gin and tonic, Nigel Lawson a mixture of wine and Malvern water but austere Scot Gordon Brown chose mineral water.

Ostensibly, the reason for secrecy is market sensitivity. In 1947, Hugh Dalton inadvertently divulged Budget information to a lobby journalist on his way to deliver his speech and later resigned. However, there have been calls for more openness and the traditional period of *purdah*, when Chancellors retreated behind a veil of silence, has been largely abandoned. Indeed, in an age of media manipulation, eve-of-Budget leaks have become almost *de rigueur*. Some of Brown's 1997 proposals greeted newspaper readers over their morning cornflakes and a substantial part of the November 1996 Budget was leaked to the *Daily Mirror*. Editor Piers Morgan piously returned the documents without publishing, but opposition leader Tony Blair was extremely well prepared when he rose to deliver his response. No police action followed a Metropolitan Police inquiry. In March 1998 the Chancellor even allowed journalists a pre-Budget interview. Moreover, he had already made a prophetic Pre-Budget Statement the previous November.

The unified budget Before 1993 the agreed expenditure was announced in the Chancellor's Autumn Statement in November and Budget Day followed in March, on the eve of the new financial year. This meant that Parliament (and the media) did not get the chance to review taxes in the light of the consequences for services. Hence, in 1993 Budget Day was brought forward so that both sides of the finance equation (figure 16.4) were considered in November as a 'unified budget'. In 1998 it returned to March.

Budget bites

In a media era Chancellors have adorned their Budgets with titles.

Sir Geoffrey Howe (1979–83)
1979   An Opportunity Budget
1983   A Budget for Britain's Continuing Recovery

Nigel Lawson (1983–9)
1987   A Budget for Success
1988   A Tax Reform Budget

John Major (1989–90)
1990   A Budget for Savers

Norman Lamont (1990–3)
1992   A Budget for Recovery
1993   (March) A Budget for Sustained Recovery and a Budget for Jobs

Kenneth Clarke (1993–7)
1993   (November) The Budget of a Responsible Government
1994   A Budget for Jobs
1996   A Budget for Lasting Prosperity

Gordon Brown (1997–)
1997   (July) Equipping Britain for Our Long-term Future
1998   (March) A Budget for Women and Children and for Economic Stability

Figure 16.4
Getting and spending: receipts and expenditure (general government spending), 1997/8 (pence in every pound, rounded off to nearest whole number).

Source: Data from Treasury (1998: tables B9 and B18).

Receipts		Expenditure	
Income tax	24	7	Defence
		1	Foreign Office and International Development
Corporation tax	10	1	MAFF
		1	Trade & Industry
Windfall tax	1	4	Transport & Regions
Petroleum revenue tax and oil royalties	1	10	Transport & Regions (Local government)a
Capital taxes	2	2	Home Office
VAT	16	5	Education and Employmentb
Fuel, alcohol and tobacco duties	10	11	Health
Other taxes, royalties and duties	5	29	Social Securityc
Business rates	5	5	Scotland
Council tax	4	2	Wales
Social security contributions	16	3	N. Ireland
		1	Legal departments
Interest and dividends	2	1	Chancellor's department
		1	Other departments and EU
Gross trading surplus and rent	2	4	Local authority self-financed
Other items and adjustments	2	7	Debt interest
Borrowing	1	5	Accounting and other adjustments

a Over half is local authority expenditure on education

b Excludes local authority education expenditure

c Includes cyclical social security expenditure, which is closely related to the level of unemployment

The budget and politics In practice, taxation is used for a variety of politically motivated purposes including redistributing income, curbing pollution, influencing behaviour (e.g. reducing smoking or car use), regulating the economy and offering election bribes. Conservatives have proclaimed themselves to be the party of low taxation while Labour has enjoyed a tax-and-spend reputation. The eighteen years of Conservative government from 1979 were partly sustained by judicious pre-election Budgets. Yet overall taxes did not fall. In 1978/9, the year before Thatcher took power, tax revenue was 34 per cent of GDP; in 1994/5 it was 36 per cent. However, there had been a significant shift from direct to indirect taxation. This is the key. Although perhaps the fairest, income tax is visible and unpopular. Hence New Labour fought the 1997 election promising no rises and one of its leading figures, Clare Short, was sternly reprimanded for suggesting that people like her should pay more. Only the Liberal Democrats promised to increase income tax (to go towards education). However, Labour's 1998 Finance Bill contained a novel feature designed to prevent future chancellors offering pre-election goodies: a Code for Fiscal Stability to promote long-term fiscal openness and bind governments to spending restraints.

The accounting process

Finally there is the accounting process, checking that the money has been used as Parliament formally agreed. In 1861 Gladstone established one of Parliament's most effective scrutiny instruments, the Public Accounts Committee (PAC). Its membership of around fifteen specialist MPs reflects party balance in the House but the chair is always taken by a prominent member of the opposition.

Since 1866 the PAC has been assisted by a unique constitutional figure, the Comptroller and Auditor General (C&AG), a servant of Parliament with the twin tasks of regulating the release of funds from the Consolidated Fund and auditing the departmental books. In 1983, the C&AG's department became the National Audit Office (NAO), its remit extended beyond Whitehall to other public bodies such as the NHS. Local government comes under the supervision of the Audit Commission.

In 1996/7 C&AG Sir John Bourn and his staff of 750 audited 465 accounts covering over £500 billion. Any department or organization which has its accounts 'qualified' by the NAO – there were twenty-eight qualifications in 1996/7 – may be investigated by the PAC, which has the power to call ministers and civil servants to explain themselves. The PAC has claimed many scalps. Headlines were prompted in September 1993 when it reported on an inquiry criticizing the royal family for lavish spending of £20 million of taxpayers' money on royal palaces.

Problems with the audit The PAC has had more success than any other part of the control process. Much of this is owed to the goodwill of the Treasury, its parsimonious concerns making it more accommodating to requests for information than is customary towards other select committees. However, it would be a mistake to conclude that the watchdogs are unfettered in their guardianship of the public purse.

The contracting out of many services to the private sector and creation of thousands of quangos create a zone of public expenditure where the NAO has no authority. In addition, the Audit Commission lost the right to monitor opted-out schools, which appoint their own auditors. Moreover, the PAC has complained that the NAO is too chummy with departments, never publishing a criticism without first obtaining Whitehall approval. Indeed, although Parliament's position was somewhat strengthened by being given a voice in the appointment of the C&AG, all have been former mandarins and, although they consult the PAC, the choice of inquiries is entirely theirs. In 1992 Sir John persuaded the PAC chairman to suppress an NAO inquiry into allegations of bribes to secure a £20 billion Al Yamamah arms deal with Saudi Arabia, leaving committee members furious. Hence, the PAC often has to rely on whistleblowers and journalists for evidence of wrongdoing. Only after a series of parliamentary questions did the NAO begin to investigate the Pergau Dam affair, four years after the event.

Turf wars are fought between the NAO and the Audit Commission. For example, the former audits the Metropolitan Police and the Department of Health, while the latter looks at local police authorities and NHS trusts. Finally there is the question of auditing the auditors. The NAO's budget is approved annually by a recently created Public Accounts Commission of nine MPs while the Audit Commission is subject to the oversight of the NAO, but in practice this has never gone beyond a cursory glance (*The Economist*, 10 Sept. 1994).

The cycle of control established by Gladstone, modified, supplemented and criticized, has tenaciously survived. Has it proved adequate for the needs of the post-war era? We examine this in the following section.

Managing Capitalism

In the *laissez-faire* liberal economy of the nineteenth century, public expenditure was a necessary evil to be constrained at all times. Despite an embryonic welfare state, the cheeseparing approach survived into the twentieth century; indeed the inter-war years are sometimes called a golden age of Treasury control. Economic depression resulting from failures of capitalism enabled it to practise a firm **monetarist** policy (controlling inflation by limiting the quantity of money in the economy) and keep down public expenditure in the belief that industry and world trade could only flourish if there was confidence that the currency would hold its value.

Yet the depression persisted, threatening the legitimacy of the state. The classical economists had argued that unemployment would automatically correct itself by precipitating a fall in wages which would restore the demand for labour. Yet although wages fell, unemployment persisted. With the spectre of the Russian revolution and the 1926 General Strike, Marx's prophecies of inevitable crisis culminating in the collapse of capitalism gained ominous plausibility.

Rescuing capitalism: the coming of Keynes

However, an alternative diagnosis and prescription was offered by John Maynard Keynes, appearing like a knight in armour as the saviour of capitalism. In his *General Theory* (1936) he argued that, contrary to the Gladstonian view, (**macroeconomic**) budgeting for the state was not the same as the (microeconomic) budgeting of firms or households. Constantly aiming for a balanced budget was inappropriate and potentially harmful to the economy and employment.

Government should use its public expenditure function as a means of **demand management**. In times of slump the state should stimulate the economy by increasing the level of aggregate demand, using its gigantic purchasing power to provide education, build roads and other public works. The effect would be to stimulate demand throughout the economy (more roads require more materials and so on in a multiplier effect). Of course, if the government merely financed its greater expenditure by increasing taxation there might be no increase in aggregate demand because citizens' expenditure would fall. However, it could be financed by borrowing from citizens, creating a *budget deficit*. Alternatively, in times of prosperity the government could run a *budget surplus*, dampening down demand by reducing public expenditure while raising taxes, thereby eliminating the debts incurred earlier (the national debt). This strategy had the momentous implication that the goal of the *balanced budget* would no longer be sacrosanct.

Although Keynes was scorned, the experience of the war years seemed to confirm his theories, massive government expenditure on arms virtually erasing unemployment. The war also saw an enormous increase in direct government intervention in various walks of life, and in the dark days of war politicians made a raft of welfare state promises.

The years of plenty: the Treasury loses its grip

Hence the post-war decades of the long boom of western capitalism saw public expenditure used for the quite new purpose of managing the national economy: stabilizing the trade cycle and maintaining full employment. In addition, key industries were brought into state control by nationalization (see chapter 18). Forceful spending ministers were able to push through costly programmes with no necessary fiscal implications. Moreover, in the expanded welfare state, people did not appear to mind paying more taxes. It seemed that the boom would last for ever; the capitalist economy could be permanently protected from its own propensity to crisis by government management. Although Britain was still a capitalist country, the market was no longer forbidden territory to the state and the nineteenth-century Treasury ideals were rendered anachronistic.

The principle of economic management was further advanced in 1961 with the establishment by a Conservative government of a National Economic Development Council (NEDC – known as Neddy). A consultative body embracing labour, capital and government, this was a timid entry into the area of **economic planning** (indicative rather than commanding) and corporatism (see p. 522) practised with success by some European rivals. In 1964, the Wilson government created a purpose-built Department of Economic Affairs (DEA) to usurp the Treasury and work with Neddy. Further intervention came in 1965, with a quango, the National Board for Prices and Incomes (PIB), to attempt to control inflation. In 1966 another quango, the Industrial Reorganization Corporation (IRC), was established with capital of £200 million to promote industrial development through state share purchase in companies with a strategic place in the economy (see p. 553).

The restoration of the Treasury However, with the end of the long boom (see p. 87), the 'hidden hand' of Adam Smith began to push up his creaking tombstone. Coming to power in June 1970, Edward Heath signalled a break with the Keynesian consensus. The 'Selsdon Man' rhetoric spoke of reducing state involvement, privatization, freeing the forces of the market, curbing union power and inducing greater efficiency in industry. However, inflation and rising unemployment led to policy reversals, branded 'U-turns', with increased state intervention and even some further nationalization. Yet by this time the long boom was ending. Inflation reached an alarming 24.7 per cent in 1975, but unemployment, defying the Phillips Curve (which postulated an inverse relationship between the two), remained on an upward path. The state appeared unable to service its existing debts and the concerted call from the IMF, the City, the financial markets, the Governor of the Bank of England and the media pundits was for a return to the Victorian principles (Keegan 1984: 88). The cry came echoing back from Whitehall, where the Treasury stood like a rock emerging glistening beneath the retreating Keynesian tide.

In 1975 Labour Chancellor Denis Healey was obliged to turn humiliatingly to the IMF for large-scale loan support. It came with strings attached; he was forced to exert further controls over the money supply, cut public spending, trim public borrowing and raise interest rates (which reached a record 15.5 per cent). In 1976 James Callaghan measured up the corpse of Keynesianism for the Treasury undertakers in his fateful declaration to the Labour conference: 'We cannot now, if we ever could, spend our way out of a recession'. Monetarism was on the agenda before Thatcherism became a word in the economic lexicon.

Public expenditure under Thatcher: the end of Keynes

When Margaret Thatcher took up residence in Downing Street, Treasury control in the Victorian sense experienced its rebirth. Despite the years of plenty, and the global nature of the crisis, the view was that Keynesianism had failed.

While Labour had reluctantly relinquished the economic reins, the New Right government dropped them with relish. The prescription was generally for less welfare spending, a curbing of union power, an easing of government 'overload', privatization of the nationalized industries and the abandonment of Keynesianism. Generally the state, and hence the area of life under democratic control, was to be 'rolled back'; the market rather than politics was to determine who got what. Collectivist tendencies gave way to individualism, balancing the books became the key budgetary consideration and public expenditure was again to be regarded as a necessary evil. In the Treasury, Keynesians were hunted like medieval witches, prudent young bureaucrats quickly deciding that they had really been closet monetarists all the time (Ponting 1986: 102).

Applying monetarism   The policy differed from that prescribed by monetarist guru Milton Friedman. He argued that the level of public expenditure and taxation did not have an important effect on the economy; the key was to control the rate of increase in **money supply**. However, the Thatcherite agenda also had moral and social goals, including a particular determination to reduce welfare state expenditure. The initial strategy had two broad thrusts: control of the money supply and, preferring the advice of Polonius in *Hamlet* that 'borrowing dulls the edge of husbandry' to that of Keynes, reducing the **public sector borrowing requirement** (PSBR). The Thatcherite objection to the PSBR was that it could be seen as increasing money supply and causing inflation. Moreover, money borrowed by government was not available to the private sector where, contrary to Keynes's view, it would be used more productively.

The failure of monetarism   Yet monetarism did not work as promised. The average growth of M3 sterling (a measure of money supply) was actually higher in the period 1979–85 than it had been at any time under the previous government. At the same time, there was a huge loss of industrial capacity and a high price to be paid in terms of unemployment (figure 16.5). Until 1984, investment and output were actually below 1979 levels, and their subsequent climb was sluggish, well below the OECD average. The balance of trade moved

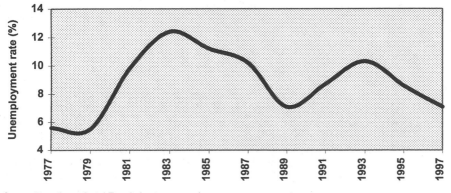

Figure 16.5
Unemployment
trends, 1977–1997.

Source: Data from *Social Trends* (various years).

> The major tenet of free market economics – that unregulated markets will of their own accord find unimprovable results for all participants – is now proved to be nonsense.
>
> Will Hutton (neo-Keynesian economist), *The State We're In* (1996: 237)

adversely and the growth in the economy actually went into reverse in 1980 and 1981; it was never significantly better than that of rival economies (*Guardian*, 29 May 1987).

By 1985, the Chancellor had effectively abandoned monetarism. Target-setting gave ground to the use of *interest rates*, which were increased to hold down money supply by decreasing borrowing and encouraging saving. Paradoxically, public expenditure rose each year throughout the 1980s as cuts in infrastructure spending and services were counterbalanced by increased welfare, health and social security costs caused by unemployment and poverty (Mullard 1997: 272). Income support for the unemployed dwarfed all other categories, reaching almost £45 billion in 1987/8 (figure 16.6).

One much-vaunted success of the government was reducing **inflation**. Yet this was an ironic achievement because it fell while the money supply was *increasing*, suggesting an accidental result of exogenous factors (and demonstrating the frailty of economists). However, even this achievement began to look less secure by the end of the 1980s, the annual rate of the Retail Price Index (RPI) climbing to 8.3 per cent by June 1989, well above the OECD average.

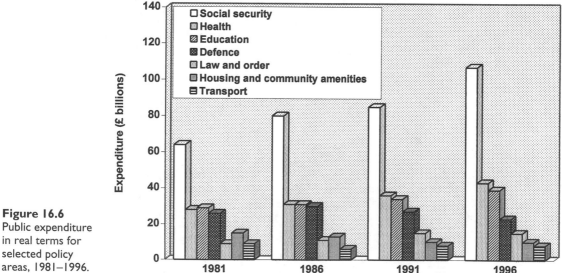

Figure 16.6
Public expenditure in real terms for selected policy areas, 1981–1996.

Source: Data from *Social Trends* (1998: table 6.20).

With tax reductions and easier access to credit, Chancellor Nigel Lawson was able to engineer a consumer boom in the economy which helped the Conservatives win the 1987 general election. However, the balance of payments plunged into deficit from mid-1987 as a decimated productive base at home caused imports to be sucked in. By 1989, Britain was running its largest ever trade deficit.

Wednesday's child is full of woe Throughout the crisis years a time-bomb had been ticking in the form of the drive towards European economic and monetary union. Although Britain had remained outside the exchange rate mechanism (ERM), business leaders felt that floating exchange rates left them at a grave disadvantage and the City, most economists and the opposition parties favoured entry. Chancellor Nigel Lawson agreed and, from the mid-1980s, had pursued a covert policy of 'shadowing' the Deutschmark; a kind of DIY ERM membership. Unneighbourly tension between 10 and 11 Downing Street led in October 1989 to Lawson's resignation over Thatcher's refusal to sack adviser Alan Walters, who declared the European monetary system 'half-baked'. Finally Thatcher conceded that sterling would enter when 'the time was ripe': when UK inflation matched that of other member states and when clear steps were being made by Italy and France in the removal of exchange controls. The 'right time' arrived under new Chancellor John Major in October 1990, the eve of the Conservative Party conference.

In the event the time was to prove quite wrong; with Britain experiencing rising inflation, a large balance of payments deficit and heading towards recession, the pound entered at an unsustainably high level. Despite government hopes that this would curb inflation by forcing down costs and prices, efforts to hold sterling's value (including high interest rates) proved disastrous to the economy. This atmosphere of panic drove Conservative MPs to the astonishing butchering of their leader. Yet her replacement was the very man who had taken Britain into the ERM. As prime minister, John Major signalled some willingness to increase public expenditure but the post-monetarist trajectory was already charted and he did little to change course. Norman Lamont's 1992 Budget provided tax cuts and public expenditure increases in time for the general election, but tumultuous events were to follow.

Selling of overvalued sterling by foreign-exchange speculators saw the Bank of England frantically buying in an effort to protect its ERM position. The doomed rescue operation cost some £18 billion and the government's economic strategy was entirely discredited on 16 September 1992, as Britain made an ignominious withdrawal from the ERM. The occasion was to enter political demonology as 'Black Wednesday'. The PSBR, which had actually gone into a surplus of £15 billion in 1998/9, sunk into a deficit of £50 billion in 1993/4, forcing post-election tax increases and high political cost.

Labour and the 'stakeholder economy'

Ironically, while doing lasting damage to the government's credibility, the effective devaluation of Black Wednesday and tax rises forced by the budget deficit assisted an economic upturn. However, John Major confounded political theory by losing the next election (having secured the 1992 victory in a recession!). One reason for this was that the improvement was not felt by everyone. In a sustained critique of economic policy, Will Hutton characterized the growing pattern of inequality as a 30/30/40 society (see p. 177).

Neo-Keynesians argued that the neoliberal era had elevated selfishness and distorted business priorities; companies aimed to grow not by increasing investment, innovating or expanding markets, but by swallowing up rivals. The willingness of shareholders to sell to the highest bidder forced companies to put short-term returns above growth. The weakening of the unions, leading to a 'flexible' workforce, had created a vast wasteland of part-time and temporary employment without worker protections. Market-testing introduced insecurity into private and public sectors at all levels (Hutton 1996: 327). Tougher rules on unemployment benefits recalled the harsh Poor Law reforms of 1834.

The deindustrialization of the early 1980s had produced a 'dual economy' with 'a substantial proportion . . . either excluded from the labour market altogether or on very low pay' (Turner 1995: 253). A furore over the 'fat cats' heading the privatized utilities, their remuneration linked to share prices, highlighted new levels of income inequality. All had taken place against a background in which direct taxation had been made much less progressive (figure 16.7) and greater weight placed on indirect taxation.

Predictably, Labour rhetoric in opposition echoed much of the critique and Tony Blair inserted into speeches the term 'stakeholder society', in which the business and financial communities accept social obligations towards their employees and society at large, as well as to shareholders (see Kay 1993; Hutton 1996: ch. 12). Upon coming to office in 1997 the new government quickly

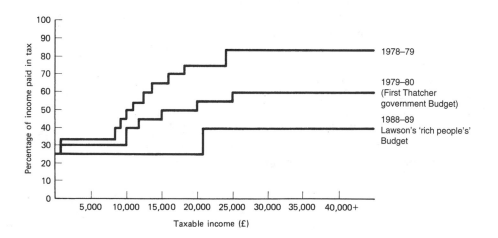

Figure 16.7
The changing income tax profile during the 1980s.

declared its intention to reverse the EU Social Chapter opt-out, legislate for a minimum wage and breathe new life into a number of corporatist-style bodies (see chapter 18).

However, desperate to appear respectable in the eyes of the City, the approach to public finance soon revealed much continuity with that of the immediate past, Gordon Brown's Budgets betraying little nostalgia for Keynesianism. Stressing the fight against inflation and tight restraints on public spending and borrowing, he revealed a Gladstonian passion to 'balance the books' and adhere to a 'golden rule' that borrowing should be limited to capital investment. Policy on capital expenditure continued to rely on the Private Finance Initiative whereby private funds would be tempted in to maintain the state infrastructure (schools, hospitals and so on). There was to be no renationalization of enterprises placed handsomely into the hands of private capital, no change in the balance between direct and indirect taxation and Labour pledged itself to stick to the Conservatives' spending targets for the next two years. Indeed, the widening gap between rich and poor was no longer seen as a problem. A 'Welfare-to-Work' scheme funded by a windfall tax on certain privatized utilities (deemed to have enjoyed excess profits) aimed to promote a work ethic. In August 1997 unemployment fell to its lowest level for seventeen years.

The March 1998 Budget redistributed income to the poorest fifth of households with children, each gaining an average of £500 per annum. However, with cash for child care and working family tax credits, the emphasis was on encouraging people to take low-paid jobs. Indeed, the minimum wage was set at only £3.60 an hour, well below what the unions wanted and the EU decency threshold. Income tax did not become more progressive and VAT rates did not fall.

Public Expenditure and Long-term Economic Decline

The Chancellor's July 1997 Budget statement reported that since 1973 GDP had grown at two-thirds the rate of the earlier post-war years. Annual growth had averaged 1.75 per cent, compared with 2.5 per cent in the major (G7) competitor economies. With the traumas of deindustrialization, restructuring and a short-lived consumer boom, the British monetarist experience had not arrested the pattern of post-war relative decline in the British economy. Various hypotheses are advanced by left and right to explain this decline. Here we consider how far the patterns and traditions of the control of public expenditure in Britain have in themselves contributed, identifying three likely suspects:

- the institutional setting;
- the competitive pattern of Whitehall decision-making;
- a failure to incorporate key economic interests into the process.

The institutional setting

The two key institutions associated with public finance – the Treasury and the Bank of England – are august establishments imbued with nineteenth-century liberal values. For critics they have lain at the heart of the problem.

The Treasury   In the Whitehall village Her Majesty's Treasury stands closest to power both geographically and functionally. Located just behind Downing Street, its political head, the Chancellor of the Exchequer, is the prime minister's next-door neighbour in their much-sought-after terrace. Controlling almost every sinew of the body politic, its permanent secretary, with the cabinet secretary, reigns supreme in Whitehall.

Notwithstanding its overweening importance, the Treasury is a small and intimate department of just under a thousand staff, its ambience creating a tightly knit community. An aroma of politics pervades each committee meeting and each information exchange in the fabled corridors of power. Personal relationships constitute key channels of communication; trust between colleagues is cemented over long acquaintance and counterpoised with mistrust and suspicion of outsiders. Within this village orthodoxies emerge as unchallengeable wisdom, contributing to a 'Treasury view' – a set of attitudes towards policy and the proper medicine for this or that malady – which will tend to influence all decision-making in Whitehall and Westminster.

Who are those with such dominance? They are called the 'Treasury men', a very special breed. Although their work sounds technical, they have been by tradition dilettantes *par excellence*, hand-picked from the very cream of civil service applicants, with no specialized knowledge of economics, accounting, or any of the policy areas in which public money is spent. Even within the Treasury the average time spent in any particular policy area is but a fleeting two years, so that they 'are clearly exposed to little danger of losing their amateur status' (Heclo and Wildavsky 1974: 65). Apologists will argue that the reason the Treasury men can move so lightly between policy areas is their renowned Rolls Royce minds; they are the exotic orchids of the Whitehall hothouse, cultivated in the fertile soil of Oxbridge.

> The good Treasury man is an able amateur . . . He relies on ability to argue, to find internal contradictions, to pick out flaws in arguments whose substance he has not fully mastered and whose subtleties he can only be dimly aware of.
>
> H. Heclo and A. Wildavsky, *The Private Government of Public Money* (1974: 60)

The Bank of England   The Treasury often works in collusion with another formidable institution which, although not part of the civil service, lies at the heart of the governing establishment. Nationalized in 1946, the Bank remains formally autonomous, nestling away from Whitehall as 'The Old Lady of Threadneedle Street' in the bosom of the historic square mile forming the City of London. Its appearance as a veritable palace, served by pink-coated flunkeys, is appropriate, for in the political life of the country its role is indeed regal.

This is the government's bank, holding its account and with a prime responsibility for implementing financial policy. On the domestic front it acts as the government's agent, managing the note issue and the national debt. In international matters it is similarly close to government, dealing in foreign currencies and maintaining the value of the pound, buying and selling gold, and engaging in international discussion on financial and trade policy. In addition, it stands at the centre of the nation's financial community. As the central bank it is the bank of banks, holding the cash reserves of the clearing banks, providing facilities that an ordinary customer might expect from the High Street bank and acting as a channel of communication between them and the Treasury.

Yet despite its overwhelming importance to the nation, the Bank has never been a passive servant of government; on the contrary, it has often appeared the master, effectively shaping policy through its advice. It can even be seen as a pressure group, using its relationship with the Treasury on behalf of the banking sector against industrial capital and pressing its preference for high interest rates (Marsh and Locksley 1987: 223). In addition, the legendary secrecy of the British state is here amplified by the claims of necessary confidentiality, keeping out any prying eyes from Parliament, the media and even the government. Generally, what is known about the Bank is what it wants known, information being purveyed through its own carefully edited publications. Some light was allowed in when, in April 1994, Chancellor Kenneth Clarke agreed to the publication of the minutes of his monthly meetings with Governor Eddie George. These revealed considerable tension between the two, with the Chancellor resisting interest rate rises.

Given this enormous power, one must ask who is in control and whether they are likely to be responsive to the needs of society. The Bank is formally under a Court, consisting of its governor, a deputy governor and sixteen directors, twelve of whom are supposed, in a quasi-democratic manner, to represent various interests throughout society. However, they come overwhelmingly from the white male establishment galaxy, with public school–Oxbridge backgrounds and top jobs in multinational giants and the world of high finance. One token trade union representative sits like the timid dormouse at the Mad Hatter's tea party. The 1997 Labour government promised to make the Court more widely representative.

The governor is a key figure, even more grand than the head of the Treasury, moving in the world of the most powerful, feted by millionaire capitalists, delivering speeches declaiming his views and theories, conferring with government and in times of crisis exerting a domineering presence. Despite the dignity surrounding the office, the position is profoundly political. The Wilson government learned very soon of this power. In its first year of office, being unpopular with the financial sector, it suffered in the face of malicious speculation against the pound, and Lord Cromer demanded that the government, notwithstanding its manifesto commitments, make all-round expenditure cuts. Wilson records:

> In January 1965 . . . I told him that Government expenditure was committed far ahead; schools which were being built, roads . . . were part-way to completion . . . Was it his view, I asked him, that we should cut them off half-finished . . . The question was difficult for him, but he answered, 'Yes'. (Wilson 1974: 62)

The political salience of the position was recognized by Thatcher, who inherited as governor Sir Gordon Richardson. A replacement was found in Robin Leigh-Pemberton, chairman of National Westminster Bank, an overtly political appointment of an 'outsider' resulting in considerable furore (Keegan 1984: 197–8). He was to be criticized by Labour for allegedly politically motivated comments. In 1993, after two stormy five-year terms, he was replaced by his deputy, Eddie George, known as 'steady Eddie' because of his cautiously monetarist views (*Guardian*, 23 Jan. 1993).

When Labour's Gordon Brown acquired the keys to Number Eleven in 1997, some major changes were made. With the line between banks, securities firms and insurance companies becoming blurred, limitations in the regulatory competence of the Bank had been humiliatingly exposed in two major banking scandals: the collapses of BCCI and Barings Bank. The Bank's supervision of the commercial banks was given to a new City 'super regulator', based on the Securities and Investments Board. It also lost the job of managing the government stock to the Treasury and there was some talk of the Governor resigning (*Financial Times*, 22 May 1997). However, it gained a crucial new responsibility: while the Chancellor would continue to set inflation targets, interest rates would be set by the Bank, to reflect expert assessment rather than political

---

Debating the single currency: the case for

A single currency eliminates the considerable expense of currency transactions, facilitates comparisons between costs and prices in different countries and eases travel. It can also inspire business confidence, stability and growth over time by removing the temptation of competitive devaluations. The absence of devaluations tends to reduce inflation since firms are forced to keep costs, wages and prices down in order to remain competitive. Of particular importance in the light of globalization, it reduces the scope for damaging currency speculation and the nightmare of Black Wednesday. A European currency would in all probability develop into a reserve currency rivalling the dollar. There are also political implications, members achieving a greater collective weight in world affairs. At an emotional level it is a potent symbol of political union. There is also the fact of the dominance of the Bundesbank and the German economy, which influences other states' economic variables with or without a single currency. For weaker economies, full EMU offers a means to gain control, not lose it (George 1991: 188).

Within the UK, supporters included the Foreign Office (with an instinct to seek membership of all prestigious international clubs), the Treasury (since joining the single currency would pose no direct threat to its powers to set or collect taxes), the unions (seeing advantages in a 'social Europe' after the Thatcherite assault), the Confederation of British Industry (recognizing the trading advantages and the fact that some 70 per cent of legislation affecting British business emanates from Brussels), the City (already doing a huge amount of business in dollars, yen and Deutschmarks) and finally the Celtic fringe (seeing the possibilities of independence as thriving statelets).

expediency. Meeting monthly and taking decisions by majority vote in the Bank's committee room overlooked by a portrait of Sir Montague Norman (a legendary but eccentric governor from 1920 to 1944), a nine-person Monetary Policy Committee led by the governor makes the decisions, which are also scrutinized by the Treasury Select Committee. There is, however, a political advantage from the Bank's independence: it relieves chancellors of responsibility.

The Bank's tendency to raise interest rates soon led to criticism from industry that only one industrialist sat on the Monetary Policy Committee. Ex-Chancellor Kenneth Clarke argued that his own opposition to rate rises had been proved right for the economy (*Financial Times*, 21 July 1997). In October 1998, amidst growing fears that economic turmoil in Asia would spread to Britain, and after strong hints from the Chancellor, interest rates began to fall, though only by a small amount. However, the Bank's power to set interest rates only remains so long as Britain has its own currency. The winds of change from Europe threaten this.

A single European currency The granting of Bank independence had another important aspect; it brought Britain into line with EU partners and reflected Maastricht Treaty requirements for joining the single currency. The latter promised considerable implications for a government's ability to manage its economy and was formally opposed by Hague's Conservative Party (see p. 295). When eleven of the EU partners formally adopted the Euro on 2 May 1998, Labour continued to wait and the nation was left to weigh up the pros and cons.

Debating the single currency: the case against

States must sacrifice autonomy, accepting common objectives such as interest rate and inflation targets. The exchange rate is no longer available to regulate international competitiveness and control over monetary and fiscal policy is surrendered. The Bank of England would cede power over interest rates to a European Central Bank. The system can threaten domination by a leader economy with costs borne largely by the weaker states.

There is also the possibility that economic convergence will lead on to convergence in social policy, justifying the right-wing suspicion of 'socialism via the back door', a fear voiced in Thatcher's notorious Bruges speech. Beyond rational argument some reservations reflect a deeper unease felt by both left and right that even shades into xenophobia. Horrific scenarios have been painted by Eurosceptics talking of German domination under a neo-Nazi regime. Indeed, Thatcher's close confidant, Trade Secretary Nicholas Ridley, was obliged to resign in June 1990 for the intemperance of his anti-German utterances.

Beyond the Conservative Eurosceptics, those against included the Bank of England, Governor Eddie George fearing to see the Bank relegated to branch-office status. In addition, the Labour government realized that the polls showed a large majority of citizens with no love for the Euro. However, arguably the most important factor in British debate was the attitude of global media mogul Rupert Murdoch, owner of *The Times* and the mass-circulation *Sun*. He stood to lose out under an increasingly powerful pan-European regulatory regime with a desire to limit cross-media ownership. Although Blair had made courtship of Murdoch a central strategy, his warm words on the Euro at the Cardiff EU summit of June 1998 earned the *Sun* headline: 'THE MOST DANGEROUS MAN IN BRITAIN'.

Heads or tails?
No Euros please,
we're British

Photo: European Parliament

Victorian institutions in a Keynesian landscape The dominance of the Treasury and Bank has meant that nineteenth-century values have lingered like the smell of stale tobacco smoke in the redecorated constitution of the post-war era. Both could be but poor instruments for Keynesianism, placing a 'dead hand' on public expenditure in general, with little thought for industry, employment, the wider economy or the welfare state. Whatever the economic problem – falling pound, rising pound, balance of payments crisis, inflation or unemployment – the response was invariably a deflationary package. The result was a series of what were termed 'stop–go' policies. When the economy expanded, imports were sucked in, the trade deficit widened and the Bank of England would step in to buy sterling with foreign currency in order to maintain its value as an international reserve currency. As the foreign currency reserves fell, deflation would be introduced (a 'stop' period) to reduce imports. However, this caused unemployment, calling for the economy to be stimulated (a 'go' period) and the cycle would begin again.

The pound in your pocket

From now on the pound is worth 14 per cent or so less in terms of other currencies. It does not mean, of course, that the pound here in Britain, in your pocket or purse or in your bank, has been devalued.

Harold Wilson's speech after devaluation of the pound (20 Nov. 1967)

Although removing the possibility of electorally motivated juggling, the independent fixing of interest rates may not in itself remedy the defects critics see in the economy. Will Hutton (1996: 298) has stressed the need for a deeper cultural change in which the financial community sees itself as 'a servant of business rather than as its master', with banks and their customers showing more commitment to the success of industry and less hunger for dividends, accepting lower rates of return on investments and allowing longer terms for repaying loans.

Competitive decision-making in Whitehall

Linked with the dominance of the Treasury and Bank has been the Whitehall method of reaching spending decisions. Despite formally accepting the Keynesian package, the basic pattern of expenditure policy-making remained and the Treasury missed its historic opportunity to become an economic coordinator. The PES reforms did not eliminate competitive infighting, with the Treasury persistently trying to reduce expenditure, regardless of the merits of individual policies. This reflected an inability to see the state as something over and above sectional interests; a manifestation of the Victorian legacy of individualism. In this respect, British government has compared unfavourably with the French, where the Commissariat Général du Plan aims to coordinate departments in line with an overall economic policy.

Failure to incorporate key economic interests into policy-making

This same ethos prevented the successful implantation of institutions designed to bring together the key interests: finance, industry and labour (see chapter 17). Remaining arm's-length quangos, Neddy and the 'little Neddies' were never well integrated into the machinery and the Cinderella DEA was killed off by the ugly sisters, the Treasury and Bank, daughters of the penny-pinching Gladstone. The Industrial Reorganization Corporation and National Enterprise Board, lacking both powers and funds, were unsuccessful in the late 1960s and 1970s respectively. Further failure came with incomes policy, union antagonism costing Labour the 1979 general election. The lack of harmony was graphically illustrated in the fate of Heath's Industrial Relations Court (see p. 621). Under Thatcher the declared policy was to end consultation with economic interests. While New Labour began to speak of forging a new consensus in a 'stakeholder society', the weakened trade unions reacted with suspicion.

The Hands-off State

All these factors lead to the conclusion that British governments have not used their financial role in the best interests of the economy at large. From the time of the Liberal social programme of 1906–14 they have been willing to help the losers in a capitalist economy but, despite the 'Keynesian revolution', have remained unwilling to interfere with the freedom of businesses to pursue their self-

> The British state is so imbued with the liberal philosophy . . . that sustained, coherent, and disinterested arbitration and sponsorship of the economy is extremely difficult, if not impossible.
>
> Will Hutton, *The Revolution that Never Was* (1986: 196)

interest. However, decisions that seemed rational to individuals (say continuing with outmoded technology rather than risking new investment) were, contrary to the claims of Adam Smith, not in the overall interest. Only governments could make decisions in the wider interest, but Britain declined to become a 'developmental' state in the manner of the dynamic economies of the post-war era (Marquand 1988: 121–3). The result is a state that has always been subservient to the market order, with a persistent legend of minimal government etched into its institutional masonry – never open enough to engage in dialogue with industry, never coordinated enough to plan, and never autonomous enough to manage.

Key points

- The public sector is held together by a financial web; few political questions can be addressed without attention to the financial dimension.
- Public expenditure is money spent by the state, its scale is enormous and most is raised by taxation.
- Public expenditure is also an expression of our propensity to live collectively in a community; paying taxes is a duty of citizenship.
- Her Majesty's Treasury presides over a set of financial controls fashioned in the nineteenth century.
- Because of its great magnitude, public expenditure cannot but influence the rest of the economy. This allowed post-war governments to intervene in the capitalist economy in pursuit of social goals.
- By the mid-1970s, with the end of the long boom, the New Right emerged to restore Victorian principles.
- The Thatcher government generally failed in its goal of reducing state expenditure: money supply grew, firms went bankrupt, and unemployment and interest rates soared.
- In retrospect it can be argued that Keynesianism was never really practised. The ethos of the minimal state and the half-hearted involvement of key interests prevented the central control found in more successful competitors.
- The New Labour government of 1997 made a virtue of continuing much of its predecessors' economic policy.
- Joining the European single currency would have considerable implications for the government's role in the economy.

Review your understanding of the following terms and concepts

Audit Commission
'Black Wednesday'
budgetary process
C&AG
capitalism
Consolidated Fund
demand management
direct taxation
economic planning
fiscal policy
indirect taxation
inflation
Keynesianism

laissez-faire
macroeconomics
mixed economy
monetarism
money supply
National Audit Office
national debt
National Lottery
prior approval
progressive taxation
Protestant work ethic
Public Accounts
   Committee

public expenditure
public expenditure
   survey process (PES)
public sector borrowing
   requirement (PSBR)
regressive taxation
single currency
stakeholder society
supply process
transfer payments

Assignment

Study the extract from the *Independent* on p. 504 and answer the following questions.

		Mark (%)
1	What are the reform priorities of David Davis and what factors may stand in his way?	20
2	Why can Davis claim that senior civil servants fear appearances before PAC hearings?	20
3	How might Davis's praise for the NAO be qualified?	20
4	Trace press reports of the PAC's review of Oflot mentioned in the extract and identify the 'events' referred to.	40

Questions for discussion

1 'Public expenditure is a reflection of our propensity to live communally.' Discuss.
2 Outline the Gladstonian cycle of financial control. What were its principal objectives?
3 How can government use its powers of spending and taxation to manage a capitalist economy?
4 How effective is Parliament in controlling public finance?
5 Explain how the monetarist approach to the economy differs from that advocated by Keynes.
6 What is meant by the 'dead hand of the Treasury'? Discuss its effect on the post-war economy.
7 Explain the shift from direct to indirect taxation since 1979. Is it likely to be reversed?

New kid on the block

The Public Accounts Committee chairman David Davis talks to **Paul Gosling**

"I am like a kid in a toy shop," says David Davis MP, the former Foreign Office minister and the new chairman of the House of Commons finance watchdog, the Public Accounts Committee. "I have been let loose from the shackles of government, but I have got all the interesting aspects of helping to make things work."

If Conservative MPs have been depressed by the election loss, it seems to have had the reverse effect on Mr Davis. By convention, the PAC must be chaired by a member of the Opposition, and Mr Davis is excited by his new role. Frustrated by the constraints imposed on a minister restricted to his own responsibilities, he now has a free rein over government spending, and is determined to make the most of it.

Initiatives are pouring out of Mr Davis. For all his generous praise for his predecessor, Robert Sheldon, he wants to do things differently – and, he says, more effectively. His top priority is to take action quicker; to look at the early stages of implementing new policy.

The second priority for Mr Davis is to enable the National Audit Office – which is autonomous but reports to the PAC – to follow public money, wherever it goes. The Royal household, housing associations, legal aid and the lottery operator Camelot are all in his sights, having escaped the NAO's rigorous auditing.

"Camelot is a private company, in every sense, but it deals with money which is almost indistinguishable from taxpayers' money. When the PAC did its review of Oflot [the lottery regulator], a rather contentious one which fed into the events of the last few weeks, one of the things it pointed out was that 11 out of 20 of the measures that Oflot was supposed to be measuring were not being measured." In future, if Mr Davis has his way, other government contractors will find themselves audited to a tougher standard.

While he has no wish for the NAO to take over commercial audits from the accountancy firms, he is clear that it must be able to ensure that all public money is being properly spent and accounted for, and that maximum value is extracted from it. This means that the NAO must have right of access to companies owned by public bodies, and must be able to instruct firms conducting audits there.

Another priority is to support the NAO doing more value-for-money work, rather than concentrating on issues of probity. "Historically, it has always been thought to be pretty bloody hard to measure the effectiveness of delivery accurately," Mr Davis says. "I think if we try a little harder we can get a lot better. We need to look more at where the rubber meets the road for the citizen. There will be a change of emphasis towards that, which is with the grain of politics. It is a new political technology, the measurement of performance. It is the way the accountancy profession is going; having more computer power helps, and it is with the grain of [public and politicians'] expectations."

The great thrill to Mr Davis is that the PAC operates across a wide spectrum. One day it examines privatisation contracts, the next it examines the inefficiency of the court system.

But he stresses that its work is possible only because of the high calibre of the 750 staff employed by Sir John Bourn, the Auditor and Comptroller General who heads the NAO. It is the quality of NAO reports that enables the PAC to conduct hearings that, says Mr Davis with some relish, are feared by even the most senior civil servants, and are prepared for days, even weeks, in advance.

For Mr Davis, losing an election has its compensations.

Independent, 18 Feb. 1998

8   What role is implied for government in the idea of the 'stakeholder economy'?

9   Examine the pros and cons of allowing the Bank of England to set interest rates.

10   Assess the political significance of 'Black Wednesday'.

Topic for debate

This house believes that the 'failure' of Keynesianism is a result of institutional factors in the British state rather than inherent defects in the approach.

Further reading

Some of the reading for chapter 4 is also relevant to the issues discussed here.

Friedman, M. and R. (1985) *The Tyranny of the Status Quo*.
Collaboration between the influential monetarist guru and his wife laments the failure of the Thatcher regime to control money supply in the manner prescribed.

Gamble, A. (1990) *Britain in Decline*, 3rd edn.
Traces various explanations for decline, stressing the importance of global influences.

Grant, W. (1993) *The Politics of Economic Policy*.
Accessible and wide-ranging account of forces shaping economic policy.

Heclo, H. and Wildavsky, A. (1974) *The Private Government of Public Money*.
A unique book, showing those involved in the public finance processes as real people.

Hutton, W. (1996) *The State We're In*.
In the traditions of Keynes and J. K. Galbraith, a sustained critique of the 'universal imposition of the market principle and decay of our political system'. Contains a comprehensive and stimulating reform agenda.

Keegan, W. (1984) *Mrs Thatcher's Economic Experiment*.
Written by an economic journalist, this account contains the flavour of the real-world politics lying behind all expenditure policy.

Marquand, D. (1988) *The Unprincipled Society*.
Erudite yet accessible critique of Britain's failure to manage its economy.

Mullard, M. (1993) *The Politics of Public Expenditure*.
Examines the political climate in which public expenditure decisions are made.

Thain, C. and Wright, M. (1995) *The Treasury and Whitehall: The Planning and Control of Public Expenditure 1976–1993*.
Monumental study explaining the structures and political forces underlying this key aspect of politics.

For light relief

Hilaire Belloc, *Pongo and the Bull*.
The power of money and the moneyed classes.

Tim Renton, *Hostage to Fortune*.
Intrigue in Threadneedle Street by ex-Conservative minister. The Chancellor of the Exchequer and Governor of the Bank of England plot downfall of prime minister.

H. G. Wells, *Tono-Bungay*.
Biting comment on an entrepreneurial society with nothing of value to sell.

Tom Wolfe, *Bonfire of the Vanities*.
Satire on the US world of capitalist high finance and its penetrating social implications.

Brassed Off
Film/video with moving account of social consequences of deindustrialization, which is seen as politically motivated.

On the net

http://www.hm-treasury.gov.uk
The Treasury's home page provides links to a wealth of information on all aspects of public expenditure, the budgetary process and the state of the economy, in addition to details of the institution itself.

http://www.bankofengland.co.uk
The Bank of England's home page will lead you to information on the Bank's history, organization and role, and an extensive range of economic and financial statistics. There is even a section entitled 'Funny Bank Stories'!

Both these sites will also lead you to information on the single currency.

Chapter Seventeen

The Politics of Influence: Who Gets What, When, How?

In this chapter we move beyond both the formal institutions of government and the overtly political structures to uncover the more shadowy forces in politics – the powers behind the throne. Where 'real power' lies is the greatest conundrum of the study of politics. We find repeatedly that the apparent puppetmasters are themselves dangling on yet further strings stretching away out of our sight in an infinite regression. The chapter falls into three main sections. The first introduces the concept of group politics and defines the types of groups to be discussed. The next identifies major theoretical approaches to this study, analysing the theories of pluralism and corporatism. We also consider the neoliberal view that the group approach distorts the political process. Finally we go beyond the group approach to examine elitist and Marxist views of power in society.

The Group Approach

In 1978, a number of protesters hurled from the public gallery of the House of Commons foul-smelling bags containing a substance later described as of 'agricultural origin' onto the heads of cowering members. In February 1988, to the alarm of the seated aristocracy, a hoard of Amazon women abseiled into the House of Lords and others appeared uninvited on a BBC news broadcast. The names 'Swampy' and 'Animal' became familiar to all but the most apathetic news followers in 1997, as they holed in beneath ground earmarked for new roads and airport runways. Such behaviour knows no class boundaries. Groups of ramblers defy enraged lords armed with shotguns, while a letter thanking the Duke of Edinburgh for his support is delivered to Buckingham Palace by protesters opposing legislation banning hand-guns. Almost daily the news media report on the activities of protest marchers, eco-warriors, parent demonstrators and hurlers of eggs at the high and mighty. The name of professional **lobbyist** Ian Greer, involved in the 'cash-for-questions' imbroglio in 1996, was probably more widely known than that of many MPs. Although the constitution makes no provision for activities such as these, they are events in politics. It is clear that our study does not end with constitutions, parties and Parliament.

Once a government has been elected the formal involvement of citizens in policy-making ends. MPs return joyfully to Westminster, the ballot boxes are stacked away in town hall vaults, and returning officers and vote counters return to their desks. To be sure, a government will take cognizance of public opinion during its reign, may even form focus groups to test ideas, but such consideration places the population in a position of passivity and can hardly be dignified as participation. Representative democracy does not formally allow people to make policy, it merely permits them to choose between elites. However, in practice popular involvement is not confined to elections, it continues through the activities of pressure groups.

A key founding figure in group theory was Arthur Bentley, an American economist who realized the limitations of studying policy only in terms of institutions and office-holders. For Bentley, the process of government was essentially about the activities of organized groups; his major work, first published in 1908, averred compellingly that 'when the groups are stated, everything is stated' (1967: 208).

Definitions

Pressure groups appear in many guises, raising various *definitional issues*, such as the following.

Interest groups and pressure groups   Although essentially different, these two terms are often used synonymously. However, an **interest group** is an association with a shared interest or concern, while a **pressure group** is one actively attempting to *influence* government. The latter term carries sinister connotations of factions seeking to subvert the democratic process and was probably coined by US journalists as a term of abuse. Some modern writers (particularly those in the pluralist tradition – see below) tend to favour the more innocent-sounding 'interest group'.

Groups and individuals   The logic of the group approach to analysis is to downgrade the role of individuals. This makes sense in that one vote is likely to have less influence than a group campaign. However, it obscures the fact that groups usually have dominant leaderships (Salisbury 1969), reflecting Michels's iron law of oligarchy. A study of the British 'poverty lobby' revealed that out of thirty-nine groups concerned with income maintenance policy, around half were controlled by a political entrepreneur (Whiteley and Winyard 1984). Similarly, leaders of economic groups are often powerful movers in the political firmament. In the early post-war decades, giants of the CBI and the TUC, as well as a variety of industrial and trade union figures, featured in the national news as visibly as ministers. Thus, groups need not eliminate personality politics, they can actually fuel it by adding to an individual's political weight, sometimes at the expense of the democratic voice of members.

> The reasonable man adapts himself to the world: the unreasonable one persists in trying to adapt the world to himself. Therefore all progress depends on the unreasonable man.
>
> George Bernard Shaw, *Man and Superman* (1903)

Groups and parties Definitions usually stress a fundamental distinction between groups and parties.

- Unlike parties, pressure groups do not seek to enter government, they wish only to influence policy.
- Pressure groups have only a limited range of policy interests; parties are concerned with the entire government remit. This is sometimes expressed in terms of different *functions*; groups *articulate* interests and parties *aggregate* them.
- Parties tend to be clearly located along the ideological spectrum but pressure groups may seek links at many points and try to gain access to a government of any political complexion.

Although useful, this distinction breaks down under scrutiny. The differences should be seen in terms of tendencies rather than clear orientations. We saw in chapter 11 that the Labour and Conservative parties have historically been wedded to particular interests. Some pressure groups do indeed fight elections: environmentalists as the Greens, anti-abortionists as the Pro-life party and Eurosceptics (in 1997) as the Referendum Party founded by Sir James Goldsmith. Some also aggregate interests as peak organizations (see below), while the Real World Coalition is a rainbow alliance of over thirty of the UK's leading environmental campaigning organizations (Jacobs 1996).

Types of pressure groups

An important dichotomy distinguishes groups on the basis of the interest they fight for. Although the nomenclature varies, the distinction is fundamental.

Promotional groups The policy goal of **promotional groups** is beyond self-interest and they are sometimes called *cause groups*. Thus, for example, the Royal Society for the Prevention of Cruelty to Children, the Society for the Protection of the Unborn Child and, say, the Antivivisection Society, fight for those unable to defend themselves. Others pursue ideological or moral goals; Liberty is concerned with civil rights while Greenpeace fights for the planet. Generally speaking, membership is open to any concerned individual and they may attract zealots. Thus members of the National Viewers and Listeners' Association (NVLA) expose themselves to long unselfish television vigils in their mission to purify the airwaves. Some groups are by their very nature limited; the Campaign for Homosexual Equality tends to attract homosexuals, while the diversity of feminist groups consists mainly of women. Many do not devote all their time to politics. The Automobile Association, for example, serves its members in a wide variety of ways, only becoming politically active when motorists' interests are threatened.

The number of cause groups rose during the 1980s and 1990s, reflecting a disenchantment with traditional politics, a greater interest in the politics of direct action, welfare cutbacks and increasing environmental concerns. The *Directory of British Political Organisations* lists over 200 concerned with the environment alone (Mercer 1994). Indeed, the groups not only aim to influence government, they may also direct their attention at other centres of power – international associations, the EU and private corporations – as when Greenpeace took on the mighty Shell over the Brent Spar oil rig. Such action became more appropriate as a neoliberal government cut back the state to leave more quality-of-life issues to the market.

Sectional groups Individual self-interest is the motive for much economic and political activity and this is reflected through **sectional groups**. Sometimes called *economic groups*, membership is generally restricted. The trade unions are a notable sub-category. Their importance was heightened by the enormous growth of the industrial public sector, making the government a large-scale employer,

World Development Movement campaigners protest against the techniques used by the tobacco multinationals in the third world

Photo: Elaine Duigenham/WDM

but has been reduced following extensive privatization. On the employers' side, there are business associations reflecting various sectors, and even multinational firms. Both unions and employers' associations combine into **peak organizations** – the Trades Union Congress (TUC), the Institute of Directors and the Confederation of British Industry (CBI) – to press their collective demands. Another category comprises *professional associations* such as the British Medical Association (BMA) and the Law Society.

The promotional/sectional distinction is blurred in practice with some promotional groups, such as Alcoholics Anonymous or the Prisoners' Wives and Families Society, concerned largely with the interests of members and some sectional groups often pursuing wider goals for society (health, education, justice and so on).

The policy bazaar: bargaining with power

Generally governments are not unwilling to talk with groups. Indeed, commissions of inquiry, consultative documents, green papers, white papers and draft bills encourage participation. This is partly because the groups themselves can have powerful bargaining counters in terms of expertise and veto power.

Expertise Many groups are expert in particular fields – farming, medicine, nature conservation – and the state bureaucracy is generally deficient in specialism. When new problems arise it is likely that voluntary organizations will be first with the expertise and information. Thus, as AIDS began its fateful march through the population, the Terrence Higgins Foundation clearly understood the problem better than the mandarins. Businessmen know how to promote trade, Sustrans can map out the best cycle routes and so on. Indeed, where expertise is not brought in the result can be policy failure, as with the poll tax, or the introduction of attainment-testing in schools.

Veto power The NHS needs doctors, education must have teachers and only farmers can implement agricultural policy. In addition, the regulatory character of much EU legislation (setting standards for companies) requires considerable cooperation. To secure compliance, government concessions may be necessary. The 1971 Industrial Relations Act, for example, failed owing to trade union unwillingness to play ball. A group's leverage increases in proportion to its monopoly status. The BMA was in an immensely powerful position when the NHS was created and threats of non-cooperation were constantly rumbling. Of course circumstances can change. The National Union of Mineworkers (NUM) appeared mighty when its strike unnerved the Heath government in 1974, but during the 1980s its power was broken by the formation (with government encouragement) of an alternative union and the exploitation of other fuel sources.

The cost of influence Bargaining is a two-way process; by permitting a group to enter the decision-making forums, a government obtains an opportunity to sell its policies. For the group representatives the price of involvement can be 'responsible behaviour' and some commitment to sell a policy to members.

Talking to power

To communicate their views to government groups require some channel of access. These range from influencing the public at large to direct talks with decision-makers. Beyond the domestic institutions there is also the path to the EU.

The public A favourable climate of public opinion is in a group's interest and there are numerous ways to achieve this. The director of the Child Poverty Action Group declared 'coverage in the media is our main strategy' (Whiteley and Winyard 1984: 35). The press is critically important, though less helpful to groups of the left, for whom biased reporting may be harmful. Some major left-wing demonstrations may even go unreported. Moreover, in an era of mass communications, power over public opinion can be a function of wealth. Rich interests may enlist the services of the advertising industry – the professional persuaders – to reach parts of the national subconscious that others cannot reach. In the early 1990s the nuclear industry assiduously massaged its public image, its infamous Windscale site became Sellafield and costly TV commercials enticed the public onto guided tours. Less well-endowed groups are usually obliged to adopt more robust tactics – marches, demonstrations and sometimes violent confrontations. Yet despite some spectacular successes, for many groups appeals to the public at large, although eye-catching, end in failure. A case of 'not waving but drowning', groups often resort to public display because they are denied access to other channels.

Parliament Groups may launch onslaughts with mass demonstrations outside the Palace of Westminster and MPs may be lobbied, besieged in their constituencies or deluged with persuasive mail. Some will be sympathetic to particular groups; deaf MP Jack Ashley campaigned with fervour on behalf of the handicapped and David Alton pursued the anti-abortionist cause. Groups try to cultivate long-term relationships with MPs and peers, even appointing them to honorary positions in their associations. The relationship can be symbiotic, a reputation for specialist knowledge serving as a basis for catching the Speaker's eye and impressing the whips. The general showpiece debates on issues chosen by the front benches afford few opportunities for backbench influence, but the committee stage of legislation can be more useful; proposed amendments, even if defeated, gain valuable publicity. Private members' bills provide a unique (though limited and expensive opportunity) to shape legislation; Friends of the Earth and the Green Party both played a significant part in the early drafting of the 1997 Road Traffic Reduction Bill. The upper house is not exempt from

1996 in United Britain, Great Kingdom...

Conservative Party	
Labour Party	
Democrats	

STREET PARTY!

Representation of the Peoples Act 1996
This ballot paper conforms to the standards laid down by the Electoral Reform Society and is registered under Subsection a), Paragraph iii) of the You Mark a Cross On a Piece of Paper Once Every Four Years Meanwhile We Make a Right Pig's Ear of Things and Get Rich Act 1996, Patent No. 37649801.

Get away from it all this Summer!

Music, children's area, info-stalls, art, magic, poetry, food, sunbathing, volleyball, clowns, acrobats, street theatre, trapeze artists, debates, instant beach & a prize for the best fancy dress...

A FESTIVAL OF RESISTANCE

**Meet 12 Noon, Saturday July 13th
Broadgate, next to Liverpool St Station
Reclaim the Streets**

attention; its function of 'tidying up' bills affords a chance for one last-ditch stand.

It is sometimes argued that promotional groups are more interested in Parliament than are the economic giants, but this is far from true. Indeed, it is possible to view the Houses as *functional* chambers where the members sit as representatives not of constituencies but of corporate interests; the 'Honourable Member for Harrods', or even 'Lord Channel Tunnel'. Wealthy interests also employ MPs as parliamentary consultants or avail themselves of the services of the professional lobbyist (Jordan 1991). The establishment of the Register of Members' Interests did little to discourage developments and in the 1980s and 1990s the British public were to learn a new piece of political terminology – sleaze – while their gaze was turned into the deeper recesses of power (see p. 365).

Parties The orthodoxy that groups will seek friends anywhere in the ideological landscape is questionable in certain cases. The ideology of many promotional groups gives a partisan leaning. Welfare groups like Age Concern or Shelter expect more from a leftish party while business interests and the

Don't let the buggers get you down.

Inscription on watch given by Michael Mates MP to fugitive businessman Asil Nadir, upon whose behalf he had lobbied.

law-and-order lobby traditionally expect a better crack of the whip from the right. Moreover, the traditional Siamese pairings of labour and capital with the two major parties demonstrate all the complications associated with the funding relationships (pp. 322–8). However, it takes two to tango and the parties themselves will attempt to court interest groups by tailoring their manifestos to their needs. In this way New Labour danced towards the business interests in the 1990s.

The government Direct lines to ministers at the heart of state power might seem the most promising of all channels. The Major government proved there was no such thing as a free lunch by creating the Millennium Club, offering businessmen (membership fee £10,000) the opportunity to meet ministers at lunches, receptions and private functions, while the Premier Club (membership fee £100,000) opened the door to the Prime Minister and senior cabinet colleagues (Cohen 1997; Fisher 1997). The discovery in July 1998 that former Labour staffers turned lobbyists, Derek Draper and Roger Liddle, were also offering access to ministers for cash caused considerable embarrassment.

The more powerful groups can *demand* meetings with ministers if so moved. Even under Thatcher, when consultation styles came to resemble that of Greta Garbo, the presidents of the royal colleges of surgeons, physicians, and obstetricians and gynaecologists demanded a summit meeting as the NHS careered towards crisis in early 1988. Again, when the 1988 Local Government Bill (Clause 28) banned the 'promotion' of homosexuality by local authorities, distinguished actor Ian McKellen sought a meeting with the arts minister.

However, although their clients often long to pass through the door of Number Ten, lobbyists advise against such close encounters. Their value is largely symbolic; they are ritualistic exchanges unlikely to result in policy change. One weakness is the incitement of media interest. Bernie Ecclestone's *tête-à-tête* with Tony Blair in 1997 may have brought home the bacon for Formula One racing but there was considerable embarrassment for both (p. 327). An increasingly sought-after channel of access is the growing number of high-profile ministerial advisers. When Labour took power in 1997 these attracted increasing interest; figures such as Dan Corry at the Department of Trade and Industry, Ed Balls at the Treasury and Geoff Norris at the Downing Street Policy Unit became increasingly popular within the shadowy world of the lobbyists, and even known to the public.

Whitehall Demonstrations may catch the headlines and lunches with ministers carry kudos, but it is dealings with the Whitehall mandarins that often prove the most potent sources of influence. The grey-suited professional lobbyists moving oleaginously about the corridors of power aim to keep out of the spotlight. It is here that the bargaining counters of the groups are most valued and where the symbiosis of mutual need is most apparent. Consultation can shape the content of official publications, green papers (putting ideas on the political agenda) and white papers (declaring government policy). This influence is greatest because it is conducted below the level of public awareness. The village of

Whitehall does not encourage sightseers and those welcomed to tea may rest assured that the curtains will remain drawn; the genteel residents will not betray their secrets even to Commons select committees (see p. 457). The group–mandarin duet sings even more *sotto voce* in the making of statutory instruments, where discussion concerns details of actual legislation.

> Recently I had to do a job on the road issue and the civil servant I wanted to talk to wouldn't meet me. So I arranged for our MP to draft something like twenty written questions, questions which I knew he would have to do the work of answering. He soon got the message. You might call that blackmail. I call it a triumph for democracy.
>
> Douglas Smith (a lobbyist of Martin Dignum Associates), quoted in the *Guardian* (31 Oct. 1978)

The European Union The EU, drawing on corporatist continental traditions, sees employers and unions as 'social partners', an approach institutionalized through the ECOSOC (see chapter 5). This offers a further focus for British pressure groups, sometimes a more receptive ear than their own government. There are many hundreds of groups lobbying at Brussels over issues such as trade, agriculture, food, commerce and the service industries. Many form transnational alliances; the CBI and the TUC operate through the European employers and unions bodies (UNICE and ETUC). As the flow of directives from the Commission increases, more and more associations are drawn into the consultative web. Interests go beyond the industrial to include human rights, children, consumer protection and the environment. Calls to Brussels for stricter regulation of drinking water and bathing beaches brought the British government before the European Court over its failings.

Groups may approach the EU institutions directly or try to influence the national government's stance at Brussels. It is symptomatic of the embryonic stage of European federalism that the indirect route is the more popular. Yet there are risks; the government may be forced to let a group down by making concessions in the Council. Groups choosing the direct line may talk to the European Parliament and ECOSOC, though it can be a mark of weakness to concentrate effort here. The key Brussels access point is the Commission – not the commissioners themselves but the 'Eureaucrats' operating within the dense committee network. Here groups will find an open door and be invited to participate at very early stages in the policy process. Like governments, the Commission has a voracious appetite for advice and expertise. In addition, talking to interests enables it to combat the charge of faceless undemocratic Euro-officialdom. However, the grave dangers of lobbyist involvement with unelected institutions was thrown into stark relief in the March 1999 report of the 'Committee of the Wise', which led to the Commission's resignation (see p. 126). Amongst this catalogue of bureaucratic shame were accounts of the corrupt awarding of contracts and even suspicions of Mafia involvement.

Explaining Group Politics

The politics of influence takes us beyond the constitutional theory of electorates, parliaments and cabinets and different theoretical perspectives are required. These take us close to the heart of the power structure within the polity.

Pluralism

Much orthodox British study in the liberal-democratic tradition subscribes to a generally **pluralist** view of politics. The operation of groups is believed to remedy some shortcomings in representative government, including the following:

- a single vote can hardly be said to constitute participation;
- the principle of one vote each fails to recognize the variation in the intensity with which views are held;
- people are denied influence between elections;
- manifesto promises can be broken mid-term;
- minority voices are generally unheeded.

The modern variant of the theory is largely a US import deriving from Bentley. Although he saw group activity as a necessary and inescapable feature of *any* political system, subsequent thinkers developed the theory as a hallmark of liberal democracy. It was not merely a *description* of the way things were, but a prescription of how they *ought* to be. Robert Dahl wrote extensively on the theory in the USA. Coining the term **polyarchy**, he regarded it as no less than a completely new theory of popular sovereignty in which groups help to exert the checks and balances so central to the US constitution (Dahl 1956). In Britain, interest in pluralism, which had been present since the rise of the trade unions (exercising thinkers like Cole, Tawney, Russell, Laski and the Webbs), was reinforced by American commentators on the British scene, such as Samuel Beer (1965), and entered into the mainstream liberal-democratic orthodoxy.

The tenets of pluralism This benign system, complementing representative democracy, may be portrayed as follows.

- The right to join groups is a mark of a free society.
- Groups provide a more effective means of participation than elections.
- Public policy is the outcome of group forces acting against each other. This resembles the mathematical vector diagram, where the *resultant* reflects the combined effect of forces (figure 17.1). Thus the system tends towards a state of equilibrium, with all forces having some effect on the outcome.
- The point where the forces act is the government, which is an impartial referee, its role 'the balancing of group pressures' (Richardson and Jordan 1979: vii).

- No single group will dominate because, as in Newton's law of motion, for every force there is an equal and opposite to counterbalance: the roads lobby will generate an anti-roads lobby and so on.
- Competition will not threaten the integrity of society because each individual tends to belong to several groups; a loss on one front will be balanced by gains elsewhere.
- The larger the group the more influence it will have, thereby maintaining the majoritarian principle while not silencing minorities.
- People with intense feelings on an issue will tend to exert more pressure than the apathetic, thereby countering the insensitivity in the one-person-one-vote principle.
- Those with a common interest, but not organized, will be accommodated because the government and other groups will regard them as *latent groups* ready to mobilize.
- Policies, as the product of bargaining and compromise, will tend to be moderate, fair to all, and conducive to social stability. Another leading pluralist, Charles Lindblom (1959), noted how a process of 'partisan mutual adjustment' resulted in **incrementalism** – small policy changes rather than great unsettling leaps.

This of course is an abstract model; the idea of government as a cypher or mere referee is unrealistic and was specifically rejected by Beer (1956) in the heyday of the theory in the mid-1950s. However, a weak role for government is necessary to the theory. Thus when the mighty Shell did a U-turn in 1996 over the disposal of the Brent Spar oil platform following action by Greenpeace, the government, although voicing disapproval, was little more than a bit player in

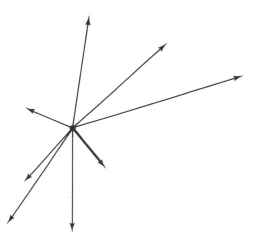

Figure 17.1
A vector diagram.

The lines represent the magnitudes and directions of forces acting at a point. They produce a resultant (the bold arrow) which is the sum of their directions and magnitudes; thus every force is taken equally into account. This is analogous to a pure theory of pluralism.

a drama where two multinational organizations competed for public support. Lively (1978: 191) suggests two interpretations of the government role: the *arbiter* model (government with enough power to ensure that the groups play by the rules) and the *arena* model (government as one of the participants in the game). Dahl and Lindblom themselves came to accept a somewhat more directive role of government under the label neopluralism.

> With all its defects, [pluralism] does nevertheless provide a high probability that any active and legitimate group will make itself heard effectively at some stage in the process of decision.
>
> Robert Dahl, *A Preface to Democratic Theory* (1956: 150)

The policy community Neopluralists give a more practical picture of the arena in which the groups bargain. In each policy area are ministers, civil servants, professional lobbyists and groups in mutual dependencies (figure 17.2) termed variously policy communities, **subgovernments** or **policy networks**. While the network image can be accommodated in other theoretical perspectives (Smith 1993: 74), it is mainly applied by those of a pluralist leaning. The communities are highly fluid, actors entering and exiting as issues change. Although in some respects members may be rivals, they also work together against other policy communities in pursuit of a greater share of public resources (Richardson and Jordan 1979; Rhodes and Marsh 1992). Communities themselves may intersect (Grant and MacNamara 1995). Over the BSE crisis communities around the Ministry of Agriculture, Fisheries and Food and the Ministry of Health presented a united front with the British beef interests (Winter 1996: 60–1).

> When I was at the [Health Education Council] . . . the Ministry of Agriculture was in there like a ton of bricks acting virtually as a lobby for the National Farmers Union.
>
> Dr David Playfair (former Director General of the HEC), quoted in the *Independent* (17 Dec. 1988)

Networks also form at EU level through vertical alliances comprising national ministries, European parliamentary committees, Eurocrats, politicians and professional lobbyists, as well as the pressure groups themselves (Scharpf 1988: 270). Close relationships develop between the favoured interest and the relevant directorates and there is rivalry between directorates in advancing the claims of their clients.

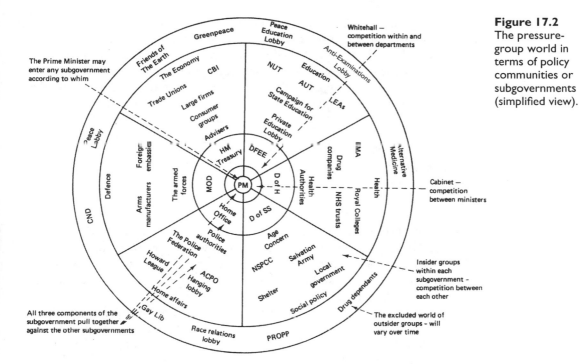

Figure 17.2
The pressure-group world in terms of policy communities or subgovernments (simplified view).

Evaluating pluralism

Few would quarrel with pluralism's stress on the role of groups in politics. However, their uniqueness to liberal democracy is questionable; they also form under totalitarian regimes. Indeed they can be seen as *undermining* democracy; Rousseau believed factions subverted the General Will. They can also be internally undemocratic with unelected leaders whose views may be at variance with those of members. Very few associations have procedures for consulting members. Moreover, the largest groups are not necessarily the winners, tightly knit associations (the City, the BMA) often having a degree of influence entirely out of proportion to their democratic weight, while groups with vast memberships – teachers, nurses and miners – have suffered successive defeats. Beyond these considerations is the geometry of the Establishment, determining which forces intersect at the centres of power and who has friends in high places.

Friends in high places Pioneering British studies, such as those of the BMA (Eckstein 1960), the CBI (Grant and Marsh 1977) and the National Farmers Union (NFU) (Self and Storing 1962) (as well as the majority of smaller case studies and various symposia on the subject), have concentrated on groups that are largely successful, respectable and legitimate. These are **insider groups**, part of the Establishment. Relationships here can be relaxed and informal, extending beyond tea and sympathy in Whitehall's corridors of power to G&T in the exclusive clubs and restaurants of London, and even to weekends in country houses where the high can meet the mighty. For the mandarins, public service can be followed by private gain when, upon retirement and duly knighted, the ex-mandarins can take up lucrative appointments with those with whom they have been doing business (p. 453). Needless to say, such a warm embrace is not extended to all; those in the underground tunnels, in raucous demonstrations or on the cold picket lines are the **outsiders**.

In practice the dichotomy between insiders and outsiders is not clear cut; there are a multiplicity of positions along a notional spectrum determined by various factors.

- *Public esteem.* The BMA has always gained mightily from the natural veneration that society accords healers. On the other hand, groups espousing causes such as, say, the legalization of cannabis or Radical Alternatives to Prison, can be safely snubbed by a government ever conscious that it will be judged by the company it keeps.

- *Stage of development.* New groups often start as outsiders, sometimes resorting to 'non-responsible' behaviour. However, insider status may well be the ultimate goal, in return for which a code of good behaviour will be accepted. By the end of the 1990s the anti-roads lobby was beginning to come in from the cold as gridlocked motorways fulfilled their prophecies.

- *Ideology.* Where group and government ideologies clash, it is likely that neither will wish to be seen holding hands with the other. By choosing to remain outside the pale a group avoids any moral burdens of self-restraint and may kick more violently against the pillars of the Establishment.

- *Social positioning.* It helps to know the right people. The middle classes are generally better placed, the representatives of some groups resembling civil servant clones, often from the same schools (public) and universities (Oxbridge). Sharing norms, values and interests, they will not only speak the same language, they will do so with the same accent.

- *Wealth.* Money can talk in many accents. Wealthy associations such as the CBI or NFU can spend much on entertaining, lobbyists, public relations consultants and image-building. Among promotional groups, unpopular causes (say ex-prisoners, drug addicts) have problems raising funds, while others (say animal and child welfare) enjoy a Midas-like touch (figure 17.3).

- *Economic leverage.* Certain interests (private industrial sectors, banks and the City) enjoy a pivotal position in the economy; governments of all complexions must therefore cater for their needs. Labour governments can be so concerned to reassure on this front that they often subordinate their social programmes.

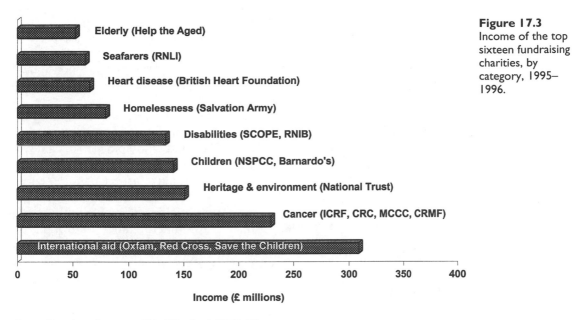

Figure 17.3
Income of the top sixteen fundraising charities, by category, 1995–1996.

Source: Data from *Britain: an Official Handbook* (1997: 46).

Governments will vary over the interests they favour but for the most part the insider groups will be those close to the heart of the Establishment. They are welcomed in by governments of the centre right, be they Conservative or Labour. The TUC experienced a back-slapping 'beer-and-sandwiches' heyday under the Wilson government, a frosty cold shoulder from Thatcher and only a stiffly formal handshake from Blair. Yet the deaf ear to unwelcome voices is one of the hallmarks of totalitarianism, for an absence of alternative views threatens democracy.

There can also be insiders and outsiders at EU level. From its inception, the idea of a federal Europe has offered a tantalizing glimpse of new forms of power to banks, international financiers and mighty multinationals. The vision of a giant market-place like that of the USA was tempting indeed; today every major company has offices in Brussels. More than other interests, these largely by-pass the European Parliament in favour of the Eurocrats, whom they fete with lunches and entertainment. The desire to contain this globalization of power is one of the reasons for calls to make the EU institutions more democratic.

Does pluralism make might right? Critics would allege that group activity does not result in equity. Like the Ancient Greek Thrasymachus, pluralism allows that 'might is right'. Anti-roads protesters proved little match for a roads lobby of hauliers, engineers, motorway caterers and the bankers behind them. Yet it can be argued that the purpose of government is to control the rich and powerful (Scattschneider 1960); weak game wardens can be profoundly dangerous when the wildlife park contains marauding beasts. In his farewell address, President

Eisenhower warned of the menacing growth in America of a 'military-industrial complex' actually threatening the sovereignty of government. Of course, this idea of weak government fits snugly within the general liberal-democratic suspicion of the state. As a kind of political *laissez-faire* it removes moral responsibility from the state for outcomes; you cannot accuse the referee if you lose the game. This culture can induce the poor to blame themselves rather than the system.

Pluralism, with its tendency towards small-scale change, can be said to produce a static society. Thus Labour governments are not able to bring about anything resembling a socialist revolution. Dahl and Lindblom (1976) came to accept in their later work theory that group politics does not take place on a level playing field. However, preserving the normative aspect of the theory, they argued that a democratic constitution should aim to counter the power of capitalist interests by maximizing group participation and listening to the weak as well as the strong (Dahl 1985). An alternative interpretation of group politics – **corporatism** – gives a much stronger role to government.

Corporatism

This is an approach to government with long European antecedents and became interesting to British scholars during the 1970s as the limitations of pluralism were exposed. Here, government works in deliberate collusion with certain major interests in society. Corporatism is identified with the fascism of the 1930s and this unpleasant aftertaste is expunged by the term **neocorporatism**. Philippe Schmitter (1974) distinguished two forms – *state corporatism* and *societal corporatism*; the latter arising naturally within a society and, unlike the former, *not* a feature of oppressive government. For some, a neocorporatist style of government is the answer to the wasteful competition generated by pluralism. It can appear as a great cure-all for national problems, engendering a classless camaraderie allegedly seen in times of war (indeed, the two world wars were great corporatist periods for Britain).

The tenets of corporatism Societal corporatism is the variant to be found in modern liberal democracies and has the following characteristics.

- Politics is seen in terms of groups but they are cooperative rather than competitive.
- Government is not a passive referee; it decides who shall be invited into the consultations and has clear views on policy.
- Groups may even be created by government to represent interests it wishes to work with.
- The interests included tend to be capital and labour, the result being **tripartism**, a *pas de trois* of government, trade unions and employers.
- Those included tend to monopolize the right to represent their interest.
- Sometimes groups join together as peak organizations to facilitate consultation.

- Special corporatist institutions can be created to bypass the formal constitution.
- The relationship is reciprocal: not only do groups influence policy, government can influence groups, forcing them to modify their demands and gaining their cooperation.

A climate of corporatism In the early twentieth century Britain encouraged institutionalization among bodies representing labour and capital as a means of securing state legitimacy. There was an attempt to set up a National Industrial Conference in 1919 and subsequently efforts were made to create a 'Parliament of Industry' (Middlemass 1979: 372). The post-war consensus saw renewed corporatist tendencies; the trade unions combined under the TUC, and the employers under the CBI. Government established a number of tripartite institutions, particularly the National Economic Development Council (Neddy) in 1961. In the mid-1970s, the Manpower Services Commission, the Health and Safety Commission, and the Advisory, Conciliation and Arbitration Service were established on a tripartite basis. In addition, there were hundreds of advisory and **consultative bodies** concerned with particular industrial sectors and policy areas. Various policies also had a corporatist flavour, particularly over prices and incomes, and the 1975–8 'social contract' gave labour and capital a voice in many domestic policies in exchange for cooperation.

The tendencies were not restricted to the capital–labour duet. In specific policy areas certain groups enjoyed particularly easy access to government while others were excluded. Thus the BMA, the NFU and the National Union of Teachers were welcomed in, while the ancillary medical professions, the environment lobby and smaller teaching unions shivered in the cold.

However, this was never fully blown corporatism and by the mid-1980s the age appeared to be past. Schmitter, who had once believed in the historical necessity of corporatism, was quick to note a dramatic revolt in Britain among Conservative and capitalist interests after the mid-1970s (Lehmbruch and Schmitter 1982). The decay came in the face of economic crisis. Heath's confrontation with the miners was a defining moment and the collapse of Callaghan's 'social contract' showed that Labour had lost its trump card – trade union cooperation.

The seeds of failure This form of corporatism was essentially a consensus-era product, the *ménage à trois* proving most fragile when it should have been most valuable – in economic crisis. Under these circumstances:

- unions were liable to opt out once the benefits of full employment were no longer available to compensate for the concessions to capital;
- employers became disenchanted with rules and constraints as profits fell;
- militants on both sides favoured confrontation over cooperation;
- large firms and unions preferred dealing directly with government rather than corporatist institutions;
- radical governments of the right found the corporatist embrace inhibiting.

Questioning the logic of group action

Some theorists question the group interpretation of politics in both descriptive and prescriptive terms, doubting whether groups are as natural as Bentley asserted or as desirable as pluralists claim. By applying the methods of classical economic theory to political analysis, public choice theory attempts to explain political decisions (public choices) in terms of self-interested actors. Olson (1968) suggests that rational individuals will not become active in a group merely because it is fighting for a collective interest that they share. They can do just as well by sitting back and letting others do the work. In the school choir it is easy enough to open the mouth soundlessly and enjoy the free meal after the concert. This is the problem of the 'free-rider'.

Thus the idea that people tend to form groups (or even parties) to protect their common interest is fallacious; groups that do exist have formed for some other reason. This, for Olson, is the explanation of the success of the capitalist interests: 'the multitude of workers, consumers . . . and so on are organized only in special circumstances, but business interests [corporations, banks, the City] are organized as a general rule' (Olson 1968: 143). Groups in the first category must develop strategies for recruiting and retaining members. They must offer **selective incentives** (insurance, free teeshirts etc.), or use coercion such as a closed-shop arrangement or intimidation. Being artificial, they lack cohesion and remain essentially weak.

However, political scientists study a real world of passion and emotion, not the abstract terrain inhabited by 'economic man'. It may be true that one more person joining, say, Greenpeace, will not alter the course of history, but it will give a psychic satisfaction. In the same way, many people join trade unions because they believe in the movement, seek camaraderie and see strength through numbers. As for the explanation of the success of capital in terms of superior organization, this is simplistic, ignoring the slope of the capitalist playing field.

On the prescriptive front Olson (1982) further argues that the presence of artificially created groups holds back economic growth. Hence commentators believed Britain to have reached a state of **'pluralist stagnation'** by the late 1970s as a result of governments' willingness to listen and bargain with union leaders (Beer 1982: 31). This thesis appealed to the New Right, with its deep antipathy towards union involvement in government.

A post-corporate era?

With talk of government overload and pluralist stagnation, as well as the demonizing of the 'winter of discontent', the 1979 Conservative government spoke a rhetoric of 'enemy within' rather than of partnership. The high steel railings erected across Downing Street were symbolic; the cosy days of beer and sandwiches at Number Ten were over. The result was bitter confrontation with the steelworkers in 1980, the railwaymen in 1982 and, most dramatically of all, the miners in 1984–5. A series of Acts weakened the unions, removing legal immunities for collective action and outlawing secondary picketing. The closed-shop laws were relaxed and compulsory secret strike ballots enabled the more deferential mass to reject the leadership advice on action. Legislation brought the courts into the arena and some unions found their funds sequestrated on a crippling scale.

By the end of Thatcher's reign the political role of the unions had virtually disappeared (Marsh 1992: ch. 4). Government policy for the once corporatist Manpower Services Commission was being made on a 'take-it-or-leave-it' basis. The breakaway Union of Democratic Mineworkers was assisted by government, and the TUC, undermined by the willingness of some unions to conclude single-union agreements, lost its right to choose union representatives on various quangos, including Neddy and the Health and Safety Executive. Figure 17.4 chronicles the decline. Not only was there no more beer and sandwiches, the government also appeared less interested in wine and pâté with the CBI. Traditional insider groups, including the Institute of Directors, the CBI, the Bar Council, the Law Society, the Royal Colleges, the BMA and the NFU all had unpalatable dishes thrust down their throats with little consultation over the menu.

Yet the anti-corporatist drive had mixed results. Ignoring the expertise of teachers, NHS workers and others in framing policy initiatives imposed high costs in terms of ill-drafted legislation and policy failure in areas such as the core curriculum and the internal market. Public criticism from alienated groups reduced public confidence further. Moreover, while it may have been possible to exclude them from the consultation chambers they remained central to the implementation process, where they could often put the brakes on radical plans (Marsh and Rhodes 1992: 181). The most dramatic failure was the poll tax; conceived with zero consultation, the outcome extracted a heavy toll on the government and the Prime Minister herself (Butler et al. 1994).

However, the exclusion was not absolute. Some post-war machinery survived, the TUC and CBI remained on a host of intermediate-level bodies and the coming of Major reduced the sense of alienation (Norton 1993a: 62). The number of consultative documents rose (though the response time was very short), access for the BMA improved and local government associations detected greater willingness to listen (Baggott 1995a: 498). The *dirigiste* Michael Heseltine became President of the Board of Trade. Yet with deep symbolism Neddy was abolished in early 1993. However, Heseltine appointed its director as his economic adviser, declaring that the Department of Trade and Industry would assume Neddy's role and revitalize industry–government relations. It was reorganized into fifteen sectoral divisions and May 1993 saw an inaugural meeting of a round table of nineteen senior industrialists. Yet the confrontational style remained, with plans for seven-day notice of strikes, postal ballots for strike action and an end to TUC regulation of trade unions (Halliday 1993: 315). Moreover, little consultation preceded a November 1992 bombshell announcing extensive pit closures. On another front, consultation was conspicuously lacking in the Sheehy Report on police pay and conditions (see p. 658).

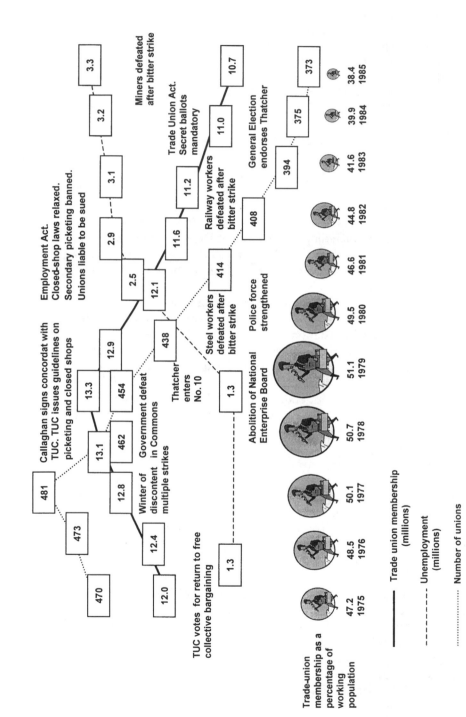

Figure 17.4 The death of corporatism.

Source: Data from *Social Trends* (1988: tables 4.19 and 11.8).

Corporatism by other means Paradoxically, the government's policies produced other forms of corporatism. Various public–private partnership schemes created a new consultative network, while compulsory competitive tendering, market-testing and the growth of the quango state (chapter 18) further extended the involvement of private business in the business of government. This exercise of patronage tended to spurn the left so that, for example, the subject groups of the National Curriculum Council excluded local authorities and teachers' unions while including independent schools and right-wing pressure groups (Baggott 1995a: 487). Further tendencies towards back-door corporatism came through consultation with think-tanks and private consultants, particularly over the privatization launches.

When one doors closes Yet developments were to demonstrate the ubiquity of groups: if denied access at one point they will seek another. One target was the EU. Encouraged by the Social Chapter and the globalizing economy, the unions looked more to Brussels, often strengthening cross-national links (Farnham 1996: 597). Other promotional groups made the journey across the channel; the European Commission's environmental directorate received many more letters from Britain than any other country (*Economist*, 13 Aug. 1994). At home there was a dramatic rise in the lobbying of Parliament, a development enhanced by opportunities to appear before select committees (Norton 1997: 360).

The denial of access also increased direct action: if the *vox populi* could not be heard in the chambers of state it would be heard in the streets. A turning point may have been marked by the successful campaigns against the poll tax, suggesting a Leviathan lying dormant in the generally inert mass. Similarly, Heseltine's pit closure programme was derailed by large-scale demonstrations, and a campaign waged by the parents of the children shot in Dunblane in 1996 resulted in the banning of handguns; even royalty could not prevent the tide of feeling. Amidst increasing disruption people not only took to the streets, environmentalists risked death on the high seas, critical-mass cyclists risked rage on the roads, and anti-motorway and airport runway demonstrators took to the trees and tunnels. Daniel Hooper (aka Swampy) emerged from underground in Devon before the TV cameras and walked unpunished from court in 1997 to

---

THANKS TO ALL THOSE WHO HELPED US DO OUR WORK IN 1998
  Shell for deciding to recycle the Brent Spar . . . at last.
  John Prescott for agreeing not to dump any oil installations in the ocean.
  Japan for becoming the 26th nation to ratify the Antarctic Treaty.
  Michael Meacher for agreeing to ban toxic and radioactive discharges from the sea by 2020.
  EU fisheries ministers for banning 'wall of death' driftnets.
  Peter Mandelson for not putting PVC on the Millennium Dome roof.
  . . . OK, so we had to run campaigns against some of them first – but thanks anyway.

Extract from front cover of Greenpeace, *Annual Review 1998* become a folk hero and a welcome guest on chat-shows. Thatcher's attempt to restrict access to government had uncovered new and perhaps dangerous regions in the complex map of power.

New Labour: old corporatism or new social partnership?

Part of Labour's modernization process had been a fundamental revamping of its relationship with the unions. The promise of 'fairness not favours' ruled out any return to the 1970s; the talk was of a new 'social partnership'. Moreover, this was a reality that the 'new unionists' – those sympathetic to 'New Labour', including TUC leader John Monks – were prepared to accept (Farnham 1996: 597). In opposition Labour had made strenuous efforts to gain the approval of establishment interest groups. The 1996 annual conference saw greater ardour than ever before, with champagne receptions and working breakfasts between business leaders and leading party figures. Stands were erected by such powerful interests as the Institute of Directors, BA, the British Bankers' Association, Lloyds, and even defence contractors. Tony Blair paid each a courteous visit before the television cameras. Within its first weeks of office Labour had made a number of corporatist-style appointments embracing establishment figures. David Simon of BP was to consider competitiveness in Europe and Martin Taylor, chief executive of Barclays Bank, was appointed to head a task-force streamlining the welfare state.

The 'social partnership' was no reincarnation of Neddy, with its alleged veto on government policy; government would remain firmly in the driving seat supervising a range of advisory groups, such as the Low Pay Commission, embracing not only the CBI and TUC but other players considered central to economic success. An advisory group on competitiveness established by Board of Trade President Margaret Beckett included Adair Turner, head of the CBI and John Monks of the TUC, as well as the heads of major companies including Nissan, Glaxo, BP and Guinness. For some of the older-thinking unionists the social partnership seemed to offer too much to business interests and did not seek sufficient influence over company management. A key area of early dissent concerned union recognition in the workplace, the government appearing loath to force the CBI to match union concessions. The access to the Prime Minister enjoyed by figures like Bernie Ecclestone and Rupert Murdoch demonstrated Labour's extraordinary respect for private power. After one year in office, an official register of firms and their clients (set up at the request of Sir Gordon Downey) revealed an exodus of former Labour staffers to the world of influence, almost all major lobbying companies employing at least one. The interests represented included arms dealing, the tobacco industry and firms involved in genetic engineering. Alarmingly, these were being wooed by party fundraisers (*Independent*, 24 March 1998).

Indication of government complaisance before right-wing pressure came when a 250,000-strong Countryside March descended upon London in February 1998, pledged to save the 'British country way of life', particularly the hunting of foxes. Organized by a 'Countryside Alliance', funding came from some of Britain's biggest companies, the Duke of Westminster and even America's shooting and hunting lobby (*Independent*, 26 Feb. 1998). In March 1998 the government refused to make time available for Mike Foster's private member's bill to ban foxhunting, despite earlier pledges.

Corporatism has never been highly developed in Britain. Some crucially important interests, particularly the City, remained outside the corporate institutions, and even those included never entirely eschewed competitive behaviour, making self-interested decisions which were bad for the economy as a whole (Marquand 1988: 121–3). Grant (1984: 130) saw 'a weakly developed system of corporatist interaction . . . coexisting with a . . . healthy and important pluralist system'. This raised the question: 'Which issues are decided in which way?' Cawson and Saunders developed the dual state thesis, suggesting that economic issues tend to be settled in a closed corporatist style affording much power to capitalist interests, while those broadly concerning welfare emerge from a more open pluralist process (Cawson 1986: ch. 7). However, the economic implications of the welfare state blunt this distinction. The 1997 Labour government justified many welfare policies in terms of Treasury, rather than social, considerations. For Middlemass (1979: 371–85) the system contains a 'corporate bias', reflecting a *desire* on the part of government to insulate itself from pluralism in order to best meet the needs of capitalist interests.

For critics the world of participation becomes like an exclusive golf club, fine for members but not so good for those beyond the fairways. Although trade unions enter this exclusive world, this may represent little more than the opportunity to act as caddies, with no invitations to the bar. For much of the time the main requirement from them was to suspend their *raison d'être* and hold down wages (Mullard 1993: 235–6). Whether corporatist or pluralist, some interests seem to come out winners and some losers. From 1979 Britain became an increasingly unequal society; by 1995 the most unequal in the western world. To some this outcome is desirable, to others it is morally defective, but regardless of the ethics, why does it happen? It is necessary to open yet another door in the labyrinthine world of influence and go beyond the group approach.

Beyond the Group Approach

Although an examination of organized interests tells us much about the politics of influence, it does not explain everything. Why are some interests more advantaged than others? Is this but a *symptom* of a more fundamental architecture of power. To search for the explanation, we must explore the dark recesses underlying the *structure* of society. Two broad perspectives which help to illuminate this are the **elitist** and the **Marxist**.

Elite theory

This approach, sometimes termed 'scientific elitism', was pioneered at the beginning of the twentieth century by a school of Italian thinkers now known as the classical elitists – Mosca, Pareto and Michels. They agreed with Marx that the institutions of liberal democracy did not work in the way claimed by apologists; the masses tended to be dominated by the few, who ruled in their own interest. However, unlike Marx, they did not see the economic base of society as the sole cause; the processes, inevitable and ineluctable like laws of nature, were present in all forms of society. The talented people in all walks of life would inevitably come out on top and, having done so, would preserve their supremacy by *collusion* with each other. This elite power is *cumulative*, new generations coming along and finding silver spoons in their mouths. The elite gains control of the state by dominating the parties, securing the elective offices and monopolizing key official positions; it becomes a ruling class. For right-wing commentators this is not only natural, it is desirable. Key positions are held by those best fitted for them. However, to critics the ever-present danger is that the elite rules in its own interest rather than that of the whole society. Elite theory was rejuvenated in the 1950s by those sceptical of pluralism. Floyd Hunter's famous (1953) study argued that a small coherent corps of wealthy people dominated both the social and political life in a US city, while C. Wright Mills argued that the pluralist belief in automatically balancing forces was more 'ideological hope than factual description' (1959: 126n).

Many chapters in this book suggest that, with its aristocracy and monarchy, public schools (still expanding), Oxbridge institutions, exclusive London clubs, the Freemasons and so on, Britain's social culture is replete with elitist features. This is both symbolized and reinforced in the unique and elaborate honours system. Titles continue to be inherited by those in the upper classes, with lesser ones bestowed upon the chosen from the upper-middle class. Peerages have enhanced elite power with seats in Parliament for those who come far nearer the royal box than the ballot box. The elite structure has been maintained by a class system which, while permitting some 'short-range' mobility (Giddens 1973: 181–2), has kept most in the same class. A study by *The Economist* (19 Dec. 1992) revealed that, despite meritocratic rhetoric from the grocer's daughter and circus performer's son who had become prime ministers, the education and social background of the top 100 people had changed very little. Two-thirds of the group had been to private schools and over half to Oxbridge. They were also overwhelmingly male and white. Only one woman had made it into the group without going to Oxbridge – Elizabeth II!

Yet the idea that the rich and successful are able to cohere and collude is questionable. There is much rivalry and bitterness within the upper and upper-middle classes, much of it arising from economic competition under the name of *individualism*. The quest to understand the balance of power and privilege is clearly not yet over.

Marxist perspectives

For Marx, the key driving force in politics was a struggle not between groups but between classes. The Marxist perspective argues that, under capitalism, the state always operates in the interests of the owners and controllers of capital. Today economic globalization means that this class is transnational and its power within any single state is amplified (see chapter 4). There are, however, many schools of thought with conflicting views on how this domination is effected. At one extreme, the state may be said to be controlled through the conspiratorial activities of the capitalist class – an instrumental perspective. At the other extreme, the structural perspective holds that the state is compelled to act in favour of the business and financial interests by virtue of the logic of capitalism.

> There is a high degree of homogeneity among the members of the dominant class ... They constantly cross each other's paths in an incessant round of meetings, lunches, dinners, functions, and ceremonies, and as members of boards, commissions, councils, committees and institutions of the most varied kind.
>
> Ralph Miliband (Marxist scholar), *Capitalist Democracy in Britain* (1984: 7)

The instrumental perspective The view of the state as an instrument of the ruling class is a feature of classical Marxist analysis and Marx's description of the government as a 'committee for managing the common affairs of the bourgeoisie' is regularly cited. The **instrumental** perspective can be supported in many ways, beginning with the manner in which, during the nineteenth century, the rising bourgeoisie reformed the state machine. Since then the senior civil service, armed forces, judiciary, and so on, have largely recruited from the same establishment soil that nurtures the financiers and businessmen. Gramsci saw the ruling class using these key positions to shape the dominant ideology so that the masses would be content and not threaten the revolution predicted by Marx. The penetration and funding of the Conservative Party (and increasingly New Labour) and the ability of a right-wing press to deliver sympathetic governments are further testimony to capitalist domination. Ministers may themselves take up company directorates upon retirement. The extensive use of patronage offers yet further ways to strengthen the influence of the business and financial communities through the quangocracy. We have seen how Labour's victory in 1997 came only after systematic courtship of capitalist interests and a loosening of its union ties (chapter 10).

Contrary to the pluralist argument that political and economic competition limit group power, there is evidence of coherence, if not collusion, within the capitalist class. At the head of Britain's largest companies are the directors, often sitting on the boards of several companies: in 1976, eleven men held 56 of the 250 top directorships in Britain, as well as many others in smaller companies (Scott 1985: 44). In 1988 the boards of the top 250 companies contained

> **Egg on the face of power**
>
> On 24 December 1988 the *Independent* revealed that the boards of the large food and poultry feed manufacturers, producing most of the eggs sold in British supermarkets, included a number of ex-cabinet ministers and top civil servants (Sir Peter Carey, permanent secretary at the DTI, 1976–83; John Biffen, former leader of the Commons and a senior Conservative MP; and former Cabinet Secretary Lord Hunt). Another big feed supplier had donated nearly £10,000 to Conservative funds in the 1987 election year. Little wonder that the government agreed to compensate egg producers for lost sales during the salmonella scare. Little wonder that the one responsible for alerting the public disappeared from the ministerial firmament.

290 multiple directors (Scott 1991: 79). Class solidarity is further promoted by intermarriage and various methods of excluding outsiders, including private education, freemasonry and inimitable accents.

In addition, although their interests can sometimes diverge (Marsh and Locksley 1983: 21–52), the split between industry and finance is now a myth: 'In terms of both ownership and control, banks, traders, and producers have come closer together the last 60 years' (Scott 1985: 45). The split is between big business and finance on the one hand and medium and small business on the other, with the former dominating (Scott 1991: 151). The fusion of finance and industry produces an 'inner circle' of finance capitalists at the heart of the state, dominating the top levels of the major cohesion-promoting institutions: the Association of Chambers of Commerce, the Institute of Directors, the British Institute of Management and the CBI. Unseem (1984) argues that world recession from the 1970s saw an intensification of the political activity of big business, with the inner circle representing a City view on behalf of the whole financial and business community on key matters of economic policy. The Thatcherite 'big bang' transformed the City, an influx of foreign capital extending links to a global financial community.

The structural perspective However, although it may capture a deep truth about the *essence* of the state under capitalism, the committee metaphor should not be taken literally. The idea that a class consciously makes the state an entirely compliant instrument is open to question. Indeed it can be argued that the very existence of state institutions (Parliament, the executive, bureaucracies, and so on) promises some degree of autonomy because these develop interests of their own. This is part of the public choice theorists' explanation for the expansion of social democracy, producing a large empire-building bureaucracy. Many public servants have a firm ideological commitment and regularly vote Labour (p. 243). In the twilight of the Major government one Conservative minister remarked ruefully that, while some top mandarins might pose problems for Labour, the grades below 'all read the *Guardian* or the *Independent*' (Timmins and Kampfner 1997).

In addition, politicians are highly ambitious and keen to remain in office. If the demands of capitalists were to threaten or inhibit their ability to do this they could be expected to resist. Some writers even believe that liberal-democratic states can actually be highly insensitive to the needs of capital. Crouch (1979: 27) argues that 'two of the most remarkable facts . . . are, first, the extent to which their ruling class mistrust the state and try to limit its activities, and second, the relative responsiveness of the polity . . . to working class demands'.

However, the state must perform certain functions if the capitalist economy is to survive. It must protect profitability and facilitate private capital accumulation. The state depends on the prosperity of capitalism for its tax income (Grant 1987: 239–40). This interpretation was advanced by the Marxist scholar Nicos Poulantzas (1973), who conducted a long-running debate with Miliband. In this view, far from appearing as an instrument of the capitalist class, the state must be able to show a degree of real autonomy in order to:

- provide services (health care, education, roads, legal services and so on) that it is unprofitable for capitalists to provide;
- promote homogeneity within the capitalist class to prevent it destroying itself, reconciling the fundamental conflict between finance capital, monopoly capital and non-monopoly capital;
- ensure political stability by absorbing potentially disruptive demands from the underprivileged and ethical pressure groups;
- keep welfare spending low enough to guarantee profitability;
- legitimate the capitalist system by promoting an ideology espousing inequality as for the good of all.

The instrumental model is *voluntaristic*, allowing individuals choice in their behaviour, while the **structural** one is *deterministic*, seeing them as puppets or role-players. In the latter case politicians are driven by the imperatives of capitalism as the actor playing Hamlet is driven by Shakespeare's script. Although both perspectives can be seen in Marx, the French philosopher Althusser (1969) believed the structural to be the more important. In real-world states we find elements of both; people have some choice but they are constrained by the system.

Questioning the Marxist perspectives

The Marxist interpretation is not welcomed by politicians and writers in the liberal tradition.

The managerial revolution thesis It has been argued in one version of elite theory that a managerial revolution has swept through the capitalist system. The old-style capitalists have been displaced by a diverse body of anonymous shareholders, allowing control of capital to pass to a new managerial class of meritocrats, well educated but of lower social origins and without the same close identification with those controlling the state (Burnham 1942).

However Marxists deny that power *has* passed to neutral meritocrats, asserting that it remains with the old dominant class, although the latter has undergone an internal transformation. In the first place, although a new ladder of meritocracy may exist, it is also open to the sons and daughters of the upper class, and they still have the best chance of ascending. Moreover, the position of meritocrats remains insecure; they can easily land upon the head of a snake and slither down to square one. Again, the meritocrats operate largely at the level of middle management, leaving the traditional elite members, with power based on ownership of property (and shares), in the boardrooms and in strategic control. Astonishingly, between the 1850s and the 1970s (when Britain was transformed into a social democracy) the proportion of chairmen of major companies with upper-class backgrounds remained stable at around 66 per cent (Stanworth and Giddens 1974). In addition, the old upper class is sufficiently permeable to absorb outstanding aspirants from the lower strata who, with artificially cultivated upper-class mores, become *'plus royaux que le roi'* and neutered as potential agents of social change. Finally, although companies are no longer in the hands of the old-style capitalists, there remains a small class with large personal shareholdings, so that control of capital remains in the hands of the few; in the view of Scott (1991: ch. 4) 'still a ruling class'.

Moreover, the managers' power is dwarfed by that of the finance capitalists, moving in the world driven not by commodities and production but by banks and ledgers. These come from various walks of the Establishment, including politics, the civil service and industry, and most have titles. Holding multiple directorships, they coordinate the business system. A mere nine individuals carried a network of thirty-nine companies in 1976 (figure 17.5). Their strength is enhanced beyond measure through economic globalization, deregulation of finance and the formation of the almighty TNCs with their ever-present threat to desert any country which does not cater for their needs (chapter 4).

Do you suppose that you and half a dozen amateurs like you, sitting in a row in that foolish gabble shop, can govern Undershaft and Lazarus? No my friend: you will do what pays us. You will make war when it suits us, and keep peace when it doesn't ... When I want to keep my dividends up you will discover that my want is a national need.

Andrew Undershaft (wealthy industrialist), addressing his MP son-in-law
in Bernard Shaw's *Major Barbara* (1907)

Bureaucratic power   The idea of class domination of government can be countered by the argument that the civil service is a neutral machine, safeguarding the public interest. Some Marxists accept bureaucratic power as a source of state autonomy. However, civil service recruitment and socialization processes have long tended towards harmony with establishment interests (see p. 449). Upon becoming Cabinet Secretary, Sir Robin Butler was immediately proposed for membership of the Athenaeum, Brookes and the Oxford and Cambridge –

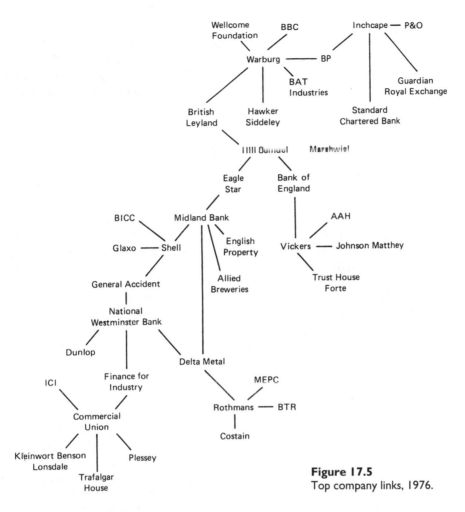

Figure 17.5
Top company links, 1976.

Source: Scott (1985: figure 2.5).

exclusive clubs that enable the great to meet the good (Paxman 1991: 313). Moreover, unlike the USA, Britain offers no public interest defence for a bureaucrat going public on an issue of concern (see pp. 459–60).

Welfare statism It may be argued that the post-war rise of social democracy, with a wide range of policies designed to ease the conditions of the working class, is hardly evidence of upper-class domination. Yet this may be countered with an argument that the **welfare state** serves the interests of capital by social-izing the costs of production, furnishing a body of healthy and reasonably well-educated workers and maintaining social harmony through legitimation (Gough 1979). Moreover, if the economy runs out of steam, a *fiscal crisis* arises as the tax-borne cost of welfare erodes profitability (O'Connor 1973); when this occurs, the capitalist interests will soon rein in the welfare state. This appeared to happen with the collapse of the long boom in the mid-1970s when doctors, for example, once insiders, found themselves on the outside as NHS budgets were squeezed in the interests of tax cuts. The New Labour government continued the squeeze, Blair proclaiming an end to the 'something for nothing culture' at the time of the 1998 Queen's speech.

Who Gets the Loot?

Explanations of power in society range from the most benign version of pluralism to class-based elitism. All devalue the role of the democratically elected government, representing an important corrective to the accounts that see formal institutions as the beginning and end of political life. Power is a complex mystery. One way to solve it is to use the technique of Hercule Poirot and see who gets the loot; to repeat the question at the beginning of this book: who gets what, when, how? Although from the late 1970s the corporatist institutions became overgrown with creepers and the path to Whitehall gathered moss, Lawson's 1988 Budget placed the loot in the wallets and handbags of the wealthy at the expense of the rest. By 1995 some 25 per cent of the male workforce was unemployed or not making themselves available for work. Between 1979 and 1996, the proportion of households with no working adult partner had risen from 6 to 16 per cent. As inequality steadily increased, Will Hutton (1996) depicted the emerging social divide as the 30/30/40 society (see p. 177).

Nothing represents communal welfare so clearly as public health, yet with powerful lobbies associated with areas as varied as agriculture, convenience foods, tobacco, drugs manufacture and trunk roads, many issues have arisen (from salmonella and BSE to railways neglect, pesticide use, pollution, road congestion and tobacco advertising) in which governments have appeared slow to defend the public interest. The case of BSE placed the issue in sharp focus. Evidence presented to the inquiry in April 1998 showed that regulations to prevent the catastrophe could have been put in place in the mid-1970s but had been thwarted by lobbying from rendering firms (*Guardian*, 30 April 1998). In 1990, Agriculture Minister John Gummer displayed rather bizarre loyalty to producer interests, giving the nation the poignant image of his small daughter munching a beefburger on prime-time television. The Southwood committee set up to investigate the issue refrained from recommending a ban on the use of cattle offal in food, not for scientific reasons but because they felt politically it was a 'no-goer' with the MAFF (Winter 1996: 163). Despite much rhetoric about establishing an independent Food Standards Agency, it was not until early 1999 that firm proposals were announced.

In broader terms governments have responded to the City preference for short-term dividends and capital gains, free international capital flows, stable exchange rates and tight monetary controls. The general economic interest is sacrificed as companies are constrained to boost share prices through wage cuts, downsizing and takeover bids rather than long-term investment. Labour came to power in May 1997 and, if the capitalist interests at home and abroad needed a sign, the government gave it in pledging to stick to the Conservatives' spending targets for the next two years. The Welfare-to-Work scheme aimed to promote a work ethic; 'life on the dole' was not to be an option. Labour had learned the lesson that socialism in a capitalist economy meant life in opposition. The party claimed it had made a new pact with the people; for critics it was a Faustian pact with capital.

Yet in the shadowy world of power, policy is made in many ways. Sometimes mass opinion can sway a government, sometimes election promises must be honoured, sometimes pluralistic bargaining takes place. Feminists and environmentalists, for example, have certainly secured some victories. However, the argument that the most important areas are under elite domination (as C. Wright Mills concluded for the USA) is compelling. The pattern of economic power moulds the space in which politics is enacted. The struggles of those representing the poor and underprivileged resemble that of Sisyphus, whose torment in hell is forever to push a great boulder to the top of a hill, from which it will invariably roll down again.

Key points

- The politics of influence takes place behind the formal scenery of the constitution; it is largely the domain of organized interests.
- Promotional groups advance broad principles while sectional groups protect their members.
- Groups have bargaining counters in the form of resources governments need.
- Points of access to the political system include public opinion, Parliament, political parties, the executive, the bureaucracy and the institutions of the EU.
- Not all groups enjoy equal access; some are insiders and others outsiders.
- Two principal theories explaining group politics are pluralism and corporatism, although there are a number of variants of each.
- Some theorists see group involvement as unnatural, distorting the allocation of resources within society.
- Elitists and Marxists look for even deeper sources of power within the polity.
- On the basis of the question 'Who gets what?', the system mainly operates in favour of the large-scale owners and controllers of capital.

Review your understanding of the following terms and concepts

bourgeoisie	Marxism	pressure group
corporatism	neocorporatism	promotional group
determinism	neopluralism	public choice theory
dual state thesis	outsider group	ruling class
elitism	peak organization	sectional group
incrementalism	pluralism	selective incentives
insider group	pluralist stagnation	structural power
instrumental power	policy network	subgovernment
interest group	policy community	tripartism
interest aggregation	polyarchy	voluntarism

Assignment

US shooting lobby funds countryside march

EXCLUSIVE

By Ian Burrell

AMERICA'S shooting and hunting lobby has been bankrolling this weekend's mass march pledged to save the British country way of life.

The Duke of Westminster, Britain's richest man, has also given more than £1m to the organisers of the Countryside March, which is intended to save rural jobs and promote fox-hunting. Other supporters include the chairmen of some of Britain's biggest companies, including Sir Alick Rankin, of General Accident, and Jonny Weatherby of Weatherby's, which runs horseracing.

Sunday's march is expected to attract 250,000 people to London. The organisers have hired 2,000 coaches and 25 trains to bring in supporters and are setting up a one-day radio station, March FM.

The Independent has established that much of the money for the £5,000,000 event is coming from overseas supporters and wealthy landowners and businessmen. The man who thought up the march and who has masterminded funding of the campaign to save country sports in Britain is Chi-cago-born lawyer Eric Bettelheim.

London-based Mr Bettelheim is secretary of the Countryside Business Group (CBG), which was formed two years ago to pay for the fight against the threat to the countryside from animal rights activists and lobby groups.

The 10-strong team set up to run the CBG included Sir Alick Rankin and Mr Weatherby as well as Nick Bannister, a senior executive of ABN Amro investment bank, and Alain Drach, chairman of the international gunmaking company Holland & Holland.

Independent, 26 Feb. 1998

Study the extract from the *Independent* and answer the following questions.

		Mark (%)
1	Would you class the Countryside Alliance as an insider or outsider group? Explain your reasoning.	10
2	What resources do you think the Countryside Alliance had access to?	20
3	What avenue of access to government is the Countryside Alliance using?	20
4	Which theoretical models of influence would you employ to analyse this case?	50

Questions for discussion

1 'In the analysis of politics, pressure groups rather than institutions are the key actors.' Discuss.

2 What problems are likely to face a group advocating a reduction in car use?

3 'Pressure groups are a natural extension of the liberal-democratic state.' Discuss.

4 'Groups that resort to loud public campaigns are revealing impotence rather than strength.' Discuss, with examples.

5 Is British corporatism dead?

6 'Rational people do not join pressure groups.' Discuss.

7 'In all societies power will tend to be held by a small elite.' Discuss in the British context.

8 'A committee for managing the affairs of the bourgeoisie'. What does this say about government under capitalism?

9 'Pressure groups distort the popular will.' Discuss with examples of government policy.

10 Compare and contrast different theories of power in society.

Topic for debate

This house asserts that direct action is the most effective way for ordinary people to participate in politics today.

Further reading

Baggott, R. (1995) *Pressure Groups Today*.
Up-to-date introductory text.

Bentley, A. F. (1967) *The Process of Government* (first published 1908).
The classic text.

Bottomore, T. (1964) *Elites in Society*.
Good introduction to elite theory.

Grant, W. (1995) *Pressure Groups, Politics and Democracy*, 2nd edn.
A comprehensive introduction, including group activity at the EU level.

Jordan, G. (1991) *The Commercial Lobbyists: Politics for Profit in Britain*.
Authoritative account of the rise of professional lobbying.

Lehmbruch, G. and Schmitter, P. (eds) (1982) *Patterns of Corporatist Policy-Making*.
Comparative insight with some seminal contributions.

Mazey, S. and Richardson, J. (1993) *Lobbying in the European Community*.
Examines the new focus for pressure-group activity.

Miliband, R. (1984) *Capitalist Democracy in Britain*.
A classic neomarxist perspective on power in society.

Olson, M. (1982) *The Rise and Decline of Nations*.
The politics of influence from a public choice theorist.

Scott, J. (1991) *Who Rules Britain?*
Asks if there is still a ruling class in Britain. Traces industrial and financial dynasties and answers 'Yes'.

For light relief

Ben Elton, *Gridlock*.
Comic novel about the nightmarish power of the roads lobby.

Jeremy Paxman, *Friends in High Places*.
Britain's most acerbic inquisitor of the high and mighty making enemies in high places.

Frederick Raphael, *The Glittering Prizes*.
A nostalgic view of a privileged world where success comes as of right to scions of the Establishment.

George Bernard Shaw, *Major Barbara*.
Explores with humour and insight government–industry relations, exposing greed and hypocrisy.

On the net

With its anarchic nature, the internet is a natural medium for all kinds of groups, from the mainstream to the more outlandish, to promote their particular viewpoints and encourage participation in their campaigns. The One World site (http://www.oneworld.org) gives access to over 350 organizations working for global justice, while the two main environmental organizations, Greenpeace (http://www.greenpeace.org.uk) and Friends of the Earth (http://foe.co.uk), concentrate on saving the world. More narrowly, the recently formed Countryside Alliance (http://countryside-alliance.org) promotes the interests of rural people (including field sports). You can also access the sites of the peak organizations representing employers (http://www.cbi.org.uk) and labour (http://www.tuc.org.uk) in their negotiations with government.

Part IV

The Outer Reaches of the State: Worlds beyond Whitehall

The media construction of British politics is generally centralist in orientation; it is around the precincts of Westminster and Whitehall that the heat of policy-making is generated. However, when we refocus through a wider-angle lens we find a variety of institutions which, while responsible for the making and implementation of much state policy, operate with varying degrees of freedom from the central institutions of government. There are a number of reasons for this administration at 'arm's-length'.

- *The evolutionary pattern.* Many important state functions (education, housing, hospitals) grew up at the periphery rather than from the centre.
- *The policy–administration dichotomy.* There is a normative belief that policy-making and implementation should be separated.
- *Commercialism.* When the state becomes involved in commercial activities the traditional institutions and rules are seen as inappropriate.
- *Artistic and technical judgement.* It has been felt that bowler-hatted bureaucrats and popularity-seeking politicians cannot make judgements in dispensing money in areas such as the arts and sciences.
- *Personal morality.* Certain areas of personal morality are felt to be beyond political judgement (such as race relations or film censorship).
- *Freedom.* A fundamental plank of liberal democracy is that some state functions must be politically neutral (such as broadcasting, policing and justice).
- *National security.* Certain matters are kept beyond the eyes and ears not only of Parliament but even of ministers. The security services operate with few restrictions, sometimes at the fringes of legality.
- *Efficiency.* It is more often rational to provide services through locally based bodies able to respond to local conditions.
- *Democracy.* If democracy is to be real, people should have a means to participate in local decision-making.

From the early 1980s the British state was subject to a radical restructuring. Some characterized this as a process of 'hollowing out' (Rhodes 1994), others as 'a casting off of an outer shell of peripheral functions' (Hogwood 1997: 714–15). Much of this was inspired, or justified, by Osborne and Gaebler's *Reinventing Government* (1992). Written in the US context, this argued that traditional public bureaucracies needed invigorating with 'entrepreneurial' values. Some spoke of a 'new public management' movement. Part of this entailed agencification of the civil service (see p. 443). However, much dramatic 'reinvention' took place in the peripheral semi-autonomous zone of the state, involving the nationalized industries, various quangos, local government and the agencies of law and order.

Yet in moving from centre stage we are by no means leaving the world of politics. We shall argue that **arm's-length administration** is often part of a strategy to 'technocratize' important matters out of politics and hence out of the public domain. In addition, we find in the grey, twilight part of the state much scope for the dangerous exercise of political patronage.

Chapter Eighteen

Arm's-length Administration: Quasi-autonomy, Quasi-democracy

We begin exploring the non-Whitehall territory with a constitutional rag-bag defying clear classification and, under the acronym 'quango', sounding more like something Alice might have encountered than part of the machinery of government. Bodies in this category share little in common other than their insulation from the machinery of ministerial control and parliamentary accountability. The chapter is something of a pot-pourri, comprising four main sections. The first introduces the category as a whole, identifying some important subgroups. In the second section we examine a very special group: the institutions comprising the National Health Service. Next we consider the lessons of the largely defunct category of nationalized industries, which were given the special constitutional status of public corporations. Their difficulties and contradictions typify those of quangos in general. The fourth section considers the programme of privatization and the new problems thrown up by the creation of a new generation of special regulatory bodies. We conclude by evaluating the implications of shadowy state territory at the fringes of democracy.

Introducing the Quango

Although not officially recognized in Whitehall, scholars and politicians use the acronym **quango** for Quasi-Autonomous Non-Government Organization. The term is employed rather loosely and often pejoratively; some might prefer the *Daily Telegraph*'s 'Quite Unacceptable And Nasty Government Offshoots'! Officials sometimes call them non-departmental public bodies. An alternative term is QGAs (Quasi-Governmental Agencies), while a report by Democratic Audit catalogued the vast panorama of what it termed 'extra-governmental organizations' (EGOs) (Weir and Hall 1994). Although set up by government, often on a statutory basis, they are bodies operating with some degree of freedom from democratic control and accountability. Usually funded from the national exchequer, they operate in industrial, social, scientific, cultural, economic and artistic areas. They are run by boards appointed by ministers from the nation's trusted worthies; not only 'great and good', they are generally white, middle class and male. Quangos may be broadly classified as follows.

Judicial These are mainly tribunals and inquiries, of which there are many hundreds (pp. 627–9).

Advisory A peculiarly British institution, known variously as advisory councils, working parties, boards, royal commissions, standing conferences or task forces, they are created to examine specific problems and make recommendations, though their use is often seen as a government ploy to avoid action. Classified as temporary or permanent, **advisory bodies** have lain thick on the ground – in 1979, the Pliatzky Report (1980: 1–2) identified over 1,500 but they were cut back under Thatcher. The temporary group includes the large, prestigious royal commissions addressing major issues such as the reform of local government or the police, their deliberations often taking several years and sometimes heralding momentous changes. The permanent category is larger and includes some major bodies advising on matters such as the safety of drugs but many, such as the White Fish Authority, have worked diligently in the cobwebbed backrooms of the state. The Blair government showed a particular predilection for task forces, which were soon looking into a host of policy areas.

Consultative These are corporatist forums such as Neddy, designed to bring together ministers, civil servants and representatives of interests. They had their heyday during the consensus era, declined under Thatcher and began to make a comeback under Blair (see p. 528).

Crown Bodies These are charged with the management of institutions such as the royal palaces, the British Museum, the National Gallery and Kew Gardens.

Commercial After the second world war a special public body was created to operate the nationalized industries: the **public corporation**. Although these industries have largely returned to the private sector, the principle of freeing state bodies to act commercially has advanced since the early 1980s.

Regulatory These agencies protect citizens from abuses such as exploitation, pollution and racial and sexual discrimination. They are common in areas such as hygiene, building standards, safety at work, the use of pesticides and quality of food. Regulation is an alternative to public ownership, particularly in conditions of natural monopoly, and a new generation of regulatory agencies grew up with privatization.

SEFRAS A new kind of body developed from the late 1980s as a result of civil service agencification: the self-financing regulatory agency. These inspect, regulate and award licences to companies, aiming to pay their own way by charging fees. Examples include the Medicines Control Agency, the Data Protection Agency and the Driver and Vehicle Licensing Agency.

*"The committee on women's rights
will now come to order."*

Reproduced by permission of *Punch*

Executive These actually administer some public service: disseminating information (tourist authorities, the Health Education Agency), distributing public
funds (the education funding councils, the Arts Council) or delivering a service
(NHS trusts). Pliatzky identified almost 500, but they became even more evident following the Thatcher creation of a 'new magistracy' (see pp. 572–4 and
Ridley and Watson 1995). Police authorities effectively belong in this category.
If housing associations, grant-maintained schools, colleges and universities are
added, the number of **executive bodies** soars to well over 4,000.

Sick of Democracy: the National Health Service

Although much political activity sees the main goals in the battle for 'who gets
what' in material terms, health is of far greater importance to the quality of our
lives. Yet curiously Britain's National Health Service (NHS), employing more people
than any other organization in Western Europe, accounting for a huge proportion
of the GDP (6.9 per cent in 1995) and likely to be used by virtually every citizen in
their journey from cradle to the grave, was placed at an arm's length from democracy. The explanation for this conundrum lay in the politics of its creation.

> Everyone – rich or poor, man, woman or child – can use it. There are no charges
> . . . no insurance qualifications. But it is not a charity.
>
> Ministry of Health leaflet, on the eve of the birth of the NHS (Feb. 1948)

The wartime consensus

In 1942 the famous Beveridge Report, *Social Insurance and Allied Services*, emerged as the blueprint for the welfare state. It espoused the New Liberal concept of freedom (see p. 31): *positive freedom* from the 'evil giants' of want, ignorance, idleness, disease and squalor in an extended social welfare system. Central to the vision was a comprehensive national health service, available to all, and free at the point of delivery. This model was supported by a broadly based consensus embracing the coalition parties, medical interests and local government. Hospitals had been pioneered by voluntary societies and local government, but during the war a national emergency medical service had brought them together under central government. A 1944 white paper envisaged its peacetime equivalent: a unified state service under local government and coordinated by a health minister. General practitioners (GPs) would retain independent contractor status but a Central Medical Board would control their spatial distribution over the country.

The consensus cracked

However, the passing of the mood of wartime emergency saw a peeling of the consensus wallpaper, revealing cracks in the social wall. Bitter fighting within the health policy community proved the 'chief headache' for Aneurin Bevan, the minister responsible for launching the NHS, and local government was a major loser. The doctors, represented by the British Medical Association (BMA), resented the idea of control by elected councillors and a draconian threat of non-cooperation finally carried the day. The result was a tripartite rather than a unified structure in which only community health functions (clinics and the schools medical service) were to be administered by local government. Hospitals and GP services would be under non-elected Regional Hospital Boards and local Executive Committees appointed by the minister and dominated by medical representatives. In 1974, the NHS was completely sealed off from local democracy, local government reform seeing its community health functions transferred to new Regional and District Health Authorities. These consisted of laypersons, local government nominees and members of the medical profession. The chairperson was the only salaried position, appointment representing a key patronage power for the health secretary.

The laypersons on the health authorities represented local interest groups

> They neither speak as elected representatives nor do they have the expertise of their own officials. And their attitude to the secretary of state and the department is necessarily pretty subservient – they want to keep their jobs.
>
> Barbara Castle (Labour Minister of Health) on health authority chairs,
> *The Castle Diaries 1974–6* (1980)

and voluntary associations. In theory they were to reflect the community in terms of factors like class, gender and race, but membership remained largely a middle-class preserve. Like Adam, they were not encouraged to taste the dangerous fruits from the tree of knowledge, receiving only a few bland documents and given virtually no training (Steel 1984: 37). The local authority nominees represented the local council and gave some semblance of democracy. As for the third category, although Bevan had argued that health authorities were not to represent any special interests, the medical profession demanded a presence on the grounds of expertise. The assumption, perhaps based upon the Hippocratic oath, was that doctors would not act to advance their own interests. Whether Hippocrates has ever revolved in his tomb is a matter for archaeological scholarship rather than political science but the NHS was to serve medical interests extremely well. Compensation for the democratic deficit came in the creation of local Community Health Councils to act as watchdogs, but like the bodies they watched, these too were unelected.

> Physicians of the utmost fame,
> Were called at once; but when they came,
> They answered, as they took their fees,
> 'There is no cure for this disease'.
>
> Hilaire Belloc (1870–1953; British essayist and poet),
> *Cautionary Tales*

The era of welfare corporatism: doctor knows best

The first three decades of the NHS saw the emergence of a closely knit health policy community. Each tier became enmeshed in a web of advisory bodies and set the doctors 'into the concrete of the institutional structure even more firmly than Bevan's design had done' (Klein 1989: 95). Other interests, from drugs companies to food producers, moved in this community, while local authorities and other health interests remained at the periphery (figure 18.1). The power structure resulted in a widespread acceptance of a 'medical model of health'. Reversing the old adage by emphasizing cure rather than prevention, it tended to play down the state's role in reducing social and environmental health hazards through public health measures. However, this comfortable world was to be jolted by the breakdown of the post-war consensus, though the result was to be less rather than more democracy.

The New Right reforms

The NHS proved to have a self-generating appetite for resources, with increasing expectations, an ageing population and undreamed of technological advances. Healers, be they witch doctors or organ transplanters, are venerated

Figure 18.1
The central arena
for health service
politics.

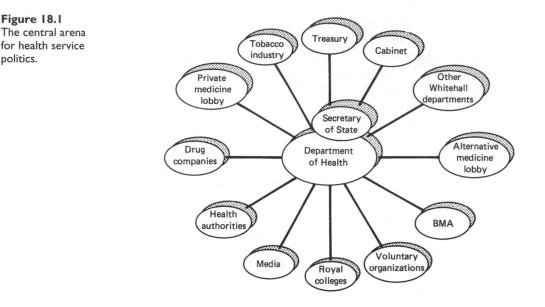

everywhere and doctors calling for resources carried irresistible political weight. Hence the government perceived a fiscal crisis of the state and from the early 1980s determined to reduce the NHS burden. The result was a major structural overhaul which, while challenging medical power, moved the NHS even further from the arms and eyes of democracy.

General management Medical hegemony was challenged in the 1983 report from Roy Griffiths, managing director of Sainsbury's. This advocated 'general management' to replace the doctor-dominated 'consensus management'. Managers, often from the private sector, were to take control at all levels of the service, their decisions reflecting economic criteria. At Whitehall a separation was made between policy-making and management, the latter entrusted to a new NHS Management Executive (NHSME) chaired by a chief executive.

The unhealth industry

Cigarettes provide government with one of their biggest and most reliable sources of revenue: they create tens of thousands of jobs in hard economic times; they present a healthy surplus on the balance of payments; they help the development in Third World countries where tobacco is grown.

Peter Taylor, *The Smoke Ring* (1984: xix)

The internal market Even more fundamental changes were announced in a 1989 white paper, which introduced the principle of the 'internal market' developed by US economist Alain Enthoven (1985). This replaced central direction of resource allocation with competition between health authorities, hospitals, GPs and other health care units, bartering as *providers* and *purchasers* of health care. Legislation made provision for hospitals and community health care units to opt out of health authority control as self-governing NHS trusts run by boards; they constituted a new kind of quango. Large GP practices were able to become 'fundholders', receiving a centrally distributed budget reflecting their patient needs for purchasing care from hospitals.

When Labour came to power in 1997 the internal market and GP fundholding were formally ended. However, the policy showed much continuity with the Conservative reforms, despite changes in terminology. Thus the purchaser/provider split was retained and the NHS was to be primary-care led, with GP group practices specifying their demands on hospitals. A proposal to allow local authority chief officers, rather than elected councillors, to attend health authority meetings did not promise much for local democracy and aroused opposition from the Local Government Association (*Municipal Journal*, 24 April 1998).

Patronage The new trusts enlarged the scope for patronage. In addition, the principle of local government nominees on health authorities was ended, the tendency being to replace them with local businesspeople (Small 1989: 69). The chairpersons were increasingly from among the latter and were given more power. In March 1986 Conservative Central Office carried out a vetting process designed to root out any who had resisted funding cuts; sixty-two were earmarked for non-reappointment (*Guardian*, 19 March 1986). There were also allegations that the government was using appointments to reward contributors to party funds.

A democratic deficit The arm's-length status of the NHS has always promoted concern. Probably no service is more fundamental to people's lives and deserving of democratic control. Community health councils and the creation of a Health Services Ombudsman have not eliminated the democratic deficit. From the beginning there has been a call for local government control, reiterated in the 1979 Merrison Royal Commission on the NHS. In June 1993, David Knowles, president of the Institute of Health Services Management, argued the case for local authorities to work within the internal market set-up by taking over the health authorities' purchasing function (Hunt 1995). In 1995 the independent Commission for Local Democracy (see p. 601) argued for directly elected health authorities. Lord Nolan has suggested that the Audit Commission should publish public interest reports on NHS bodies at its own discretion.

Power in the NHS: who gets healthy, how, when?

The example of the NHS illustrates how the use of quangos has implications for the exercise of power in society. The structure permitted a closed form of corporatism in the early post-war decades which enhanced the medical dominance. Some interpreted this in neo-elitist terms as demonstrating professional power in modern society (Illich 1975: 165). A medical establishment enjoyed wealth and privilege linked through family, educational and social ties to the broader social elite.

> As to the cause of our illness
> One glance at our rags would
> Tell you more. It is the same cause that wears out
> Our bodies and our clothes.
>
> Bertolt Brecht (1898–1956; German dramatist and poet),
> 'A Worker's Speech to a Doctor'

However, the medical model of health accorded well with capitalist interests. Polluting industries imposing mental and physical stress upon workers and even manufacturing products (such as cigarettes, alcohol and 'junk food') known to damage health would not welcome a regulatory preventative regime. A Marxist explanation would see the power of the profession deriving largely from its ability to serve the interests of capital (Navarro 1976). If these interests were to diverge one would get a clearer picture. This happened with the fiscal crisis of the 1970s as welfare expenditure began to threaten profitability; the result was a challenge to medical hegemony. The internal-market policy was made in the absence of health professionals but with the involvement of right-wing think-tanks and business interests. Patronage strengthened these voices at all levels. BMA and royal college objections fell on deaf ears and, by the late 1980s, the once-favoured insiders were beginning to take on the appearance of an outsider group, demonstrating, criticizing ministers and appealing to the public with advertisements.

Nationalizing Industry

Health care was not the only area to be nationalized and placed beyond the conventional mechanism of accountability in the post-war years. Large-scale advances in the state ownership of industry occurred in two waves. The first, immediately following the war, encompassed coal, electricity, gas, rail, road haulage, air transport and steel. (The Bank of England was also nationalized at this time.) The second began in the mid-1960s under both Labour and Conservative governments, largely through state purchase of shares in a wide range of undertakings. The economy was not capitalist but 'mixed'. The motives for state ownership were also mixed, and by no means all anti-capitalist.

Motivations for state ownership

The reasons for **nationalization** were partly ideological principle and partly political expediency, the left being more favourably disposed for a number of reasons.

- *Socialist doctrine*. Nationalization represents an attack on capitalism; central to the Labour Party constitution until expurgated by Blair.
- *Market imperfections*. Keynes showed that the free market did not produce the optimum allocation of resources. Nationalization is one means of regulating the market.
- *Power within society*. Large-scale owners of capital have great political power. Public ownership is a means of strengthening the democratic voice.
- *Protection of workers*. Industrial relations in the coal and rail industries were particularly bad. The state could prove a model employer.
- *Security*. Certain industries were adjudged too important for state security to be left in private hands. Similar considerations applied to atomic energy and the exploration of the North Sea for mineral fuels.
- *Natural monopolies*. Some industries (such as power and railways) were regarded as necessarily monopolistic and therefore the public had to be protected from exploitation.

Although the principle was ideologically anathema to capitalist interests, in practice there were advantages. The owners of outdated plant and machinery were not only relieved of the responsibility for modernization, they received generous compensation. Moreover, in an era that was Keynesian rather than socialist, most industry still remained in private hands and could benefit from state control of the **natural monopolies**. Table 18.1 shows the extent of the mix in the economy on the eve of the collapse of the post-war consensus.

However, in the gestation period the question of management became a key issue and an orthodoxy emerged that this could hardly be entrusted to Whitehall mandarins with little knowledge of industry, trussed in red tape and socialized in a culture of detailed parliamentary accountability. The quest to combine public accountability with commercial freedom led to the evolution of a new kind of agency – the public corporation.

The concept of the public corporation

In 1908 a Port of London Authority had been set up to manage London docks and the Labour government of 1929–31 had created a London Transport Passenger Board; both had considerable autonomy. A prominent figure in establishing the latter was Transport Minister Herbert Morrison, who outlined the model of the public corporation in *Socialism and Transport* (1933). Although relating to government through a sponsoring department, it was not subject to the full rigour of ministerial control or parliamentary accountability. Its management structure would broadly resemble that of a private industrial

Table 18.1 The mixed economy at its height: the share of the big nine nationalized industries in the UK economy, 1975 (percentages of total)

Industry	Output	Employment	Investment
Post Office and Telecommunications	2.8	1.8	4.5
Electricity Board	1.5	0.7	2.9
British Airways	0.3	0.2	0.4
Coal Board	1.5	1.2	0.9
British Rail	1.2	1.0	1.0
National Bus Company	0.2	0.3	0.1
National Freight Corporation	0.2	0.2	–
British Gas	0.8	0.4	1.7
British Steel	0.8	0.9	2.0
Total	9.3	6.7	13.5

Source: Data from McIntosh (1976).

undertaking, the board being appointed by ministerial patronage and responsible not to shareholders but to the nation. The key actors in this set-up were the minister of the sponsoring department, the chair of the board, Parliament, and a set of consumer councils established as watchdogs.

Celestial orbits

Barbara Castle's diaries (1980: 295–6) give an insight into the politics of patronage in the nationalized industries. In 1967, as the sponsoring minister, she wanted to get rid of British Rail Chairman Sir Stanley Raymond. Feeling that it would be politically dangerous to sack him outright she decided she would 'have to blackmail him into resigning'. Prime Minister Wilson chipped in by offering to give him a peerage 'if it will help'. The removal of the chairman was finally effected by making him head of another quango, the Freight Integration Council. Thus do the great and the good move about their celestial orbits.

Problems with the nationalized industries

The key was to combine commercial freedom with public accountability; to secure that most illusory of human desires – the best of both worlds. Ministers were responsible for broad policy but the boards were to be free to make day-to-day management decisions. However, ministers were empowered to intervene in the 'national interest' and this meant that chairmen were to be frustrated in their commercial designs. Factors leading governments to interfere included:

- the initial need to promote rapid post-war economic reconstruction;
- a desire to use the industries for economic management;
- a tendency to emphasize social interest at the expense of commercial performance, leaving some in need of huge government subsidies;
- a tendency to manipulate the industries for political advantage (such as holding down prices before elections).

The result was a blurring of the roles of boards and ministers. Successive attempts to distinguish between broad policy and day-to-day management failed, making it difficult for Parliament to pin ministers down.

State shareholdings

An alternative form of nationalization was to become the main instrument after the initial phase. The principle was by no means new; government had acquired an interest in the Suez Canal in 1875 and shares in British Petroleum (BP) were used to guarantee naval oil supplies during the first world war. Such arrangements were more congenial to private capitalists, allowing maximum managerial independence to company directors.

The most important motive for this wave of nationalization was rescuing capitalist disasters rather than public control over industry. In 1966 Labour established an Industrial Reorganization Corporation (IRC) with capital of £200 million to promote industrial development through state share purchase, but much of its effort went into merely supporting lame ducks. It was abolished in 1970 by the Conservatives but economic problems forced Heath's notorious 'U-turns' and the 1972 Industry Act offered assistance to industries (British Leyland, Cammell Laird and Rolls Royce) considered vital to the economy.

The end of the long boom and the mid-1970s oil crises added to the problems and, returning to office in 1974, Labour established an even more comprehensive policy of state aid. A National Enterprise Board (NEB) was set up in 1975 as a more powerful successor to the IRC and shares were acquired in over twenty companies. However, the Thatcher government again reversed the trend, giving lame ducks specific time limits to restore their plumage and winding down the NEB.

State share purchase: the problems This policy was always controversial and subject to criticism from both political extremes. The left saw it as propping up capitalism at a time when its frailties were being exposed, while the right viewed it as creeping statism. The firms themselves found it difficult to pursue profits when the government was seeking social (employment) as well as commercial objectives. Finally, the passage of substantial funds to the private sector raised constitutional questions of responsibility, since Parliament had little ability to scrutinize private companies (Mitchell 1982).

Privatization: the Full Circle

The 1979 general election introduced a government committed more firmly than any of its predecessors to the view that public corporations should function profitably. State ownership was at a peak, producing 10.5 per cent of GDP, employing some 1.75 million, with an annual turnover of £55 billion and annual investment of around £7.5 billion. As part of the general strategy to reduce the PSBR and control inflation, medium-term financial targets were set and tight restrictions placed on grants and borrowing through setting 'external financing limits'. Ministers took a Pontius Pilate interest in a number of disputes over wages and job losses.

The power of patronage was used to replace Labour appointees with ideological sympathizers. Ian MacGregor was brought (at enormous expense) from the pinnacle of the capitalist world, first to head British Steel and then the National Coal Board. In each case he waged bitter wars with the unions. Sir John King took charge of British Airways and the tough Sir Michael Edwardes became chairman of British Leyland. The Post Office and the Electricity Council were placed under safe ex-civil servants. Yet tinkering with the fundamental problem of reconciling public accountability with commercial efficiency did not go far enough. A radical solution began to brew in the cauldrons of the New Right think-tanks that was to redraft the political agenda – **privatization**.

The case for privatization

Privatization offered the following advantages:

- consumer sovereignty through breaking the state monopolies;
- greater efficiency through the profit motive and shareholder pressure;
- reduced public expenditure through the ending of state subsidies;
- reduction in the PSBR;
- worker ownership through shareholding;
- no political interference in management;
- a sense of *real* ownership for the shareholding public rather than the *illusion* of ownership given by nationalization.

Generally these arguments came from the right, the policy having several political advantages for the Conservatives. By increasing the private sector it served the interests of capital. Furthermore, short-term cash gains from the sales generated colossal government income (almost £90 billion by 1997) to fund tax reductions (figure 18.2). The beneficiaries were largely in the higher tax brackets; those buying the lion's share were twice blessed. In addition, the policy offered a populist power base for the Conservatives by claiming to transform society into a *shareholding democracy*.

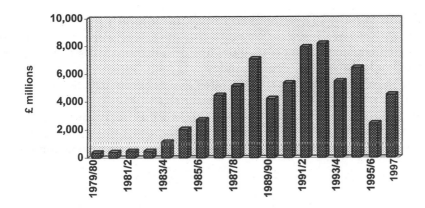

Figure 18.2
Un embarras de richesses?
Privatization proceeds, 1979–1997.

Source: Data from Treasury (1997: table 3.13).

The pattern of privatization

The steel industry had been denationalized by the Conservatives as early as 1951 but had been reclaimed by Labour. In 1970, the Heath government had sounded much rhetoric about reducing the state but the dissolution of the IRC and the sell-off of Thomas Cook and some pubs and a brewery in Carlisle were no more than the thin gruel of symbolism. Even the Labour government made nods in the privatization direction when, during the 1976 sterling crisis, it sold part of the stake in BP to avert some of the public expenditure cuts demanded by the IMF.

In 1979 the government further reduced its BP holding, followed in 1981 by the disposal of its Cable and Wireless holdings as well as its majority stake in British Aerospace. The next year the National Freight Corporation went to a management-led buy-out. A major watershed was reached with the sale of 50 per cent of the equity of British Telecom (BT). At a cost of £4 billion, this was the first large-scale public monopoly to be shifted and much expensive political advertising paid off in a clamorous demand from small investors. Jaguar Cars, Enterprise Oil, Sealink Ferries and the British Gas onshore oil wells followed.

The sale of British Gas in 1986 represented an even bigger operation than BT. It was trumpeted in a massive campaign, with TV commercials, mailshots and newspaper double spreads, taking as its theme the patronizing image of 'Sid', an advertiser's vision of an 'ordinary bloke'. The only cloud on the horizon was the intense opposition to the privatization of the water industry, postponed until after the 1987 general election (ostensibly for 'technical reasons'). The bill eventually went through Parliament in 1989 amidst prolonged controversy.

The 1987 stock-market crash did not stay the fall of the auctioneer's hammer or stem the cascade into the Treasury vaults. Only the Post Office remained stubbornly in the public sector after a government retreat in November 1994 following a backbench revolt. Ten years after gas privatization, the number of private shareholders had more than trebled to 10 million (Miles 1996) and the programme had generated a growth industry in itself. Merchant bankers, stock-brokers, advertisers and lawyers grew fatter and richer from lucrative opportunities to advise, conduct sales and underwrite share issues.

The privatization trawl went well beyond the industrial to the very fabric of the state (figure 18.3). In the civil service and local government, market-testing and compulsory competitive tendering saw a large range of functions (from

Figure 18.3
The privatization
trawl into
the 1990s.

catering to financial services) move into the hands of private companies. In the 1990s one would not have been surprised to wake up to find Britain conducting war by means of a contract with the British Army PLC, or receive a parking ticket from British Police Ltd. After 1992 it became possible to be 'sent down' to a private sector prison rather than one of Her Majesty's. The question asked was not 'Why should this industry be privatized?' but 'Why should it not be?'. For enthusiasts the early years were euphoric, with soaring profits (table 18.2) for the privatized concerns (some with debts written off). However the public were becoming more sceptical. A May 1989 MORI poll showed popular enthusiasm to be waning, almost all the prospective privatizations evoking more hostility than support.

When Labour came to office in 1997 the architecture had been redrawn and, despite promises in opposition, renationalization was ruled out. Indeed, the new government followed the same trajectory, pushing ahead with privatizing the Tote, the Royal Mint and Air Traffic Control and partially privatizing Lon-

> Our air is not for sale.
>
> Andrew Smith MP (Labour transport spokesman) on the proposed sale of Air Traffic Control, speech at Labour Party conference (Oct. 1996)

Table 18.2 Shareholder profits in the privatized industries: average annual percentage increase in share prices from launch date to November 1996

Year of launch	Company	Annual % increase (mean)
1981	British Aerospace	45
	Cable & Wireless	108
1982	Amersham International	39
1983	Associated British Ports	142
1984	Enterprise Oil	18
	BT	15
1986	British Airways	44
	Rolls Royce	5
	British Airports Authority	33
1988	British Steel	4
1989	Water companies	23
1990	Electricity companies	33
1991	National Power	32
	PowerGen	46
	Scottish Hydro-Electric	5
	Scottish Power	8
1992	Forth Ports	128
1993	Northern Ireland Electricity	15
1996	British Energy	14[a]
	Railtrack	31[a]

[a] Share price increase in first 6 months
Source: Data from the *Guardian*, 23 Nov. 1996.

don Underground. There was even to be some privatization of the Post Office, something that even Thatcher had balked at.

Mammoths and fat cats: problems with privatization

Critics saw the policy broadly as serving elite interests: giving to a few that which belonged to the many. Early in the programme Samuel Brittan (1983) had argued that an ethical form of privatization would be the equal distribution of free shares to the public, who already owned them. In addition, the sheer cost of the programme was another cause for concern; at £1.4 billion, rail privatization topped the bill (*Guardian*, 3 Aug. 1998).

In the case of the natural monopolies there are special problems. In April 1995 the combined profits over the previous year for gas, electricity and water jumped by 40 per cent, to a record level estimated at £7.7 billion (Smith 1995), suggesting an abuse of monopoly status. Share prices soared (table 18.2) and public indignation was further roused by share options and fat-cat salaries with which the executives rewarded themselves. A high-profile case was the 75 per cent pay rise (£475,000) received by Cedric Brown, British Gas chief executive, in 1994. Trade and Industry Secretary Michael Heseltine supported this as a tribute to a 'world class company', though unions claimed that profits had been raised through redundancies. The water companies incurred particular public anger as reservoir levels fell while dividends and top salaries rose. In 1995 Yorkshire Water was losing 103 million gallons a day through leakage, almost one-third of the total distributed, while its chairman had enjoyed a pay rise and perks of 169 per cent since privatization; the £11 million being spent to control leaks appeared meagre. Rail operating companies were widely criticized for late running, cancellations and dirty carriages and in 1998 some of their new owners became millionaires by doing no more than selling on their companies, which had been offered at knock-down prices by a government desperate to sell before the general election.

Clearly, the release of these mammoths from state ownership does not remove them from political controversy. Paradoxically it has led to the birth of a new generation of arm's-length agencies. It is to these that we now turn.

Regulating the Natural Monopolies

The moral justification of *laissez-faire* is that the operation of the market will result in the optimum use of society's resources. However, the theory collapses once a **monopoly** emerges. Without competition consumers will be exploited, with poor services and high prices. Hence, when natural monopolies are privatized government must find other ways of protecting the national interest. Significantly, this question of regulation remained well away from the front pages during the privatization process. However, it was to become increasingly salient as problems emerged. Various regulatory instruments are available to government.

Creating competition

In some areas competition can be introduced. For example, the Department of Transport's road construction designs department was hived off to fifteen private consultancy firms and a competitor for BT's business services emerged in the form of Mercury, a consortium formed by the privatized Cable and Wireless, BP and Barclays Merchant Bank. Other cable companies also began to make inroads into the telecommunications market.

However, being less attractive to buyers and likely to lower the sale price, breaking the natural monopolies into competitive units was not initially favoured. Hence, British Aerospace, where fragmentation would have been feasible, was offered as a job lot. The controllers of the industries themselves showed little appetite for such a solution, Sir Dennis Rooke fighting a long and bitter battle to keep British Gas intact. Yet after privatization there were soon loud squeals from industrial users about overcharging. Similarly BT, also kept as a single company, came under fire for lazy monopolistic behaviour, with low service standards and failure to maintain its call-box network.

It became clear that the government would have to use a different model. In 1988 the electricity industry was offered as two separate operations, generation and transmission, the former sold as two companies and the latter parcelled out regionally. Similarly, the water industry was offered as ten separate regional companies and British Rail was broken up by separating track from train operation. The former became Railtrack, freight and parcels services were sold outright and passenger services were leased to a number of private train operating companies by a franchising authority. In early 1996 British Gas split into two, Transco dealing with the pipeline business while British Gas Energy embraced retailing and supply.

However, artificial fragmentation can never produce the degree of competition demanded in the perfect market model. Moreover, even when split up the gravity of natural monopoly tends to draw them back together through amalgamations or hostile takeovers. Vertical integration within the electricity industry began to take place between generators and distributors and there were even mergers between gas and electricity suppliers, threatening a wider monopolistic hold than under public ownership. Hence, state regulation is required.

Existing regulatory machinery

At the time of privatization there were several regulatory instruments available.

- *Regulatory quangos.* A number of watchdog bodies (consumer councils, ombudsmen, the Office of Fair Trading and the Monopolies and Mergers Commission – the MMC) could police the new leviathans. Under the 1998 Competition Act the MMC was to be replaced by a Competition Commission to toughen controls and bring the UK into line with EU competition law. However, with their wider-ranging remits, such bodies cannot develop the necessary level of detailed understanding.

- *Fiscal instruments*. The taxation system can provide carrots and sticks to companies. The objection to this is the heavy reliance upon the concerns themselves for information, together with the problems and costs of analysing it.
- *Special laws*. Although privatized companies are legally indistinguishable from private ones, it is possible to prescribe a special framework within which they operate. However, critics see this as blunting commercial instincts.
- *Special articles of incorporation*. It is possible to amend certain articles of company law, say by outlawing takeovers in early life, proscribing foreign ownership and blocking disposal of assets without ministerial consent. Such arrangements were made in the cases of Cable and Wireless and British Aerospace.
- *Ministerial intervention*. In the final analysis ministers can step in. Thus in April 1996 President of the Board of Trade Ian Lang vetoed proposed takeovers of electrical companies by Powergen even though the MMC had been satisfied.

The golden share A government may retain one special share in a privatized industry. Although nominally only worth £1, the **'golden share'** gives it the power to outvote all others on national-interest issues. This was used from the early days of the privatization programme. However, it is not in the free-market spirit; it could even be used by a left-wing government to restore state control without the inconvenience of renationalization. By 1997 golden shares remained in National Power, PowerGen, British Energy, Rolls Royce, British Aerospace, National Grid, Transco, Cable and Wireless, Scottish Power, Scottish Hydro and Northern Ireland Electric. However, governments seem loath to use them and the 1997 Labour government actually relinquished its golden share in BT.

New regulatory bodies

In 1985, Financial Secretary to the Treasury John Moore (1985: para. 23) declared that in order for privatization to move into the heartlands of the public sector 'novel techniques' should be developed, entailing the creation of ad hoc regulatory agencies. The first to be established was the Office of Telecommunications (OFTEL) to watch over BT by laying down conditions (a universal service including uneconomic rural areas, emergency services and the call-box network) and controlling price increases.

The early auguries did not suggest a firm regime; the government's avowed intention was to keep the regulation as light as possible (de Jonquieres 1983). With a modest staff of only fifty, OFTEL had to rely heavily on BT itself for information. In the gas privatization, chairman Sir Dennis Rooke declaimed:

'Regulation should be as light as possible and cover the smallest area' (Hargreaves and Lawson 1985). When the licence was published in December 1985 it gave a decidedly hands-off role for OFGAS. Apart from abuse of monopoly powers and serious miscalculation, the setting of prices was left entirely to the company, constrained only by a price formula in the domestic market (to be revised every five years):

$$RPI - X + Y$$

where RPI = retail price index;
        X = an arbitrary figure designed to squeeze efficiency from the company;
        Y = an allowance for increasing costs as North Sea supplies become tighter.

These agencies began to proliferate. OFFER was created to regulate the electricity industry and OFLOT to regulate Camelot, the lottery operator. The water industry posed particularly difficult problems because of public health considerations. An Office for Water Services (OFWAT), headed by a director general, was established and the National Rivers Authority (later taken over by the Environment Agency) given a remit to monitor pollution.

Debating regulation

Debate over the role of the new regulatory bodies now replaces that over the public corporations or privatization (see Thatcher 1998). Are the regulators too timid or too interfering? Either way, there is the underlying issue of the accountability of this new breed of unelected officialdom.

Agency capture Regulators are vulnerable to becoming not watchdogs but tame guard-dogs of the industry. Even before the lottery came into operation

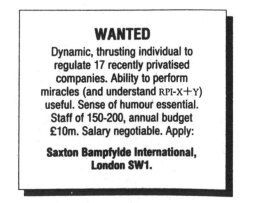

THE ECONOMIST FEBRUARY 25 1989

Friends of the Earth protest outside the Environment Agency to draw attention to the cosy relationship between polluters and regulator

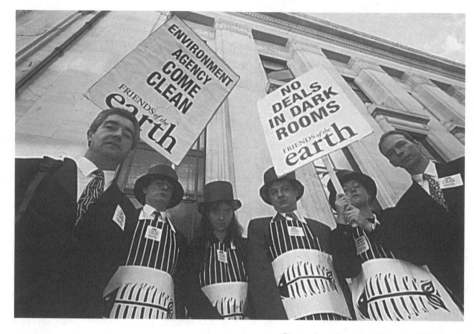

Photo: Jennifer Bates/Friends of the Earth

Camelot was feting the regulator. When Ian Byatt, director general of OFWAT, urged the government in July 1993 to renegotiate EC sewage and drinking water standards for fear of putting up water prices, Friends of the Earth accused him of 'using legitimate public concern about rocketing water bills as an excuse to . . . let the water companies off the hook' (Bannister 1993). Similarly, his advocacy of water meters in May 1998 was seen by critics as supporting companies rather than users. Again, when South West Trains imposed a spate of cancellations in February and March 1997 as a result of its earlier redundancies policy, franchising director John Swift did not impose the £1 million fine threatened. The danger of **agency capture** could be reduced by replacing individual regulators with boards or a regulatory commission covering a number of utilities.

Bullying When regulation bites, the companies can often feel they are being treated unfairly and retaliate. The proposal by gas regulator Claire Spottiswood for new controls aiming to cut some prices by up to 20 per cent within a year led to an angry reaction from the company, with loud protestations and exhortations to shareholders to complain. She was forced to retreat. The vertical integration in the electricity industry was opposed by the regulator but the companies appealed successfully to the MMC; it was left to the minister to override the ruling and shares fell by £1 billion. The kind of reform proposals favoured by the companies include reducing the regulators' discretion, restricting the range of objectives, rights of appeal against decisions, greater openness and a requirement that regulators give reasons for their decisions. Some argue for the removal of specific industry regulators and a strengthened system of competition law, with the utilities being treated like any other company.

Accountability Regulators are appointed through ministerial patronage and, as always, this raises problems of cronyism, politicization and impartiality. Thus, in 1986 the vice-chairman of the Health Education Authority, often concerned with regulating industries likely to harm health, was also director of a market research firm with interests in the tobacco and alcohol industries, and with the distinction of having made the eighth largest company donation to the Conservative Party (*Guardian*, 19 Feb. 1987). More fundamentally, unelected regulators escape democratic accountability. The Comptroller and Auditor General has argued for greater openness and a right of appeal for dissatisfied consumers (National Audit Office 1996: 38–40). Other reform proposals include increased ministerial powers to overrule regulators, defined appointment procedures, greater parliamentary powers over appointments and a select committee to scrutinize the system.

The Government has never made any secret of the fact that it would consider relaxing the law if authorities are having temporary problems . . . The water authorities cannot meet the [anti-pollution] standard overnight.

Department of the Environment spokesman, quoted in the *Daily Telegraph* (12 Nov. 1988)

Government attitude Government ideology will set the climate in which the regime operates. Free-market enthusiasts have little appetite for it, even when health is involved. Speaking in Parliament on the tobacco industry, Thatcher stressed that 'we should be very slow indeed in thinking of imposing statutory regulation' (Goodin 1986). The whole purpose of privatization is to prise the fingers of the state off the ball. In late 1989, when the US giants General Motors and Ford were bidding for Jaguar, Nicholas Ridley, as Industry Secretary, threw in the government's golden share gratis, surprising even the bidders. Under Labour there were suggestions of a tougher line; the water authorities were ordered to reduce leaks, with new targets being set by OFWAT, while the rail regulator's powers were to be reviewed and a tighter licensing regime imposed on Railtrack. However, the 1998 Queen's Speech omitted a bill on a coordinated transport policy, despite lengthy consultations and a major white paper earlier in the year.

The reason the important function of regulation is placed in the hands of non-elected appointees is to take matters out of politics. Perhaps the most important conclusion for students of politics is the impossibility of such an ambition. The networks around different services and functions contain producers, consumers, ministers, officials, MPs and the regulators themselves. In addition, a host of groups call for cleaner air, purer water, better public transport and so on. There are also directives from the EU, itself the centre of a further lobbying network. All is watched by the media, keen to report late trains, polluted drinking water and fat-cat salaries. It is impossible to argue that privatization has depoliticized the operation of the public utilities.

Quangos in Politics

It is clear that a system of government that has set great store by secrecy and evading accountability is attracted by the concept of a shadowy world of quasi-democracy. It is 'a means of farming out government functions based on distrust of the public, the belief that they are best left as passive consumers' (Hirst 1995: 358). Yet any idea that quangos can take matters out of politics is fallacious. Indeed, they tend to operate in acutely sensitive areas: unemployment, race relations, atomic energy, inner-city riots, police violence, local government reform, education, the NHS, university grants, the arts, railways, water supply, broadcasting and so on. Quasi-democracy is criticized from left and right. The left view with misgivings the reduction in accountability while the right fear the insidious extension of state tentacles. Key areas of concern include the following.

Scale The unending debate over what is, or is not, a quango arises in part from attempts by government to minimize and of critics to maximize the number, the latter frequently evoking the term 'explosion'. Conservative MP Philip Holland established a reputation as a quango hunter, publishing *The Quango Explosion* in 1978 and *Quango, Quango, Quango* in 1981. In 1992/3 conservative estimates suggested a figure of 5,573, but if advisory bodies, Next Steps agencies and tribunals were included the figure approached 7,000 (Weir 1995: 306). Scale is not only a question of numbers; in 1992/3 quangos were responsible for some £46.6 billion, almost a third of central government expenditure (Weir 1995: 306).

Accountability The Democratic Audit report revealed the accountability shortcomings of quangos (Weir and Hall 1994). Not subject to the Access to Meetings Acts, most can assemble behind closed doors and their documents need not be exposed to the withering sunlight of democratic scrutiny. Some high-profile cases of mismanagement and corruption (the Welsh Development Agency, Wessex and West Midlands health authorities) linked the world of quasi-democracy with the wider allegations of sleaze and venality gnawing at the heart of the British state.

Representation Generally members are chosen from the great and the good – those white, middle-class, middle-aged males carrying the 'safe pair of hands' kitemark. This bias obviously discriminates against the lower social classes and ethnic minorities. It has also tended to ignore women, though moves to strengthen their representation resulted in an increase from 23 to 30 per cent between 1991 and 1993. By the mid-1990s, NHS trusts comprised 39 per cent women, one-third of them holding the chairs. However, some were wives of prominent Conservatives, likely to represent party and husband rather than women. Moreover, only 2 per cent of TECs were chaired by women and no UDCs (Sperling 1997). Lord Nolan argued that quango membership should be representative of the whole community.

Packing Labour had been criticized for packing public bodies with its supporters; in 1977 the 39 members of the TUC General Council shared 180 public appointments (Stewart 1995: 229). By the 1990s, it was the Conservatives in the dock. Lady Denton, a junior trade and industry minister with responsibility for 804 public appointments, confessed to never knowingly appointing a Labour supporter (*Independent on Sunday*, 23 March 1993). The press became replete with stories of party placemen, while academics (Morgan and Roberts 1993) declared Wales to be under an 'inner circle' of Conservative quango kings.

Rewards: 'snouts in the trough' Critics allege that patronage is used to give rewards. Of the 450 directors on the boards of the companies in the FTSE-100 Index making donations to the Conservative Party, as many as 150 were appointed to quangos. Only 50 appointments had been made from the remaining 480 directors of companies *not* making donations (Fisher 1997). After May 1997, Labour too was accused of cronyism as its supporters, often 'celebrities' in their own right, began to sit on its many task forces. Indeed, its House of Lords reforms promised to create the biggest quango of all.

Who's afraid of the quango?

Concern over quangos led to a House of Commons Public Accounts Committee investigation, its report (1994) lamenting falling standards. The issue was placed within the remit of the Nolan Committee and its detailed recommendations included the following:

- all appointments to executive non-departmental public bodies or NHS bodies should be made after advice from an independent panel;
- at least one-third of a body's membership should be independent;
- an independent Commissioner for Public Appointments should regulate departmental appointments procedures and publish annual reports;
- the Public Appointments Unit should be taken out of the Cabinet Office and placed under the Commissioner;
- all secretaries of state should make annual reports on their appointments;
- candidates should report any political activity undertaken during the previous five years (Committee on Standards in Public Life 1995).

The government's response was to produce a code of practice and create a

Commissioner of Public Appointments situated within the Cabinet Office. With some irony the first incumbent was one of the great and the good – Sir Len Peach, former NHS Chief Executive. He made an early appearance before Parliament's Public Service Committee to state that from July 1996 over 8,000 ministerial appointments to quangos would be made on merit through open competition, and political allegiance would be a matter of public record. For critics this did little to really address the problems of the unelected untouchables of the quango state (Hall and Weir 1996).

> Is he really suggesting that one should engage in a series of silly questions to all the people on quangos as to what their political affiliation might be? Are you or have you ever been a Conservative – is that the sort of society the Hon. Gentleman wants?
>
> John Major on the Nolan Report, quoted in the *Guardian* (12 May 1995)

The problems of quangos have led to a reform debate (see Skelcher 1995), with various models suggested that go beyond the Nolan principles. Although the diversity of quangos means there is unlikely to be any single answer, various ideas have been canvassed.

- More functions given to a revitalized elected local government.
- The establishment of a regional tier of government. It was hoped that Welsh devolution would lead to a 'bonfire of the quangos'.
- Greater powers for the voluntary sector.
- Limitations on the number of public positions an individual may hold.
- Public advertisements for posts.
- A register of interests and affiliation of appointed members.
- A written constitution to reduce executive manipulation.

Whatever happens, quangos are unlikely to become an endangered species. They offer governments some extremely useful facilities, enabling them to wash their hands of embarrassing matters, disclaim responsibility for unpopular policies, evade parliamentary scrutiny and keep areas off the political agenda. Patronage power also provides a large bag of goodies with which to encourage and to repay favours.

We find that the great, the good, and the sometimes pompous move in and out of quangos from the other peaks of social, academic and economic life, names tending to reappear on this or that council, working party and advisory body with some predictability. Virtually all can be counted upon to favour an establishment line; if they develop a maverick streak they can be removed as easily as they were appointed. Even the Director General of the BBC is not immune, as Alasdair Milne found to his cost. Hence there remains in British public life today more than a little whiff of early-nineteenth-century corruption and nepotism (Hood 1979: 40).

Key points

- Quangos are state-created bodies deliberately placed at arm's length from the institutions of democracy. They may be broadly classed as judicial, advisory, consultative, commercial, regulatory and executive.
- There are various reasons for the view that certain areas are best placed outside politics.
- The Thatcher government came to power promising a large-scale cull but ended up presiding over a quango explosion.
- The creation of the NHS as a quasi-autonomous system was an institutional recognition of medical resistance to political control.
- Nationalization of industry represented a major experiment in arm's-length administration.
- The public corporations were intended to combine state control with commercial freedom but were never entirely successful.
- The Thatcher government tried to erase the problems associated with nationalized industries by privatization, but this solution bequeaths a new set of problems of regulatory quangos.
- Quangos survive despite much criticism because governments of all complexions find them politically useful.

Review your understanding of the following terms and concepts

accountability
advisory body
agency capture
arm's-length
   administration
consultative body
EGO
executive body

golden share
health authority
medical model of health
nationalization
natural monopoly
NHS trust
patronage
privatization

public corporation
public health
QGA
quango
regulation
regulatory agency
state shareholding

Assignment

Refer to *Hansard* for 19 November 1998 (either via the internet or in your library). Look for the questions to Dr David Clark on the accountability of non-departmental public bodies (beginning in column 316) and answer the following questions.

Mark (%)

1 How true is the statement that the quango state 'was created by the previous Government'?   20

2   How does Dr Clark propose to ensure greater openness and
     accountability in the operation of quangos?   40
3   Identify the more radical proposal for accountability made by
     Mr Baker. What problems might this pose?   40

Questions for discussion

1   Compare and contrast right-wing and left-wing attitudes towards
     quangos.
2   Discuss the problems associated with the use of patronage in appoint-
     ments to public boards.
3   How has the autonomy of the NHS influenced its policy-making style?
4   'The diversity in quango forms makes it impossible to consider them as
     a single category.' Discuss.
5   Outline the basic structure of the public corporation. Why was such a
     model considered necessary?
6   'Regulation of the natural monopolies must encounter the same conflict
     between commercial pressures and the public interest as did the public
     corporations.' Discuss.
7   Evaluate the role of advisory bodies in British government and politics.
8   Account for the longevity of the quango in British public life.
9   How could the 'quango state' be made more democratic?
10   'The use of quangos brings expertise into the service of the state which
     would not otherwise be available.' Discuss.

Topic for debate

This house believes that while the people of Britain voted for Tony, they did not
vote for his cronies.

Further reading

Bishop, M., Kay, J. and Mayer, C. (eds) (1995) *The Regulatory Challenge*.
Readings on an increasingly important topic.

Holland, P. (1981) *The Governance of Quangos*.
Quangos seen as an insidious extension of the state tentacles.

Jenkins, S. (1995) *Accountable to None: The Tory Nationalisation of Britain*.
Sharp polemic exposing an impatient *dirigisme* leading to the destruction of local government and the extension of the quango state.

Klein, R. (1989) *The Politics of the National Health Service*, 2nd edn.
Lively account stressing how NHS structure serves medical interests.

Weir, S. and Hall, W. (eds) (1994) *Ego Trip: Extra-Governmental Organisations in the United Kingdom and their Accountability*.
Articles on the contemporary quango threat.

For light relief

George Bernard Shaw, *The Doctor's Dilemma*.
Written forty years before the creation of the NHS, this play explores the power of the medical profession.

On the net

http://www.open.gov.uk/ofwat/index.htm
http://www.open.gov.uk/offer/offer.htm
http://www.ofgas.gov.uk
http://www.oftel.gov.uk
http://www.rail-reg.gov.uk
These are just some of the web sites of the regulatory agencies, outlining their activities in curbing the natural monopolies. Using the organizational and functional indexes on the open government site (http://www.open.gov.uk), you can access a vast range of agencies and non-departmental public bodies.

Chapter Nineteen

Local Government: the Grass Roots of Democracy

> The media construction tends to see in Westminster, Whitehall and the Cabinet the holy trinity of political life, but this places the political thermometer too near the radiator of London. Throughout history it is in local rather than central government that ordinary people have encountered much of the reality of the state. A vast range of important services (roads, law and order, education, water supply, housing, hospitals, social security) were pioneered here. This is also a level of government where people can experience democracy at first hand through participation. The first two sections of the chapter examine the nature of local governance and its evolution. The third section considers local politics, identifying the principal actors in the drama. Next comes the issue of management, which leads to the crucial question of who pays the piper. Throughout, we will be conscious that every breath local authorities take is polluted with a Dickensian fog drifting from London and we conclude with the controversial question of central–local relations.

Local Government and Democracy

Defining local government

Local government is the self-government of subnational territorial units of the state. It is found in virtually all developed polities as a complement to central government and is generally seen as a sign of a healthy democracy: a check on state power. Indeed, its elimination is generally taken as a symptom of totalitarianism; it was one of the first casualties of Hitler's rise in Germany. Modern local government has the following characteristics:

- democratic control by locally elected representatives who form the council – a local parliament;
- power to levy taxes;
- clearly delineated territorial boundaries;

- large permanent bureaucracies – local civil services;
- responsibility for a wide range of services;
- a legal *persona* as a **body corporate** – the **local authority** in the name of which all activities are carried out.

Local politics is the process of settling differences and reaching compromises over local issues and can take place in the streets as well as in the town hall. It involves local elections, parties, pressure groups, media and local opinion. It can also involve a world of intrigue within the corridors and debating chambers of the town hall.

What does local government do?

Local authorities are by no means entirely free. They are subject to the legal doctrine of *ultra vires* (beyond the power), which means that, however well intentioned, they cannot exceed those powers given to them by Parliament. An action that may be legal for an individual (say giving children free ice-cream) will not be legal for a council. This is largely an Anglo-Saxon model; in many countries authorities have a 'general competence' to act on their own initiative. There is some mitigation in that Section 111 of the Local Government Act (1972) does allow authorities to do things 'incidental, conducive or calculated to facilitate the discharge of their functions'. However, doubts over how far this may go restrict its application.

Yet local democracy is meaningless if it is not linked with important services. Parish government today is of little more significance than maypole dances performed on village greens. Yet if it had important functions, it would be, as in France, a central feature of communal life. Although interesting the Webbs in the 1920s, few studies of local government stressed the political importance of function; today this complacency is being shattered in politically charged debate.

> The strength of free peoples resides in the local community. Local institutions are to liberty what primary schools are to science.
>
> Alexis de Tocqueville (1805–59; French writer and politician),
> *Democracy in America* (1839)

Classifying functions Local authorities are *multi-functional*, to be distinguished from *ad hoc* single-purpose bodies. They can provide most state services required by ordinary people from womb to tomb, which may be broadly classified as follows:

- *protective* – fire, police, consumer protection;
- *environmental* – roads, transport, planning, refuse collection and recycling;

- *personal* – schools, social services, housing;
- *recreational* – parks, sports facilities, theatres, art galleries, libraries;
- *commercial* – markets, restaurants, transport;
- *promotional* – employment creation, tourism, economic regeneration;
- *regulatory* – implementing regulations and monitoring standards (national and European).

Allocating functions within the state Is there any clear rationale explaining the division of functions between local and central government? There are few theories to underpin such a discussion. A basic premise of any rational explanation must be that services where the special qualities of local government (local knowledge, local participation, sensitivity to the popular will) are of particular importance should be provided locally. However, other rational arguments might dictate otherwise. For example, from a socialist perspective, it would be unfair if the hospitals in one area were better than those in another. This calls for central administration to ensure equality.

In his 'dual state' thesis, Saunders (1984: 25–8) associates the two levels of government with two key functions of the capitalist state: **collective investment** (roads and telecommunications, for example) lying with the centre and **collective consumption** (social services, education, and so on) being provided locally. Hence the great Victorian city governments emerged to house the labour force needed to feed the voracious appetites of the new factories. Public health, law and order, education and other policies all served the same master. They were desperately needed but too unprofitable for the capitalists to provide for themselves. Another reason is political rather than rational; central government may use its power to shape the allocation to its own advantage, perhaps to curb local democracy, seen as a potential rival.

A new magistracy? While it is self-evident that some state functions are best administered within the community, not all lie with the elected authority. Some are provided by unelected local boards or civil service branches. Historically, electricity and gas supply, water and sewerage, hospitals and income maintenance were all in the hands of elected local authorities. Some writers use the term **local governance** to encompass the wider range of local providers. From the 1980s a major development was the passing of much local authority responsibility to unelected bodies, forming what John Stewart (1992, 1995) termed a 'new magistracy' in evocation of an earlier age. This emerged in three principal ways:

- removing local authority appointees from boards upon which they had previously sat;
- transferring functions from local government to appointed quangos;
- allowing bodies to opt out of local authority control.

By the late 1990s local authorities had ceased to make appointments to health authorities or the family health service agencies running the GP services. Self-governing trusts had been created to run hospitals and community health care services. Housing Associations had to a considerable extent taken over public housing while Housing Action Trusts and Urban Development Corporations had assumed many urban development functions. Training and Enterprise Councils were responsible for many educational and economic development responsibilities. Grant-maintained schools, sixth-form colleges, colleges of further education and what were once the polytechnics had come under appointed boards to be financed by nationally appointed funding bodies. Control of the police had been lost to new police authorities (see chapter 21). In 1997 there were over 5,000 local quangos but only 445 local authorities, a situation reflected in the employment pattern (figure 19.1).

What kind of people formed this shadowy magistracy? Estimated at around 66,000, they outnumbered elected councillors by three to one (Hall and Weir 1996). Broadly they shared many of the characteristics of councillors though of course they were not elected; one in ten had stood in a local election (Skelcher and Davies 1996: 20). They have fewer similarities with the populations they serve, tending to come from local business communities. Politically many claimed to be independent but critics alleged Conservative jobbery: 'patronage . . . as well as the desire by the government to see greater private sector involvement, all contribute to the possibility of one set of political interests predominating' (Skelcher and Davies 1996: 20). Critics alleged a 'democratic deficit' and loss of popular accountability. Those serving on the boards look to central government for their reappointment, further promotion, or even a CBE. The local electorate pass no judgement on their stewardship

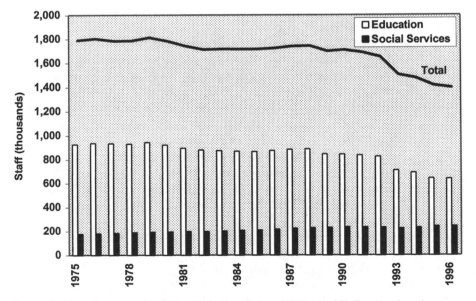

Figure 19.1
Local authority staffing (England only), 1975–1998.

Source: Data from *Local Government Financial Statistics England* (1996: table 8.2). Totals and numbers employed in education and social services departments.

so that the new magistracy has no particular reason to satisfy the communities they serve.

These developments took place on a salami-style basis: a constitutional revolution by stealth resulting in a hotch-potch of organizations with little overall coordination – the very thing the nineteenth-century municipal reformers had sought to eradicate. Local councillors looked to the 1997 Labour government for some restoration of functions. Various consultation documents were followed in July 1998 by a white paper, *Modern Local Government: In Touch with the People* (DETR 1998a). All spoke of the duty of elected local authorities to 'promote the economic, social and environmental well being of their areas'. The white paper promised a scheme of about 100 'beacon councils' as examples to the rest, stating that 'the more a council demonstrates its capacity for effective community leadership, the greater the range of extra powers which should be available'. However, the emphasis was on working in partnership with private agencies rather than returning functions to local government.

Evolution

The spirit of local government

The history of local government extends from early times and from the first there has been a tension between the centre and the locality. Evolution saw a twin-track development, with two traditions – centralist and localist – which continue to colour modern debate.

- The *centralist tradition* arose from the ruling needs of royal authority. The key territorial unit was the **county** (sometimes small kingdoms). Kings would impose local agents, sheriffs and Knights of the Peace, who became Justices of the Peace (JPs), to collect taxes, recruit for the army, keep order and dispense justice.
- The *localist tradition* developed in an organic, evolutionary way as communities sought to provide collective services such as roads and poor relief for themselves in the **parishes** and **boroughs**. Also part of the localist tradition were guilds, which developed from the twelfth century as associations of craftsmen and merchants. Their interests lay in orderly, well-conducted town life and they lent a strong dynamic to civic administration to the extent that guild halls often became in effect town halls.

By the mid-eighteenth century local government was a patchwork counterpane. The centralist and localist traditions had coalesced into a two-tier system, with counties containing parishes of various sizes and status, operating under the eye of the JPs and local landed interests, and boroughs (often controlled by the guilds) with royal charters granting them independence from the county jurisdiction.

The industrial revolution

The social upheavals of industrialization destroyed this pattern as massive urbanization drew people from the countryside to spawn huge teeming communities around the factories, the like of which had never been seen before. This did not necessarily happen in those market boroughs where municipal institutions were well established. Often sleepy rural hamlets were traumatized by a range of social and economic problems quite beyond the administrative capacity of the *ancien régime* of squirearchy and JP. Housing was hastily erected with little thought for comfort or sewerage. Privy middens made the urban ecology better suited to bacteria than to people; disease of epidemic proportions was as much part of life as the dense smoke belching from the factories. Gross inequalities generated by the new economic system promised crime (dark alleys were fertile ground for footpads and prostitutes) and threatened public order. The harrowing spectre of the French Revolution and its aftermath haunted the bourgeoisie, leaving them in a state of perpetual fear of the Frankenstein's monster they had created – a vast new social force, the urban working class.

The initial response was necessarily localist. The capitalists required a strong passive workforce, good roads, freedom from disease, public transport, a degree of education, street lighting and law and order. This was accomplished by establishing a range of ad hoc bodies and reforming the system of local government.

Ad hoc bodies These were essentially boards (often elected by ratepayers) of leading citizens established to provide some particular service (sometimes gaining the statutory right through private Acts of Parliament, sometimes following a public Act). The movement gained momentum, producing a network of boards responsible variously for services such as the poor law, burial, gaols, asylums, sanitation, water supply, roads, street lighting, hospitals, civic improvement and education.

Reform of existing municipal institutions This had a more lasting effect. Following the 1832 Reform Act, which increased the power of the Liberal Party, a number of important official inquiries were conducted into the state of the municipal institutions. The Elizabethan poor law was reformed in 1834 to reflect Benthamite 'less eligibility' principles. An inquiry into local government was deeply critical of administration by the old landed classes and the Municipal Corporations Act (1835) modernized the system with prudent accounting, elections and a widening remit of efficient services.

The truth, Sir, is that we have a chaos as regards authorities, a chaos as regards rates, and a worse chaos than all as regards areas.

G. J. Goschen, House of Commons speech introducing bills to
reform local government (3 April 1871)

Later Local Government Acts (1888 and 1894) extended the modern model to the counties. The original intention was for a unified system covering the whole country based upon counties, with a second (subordinate) tier responsible for certain defined functions. However, the efficient (mainly Liberal) municipal corporations resented losing autonomy to the (mainly Conservative) counties and lobbied strongly to amend the 1888 bill, with the result that all boroughs with populations over 50,000 were permitted to remain independent as county boroughs (figure 19.2). The Act met the unique needs of the huge London conurbation with an entirely new administrative county, under a London County Council (LCC) (figure 19.3), with a second tier of twenty-eight metropolitan boroughs (established in 1899) and three county boroughs. The curious system was a recognition of the facts of social and economic life. It was, as Redlich and Hirst stated in a classic work of 1903, 'a system . . . condemned by logic . . . [but] approved by experience' (1970: 115).

> The County Councils are likely to prove stronger and more exacting than local sanitary authorities have been, though here it must be recollected that manufacturers who find it convenient to pour their refuse into the nearest rivers will be very apt to seek a place on the County Councils.
>
> Leading article in *The Times* on the prospects for the new county councils (23 Oct. 1888)

The 'Golden Age' As the modern pattern became established, the responsibilities of the ad hoc bodies and voluntary societies were gradually taken over (not without resistance and infighting). In addition, the authorities bought out the various utility companies (water, tramways, electricity and gas). With municipal schools, hospitals, bathhouses, parks, improved roads and pave-

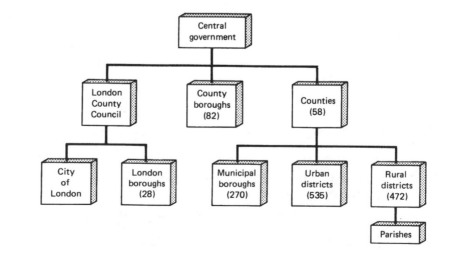

Figure 19.2
The local government structure in England and Wales at the end of the nineteenth century (numbers varied over time).

ments, libraries, museums, art galleries and even public conveniences, the late nineteenth century can be seen as the high point of local government, when the energy of capitalism was harnessed with municipal endeavour. Joseph Chamberlain was able to build a national reputation through his modernization of the city of Birmingham. The economic elite were also its political leaders and Gothic town halls, the cathedrals of the age, testify to the importance placed by the Victorian capitalists upon their municipalities and, indeed, upon themselves.

Into the twentieth century: reappraising the pattern

Although the nineteenth-century boundary pattern reflected the prevailing patterns of life, there was no mechanism to accommodate subsequent demographic development and it remained in a Victorian time warp. As the twentieth century progressed, railways, trunk roads, aeroplanes, telecommunications, radio and television enlarged the territory in which people lived their daily lives. The traditional heavy industries that urbanization had served went into decline and the urban–rural dichotomy was blurred as towns increasingly interacted with their hinterlands.

Figure 19.3
The Greater
London reforms.

Reforming the Great Wen The problems of London were the most acute; the LCC area and surrounding counties experienced enormous population growth, imposing heavy housing demand and traffic congestion. In 1957 the Conservative government set up a Royal Commission under Sir Edwin Herbert to drive through a wall of intransigence erected by the local authorities and the Labour Party (fearing loss of its control over the LCC). This recommended a drastic redrawing of the 1888 boundaries, massively expanding the area from 75,000 to 510,000 acres, raising the population from just over 3 million to well over 8 million, and engulfing parts of Kent, Surrey and Essex as well as the whole of Middlesex (figure 19.3). The newly staked territory would be divided into boroughs, with functions shared between two tiers. In 1963 a new Greater London Council (GLC) emerged with responsibility for area-wide functions (housing, major roads and traffic management), soon gaining public transport by taking over the London Passenger Transport Executive.

The 1974 reform In 1964 Labour came to office and Richard Crossman, Minister of Housing and Local Government, set up the Royal Commission on Local Government chaired by mandarin Lord Redcliffe-Maud. Reporting in 1969, it criticized the complex maze of over a thousand authorities, recommending its replacement with a simple **unitary system** (figure 19.4). However, the 1970 general election gave an unexpected victory to the Conservatives, who sniffed out a number of malodorous political rats in the scheme. In particular, a single-tier model, integrating rural areas with the densely populated urban strongholds, risked the new areas falling under Labour control. In a new white paper, the government recommended preserving the two-tier principle.

The result was the Local Government Act (1972) and in 1974 the 58 counties of England and Wales were recast in the form of 47 shire counties and 6 metropolitan counties covering the major conurbations of Greater Manchester,

Figure 19.4
Redcliffe-Maud's recommended structure and the 'city-region' alternative proposed by dissenting commission member Derek Senior.

Merseyside, Tyne and Wear, West Yorkshire, South Yorkshire and the West Midlands. With populations of 1–2.7 million, these were based on the GLC model. For those favouring radical nostrums these reforms were seen as a missed opportunity of monumental proportions. The new counties were remote and many ancient county boroughs were relegated to district status, robbed of prestige and power. The vital functions of water supply, sewerage and personal health were lost to new water and health authorities.

A further revision was even more overtly political. The metropolitan counties and the GLC were seen during the 1980s as hotbeds of socialist insurrection. Conservative patience finally snapped and the decision was taken to 'streamline' them (Department of the Environment 1983). This meant abolition, their functions being absorbed by their districts, which became single-tier authorities, and by appointed boards. London became unique in the world as a capital city without a strategic authority.

Wiping away the tiers

During the 1980s, changes in capitalist production patterns (large-scale undertakings replaced by smaller, more flexible units – post-Fordism) had led to a process of *counterurbanization* in which people and industries were deserting the cities for smaller towns. The local government map was again lagging behind the reality of life. It was Michael Heseltine who placed structural reform back on the agenda. At the fall of Thatcher he made it part of his party leadership manifesto, continuing the drive as Major's Environment Secretary. In 1992 a Local Government Commission was established under Sir John Banham, while Wales and Scotland were to be examined by their respective Secretaries of State. The government's hope was that reform would end 'Labour's perpetual domination of the massive Strathclyde region of Scotland, of Derbyshire, Nottinghamshire, Humberside and their like and their replacement by either Conservative winnable, or at least smaller and less provocative, unitary councils' (Game 1997: 6).

However, things did not go according to plan. The commissioners worked on the basis of local consultation and opinion polling.

Stage 1: research to ascertain local feelings in each community.
Stage 2: draft plans produced.
Stage 3: further consultation on the proposals.

The second-stage proposals varied according to demography, local opinion and reorganization costs; some were two-tier, some hybrid but 99 were unitary. However, when returned to in stage 3, people showed a marked preference for the status quo, as did many Conservative MPs in the shires. Hence the number of proposed unitary authorities was cut to 38, angering the government, with its preference for a unitary structure. Sir John was sacked by

Environment Secretary John Gummer and the process reopened for 21 of the review areas under a new chairman, Sir David Cooksey. With less weight placed on public opinion (Game 1997: 8–9), the final result was eight more unitary areas.

On 1 April 1996 the move to a unitary system was made in Scotland and Wales, the counties (such as Gwent) and regions (including Strathclyde) disappearing overnight. Sir David Steel declared the proposals the most corrupt he had ever encountered. For England, the result was more disparate and emerged gradually. By 1998 there were 34 counties divided into 238 districts and 46 new unitary authorities (table 19.1). The government claimed that services would be closer to the citizen but job losses of over 7,000 were foreseen (*Local Government Chronicle*, 29 March 1996). There had been little rationality in the process. Goals and the means of achieving them were fuzzy, clouded by the vast and changing number of participants (Stoker 1993: 4). One commentator pondered whether the whole exercise was a government smoke-screen to obscure a fundamental weakening of local government (Leach 1993: 35). In addition, the decline in the number of authorities reduced the number of councillors by almost a third; the ratio to population already compared unfavourably with other European countries (see figure 19.6).

Full circle London and the metropolitan boroughs (already unitary) had remained untouched. However, the great wheel of reform moved to complete a circle when, on 7 May 1998, the Labour government held a referendum on a new elected strategic top-tier authority for the Greater London area – effectively restoring the GLC and, even more radically, introducing an elected mayor (see p. 591). Supported by the three main political parties, the people voted 'Yes'. The issue was not seen as particularly controversial and turnout was distinctly underwhelming.

Table 19.1 The decline in the number of local authorities, 1994–1998

| | England | | | | | | | | |
| | Non-metropolitan | | | Metropolitan | | | | | |
Year	Counties	Districts	New unitaries	London	Metrop. boroughs	Scotland	Wales	NI	Total
1994	39	296	0	33	36	65	45	26	540
1995	38	294	1	33	36	65	45	26	538
1996	35	274	14	33	36	32	22	26	472
1997	35	260	27	33	36	32	22	26	471
1998	34	238	46	33	36	32	22	26	467

Almost forty years of structural reforms had done little to revitalize local government. Structure was probably never the real problem, which was the relationship between local and central government (Leach 1998). We return to this later.

The Local Political Environment

Each local authority is a miniature political system populated by politicians, bureaucracies, electorates, parties and interest groups.

The council

Sitting as local parliaments, councils are formally the linchpins of local politics. Full meetings in the council chamber usually take place once a month although, like Parliament, any idea that this is a decision-making body is a myth. Much of the work is done in committees. Today many council chambers split along party lines, disciplined Westminster-style voting reducing many to backbencher status. However, unlike their central counterparts, officials are legally responsible to the full council, not merely the ruling party. This has created a different working culture and, as we shall see below, is an aspect where change is expected.

Choosing councillors: local elections

Local elections are of great constitutional significance. Dicey justified parliamentary supremacy on the basis of the popular election and, unlike any other

Municipal pomp: the first council of the Royal Borough of Kensington – elected November, 1900

Source: Mary Evans Picture Library

state actors, councillors can claim a similar legitimacy. They serve four-year terms and are elected by first-past-the-post to represent subdivisions of the area (wards), which often return three members. Counties, London boroughs, some unitary and shire districts, and all parishes have whole council elections every four years. Metropolitan districts, some unitary authorities and some shire districts have elections by thirds, electing one-third of the council each time, with three elections in every four-year cycle.

Local electoral behaviour Local electoral behaviour betrays the centralism within British politics (Newton 1976: 19). People often cast a judgement on central government and the media tends to emphasize this aspect. Because national governments are often at their lowest ebb in mid-term, local elections tend to show a swing to the opposition party at this time. Hence, the unusually long period of Conservative government subjected the party to a painful near death by a thousand cuts at local elections, with heavy losses (often to the Liberal Democrats) in their traditional south-eastern heartlands. In 1996 they were left bereft of any representation whatsoever on more than fifty councils and, on many others, including six metropolitan authorities, they were down to one solitary member. After the May 1997 local elections there was serious doubt for the party's local future and the door stood ajar for a Liberal Democrat surge to become the principal municipal opposition (Rallings and Thrasher 1997).

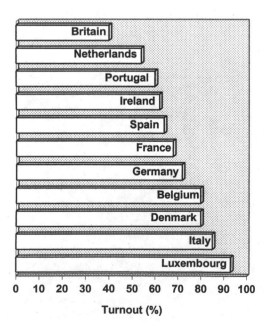

Figure 19.5
Average turnout in sub-national elections in the EU.

Source: Data from Rallings and Thrasher (1996).

Turnout A much-discussed issue is the relatively low turnout (often below 40 per cent), particularly in comparison with other EU countries (figure 19.5). Those favouring centralism invariably take this as evidence that people do not want local democracy. However, in many areas one party enjoys so entrenched a position that a rational voter would not bother to vote. In urban areas Labour dominates while Conservatives have traditionally had green wellies securely planted in the mud of the shires. Lack of publicity, the rise of the 'new magistracy' and central domination also help to explain low turnouts. A further factor is the relatively large size of ward populations (figure 19.6). Rallings and Thrasher (1994) conclude that factors helping to increase turnout include a close contest, elections by thirds, single-member wards, small ward populations and middle-class social profiles. However, these effects were very small, suggesting deeper causes than electoral arrangements.

High turnout is generally seen as a sign of a healthy democracy and the 1997 Labour government opened debate on ways to improve matters. Various suggestions have been canvassed such as the following:

- annual election (by thirds) in *all* authorities;
- more effective means of registering voters;
- mobile polling stations located at places of work, colleges, hospitals, super-markets, railway stations and other places where people are concentrated;
- electronic voting;
- weekend polling;
- proportional representation.

The reform that might prove most significant is proportional representation, which would produce more close contests (Rallings and Thrasher 1994). However, a February 1998 consultation document steered clear of this, arguing that 'changes to the voting system are not a panacea for the current weaknesses in local government'.

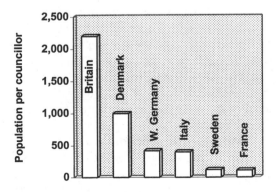

Figure 19.6
Ratio of councillors to population in selected West European countries, 1994.

Source: Data from Wilson (1994).

Beyond the ballot box It is also possible to increase popular interest through various other forms of participation including:

- citizens' juries, bringing together groups of twelve to sixteen selected as representative of the community to consider an issue in depth (usually over three to five days);
- focus groups of approximately twelve to twenty people brought together to give in-depth responses to a particular question;
- deliberative opinion polls involving debate on an issue prior to voting;
- standing citizens' panels comprising a stable sample, statistically representative of the population, to act as sounding boards;
- area-based neighbourhood committees;
- interest- and user-group forums;
- tenants' and residents' groups;
- referendums;
- public question times at council meetings;
- interactive technology using the internet to inform and ascertain people's views.

Such methods bear much resemblance to market research. In opposition the Labour Party had made extensive use of them in tailoring its popular appeal and saw a continuing use for them in government. The 1998 white paper stressed councils' 'duty to consult local people about plans and services' and promised 'power to hold local referendums'. Indeed, several councils had been pioneering such approaches long before the white paper.

The calibre of councillors The question of councillors' calibre is frequently addressed (it is less commonly asked about MPs). The subtext of this enquiry suggests a traditional elite suspicion of the entry into politics of ordinary folk: like the dog walking upright, an unnatural occurrence requiring some explanation. These issues were addressed by the Maud Committee on management in local government (1967) and the Widdicombe Committee (1986a) (see also Barron et al. 1991).

The belief that the calibre of councillors has fallen since the nineteenth century unites middle-class politicians, academics and Whitehall mandarins. It has two basic strands – *class* and *centralism*. The class case notes the retreat of the old landed and industrial elites from local affairs. Academic case studies (such as Birch 1959) argued that the managerial revolution in British capitalism meant that local industry was no longer controlled by local people, separating economic leadership from political leadership to the detriment of quality. It was this local vacuum that allowed socialist activists to enter politics. Hence the lament is in part an attack on increased mass participation (Kingdom 1991: 119–36). The centralist case, put by J. S. Mill amongst others, is that local activists lack the sophistication of their Westminster counterparts. This concern is certainly not dead. In 1998 Labour introduced interviews and tests for sitting and would-be councillors. Thus in October 1998 Rotherham mayor Ron

Windle, despite over twenty years' council service, was one of those who failed the test and agreed not to stand for re-election.

> Labour representatives usually make excellent councillors, because they are much more severely criticised than their middle-class colleagues. It is possible for a middle-class councillor to sit on a municipality for twenty years in a condition of half-drunken stupor without exposure and defeat at the polls; but Labour councillors receive no such indulgence.
>
> George Bernard Shaw, *The Commonsense of Municipal Trading* (1908)

A new breed The 1974 local government reform signalled a change in the composition of many urban councils and a new breed of councillor emerged – younger, more self-confident and better educated. They began to challenge some of the traditional expectations during the 1980s as a New Urban Left movement. A number of councillors in all parties became well known through news and current affairs programmes and chat shows, going on to pursue parliamentary careers. John Major himself had risen from humble origins through the municipal ranks.

Political parties

Although modern local government is dominated by parties, study of them has been rather neglected. The Maud Report (1967) went so far as to conduct a survey on whether or not councillors belonged to parties but did not consider it necessary to ask *which* party, leaving the data antiseptically apolitical. The Bains Report (1972) was reticent on the subject but where it did speak it suggested parties undermined the 'efficiency and morale' of the officers (1972: 37). However, by 1986 the Widdicombe Committee was able to report high levels of party dominance in the town halls, with strict party-line voting in council and committee (1986b: tables 2.3 and 2.5).

Opponents of local parties often evoke a mythical age when independents supposedly ran councils, yet local parties have long existed. Even before the nineteenth-century reforms, electoral battles would take place to secure control of both ad hoc boards and boroughs. However, it was Labour, without the advantages of wealth and position, that needed local organization. This was deeply feared; the old Liberal and Conservative adversaries sometimes formed anti-Labour alliances, behaving like Tweedledum and Tweedledee when confronted by a

> monstrous crow as black as a tar-barrel,
> Which frightened both our heroes so,
> They quite forgot their quarrel
>
> (Lewis Carroll, *Through the Looking-Glass*: ch. 4)

Local national parties Today the term 'local party' is largely a misnomer. Although some are genuinely local, most are effectively branches of national parties, the same army of canvassers fighting both local and parliamentary elections. This has three compelling centralizing implications:

- close ideological identification between national and local politics;
- local politicians often look to the national party for inspiration and guidance;
- national leaders expect to dominate local parties, even suspending the membership of councillors of whom they disapprove.

However, local parties can sometimes be ideologically more extreme. In the 1980s, a tough breed of New Right councillors (as in Bradford and Westminster) seemed intent on outdoing their central counterparts in 'dryness', while local socialism moved further to the left than the Westminster party. Local Liberal Democrat parties tend to be less ideologically focused and more pragmatically active in community issues.

Party animals Most politically active people operate through parties. The impact on local politics can be examined at two levels. Within the community they can act as catalysts, mobilizing electorates, educating the public, stimulating interest in issues, improving accountability, aggregating and articulating interests, recruiting members and promoting citizen participation. Within the town hall the language is of party control and discipline. Such domination, particularly in urban areas, increased considerably after the 1974 reorganization and is manifest in a number of ways.

- *The party group*. The local government equivalent of a parliamentary party, groups can meet behind closed doors to plan strategy.
- *Council committees*. These generally reflect the balance in the council chamber, all policy carrying the stamp of the majority party.
- *Chairs*. Analogous to ministers, the committee chairpersons have traditionally been powerful figures. The majority party can monopolize these positions.
- *Local 'Cabinets'*. Senior councillors from the majority party can form a Policy and Resources Committee, rather like a Westminster-style Cabinet.
- *Council leaders*. Similarly, the majority party leader can become a kind of local prime minister.
- *Political appointments*. Officers and advisers can be chosen with sympathetic views.

The establishment of the Widdicombe Committee on the Conduct of Local Authority Business was prompted by concern over what was seen as excessive party politicization. It reported in 1986 with legislation following in 1989. This limited party dominance in certain ways by extending the rights of minority parties, limiting the use of political advisers to one per party and ending a practice known as 'twin-tracking' whereby leading councillors could effectively become full-timers by holding sinecures in friendly adjacent authorities.

No overall control Recent years have seen an increase in the number of 'hung councils', largely resulting from the Liberal Democrat surge at the expense of the Conservatives. Here the parties must work together. Sometimes a formal coalition between two or more parties will see committee chairs shared and even cross-party agreement on policy. However, in most cases the largest party takes the lead, holding the chairs but making policy concessions to other parties. In a minority of cases no effective power-sharing arrangement is found and the result is prolonged wrangling (Leach and Stewart 1992).

Local interest groups

In several respects local interest group behaviour resembles that at national level. Although only a small proportion may be active at any time, the potential is enormous; Newton identified over 4,000 organizations in Birmingham alone (1976: 38). The rise of single-issue politics from the 1980s has added to the number. Local groups seek channels of access to officers, leading councillors, backbench councillors and local opinion. As with groups operating in the central government arena, there are insiders and outsiders and evidence of pluralism, corporatism and elitism.

Insiders This category includes chambers of commerce, companies, professional bodies and sometimes trade unions. Saunders (1980) showed councillors of the London borough of Croydon hand in glove with private business interests in facilitating the commercial development of the town centre, confirming Dearlove's findings in Kensington and Chelsea (1973). Here we find local corporatism of the 'gin-and-tonic' kind. However, councils are not always captured exclusively by capitalist interests. In Sheffield, for example, the local trade unions, through the Trades and Labour Council, for long enjoyed a close relationship with councillors (Hampton 1970). But councils cannot ignore the structural imperatives of locally based capitalism, particularly if they are concerned about employment. By the late 1990s Labour councils were offering incentives to manufacturers and retailers to set up camp in their business parks and development sites.

Outsiders Movements representing squatters, ethnic minorities, one-parent families and other dispossessed sections of society can all be on the outside when the municipal banquets are held. Radical groups concerned with, say, environmental issues, may also encounter the cold face of officialdom. Even citizens' groups can be excluded in favour of establishment interests in areas such as housing (Dunleavy 1981). Although great efforts were made by left-wing councils to work with the underprivileged during the 1980s, they were often branded the 'loony left', suffering at the hands of the media and the modernizing wing of their own party.

The extent to which local groups play a part in policy-making is conditioned by the central–local government relationship. Sometimes it is better for a group to turn attention to Westminster or even Brussels. As Cockburn's study of Lambeth noted: 'Deals that matter most to [local capitalist interests] over taxation and employment policy, grants and control, are deals done at Westminster and Whitehall' (1977: 45).

'Yes Councillor': municipal mandarins

Local government has traditionally worked through large permanent bureaucracies, raising the Weberian problem of the dictatorship of the official. Formally, councillors make policies which the officers implement, but in practice matters are more complex. Councillors are essentially laypeople while the officers are bureaucrats with all the tricks of a poor man's Sir Humphrey Appleby. Indeed, the bureaucratic threat can be greater than that in Whitehall. Ministers are full-time politicians while most councillors are part-timers. Moreover, unlike civil servants, the top administrators are not *generalists* but professionally qualified *specialists*, their authority enhanced by professional associations.

The view of the expert can become too narrow. Professional enthusiasm can carry the expert beyond the bounds of good judgement, and 'Bumbledom' can be a real danger . . . The control of the expert by the amateur representing his fellow citizens is the key to the whole of our system of government.

Report of the Royal Commission on Local Government in Greater London, 1957–60, Cmnd 1194 (1960)

There is often an underlying class dimension. Officials are generally middle class and much of their work entails informal consultation with local elites, where they 'believe that they are behaving quite properly and [do] . . . not see that they are consulting a minority opinion' (Hill 1974: 87). Some local bureaucrats resent working-class councillors, whom they see as managers *manqué*, with delusions of grandeur (Henney 1984: 321–41). As in other parts of the state, the culture is male-dominated although women's particular managerial skills are increasingly recognized in some authorities (Maddock 1993).

Local bureaucrats can sometimes be Whitehall Trojan horses through informal networks. Councillors have discovered 'moles' keeping civil servants informed about their plans. In addition, a constant flow of demands and regulations, in the form of official circulars, emanates from Whitehall and Brussels, setting standards and telling officials how to proceed under particular circumstances. The councillor–officer relationship takes us to the heart of a key modern debate about local authority management.

In general we suffer from too much government – especially local government.

Norman Tebbit, *Unfinished Business* (1993)

Management and Leadership

The traditional style of management in local government entailed departments responsible for different services headed by chief officers and responsible to council committees. Post-war critics have alleged this to be cumbersome and lacking central control and direction, the issue of **corporate management** becoming a particularly salient area of debate in the 1960s. To the reformers managerial issues often seemed more important than democracy; a Committee of Enquiry under Whitehall mandarin Sir John Maud (1967: vol. I, p. 68) recommended more centralized structures, asserting that 'the local administration of public services is essential, that the organs of administration should be democratically elected bodies is not'. The report of the officer-dominated Bains Committee (1972) recommended that the key locus of power within each authority should be a *management team* of chief officers, a *policy and resources committee* of senior councillors and a *chief executive*, rather like the managing director of a private company (figure 19.7). A hymn to bureaucracy, the report warned councillors that 'the skilled professional officer is not just a servant who is paid to do as he is told' (1972: 8).

Enthusiasm for corporate management peaked in the 1970s. In the changed climate of the 1980s, 'New Public Management' became a recognizable inter-

Figure 19.7
The Bains-style management structure.

national movement (Lowndes 1997) which suggested that mere tinkering with age-old machinery would not suffice (Hambleton 1996: 94). Questioning the traditional basis of local government management the New Right regime introduced the concept of the 'enabling authority', the implications of which went to the very nature of local democracy.

The enabling authority: government by contract

The fact that local government is responsible for a service does not necessarily mean it should deliver it; responsibility may be '**contracted out**' to the private or voluntary sectors. Such a practice was by no means new but, following the 1988 Local Government Act, it became a principal goal of central government policy, with compulsory competitive tendering (CCT) required for an ever-widening range of functions, from refuse collection to professional, legal and accounting responsibilities. A foretaste of the market-testing wave to hit civil servants, it meant that council employees had to compete with the private sector. Sharing the same roots as privatization the policy had a clearly ideological thrust and was strongly advocated by New Right think-tanks (Greenwood and Wilson 1994: 406).

Local responses varied with political disposition. Conservative flagships, such as Westminster, were enthusiastic while others resisted, preferring to award contracts to the 'in-house' teams. Yet in virtually all authorities the culture was changed: officials were placed in competitive relationships, some becoming contractors and others providers (Audit Commission 1993b). The policy of 'care in the community' coming into force in April 1993 added impetus by asking local authorities to make use of private and voluntary-sector residential homes in taking over NHS responsibility for a range of patient categories, including the chronically sick, the elderly and the physically and mentally handicapped. In 1996 the enabling principle was extended to the provision of social services.

Supporters argued that services would cost less and that contracts and various citizen's charters would safeguard the public interest. Critics, including the local authority associations and various professional bodies, feared job losses, worsening conditions of work, damage to the corporate approach and a loss of accountability. There were also worries that the search for profit would lower the quality of services and increase risks of fraud and corruption (Doig 1995: 104).

Prior to the 1997 general election the government was promising draconian measures to press CCT further. However, although disagreeing with the approach in opposition, Labour in government maintained the principle, renaming it 'Best Value' and requiring authorities to consider new national performance indicators when awarding contracts.

We can't go on meeting like this

There were profound managerial implications in the new approach. CCT was largely a job for lawyers and accountants, with little room for social or democratic considerations; the councillor's job could more easily be seen as part-time. Indeed, Conservative minister Nicholas Ridley (1988) envisaged them meeting only a few times a year.

In September 1990 the Audit Commission published *We Can't Go On Meeting Like This*, its punning title condemning labyrinthine committee structures that were ill equipped for speedy decision-making. Environment Secretary Michael Heseltine followed this up with a consultation document on internal management (Department of the Environment 1991). Its broad thrust fitted snugly with the enabling vision, arguing that the control and coordination of large workforces would no longer be the management task. It looked for speedy decision-making at the top, with local cabinets, appointed council managers or directly-elected US-style mayors with high public profiles and thrusting leadership styles.

Heseltine's successors tried to continue the thrust. A report issued by John Gummer (Department of the Environment 1993) suggested that leaders were to concentrate on policy while most councillors would devote rather more time to their constituency roles, if not their families. In addition, the government opened the radical possibility of forms of management not permitted under current legislation which might be tested in pilot authorities. Four models were canvassed:

- the single-party executive committee with delegated powers over strategy subject to full council scrutiny;
- the leader–member system with power delegated to key individuals rather than a collective executive;
- the cabinet system formed by the leaders of the majority party acting with collective and individual responsibility;
- the legally separate political executive, perhaps directly elected and with power held independently of the council.

Towards elected mayors The last of these pointed to directly **elected mayors,** a radical possibility offering clear mandates and perhaps more popular interest. The *Municipal Journal* (14 June 1996) reported an astonishing 70 per cent of the public supporting the principle. However, the government fought shy of the prospect of all-powerful Ken Livingstone clones in the town halls. Yet a head of steam was building up, with support from an independent Commission for Local Democracy (see p. 601) and the Labour Party. In its February 1998 consultation paper (Department of the Environment, Transport and the Regions 1998b: para 5.14), the Labour government declared itself 'very attracted to the model of a strong executive directly elected mayor'.

The Greater London area, without an elected authority since GLC abolition, was seen as a particularly suitable launch-pad. After much speculation proposals emerged for an assembly elected by the additional member system, with fourteen members elected by first-past-the-post and eleven from London-wide party lists, plus a mayor elected by the supplementary vote system. The mayor, with three or four deputies and a bureaucracy of around 250 (much smaller than the 25,000 serving the old GLC), would set policy objectives and an annual budget of some £3.3 billion to be approved by the assembly. Responsibilities would include public transport, the fire brigade, strategic planning, trunk roads, traffic management, the ambulance service and possibly the arts. In addition, the Metropolitan Police force would cease to be the responsibility of the home secretary and come within the system (p. 641). In the USA, elected mayors are powerful figures (Elcock 1995) and, with a salary in excess of £100,000 per annum, the expectation was that formidable personalities would be attracted to the new position (Lord Archer, Ken Livingstone and Tony Banks, along with other non-political figures, featured in speculations).

This represented a radical break with tradition and there was speculation that it would be extended to other major cities. In April 1997, with government approval, a private member's bill (the Hunt Bill) had been introduced in the Lords to allow local authorities to make such experiments but it was talked out by Conservatives on its second Commons reading on the grounds that so important a measure should not have been introduced in the other place. Subsequently a July 1998 white paper (DETR 1998a) required all 494 councils to separate councillors' decision-making and local representative roles. They were to be given three options:

- a directly elected executive mayor who can then appoint a cabinet from among councillors;
- a leader elected by the council who then appoints a cabinet;
- a directly elected mayor working in tandem with a full-time manager appointed by the council.

Councils choosing elected mayors would need public support through a referendum. If councillors were to reject such a system, local people would be able to demand a referendum.

The fear of the Local Government Association (the LGA, representing the local authorities) was that so powerful a position would downgrade the role and status of other councillors. Indeed, the February 1998 white paper had noted that 'being a "backbench" councillor . . . could be less time-consuming' (DETR 1998b: para 5.21) – like a Westminster backbencher, scrutinizing the executive and holding constituency surgeries. For other critics the divide between the policy and constituency roles was itself artificial (Wilson and Game 1994: 318). Moreover, there seemed little argument to show why speedy decisions would be better decisions.

Finance

The world of local government finance is mysterious and arcane. However, its study provides an important key to our understanding for nothing more clearly betokens local government's relationship with the centre. Local expenditure (figure 19.8b) is by definition public expenditure (comprising around 25 per cent of the total) and any central government will take great interest. The scale (£72 billion in 1994/5) is huge, for the services traditionally provided tend to be labour intensive, with no easy technological routes to savings. From the 1980s central government pursued local government like a Victorian father cursed with a profligate son.

Gross expenditure falls into two categories.

- *Capital expenditure* covers items of lasting value.
- *Revenue expenditure* covers current expenditure incurred in the running of services (payments to contractors, wages) and non-current expenditure (loan charges).

Local authority income comes from three principal sources: fees and charges, local taxation and grants from central government (figure 19.8a). In addition, money can be borrowed and paid back from future current income. Each source has been made subject to increasing central control.

Fees and charges

Local authorities have provided many services where charging is possible. In the nineteenth century, they were able to raise large amounts from water, electricity, gas, roads and public transport but nationalization reduced these opportunities. Labour Party ideology also contributed to a reduction, seeing local government as a vehicle for socialism.

The hand of the centre At first sight it might appear that central government has little interest in local charges. However, if a service is offered below cost a subsidy is required from some other source – ultimately taxpayers. The Thatcher government favoured **deregulation** and commercial pricing; public transport fares and housing rents were raised and the 1989 Local Government and Housing Act gave the centre the right to designate further areas for charges.

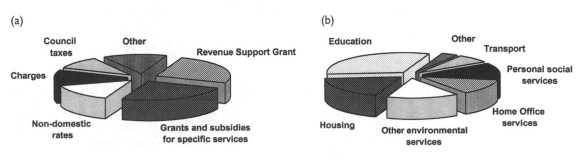

Figure 19.8 Local authority income (a) and expenditure (b), 1994/5.
Source: Data from *Local Government Financial Statistics England* (1996: table 2.2). *Note:* 'Other' expenditure includes agriculture and fisheries, arts and libraries, and urban and regeneration departments.

Borrowing

Like individuals and organizations, local authorities have the right to borrow and they do so for the same kinds of reasons. If we cannot afford a holiday in Disneyland we do not go, but when we purchase a car or a house, we borrow because there is a tangible asset to act as collateral. Thus, local authorities generally only borrow for *capital expenditure* (schools, houses, machines and the like). Borrowing has the additional advantage of spreading costs over the successive generations using the asset.

The hand of the centre However, authorities do not have complete freedom. Before 1981 they required central loan sanction. Originally this was to ensure prudence but in the post-war era it became an instrument of demand management. When the Thatcher government renounced Keynesianism there was promise of a bonfire of borrowing controls, but the Local Government Planning and Land Act (1980) introduced a general power for the centre to set ceilings on capital expenditure. The regime was further tightened in the 1989 Housing and Local Government Act. Moreover, local authorities were restricted in the use of capital receipts (from the sale of council housing) for purchasing new housing (or renovation). This was relaxed when Labour returned to power in 1997, though the regime remained tight.

Local taxation

In both political and constitutional terms local taxation has been by far the most significant element of local government income, the essential guarantee of local autonomy. The original instrument was through rates – a tax with liability based on the occupation of domestic and non-domestic property. Broadly speaking, the greater a property's desirability, the higher the tax. The system came increasingly under criticism, accused of being:

- regressive (see p. 484);
- outdated (introduced in 1601 to finance the poor law);
- a disincentive to property improvement;
- lacking buoyancy (not rising automatically with inflation);
- insufficient in yield.

In addition, the non-domestic rate appeared unfair to commerce and industry; although contributing around 50 per cent of income they had no corporate vote. Moreover, the system seemed fiendishly designed to penalize the middle classes, over 50 per cent of adults in lower income groups benefiting from rebate schemes.

The hand of the centre Central interference in local taxation was to provide one of the greatest policy dramas of the post-war era. The system had traditionally lain in neutral waters in the central–local battle. Yet in 1984 the government broke the rules of engagement, introducing a system of rate limitation, soon to be known as rate-capping. The move was of great constitutional significance because it denied a community the right to spend its own money. Of the eighteen authorities affected in the first year, sixteen were Labour controlled. However, Conservative councils were also to suffer.

After their 1987 election victory the Conservatives were so emboldened as to replace the rates with a flat-rate community charge. Apart from some concessions to the very poor, the same demand fell on the doormats of rich and poor alike and it was quickly dubbed a **poll tax**. The goal was to make councils accountable to more people for their spending. Arousing unprecedented levels of hostility, the bill negotiated the Commons with heavy whipping, surmounting the Lords only with a summons to the backwoodsmen. The previous poll tax had led to the Peasants Revolt of 1381; in 1990 it was the middle classes revolting, with stormy and sometimes violent scenes outside council chambers (Butler et al. 1994).

The poll tax helped bring down Thatcher and on April Fool's Day 1993 it followed her off the stage. Costing taxpayers an estimated £2.1 billion, critics felt it to have been a complete waste of public money, contributing nothing towards the services local government is supposed to provide. Its successor, the council tax, returned to property values (allocating property into bands) and slipped into place relatively quietly (Keen and Travers 1994).

The non-domestic rate had also been reformed as a national business rate (about £12 million in 1998), with central collection and redistribution according to a

"We're in Band C!"

formula making it more like a central grant. This survived the poll tax, as did the capping regime, which was actually tightened. In opposition Labour promised to end this, but once in government it assumed new powers to 'protect' local tax-payers, which suggested capping by other means. It also retained the national business rate, although councils were allowed to raise a supplement of 1 per cent if they obtained the backing of local businesses. The LGA was disappointed, claiming 'the shackles' had not been loosened (*Guardian*, 31 July 1998).

Central grants

Central government commands the heights of the taxation system with an un-paralleled fundraising capability through income and sales taxes as well as other forms of duty. Local government has been obliged to rely upon some of this revenue being passed back in the form of grants. There are in principle two types:

- *specific*: for particular services (housing, education, police, etc.), usually with the centre contributing a given percentage of expenditure incurred;
- *general*: currently known as the Revenue Support Grant (RSG), this sup-plements a local authority's general income and allows local discretion in spending. Central grants can also facilitate a redistribution of the nation's wealth in favour of the poorer areas, through a process of equalization.

In 1996/7 the RSG accounted for just over half of all 'aggregate external finance' (AEG), the remainder comprising non-domestic rates (36 per cent) and specific and special grants (13 per cent).

The hand of the centre The complex system entails two basic operations: de-termining the overall size of the cake and sharing it between authorities. In the first task the secretary of state works with an advisory body, the Consultative Committee on Local Government Finance (CCLGF), bringing together minis-ters, civil servants and local government representatives. However, the final decision is a political one taken by the Treasury and Cabinet. The second op-eration is no matter of simple division; like a just parent with different-sized children, central government is supposed to ensure that the slice on each authority's plate reflects its own resources and responsibilities.

During the 1980s, the partners on the CCLGF felt they were meeting to hear rather than shape the decision (Rhodes et al. 1983). Beginning with the 1980 Local Government Planning and Land Act, a series of reforms toughened the regime with increasingly severe 'holdback' penalties for 'overspending'. By the 1990s, in harness with the capping regime, it had become a razor-sharp tool of central control, its complexity bewildering to officers and councillors alike. The system was castigated by the Audit Commission (1993a) for its lack of account-ability and failings in terms of economy, efficiency and effectiveness. In 1998 Labour promised greater stability by setting the AEG distribution formula for a three-year period.

By the mid-1990s, capping and the centralization of the non-domestic rate meant that local tax covered only some 10 per cent of local government spending in England (figure 19.8b) and only about 7 per cent in Wales. This could be compared with some 53 per cent in 1989/90 (Wilson and Game 1994: 161). Producing a 'gearing effect', whereby a 1 per cent rise in an authority's spending required a council tax rise of some 10 per cent, it meant a considerable curtailment of local discretion. A June 1997 meeting of European local government finance specialists in Rome revealed that local taxes in Britain, as a percentage of local authority revenue, were just one-fifth of those in France and Germany and less than half the level in Italy. The degree of detailed central control would, in the view of Tony Travers (1996), have impressed Stalin. Local authorities are bound to the central state with chains of gold. This will shortly lead us to one of the major debates in British politics.

Auditing the books

Sleaze is not confined to the Palace of Westminster. Revelations in the 1970s of the Poulson affair exposed the corrupt awarding of contracts and *Private Eye* has for long logged a catalogue of 'rotten boroughs'. A number of characteristics leave local government open to corruption. Single-party rule produces local oligarchs who may make the authority their fiefdom, doing favours to themselves and their friends. The appointment of senior officers and policy advisers is a patronage power that can be abused, council 'newspapers' can promote party propaganda, attendance allowances can be claimed for token appearances, CCT offers temptations of bribery, and 'fact-finding' can be junketing in sunny climes or even fleshpots (Doig 1995: 104).

Like other organizations, local authorities must submit their accounts for annual audit. Originally this aimed to ensure good accounting practice, prevent corruption, and identify *ultra vires* expenditure. In 1983 the system was toughened up with the creation of the Audit Commission, a centralized watchdog quango with its fifteen members appointed by the government. This was to add special 'value-for-money' audits to the function. It soon claimed some notable scalps. In 1993 Lambeth Council was accused of fraud and malpractice, including over £20 million of unauthorized highways expenditure. In 1994 a damning report came from District Auditor John Magill concerning Westminster Council under Dame Shirley Porter. Officers and members were accused of 'wilful misconduct' and gerrymandering through the sale of council houses prior to the 1990 elections; surcharges were put at some £31 million (*Guardian*, 26 March 1997).

Post-Widdicombe legislation outlawed a number of questionable practices, recommending the appointment of 'propriety officers' to oversee appointments and requiring councillors to sign a National Code of Conduct. In 1994, the local authority associations published a code for officers. The Nolan Committee also recommended codes for councillors and the 1998 white paper promised a new ethical framework, the Secretary of State proclaiming: 'There will be no hiding place for dishonesty, corruption or sleaze' (*The Times*, 31 July 1998).

Local Government in a Centralist State

> The fundamental idea of Centralisation is, *distrust*. It puts no Faith in Man; believes not in Hope, nor in the everlastingness of truth; and treats charity as an idle word. Its synonyms are, irresponsible control; meddling interference; and arbitrary taxation.
>
> J. Toulmin Smith, *Local Self-Government and Centralization* (1851)

Although a steady erosion of local autonomy by central government has been a persistent post-war trend, it was to be accelerated in the 1980s. New Right policies, centring upon public expenditure cuts and rolling back the social democratic state, had stern implications for local government, the major arm of the welfare state. The outcome was fierce central–local battle. Many left-wing authorities began to resist central cuts and when Ken Livingstone became leader of the GLC, in 1982, he widened the vision of what an authority with limited powers could do, with public transport subsidies, cycle lanes, arts subsidies and help for disadvantaged groups such as homosexuals, women and racial minorities. Movements of the far left, churches, community organizations, women's movements, radical sections of the public-sector workforce, black rights groups, the CND and environmentalists began to forge the kind of alliance that scholars such as Eric Hobsbawm had long advocated as a panacea for the British left. It was termed the New Urban Left.

> **The things they said**
>
> Local government can be a tool for achieving socialist change. This has been submerged in parliamentary, centralist views of progress.
>
> David Blunkett (as leader of Sheffield City Council), interviewed in M. Boddy and C. Fudge, *Local Socialism: The Way Ahead* (1984)

Central government responded with a legislative fusillade, much of it through the financial instruments already discussed. The intergovernmental relationship was even dragged into the courts as, for example, when Lord Denning ruled against the GLC's 'Fares Fair' policy. The Widdicombe Committee reminded councillors that the fact that a local authority is elected

> may lend political authority to its actions within the law, . . . but does not provide a mandate to act outside or above the law. Its continued existence . . . depends on the contribution it can make to good government. (Widdicombe 1986a: ch. 3, para. 49)

However, the 'law' is anything the central government wishes to drive through Parliament, and 'good government' is whatever the Cabinet or prime minister approve of.

Conceptualizing central–local intergovernmental relations

The decline in the autonomy of local government has given rise to a number of theoretical models explaining the **central–local relationship**.

Agency The idea that local government should be an agency of the centre, with little will of its own, is essentially the Benthamite position, justified on grounds of efficiency rather than democracy. From the 1930s, W. A. Robson (1966) lamented the loss of the latter. Writing in the 1990s, King (1993: 196) could still employ the agency terminology, likening the central–local relationship to that between government and its Next Steps agencies.

Partnership In the early 1970s, scholars refuted the agency model by noting that differences in per capita spending on particular services (education, housing, social services) between authorities demonstrated local autonomy (Boaden 1971; Davies 1972). It was argued that central and local government existed together in a largely harmonious social democratic partnership.

Power-dependence Rhodes (1981) offered a power-dependence model, stressing that local authorities, like other organizations, were engaged in a pluralistic bargaining process with the centre. In this they had a number of resources (expertise, organization, information) and there was no reason to believe that the wishes of the centre must always prevail. This was underlined throughout the 1980s as the centre was repeatedly forced to pass new legislation following successive failures to impose its will.

However, certain less novel policies, such as selling council houses, worked well, leading John (1994a) to argue that the power-dependence model tended to ignore central government's capacity to learn and ultimately dominate. More generally, Hogwood (1997: 715) notes that a party's duration in office is a key factor in explaining radical change. Thus the Major years, following so long a period of Conservative rule, saw a more effective marginalizing of local government.

Stewardship Chandler (1988: 185–6) argued that the power-dependence model ascribed too much autonomy to local authorities. He suggests the idea of the stewardship of an estate as an analogy for the relationship. The steward has discretion because he is on the spot but any sense of independent power is illusory; ultimately the steward must defer, or face removal.

Dual state This neo-Marxist model (see p. 572) depicts central government as a closed system of corporate decision-making (concerned with collective investment) and local government as relatively open (concerned with collective consumption) (Saunders 1984: 24). Central–local conflict can occur along four dimensions: *organizational* (bargaining between central and local officials), *functional* (investment versus consumption policy), *political* (corporatism versus open participation) and *ideological* (market allocation versus collectivist provision). In a capitalist society the logic in each case favours central domination, because the interests of capital come first.

Marxist A Marxist view portrays local authorities as the mandataries of a greater power – not central government but the forces of wealth and capital (Cockburn 1977). The history of local government can indeed be read as a series of responses to the needs of the capitalist economy (Castells 1977). Paradoxically, from the 1980s, as communist systems collapsed throughout the world, the Marxist analysis of power in capitalist society became more compelling. Under conditions of fiscal crisis (O'Connor 1973), the business voice was amplified at the expense of elected representatives in the ways described above.

The local government network

The model of a single central–local relationship is simplistic. The real-world is messy and bewilderingly complex, with relationships varying from one authority to another and arising around different policy areas and issues within policy networks of interested parties (Rhodes 1988). Thus, for example, the poll tax issue would engage one network, local management of schools another. Voluntary societies, environmentalists, private-sector providers and large business interests move on and off the stage in an ever-changing policy drama. The contentious events surrounding the Banham reforms provided some insight into the intricacies of this world of pressure and counter-pressure (Wilson 1996: 442). Moreover, the relationship is not static over time. In the immediate post-war years the vocabulary of partnership seemed appropriate, while the 1980s were characterized by antagonism and mistrust. Indeed, according to Major's former adviser, Baroness Hogg, in 1990 ministers had seriously considered abolishing local government altogether (*Observer,* 14 July 1996).

   EU membership introduces further complexity. Authorities can lobby at Brussels, arguing the case for subsidiarity to reclaim responsibilities (thereby hoisting the British government – the leading advocate of the principle – with its own petard). Indeed, the European Commission successfully brought an enforcement action against the UK government for failing to implement a directive protecting workers in conditions of CCT (preventing them being rehired at a cheaper rate) (Woodhouse 1995: 413). Authorities have not themselves responded uniformly; some have created special EU units, some have even established a lobbying presence in Brussels, sometimes in consortia, while others have remained minimalist (John 1994b). With devolution for Scotland and Wales and a greater regional focus in other EU countries, EU membership could set the cat amongst the central–local pigeons, strengthening calls for English regionalism (see pp. 148–9).

Local Democracy in Crisis

It is but a small proportion of the public business of a country which can be well done, or safely attempted, by the central authorities; . . . the legislative portion at least of the governing body busies itself far too much with local affairs.

J. S. Mill (utilitarian philosopher), *On Representative Government* (1861)

There is in British politics what Andrew Marr (1995: 65) has called a 'malign dynamic' – the more unpopular a Westminster government becomes the more the people vote for its opponents locally, giving the centre ever more reason to reduce the power of local government. Throughout the 1980s and 1990s there was a feeling that local democracy in Britain was in crisis, perhaps near extinction.

Concern led the public service union UNISON and the local authority associations to establish in 1993 a Commission for Local Democracy, including representatives from the major parties, local officials and academics. Chaired by Simon Jenkins, former editor of *The Times*, it reported in 1995 with over forty proposals, including elected mayors, directly elected health and police authorities, proportional representation, more councillors, citizen rights to call for referendums, the end of capping and a new settlement for the central–local financial relationship (Commission for Local Democracy 1995).

Added impetus comes in the EU *Charter of Local Self-Government*, signed by the UK government on 3 June 1997. In its February 1998 consultation paper (DETR 1998b) the government talked the language of reinvigoration. It was the first of a series designed to stimulate debate around democratic renewal, best value, ethics and finance. Yet despite the rhetoric local councils saw continuing cuts in their grants, their control over schools and social services further threatened and their spending caps screwed down. Quangocracy continued to flourish and managerialism squeezed out democratic accountability. Centralism was underlined in a March 1998 pamphlet published by the Institute for Public Policy Research, in which Tony Blair warned local government:

If you are unwilling or unable to work the modern agenda then government will have to look to other partners to take on your role.

With fast-food chains operating in Education Action Zones there could be little doubt who the new partners would be. The 1998 white paper, while promising changes, stopped short of any new powers; it was criticized by LGA chairman Sir Jeremy Beecham.

Finally we may ask whether the doctrine of the supremacy of Parliament leaves local democracy shorn of any legitimate claim to autonomy. Has it any constitutional defence against central government? The answer to this is very clearly 'Yes', providing we go beyond the lawyer's wig and gown and address the spirit of democracy. Throughout history there has been a spontaneous

> When you have provided the proper constitution of local authority you must provide that the local authority must have sufficient powers; and that it gets these powers by diminishing the excessive and exaggerated powers that have been heaped on the central authorities in London.
>
> Lord Salisbury (Conservative prime minister) speaking on his government's creation of the LCC (1888), quoted in K. Young and P. L. Garside, *Metropolitan London* (1982)

desire by communities to provide services collectively. The idea that local government is nothing more than a creation of Westminster is a myth established by nineteenth-century legislation and perpetuated by centralist politicians of all shades. There is nothing morally superior about central government. Localism can be said to be embedded in the evolution of the constitution. Aristotle declared that one who lives without politics is either a god or a beast. Local democracy, by permitting ordinary people to participate in politics, enriches democracy and the quality of life.

Key points

- Local government is the self-government of territorial units of the state.
- Britain has a long history of local government, combining both localist and centralist forces.
- Industrialization promoted urbanization and marked a traumatic break with the past. The new bourgeoisie advanced the municipal institutions.
- The significance of local government lies in the services for which it is responsible.
- Generally local government has provided consumption rather than investment functions.
- Modern local government is essentially political and cannot be understood without reference to political parties and interest groups.
- The 1980s and 1990s saw some dramatic revamping of local government in terms of areal pattern, management and functions.
- Today a number of local services are provided by unelected bodies – a 'new magistracy'.
- Local government operates in the shadow of central government, not least because of the latter's financial control.
- Despite the legislative supremacy of Westminster, local government retains a moral justification derived from the ancient traditions and conventions of communal life.

Review your understanding of the following terms and concepts

body corporate	council officer	metropolitan county
borough	council leader	New Urban Left
CCT	council tax	parish
central–local relations	county	rate-capping
centralism	county borough	rates
collective consumption	elected mayor	Revenue Support Grant
collective investment	enabling authority	shire county
community charge (poll	local authority	single-tier system
tax)	local bureaucracy	specific grant
corporate management	local governance	*ultra vires*
council	localist tradition	unitary system

Assignment

Study the extract from *The Times* on p. 604 and answer the following questions.

	Mark (%)
1 Why do you think senior Labour figures wanted to block Ken Livingstone from becoming mayor of the new London authority?	25
2 What are the arguments against a central party machine dictating to local government who should stand as mayor?	25
3 To what extent could an elected mayor of the new London authority provide opposition to the central government?	25
4 Nominate a possible mayor for the new London authority and write his or her manifesto.	25

Questions for discussion

1 What were the implications of the industrial revolution for the development of English local government?
2 Suggest and evaluate some ways of increasing the turnout at local elections.
3 'It is impossible to understand the internal working of local government without reference to parties and interest groups.' Discuss.
4 'The professional expertise of senior local government officers means that they must inevitably dominate councillors.' Discuss.
5 Examine the problems faced by the Banham Commission.
6 What constitutional problems are posed by the concept of the enabling authority?

Blair is urged to block Livingstone for mayor

BY PHILIP WEBSTER
POLITICAL EDITOR

FEARS of perpetual conflict between Downing Street and London's new authority were raised by senior Labour figures last night as they urged Tony Blair to "bite the bullet" and block Ken Livingstone from becoming the party's candidate for mayor.

As Labour looked back on satisfactory local elections in which they finished comfortably ahead of the Tories and Liberal Democrats and secured a runaway majority in favour of an elected mayor, the possibility that Mr Livingstone might get the job was described by Cabinet sources as "the worst problem facing Blair".

Some senior Labour politicians even suggested tongue in cheek that the Prime Minister should offer Mr Livingstone a job in the Government, sidelining him from a position where he could do far more damage.

They said that Mr Livingstone would undoubtedly use the post as a vehicle for his own political ambitions and "he and not William Hague or Paddy Ashdown would be seen as the main opposition to the Labour Government".

Mr Livingstone's call yesterday for a wealth tax on London "fat cat" directors – he called it a "special Cedric Brown greedy bastard rate" – was cited by Blair circle members as an example of the trouble he would cause.

The key question for Mr Blair is to decide in the next 10 days whether the National Executive Committee should draw up a shortlist excluding Mr Livingstone.

The Livingstone "problem" overshadowed yesterday's inquest into Thursday's poll, in which Labour's share of the vote was 38 per cent, the Tories 32 per cent and the Liberal Democrats 25 per cent.

---

7   'A system of popularly elected mayors would revitalize local government in Britain.' Discuss.

8   'Central government dominates local government, not because of the constitutional supremacy of Parliament, but because it stands for the interests of capital while local government stands only for the community.' Discuss.

9   Why can local government be said to be in crisis?

10   Present the case against central government capping of local taxation.

Topics for debate

This house believes that a system of elected mayors will further reduce the role of ordinary people in local politics.

Further reading

Local libraries contain much information on local government in the area. This can furnish material for local projects.

Chandler, J. A. (1996) *Local Government Today*, 2nd edn.
Up-to-date view of the rapidly changing structure and processes of local government.

Checkland, S. G. and E. O. A. (eds) (1974) *The Poor Law Report of 1834.*
Unique insight into the utilitarian and moralistic outlook that was central to industrialization.

Commission for Local Democracy (1995) *Taking Charge: The Rebirth of Local Democracy, Final Report.*
Details an extensive and thought-provoking reform agenda covering local government and quangocracy.

Dunleavy, P. J. (1980) *Urban Political Analysis.*
Lively and provocative, though introducing some highly sophisticated analysis. Not for beginners.

Elcock, H. (1994) *Local Government*, 3rd edn.
Insight into policy-making and administration under the Thatcher reforms.

Kingdom, J. (1991) *Local Government and Politics in Britain.*
Stresses the political motives in many of the Thatcher reforms.

Rhodes, R. (1988) *Beyond Westminster and Whitehall: The Sub-central Government of Britain.*
Clear exposition of the power-dependence analysis and much else.

Wilson, D. and Game, C. (1997) *Local Government in the United Kingdom.*
Well-set-out and readable analysis providing good introduction to theory.

For light relief

Roy Hattersley, *A Yorkshire Boyhood.*
Labour ex-politician recounts his local government years.

Winifred Holtby, *South Riding.*
Few novels take county government as their background, but here by-laws and drainage are entwined with the passions of ordinary people.

On the net

http://www.detr.gov.uk
The web site for the government department concerned with local government.

http://www.lga.gov.uk
Much of the Local Government Association's site is open to the public as well as to its members (councillors and officers). In addition to a wide range of news and up-to-date statistics, it covers local government relations with central government and other organizations.

http://www.open.gov.uk
From the open government site you can locate the web sites of many local authorities.

Chapter Twenty

Justice and Politics: Trials and Errors

In this chapter we turn to the institutions applying the laws that emerge from the political process. We begin by mapping the institutional stage upon which legal dramas are enacted: the system of courts. Next we examine the *dramatis personae*, the members of the legal profession and the judges, and place a critical lens upon the constitutional principle of judicial impartiality. Section three examines the role of judges in the political process and the final section considers certain special institutions concerned with administrative justice, the protection of citizens from the state itself. The law is supposed to be above politics and the judges are its high priests, set outside party, class and faction, dispensing justice to weak and powerful, rich and poor, without fear or favour. However, we find that the judicial process and those working within it are by no means insulated from the controversies and vicissitudes of political life.

The Legal System

The administration of justice is shared by the Lord Chancellor's Department, responsible for administering the courts and appointing judges, and part of the Home Office. Under John Smith the Labour Party was committed to amalgamating these into a single Ministry of Justice and, although this was dropped from the 1997 manifesto, the new Lord Chancellor, Derry Irvine, was credited with it as a long-term ambition (*Sunday Times*, 8 Feb. 1998). Home Office responsibilities for examining suspected miscarriages of justice were transferred in March 1997 to a new quango, the Criminal Cases Review Commission.

The courts

Of all our constitutional institutions, none is as august and dignified as those associated with the administration of justice. Judges deck themselves in the

Hogarth's 'The
Bench'

Source: Mary Evans Picture Library

regalia of another age as necessarily as plumbers wear boiler-suits, and the
most venerable members of the judiciary sit in the House of Lords. In court,
judges expect impeccable courtesy and deference (indeed, failure to display this
can be punished as *contempt*), enshrined in archaic forms of language. When
Lord Chief Justice Taylor tried to abolish wigs in 1996, he met with obdurate
opposition from barristers addicted to 'pantomime flummery' (Robertson 1997).
Yet the pageantry and splendour has a purpose: it is intended to bestow upon
the system an aura of power, wisdom and integrity. Through these legal custodians the principle of the rule of law is manifested. This is the orthodox view; in
this chapter we put it to the test.

The structure of the courts in England and Wales is hierarchical (figure 20.1);
superior courts check the actions of those below through a process of appeal.
The organization reflects a fundamental dichotomy between **civil jurisdiction**
(citizen versus citizen using such laws as tort and contract) and **criminal jurisdiction** (state versus citizen as in crimes such as burglary or murder).

Civil jurisdiction   Minor cases begin in county courts, presided over by itiner-
ant circuit judges, while more serious ones are heard in the High Court. Ap-

> Judgement must always be passed with complete solemnity – because it's such rot. Suppose a judge throws a woman into clink for having stolen a corncake for her child. And he isn't wearing his robes. Or he's scratching himself while passing sentence . . . then the sentence he passes is a disgrace and the law is violated. It would be easier for a judge's robe and a judge's hat to pass sentence than for a man without all that paraphernalia.
>
> Azdak in Bertolt Brecht's *The Caucasian Chalk Circle* (1948)

peals go on to a Court of Appeal (civil division) and thence, upon further appeal, to the House of Lords, the highest court in the land.

Criminal jurisdiction   Minor criminal cases are tried summarily (without a jury) in a magistrate's court. For serious criminal cases the magistrate's court conducts committal proceedings, which merely decide whether there is a case to answer. If there is, it will go to a Crown Court to be tried before a jury and presided over by a High Court judge or circuit judge. Appeals from the Crown Court may be taken to the High Court (on a point of law) or the Court of Appeal (Criminal Division), and thence to the House of Lords.

'Re-inventing' the system   In the 1990s came a taste of the 're-inventing' that had been visited on other parts of the state; the courts were given performance targets and citizen's charters, and managerialism came to the Lord Chancellor's

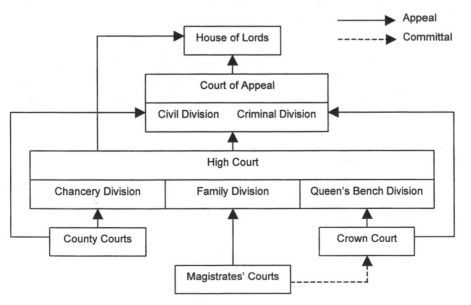

Figure 20.1
The courts in England and Wales.

Department. Critics began to imagine the courts peopled by consultants with clipboards rather than bewigged lawyers. There was concern that justice and accountancy did not mix, that judicial considerations were giving way to politically motivated cost savings. In April 1995 the Courts Service Agency took over the administration of justice, with the usual constitutional problems of agencification (Woodhouse 1995: 404). In 1996 Lord Woolf's report, *Access to Justice*, proposed a radical overhaul of civil justice to reduce delay. However, the government refused to make the necessary resources available, announcing that the system should be made to pay for itself through increased court fees. In addition, the discretion of the courts to waive or reduce fees in cases of financial hardship was withdrawn. Angered judges argued that this would restrict access to justice and in *R. v. Lord Chancellor ex parte Witham*, in 1997, the High Court ruled it illegal.

The European dimension

To the domestic system must be added two European courts.

The European Court of Human Rights The European Convention on Human Rights (ECHR) was signed by a number of European countries in 1950. Alleged breaches are investigated by the European Commission on Human Rights and cases appear before the Court. Although ratified by the UK the Convention was not incorporated into domestic law until 1998 so judges were unable to apply it in domestic courts. However, since 1966 UK citizens had been enabled to petition the Commission and a number of cases against the British government were upheld (see p. 72 and Lester 1994). Particularly controversial was the 1994 judgement that the shooting by the SAS of three IRA suspects in Gibraltar was unlawful. Incorporation of the Convention can be expected to increase the area for controversy by making the courts more political (p. 625).

The European Court of Justice (ECJ) As the importance of the EU increases in the lives of states and citizens so does its court. All UK courts must take notice of its decisions and lower courts may seek definitive rulings on the meaning of European law and treaties (see p. 62).

Access to the law

In England, Justice is open to all, like the Ritz hotel.

Attributed to James Matthew (1830–1908; British judge)

A prerequisite of a just legal system is that all have equal access. Yet in practice this is by no means the case; the lawyers' clientele remain predominantly middle class (Zander 1969). There are various reasons for this.

- *Cost*. Lawyers' fees, protected by the monopolistic practices of the Law Society, mean that the law does not come cheap. For many it is better to suffer a wrong than risk an expensive lawsuit.

- *Legal expertise.* It is in the nature of the legal profession to take a greater interest in the problems of the wealthy than the poor. The intricacies of business and commerce tend to preoccupy the legal mind, to the exclusion of problems with landlords, local authorities and social security agencies.
- *The nature of the law.* The law places its greatest emphasis on the management and protection of property.
- *Class.* The upper-middle-class image of the profession is itself a deterrent. A yawning gulf exists between working-class people and the typical smooth-talking, self-confident lawyer. Fear of embarrassment, of appearing foolish, tends to keep the ordinary person away from the intimidating consulting room.

Attempts have been made to improve access. First, there is a system of *legal aid*, whereby the state gives financial assistance to litigants. Introduced in the Legal Aid and Advice Act (1949) it represented a significant development, both for the law and for democracy. Generally aid depends upon income and the merits of the case. However, it is subject to abuse both by wealthy individuals finding a technical means to qualify and by 'fat cat' barristers claiming huge fees; earnings for the year 1995/6 totalled £286 million (*Independent*, 18 June 1998).

With unemployment driving more people into debt and mortgage difficulties, the 1980s saw a great rise in the number of claimants and the government attempted to ease the cost by reducing eligibility. The Legal Aid Act (1988) transferred administration from the Law Society to a new quango, the Legal Aid Board. In 1995 the system was cash limited and solicitors and advice agencies were to compete for contracts to hold legal aid budgets; regional boards, rather than the courts, were to decide who qualified. The government continued the quest for cuts in the £1.5 billion bill by excluding personal injury cases, extending the 'no win, no fee' principle throughout civil proceedings and involving the private insurance market. To critics this compromised the government's professed commitment to human rights.

The *Dramatis Personae*

> I dined at my Lord Chancellor's, where three Sergeants at law told their stories, how long they had detained their clients in tedious processes by tricks, as if so many highway thieves should have met and discovered the purses they had taken.
>
> John Evelyn (1620–1706), *Diary* (26 Nov. 1686)

The courts are rather like churches – nothing without the people inside them. Control is jealously guarded by a veritable priesthood of curates, vicars, bishops and even an archbishop in the form of the Lord Chancellor. The law, perhaps the oldest and most venerable of the professions, saw its heyday under

> The Law is the true embodiment
> Of everything that's excellent.
> It has no kind of fault or flaw,
> And I, my lords, embody the law.
>
> The Lord Chancellor in Gilbert and
> Sullivan's *Iolanthe*

the Victorians. The capitalist bourgeoisie based their claim to wealth, prestige and power on property and needed lawyers to secure these. The reform of the law along Benthamite lines, through Acts of Parliament, was the basis for establishing the new order, and the huge increase in private and public legislation made Parliament an earthly paradise for the great Victorian lawyers. The natural partners of the capitalists, like them the lawyers were hard working, generally became immensely wealthy and registered this with a profound sense of their own dignity and importance. Respect for the law became, in practice, a veneration of lawyers that endures to this day.

In the administration of justice lawyers fall into three categories: solicitors, barristers and the judiciary. Although bound together with dense legal bindweed, they have long practised a strict division of labour. While not entirely unique to Britain, the system is relatively unusual and not much admired by lawyers from other countries.

> The Lawyer is exclusively occupied with the details of predatory fraud either in achieving or in checking chicanery, and success in the profession is therefore accepted as marking a large endowment of that barbarian astuteness which has always commanded men's respect and fear.
>
> Thorstein Veblen (1857–1929; American social scientist),
> *The Theory of the Leisure Class* (1899)

Solicitors Solicitors can be employed in various contexts, including national and local government, but they mainly practise privately, usually in partnerships, dealing directly with the public. They are collectively represented by their 'trade union', the Law Society, which has enjoyed considerable influence as an 'insider' pressure group *par excellence*. Although they may work very closely with clients, perhaps understanding every nuance of their cases, they were by convention prohibited from appearing in a superior court, having to instruct a barrister, their superior in the legal pecking order.

In January 1989 the Lord Chancellor, Lord Mackay of Clashfern, unveiled three green papers proposing reforms of the profession which placed some very lively cats among the legal pigeons. The goal was to introduce free-market disciplines into the cloistered world of wig and gown; breaking the barristers' advocacy monopoly, allowing lawyers to take cases on a US-style 'no win, no fee' basis, to advertise their services and to publish fees. The profession was enraged, even Lord Hailsham, recently retired Lord Chancellor and once staunch member of the Thatcher Cabinet, expressed hostility. After much lobbying a white paper appeared (Lord Chancellor's Department 1989), with the original proposal modified in certain important respects. The most innovative feature of the resulting Courts and Legal Services Act (1990) was the right of audience for lawyers provided they had gained a certificate of advocacy. However, barristers could expect to maintain their hegemony in the rarefied atmosphere of the upper courts.

Barristers Known collectively as 'the Bar', barristers are far less numerous than solicitors and, despite their superior status, dependent on the latter for business. They may advance to a higher grade by 'taking silk', when they are formally appointed a Queen's Counsel (QC) by the Lord Chancellor. At the apex stand two political appointees: the *Attorney General* (the government's attorney) and the *Solicitor General* (the government's solicitor). A number of them become MPs, their allegiance going predominantly to the Conservative Party or Labour's right (such as Clement Attlee, John Smith and Tony Blair).

As a group, barristers remain socially insulated, over half operating in the hothouse of London in one of the four great Inns of Court, marked by much tradition, ritual and perhaps snobbery. Controlling the profession through the General Council of the Bar and a Bar Secretariat, the Inns of Court have an ancient lineage, being well established in the fifteenth century. They were originally concerned with training barristers through lectures and 'arguments', and successful students would duly be 'called to the Bar'. This training gradually declined until, by the early nineteenth century, the call was a formality, the student being merely required to pay an appropriate fee and symbolize attendance for twelve terms by consuming a prescribed number of dinners. Nineteenth-century reforms added to wealth and gastronomic capacity a requirement to pass examinations. The organization continues to reflect that of the ancient Oxbridge colleges (Jackson 1960: 217). The Bar has been no place for a woman. In 1995, they accounted for 16 per cent of the pool of suitable candidates for silk, 8.5 per cent of applicants and only 5.8 per cent of QCs appointed, a rate of appointment only 0.8 per cent higher than in 1991 (*Independent,* 27 June 1996).

A client is fain to hire a lawyer to keep from the injury of other lawyers – as Christians that travel in Turkey are forced to hire Janissaries, to protect them from the insolencies of other Turks.

Samuel Butler (1835–1902; English satirist), *Prose Observations*

The judiciary For historical reasons it is mainly from the Bar that judges have been chosen. This has an important implication for the legal system because judicial office is seen as legal business rather than as an aspect of public service. It helps to legitimate the law by reinforcing the impression of independence. In the sense that appointment is seen as promotion (although one which the richest barristers will spurn), the judiciary may be regarded as the top of the legal hierarchy (figure 20.2).

Appointments, made by the Lord Chancellor, have long been based on secret 'soundings' or 'consultations' among existing judges and senior lawyers. The system was given a resounding vote of confidence by the Commons Home Affairs Select Committee in 1996, which agreed that practical difficulties prevented using advertisements, competition and interviews to fill the vacancies on the High Court bench and above. Reformers have long argued for an independent Judicial Appointments Commission, staffed with lay people as well as representatives from both sides of the legal profession. Such a reform was under consideration soon after Labour came to power in 1997, but after stern judicial opposition it was rejected. However, for the first time, High Court vacancies were to be advertised within the profession.

Magistrates At the bottom of the hierarchy are the unpaid magistrates sitting in the local courts as Justices of the Peace (JPs), most of whom are not lawyers (they are advised by clerks who are qualified lawyers). In large cities there are also stipendiary (professionally qualified and paid) magistrates. JPs were key figures in local government until the municipal reforms following industrialization swept them from centre stage. They retained a legal role, which was increased with responsibility for juvenile cases after 1908. Despite the reforming hand of the Attlee government the system remains elitist. Formal appointment is by the Lord Chancellor acting on the advice of local committees. Technically anyone can become a magistrate but the process is often in the hands of secretive local oligarchies within political parties, chambers of commerce and the Freemasons.

Figure 20.2
The judicial
hierarchy, 1997.

8   Lords of Appeal in Ordinary
Lord Chancellor
Lord Chief Justice
Master of the Rolls
President of the Family Division
Vice Chancellor
35   Lords Justices
96   High Court Judges
523   Circuit Judges

Source: Data from *Judicial Statistics* (1997).

Twelve men good and true: the jury system

Although we have introduced the highest and most mighty we have not encompassed the full judicial *dramatis personae* until we consider the twelve ordinary people forming the **juries** in many trials. Juries are made up of people selected randomly from the population. This is without doubt the most democratic aspect of the legal system; perhaps the most democratic aspect of the whole political system. In the eighteenth century Lord Camden stated: 'trial by jury is indeed the foundation of our free constitution; take that away and the whole fabric will soon moulder into dust' (Jackson 1960). Here it is possible for ordinary citizens to speak so authoritatively that the most lofty in the land must heed their words. It was a jury that acquitted Clive Ponting of charges of treason, against the direction of the judge.

However, juries live under threat. The police in particular find them tiresome, conducting an unceasing campaign for their abolition or limitation. In 1965 Robert Mark (as Chief Constable of Leicester) called for majority verdicts (rather than unanimity) and in the 1967 Criminal Justice Act the Labour government duly obliged. In 1989, Metropolitan Police Commissioner Sir Peter Imbert argued in a lecture to the Police Foundation that British courts could usefully move away from the adversarial method of barristers arguing before a jury to a French-style inquisitorial system, whereby an examining magistrate takes charge of the investigation at an early stage and the judge questions the witnesses, leaving juries less leeway to form judgements on the basis of arguments. The tendency of professional people to escape jury service on the grounds of work commitments can lead to a preponderance of the working-class or unemployed and tabloid horror stories report jurors celebrating 'over a pint' with the defendants after their acquittal (Gibb 1988). When juries acquit on the grounds of a 'lurking doubt', they are 'frequently disparaged as unfit for the task' (Kennedy 1992: 9).

"*The jury will ignore that last remark…*"

Reproduced by permission of *Punch*

Today juries are only employed in a minority of cases, no longer being used in Crown Courts where the accused pleads guilty – which most do. Yet the demise of the system would constitute a grave threat to democracy. In Northern Ireland fears of intimidation led, in 1973, to juries being dispensed with in certain terrorism cases. In these 'Diplock courts' convictions were often based on confessions obtained during long hours of police interrogation, where allegations of ill-treatment were subsequently proved. Radical lawyer Michael Mansfield (1997) argues that far from being contracted, the system should be extended, with all crimes susceptible to jury trial.

Social characteristics

The British judiciary has for long been tied by silken threads of class to the Establishment, one important condition being success as a barrister. The career path ensures that judges will be relatively old and predominantly male, and the likelihood that their faces will be white is almost as certain as that their wigs will be so. There were no black or Asian judges on the High Court bench (Dyer 1995). In 1995 the sex balance of judges in England and Wales was 2,804 men to 312 women (*Independent*, 27 June 1996). Only 6 of the 94 High Court judges, and only 1 of the 32 Appeal Court judges, were women. After two years in office Labour's relatively reformist Lord Chancellor, Derry Irvine, had still not been able to appoint a single woman to high judicial office.

This soil does not nourish radical saplings; the hand of patronage will not be laid upon any suspect characters. From the beginning, selection is by their seniors, who fashion the clay in their own image before administering the breath of life. When those from less propitious backgrounds receive the call – and there is evidence of a widening entry to the Inns of Court School of Law (Bar Council 1989: 51), they are unlikely to make any impression on the impassive face of tradition. Characteristically motivated by social aspiration, with little desire to challenge the status quo, they will already have been subject to a battery of socializing pressures and will make sure they join the right clubs and say the right things with the right accents. One club has appeared particularly attractive: the Freemasons, a shadowy organization involving strange rites, secret handshakes and rolled-up trouser-legs. Even the chair of the new Criminal Cases Review Commission was reported to be a member. Rumours regularly circulate that membership interferes with judicial impartiality and in 1997 Home Secretary Jack Straw announced that all new recruits to the criminal justice system should declare their membership, existing members being invited to sign a voluntary register. Judicial hostility was palpable, with even the Lord Chancellor in full cry.

In 1994 a less secretive process was introduced for appointments below High Court level, with open advertisements in newspapers. Yet despite protestations from Lord Chancellor Lord Mackay that the 'old boy network' no longer operated, figures released by his department in 1995 revealed that 80 per cent of Lords of Appeal, Heads of Division, Lords Justices of Appeal and High Court judges had Oxbridge backgrounds, as had over 50 per cent of middle-ranking circuit judges. Only amongst the lower-ranking district judges was social composition more mixed. Yet even here 12 per cent had travelled by this route.

In May 1995 Sir Thomas Legg, Permanent Secretary in the Lord Chancellor's Department, told the Commons Home Affairs Committee: 'it is not the function of the professional judiciary to be representative of the community'. However, reformers argue that they should reflect the heterogeneity of the society they judge in order to bring some sympathy with the unemployed, unqualified, discriminated against and dispossessed. The judiciary are the high and the mighty and, if the Sermon on the Mount is to be believed, such worries that they may have concern the next world rather than this.

Questions of impartiality

The iconic statue above the Central Criminal Court (the Old Bailey) shows Justice blindfolded, not knowing who sits on the balance she holds. Judges favour neither rich nor poor, neither right nor left. This picture of **judicial impartiality** is essential to the legitimation of liberal-democratic government. Judges must appear to stand above the confused mêlée of classes, parties and interests. But do they?

Class Generally judges are more lenient towards members of the professions than they are towards the working class or the unemployed (Box 1971). Prudent solicitors recognize this when advising clients to wear a conventional middle-class uniform in court. This is not to deny that there are liberal judges (Lord Justice Woolf, for example, has expressed publicly his desire for reform), but they tend to stand out as the exception. Radical lawyers such as Helena Kennedy, Lord Lestor and Michael Mansfield point to inequity, campaigning for the rights of the disadvantaged and wrongly imprisoned. In large cities, law centres financed by charities and local authorities have been established to combat the bias, by directing legal attention away from business and property matters to concerns affecting ordinary people, such as welfare legislation, consumer affairs and employment problems.

Framing Eve The male domination of the legal profession and judiciary is manifest in the way women are treated. Sexism is institutionalized into the law itself as well as its practice. Until the late nineteenth century, marriage meant that a woman surrendered all separate legal and property rights and until very recently wives could not be raped by their husbands, who had contractual rights to sex upon demand.

Helena Kennedy, one of the few women QCs, found herself in a world of sexist innuendo and jokes about prostitutes and rape cases. To her, journalist Andrew Neil's libel action against a newspaper that had suggested he had consorted with a prostitute resembled a 'stag party', with amusing definitions of terms such as 'bimbo' (Kennedy 1992: 141–2). Judges regularly display excessive leniency in rape cases, the women said to have been 'asking for it'.

Although far fewer women commit crimes than men, it is often said that, like Eve, they lie behind them. They can receive harsher sentences than men because, as mothers, community service is less suitable. Indeed, 53 per cent of women in prison have fewer than two convictions compared with 22 per cent of men (Kennedy 1992: 22–3). Women also have problems in obtaining realistic damages for personal injuries because the economic value of housework is not acknowledged.

Compensation for rape is particularly difficult. For example, a man who had suffered brain damage in a road accident was left with an increased propensity for sexual violence. In two cases he subjected women to brutal assaults, forcing one to strip, trussing her up 'like a chicken', raping and stabbing her. For their ordeals, the women subsequently received £1,000 and £3,600 from the Criminal Injuries Compensation Board. After suing in the High Court they received £7,080 and £10,480 respectively. Although sentenced to life imprisonment in 1983, the man was later to receive £45,750 in compensation for the car accident (Kennedy 1992: 28).

Prosecuting Counsel: And you say she consented?
Defendant: I didn't say she consented.
PC: Did she agree?
D: She didn't agree.
PC: Having said no at first, she just gave in?
D: She enjoyed it.
Judge: The enjoyment wiped out her initial resistance – is that what you are saying?
D: Yes.

From a trial at the Old Bailey, reported by Sue Lees in *New Statesman* (December 1989)

Black justice Judges will hotly deny that decisions are influenced by racial factors. However, Home Office statistics reveal that while black people constitute less than 6 per cent of the population they constitute 22 per cent of the prison population. Although social deprivation must account for some of this there are other factors. Kennedy (1992: 162) reports research by probation services showing that black defendants are more likely to receive immediate custodial or suspended sentences. Average sentence length for a West Indian male is some eight months longer than for his white counterpart (*House of Commons Debates*, 11 Nov. 1991). Various forms of racial stereotyping emerge in court; Asians are more likely to get bail than those of Afro-Caribbean descent because they are thought to be more hard working. West Indians are assumed to be more violent and sexually insatiable. Black women are held to be inherently promiscuous, making it doubly difficult for them to bring rape cases (Kennedy 1992: 161–89). In the area of race relations, judges have proceeded 'on the basis that legislation is primarily an interference with the rights of individuals to discriminate and that the public interest is best served by restricting the impact of that legislation as far as possible' (Griffith 1981: 225).

Party *Prima facie* the evidence suggests a natural bias of the judiciary towards the right. It has appeared that Labour governments have been more likely 'to act in ways which offend the judicial sense of rightness, the judicial sense of where the public interest lies' (Griffith 1981: 236–7). However, as we will see, from the mid-1980s reforms to the legal profession and policies towards crime, sentencing and punishment soured relations with the Conservative Party and contributed to increased judicial political activism.

Moral Issues Members of sexual minorities, prostitutes, holders of unorthodox views, squatters, student protesters and so on can all expect rough justice. In 1976, for example, the House of Lords opined, in dispensing with his right to refuse the adoption of his child, that a homosexual had nothing to offer his son. According to gay rights campaigner Peter Tatchell, men having consensual sex with males over sixteen are five times more likely to be prosecuted than those having sex with girls under sixteen and three times less likely to get off with a caution.

Police actions The judiciary has generally supported the police in areas such as questioning, seizure, obtaining 'confessions', conduct of identification parades, and telephone tapping, when legal powers have been exceeded. It is generally recognized by the Director of Public Prosecutions, in deciding whether or not to proceed against the police, that it is exceedingly difficult to secure a conviction. Even the five-year inquiry under retired High Court Judge Sir John May into the wrongful imprisonment of the Guildford Four on the basis of false confessions was only mildly critical of the police. Helena Kennedy (1992: 6) reports that criminal lawyers will present cases on the assumption that 'the judges will always prefer the police account unless the defence case is overwhelming'.

Security In matters of national security the judiciary is willing to set most other considerations aside in siding with the state. In the *Hosenball* case (1977), an American journalist was ordered to be deported by Merlyn Rees, the Labour Home Secretary, for obtaining for publication material said to be harmful to UK security. Lord Denning, in dismissing an appeal, said 'when the state is in danger . . . even the rules of natural justice had to take second place' (*The Times*, 30 March 1977). In the case of Sarah Tisdall (p. 456), a severe sentence was imposed for leaking a memo, while in the Ponting case (p. 455) the judge equated the interests of the state with those of the government. In IRA cases, judicial enthusiasm to convict has resulted in serious miscarriages of justice, such as the cases of the Guildford Four, the Maguire family and the Birmingham Six.

Property rights versus civil rights The rise of the bourgeoisie was dependent upon property rights. These are legally vested in individuals through contracts and leases, their protection being one of the primary purposes of the law. In the absence of a Bill of Rights or a written constitution, human rights are not vested, so that judges have been asked not to *protect* a right but to *assert* it, often against a powerful private interest (Griffith 1981: 222). Judicial reaction to the incorporation of the ECHR remains to be seen.

The state versus property If the state threatens property rights the judiciary has appeared more zealous. In the *Amisminic* case (1969) a company was aggrieved by the refusal of the Foreign Compensation Commission to recompense it for the forced sale of its Egyptian property to the Egyptian government at a loss. Although there was no right of appeal to the courts, the House of Lords insisted on hearing the case and found in favour of the company. In another case, in 1976–7, a minister instructed the Civil Aviation Authority to refuse a permit for entrepreneur Freddie Laker to offer cut-price fares over the Atlantic. The courts supported Laker. In both cases the government was Labour.

Trade unions Trade unions have since their inception been opposed by judges. In the nineteenth century, when a series of Combination Acts sought to restrict their growth, the judiciary assisted with statutory interpretation and through common-law decisions. Indeed, towards the end of the century, when Parliament began to doubt the value of legal penalties, it was necessary to curb judicial anti-unionism with legislation. Hence the 1875 Conspiracy and Protection of Property Act effectively legalized strikes and the 1906 Trade Disputes Act reversed the notorious Taff Vale Judgement (p. 270). In 1913 further judicial zeal was curbed with the Trade Union Act to reverse the 1910 Osborne Judgement, which prevented the fledgling Labour Party from using union funds.

More recently Parliament was obliged to nullify a vicious House of Lords judgement in *Rookes* v. *Barnard* (1964), which was seen as a direct attack on the right to strike. In 1972, five dockers who refused to comply with a ruling of the National Industrial Relations Court (created by the Heath government) were imprisoned for contempt. The resulting furore prompted widespread threats of industrial disruption and, in a Machiavellian manoeuvre, the House of Lords delivered an unprecedentedly speedy judgement on an unconnected case which presented an excuse for the dockers' hasty release, thereby foiling their willing martyrdom.

Conservative legislation during the 1980s was designed to push more industrial relations issues into the courts, which were not laggardly in responding, interpreting it in a way that cut union protection to a minimum (Marsh 1992: 109). The miners', printers' and seamen's unions all suffered from large-scale sequestration of funds under court orders. In the dispute between press baron Rupert Murdoch and the print union SOGAT 82, the courts, in finding members guilty of secondary picketing, refused to consider that Murdoch had forced this upon them by splitting his newspaper holding into separate companies.

Central–local relations In this political minefield the courts have frequently been friendly to the right, as a number of *causes célèbres* show. In the 1976 *Tameside* case a newly elected Conservative council cancelled a plan for comprehensive education prepared by its Labour predecessor. The Labour Secretary of State intervened under powers in the 1944 Education Act but the House of Lords supported the council on the grounds of a local mandate for its actions. However, in the 'Fares Fair' case, although the High Court upheld the Labour-controlled GLC's right to reduce London Transport fares, the Appeal Court and House of Lords ruled that the statutory duty to provide 'economic' transport ruled out the policy. This time the local mandate was rejected (Griffith 1991: 301–7).

Judges are constantly asked to decide what is in the *public interest*. However, they see this from a narrow perspective, consistently exercising a conservative bias and led ineluctably to the view that 'stability above all is necessary for the health of the people and is the supreme law' (Griffith 1981: 235). However, beyond this judges also operate more overtly in the political world.

Judges and Politics

The principle of the separation of powers would exclude judges from the political process. However, in the real world the judiciary dips more than a toe in the murky swamp. This is institutionalized in the constitutionally anomalous position of its head, the Lord Chancellor. Appointed through prime ministerial patronage rather than elected, he is also a key member of the executive and of the legislature (p. 65). Lord Hailsham was a controversial politician before his appointment and Lord Mackay became increasingly political as he backed the New Right reforms. The position became even more political under Blair's appointee, Lord Irvine. Noted for an overbearing style, he was soon chairing three key cabinet committees driving through constitutional reforms. Informed critics increasingly question so anomalous an office (Steyn 1997).

The Attorney General and Solicitor General are also political appointees. Blair's Solicitor General, Lord Falconer QC, was a personal friend who had to be persuaded to leave a £500,000 commercial practice at the Bar (*The Times*, 27 June 1997). Also appointed through the secretive machinery of political patronage are the Law Lords, able to pronounce on issues of the day from the upper house. Beyond this formal proximity to power there are several further means whereby the judges enter the world of politics.

Judges making law

Parliamentary sovereignty decrees that judges should discover and apply the law rather than make it. However, in reality they play an exceedingly important law-making role.

Evolving the common law Much British law is no more than a body of past judgements, a great coral reef of wisdom from successive ages. In trials lawyers will delve into the records to find *precedents* to guide current decisions. This body of **case law** is continually evolving. Where two or more cases appear to have been resolved differently, or where social conditions have changed, the judge will exercise discretion and so create a further precedent.

Interpreting statute law In the nineteenth century the new capitalists were impatient with a slowly evolving law, which could be seen as a recipe for the maintenance of the status quo. Bentham argued from his utility principle that each generation should fashion its laws in accordance with the needs of the age.

The result was a vast increase in statute law, made by politicians in the re-formed Parliament, which was given precedence over the common law. However, this change of emphasis did not rule out the creative role of the judiciary. No Act of Parliament can take into account all the circumstances of any particular case and invariably some interpretation, or *statutory construction*, is required. Although judges try to reflect the legislators' intentions, they do not always succeed. For example, the Law Lords decided that the race relations legislation (intended to outlaw discrimination generally) did not apply to private clubs. Again, much legislation invokes the concept of 'reasonableness' in determining standards of acceptable behaviour, which in practice means what *judge*s regard as reasonable. Moreover, where loopholes exist in legislation (which they often do), judges can show great ingenuity in inserting their own policy judgements.

The Common Law of England has been laboriously built about a mythical figure – the figure of the 'reasonable man'.

A. P. Herbert (1890–1971; British writer and politician), *Uncommon Law* (1935)

The Law Commission This quango, composed entirely of lawyers, is responsible for revising the law. Its role is defined formally as technical and non-political, concerned with clarifying obscure language, repealing obsolete statutes, and consolidating and codifying masses of complicated statute or common law. However, it can make major recommendations with more than a cosmetic impact. For example, the controversial 1986 Public Order Act (replacing that of 1936 and consolidating various other pieces of relevant law) incorporated most of the recommendations of a report made by the Commission three years earlier.

Judicial activism

In the great debates of the day, judges are by no means shrinking violets. When delivering judgements their exegesis will often pass comment on various matters of social concern, such as the role of the family, discipline in schools, moral standards, and so on. However, they can also take off their wigs and gowns and enter the political fray.

Lunchtime sandwiches Restrictions on judicial pronouncements came in the form of the Kilmuir guidelines laid down in 1955, though observance of these has varied with Lord Chancellors and they were relaxed by Lord Mackay in 1988. Judges even began to discuss issues over lunchtime sandwiches with journalists (Dyer 1995). Lord Chief Justice Taylor gave regular press conferences and speeches, including the Dimbleby Lecture, in which he attacked the Conservative government's handling of the criminal justice system.

Flattering invitations Governments can invite judges into the political realm in various ways. Legislation can be drawn up that asks them to adjudicate in controversial social matters, as in Heath's IRC. Restrictive union legislation during the 1980s also brought judges into some bitter political struggles. In addition, leading members of the judiciary are frequently asked to head inquiries into controversial questions. Reports such as Scarman (race relations), Nolan (sleaze) and Taylor (the Hillsborough disaster) make their authors' names household words. This places them in the front line of controversy and open to political attack as, for example, when Lord Howe publicly denounced Sir Richard Scott's inquiry into the Matrix Churchill affair.

Judicial review In many countries (including the USA and France) judges are responsible for reviewing legislation in the light of the constitution and basic civil rights. The doctrine of parliamentary supremacy renders this abhorrent to the British constitution. However, while unable to strike down the legislation itself, judges have the power to quash executive actions under it when challenged in the courts. This can produce a serious check since, in reality, it may be dissatisfaction with the legislation itself that produces the action. Traditionally, judges had been content to confine such review to the principle of *ultra vires*. Where they brought in other considerations (reasonableness, fairness) they did so only on the basis of legislative intent, thereby respecting parliamentary sovereignty. However, calls for judicial review were to rise sharply from the mid-1980s (figure 20.3) as lawyers, individuals and pressure groups became more aware and judges, concerned about a growth in executive power since 1979, became more willing to consider the spirit as well as the letter of the law. Mr Justice Laws asserted that political controversy should not be grounds for believing a decision to be outside the courts' jurisdiction (Woodhouse 1995:

Figure 20.3
The increase in the number of applications to apply for judicial review of administrative action.

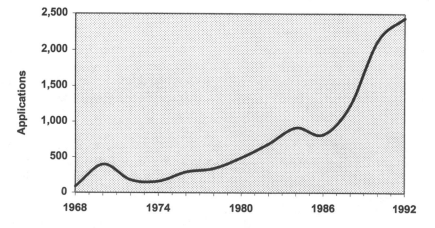

Source: Data from Butler and Butler (1994: 318).

405–6). The more robust approach caused such alarm in official circles that a highway code was produced in 1987 (*Judge Over Your Shoulder*) to keep bureaucrats on the right side of the road.

All departments were vulnerable. The Foreign Secretary was declared at fault in the Pergau Dam affair and the Transport Secretary was found to have abused his powers over night-flying restrictions at Heathrow, Gatwick and Stansted. The Department of Health was in trouble over availability of beds and the Ministry of Defence was found to have acted unlawfully in requiring women to leave the armed forces on becoming pregnant. The December 1992 decision to close thirty-one pits, with 30,000 job losses (to make the industry more attractive for privatization), was outlawed. There were also calls for greater openness. The Matrix Churchill case in particular made the courts sceptical of ministerial use of public interest immunity certificates (p. 456).

However, the department proving most susceptible was the Home Office, with a long-running series of clashes over asylum, the rights of prisoners, sentencing policy (including Michael Howard's intervention in the James Bulger case where the convicted were children), the handling of miscarriages of justice (the Guildford Four, the Birmingham Six, the Broadwater Three, Judith Ward, Stefan Kisko, the Taylor sisters) and victims' compensation. In finding Home Secretary Kenneth Baker in contempt (in July 1993) for deciding to deport a Zairean asylum seeker in defiance of a court order, the courts were challenging ministers' claims to the protection of Crown immunity.

Europe Membership of the EU increases the scope for judicial activism, judges acquiring the powers held by constitutional courts in other countries in a process of 'constitution creep' (Thompson 1997: 186). Indeed judges appeared ahead of politicians in accepting the full implications of EU membership, entailing a responsibility to review domestic legislation in the light of EU law. The courts' powers to suspend an Act of Parliament breaching EU law was revealed in the *Factortame* case (see p. 68). EU law can also be a basis for judicial review. The Equal Opportunities Commission (EOC) claimed that, in denying certain rights to those working less than eight hours a week, the 1978 Employment Protection Act conflicted with EU law. In finding for the EOC the House of Lords demonstrated its unequivocal acceptance of the supremacy of EU law.

Perhaps more importantly, EU membership liberalized judicial attitudes towards statutory interpretation. The courts now refer to *Hansard* in determining the intention behind legislation. Originally prohibited, this first became necessary to establish whether national law was intended to comply with EU law, and it has since been extended to all cases of ambiguity.

Moreover, even before its incorporation as the Human Rights Act a greater willingness had emerged to use the ECHR. In finding against a health authority wishing to discontinue treatment of a ten-year-old girl with leukaemia, Mr Justice Laws ruled that the ECHR could be taken as 'persuasive legal authority' (Woodhouse 1995: 412–13). However, cases of conflict obliged judges to uphold domestic law. The Human Rights Act, operative from the year 2000, thus opens up new vistas of judicial activism.

Open conflict with government

In 1990, crime rates reached the highest levels since records began in 1851 (*Criminal Statistics*, 1993). In September 1991 Archbishop of Canterbury George Carey declared that 'human wrongdoing is inextricably linked to social deprivation, poverty, poor housing and illiteracy'. The government was unwilling to accept that its policies were implicated and blame was placed on judicial liberalism. There were even attacks from the podium at the 1995 Conservative conference, party chairman Brian Mawhinney urging members to write to judges to complain about light sentences.

> **Tabloid justice**
> If you can't do the time, don't do the crime.
>
> Home Secretary Michael Howard's 'prison works' soundbite

The government began to meddle with judicial discretion. The 1994 Criminal Justice and Public Order Act contained several controversial measures, including an end to the traditional right of silence. A suspect's refusal to speak could now be cited in court as a suggestion of guilt. Lord Chief Justice Taylor expressed open opposition, arguing that this undermined a cornerstone of British justice: the presumption of innocence. The 1997 Crime (Sentences) Bill aimed to deal with 'soft' judges with mandatory prison sentences for certain offenders (see p. 650), the judiciary complaining that the government was taking more notice of the tabloids than the judges.

In the Lords, former Master of the Rolls Lord Donaldson condemned the lack of trust in the judiciary, while Lord Williams, former chairman of the Bar Council, spoke of 'a perversion of justice'. Lord Chief Justice Taylor took the unprecedented step of issuing a public condemnation. Perhaps the only succour for the government was Her Majesty's Opposition, determined to show it too could be as tough as the tabloids demanded.

How far do the tensions of the Thatcher and Major years call into question the thesis of Conservative bias? To some extent the House of Lords began to appear as a liberal court and 'soft judges', concerned about harsh sentencing, human rights and the welfare of asylum-seekers, appeared more in tune with radical pressure groups. Yet much of the judicial opposition was constitutional rather than ideological. Judges may well have felt that so long a period of single-party rule was itself unconstitutional, producing 'arrogance . . . with regard to the law and judicial decisions' (Woodhouse 1996: 424). The battle was for judicial independence. Again, in some cases, as when adjudging Howard to have acted unlawfully in April 1994, by introducing a scheme for compensating victims of violent crimes without parliamentary approval, the courts could be said to be protecting Parliament's rights in a way the House was no longer able to. Labour's return to office did not promise to reduce the executive–judicial tension. Although promising constitutional reforms there was resonance with the tough-on-crime rhetoric, 'zero tolerance' and a commitment to the neoliberal economic agenda.

Administrative Justice

The threat of the state

The twentieth century has witnessed a burgeoning of the welfare state, an extensive road-building programme, intensified activity by coercive forces such as police and immigration control, and increased regulation of social life in areas ranging from rent control and race relations to gender equality. All this heightens the chances that citizens may need to seek **redress of grievance** not from a fellow citizen but from the state itself. Some countries face this contingency with separate systems of courts and a body of **administrative law** such as the French *droit administratif*. However, in Britain most of the relevant law is in the form of general statutes and a haphazard body of common law. This is supplemented by a system of administrative tribunals and public enquiries and the office of ombudsman.

Administrative tribunals

Although taking multifarious forms, **administrative tribunals** are generally bodies adjudicating in various categories of cases where a citizen feels aggrieved by some action of a government official or fellow citizen (employer or landlord). They offer the advantages of speed, informality and expertise. Most are standing bodies, concerned with areas such as rents, social security, pensions, benefits, immigration, housing and the NHS, though others arise on an ad hoc basis for particular cases. They hardly constitute a system, more a motley counterpane, defying precise enumeration. Some are so closely woven into the state fabric that it is difficult to discover whether they are tribunals or merely committees. However, with over seventy different systems, the network is extensive (Pliatzky 1980: 2), some 2,000 tribunals hearing many thousands of cases each year (figure 20.4) (Madgewick and Woodhouse 1995: 291).

The Crichel Down affair

This famous 1954 case highlighted the question of minister–civil servant relationships. It concerned the restoration of land previously requisitioned by the government for military purposes. Although the former owners wished to regain possession, Ministry of Agriculture officials thwarted them with underhand tactics. The owners, well-connected members of the upper-middle class, were able to fight for their rights and after a public inquiry the officials were severely censured and Minister Sir Thomas Dugdale resigned.

Dissatisfaction following the Crichel Down affair led to the establishment in 1954 of the Franks Committee on Administrative Tribunals and Inquiries. Reporting in 1957 it contained a number of indictments.

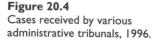

Figure 20.4
Cases received by various
administrative tribunals, 1996.

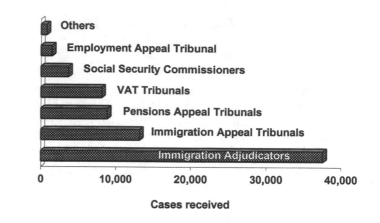

Source: Data from *Judicial Statistics* (1996: 71).

- The minister whose department was subject to the complaint appointed the tribunal, making it judge in its own cause.
- Members were not legally qualified and in many cases legal representation was denied.
- The methods of hearing evidence were not strictly controlled.
- Decisions were often given without reasons.
- Justice was not *seen* to be done, hearings often being conducted like masonic rituals.
- There was no appeals machinery.

Franks wanted chairpersons appointed by the Lord Chancellor and an independent body to create tribunals and keep them under constant review. He also argued for greater openness, legal representation, reasoned decisions and a right of appeal to the courts. Some reform followed: proceedings became public unless personal privacy was involved, limited appeals machinery was introduced (appellate tribunals and the courts) and some legal representation permitted.

In 1958 a Council on Tribunals of ten to fifteen members was created as a watchdog appointed by the Lord Chancellor. However, with less power than Franks envisaged, it could not appoint tribunals, award compensation, hear appeals, or overturn decisions. Its pleas for more powers have been unheeded by bureaucrats keen to cocoon themselves against the winds of justice. The Council has also complained at the lack of government consultation when relevant legislation is being drafted. Although some tribunal chairpersons are now legally qualified, appointment still remains within the patronage of the minister, selecting from a list approved by the Lord Chancellor. Members are also appointed by ministers, which means in practice by officials of the interested department.

Apologists have made much of the informality of tribunals but this has been reduced, the Council on Tribunals publishing *Model Rules of Procedure* in

1991. The virtue of expertise is also questionable; in practice this can mean the opportunity for officials to obfuscate with fog, which a skilled judge would dispel. To citizens tribunals can appear as a Kafkaesque part of the Establishment, often more anxious to protect bureaucrats than pursue justice.

Public inquiries

Government and officials have another alternative to the courts in the **public inquiry,** particularly in cases of collective grievance in areas such as planning and state acquisition of land. Hearings, sometimes dragging on for years, are conducted before interested parties and voluminous reports issued. The Franks Report led to more stringency in their operation; the reports are now published and reasons given for recommendations. Increasingly, major inquiries are chaired by eminent lawyers (p. 624). However, they remain heavily dominated by officials. Although not bound, ministers tend to follow their recommendations, which is not surprising, since the inspectors are from the heavenly list of the great and the good, chosen as a 'safe pair of hands'.

As with tribunals, bureaucrats like to see these exercises as administrative operations (Wraith and Lamb 1971: 13) but the siting of airports, nuclear power stations and motorways affects the quality of people's lives and incites intense feeling. Large-scale public hearings, such as that considering the siting of the nuclear reactor at Sizewell, attract considerable media attention and involve pressure groups, local authorities and private companies. However, the general feeling of those who attend is often one of impotence before a bland wall of polite bureaucratic intransigence. Where protesters give vent to their feelings they may be removed by the inspector's ever-present henchmen in blue. As a result there is an increased tendency for protesters to ignore this avenue and resort to direct action (see chapter 17).

The ombudsmen

A limitation of the tribunal system is its uneven spread. Some departments, such as Social Security, are heavily tribunalized, while others, such as the DfEE, have few. In addition they are limited to certain categories of complaint and cannot cover the full scope of administrative discretion. A 1961 report by the British section of Justice, the legal reform group, recommended the introduction of an **ombudsman system** based on the Scandinavian model of a troubleshooter to investigate citizens' complaints concerning **maladministration** (Whyatt 1961). The idea was received frostily by both officials and government, arguing that it would undermine the quintessential genius of the British constitution, with its supremacy of Parliament and ministerial responsibility.

A very British ombudsman The Labour government proved more sympathetic but the British version created in 1967 was so locked into existing institutions that it was but a pale shadow of the Nordic prototype. Even the term 'ombudsman' (people's friend) was translated through Whitehallspeak into 'Parliamentary Commissioner for Administration' (PCA), who was to be a servant not of the people but of Parliament. The principle was guardedly extended in 1969 to Northern Ireland, the NHS in 1973 and local government in 1974.

In 1977 Justice published another report assessing the impact of the new institution. Its title, *Our Fettered Ombudsman*, betrayed its conclusion (Widdicombe 1977). Britain's PCA is shackled by heavy chains forged by the unharmonious blacksmiths of Whitehall.

- *Access.* The British cannot address their ombudsman directly; they must go through their MP. This protects the traditional role of MPs in the redress of grievances. However, beneath all is the bureaucracy, ever sensitive to the prying eyes of outsiders. A number of critics, including Justice and the PCA himself, have argued for direct access but this has only been permitted for NHS and local government ombudsmen. The latter receive by far the lion's share of complaints (figures 20.5 and 20.6).
- *Maladministration.* Meaning no more than bad administration, the term has proved restrictive. Richard Crossman, when introducing the bill, provided a catalogue of bureaucratic natural shocks to lengthen Hamlet's soliloquy, including 'bias, neglect, inattention, delay, incompetence, ineptitude, perversity, turpitude, arbitrariness, and so on'. Generally the PCA is permitted to consider only the *procedure* of decision-making, not the actual decision. However, it is often the latter that causes the suffer-

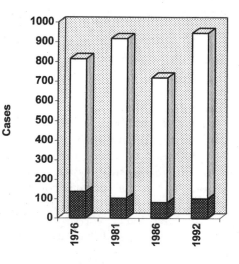

Figure 20.5
Complaints received by the
Parliamentary Commissioner for
Administration, 1976–1992.

Source: Data from *Social Trends* (1994: table 11.17). The shaded portion indicates the cases in which maladministration leading to injustice was found.

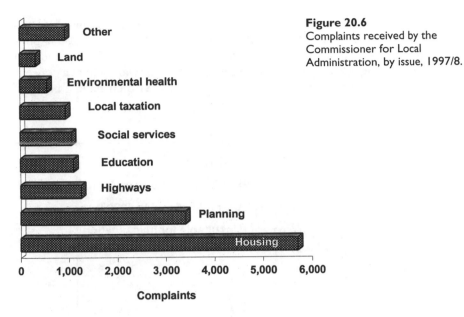

Figure 20.6
Complaints received by the Commissioner for Local Administration, by issue, 1997/8.

Source: Data from *Annual Report of the Commission for Local Administration* (1997/8).

ing. Widdicombe recommended that 'unreasonable, unjust, or oppressive decisions' should be investigated, as in other countries. With the support of their select committee, successive ombudsmen have managed to widen their scope.

- *Limited jurisdiction.* Complaints that may be pursued through the courts or tribunals are excluded, as is sensitive public-sector territory such as the armed forces, police and government contracting. The result is rejection for a large proportion of cases (figures 20.5 and 20.7).

- *Limited autonomy.* Although formally independent, the ombudsman's real autonomy is questionable. While the executive cannot sack him, it appoints him in the first place, along with his staff. Moreover, legal advice comes from the Treasury Solicitor rather than from the courts (although since Widdicombe sources of advice have broadened). Until the appointment of the ex-judge Cecil Clothier in 1979, the first three incumbents were ex-civil servants; justified on the grounds that, as ex-poachers, they would be best able to stalk their prey along the burrows of Whitehall. However, they were never particularly zealous gamekeepers, acting more like civil servants, sidling shyly out of the media limelight, denying any political role and delivering pious apologias for their position.

- *Enforcement.* Following an investigation, the PCA submits a report, not to the citizen but to the MP and department concerned. Although this may contain recommendations, there is no power of enforcement. However, departments have generally tried to comply to avoid adverse publicity. In his first major case, in 1968, the PCA scored an impressive goal by securing compensation for four ex-prisoners of war, held at a concentration camp at Sachsenhausen in Germany, after their having been refused by three Foreign Office ministers.

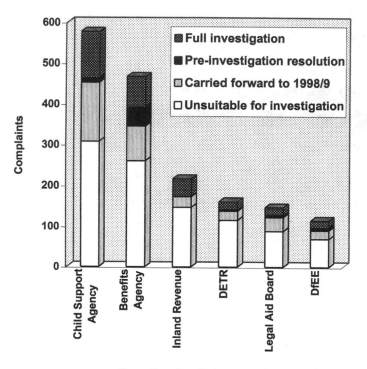

Figure 20.7
The outcome of complaints to the PCA for the departments and agencies subject to the most complaints, 1997/8.

Source: Data from Parliamentary Commissioner for Administration, *Summary Annual Report* (1998).

Ombudsman or ombudsmouse? Designed for a deferential and secretive polity, these are very British ombudsmen. Remaining on the sidelines of political life; few know of the system and few use it. Their value lies perhaps more in legitimating bureaucracy than in providing redress of citizens' grievances. Sir Edmund Compton told the select committee of the excellent standards achieved, taking pride in his many failures to find in favour of complainants.

The Citizen's Charter: freedom, equality and fraternity – or your money back

Citizens' rights were supposed to be further augmented with the issue by the Cabinet Office (1991) of *The Citizen's Charter*. It was soon followed by numerous glossy progeny covering specific services (patients, passengers, parents), setting performance targets and telling people how to complain. Hailed as John Major's 'big idea', this laid down standards for various services, allowing the public to complain, and in some cases receive compensation, much as they might in a supermarket. The initiative was given status with a special unit in the Cabinet Office, the Office of Public Service and Science, and was used by government to rebut criticisms that agencification had undermined democratic accountability.

However, critics saw the charters as fig leaves to conceal falling standards: 'It is perverse and futile . . . to impose financial penalties for delays to services which are delayed in the first place because of lack of finance' (Wilson 1992: xiii). Certainly they were not charters in the sense understood in political history – people's demands to rulers for rights (Kingdom 1996). Neither could they be seen as substitutes for the redress offered through Parliament or the courts. Apart from puzzling motorists with invitations to ring the 'Cones Hotline' (which was apparently merely the Whitehall switchboard number), there was little public reaction. In 1993 a 'Charterline' established to hear complaints was scrapped for lack of calls. A *Guardian* poll (18 Oct. 1994) revealed that 66 per cent of the population regarded the initiative as a public relations stunt.

Judicial review

As we have already seen (p. 624), judicial review is increasingly used for checking the actions of the executive. However, despite a number of high-profile cases, it remains discretionary, striking intermittently and unpredictably and leading some to doubt whether it can be regarded as meaningful control over government (Rawlings 1986). Despite the burgeoning number of cases only a minority concern central government. Moreover, being an expensive process it is unavailable to many individuals and groups.

Towards an administrative court

In 1971 Justice suggested creating a special division of the High Court to provide an avenue to appeal from tribunals on points of law. This would have resembled the prestigious French *Conseil d'Etat*, a supreme administrative tribunal through which ordinary citizens can, at small cost, obtain a wide range of remedies against officialdom. The suggestion meets bureaucratic opposition on the grounds that such a court would lack expertise – a weak objection given that technical cases in the ordinary courts are routinely dealt with by means of expert witnesses. However, increasing use has been made of the Queen's Bench Division for judicial review of tribunal *procedure*, some twelve judges specializing in administrative law. With this growing expertise the demands that the British government drop its objection to a formal system of administrative courts become more compelling.

Law and Politics

Writing in 1998 Nevil Johnson noted how 'during the past 20 years or more the decisions of judges and of other office holders and institutions with adjudicatory functions have begun to impinge more often and more insistently on the spheres of political and administrative discretion in Britain' (1998: 148). This chapter bears this out. While the confrontational style of the post-1979 governments may well have stimulated judicial activism, there are other contributory factors: a political culture that, perhaps because of sleaze scandals, is less willing to trust its leaders; more judicial review; the enlarging presence of the EU in daily life; a growth in tribunals, and the regular use of judges in inquiries. Significantly, the Blair government, by incorporating the ECHR, accepting the EU Social Chapter, setting devolution in motion and promising freedom of information legislation is increasing this tendency. Should Britain take the final step to a written constitution, the involvement of judges would increase even more.

However, while many of these developments proceed in the name of freedom and rights, the greater involvement of judges at the expense of the discretionary power of ministers narrows the area under democratic control and accountability; the people do not appoint judges and they cannot remove them. Judicial involvement may be supported by the argument that the law protects the 'public interest'. However, when judges consider the public interest, the public they have in mind is perhaps more that in the public school than in the public convenience. When the state agencies claim to be enforcing a neutral law, through neutral machinery, they are walking a perilous psychological tightrope. That they have been able to defy political gravity with such conspicuous success is testimony to the forces of socialization that shape popular attitudes.

Key points

- Within the British state the legal institutions are the most august and venerated.
- The organization of the courts is hierarchical and reflects a fundamental dichotomy between civil and criminal jurisdiction.
- The European Court of Human Rights and the European Court of Justice are playing an increasing part in British justice.
- The jury system is the only democratic chink in the legal system.
- High costs mean that for many people access to the law is restricted.
- The legal profession assumed particular importance during the eighteenth and nineteenth centuries as the industrial bourgeoisie sought to safeguard property and wealth.
- Lawyers and judges are generally from the upper-middle classes, predominantly male and white. These factors call into question their impartiality.

- Although the role of judges is formally seen as interpreting and applying the law, they are in reality able to shape it in a number of ways.
- The New Right reforms were to create considerable and uncharacteristic tension between the Conservatives and judiciary.
- Britain does not have a special set of administrative law and courts. The vacuum is filled with administrative tribunals, ombudsmen and citizen's charters.
- Law and the legal system cannot be regarded as above politics and lawyers are increasingly entering the political sphere.

Review your understanding of the following terms and concepts

administrative law
administrative tribunal
barrister
case law
citizen's charter
civil jurisdiction
common law
criminal jurisdiction
European Court of
  Human Rights

JP
judicial activism
judicial impartiality
judicial review
judiciary
jury
legal aid
Lord Chancellor
magistrate
maladministration

ombudsman
Parliamentary
  Commissioner for
  Administration
  (PCA)
public inquiry
redress of grievance
rule of law
solicitor
statute law

Assignment

Study the extract from *The Times* on p. 636 and answer the following questions.

		Mark (%)
1	Why do you think senior members of the judiciary strongly oppose the idea of a judicial appointments commission?	20
2	Are there any grounds for suspicion that Lord Irvine's change of mind resulted from judicial opposition?	20
3	What would you see as the advantages and disadvantages of involving lay people in the selection of judges?	30
4	How might open advertising of senior posts within the legal profession alter the nature of the judiciary?	30

Irvine drops plan for lay people to help pick judges

BY FRANCES GIBB, LEGAL CORRESPONDENT

The Lord Chancellor has ditched controversial plans for a judicial appointments commission, in which lay people would have helped in the selection of judges.

Lord Irvine of Lairg said yesterday that he had decided not to consult on the idea of setting up a commission because of the "very heavy workload" facing his department.

Instead, he announced other reforming measures aimed at modernising the judiciary in the run-up to the millennium and improving "openness, flexibility and effectiveness" of the system.

Vacancies for High Court judgeships will be advertised for the first time within the legal profession, ending the system of appointment to the senior judiciary by invitation only. There are currently 93 High Court judges on a salary of £108,192. Under the previous Lord Chancellor, advertising of vacancies of lower judicial ranks such as circuit and district judges was introduced.

Lord Irvine is also to consider setting up a judges' ombudsman to handle complaints from aggrieved candidates for judicial posts. The proposal for a judicial appointments commission, Labour policy for some years although omitted from the election manifesto, is strongly opposed by the senior judiciary.

But Lord Irvine is understood to have changed his mind about a commission without the need for lobbying by senior judges. A Lord Chancellor's Department spokesman said: "It is his decision entirely. Obviously he talks to senior judges, but he feels that a commission is really not necessary at the moment. One can never say 'never', but it is really on the backburner. He would rather get on with the changes he thinks should be made."

© Times Newspapers Ltd (10 Oct. 1997)

Questions for discussion

1   Why did the nineteenth century see important developments in the legal profession?
2   Evaluate the principle of trial by jury. Why do you think bodies such as the police are unhappy with it?
3   Assess the role of British judges in shaping the law.
4   'The way judges are appointed means that they must nurse conservative leanings and have little sympathy with working people or left-wing movements.' Discuss.
5   What likely problems face women bringing rape charges in our courts?

6   'The British ombudsmen do little more than legitimate bureaucratic power.' Discuss.
7   How might the incorporation of the ECHR change the role of British judges?
8   How far is Britain's system of administrative tribunals an adequate substitute for a full-scale system of administrative law?
9   Discuss whether judges should be Freemasons.
10 'The political involvement of judges has increased, is increasing and should be curtailed.' Discuss.

Topic for debate

This house gives a black mark to white justice.

Further reading

Griffith, J. A. G. (1997) *The Politics of the Judiciary*, 5th edn.
First published 1977. Lively critique of the judiciary and its alleged political neutrality. Continues to irritate in establishment circles.

Harris, P. (1997) *An Introduction to the Law*, 5th edn.
Introductory text portraying the law and the legal system as living institutions.

Kairys, P. (ed.) (1982) *The Politics of Law: A Progressive Critique*.
Readings on law in society.

Kennedy, H. (1992) *Eve was Framed*.
Searching, semi-autobiographical polemic by woman barrister criticizing the legal profession, with special emphasis on its sexism.

Lee, S. (1988) *Judging Judges*.
Defends judges against critics of the left.

Rosenberg, J. (1997) *Trial of Strength*.
Details the battle between ministers and judges over who makes the law.

Thompson, E. P. (1975) *Whigs and Hunters*.
Explores the relationship between the law and economic power.

For light relief

Charles Dickens, *Bleak House*.
Satire on the Court of Chancery. Tells of *Jarndyce and Jarndyce*, a case which continues interminably for the profit of the lawyers and the ruin of others.

Franz Kafka, *The Trial*.
A nightmare vision of a judicial system. Begins: 'Someone must have slandered Joseph K., because one morning, without his having done anything wrong, he was arrested'.

John Mortimer, *Rumpole of the Bailey*.
Humorous tales by famous playwright/barrister. Also available as videos.

David Pannick, *Advocates*.
Thought-provoking and amusing account of the practices and morality of the Bar.

Twelve Angry Men.
Classic film in a jury room, starring Henry Fonda.

On the net

http://www.ombudsman.org
This site includes the PCA's annual reports and extensive statistics on the cases reviewed.

http://www.open.gov.uk/lcd
The Lord Chancellor's Department is at the heart of the criminal justice system. A vast amount of information is available on this web site, which also includes links to related sites, from the European Court of Justice to the Law Society.

http://www.ccrc.gov.uk
Find out about miscarriages of justice investigated by the Criminal Cases Review Commission.

http://www.open.gov.uk/lawcomm/homepage.htm
If you are interested in the Law Commission's role in law reform, take heed of the warning that some of the documents available on this web site can be very large.

Chapter Twenty-one

The Coercive State: the Politics of Law and Order

One of the defining characteristics of the state is the right to use violence. Although a necessary power, it is one fraught with danger, evoking fears of a 'police state' or military dictatorship. The world is full of examples of how real this threat is. Clearly debates around issues of law and order must be central to politics. This chapter begins with the evolution of the police service, and its organization and culture. We then focus on its twin functions of fighting crime and maintaining public order. This leads to a consideration of four trends in modern policing – centralization, militarization, politicization and the increasing involvement of the private sector. This is followed by an examination of the crucial function of monitoring – the police complaints procedure. We also go beyond the police to consider the more shadowy world of the military and the security services. We conclude by asking whether the coercive policing of modern times should or could revert to a more consensus style.

There are grounds for believing that policing in the UK is a model for the world. Certainly many men and women in all ranks serve with dedication, tact, and often great bravery. Yet the position they are in is necessarily one of acute political sensitivity. Policing can only enjoy legitimacy in a society that constantly debates its role and evaluates its operation. It is a measure of the success of British policing that a number of associated issues feature openly in modern political debate. We turn to these after briefly reviewing the evolution of the police service.

Evolution

Although the history of policing may be traced back before the Norman Conquest, lying in the principle that a community accepted a joint responsibility for maintaining the peace, like most of the apparatus of the modern state, the police service was largely a nineteenth-century creation of the bourgeoisie. In the dense unholy urban communities, lawlessness could thrive and an ever-present threat of civil unrest was made more terrifying to the propertied by the spectre of the French Revolution and its terrible aftermath. An early move to strengthen law and order was made in the eighteenth century by Henry Fielding (author of the classic *Tom Jones*), a justice at London's Bow Street Court, who gathered together a group of upper-class vigilantes – the celebrated Bow Street Runners.

Radical agitation in the 1815–19 period saw magistrates bringing in the cavalry to break up a large but peaceful working-class demonstration in Manchester in August 1819. Known as the Peterloo Massacre, it created a scandal and was clearly no way to legitimate the political order. As Home Secretary, Sir Robert Peel secured a number of important penal reforms, introducing the concept of modern policing in the Metropolitan Police Act (1829). This was a paid, uniformed, full-time, disciplined and specially trained corps. It became the model for other municipalities, consolidated under the 1856 County and Borough Police Act.

Structure, accountability and control

There are forty-three police services in England and Wales employing around 250,000 police officers as well as over 50,000 civilians (figure 21.1). Although nominally under local government this image has always been misleading and recent reforms have left it even more removed from community control. The key figures in the chain of command and accountability are the local police authority, the chief constable and the home secretary. Parliament also has a part to play, though a smaller one than might be expected.

The police authority Supposed to represent their communities, police authorities cover single counties or joint areas formed by adjacent unitary authorities. Their forebears, the nineteenth-century watch committees, exercised considerable control and could dismiss officers and demand weekly reports (Baldwin and Kinsey 1982: 106). However, their role has been gradually reduced so that today it is mainly limited to consulting the local community about their concerns and priorities, identifying local objectives and setting targets within objectives set by the home secretary.

Membership was also changed, reducing the role of councillors. Before April 1995 police committees comprised two-thirds local councillors and one-third JPs. However, under the 1994 Police and Magistrates Court Act police authorities were made independent precepting bodies (effectively quangos). The government wanted them to have sixteen members, regardless of area, with the chair and one-third of members in the patronage of the home secretary and eight members from the local authority. However, this aroused considerable hostility and the House of Lords forced concessions, the size increasing to seventeen: nine councillors, three JPs, and the rest appointed from a shortlist by

Figure 21.1
Size of the police force in England and Wales, 1971–1996.

Source: Data from *Social Trends* (1988: table 12.27) and *Annual Abstract of Statistics* (1998: table 4.2).

the home secretary. The authorities appoint their own chairs.

London's Metropolitan Police (the 'Met') had been the direct responsibility of the home secretary. However, Labour's reform of London government in 1999 brought policing in line with the rest of the country, with a new Metropolitan Police Authority under the directly elected mayor. The membership of twenty-three was to comprise eleven (including the deputy mayor) drawn from the new Assembly, one from the district councils outside London which came under the Met, with the remaining eleven being magistrates and independent members, one of them appointed by the home secretary to reflect the authority's national and international functions.

The chief constable In day-to-day policing the key figure is the chief constable who, as a servant of the Crown, is not under the direction of the police authority. Although the chief constable usually presents an annual report to the police authority, this is not obligatory. One element of control the authority does have is over funding, though this is limited (see below).

The home secretary The home secretary is in a sense the minister for the police. Although having considerable formal powers, incumbents have generally been timid. In the 1980s Douglas Hurd was admired for the way he was able to cultivate 'an appearance of almost deliberate powerlessness when it comes to police operation' (Evans 1986a). When power has been used it has more often been to direct police authorities than chief constables. During the 1984 miners' strike, South Yorkshire tried to withhold the supply of funds for policing the strike. They were opposed by the Chief Constable, who sought the support of both Home Secretary and Attorney General, the latter applying to the High Court for powers to coerce the authority (Oliver 1987: 215–21). However, as we shall see below, in the 1990s Kenneth Clarke and Michael Howard began to take a stronger line.

> Not only can the chief constable do what he likes, but he can spend all our money doing it.
>
> Gabrielle Cox (Manchester Police Committee chairperson), quoted in the *Guardian* (11 Aug. 1984)

Parliament Since, as officers of the Crown, the police escape local accountability, it might be thought that they are accountable to Parliament through the home secretary. However, a 'catch 22' situation obtains: the Speaker has ruled that, because the police administration lies with police authorities, the home secretary is *not* answerable (*House of Commons Debates* 1958: col. 1259).

Who controls? The lack of accountability can be defended on the grounds that it insulates the police from corrupt politicians and prevents the rise of a **police state**. However, it can be argued that evils are more likely in the absence of democratic accountability. We explore this later in the chapter.

> Had the Metropolitan Police been influenced over the past ten years by elected representatives . . . many of the mistakes would have been avoided and its reputation would stand far higher.
>
> Roy Hattersley (Shadow Home Secretary), quoted in J. Benyon (ed.),
> *Scarman and After* (1984: 108)

Culture and the Policing Function

Policing entails two broad functions – fighting crime and maintaining public order. Both require considerable discretion and the way this is exercised shapes society, making policing an essentially political role. Hence it is important to study the ideas and attitudes informing actions – the **police culture**.

Police culture

Policing is an all-consuming occupation and can create an incestuous professional community. Socializing in the community being policed is obviously difficult, officers often spending their leisure hours with each other, reinforcing attitudes and creating strong pressure to conform. This culture is secretive, as is shown in a tendency to join the Freemasons. In 1988 the *Sunday Times* acquired a list of no fewer than a hundred senior Scotland Yard officers who were active members. There were believed to be some 5,000 Masons in the Metropolitan force alone and allegations circulated that membership enhanced promotion prospects, influenced investigations and led to cover-ups (Chittenden 1988). Although the Home Affairs Select Committee concluded in March 1997 that the problem was exaggerated, serious public concern led Home Secretary Jack Straw to follow their recommendation that new recruits to the police, probation and prison services, as well as judges, should register Freemason membership.

Characteristically the police are associated with certain attitudes towards race, gender, class and ideology.

"Look, this is damn silly if we're both masons."

Race A traditional reluctance to employ black people, and their disinclination to apply, reinforces white police culture. Attracting increasing attention since the 1970s it is one of the major problems of policing today. Research by the Policy Studies Institute in the 1980s found the casual manner in which racist language was used its most telling feature. West Indians were regularly referred to as 'nigger', 'sooty', 'coon', 'spade', 'monkey' and 'spook', while Asians were invariably 'Pakis', regardless of origins. These norms led officers who did not think of themselves as racists to use the terms (Smith and Gray 1985: 390–3). The Police Complaints Authority's 1993 annual report recorded 172 complaints of racism, but in only a single case were charges recommended.

Such attitudes have helped to precipitate race disturbances in several cities. The 1986 Broadwater Farm riots, during which a policeman was brutally murdered, illustrated the intensity of feeling. Subsequent research revealed that 75 per cent of young blacks perceived the police as being unjust towards them; as many as 67 per cent of young whites agreed (Lea et al. 1986). Confidence was not restored in the Stephen Lawrence case, in which five white youths were accused of murdering a black student. The Met failed to convict and displayed a profound lack of sympathy towards the Lawrence family. During the public inquiry begun in May 1998 under Sir William Macpherson, Home Office expert Paul Pugh declared police racial awareness training to have been a waste of

> Reading isn't an occupation we encourage among police officers. We try to keep the paperwork down to a minimum.
>
> Joe Orton (1933–67; British dramatist), *Loot* (1965)

money. Home Office statistics revealed that 108 black people had been arrested in every 1,000, compared with 14 per 1,000 for white people. Although apologizing for his force's handling of the case, Commissioner Paul Condon resisted resignation calls and refused to concede institutional racism. However, David Wilmot, Chief Constable of Greater Manchester, created a stir in October 1998 with a dramatic admission that institutional racism infected his own force. Despite damning reports from both the Police Complaints Authority and the Macpherson inquiry, no officer faced disciplinary charges and all left with pension rights fully intact.

> We've got a young lad in there, he's dead, we don't know who he is and we'd like to clarify that point. If he's not your son, all well and good, but we need to know and I'm sure you'd like to know too.
>
> Inspector Ian Little, senior police officer, to Stephen Lawrence's parents at the hospital after their son had been pronounced dead, quoted in the *Independent* (8 April 1998)

Sexism The police ethos is overtly masculine, similar to that found in other predominantly male preserves like the army or rugger clubs (the police field formidable teams, often including internationals). Women often experience great difficulty in developing a career, constituting only a small proportion of the service (see figure 21.1). The conversation and jokes mock women colleagues ('plonks'). Smith and Gray (1985: 373), choosing a deliberately mild example, report an older constable enthusing over the practice whereby new WPCs were always 'stamped on the bare bum' with the official rubber stamp. The absence of women is a question not merely of unequal opportunity, it has deep operational and political implications. The non-consensual pattern of policing (see below), which can actually incite violence, is a product of the macho culture.

In February 1993 the Home Office released a report by academic researchers on sex discrimination in the police service, disclosing that nearly all policewomen experience sexual harassment ranging from 'groping' to rape. Women were also twice as likely as men to take sick leave because of frustration over career development (*Guardian*, 12 Feb. 1993). Alison Halford, who rose to become one of Britain's seniormost policewomen, brought a celebrated case to the Equal Opportunities Commission after being rejected for promotion to deputy chief constable nine times while less qualified men advanced. The service responded by bringing disciplinary charges against her. Both cases were dropped and a financial settlement accepted by Halford; her subsequent book title summed up her career – *No Way Up the Greasy Pole* (1993).

Attitudes towards women in general are similarly sexist. A particular problem arises with rape. In the first place, victims are loath to report, and those that do so (about one in four) have been subject to humiliating scepticism (Benn et al. 1983). The Greenham Common demonstrations, where women stepped outside traditional structures of protest to express a particularly female view of the arms race, widened awareness of the problem with a huge number of arrests for trivial offences, intimidating dawn raids, many injuries, sexual harassment, strip searching and photographing. Similarly, wives who became involved in the miners' strikes experienced humiliation and abuse: mocked for their poverty, locked in vans for up to two hours and 'refused access to a toilet . . . offered a milk bottle instead' (Benn 1985: 132).

Class The police stand in a curious position socially; approved of by the middle classes, whose privileges they work to protect, they have traditionally recruited from the working class (Reiner 1982). The class basis is not surprising, because the job can be variously onerous, boring and dangerous; between 1981 and 1987, 111 police officers in England and Wales were killed on duty (Lambert 1988). Hence the police are among the most oppressed of the working class, suffering from an alarming rise in stress-related illnesses (Evans 1986a). Yet paradoxically the police oppress working-class people. In the Met, officers divided the citizenry broadly into two categories – on the one hand 'slag' or 'rubbish' and on the other 'respectable people' – defined largely in terms of social class (Smith and Gray 1985: 434).

Political complexion Although officially neutral, the police service is clearly right wing, as many as 80 per cent designating themselves Conservative (Kettle 1980: 31; Reiner 1993). Indeed, the National Front experienced little difficulty in seducing 'chief constables and even the Home Office into providing the movement with the necessary facilities for its public campaigns' (Walvin 1984: 142).

Police culture exerts a constant socializing effect. As recruits work their way up the pressure is to conform, to become more macho, more racist and more right wing. Indeed, higher-class recruits may even affect lower-class accents (Smith and Gray 1985: 435). The successful officer will not usually be one who stands out against prevailing norms, and those in positions of authority will tend to promote in their own image. However, the culture affects the pattern of policing in both fighting crime and maintaining public order.

Fighting crime

The image of the police treating all equally belongs largely to a fantasy world of cops and robbers. Police culture tends to favour the white and the wealthy and offences relating to property dominate crime statistics. The weight of police suspicion bears most heavily on the lower sections of the working class (unskilled workers, the unemployed and the young), who are more likely to receive contempt and abuse. Researchers listened to an officer, not considered unusual, addressing a boy in the absence of his parents:

> 'You're a fucking little cunt aren't you? You've been at it again haven't you, you little bastard? . . . I'm going to nail your fucking hide to the wall'. (Smith and Gray 1985: 420)

It is unlikely that a stockbroker would be addressed in such terms. The evidence is that black people, particularly West Indians, are far more likely than others to be stopped and even arrested on the grounds of intuition. Yet the popular view that blacks are more prone to commit violent crime is unjustified (figure 21.2).

Various areas have caused concern, including brutality, false confessions and the decision to prosecute.

Police brutality The macho style has resulted in a harrowing catalogue of atrocities. For example, in 1971 in Leeds, David Oluwale, a Nigerian, was singled out for 'special treatment' in which he was urinated on, beaten severely and abandoned dead in the countryside; in an ensuing cover-up notebooks were doctored. In 1976, Liddle Towers was set upon by police outside a Gateshead club, subsequently dying from injuries received; although his doctor described his body as 'pulped', a Labour home secretary refused to set up an official enquiry. In June 1979, Jimmy Kelly was set upon by police as he walked home from a pub in Huyton, Liverpool, subsequently dying in police custody. Further journalistic investigations into this force disclosed a long trail of beatings and sadism.

In July 1990 Oliver Price died after being held in a necklock by police. In August 1993 Joy Gardener died of suffocation after police taped over her mouth when attempting to deport her. The three police officers charged with her manslaughter were subsequently acquitted. In May 1995 Brian Douglas died after being struck on the head with a long-handled police baton; no disciplinary action followed. While not all deaths in custody are the result of police treatment, the trend is disturbing, more than doubling from twenty-seven in 1993 to fifty-seven in 1996/7.

Figure 21.2
Sentenced adult male prison population by offence and ethnic group, 1995.

Source: Data from *Social Trends* (1997: table 9.23).

False confessions and miscarriages of justice Formal protection for suspects was based on the famous though ill-understood Judges' Rules, permitting the right to silence and access to a solicitor or friend. These did not carry statutory force, were applied capriciously and subject to abuse. In addition, 'confessions' extracted by police officers appeared to reflect the talents of Agatha Christie rather than Sherlock Holmes. A major *cause célèbre* was the *Confait* case: three boys convicted of murder and arson on the basis of false confessions after a male homosexual had been found dead in his blazing home in April 1972. This led in 1977 to a Royal Commission on Criminal Procedure, set up against police wishes, which reported in 1981. Sir David McNee, Metropolitan Police Commissioner, argued that the things the police did were necessary and should therefore be legalized (Koffman 1985: 15).

The resultant Police and Criminal Evidence Act (1984) (PACE) made provision for restricting police power: all interviews were to be taped, suspects given the right to have a solicitor present and confessions were to be unforced and only used as evidence if taped. Yet in reality little changed; indeed suspects were arrested more often, detention was authorized as a matter of routine, the law on interrogation remained unclear, the right to legal advice proved difficult to enforce and the taping of interviews was easily evaded. Police could also pressurize suspects (Sanders and Young 1995). The Act actually *increased* police powers.

Public concern about miscarriages of justice continued to hit the headlines. In 1989, the West Midlands serious crime squad was suspended, pending an inquiry, after a series of trials collapsed amidst allegations of fabricated evidence. Officers from the squad had been involved in the controversial conviction of the 'Birmingham Six', imprisoned for the pub bombings of 21 November 1974. In January 1990 the 'Guildford Four', convicted on the basis of false confessions for the pub bombings of 5 October 1974, walked free. In 1997, the 'Bridgewater Three' were released after being imprisoned for the murder of newspaper boy Carl Bridgewater on the basis of improper methods by Staffordshire police.

In 1991 a Royal Commission on Criminal Justice was established 'to examine the effectiveness of the criminal justice system in England and Wales in securing the conviction of those guilty of criminal offences *and the acquittal of those who are innocent*' (emphasis added). However, it simply recommended fine tuning, suggesting no fundamental reforms and offering 'little comfort to those now languishing in jails for crimes they did not commit, convicted on the basis of confessions they did not want to make' (Sanders and Young 1995: 140). Concern led to the Criminal Appeal Act (1995) establishing the Criminal Cases Review Commission (see chapter 20). However, with its chair a Freemason and its membership heavily weighted towards the prosecuting authorities, its independence appeared questionable (Mansfield 1997).

The decision to prosecute Arrest does not in itself mean that a criminal prosecution will follow and traditionally the police enjoyed discretion over this decision. This unsatisfactory state eventually led in 1986 to the creation for England and Wales of a Crown Prosecution Service (CPS), under a Director of Public

Prosecutions. Many problems dogged the new service, including inadequate funding, police scepticism, some very expensive trials ending in acquittals, such as those of three footballers accused of taking bribes (two trials and the police investigation costing £12 million) and a failure to prosecute police accused of offences. Of the eight most serious cases of deaths in police custody between 1990 and 1995, only two resulted in prosecution. The relatives' support group, Inquest, argued that 'the perception is that the police are above the law and that those deaths are not taken seriously' (*Guardian*, 5 Oct. 1996). The same New Right managerialism that had affected much of the state was also apparent in the CPS. In 1998 its director, Dame Barbara Mills, abruptly retired, having 'become synonymous with the worst aspects of the service; its overblown bureaucracy, its poor morale and its civil service mentality' (*The Times*, 21 May 1998).

Maintaining public order

Despite the increase in powers (under the 1984 Act), the police record in crime-fighting is questionable. The prolonged failure to catch the 'Yorkshire Ripper' in the 1980s provided bizarre evidence of ineptitude. However, in the second of their functions they can appear more effective. Maintaining **public order** is a more overtly political function. Indeed the police can sometimes be cast as instruments of government policy; they often act as if they are protecting not public order but the state itself, working through the Special Branch and in

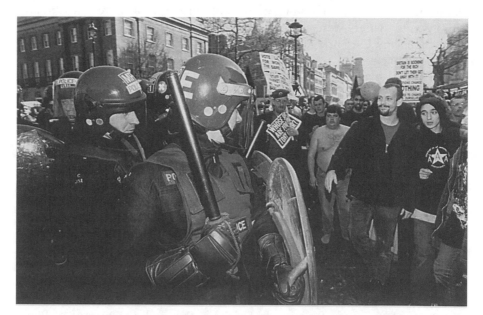

Bobbies on the beat: policing the social justice march, April 1997

Photo: *The Socialist*

liaison with MI6. It is here that some of the worst police violence has been seen.

In making public order decisions police culture leads officers to have little empathy with the people who march in support of causes such as anti-fascism, gay rights, CND, Irish republicanism or Greenpeace. They can see such people as unpatriotic enemies, expressing views such as: 'It's the scum of the earth. Why should we protect that?' (Smith and Gray 1985: 436). Legislation tends to support police action. In the early 1980s powers rested mainly on the 1936 Public Order Act. This was replaced by a designer Public Order Act (1986) intended to legitimize many of the powers they had already been assuming without authorization. The 1994 Criminal Justice and Public Order Act contained a number of new measures roundly criticized by civil liberties groups. Powers to stop and search were increased and police were enabled to restrict travellers, squatters, protesters and those attending raves. A new offence of 'aggravated trespass' made trespass a criminal rather than a civil offence, giving the police the right to act against those protesting against, say, new roads, airport runways or foxhunting. It was easy to find grounds to act against protesters offending the government and critics feared a police state. Days before Easter 1996 the Home Secretary gave the police new stop-and-search powers under the Prevention of Terrorism Act.

The change of government in 1997 did little to stop the momentum. In 1998 Jack Straw unveiled his Crime and Disorder Bill, which promised night-time curfews for children under ten and orders making parents of delinquent children attend special parenting classes. Straw's rhetoric proudly highlighted the tough side of the bill: 'This is about implementing a zero-tolerance strategy'. It was aimed at gangs, drug dealers, criminal families and bad neighbours. However, it had a softer side with plans for the early release of minor offenders and electronic tagging and community-service orders as alternatives to prison.

Making the punishment fit the crime: penal policy

> My object all sublime,
> I shall achieve in time,
> To let the punishment fit the crime,
> The punishment fit the crime.
>
> *The Mikado*, W. S. Gilbert

The treatment of the convicted is a major cause for debate, with two polar extremes: a tough retributive approach which can even include death (capital punishment), or punishment as a means of rehabilitation. Those arguing the latter case characterize prisons as 'universities of crime', some 60 per cent of their 'graduates' reoffending within two years.

For most of the twentieth century, home secretaries aimed to limit or reduce the prison population. However, Conservative Michael Howard reversed the thinking with his 'prison works' mantra. An October 1993 promise to expand the prison building programme was followed in September 1995 with plans for Britain's first 'boot camp' for young offenders. The Crime (Sentences) Act (1997) established mandatory prison terms, including 'life' for anyone aged eighteen or over convicted for a second time of a serious violent or sexual crime. Labour generally supported the policies and its own Crime and Disorder Act (1998) toughened up the treatment of young offenders. They would be forced to make reparations to their victims and the principle of *doli incapax* (presuming that children under fourteen do not know right and wrong) was abolished.

Whether or not prison works, Britain places a higher proportion of its population behind bars than any comparable nation. Between 1980 and 1995 the average prison population rose from 43,109 to 51,231 and was projected to reach 74,000 by 2005. However, this produced an overcrowding crisis (figure 21.3) and a series of damming reports from Her Majesty's Chief Inspector of Prisons, Judge Stephen Tumim, detailed grim and insanitary conditions. The 1995 Learmont Report on the Parkhurst Prison breakout chronicled 'mind-numbing bureaucratic incompetence' (*The Times*, 18 Oct. 1995). The following year forty-six prisons were classed as overcrowded and a record number of prisoners (forty-six) committed suicide.

Tough penal measures provoke opposition from the judiciary and prison reform groups. Research evidence suggests that the likelihood of being caught is the more serious deterrent (Downs 1997), though of course this requires more police resources and hence higher taxes.

Figure 21.3
A punitive society? Prison population, 1901–2005 (using lowest estimated projection for 2005).

Source: Data from Butler and Butler (1994: 320) and Home Office Research and Statistics Directorate.

Trends in Modern Policing

Traditionally the British police service was decentralized, non-militaristic and apolitical. This remains the official picture but, like so much of the constitution, the formal principles mask reality.

Centralization: a national police service?

> The combination of a centralised police system and an unwritten constitution is the stuff that dictators dream about.
>
> John Alderson (retired chief constable and academic), *A New Cromwell: The Centralization of the Police* (1994)

Local policing and a plurality of forces were justified in terms of local democracy and responsiveness to local conditions. Moreover, the absence of a single national service is a crucial bulwark against the growth of a monolithic police state. The police themselves have consistently resisted the idea of a single service under the home secretary and responsible to Parliament. However, throughout the twentieth century insidious **centralization** has taken place beneath a pluralistic facade through amalgamation, centralized staff organizations, communications technology, specialist units and the strategy of central government.

> I am inclined to the view that we are witnessing a move, perhaps unintended, for national control of the police by central government.
>
> Sir John Smith (ACPO President), speech (4 Feb. 1994)

Amalgamation From the outset, central government was concerned to enlarge police areas. An 1882 Act forbade new boroughs with populations less than 20,000 from establishing their own forces and the 1888 Local Government Act insisted that those with populations below 10,000 merge their forces with those of the parent county under joint committees. Amalgamation was further advanced under the emergency conditions of the second world war.

A royal commission reviewing the constitutional position of the police argued in 1962 that a single force would be more efficient and offer a clear line of accountability. Although the 1964 Police Act stopped short of unification, it increased the home secretary's power to effect amalgamations and strengthened the system of central inspection. Governments did promote amalgamations and the Local Government Act (1972) created some joint forces (such as Thames Valley and West Mercia). A 1993 white paper questioned whether forty-three separate organizations made 'the most effective use of resources available for policing' (Home Office 1993: 41–2) and Home Secretary Kenneth Clarke favoured massive reductions down to twenty-two authorities (Loveday 1996). The reorganization of local government and increase in the number of unitary authorities suggested further scope for amalgamation.

Centralized staff associations *De facto* centralization of the police service has occurred through the development of national associations. Important among these is the Police Federation, a kind of union representing all officers up to the rank of chief inspector (officially the police cannot join a union). It speaks for members in negotiations with government and through public pronouncements as if for a single force.

Of even greater significance is the Association of Chief Police Officers (ACPO) representing senior officers, including chief constables. ACPO does more than speak for its members, it organizes policing nationally, particularly through the National Reporting Centre (NRC), which coordinates policing throughout the country and liaises with the Home Office and MI5 (Boateng 1985: 240). It was established at Scotland Yard in response to fears for public order in the early 1970s. ACPO also operates the Mutual Aid Coordination Centre set up by the 1964 Police Act, whereby police may be deployed anywhere in the country like a national force. The system was particularly visible during the 1984/5 miners' strike, when convoys of blue minibuses became a familiar sight on the M1.

Advanced communications technology Forces now operate sophisticated computer and electronic communications systems. These assist in the collection and collation of vast quantities of data for national records, offering 'precise and rapid central control' (Campbell 1980: 65). In 1959 the Home Office, the Metropolitan force and the Prison Commission set up a Joint Automatic Data Processing Unit, which led in 1969 to the establishment of the Police National Computer Unit at Hendon to supervise a complex communications network of almost a thousand terminals located throughout the country. Liberty estimated that in 1991 at least 70,000 individuals were under surveillance in the national computer (*Independent*, 18 Dec. 1991).

Specialist units Further centralization comes from the development of specialist CID squads, including regional crime squads, the National Drugs Intelligence Unit, the National Identification Bureau and the Serious Fraud Office. In addition, there are the specialist squads of the Metropolitan force such as the Special Branch, concerned with national security and working with MI5, and the Royalty and Diplomatic Protection Service. Even the Crown Prosecution Service can be seen as part of the centralizing tendency.

Central government strategy Finally, there is the role of central government. Whitehall's ability to influence policing is by no means new; it has been part of the hidden constitution since the early twentieth century, particularly in class disputes (Morgan 1987). The policing of the miners' strike gave a number of important insights into this. Strategy was coordinated by a high-powered cabinet committee (Misc 101) chaired by Thatcher and including leading ministers and a representative of the armed forces. It received regular reports from the NRC. The Cabinet Office also played a part, by word of mouth to mask a link between the Coal Board and police (Boateng 1985: 239).

The Police and Magistrates Court Act (1994) aimed to increase Home Office control over policing (Jones and Newburn 1995). Ex-chief constable turned academic, John Alderson (1994), saw the legislation creating Britain's first 'Minister of Police'. Senior officers were placed on fixed-term contracts renewed by the home secretary, putting them under pressure to act in a manner likely to gain ministerial approval. Ian Oliver, chief constable of Grampian, who voiced objections, was effectively sacked in 1998 by Scottish Secretary Donald Dewar. Moreover, police authorities began to complain of excessive interference with the shortlists for their independent members (*Police Review*, 18 Nov. 1994); in Warwickshire, both chief constable and police authority alleged that the Home Office had removed women and ethnic minority representatives, replacing them with businesspersons (*Independent*, 27 Jan. 1995).

Central government also sidelined local government in crime prevention. Programmes such as Safer Cities, Crime Concern, Inner City Task Forces, Neighbourhood Watch and schemes for Citizen Patrols were developed by the Home Office and other central departments. Where they looked for local involvement, the preference was again for the business community (Loveday 1994).

Towards a British 'FBI' In July 1989, Metropolitan Police Commissioner Peter Imbert, in a lecture to the Police Foundation, called for an even tighter degree of central control with the creation of a single, national detective force along the lines of the US Federal Bureau of Investigation (FBI). Comprising police, customs officers, lawyers, accountants, computer experts and immigration officers, the new body would be centrally funded, responsible to Parliament through the home secretary and with access to a national computerized intelligence system. Local forces would exist alongside but be required to yield some of their sovereignty. A move in this direction was seen in the 1997 Police Act, which made provision for a National Crime Squad for England and Wales (launched in April 1998 with 1,450 detectives seconded for three- to five-year terms) and put the National Criminal Intelligence Service on a UK-wide statutory basis.

With such centralizing forces at work, why does government resist the formation of a single police service? Official arguments are couched in terms of democracy and local control and accountability, yet the reality of these is highly questionable. Moreover, British democracy has never depended upon such a principle. Hence critics argue that the formal fragmentation of the service serves as a convenient fiction to permit a *de facto* centralization which can evade inconvenient accountability to Parliament.

Militarization

The economic problems of the 1970s saw waves of unrest with much of the 'goodwill' between the police and the people breaking down. The policing of demonstrations and strikes began to show signs of **militarization**, with marching in troops, charges, visors, CS gas and intimidation such as the rhythmic beating of riot shields. Forces now have grim arsenals of rubber bullets, riot shields, water cannon and armoured vehicles. New recruits receive training in their use and forces have special crack firearms squads. In the period 1970–2, police were issued with guns on 5,244 occasions; during 1975–8, this happened 14,574 times (Rollo 1980: 166–7). In 1983, an innocent man, Stephen Waldorf, was shot in his car by police mistaking him for someone else.

Policing of the industrial dispute between print unions and Murdoch's News International at Wapping led to some 440 complaints, many concerning the mounted police who charged like the cavalry (*Independent*, 10 Dec. 1988). The miners' strike introduced strikers (and television viewers) to specialized paramilitary forces. Following experiments, the use of special US-style two-handed collapsible batons was authorized by Michael Howard in 1993. In May 1995 he urged the Police Federation conference at Blackpool to follow the example of the Metropolitan Police and use body armour (*Guardian*, 18 May 1995).

A third force? In some countries there exists within the coercive apparatus of the state a third force, poised between the police and the military. This avoids using the military to quell civil disturbance, while protecting police relationships with citizens. However, the hallmark of such forces is savagery. In France, for example, the Compagnie Républicaine de Sécurité is dreaded; in the Paris riots of 1968 it injured 1,500 in a single night. Britain traditionally eschewed such a force but today we are witnessing the appearance of **paramilitary** units.

In the early 1970s, establishment fears of left-wing movements led to the creation of a National Security Committee, with representatives of the military, intelligence services, Home Office, Department of Trade and police, to prepare for nothing less than an internal attack on the state (Bunyan 1977: 293). It recommended better training in riot control, the use of firearms and regular joint police–military exercises. Additionally, a Special Patrol Group (SPG), established in London by the Labour government some years earlier to combat crime, was given a paramilitary remit while remaining formally within the police service. A key mover was Metropolitan Commissioner Sir Robert Mark, who had made detailed studies of the methods of the RUC and B-Specials in Northern Ireland. The new elite corps was to have an independent command structure based on Scotland Yard. Members, selected from young volunteers from the London police divisions, distinguished by the letters CO on their shoulders, served for two-year terms.

The SPG's existence remained largely unknown until the India House incident in 1973 when, in a religious protest, two Pakistanis from Bradford invaded the Indian High Commission with toy guns. Within four minutes, and

> His tongue was stuck to his upper jaw, and the upper part of his head was all red as if he was bleeding inside.
>
> Local resident who attempted to administer aid to Blair Peach, quoted in J. Rollo, 'The Special Patrol Group', in P. Hain (ed.), *Policing the Police* (1980: 158)

without being asked to drop the guns, they were shot dead by SPG guards who became overnight heroes. Another celebrated operation was the Grunwick industrial dispute of 1977, where an employer sought to deprive his employees (Asian women) of trade union rights. When mass picketing took place, the SPG moved in and their brutality astonished prominent figures present. However, the Labour government ignored TUC demands for a Home Office enquiry and Home Secretary Merlyn Rees supported the SPG.

The Blair Peach affair in April 1979 brought home the extent to which the SPG operated in a realm above the law. Peach, one of the objectors to a National Front demonstration (held with extreme provocation in the largely black area of Southall), was struck on the head with a rubber cosh filled with lead (an unauthorized weapon) by an SPG officer. Before long he was dead. The events following this had all the characteristics of a cover-up and no prosecutions were made (Rollo 1980: 165).

Militarism quickly spread; today most forces have some kind of SPG clone under an independent chain of command. Known variously as Mobile Support Unit, Special Operations Unit and Tactical Aid Group, some have themselves been involved in *causes célèbres*, such as the James McGeown case (1978) in Strathclyde, in which a man with hands tied behind his back was kicked to death by members of the Strathclyde Support Unit.

Politicization

Although formally outside politics, it has already been shown that policing has political consequences. Where there is inequality, the police must constantly seek to restrain the 'have nots' from threatening the 'haves' and it is not surprising that they feel an affinity with the political right. However, involvement in politics goes beyond this to an overt presence as a political pressure group.

Publicity campaigning Although the Police Federation and ACPO are statutorily restricted, they have broken out of this straightjacket to become mouthpieces of collective police views. Unlike the civil service, the police do not subscribe to the Trappist monk school of public relations; they have argued against light sentences, juries, community policing and a suspect's right to silence. They also make strong moral judgements about schools, drugs, parents, the church, industrial relations and homosexuality.

The politicizing of the police was never better illustrated than when the

Police Federation actually launched a Law and Order Campaign in 1975. The movement arose over frustration that 'soft' groups were having a liberalizing effect on the law, policing and penal policy. Their campaign copied the methods of other pressure groups with public speaking engagements, feeding the media and lobbying. After some confrontation with the government, the Federation announced in February 1978 its intention to make law and order an issue in the forthcoming general election, even sponsoring large newspaper advertisements. The Conservatives became enthusiastic, pledging 'unstinting backing' for the police. However, this relationship was to sour under Home Secretaries Clarke and Howard in the 1990s with their managerial reforms (see below).

Police superstars Leading police figures have sought to project themselves as national celebrities. In particular, Metropolitan commissioners have found a unique platform. Notable was Sir Robert Mark, brought in by the libertarian Home Secretary Roy Jenkins, in 1967, to clear up internal corruption. He soon revealed a fiercely anti-libertarian stance on many social issues (Kettle 1980: 13). In 1973 he delivered the BBC Dimbleby Lecture, giving him the largest audience any policeman had ever had. This has been seen as the coming of age of politically assertive policing in Britain.

Following this a number of senior officers have enjoyed celebrity. James Anderton, Chief Constable of Greater Manchester, was particularly prominent during the 1980s, proclaiming that AIDS sufferers and drug addicts dwelt in 'a cess-pit of their own making'. He charmed the Establishment on television and radio current affairs programmes and chat-shows', though was eventually restrained after proclaiming that he heard 'voices'.

Rising crime rates have helped keep chief constables in the political limelight with statements upon the state of society. Paul Condon caused an outcry in July 1995 by suggesting that most London muggings were committed by young black males. West Yorkshire Chief Constable, Keith Halliwell, made contributions to the drugs debate (often sounding more liberal than politicians) and in 1998 became the government's 'Drugs Tsar'.

A climate of corporatism Senior officers enjoy direct links with Whitehall. When Michael Foot put forward proposals to amend the law on picketing, Sir Robert Mark told 'Jimmy Waddell [Sir James Waddell, high-ranking Home Office civil servant] in no uncertain terms' that he would conduct a vigorous public campaign against such laws. 'Happily they were abandoned and no harm was done' (Mark 1978: 151–2). Today the police service may be seen unequivocally as a pressure group, enjoying close insider status. Whenever there is a proposal for a change of law relating to criminal or judicial procedure, or whenever there is a *cause célèbre* involving the police, a well-maintained network springs into life.

The politics of confrontation However, as with a number of corporatist relationships, that between police and government soured from the 1980s. The

Figure 21.4
Crime rates and
expenditure on
police and prison
services, 1989–
1996.

Source: Data from *Key Data* (various years) and Home Office Research and Statistics Directorate.

key problem was crime rates which, between 1981 and 1995, rose by 91 per cent (figure 21.4) (Mirrlees-Black et al. 1996). Having made substantial increases in policing expenditure the government, according to former Home Secretary Kenneth Baker (1993), felt let down. Abandoning the 'adulation towards the police demonstrated by Mrs Thatcher' (Loveday 1996: 23), the Major government alleged inefficiency and sought to 'destabilise established police interests'. A critical report compiled by businessman Sir Patrick Sheehy was published in 1993 (see below) but the police associations responded with outspoken condemnation of Conservative home secretaries. On 30 July 1993, 20,000 officers congregated in an unprecedented protest rally. At the same time, Shadow Home Secretary Tony Blair recognized the political power of the police and used his 'tough on crime and tough on the causes of crime' soundbite to suggest that poor policing was not the reason for rising crime rates. Soon it was he who began to receive the applause of the Police Federation.

The politics of policing became a party fighting ground as both began competing as Vlad the Impaler impersonators (Reiner 1996). At the Conservative Party conference in October 1993 Michael Howard made twenty-seven proposals for a tougher line on law and order. Labour did not substantially oppose this policy and in office continued the tough line. The public appeared to approve, the 1997 British Social Attitudes Survey indicating considerable support for greater police powers and stiffer sentencing, as well as firmer discipline in home and school (Tarling and Dowds 1998).

The time is ripe for taking on the boys and girls in blue.

The Sheehy Report (1993)

Helping the police with inquiries: suspicious customers

While the police service itself has not been privatized and suspects are not yet seriously referred to as 'customers', the New Right reforms did not pass them by. Private-sector involvement was stimulated and attempts made to import managerial practice.

DIY crime fighting The rise (and perceived rise) in crime rates led, during the 1980s and 1990s, to calls for citizens to become more active in crime prevention and even detection. They were encouraged by 'crime-busting' television programmes, often relaying footage from a steady accretion of CCTV cameras on urban buildings. Domestic alarms became almost as ubiquitous as television aerials and the Neighbourhood Watch movement saw thousands of suburban community groups coming together to keep a watchful eye over their cars, houses and garden gnomes. To critics this is not far removed from vigilantism – individuals taking the law into their own hands, making citizen's arrests and even using violence. Jack Straw's curfews and parenting classes even suggested a policing role for families. The danger of DIY policing is of a lynch-mob mentality, seen in the hounding of paedophiles. However, the courts often find against over-zealous amateur law enforcers.

Privatization The 1980s saw considerable expansion of the private security industry, with militaristically uniformed guards patrolling shopping malls, car parks and even residential areas. Sometimes private security firms work in conjunction with the police. By 1997 the £2-billion-a-year industry of some 8,000 firms with 170,000 employees was dwarfing the state police service (*Observer*, 14 Feb. 1993). When firms such as Group Four took over the transport of prisoners, embarrassing escapes led wags to comment on Thatcher's desire to set the people free! However, the industry remains largely unregulated (Loveday 1994). Its employees (some of them convicted criminals) are themselves responsible for an estimated 2,000 crimes a year (*Evening Standard*, 15 July 1997).

From 1993 major privatizations were seen in the prison service, with contracts awarded to build and run new prisons. Jack Straw, to boos and cries of 'rubbish' at the 1998 Prison Officers' Association conference, declared himself, despite his earlier opposition, a 'convert' to the idea (*Independent*, 20 May 1998). The Adam Smith Institute has envisaged a future in which the state police operate in competition with private-sector agencies. Neoliberal ideologues would extend CCT to all aspect of policing.

Managerialism The 1993 Sheehy Report was highly critical of 'cosy relationships'; recruits could expect a job for life, there was little performance appraisal and the service was top heavy with senior grades. Its proposals included performance-related pay, fixed-term contracts, the abolition of certain senior ranks, limitations on pension rights, compulsory redundancies, the removal of certain allowances and a ban on overtime. There was also to be a cut in starting salaries. The proposals incurred the bitter wrath of the police and lower starting salaries were rejected outright. Home Secretary Michael Howard also agreed to drop other key recommendations, including performance-related pay, short fixed-term contracts and a higher age for full retirement pension entitlements. However, the management culture of the service was changed.

Quis Custodiet ipsos Custodes? Who Guards the Guards?

Being subject to only weak democratic control, modern policing raises the age-old question: 'Who guards the guards?'

The complaints procedure

One safeguard against improper policing is a mechanism whereby members of the public can have complaints investigated. The Police Act (1964) placed an obligation on chief constables to investigate all complaints, bringing in officers from other forces if they so wished. If the chief constable believed that a criminal offence might have occurred, a report was sent to the Director of Public Prosecutions. The system left many unhappy. In the 1970s, investigations into allegations of police brutality and deaths in police custody seemed unsatisfactory to victims' families. The police response complained of agitation by left-wing extremists. However, the 1976 Police Act established a quango, the Police Complaints Board (PCB), a lay body with a limited supervisory role over the process. The system had many weaknesses, the greatest being that the investigation remained in police hands, justified on the grounds that only they could do the job. However, calls for independent investigation continued from many quarters, including Liberty, Justice, the Law Society, the Runnymede Trust, the local ombudsman and the Labour Party. In 1980, the PCB itself recommended investigation by an independent team of seconded police officers.

Following serious race and anti-police riots in Brixton, Lord Scarman's report (1981: para 4.2) cited the absence of an independent **police complaints procedure** as one of five crucial factors contributing to the breakdown of police–community relations. Cynicism meant that people did not even bother to lodge complaints. The Police and Criminal Evidence Act (1984) established a three-tiered approach, adding to the existing system a conciliation mechanism for non-serious complaints and independent supervision of police investigation into serious ones by a Police Complaints Authority (PCA), which replaced the PCB.

Although the first chairman, Sir Cecil Clothier, had formerly been the ombudsman the reform fell short of truly independent investigation. Initially the chief constable (or police authority if senior officers were involved) would decide whether the matter could be solved by informal conciliation. If not, an officer would be appointed to conduct an enquiry under PCA supervision. However, the PCA's 1987 report castigated the Metropolitan force (which received a quarter of all complaints) for making it difficult to achieve 'a dialogue at senior level'. In November 1988 the Commons Home Affairs Committee, following a suggestion from Sir Cecil himself, recommended regular parliamentary scrutiny of the procedure. It also advocated strengthening the PCA's ability to acquire evidence. The response of the Police Federation in its 1989 annual conference was a vote of no confidence in the PCA, which was accused of siding with complainants.

The 1994/5 PCA report highlighted concern about the number of deaths in police custody and deaths associated with police vehicles (twelve involving pursuits). Moreover, some forces had failed to implement PCA recommendations that service in specialist squads be subject to time limits. The report for 1996/7 revealed that, despite a steady increase in complaints, the number substantiated remained very low (figure 21.5), falling from around 4–5 per cent in the mid-1980s to only 2 per cent in the late 1990s. However, an increasing proportion were resolved informally. In 1996/7 disciplinary charges were proved against 377 officers, resulting in 77 dismissals. A further 65 retired or resigned before proceedings had been completed.

> If one of the boys working for me got himself into trouble, I would get all of us together and I would literally script him out of it. I would write all the parts out and if we followed them closely we couldn't be defeated.
>
> Metropolitan Police sergeant quoted by D. J. Smith and J. Gray,
> *Police and People in London* (1985: 355)

In March 1998 Jack Straw responded to a Home Affairs Select Committee report on police complaints and discipline. While agreeing to some tightening

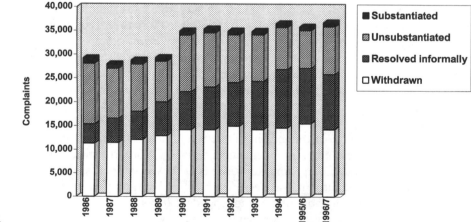

Figure 21.5
The outcome of complaints received by the police, 1986–1997.

Source: Data from *Home Office Statistical Bulletin* (No. 21/97: table 1). The number of complaints is greater than the number of cases received since each case may represent several complaints. In 1996/7, 22,500 cases were received.

of disciplinary procedures, a key recommendation that powers be given to the PCA to commission independent investigations was rejected on 'resource implications' grounds. He stressed his intention not to make the police 'more vulnerable to malicious complaints', promising little to deal with the police tradition of sticking together when under attack, which had prevented the identification of Blair Peach's killer.

Beyond the Blue Horizon

It is not only through the police service that the state exerts its coercive power. Although less overt than they have been in Northern Ireland, there are other fingers on the iron hand which can operate on the home front, including the military and the security services.

The military

Ostensibly states have a military arm to defend themselves from invasion or to subjugate other states. During the imperialist era Britain's military was a feared world power. In two hellish world wars it became even more central but with the post-war dismantling of empire it was anticipated that the men on horseback would retire to their barracks. However, they were to seek a role rather nearer home to confront the 'enemy within'.

Policy-making for the military Control of the military is vested formally in government ministers responsible to Parliament, which grants its funds. The modern history of political control dates from the creation of the Committee of Imperial Defence in 1902 after the Boer war. During the second world war this was replaced by the War Cabinet and a Ministry of Defence established. In 1964 the three service departments were amalgamated under the Secretary of State for Defence and a Defence Council.

The service chiefs are, like civil servants, heavily involved in decision-making. Sometimes appearing as the more arrogant of the British upper class, they take it hard if politicians resist their 'advice'. Here is another corporatist enclave where the select influence the destiny of the nation away from the prying eyes of democracy. Few outsider groups were as 'outside' as the CND. Parliament and the full Cabinet have very little hold on the reins; thus defence spending reached astronomical heights (figure 21.6) and the arms industry grew fat. Talk of a post-cold-war peace dividend proved over-optimistic as new flashpoints were identified the world over.

Class and the military The majority of those marching to venues like the Somme were from the working class but the people who matter in the military, the top brass, follow very much in the traditions of British elitism. Today members of the royal family continue to hold high military rank. Before the rise of the industrial

Figure 21.6
Defence expenditure, 1900–1996.

Source: Data from Butler and Butler (1994: 393–5) and *Annual Abstract of Statistics* (1998: table 7.2).

bourgeoisie, commissions in the army and navy were reserved for the sons of the aristocracy and wealth was needed for their purchase and subsequent promotion. However, the worldwide policing necessary to protect free trade made the bourgeoisie more than a little concerned and a modernization programme placed the military in the hands of the new elite. The social prestige is such that, unlike privates or sergeants, retired officers retain their titles like honours, even having them engraved on their tombstones to proclaim their stature long after the worms have digested their entrails. However, to admit the existence of elitism in the service is tantamount to taking voluntary redundancy – after writing a Fabian Society pamphlet accusing the army of sexism, racism and elitism, in January 1999 Major Eric Joyce was asked to resign or face compulsory discharge.

Race and the military   The British army probably has a worse record of racism than any other state institution, remaining largely untouched by the post-1970s anti-discriminatory laws. In 1997 only 1 per cent of military personnel came from ethnic minorities, compared with more than 5 per cent of the civil service (*Financial Times*, 14 Oct. 1997). Prince Charles himself expressed concern at the milk-white complexions of his royal guards. Given the role of the army in subduing foreign enemies, a racist culture is not entirely surprising. This was confirmed in March 1996 by a highly critical report from the Commission for Racial Equality. A 1997 review of ethnic minority initiatives commissioned by the Ministry of Defence revealed racial insults, harassment and physical injury, leading most black recruits to an early return to civvy street.

The military on the home front The military in any state contains a fearsome potential for violence. Most *coups d'état* are military backed and it is not unusual for a state to direct such power on its own citizens. In Britain, the 1714 Riot Act enabled magistrates to call in the military to quell disturbances, while today governments can make 'reasonable' use of troops in riotous situations. In the confrontation with the miners there were rumours of soldiers in police uniforms, distinguishable by the absence of a number. Perhaps the most telling post-war use of the army in civil situations has been in Northern Ireland from 1969 (see chapter 6).

> There is no horror, no cruelty, sacrilege, or perjury, no imposture, no infamous transaction, no cynical robbery, no bold plunder or shabby betrayal that has not been ... perpetrated ... under no other pretext than those elastic words, so convenient and yet so terrible: 'for reasons of state'.
>
> Mikhail Bakunin (1814–76; Russian anarchist)

Overt military involvement in civil affairs can be conducted by a special elite corps – the Special Air Service (SAS) – which first caught the public imagination in 1980 when, under the eyes of television cameras, it daringly ended a siege of the Iranian Embassy. It also operated under cover in Northern Ireland, where codes permitted extra military freedoms, buttressed by special emergency powers granted by Parliament.

Although conventions restrict the use of troops in mainland Britain, there is nothing to prevent these changing. The Crown prerogative means that in a state of emergency troops can be used in any way at all. An army–police anti-terrorist operation at Heathrow airport in 1974 greatly alarmed Prime Minister Wilson, who realized how easily troops could be turned against the government (James 1987). It was chillingly explained afterwards that the purpose of the exercise was 'to accustom the public to the reality of troops deploying through the high street' (*Guardian*, 8 Jan. 1974).

The security services: the 'cloak and dagger' of the state

Courses on British government often ignore the **security services**, not because such matters should not be discussed in front of children but because they are things that nobody is supposed to talk about. Here we meet agencies operating below the level of public accountability and consciousness. People have some vague notion from the novels of John Le Carré and Ian Fleming that they exist, but these are chauvinistic fantasies about superhuman figures like James Bond.

The services are not new. The Home Office, with an historic responsibility for state security, has maintained an ad hoc network of spies and informers, partnering the industrial capitalism rising in the eighteenth century (Bunyan 1977: 153). They comprise a number of agencies.

- The *Special Branch* of the Met was created in 1883 to be concerned mainly with criminal offences against the state and subversive organizations. It has always been heavily involved with Irish affairs. The emphasis is on intelligence gathering and 'watching', with 'political policing' (Bunyan 1977: ch. 3).
- *MI5* was established in 1909 to root out subversive activity at home. Today it works closely with the Special Branch, calling on police powers (of arrest and so on) when required.
- *MI6*, the *Secret Intelligence Service*, is concerned with organizing espionage overseas. In 1919 it 'poured in agents and several million pounds in a vain effort to subvert the [Russian] revolution' (Bunyan 1977: 155).
- The *Government Communications Headquarters* (GCHQ) at Cheltenham is concerned with worldwide electronic surveillance.
- The *Defence Intelligence Staff* of the Ministry of Defence oversees the work of the intelligence staffs of the armed services.
- The ordinary *police service* (liberally interpreting its public order function) is increasingly concerned with matters of security.

Although separate organizations, they work together at various levels, coordinated by Scotland Yard (Campbell 1980: 116). The paranoid secrecy of the state is never more tight lipped than here, serving not merely to safeguard Brit-

"None of you knows each other, I trust."

Reproduced by permission of *Punch*

ain's secrets from potential enemies, but to conceal the fact that the agencies can sail extremely close to the wind. When joining MI5, Peter Wright (1987: 31) was told that it could not be part of Whitehall because its work 'very often involved transgressing propriety or the law'.

The British government long fostered the idea that the security services did not actually exist: the Head of MI6 in 1956 (and former head of MI5), Sir Dick Goldsmith White, was officially listed as Deputy Under Secretary at the Foreign Office and Superintending Under Secretary of the Library and Records Department (Bunyan 1977: 189–90). However, a surprising break with tradition came in 1991 with the appointment of Stella Rimmington as MI5 head; not only was she a woman but she was named. In July 1993 MI5 published a booklet on the security service, revealing some 2,000 people operating in its secretive world.

The class factor Unlike the police service, the security services remain very much a bastion of the lordly amateur male establishment world of John Buchan, even to the extent, according to Peter Wright (1987: 36), of closing down MI5 once a year for the Lord's test match, where they have an unofficially reserved patch in the Lord's Tavern. The girls managing the files are debutantes recruited from the aristocracy, perhaps the best vetting of all. Despite some attempts to advertise in the late 1990s, recruitment is traditionally conducted on an informal basis and most members (including the spies) have come from the public school–Oxbridge hothouse.

What are the buggers up to? The security services protect the state from subversion and espionage. Their activities are potentially infinite in their variety. After the first world war, fear of communism saw working-class activists harassed and even imprisoned. The National Unemployed Workers' Movement was kept under constant surveillance by the Special Branch, its leaders eventually arrested and its documents confiscated. One notorious act concerned the Zinoviev letter.

In the soft-focus days of the 1960s, when the Beatles, Mary Quant and student uprisings seemed to symbolize a new era, and Harold Wilson appeared to be making Labour a natural party of government, members of the Establishment talked long into the nights of *coups* to prevent the drift. In 1965, the Lord Chancellor was reduced to driving around Green Park when holding discus-

---

The Zinoviev letter

This letter was reputedly uncovered during the 1924 general election campaign. Apparently sent by Gregory Zinoviev, president of the Communist International, to a prominent member of the British Communist Party, it urged armed revolution. The resulting paranoia effectively ruined Labour's election chances. A middle-man named Thurn, who received £7,500 from the Conservative Party, touted the letter around and ensured its publication in the *Daily Mail*. Its authenticity was never proved and it appears to have been the product of a dirty tricks operation involving 'members of MI6 and MI5, the top personnel at the Foreign Office, and the Tory party' (Bunyan 1977: 159).

sions with the Attorney General, believing it 'more likely than not that MI5 were bugging the telephones in my office'. In this Orwellian scenario he could hardly complain to the Prime Minister, who believed he too was under surveillance (Knightly 1986).

Clearly the definition of **subversion** must have a considerable bearing on whom the security services fix their attentions upon and it was a Labour home secretary who threw the gates open. The definition given by Lord Denning in his 1963 report on the Profumo scandal was contemplating 'the overthrow of the government by unlawful means'. However, in 1978, Merlyn Rees dispensed with 'unlawful', redefining subversives as those who 'threaten the safety or well being of the state, and are intended to undermine or overthrow parliamentary democracy by political, industrial, or violent means'. This gave the green light to the security services (Kettle 1980: 52–3), allowing them to turn inward on the body politic like a virus, investigating left-wing politicians, trade unionists and anyone expressing an unorthodox political opinion, despite their innocence of any crime. In 1990, Colin Wallace claimed that, as an army public relations officer in the 1970s, he had been involved in MI5 operations ('Clockwork Orange') to smear British politicians, including David Owen, Jeremy Thorpe, Edward Heath, Denis Healey, Merlyn Rees and Harold Wilson (*Observer*, 4 Feb. 1990).

> "There are also certain matters of personal conduct which could quite possibly leave you open to blackmail."
> *Shit!! . . .*
> I thought about it for a little while. They must have been bugging my phone. There was no other explanation. And for ages.
>
> Alan Clark on meeting with Cabinet Secretary Sir Robert Armstrong,
> shortly after becoming a minister, *Diaries* (24 June, 1983)

The advance of technology lifts the capability to gather, collect and collate information to truly Kafkaesque levels. An unprecedented bank of computer data was built up, focusing on leaders of groups like CND, Greenpeace, the trade unions, schools and universities, hospitals, the theatre and the media. MI5 tried to have newsreader Anna Ford sacked on the grounds that a former boyfriend had once been a communist. The *Observer* showed the service to have had long-standing links with BBC management in order to blacklist left-wing journalists (Leigh and Lashmar 1987). Phones are tapped, people photographed and mail opened by the Post Office or by MI5. During the miners' strike, a complex operation involved informers, spies and *agents provocateurs*. From the early 1970s the security services found an increased role in Northern Ireland, where they saw the IRA as part of a communist threat (Pilger 1998: 516–17).

The ending of the cold war left MI5 casting around for a *raison d'être* but by 1993 some 70 per cent of its resources were devoted to 'counter-terrorism'. Stella Rimmington was well equipped for tackling the 'enemy within', having been active during the battle with the miners in 1984 and monitoring trade unions under the brief to target 'domestic subversion'. This thinking had led to

> Diana, to her dying day, thought it was MI5 on behalf of the establishment at the height of the 'wars of the Wales' who bugged her and were responsible for the Squidgy tapes.
>
> Anthony Holden, 'Royal Blues', in *Red Pepper* (Oct. 1997)

the ban on union membership at GCHQ, which John Major refused to lift in December 1993. Ironically, civil liberties groups have alleged that GCHQ bugged trade unionists and there were even suspicions that it was responsible for the 'Squidgygate' and 'Camillagate' tapes. During the Gulf war MI5 embarrassed the Foreign Office by arresting a number of innocent people of Middle Eastern origin (*Guardian*, 17 Dec. 1991). In December 1996, a former IRA officer was 'turned' by MI5, given media training and released from prison to denigrate the IRA ceasefire and attack the moderate SDLP leader John Hume (Pilger 1998: 516–17). In August 1997, David Shayler, a former MI5 officer, disclosed in a newspaper article that Home Secretary Jack Straw's file was still held, and that files existed on ministers Peter Mandelson and Harriet Harman. In July 1998 Straw opened a window of light, but did little to allay fears, by revealing that MI5 currently held nearly half a million files (*The Times*, 30 July 1998).

Even objectors to road and airport development have become seen as targets. On 17 February 1993 Channel 4's *Dispatches* showed extraordinary levels of surveillance of protesters against a motorway through Twyford Down by police, private security firms and even a detective agency, with names faxed to the Department of Transport. John Alderson saw MI5 involvement in policing as the acorn of a police state (*Red Pepper*, April 1996).

> The tragedy of the Police State is that it always regards all opposition as a crime, and there are no degrees.
>
> Lord Vansittart (1881–1957; British diplomat), House of Lords speech (June 1947)

Who watches the watchers?

Dissatisfaction with the current state of affairs led in 1989 to a Security Services Act; for the first time, official recognition was given to the existence of MI5 (though not of MI6) and a tribunal was created to hear complaints. In addition, a commissioner (a Law Lord) would oversee warrants for bugging and entering and make an annual report to Parliament, though this could be edited by the prime minister. Critics such as the Campaign for Freedom of Information regarded this as rather little rather late and well short of full parliamentary oversight.

A report from the House of Commons Home Affairs Committee (1993) noted that, while all the country's closest allies had independent oversight of their security services, Britain's operated beyond the realm of parliamentary

> The club of ex-Home Secretaries is, in my view, one of the worst features of British public life: they all compliment each other . . . but nobody believes [they] are really kept informed by the security services.
>
> Tony Benn, *Diaries* (1991: 587)

scrutiny. Among elected politicians, only the prime minister is formally in the know, but even this is doubtful. The British tradition of the neutral civil service has created a situation in which 'Ministers, and Prime Ministers, increasingly become putty, on questions of "security", in their senior adviser's hands' (Thompson 1980: 157). The Blunt case in particular called into question the relationship of the security services to their elected masters. In 1964 this aristocratic self-confessed spy, a former member of MI5, struck a secret deal with the security agencies, guaranteeing immunity from prosecution (and allowing him to retain his prestigious royal appointment as Surveyor of the Queen's Pictures) in exchange for information. Despite promises, Labour governments have never conducted a scourge of the security services. David Shayler, after blowing the whistle on what he saw as MI5 inefficiency and bungling, came under investigation for suspected breach of the Official Secrets Act, the government attempting to have him extradited from France to face prosecution (see p. 456).

The spies Although the security services have an impressive record of probing and harassing the left, they have enjoyed rather less success in catching real spies. The result has been some embarrassing post-war scandals, including those of Blake, Burgess, Maclean, Philby, Vassall and Blunt. Of course, the spies have come from upper-class backgrounds because of the security services' recruitment practices. The Establishment cannot tolerate such behaviour from within its ranks; they are not merely traitors, they are class traitors.

> If you ask me to strike a balance in my own life, I'd say that the right I've done is greater than the wrong I've done.
>
> Kim Philby (civil servant who spied for the Russians), interview in Moscow in the *Sunday Times* (27 March 1988)

The Coercive State and the Community

It would of course be absurd to expect policing and other forms of state coercion to operate without force and violence; this is why they are created. While it is not the only cause of disharmony, capitalism, with its tendency towards inequality, needs a strong state (Gamble 1988). Hence the emergence of the modern police service was tied to the industrial revolution. Yet the service managed to develop an ethos of community spirit linked with the gradual assimilation of the working class into the system, reaching a peak in the post-war

> PC Attilla Rees, ox broad, barge booted, stamping out of Handcuff House in a heavy beef-red huff, blackbrowed under his damp helmet . . . limbering down to the strand to see that the sea is still there.
>
> Dylan Thomas (1914–53), *Under Milk Wood* (1954)

corporatist decades. Dixon of Dock Green, a caring 'bobby' featuring in a long-running television series, did not seem grossly at variance with reality.

Yet the neoliberal right was never entirely at ease with the idea of **consensus policing** and from the late 1970s it was explicitly rejected with the 'enemy within' rhetoric. Thatcher recognized the key role that would be given to the police, promising in the 1979 Conservative manifesto to 'spend more on fighting crime even while we economize elsewhere'. In the bitter events of the miners' strike, while criticism of police tactics reached a crescendo, the government refused to encourage a negotiated settlement. Since then society has continued to be darkened by the spectre of violence.

The alternative to the strong arm

Against the trend came the Scarman Report, which saw the roots of crime, riots and public disorder in the social environment (1981: para. 2.38). It aroused considerable public and official interest, with recommendations favouring **community policing** including:

- new recruitment procedures to screen out racism and sexism and encourage more black people and women to apply;
- outlawing of discriminatory practices;
- increased community consultation;
- reduction in police discretionary powers;
- increased accountability by means of lay visitors to police stations.

The law-and-order lobby were sceptical and responses to Scarman often involved cosmetic reforms such as employing 1 or 2 per cent of the service in community policing. These officers were isolated, often ridiculed and given nicknames like 'Sambo'. One of the most prominent advocates of community policing has been John Alderson (a former barrister) who, as Chief Constable of Devon and Cornwall, sought to concern *every* officer with community relations. However, in the neoliberal environment the approach could not flourish. He was consistently opposed by the Police Federation, which sent deputations to question his use of resources, and he finally left to take up an academic post.

Conservative Home Secretary Howard had stressed the 'tough cop' approach and his successor, Labour's Jack Straw, followed a similar line in several ways. However, after visiting Baltimore, where the police run youth clubs, he was to

I never saw any of them again – except the cops. No way has yet been invented to say goodbye to them.

Philip Marlowe in Raymond Chandler's *The Long Goodbye* (1954)

announce a softer approach, criticizing entrants seeking an 'adrenalin rush' from police work (*Sunday Times*, 8 Feb. 1998).

Policing at arm's length

In March 1990, a report commissioned by ACPO from the Harris Research Centre revealed that 74 per cent of those questioned preferred the friendly 'bobby on the beat' to the 'Sweeny' image of fast cars and tough policing (*Guardian*, 9 March 1990). Yet hurdles stand in the way of a return to a community approach. The Scarman Report did not recognize all the problems. It ignored the contradictions between the community approach and increased centralization, militarization and incorporation of the security forces. It also failed to emphasize democratic control through elected councils as the way to local accountability. Without this, community policing can become community control (Gordon 1984: 56). Yet today the 'long arm of the law' is probably at a longer 'arm's length' from the democratic state than ever before.

Key points

- Every state requires a right to use physical force and coercion. The liberal-democratic state is no exception; indeed the market freedom requires a strong state.
- The modern police service in Britain was a creature of the industrial revolution. Previously policing was undertaken on a voluntary basis by local communities.
- Britain formally has a number of separate police authorities upon which local government is represented. However, forces are under the firm control of their chief constables.
- It is sometimes said that policing is outside politics, but this is untenable.
- There are acute problems in policing associated with sexism and racism.
- Since the 1970s British policing has become increasingly centralized, militarized and politicized.
- Through ACPO the police can enjoy most of the advantages of a national force without responsibility to Parliament.
- The police complaints process is controversial because the police themselves conduct any inquiries.
- Britain imprisons a higher proportion of its population than any comparable country.
- The military and security services play a policing role, though they do so covertly and with less accountability than the police themselves.
- There is an alternative to coercive policing in community policing.

Review your understanding of the following terms and concepts

Association of Chief
   Police Officers
   (ACPO)
centralization
chief constable
community policing
consensus policing
crime-fighting
Crown Prosecution
   Service

Judges' Rules
'Met'
MI5 and MI6
militarization
paramilitary unit
penal policy
police authority
police committee
Police Complaints
   Authority

police complaints
   procedure
police culture
Police Federation
police state
politicization
public order
security services
Special Patrol Group
subversion

Assignment

Study the extract from the *Independent* on p. 672 and answer the following
questions.

		Mark (%)
1	Explain the meaning of the term 'institutional racism'.	10
2	Why was the Stephen Lawrence inquiry holding a hearing in Manchester?	10
3	Assess the significance of David Wilmot's admission in dealing with the problem of police racism.	40
4	Why do you think Sir Paul Condon 'steadfastly refused to recognize institutional racism within the Met'.	40

Questions for discussion

1   Why did the industrial revolution threaten a breakdown in traditional methods of policing?
2   Evaluate the role of the local police authority.
3   How could the rise of the private security industry threaten liberal democracy?
4   'Allegations of police brutality and false confessions only undermine the morale of police officers and reduce their effectiveness.' Discuss.
5   'The security services stand outside the political system.' Discuss.
6   Examine the proposition that Britain has a national police service in all but name?
7   Identify the weaknesses in the police complaints procedures. How could they be improved?
8   What is meant by 'community policing'? What factors inhibit it?
9   Is it true that 'prison works'?
10   How do the police influence government policy? Is this desirable?

Police chief admits to racism in ranks

BY KATHY MARKS

IN AN unprecedented admission by a senior officer, the Chief Constable of Greater Manchester acknowledged yesterday that his force was infected by institutional racism.

David Wilmot, head of the second-largest force in England and Wales, made the declaration at a hearing of the Stephen Lawrence inquiry in Manchester. His attitude was in stark contrast to that of Sir Paul Condon, the Metropolitan Police Commissioner, who steadfastly refused to recognise institutional racism within the Met when he appeared before the inquiry two weeks ago.

Mr Wilmot told the public inquiry: "We live in a society that has institutional racism, and Greater Manchester Police is no exception. We accept that we have a problem with some overt racism, and certainly that we have a problem with internalised racism."

Sir William Macpherson of Cluny, the inquiry chairman, responded with an oblique but unmistakable criticism of Sir Paul. "There is a reluctance to accept that it is there, which means that it will probably never be cured," he said.

Manchester was the inquiry's first stop on a regional tour aimed at taking the temperature in racially sensitive cities outside London and identifying lessons to be learnt from the Met's abortive investigation of the racist murder of Stephen Lawrence, an 18-year-old student, in 1993.

Manchester's large Afro-Caribbean and Asian Communities suffer a high level of racial crime and harassment – an estimated 21,000 become victims each year – and have a history of chequered relations with the police.

Mr Wilmot is the first chief constable to have acknowledged institutional racism within his own force.

Independent, 14 Oct. 1998

Topic for debate

This house believes that policing is no job for a woman.

Further reading

Baxter, J. and Koffman, L. (eds) (1985) *Police, the Constitution and the Community*.
Book of readings. See especially M. Benn, 'Policing women' and P. Boateng, 'Crisis in accountability'.

Benn, M. et al. (1983) *The Rape Controversy*.
Looks at the area where the macho police culture is at its most destructive.

Hain, P. et al. (eds) (1980) *Policing the Police*.
Critical book of readings. See especially the chapters by M. Kettle and D. Campbell.

Halford, A. (1993) *No Way Up the Greasy Pole*.
Inside account of sexism in the police service by its most celebrated victim.

Knightly, P. (1986) *The Second Oldest Profession: The Spy as Bureaucrat, Fantasist and Whore*.
Specialist journalist's account of a field too boggy for most academics.

Newburn, T. (1995) *Crime and Criminal Justice Policy*.
All aspects clearly presented in historical context.

Reiner R. (1993) *The Politics of the Police*, 2nd edn
Clear treatment of the central points of analysis.

Reiner R. (ed.) (1996) *Policing*.
Collection of significant articles.

Smith, D. J. and Gray, J. (1985) *Police and People in London*.
A powerful study of the Metropolitan Police Force at work.

Urban, M. (1997) *UK Eyes Alpha: The Inside Story of British Intelligence*.
BBC journalist reports wide range of interviews with those involved. Title is the security term for highly sensitive intelligence.

For light relief

Bertolt Brecht, *The Threepenny Opera*.
Satirical musical play on the relationship between capitalism and law and order.

Robert Harris, *Enigma*.
Tense novel of code-breaking and spying based on second-world-war events.

Stephen Knight, *The Brotherhood*.
An exposé of freemasonry in Britain in the higher reaches of the Establishment, including MI5, judiciary and police.

G. F. Newman, *Law and Order*.
A powerful and realistic novel exploring police–Establishment relations.

Prime Suspect.
TV series available on video. Shows in dramatic form some of the problems facing women in the police service.

On the net

http://www.homeoffice.gov.uk
http://www.mod.gov.uk
The Home Office and MoD web sites are good starting points for many of the issues dealt with in this chapter.

http://mi5.gov.uk
Once so secretive that its very existence was denied, the security service now has its own web site.

Chapter Twenty-two

Concluding Note: Thinking Holistically

An important theme of this book has been the interconnected nature of the subject matter. Government is deeply enmeshed in a dense biomass of political life, and politics is a process involving not merely the institutions of state but also those of the economy and civil society, and subject to a range of influences emanating from the global context. Political energy has been shown to issue from multifarious sources including differences in ideology, wealth, education, employment status, class, gender, race, geographical location, and so on. More-over, the process embraces institutions well beyond the formal Westminster–Whitehall terrain, encompassing the judiciary, the police, the military, the secret services, trade unions, private firms, thousands of pressure groups espousing an infinity of causes, and giant peak organizations like the TUC and CBI. Yet despite this seamless cohesion the previous chapters have been characterized by distinct focuses. There are two principal reasons for this.

- *Verisimilitude.* The world of government and politics really is to some extent formally compartmentalized through the organizational structures of the state. Thus, for example, the judiciary is distinct from the civil serv-ice, Parliament is distinct from local government, and so on. We saw in chapter 3 that this division is actually part of the constitution: the division of authority is seen as a protection from overpowerful government.
- *Pedagogical necessity.* It is a natural characteristic of the human intellect to split up, compartmentalize and classify any subject matter under study; it is only by doing this that we can make sense of the complexity of the world surrounding us. This is partly what we mean by 'analysis'. Thus, for example, actors will split up a play into its scenes, acts and dialogues in the process of mastering it.

However, ultimately the actors will want to rebuild the play in its entirety to reveal its dramatic intent. When we take a **holistic** perspective we view our subject as a whole **system**, rather than in terms of its parts, and it may be argued that it is only from such a perspective that the political drama can be fully understood. To take another analogy, a football team is something qualitatively different from the eleven individuals who comprise it. To assess its likely success we need to understand how these individuals relate together. The potential energy of the team as a goal-scoring machine may be greater than the sum of that of each individual; this increase gained from working together is termed synergy.

There are various ways of conceiving politics in holistic terms. We shall introduce two which are closely related and which underlie much political study and debate: the organic and the systemic.

Organic theories of the state

> States, like men, have their growth, their manhood, their decrepitude, their decay.
>
> Walter Savage Landor (1775–1864; English writer), *Imaginary Conversations* (1824–9)

A long-prevailing view of the state has pictured it as a living organism (usually the human body), with its various organs fulfilling particular functions but bound together in mutual dependence. This goes back to the Ancient Greeks, but a particular version flourished in the nineteenth century amongst a school of biological political theorists. The notion of the organism was not merely metaphor; the state was believed to be a life form, capable of birth, life, disease and death. They also spoke of the state's adaptation to its environment through a slow process of evolution in which some organs became more important and others (like the human appendix) became unwanted and withered away.

Functionalism The organic view was to underlie an approach to the study of society and the state termed **functionalism**. This argued that state structures and institutions must, like the organs of the body, perform certain necessary functions (respiration, reproduction, digestion, and so on) for it to survive. The approach was applied by influential anthropologists like A. R. Radcliffe-Brown (1881–1955) and Bronislaw Malinowski (1884–1942) to explain and compare primitive societies in which formal institutions did not exist. Thus while a society might not have a parliament in the sense understood by western culture, it would necessarily require the function of making rules.

A function only has meaning in terms of the *whole* and, by the same reasoning, if an institution acts in a manner harmful to the whole then it is, like a disease in an organism, dysfunctional. The sociologists Talcott Parsons (1902–79) and Robert Merton (b. 1910) adapted the anthropologists' ideas more specifically to industrialized societies, revealing that even here it is possible to ask questions based on functional analysis. Thus we may enquire whether an institution really fulfils the function it is supposed to (does Parliament really

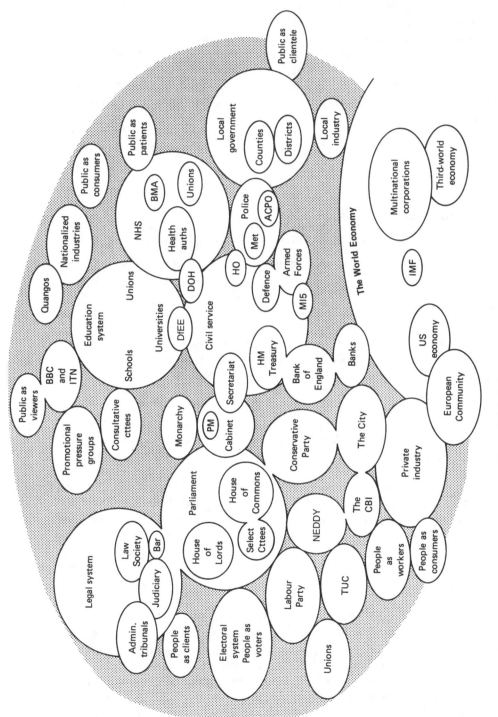

Figure 22.1 Politics as a system.

make laws?), or whether it is fulfilled elsewhere (the civil service, the Cabinet, and so on). It can be seen that questions such as these, which seek to look behind the institutional facade, arise throughout this book.

Ideology and the organic view However, the organic view has ideological implications. It leads to a Burkean form of conservatism that institutions should be allowed to grow naturally and not be tampered with – a veneration of the status quo. On the other hand, the organic view can also entail the idea of *death* followed by *rebirth* – in other words, *revolution*.

Systems theory and the political system

The organic view demanded a degree of metaphysical faith and fell out of favour. However, it was replaced with the idea of the **political system** (figure 21.1). Although the term is often used loosely to denote little more than 'where politics takes place', the concept is essentially holistic. Systems theory was pioneered by the biologist Ludwig von Bertallanfy, who stressed that 'Each part depends not only on conditions within itself, but also . . . on conditions within the *whole* of which it is part' (1952: xix). The concept was introduced into political science by the American scholar David Easton, who entitled a seminal work *The Political System*, on the holistic premise that 'the phenomena of politics tend to cohere and to be mutually related' (1953: 97).

The systems approach advanced thinking by adding to the long-standing (and out-of-favour) organic view a mechanical one. The two may be distinguished as follows. The system differs fundamentally from the organism in that it does not evolve under some internal dynamic of its own; it is conceived as a machine *designed* to fulfil a particular purpose. Thus a car is designed to transport us; it will never seek to place its own interest before its rider as might a horse (an organic system). Perceived in this way the state becomes something that can be *changed* on the basis of *reason* – an Enlightenment belief. Bentham and the Philosophical Radicals saw the state as a constitutional Meccano set to be constructed at will. We have seen throughout this book how the rising bourgeoisie made prolific use of the idea of deliberate change, to the extent of sculpting the modern British liberal-democratic state.

The approach has been extended by some political scientists into the new field of cybernetics, the study associated with the science of information technology, which looks at the internal control mechanisms through communications networks. Karl Deutsch, for example, in *The Nerves of Government* (1964), characterized government in terms of a complex network of internal informational channels binding all parts together like the printed circuits of a computer. For Deutsch, communication, rather than power, is the key to understanding the process of government. Today the concept of the network is central to academic thinking about politics.

A holistic study strategy

If politics is perceived holistically, one is drawn to conceptualize the parts of the political system in terms of their relationship to the whole and to each other (figure 22.1). This can open the doors to a level of understanding far deeper than that gained from compartmentalized knowledge. We realize that the behaviour of some element (say a pressure group) cannot be fully explained without understanding its relationship with other elements (other pressure groups, the mass media, Parliament, public opinion, the civil service, international organizations, its own rank and file, society at large, and so on).

There is no limit to the level at which the holistic perspective may be focused. Systems may be conceived as consisting of *subsystems* (for example, the select committee system may be seen as a subsystem of the House of Commons and the latter as a subsystem of Parliament) and may themselves be seen as part of larger systems (for example, the political system itself can be seen as a subsystem of the British social system, or of the national economy or of the world economy) *ad infinitum*.

Some lessons on holistic thinking come from science in general and particularly from meteorology, where it is crucially necessary to take a global perspective. The range of influences which shape our weather are so complex that, even with computers capable of performing hundreds of millions of calculations a second (the present state of the art), it will always be impossible to include every causal factor; hence we will never be able to predict weather with complete accuracy. Scientists speak of the 'butterfly effect' wherein a butterfly flapping its wings may set in motion a chain of events which will alter the course of a tornado on the other side of the globe. Politics is full of such causal chains. Clinton's election in the USA may have contributed to the election of Blair in Britain, a currency speculator in one part of the world may precipitate something like Black Wednesday in Britain. To think in a consciously holistic way is constantly to pose a battery of relevant questions about any particular part of the political system. When you think about any political question try to conceptualize the overall system in the way depicted in figure 22.1 and try to think how the particular part of the system you are concerned with relates to all other aspects. Never imagine that you can fully understand one part without appreciating its place in the whole system.

Further reading

Dunleavy, P., Gamble, A., Holliday, I. and Peele, G. (1997) *Developments in British Politics 5*.
Latest in regular series in which eminent scholars concentrate on contemporary development.

Harrison, B. (1996) *The Transformation of British Politics 1860–1995*.
Charts the history of British politics from the time of Bagehot, noting the significance of social and economic change.

Marr, A. (1995) *Ruling Britannia*.
Thought-provoking 'constitutional audit' of the past two decades.

For light relief

Anthony Burgess, *Clockwork Orange*.
An alarming vision of a future dominated by technology, violence and authoritarian government. Made into a film by Stanley Kubrick in 1971.

Aldous Huxley, *Brave New World*.
A fable set in the seventh century AF (after Ford), where life is subjugated by science, all under World Controller Mustapha Mond. In *Brave New World Revisited*, Huxley believes his prophecies are already (1958) coming frighteningly true.

William Morris, *News from Nowhere*.
A utopian socialist fantasy.

George Orwell, *Nineteen Eighty-Four*.
A nightmare of totalitarianism with 'newspeak', 'doublethink', where war is peace, freedom is slavery and ignorance is strength.

Alvin Toffler, *Future Shock*.
The effects of the communications technology revolution.

Chronology of Events

427 BC Birth of Plato.
384 BC Birth of Aristotle.
1066 Norman Conquest.
1086 Domesday Book.
1154 Henry II first Plantagenet English king.
1170 Thomas Becket murdered.
1215 Magna Carta.
1258 Simon de Montfort forces reforms on Henry III.
1265 De Montfort's Parliament; defeat and death of de Montfort.
1284 Edward I completes conquest of Wales.
1290 Edward I begins conquest of Scotland.
1295 Edward I's 'Model Parliament'.
1314 Robert the Bruce secures Scottish independence.
1327 Edward II deposed and murdered.
1338 Hundred Years War begins.
1362 English becomes official language in Parliament and courts.
1381 Peasants' Revolt.
1399 Richard II deposed by Henry IV.
1400 Welsh revolt under Owen Glendower.
1415 Battle of Agincourt.
1450 Jack Cade's rebellion against Henry VI.
1453 Final English defeat and end of Hundred Years War.
1455 Wars of the Roses begin.

1476 Caxton sets up printing press.
1485 Battle of Bosworth Field; Tudor dynasty begins.
1493 Vasco da Gama finds sea route to India.
1515 Thomas Wolsey becomes Lord Chancellor and Cardinal.
1517 Martin Luther begins Reformation.
1534 Act of Supremacy; Henry VIII takes control of Church in England.
1535 Thomas More executed.
1536 Ann Boleyn executed.
1558 Elizabeth I becomes Queen.
1577 Drake begins circumnavigation.
1588 Spanish Armada defeated.
1600 English East India Company founded.
1601 Elizabethan Poor Law; rates introduced.
1603 Irish revolts suppressed. Death of Elizabeth I; accession of James VI of Scotland as James I of England.
1605 Gunpowder plot.
1611 English and Scottish Protestants settle in Ulster.
1620 Pilgrim Fathers settle in New England.
1628 Petition of Right to Charles I by Commons.
1629 Charles I tries to rule without Parliament.

1635 John Hampden refuses to pay ship money.

1642 Charles I attempts to arrest five members of Parliament. Outbreak of civil war.

1644 Battle of Marston Moor. North lost to Charles I. Royalist campaign in Scotland.

1645 New Model Army formed. Royalist army crushed at Naseby.

1646 Charles I surrenders to Scots.

1647 Charles I handed over to Parliament, seized by army, flees to Carisbrooke Castle.

1648 Second civil war; New Model Army defeats Scots and Royalists.

1649 Charles I executed; England governed as republic under Cromwell. England suppresses Ireland.

1651 Cromwell becomes supreme in all Britain after the Battle of Worcester. First English Navigation Acts. Thomas Hobbes publishes *Leviathan*.

1655 English take Jamaica.

1658 Cromwell dissolves Rump Parliament, becomes Lord Protector.

1660 Restoration of monarchy; Charles II returns from exile.

1665 Great Plague of London.

1666 Great Fire of London.

1681 Charles II tries to rule without Parliament; establishes Oxford Parliament.

1685 Monmouth's rebellion crushed by James II at Sedgemoor.

1688 William of Orange lands with army in England; flight of James II. The 'Glorious Revolution'.

1689 Bill of Rights limits monarchy.

1690 Locke's *Two Treatises on Government*. Battle of the Boyne; William crushes Irish.

1693 National Debt begun.

1694 Bank of England founded.

1701 Act of Settlement establishes Hanoverian succession.

1707 Act of Union of English and Scottish Parliaments.

1714 Death of Queen Anne; accession of Elector of Hanover as George I.

Riot Act enables magistrates to call in military to quell civil disorder.

1715 Septennial Act; Parliament prolongs its life from three to seven years.

1720 'South Sea' bubble.

1721 Robert Walpole seen as first prime minister.

1733 John Kay invents flying shuttle. Jethro Tull advocates new agricultural technology.

1742 Walpole falls.

1748 Montesquieu publishes *L'Esprit des Lois*.

1757 Pitt as Secretary of State is main force in British government. Clive conquers Bengal.

1759 Canal age begins.

1760 Beginning of 100-year period termed industrial revolution.

1763 First British empire at its height.

1764 John Wilkes expelled from Commons.

1769 Richard Arkwright invents water frame for spinning.

1770 James Cook discovers New South Wales.

1774 Warren Hastings appointed first Governor General of India.

1776 American Declaration of Independence. Adam Smith's *Wealth of Nations*.

1783 Treaty of Versailles; American independence recognized. Pitt the Younger becomes PM.

1784 Last appearance of monarch in Cabinet.

1785 Cartwright invents power loom.

1787 American Constitution drafted. Consolidated Fund established. Creation of Royal Ulster Constabulary.

1789 Washington first US President. French Revolution begins with storming of the Bastille (14 July). Bentham's *Introduction to the Principles of Morals and Legislation*.

1792 Denmark first country to prohibit slave trade. France becomes republic.

1798 Battle of Vinegar Hill.

1800   Parliamentary union of Great Britain and Ireland.
1804   Napoleon Bonaparte becomes French Emperor.
1805   Battle of Trafalgar; victory and death of Nelson.
1807   Slave trade abolished in British empire. Napoleon in control of all Europe. Britain blockaded by continent.
1811   Luddite riots against new machinery.
1812   Napoleon retreats from Moscow.
1814   Napoleon abdicates; Louis XVIII King of France.
1815   Napoleon escapes from Elba. Battle of Waterloo. Corn Law protects British agricultural interests at expense of commerce.
1819   'Peterloo Massacre'.
1823   USA announces 'Monroe Doctrine'.
1824   Repeal of Combination Acts legalizes trade unions.
1829   Metropolitan Police formed.
1832   First Reform Bill.
1833   First British Factory Act. First government grant for education.
1834   Poor Law Amendment Act. 'Tolpuddle Martyrs' transported to discourage working-class association.
1835   Municipal Corporations Act. Peel's 'Tamworth Manifesto'.
1836   Chartist movement formed.
1837   Queen Victoria's accession.
1839   Anti-Corn-Law League formed.
1842   Chartists present second Charter.
1845   Irish potato famine.
1846   Corn Laws repealed; Peel resigns; Conservatives split; Disraeli becomes leader.
1848   Revolutionary movement throughout Europe. French Republic proclaimed. Marx and Engels produce *Communist Manifesto*.
1851   Great Exhibition.
1854   Crimean war; France and England declare war against Russia. Much British bureaucratic incompetence exposed; Northcote–Trevelyan Report.

1855   Crimean War ends.
1856   Bessemer process invented.
1858   British Crown assumes sovereignty over India.
1859   Darwin's *Origin of the Species*. J. S. Mill's *On Liberty*.
1861   American civil war begins. J. S. Mill's *Considerations on Representative Government*. Public Accounts Committee established.
1864   First Socialist International.
1865   American civil war ends.
1866   Office of Comptroller and Auditor General established.
1867   Second Great Reform Bill. Bagehot's *The English Constitution*. Volume I of Marx's *Capital*.
1868   Disraeli succeeds Lord Derby as PM; later defeated by Gladstone in general election.
1870   Forster's Education Act sets up school boards.
1872   Secret ballot introduced.
1874   General election; Disraeli succeeds Gladstone as PM.
1880   Gladstone returned as PM.
1883   National insurance introduced in Germany. Special Branch of the Met. established.
1884   Third Parliamentary Reform Bill. Fabian Society founded.
1885   Dicey's *Law and the Constitution*.
1886   First Irish Home Rule Bill defeated in Commons. Unionist defectors from Liberals join Conservatives.
1888   County Councils Act.
1889   Second Socialist International. Great strike at London Docks. First Official Secrets Act.
1890   Parnell ruined by divorce case.
1893   Second Irish Home Rule Bill rejected in Lords. Independent Labour Party formed.
1894   Manchester Ship Canal opens. Gladstone resigns.
1899   Boer war starts.
1900   Labour Party formed. 'Khaki Election'.
1901   Queen Victoria dies. Taff Vale judgement.

1902   Boer war ends. Committee of Imperial Defence established.

1903   First flight of heavier-than-air machine at Kitty Hawk, USA. Emmeline Pankhurst forms Women's Social and Political Union.

1905   Liberal landslide; first Labour MPs.

1906   Suffragette activism. Trades Disputes Act reverses Taff Vale judgement.

1908   Asquith becomes PM.

1909   Old age state pension scheme introduced. Lords reject 'People's Budget'. Henry Ford begins manufacturing cheap motor cars. MI5 established.

1910   Edward VII's death; accession of George V. Labour exchanges established. Liberals battle with House of Lords, win two general elections, but become dependent upon Irish MPs. Osborne Judgement.

1911   Parliament Act reduces Lords' power. MPs to be paid. National Insurance introduced. Second Official Secrets Act passed with notorious Section 2.

1912   Third Irish Home Rule Bill. *Titanic* disaster.

1913   'Cat and Mouse Act'.

1914   Archduke Ferdinand assassinated; war in Europe. Britain declares war on Germany. Coalition government formed. Irish Bill passed but put in cold storage.

1916   Lloyd George becomes PM. New coalition reduces role of Liberals. Easter uprising in Ireland. Battle of the Somme; 420,000 British soldiers killed ('lions led by donkeys').

1917   USA declares war on Germany. Russia proclaimed a republic; Bolshevik revolution. Balfour Declaration.

1918   Armistice signed. Women given vote. 'Coupon Election'. Sinn Fein MPs win majority of Irish seats but set up own Parliament (Dáil).

Michael Collins forms IRA. New Labour Party constitution.

1919   Versailles Treaty. League of Nations established (Germany excluded).

1920   Black and Tans sent into Ireland.

1921   Irish settlement; Irish Free State set up; Ulster to remain in UK.

1922   1922 Committee formed. Conservatives win general election.

1923   Baldwin dissolves Parliament over tariff reform. General election makes Labour second largest party; they rule for 10 months with Liberal support.

1924   Liberals withdraw support over Campbell case. Zinoviev letter affair. Conservatives return triumphantly to office.

1925   Winston Churchill puts Britain back on gold standard. Drastic cuts in wages and industrial unrest.

1926   General strike.

1928   Equal Franchise Act; voting age for women lowered to 21.

1929   Labour wins election as largest single party for the first time. Second Labour government under MacDonald. Liberal decline becomes inevitable. Wall Street crash. BBC established.

1931   Economic depression; Cabinet split over public expenditure cuts. MacDonald resigns. Surprise formation of coalition under MacDonald, who is denounced by his own party. Coalition overwhelmingly endorsed by electorate. Henderson becomes Labour leader.

1932   Lansbury becomes Labour leader.

1933   Hitler appointed Chancellor by Hindenburg and begins to gain iron control in Germany.

1934   Hitler becomes dictator. Foundation of NCCL.

1935   Baldwin succeeds MacDonald as PM. Attlee becomes Labour leader. Conservatives win election.

1936   Spanish civil war breaks out.

Public Order Act. Keynes's *General Theory of Employment, Interest and Money*. BBC TV begins.

1937 Chamberlain forms coalition.

1938 Germany annexes Austria. British navy mobilized. Chamberlain signs Munich Agreement with Hitler.

1939 Britain recognizes Franco government in Spain; civil war ends. Conscription introduced. Germany invades Poland. Britain declares war on Germany. Third Official Secrets Act.

1940 Labour joins coalition; Churchill forms National Government. Army evacuated from Dunkirk. Italy declares war on Britain and France. Germans capture Paris. Battle of Britain. Attlee recognized as deputy PM.

1941 Japanese attack Pearl Harbor.

1942 Beveridge Report.

1943 Mussolini overthrown. Italian Fascist Party dissolved.

1944 D-Day invasion of Europe. Paris liberated. Bretton Woods Agreement; IMF and World Bank established. Great Education Act.

1945 Mussolini and mistress shot by Italian partisans. Suicide of Hitler and mistress. End of second world war against Germany (2 May). UN Charter signed. Landslide Labour victory; Attlee becomes PM. Britain begins to create modern welfare state; accepts Keynesian principles. Atomic bomb against Japan. Russia declares war against Japan. Japan surrenders. Lend–Lease terminated. Nuremberg Trials of major war criminals. UN formed. Attlee takes decision that Britain shall manufacture atomic bombs.

1946 US eventually approves loan to Britain.

1947 Nationalization begins (coal). Marshall Aid plan begins. India and Pakistan become dominions. Marriage of Princess Elizabeth.

1948 End of British mandate for Palestine; partition into Jewish and Arab states. NHS established. Electricity nationalized. Republic of Ireland Bill signed.

1949 Parliament Act reduces Lords' power. NATO formed after Russians blockade Berlin. Gas nationalized.

1950 Rebuilt House of Commons opened. Labour secures narrow election victory.

1951 Resignation of Bevan over NHS charges. Attlee dissolves Parliament. Labour defeated in election, despite receiving most votes; Churchill becomes PM.

1952 George VI's death.

1953 Elizabeth II's coronation; ceremony televised. Steel de-nationalized.

1954 Crichel Down case. Food rationing ends.

1955 Churchill resigns as PM; succeeded by Eden. Conservative general election victory. Independent TV begins. Gaitskell succeeds Attlee as Labour leader.

1956 Britain's first atomic power station starts working at Calder Hall. Suez crisis. Anthony Crosland publishes *The Future of Socialism*.

1957 Eden resigns as PM; replaced by Macmillan. Franks Report on tribunals and inquiries.

1958 EEC treaty comes into force; Britain stays out. CND launched under Bertrand Russell; first London–Aldermaston protest march. Life Peerage Act. First women peers in House of Lords.

1959 Conservatives' third successive election victory.

1960 Macmillan's 'wind of change' speech; Conservatives form Monday Club. Plowden Report on public expenditure; PES system begins. Kennedy elected US president. Herbert Report on Greater London. Momentous Labour conference; Gaitskell makes 'fight, fight, and fight again' vow.

1961 Justice Report, *The Citizen and the Administration*. Neddy established.

1962 Cuban missile crisis. 'Beeching axe' reduces British Rail network. 'Night of the Long Knives'. First post-war Immigration Act, limits entry to those with jobs. Vassall spy scandal. Royal commission on police reports.

1963 British application to join EEC rejected. Harold Wilson becomes Labour leader after Gaitskell's death. Profumo scandal. Peerage Act enables peers to renounce hereditary titles. Macmillan resigns as PM; succeeded by Sir Alec Douglas-Home. Kennedy assassinated.

1964 First elections for new GLC; Labour victory. Nelson Mandela sentenced to life imprisonment. Labour gains narrow general election victory; Wilson PM. DEA created. Import surcharge and export tax introduced to improve balance of payments. Government, TUC and employers agree policy on productivity, prices and income. Police Act limits local control of police forces.

1965 Douglas-Home resigns; Heath elected Conservative leader under new procedure. BP strike North Sea oil. Death penalty abolished. Prices and Incomes Board created.

1966 Election increases Labour majority to almost 100. Frank Cousins resigns from government over incomes policy. Industrial Reorganization Corporation created. Prices and incomes freeze. Post Office becomes public corporation. Sir Edmund Compton becomes first ombudsman.

1967 Jo Grimond resigns as Liberal leader; replaced by Jeremy Thorpe. Britain makes another application to join EEC. Criminal Justice Act allows majority verdicts from juries. *Rookes* v.

Barnard judgement attacks right to strike.

1968 NHS prescription charges re-introduced. France vetoes British entry into EEC. Northern Ireland disturbances begin. Enoch Powell's 'Rivers of Blood' speech. Fulton Report on civil service.

1969 British army units to be deployed in N. Ireland. Voting age lowered to 18. Government seeks TUC voluntary agreement to curb unofficial strikes. Redcliffe-Maud Report on local government.

1970 Heath gains surprise election victory. Third application to join EEC. Army uses rubber bullets in N. Ireland. Heath's economic policy a 'dash for growth'.

1971 Currency decimalized. Immigration Act reduces status of Commonwealth immigrants to that of aliens. Both Houses of Parliament vote to join EEC. Compton Report on interrogation of IRA suspects finds evidence of ill treatment. US balance of trade slides into deficit with major consequences for world capitalism.

1972 'Bloody Sunday' in Londonderry; 13 civilians killed. Power crisis; state of emergency and power cuts. Increased IRA bombing. Direct Westminster rule over N. Ireland introduced. Decision taken to float pound. Local Government Act to reorganize system.

1973 Britain, Ireland and Denmark join EEC. Heath U-turns on economic policy; nationalization of lame ducks. N. Ireland referendum strongly supports retaining link with Britain. VAT introduced. First sitting of new Ulster Assembly collapses in chaos. Diplock Courts introduced in terrorist cases. Arab–Israeli war; oil prices quadruple. Fuel conservation measures include three-day week. Collapse of long boom becomes apparent. 'Snake in the Tunnel' agreement in Europe. India House incident brings existence of Special Patrol Group to public attention. Sir Robert Mark delivers BBC Dimbleby Lecture.

1974   End of direct rule in N. Ireland. Parliament recalled for two-day debate on energy crisis. Miners' strike. Reorganized local government and NHS systems come into operation. Heath calls election to decide 'who governs'; no clear result; Labour becomes minority government. Miners return to work. Ulster assembly collapses; direct rule resumed. Red Lion Square disorders. End of statutory incomes policy. Guildford pub bombing kills five. Second election in October returns Labour (majority 3). Birmingham pub bombing (21 killed). Anti-terrorist bill rushed through Parliament proscribes IRA. IRA bombs in London.

1975   Heath forced by 1922 Committee to resubmit to election; defeated by Margaret Thatcher. Referendum on remaining in EEC; 2 to 1 majority 'Yes'. First live broadcast of Commons. Unemployment exceeds 1 million. Balcombe Street siege; two Londoners held in flat by IRA. National Enterprise Board established. Anti-sex discrimination and equal pay legislation come into force. Ombudsman system extended to NHS.

1976   Wilson's unexpected resignation; Callaghan becomes PM. Britain begins exporting North Sea oil. David Steel elected Liberal leader. Britain found guilty by European Commission on Human Rights of torturing detainees in Ulster. Lord Hailsham expounds 'elective dictatorship' thesis. Blunt spy scandal. Police Complaints Board established; Sir Robert Mark resigns. PM announces death of

Keynesianism: 'we cannot . . . spend our way out of a recession'.

1977   Government loses absolute majority; Lib–Lab pact. Grunwick dispute. Violent racist clashes in Lewisham. *Hosenball* case.

1978   Special Liberal assembly votes to continue Lib–Lab pact until July. Regular broadcasting of parliamentary proceedings begins. Publication of *The Times* suspended in year-long dispute over new technology. IRA bombing in British cities. IMF Articles redrawn to mark end of Bretton Woods Agreement. Public-sector strikes bring 'Winter of Discontent'.

1979   Scottish and Welsh referendums reject devolution proposals. Government defeated on no-confidence motion; PM announces general election. Blair Peach dies in clash with police. Thatcher wins election, becoming first woman PM. Conservatives also dominate in European elections. Earl Mountbatten and others killed by bomb on boat in Sligo. Lancaster House talks to settle Rhodesia's (Zimbabwe's) future. All foreign exchange controls removed. New system of Commons select committees introduced.

1980   Bristol race riots. Zimbabwe becomes independent with Robert Mugabe as PM. National Front and Anti-Nazi League clashes at Lewisham. Iranian Embassy seized; later stormed by SAS. Bombings and violence in Ulster mark 10 years of internment. Callaghan retires as Labour leader; replaced by Foot. Reagan becomes US president. Alan Walters appointed PM's personal economic adviser. Local Government Planning and Land Act reforms block grant system, giving more central control.

1981   Special Labour conference changes leadership election method to give unions and constituencies a say. 'Gang of Four' establish Council for Social Democracy; SDP formed. Rupert Murdoch buys *The Times*. Engagement of Prince Charles and Lady Diana Spencer. Racial anti-police violence at Brixton. Death of Bobby Sands after 66-day fast; other IRA hunger strikers. Blanks fired at the Queen during Trooping of the Colour. SDP alliance with Liberals. Public expenditure cuts across a wide front. Inner-city riots and savage confrontations with police. Lonrho take over the *Observer*. Wedding of Lady Diana and Prince Charles. Benn unsuccessfully challenges Healey for Labour deputy leadership. Government announce privatization of state North Sea oil assets. OPEC unify oil price structure. Anglo-Irish summit agrees on Intergovernmental Council; uproar in Commons; Ian Paisley promises to make province ungovernable. Benn elected off Shadow Cabinet. Scarman Report on Brixton riots. Arthur Scargill elected NUM leader. Labour NEC investigates Militant Tendency. Law Lords rule against GLC's 'Fares Fair' policy. British Nationality Act closes door to non-whites.

1982   Unemployment reaches 3 million; Thatcher's popularity at all-time nadir. Falklands war; Carrington resigns as Foreign Secretary. Thatcher's popularity soars. Roy Jenkins becomes SDP leader. IRA bombs in Hyde Park and Regent's Park; 11 killed. Greenham Common anti-nuclear, feminist protest by 30,000 women.

1983   Labour NEC expels 5 members of Militant. Ian MacGregor appointed NCB chairman. 'Falklands election' gives Conservatives majority of 144. Bernard Weatherill elected

Speaker against Thatcher's wishes. Jenkins resigns as SDP leader; succeeded by Owen. Chancellor Lawson announces public expenditure cuts of £500 million. 38 IRA prisoners escape from Maze prison; governor resigns. Kinnock replaces Foot as Labour leader. First US Cruise missiles arrive at Greenham Common. Massive bomb outside Harrods. US invades Grenada. Audit Commission established.

1984   Government announces ban on trade union membership at GCHQ. NCB announces 20,000 job losses and 21 pit closures. Miners' strike begins; High Court injunction prevents flying pickets. Sarah Tisdall jailed for 6 months for leaking documents about Cruise missiles. Greenham Common women evicted by bailiffs. Michael Bettaney jailed for 23 years for espionage. Labour gains in European Parliament elections; Conservatives retain majority.
   Immigration rules further toughened. Mirror Group Newspapers bought by Robert Maxwell. High Court rules ban on union membership at GCHQ illegal. 18 councils rate-capped. Clive Ponting charged under Official Secrets Act. Police and Criminal Evidence Act. Police Complaints Authority replaces Police Complaints Board. IRA bomb in Brighton hotel housing Conservative leaders for party conference. High Court orders sequestration of NUM assets. Talks between NUM and NCB repeatedly break down. Law Lords support ban on unions at GCHQ. High Court appoints receiver to control NUM funds. BT privatized; massive profits on first day's trading.

1985   House of Lords televised live. Oxford University refuses Thatcher honorary degree. Clive

Ponting acquitted by jury. Miners drift back to work after repeated failures of talks. Fourth government defeat in Lords over GLC abolition. European Court of Human Rights holds that British immigration rules discriminate against women. Violent rioting in Brixton after police accidentally shoot Mrs Cherry Groce. Policeman killed during Broadwater Farm riots (Tottenham). Miners in Notts and South Derbyshire join Union of Democratic Mineworkers. Anglo-Irish agreement signed; mass resignation of Ulster Unionist MPs. Control of *Daily Telegraph* passes to Canadian, Conrad Black. Westland affair begins. Church of England *Faith in the City* report.

1986 Heseltine resigns criticizing Thatcher style. Brittan resigns over part in leak of Solicitor General's letter in Westland affair. Murdoch prints *Sunday Times* and *News of the World* at Wapping despite opposition from print unions; violent demonstrations. GLC and metropolitan counties abolished. Labour NEC begins disciplinary action against 16 Militants at Liverpool. John Stalker suspended and taken off N. Ireland inquiry into RUC 'Shoot to Kill' policy. Derek Hatton (Liverpool Militant leader) expelled from Labour Party. Gifford Report on Broadwater Farm riots.

Appeal Court imposes ban on *Spycatcher* by former MI5 officer, Peter Wright. Stalker reinstated by Greater Manchester police force. Marmaduke Hussey appointed by Thatcher as BBC Chairman. Launch of new quality national broadsheet, the *Independent*. 'Big Bang' in City as computers are introduced. *Spycatcher* case begins in Australian court. British Gas privatized. US air attack on

Libya from British bases. Crown Prosecution Service comes into operation. New Public Order Act increases police powers.

1987 Privatization of BA. Large-scale redundancies on Tyneside. Home Secretary refers 'Birmingham Six' case (pub bombing) to Court of Appeal after much campaigning; they will not be acquitted. SAS shoot 8 IRA men and a civilian in County Tyrone. European Court of Human Rights dismisses case of GCHQ workers. Government obtains injunction to prevent showing on BBC of Zircon spy satellite.

Relaunch of formal Liberal–SDP Alliance. Enforced resignation of BBC Director General Alasdair Milne. Police raid on BBC offices in Glasgow to remove film *Secret Society*. Sir Kenneth Newman retires as head of Metropolitan Police; replaced by Peter Imbert. President Reagan admits 'arms for hostages' deal with Iran ('Irangate' scandal).

Three men convicted of murder of PC Blakelock on Broadwater Farm estate. Moscow talks between Thatcher and Gorbachev. Thawing of cold war; Gorbachev offers to abolish short-range missiles in Europe. Third successive general election triumph for Thatcher but great vote of no-confidence in Conservatives from Scotland, Wales and north.

1988 Thatcher becomes longest-serving PM of century. Budget creates uproar in Commons; top rate tax reduced to 40 per cent (lowest in Europe); £2,000 million of tax cuts go to wealthiest. Imports begin to rise faster than exports; fuelled by consumer credit boom. Ibbs Report on civil service. SAS gun down suspected IRA members in Gibraltar. Free vote in Commons decides to admit television cameras. Clash between PM and Chancellor over return of economic adviser Sir Alan Walters.

Trade deficit rises to record £2,150 million. Inflation begins upward spiral. Poll tax bill receives royal assent after stormy passage. Church continues to attack Thatcherite policies. SDP and Liberals form Social and Liberal Democratic Party; Paddy Ashdown emerges as leader. Benn and Heffer challenge Kinnock/Hattersley leadership but easily defeated. Fall in NUM membership means Arthur Scargill no longer entitled to automatic place on TUC's General Council; fails to get elected.

TUC becomes more favourably disposed towards EC after European Commission President Jacques Delors declares that 1992 single market drive means workers' rights and social reform. Thatcher resists French and German call for Britain to join EMS; Bruges speech encapsulates her Euroscepticism.

Last act of *Spycatcher* drama; High Court rules newspapers free to comment on and publish extracts. Legislation to replace Section 2 of Official Secrets Act; critics say no improvement. Broadcasting Standards Authority set up under Sir William Rees Mogg; fears of censorship. British Steel privatized. Police Federation passes vote of no confidence in Police Complaints Authority. Government imposes ban on media interviews with members of Sinn Fein. Formation of Charter 88. Salmonella crisis; Health Minister Edwina Currie forced to resign.

1989 White paper on NHS reforms threatens doctors' autonomy. White paper on reforms to legal system. Ayatollah Khomeni passes 'death sentence' on Salman Rushdie; some British Muslims demonstrate against the author. European election results bad for Conservatives; Greens gain 15 per cent of votes but no seats. Televising of Commons begins. Chief Constable of West Midlands disbands Serious Crime Squad after allegations of falsified confessions; largest investigation into police corruption for 10 years begins. Water industry privatized. Lawson's dramatic resignation when Thatcher refuses to sack Alan Walters; John Major replaces him.

1990 Nelson Mandela released from prison. Thatcher's calls for ending of sanctions resisted by rest of world. Release of 'Guildford Four'; doubt about their 'confessions'. Ending of cold war and dramatic changes in Eastern Europe make future shape and role of NATO and the EC problematic. Massive anti-poll-tax demonstrations. Labour's popularity over Conservatives higher than ever before (24 per cent). Iraq invades Kuwait; condemned by UN; US and British troops sent.

Interest rates rise in attempt to control inflation; many council house buyers suffer. Conservatives lose safe seats to Labour and SLD in by-elections. Local elections débâcle for Conservatives. Cabinet splits over Thatcher's vision of Europe; Geoffrey Howe resigns and makes devastating Commons speech. Conservative leadership contest. Heseltine forces second ballot; Thatcher resigns; John Major emerges as party leader and PM.

1991 Gulf war. IRA bombs in London. Woolf Report into prison riots. Electricity privatization. 'Birmingham Six' freed by Court of Appeal. Major NHS reforms. N. Ireland talks begin. Citizen's

Charter launched. Robert Maxwell drowns.

1992   Maastricht Treaty signed. Unexpected Conservative general election victory; majority only 21. Intensification of IRA campaign on British mainland with bombs in Whitehall, other parts of London and elsewhere. Betty Boothroyd first woman Speaker of Commons. Kinnock resigns; John Smith elected Labour leader. Britain assumes EC presidency. 3,000th death in N. Ireland since 1969.

'Black Wednesday'. Labour conference reduces union power in party. Criminal Justice Act comes into force. Pit closure plan (31 pits) hastily modified after public outcry. Matrix Churchill trial collapses. Uncomfortable disclosures on the private lives of Conservative politicians. Separation announced of Prince and Princess of Wales. Queen's '*annus horribilis*'.

1993   Single European Market comes into force. Inflation lowest for 25 years; unemployment 3 million. James Bulger murder. Maastricht Bill defeated in Commons. Sheehy Report on police. Care in the Community programme instigated. Massive IRA bomb in City of London. Scott Inquiry into arms-to-Iraq begins. Conservatives lose Newbury by-election to Lib Dems. Council tax replaces poll tax. Extensive Lib Dem and Labour gains in local elections. Further defence cuts announced.

In highest twentieth-century turnout, Lords vote against referendum on Maastricht by 445 to 176. Government defeated on Social Chapter opt-out by 324 to 316 but wins subsequent no-confidence vote by 339 to 299. ERM effectively suspended. Britain ratifies Maastricht Treaty. BNP wins local council seat in Isle of Dogs. Labour agrees to OMOV for candidate selection. Major calls for 'back to basics'. First November unified Budget; tax increases and public-spending cuts. Anglo-Irish 'Downing Street Declaration'.

1994   District auditor alleges gerrymandering by Conservative Westminster Council. Sleaze allegations and government resignations. Free votes reduce homosexual age of consent to 18; death penalty not re-introduced. Ordination of women priests approved amidst controversy. UK reluctantly accepts modified rules on QMV in an enlarged EU. Rail privatization begins. Further Conservative losses in local elections. Channel tunnel opens. John Smith dies.

Conservative setbacks in Euro elections; Lib Dems gain first two seats. Prince of Wales admits adultery on TV. Two Conservative PPSs resign after *Sunday Times'* allegations of cash for questions. Jacques Santer succeeds Delors as EC president. Pergau Dam affair. Blair elected Labour leader; Prescott deputy. Demonstrations against Criminal Justice Bill. Kinnock appointed European Commissioner. IRA ceasefire.

Neil Hamilton resigns over sleaze allegations. Nolan Committee established. Criminal Justice Act comes into force. Post Office privatization postponed. National Lottery launched. Public outrage over British Gas chief executive's 75 per cent pay rise. Gerry Adams visits mainland. Whip withdrawn from eight Conservative rebels; Government becomes dependent on Ulster Unionists. Government defeated on VAT increases on domestic fuel.

1995   Austria, Finland and Sweden join EU. Resignations of ministers, PPSs, etc. continue due to sleaze etc. Joint framework document on

N. Ireland. Baring Bank collapse. Former Chancellor Lamont votes with Labour on EMU. Conservatives win only 81 seats in Scottish local elections; Labour control 20 of 29 new unitary authorities. 'Cash for questions' MPs suspended; 'whipless Tories' reinstated. Special Labour conference approves new Clause Four.

Further Conservative losses (1800 seats) in local elections (England and Wales); Labour gain control of 39 councils. First direct talks between British government and Sinn Fein for 23 years. First report of Nolan Committee. Harold Wilson dies. New parliamentary boundaries approved. Shell UK abandons plan to dump Brent Spar oil rig at sea.

Major throws down gauntlet over party leadership; John Redwood stands against him but defeated. Labour reduces union conference vote to 50 per cent. David Trimble elected leader of Official Unionists. ECHR rules British soldiers acted unlawfully in 1988 Gibraltar killings. Conservative MP Alan Howarth defects to Labour. Lord Home dies aged 92. Home Secretary announces 'boot camps' for young offenders and tougher penalties for criminals. Prison Service director Derek Lewis sacked after Learmont report.

Referendum Party launched. MPs agree to reveal outside earnings. Blair assures CBI Labour will not automatically adopt EU social legislation. Princess of Wales gives frank TV interview. Major and John Bruton sign agreement on N. Ireland talks and weapons decommissioning. Bill Clinton visits Belfast and Dublin. Eurosceptics cause government defeat on EU fishing quotas. Conservative majority

falls to 3 as Emma Nicholson defects to Lib Dems.

1996 Labour's all-women shortlists ruled illegal. Gerry Adams meets Bill Clinton. Privatized rail services begin. Canary Wharf bomb ends IRA ceasefire. Scott Report on Arms-for-Iraq affair. New N. Ireland peace talks boycotted by most participants. Dunblane shooting. Link between BSE and CJD admitted. EU ban on British beef exports.

After by-election Conservative majority down to one. Arthur Scargill launches Socialist Labour Party. Further substantial Labour and Lib Dem gains in local elections. Revised register of MPs' interests published. Westminster councillors surcharged for gerrymandering. Government promise to block EU decisions requiring unanimity in retaliation for beef ban.

Former US Senator George Mitchell to chair N. Ireland peace talks; Sinn Fein excluded in absence of IRA ceasefire. Manchester bomb injures nearly 200. Labour pre-manifesto statement *New Labour, New Life for Britain*. Violence following Orange Order marches in N. Ireland. SNP publish plans for Scottish independence; Scottish Labour Party advocates referendum on Scottish parliament. Multi-party talks re-open at Stormont. TUC call for national minimum hourly wage of £4.26.

Prince and Princess of Wales divorce. Standards and Privileges Committee launches cash-for-questions inquiry. Labour and Lib Dems announce joint talks on constitutional reform. Budget details leaked to *Daily Mirror*. David Willetts resigns as Paymaster General after Commons report criticizing behaviour in cash-for-questions affair. By-election eliminates government's majority. European Council meeting in Dublin outlines details of 'Euro'.

1997 Major government becomes increasingly fragile. N. Ireland situation deteriorates. Labour win Wirral South by-election with 17.2 per cent swing from Conservatives. Government secures Ulster Unionist support by promising a N. Ireland Grand Committee. MoD failures over Gulf war syndrome admitted. Bridgewater Three released by Appeal Court. Stephen Lawrence inquest returns verdict of unlawful killing; public criticism of police failure to achieve convictions. EP blames UK government for BSE crisis; worldwide ban on UK beef exports.

Major calls general election for 1 May, heralding longest-ever campaign. Conservative campaign sharply contrasted with Labour's. Arrival of prison ship at Portland (first since 19th century). Multi-party N. Ireland talks adjourned. Rail and road transport disrupted by bombs and bomb threats. Labour election landslide on 1 May; overall swing 10.6 per cent but lowest turnout since 1935. Conservatives wiped out in Scotland and Wales and lose many seats in south-east heartlands. Number of women MPs and Lib Dems doubled. Blair youngest PM since 1812; five women in first Cabinet. Mandelson given powerful role as Minister without Portfolio.

Chancellor Gordon Brown relinquishes power to set interest rates to Bank of England. UK signs up to EU Social Chapter. Major resigns; William Hague elected Conservative leader. Blair announces renewed contacts with Sinn Fein, providing ceasefire maintained. Amsterdam Summit

fails to resolve key issues prior to EU expansion; proposal to integrate WEU into EU defeated. Brown's first Budget maintains Conservatives' overall spending plans. Windfall tax on privatized utilities to subsidize welfare-to-work programme. Senior Lib Dems on joint cabinet committee.

Downey Report published but Standards and Privileges Committee cannot discipline those criticized because they are no longer MPs. Nolan Committee recommends new criminal offences covering misuse of office by public servants. NATO invites Poland, Czech Republic and Hungary to join. Agenda 2000 presented to European Parliament details plans for enlargement, budget and CAP reform. Opinion poll indicates declining support for monarchy. Former MI5 agent David Shayler questions accountability of the service. N. Ireland Secretary Mo Mowlam invites Sinn Fein to multi-party talks.

Death of Princess of Wales provokes unprecedented public grief and debate on monarchy. Scottish and Welsh referendums approve devolution proposals, but very close in Wales. Chancellor announces commitment to single currency, but not in first phase. Keith Halliwell appointed 'drugs tsar'. Blair holds historic meetings with Gerry Adams. Talks continue, despite setbacks, including bombs.

Formula One tobacco sponsorship controversy. Chancellor's autumn statement unveils welfare-to-work plans. Jenkins Commission on electoral reform established. Cabinet committee on Lords reform established. Kyoto climate summit. 47 Labour MPs defy three-line whip over lone-parent benefit cuts. High Court supports surcharges on Westminster City Council. Inquiry into the BSE crisis begins. Hague marries former Welsh Office civil servant Ffion Jenkins.

1998   N. Ireland Secretary Mo Mowlam meets imprisoned Protestant paramilitaries. Blair announces new inquiry into Bloody Sunday. Sinn Fein temporarily expelled from peace talks after IRA blamed for two murders. Countryside March against fox-hunting ban. European Commission rules 11 countries eligible to join single currency. EU begins entry negotiations with five former East European countries. France and Britain ratify nuclear test ban treaty.

Historic Good Friday peace agreement over N. Ireland; creation of new assembly and north–south institutional links. Row continues over arms shipments to Sierra Leone in contravention of UN arms embargo. G8 summit in Birmingham calls for further global trade liberalization. Referendums in N. Ireland back Good Friday Agreement. Lords defeat legislation to lower homosexual age of consent to 16. N. Ireland Assembly inaugural meeting; David Trimble chosen as 'first minister'. Extra 800 British troops sent to N. Ireland. Protestants insist on right to march through mainly Catholic areas against Parades Commission ruling. Omagh bomb kills 29; worst atrocity in nearly 30 years. IRA splinter group (Real IRA) admits responsibility.

Conservative party conference reveals deep divisions over Europe; Heseltine says party becoming 'unelectable'. Lords defeat Euro-elections bill five times. Welsh Secretary Ron Davies resigns after Clapham Common incident; withdraws

candidacy for first Minister of Welsh Senedd. Two Cabinet members (Mandelson and Nick Brown) 'outed' as homosexuals. BBC criticized for attempting to censor reporting on Mandelson.

Neill Report proposes reform of rules governing party financing and campaigns. Jenkins Report recommends PR; government gives cautious welcome but declines commitment on referendum before next general election. Bank of England makes first interest rate cut after six increases since gaining the power.

Met. Commissioner Sir Paul Condon apologizes to Lawrence inquiry but denies institutional racism. Official inquiry into BSE/CJD affair reveals serious government and civil service shortcomings. Queen's Speech attended by slightly less ceremonial. Spain calls for extradition of former Chilean dictator Pinochet undergoing medical treatment in London. EU lifts ban on British beef exports.

Hague sacks leader in Lords over secret deal with Labour over Lords reform. Paris court refuses request for extradition of former MI5 officer David Shayler, to face charges under the Official Secrets Act. Prince Charles's 50th birthday party hosted by Camilla Parker-Bowles. Royal assent for Human Rights Bill. Joint Lab–Lib Dem cabinet committee has remit broadened. White paper recommends greater parliamentary control over EU legislative proposals. Government publishes first 'quality of life barometer' recognizing green factors. Shock resignation of Mandelson from Cabinet after revelations of undeclared loan from colleague Geoffrey Robinson (who also resigns).

1999   Bill introduced to end sitting and voting rights of hereditary peers;

royal commission to consider further reforms of upper house. Paddy Ashdown stuns Lib Dems by announcing forthcoming retirement after local and Euro elections; future of alliance with Labour in jeopardy. Violence in N. Ireland continues with brutal 'punishment beatings'. Commons supports legislation to lower age of homosexual consent to 16. Damning report from Foreign Affairs Select Committee on arms-to-Sierra Leone affair; scandal over leaks from select committee to ministers. In contest for Labour leadership in Wales (and therefore First Minister of Senedd), Rhodri Morgan defeated by Alan Michael, Blair's choice. Macpherson Report on Stephen Lawrence inquiry a damning indictment of Met. Dramatic resignation of EU commissioners after report on corruption. Law Lords reconsider the Pinochet extradition case but put ball back in Home Secretary's court, prompting further debate on politicization of judiciary. After failure of negotiations, NATO begins bombing Yugoslavia on humanitarian grounds, in its first ever attack on a sovereign state.

Glossary

Words in **bold** type within entries refer to terms or concepts found elsewhere in the Glossary. Remember to consult the Index to locate more information and for terms (especially institutions and organizations) not included here.

absolute majority   A majority greater than 50 per cent.

abstention   Deliberate non-voting.

accountability   Answerability to a higher authority (the people, in a **democracy**).

Act of Parliament   Law passed by Parliament.

administrative law   Concerned with cases between the citizen and the state.

administrative tribunal   Deals with citizens' grievances against the state.

advanced capitalism   Modern, hi-tech, multinational **capitalist** economy. Distinguished from late capitalism (capitalism in crisis and decay). Technology makes workers less important, increasing opportunities for the few to amass wealth.

adversary politics   Description of British **two-party system**, seeing it based on argument rather than compromise between parties.

advisory body   Set up by government to conduct an inquiry and come up with recommendations.

agency capture   Control of an agency by the enterprise it is supposed to be regulating.

anarchy   Society without government.

anthropocentrism   Seeing human life as the principle criterion of value.

aristocracy   Government by an enlightened elite.

arm's length administration   Quasi-autonomous agencies running various state services with little government interference.

art of the possible   Classic aphorism used to define politics, drawing attention to compromising and wheeling and dealing evident in real world.

authoritative allocation of values   Definition of politics. May be contrasted with **market** allocation in that allocation is on the basis of political authority, rather than ability to pay.

authority   Form of **power** distinguished by the fact that it is accepted by those over whom it is held.

autonomy   Self-determination; usually of a state.

behaviouralism   Approach to social sciences, including political science, taking only observable phenomena as its data.

Bill of Rights Constitutional document guaranteeing citizens' rights.

bils The form in which legislation is introduced into Parliament (when passed it becomes an **Act**).

bipartisan Consisting of two parties.

block vote Large number of votes tied together and cast at one go; a controversial feature of the Labour Party conference.

body corporate Organization with a persona in law (e.g. local authority).

borough Historic **local government** area based on a town which had gained a royal charter entitling it to certain freedoms.

bourgeoisie French term for town-dweller appropriated by Marx to denote a capital-owning social **class** spawned by the industrial revolution; to Marx, the ruling class.

broadsheet Quality newspaper.

budgetary process Method whereby government determines its annual expenditure and sources of income.

bureaucracy Strictly speaking, rule by officials. Weber argued that the growth of **socialism** would result in such rule. Used without pejorative connotations to denote a large hierarchical organization.

by-election Election held following death or retirement of sitting member.

Cabinet Group of leading ministers heading the government.

cabinet government Government by a team rather than a single ruler; *see also* **collective responsibility**.

Cabinet Secretariat Special part of **civil service** responsible for servicing the Cabinet and its committees; can be influential in policy.

Cabinet Secretary Head of **Cabinet Secretariat** (and of civil service).

cadre party Party in Parliament consisting of MPs; may or may not have a mass membership outside Parliament.

capitalism Mode of production in which private individuals, rather than the state, own materials necessary to produce what society needs for its survival.

case law Law resulting from previous judicial decisions (precedent).

central–local relations Relationship between central government and its territorially based agencies; most often in connection with **local government**.

centralization Central government's dominance over other state agencies.

ceremonial Ostentatious aspects of government usually with little importance for decision-making, but often crucial for **legitimation**.

Chartism Working-class organization founded in 1836 demanding universal male suffrage without property qualification.

citizen Member of a **state**, with rights and obligations.

city-state Political unit about which most Ancient Greek political thought was written; very small and not comparable with complex modern **nation-states**.

civic culture Political culture in which people have confidence in, and will cooperate with, government.

civil jurisdiction Pertaining to that part of the legal system concerned with cases involving one citizen against another.

civil rights Rights accruing to individuals as **citizens** which may not be infringed by other citizens or by the state.

civil service The central government **bureaucracy**.

civil society That part of social life outside the control of the state.

class Section of population sharing a common social status; almost invariably associated with socioeconomic factors. Usually divided into upper, middle and lower. In Marxist terms, seen as a dichotomy arising from the position of individuals in the productive process; *see also* **bourgeoisie** and **proletariat**.

coalition Parties working together as a government.

cold war State of East–West tension beginning after the second world war.

collective consumption Services

consumed collectively by the population (e.g. education).

collective investment State role in investing in the economy (e.g. road building).

collective responsibility Constitutional convention reflecting the idea of **cabinet government**; entails various things including the idea that ministers participate in collective **policy-making**.

collectivism Sees the collectivity, rather than the individual, as the essential human unit.

colonialism Form of domination of one state over another associated with **imperialism**; may be established after military conquest or economic penetration of a weak economy (**neocolonialism**).

common law Law formed on the basis of precedents set in previous cases; reflects the accumulated wisdom of the past rather than legislation.

communism Ideology of equality and the common ownership of property.

community policing Form of policing in which the force becomes deeply involved in community affairs to establish mutual trust.

comparative advantage Economic theory underpinning the philosophy of **free trade** associated with Adam Smith, arguing that if each nation produces that which it does most efficiently, the world will maximize its wealth.

consensus Harmony between possibly opposed factions. The era of consensus politics in Britain (late 1940s–mid-1970s) saw Labour and Conservatives in agreement over a wide range of policies.

consensus policing Policing based on gaining the consent and cooperation of those policed rather than force.

conservatism View of politics, society and the constitution which believes in the wisdom of the past and is suspicious of radical change. Has deep intellectual antecedents; associated particularly with Edmund Burke and the ideology of the Conservative Party.

consociationalism Two or more communities living harmoniously in the same state (as in Belgium).

constituency Territorial electoral division (e.g. Glasgow Hillhead). Can also denote the nature of a politician's support (e.g. 'small businessmen are the natural constituency of the Conservative Party').

constitution Set of rules, customs and conventions defining the composition and powers of state institutions and regulating their relationships to each other and to private **citizens**; unwritten constitutions do not exist as a single document but in the form of custom and practice and various laws.

constitutional amendment Formal change to the **constitution**.

constitutional convention Regularly observed practices regarded as part of the **constitution**.

constitutional government Government constrained by rules and procedures laid down in the **constitution**; contrasted with arbitrary government.

constitutional monarchy Political system in which a **monarchy** is so constrained by the **constitution** that it plays no part in decision-making.

consultative body Set up by government to bring together interested parties for policy discussions.

consumer voting model Voting behaviour model seeing voters as shoppers in a political market-place, choosing parties on the basis of their shop windows (**manifestos**, etc.).

contracting-out Privatization of work previously done by the state, often enforced, as in CCT (compulsory competitive tendering in local government) and market-testing (civil service).

core executive The complex network of people, relationships, structures and procedures around the **Cabinet**.

corporate management Form of management urged upon **local government** which seeks to unify control of its services under a single chief executive.

corporatism Theory of **pressure group** activity in which the government incorporates certain groups into the **policy-making** process.

county   Top-tier **local authority** with ancient lineage.

criminal jurisdiction   Pertaining to the criminal law in which the crimes are against the state rather than against a particular person.

cross-bencher   Member of House of Lords disdaining allegiance to any party.

cross-border body   Body set up to consider certain policy areas across national boundaries (e.g. northern and southern Ireland).

cross-class voting   Phenomenon whereby individuals belonging to one social class vote for a party ostensibly supporting the interests of another.

D-notice system   Voluntary code whereby the press restrains itself from publishing material on defence which officials want kept secret.

de facto   In actuality.

de jure   According to law.

deference   Belief amongst citizens that they should not play much part in government; they are happy to leave things to those whom they believe to be superior.

delegated legislation   Laws made by **bureaucrats** with power delegated by Parliament.

demand management   Keynesian principle whereby government uses its financial influence in the economy to manipulate the level of aggregate demand to maintain full employment.

democracy   Rule by all **citizens** in a community.

demos   Greek word for the people as a collectivity (hence **democracy**).

deregulation   Removal by the state of controls tending to protect state services from competition (e.g. local authority transport services).

détente   Reduction of tension between states; used particularly of East–West relations during the **cold war**.

determinism   Doctrine that everything that happens does so because of other forces; downgrades human free choice (**voluntarism**) as a factor explaining

events.

devolution   State authority passed down from a higher level of government to sub-national areas; *see also* **federalism**.

dignified and **efficient elements** Distinction between those elements of a **constitution** which have no direct impact on **policy-making** and those which do; does *not* mean that the dignified elements are unimportant.

direct democracy   Form of **democracy** in which **citizens** actually take part in making decisions; almost impossible in the real world.

ecocentrism   Placing nature in general before human life as a criterion of value.

economic and monetary union (EMU) The linking of economies and currencies of a number of states; a major project of the EU.

economic planning   Government intervention in the economy to achieve certain future goals, such as full employment, economic growth, balance of payments; opposed by **monetarists**.

elected mayor   Politician elected by all citizens in a local government area to lead the authority.

election campaign   Efforts made by **political parties** in the run-up to an election to win voters' support.

electoral quota   Number of votes a candidate requires to be elected under certain systems of **proportional representation**.

electoral swing   Calculation measuring the percentage shift of party support across the country; may or may not be uniform.

electoral volatility   Condition in which the electorate cannot be relied upon to vote regularly for the same party.

elitism   Body of thought on **power** in society which sees as inevitable the formation of elites which will consolidate their positions, collude with each other and control government in their own interests.

embourgeoisement   Process whereby members of the working class acquire middle-class habits and characteristics.

endogenous explanation   Explaining national political events solely in terms of factors internal to the country.

Enlightenment   Seventeenth-century European intellectual movement which saw a flowering of science and faith in rational thought and progress in social and political life.

entrenchment   Often used of **constitutions** to denote provisions that cannot be changed by the normal process of law-making; absent in the UK.

environmentalism   Ideology derived from ecology aiming to prevent human despoilation of life forms.

Establishment   Imprecise term used for a narrow, upper-middle-class elite with much power in society.

Eurosceptic   Those opposed to European **federalism**.

exchange rate   Value of one currency in terms of that of another country.

exchange rate mechanism (ERM)   A system of fixing currencies against each other on the way to complete **economic and monetary union**.

executive   That part of an organization responsible for policy-making; in politics usually with reference to the **government**, or more narrowly, the **Cabinet**; *see also* **core executive**.

executive agency   Civil service body created to administer functions hived off from the main body of the civil service (often referred to in the UK as Next Steps agencies).

executive body   Quango responsible for actually administering some state function (e.g. Arts Council).

exogenous explanation   Explanation of internal political events based on external factors.

Fabianism   Approach to social and political reform advocated by the Fabian Society, stressing small incremental advances rather than revolution.

faction   Segment within a party; usually considered more hard edged than a **tendency**.

false consciousness   Errors of perception concerning one's self-interest; may explain why working-class people support the Conservatives.

fascism   Ideology espousing nationalism, militarism and demagoguery.

federalism   Process whereby states voluntarily pool their **sovereignty**, thereby creating a higher level of government.

feminism   Ideology supporting equal rights for women.

fiscal policy   Taxation policy; may be used in pursuit of various objectives (e.g. full employment or pollution control).

floating voter   Member of electorate who easily changes party allegiance.

franchise   The right to vote in elections.

free press   Doctrine that newspapers should be free to print what they like without government direction or censorship.

free trade   Free flow of goods in international trade, unimpeded by tariff barriers; has fuelled much political controversy.

Freedom of Information Act   Legislation giving citizens a legal 'right to know' much of what happens in government.

functionalism   Body of theory looking primarily at the way institutions and practices contribute to the working of a social or political system; may be contrasted with an institutional approach.

Gemeinschaft* and *Gesellschaft   German terms meaning community (based on bonds of affection, kinship, etc.) and association (based on contract), respectively.

General Will   A shared feeling/view amongst people, beyond self-interest, of their common good; central to thinking of Rousseau.

generalist   Civil servant with no special or professional skill; often holding a high position within the British service.

globalization   Growing interdependence of individual, countries and regions of the world.

'Golden Age' of Parliament   Period approximately between the 1832 and 1867 Reform Acts when Parliament appeared to have the power to bring down governments; ended by the rise of party discipline.

golden share   State-owned share in a privatized company enabling it to have control over certain key decisions.

government   (verb) The process of ruling a community; (noun) an elite group formally recognized as being in control of the community.

green paper   Government document to stimulate public debate; *see also* **white paper**.

Hansard   Official record of parliamentary proceedings.

hegemony   Rule or domination often of one state over others; used by neo-Marxists of a class dominating society by holding leading positions in various walks of life.

hidden hand   Used by Adam Smith and neoliberal economists to account for the order which comes out of an unregulated **market**.

historical materialism   Marx's 'scientific' theory of history, which sees it shaped by the means of production.

hiving off   Chopping off pieces of public **bureaucracy** to form semi-autonomous **executive agencies** responsible for some clearly defined block of work.

holism   Theory stressing the *whole* of the object of study rather than the parts.

ideology   Political doctrine claiming to give a universally applicable theory of people and society from which may be derived a programme of political action.

imperialism   Extension of the **hegemony** of one country by conquest (military or economic) and imposed rule over others.

incrementalism   Theory of government decision-making holding that radical steps are impossible or undesirable.

individualism   Doctrine seeing the individual as the prime unit in morality and politics; underlies the theories of classical economists in which individuals pursue their own self-interest.

industrial revolution   Period between 1760 and 1860 (approximately) based on multiple innovations in production methods and technologies; revolutionary in the social transformation it induced.

inflation   General rise in prices throughout the economy; often measured by the Retail Price Index (RPI).

inner cabinet   Unofficial **Cabinet** consisting of the PM and a few chosen members of the government.

insider group   **Pressure group** with a close, secretive relationship with government.

institutional racism   Entrenched practices reflecting **racist** attitudes, such as discrimination in job appointments or immigration procedures.

instrumental explanation   An interpretation of politics seeing the state as an instrument of some greater power behind the throne; in **Marxism**, this is the **bourgeoisie**.

interest aggregation   Bringing interests together to construct a body sufficiently large (party or group) to have political clout.

interest group   Association of people with some common concern; *see also* **pressure group**.

intergovernmental organization   Association of governments in which each retains its **sovereignty**; *see also* **supragovernmental**.

international associations   Associations formed across nations such as NATO and the United Nations Organization.

internet   Global system of connections between computers.

Iron Curtain   Powerful image employed by the West to describe the separation between the communist East European bloc and the capitalist West.

iron law of oligarchy   Sociological 'law' postulated by Michels stating that in any **political party** a small elite would eventually gain control.

jingoism   Chauvinistic militarism (from an anti-Russian music-hall song of 1878).

judicial impartiality Constitutional principle that judges are impartial with regard to the interests within society.

judicial review Part of the principle of the **separation of powers**. The **judiciary** is able to review legislation and actions of the **executive** in terms of their constitutionality. In Britain this is restricted to actions of the executive.

judiciary The body of judges.

jury Part of judicial system; highly democratic in that the jury is selected at random, so does not include power-seekers in the way electoral politics does. Used by the Greeks not only for legal decisions.

Keynesianism Economic theory arguing that the free **market**, left to itself, will not automatically work for the benefit of all. Consequently the state must intervene to achieve desirable social ends, particularly full employment.

laissez-faire Slogan adopted by classical economists; the state should keep out of the private **capitalist** economy.

legislative process Series of stages by which a **bill** becomes an **Act**; entails passage through Parliament.

legislature Institution formally charged with making laws – Parliament.

legitimacy Quality of being popularly accepted as rightful and just.

legitimation Actions and processes designed to secure **legitimacy**; may entail deception.

Leviathan Huge sea monster – Hobbes's term for the all-powerful ruler.

liberal democracy Form of **democracy** based upon elections and representative institutions which places great stress upon the idea of individual freedom defined in terms of a *limited* role for government and the state; linked with idea of **market** economy.

liberalism **Ideology** seeing minimum government and individual freedom as its prime virtues; attractive to **capitalism** by permitting the operation of the free **market**.

limited government Government restrained from arbitrary rule; accomplished variously by **rule of law**, separation of powers, or a **constitution**.

lobby (verb) Act of seeking the ear of a member of government; (noun) the 'club' of parliamentary correspondents who receive unattributable briefings from government.

lobbyist One practised in the art and craft of dealing with MPs and ministers on behalf of **pressure groups**.

local authority Body responsible for delivering local government services; comprises a work force, a **bureaucracy** and an elected council.

local governance Broadly, the function of various locally based public bodies, elected *and* unelected.

local government Self-government by the people of some subnational territorial unit within the state through an elected council.

long boom Period from the end of the second world war to the beginning of the 1970s when the developed **capitalist** countries enjoyed rising standards of living and a great rise in material wealth.

machinery of government Institutions through which **government** works; **civil service** departments, **local authorities**, etc.

macroeconomic policy Policy concerning the aggregate performance of the national economy.

maladministration Bad administration causing inconvenience or suffering.

managerialism Approach to government in which the public sector tries to ape private-sector methods; tends to reduce elected politicians' authority.

mandarin Term used to describe members of the upper echelons of the **civil service**. Originally used of officials in imperial China.

mandate Approval for a set of policies gained by a party elected to office on the basis of a **manifesto**.

manifesto Set of policy promises made by the parties to entice electors.

market Key mechanism (based on price) in classical economic theory; it is said to work as if controlled by a **hidden**

hand to achieve optimum allocation of the resources in society.

market-testing Examination of public-sector functions to see if they can be **contracted out** to the private sector.

Marxism Body of thought with many strands deriving from the ideas of Marx; sees the private ownership of materials needed for production as the key explaining society and politics.

mass party **Political party** organized throughout the country with thousands of members.

media mogul Owner of newspaper and broadcasting empires; often global in scope.

MEP Member of the European Parliament.

mercantilism Economic doctrine favoured in the sixteenth and seventeenth centuries. Argued that a country should seek to export as much as possible, while restricting imports. Did not suit the **capitalists** of the **industrial revolution**, who favoured **free trade**.

meritocracy Literally, rule by the most able; more colloquially, refers to a system (educational or social) where promotion is based on merit, usually measured by examination performance.

militarization Used of police to refer to greater use of defensive and offensive weapons and militaristic tactics.

mind politics Term used in this book to denote an arena of political activity concerned with influencing what people think, rather than allocating values.

ministerial adviser Expert from outside the **civil service** who advises ministers on policy; may adopt openly partisan stance and is not welcomed by the **bureaucrats**.

ministerial responsibility Doctrine declaring that the minister in a government department is the only one who should be questioned, praised and blamed. May be expected to resign where extreme shortcomings are revealed (e.g. Lord Carrington over the Falklands war).

minority government Government by a party without an **absolute majority**, relying on support from other parties.

mixed economy One in which **capitalism** is modified so that some of the productive capital in society is owned by the people (e.g. Britain before the **privatization** programme).

mob rule The down side of **democracy**; term used by opponents of democracy.

monarchy Rule by a single person; usually hereditary.

monetarism Economic doctrine holding that governments should do little in the economy, being content to control the rate at which the quantity of money in circulation rises. Everything else is then said to take care of itself through the **market**.

money supply Quantity of money in the economy, believed to be causally linked with **inflation**.

monopoly An industry in which a single firm exists with no competition to keep its prices in control.

multi-member constituency Electoral district returning more than one candidate; a prerequisite of **proportional representation**.

multi-party system **Political system** in which three or more parties contest elections and gain seats in the assembly. Often associated with coalition government.

multinational corporation Giant private firm located throughout the world; often producing a wide range of unrelated products.

nation-state The state as understood today; to be contrasted with the **city-states** of Ancient Greece.

nationalism Ideological attachment to the nation and its interests.

nationalization State acquisition of private property or a business within its territory.

natural law System of law deriving from human nature, rather than invented by reason; an idea present in political thought from the time of the Ancient Greeks. The great Roman statesman Cicero (106–43 BC) spoke of 'right reason – which is in accordance with nature, and is unchangeable and eternal' (*Republic*, III, 22).

natural monopoly   An industry where the technical problems of competition are so great that it is better for society if **monopoly** is permitted (e.g. telecommunications, railways).

natural rights   Rights (say to life or property) that some philosophers believe to come from nature rather than from government.

neocolonialism   Form of domination characteristic of the post-war era in which **capitalists** from the developed world effectively dominate the less-developed economies through **multinational corporations**.

neocorporatism   Used to distinguish the practice of post-war **corporatism** from the pre-war fascist variant.

neoliberalism   Ideology aiming to replace **social democracy** by returning to *laissez-faire* principles; *see also* **New Right** and **Thatcherism**.

New Right   Term for a resurgence of anti-social-democratic thought; in many ways restating the free-market ideas of the nineteenth-century economists.

New World Order   Term used by President Bush to donate the post-cold-war world based on **capitalism**.

news management   The practice of politicians and their press secretaries attempting to influence the reporting of politics; *see also* **spin doctor**.

non-aligned world   Group of nations professing neutrality during the **cold war**.

north–south divide   Political gulf between the north and south of Britain emerging from the late 1970s.

official censorship   Government restriction on what people can see, hear or read.

official secrecy   The keeping of state secrets; justified on the grounds of national security.

oligarchy   Oppressive rule by a small group.

ombudsman   Common term for **citizens'** trouble-shooter (e.g. the Parliamentary Commissioner for Administration)

who investigates complaints of **maladministration**.

opinion poll   Survey of public opinion on some issue by use of sampling techniques.

organic system   System which has grown naturally rather than having been designed by people.

outsider group   Pressure group that government is unwilling to listen to.

paramilitary   Militaristic methods and equipment used by non-military organizations (e.g. Special Patrol Group).

parish   One of the oldest units of **local government**; very small and based on the area around the church.

parliamentary privilege   Set of privileges accorded to MPs; supposed to enable them to perform better as representatives, without fear of, say, libel.

parliamentary questions (PQs)   Questions from MPs to members of the government on a rota system.

parliamentary sovereignty   Belief that Parliament is the supreme source of **sovereignty** in the **constitution**. Dicey believed this to be the only morally defensible version of sovereignty in a **democracy**.

partisan dealignment   Tendency of voters to break away from stable (especially **class**-based) identification with a **political party**.

partisanship   Political bias, as in newspaper reporting and editorial comment.

partition   Political division of a country; as in Ireland.

party conference   Usually the highly publicized annual meeting of all elements of the mass party organization.

party discipline   MPs' obedience to their party leadership.

party identification   Used by psephologists to describe voters who always vote for the same party regardless.

party list   Feature in **proportional representation** electoral systems; displays the candidates of a party, sometimes in order of preference.

party system   Usually defined in terms of the number of parties taking part in the political fray.

patriarchy   Society in which men dominate women.

patronage   Making appointments on the basis of favour rather than electoral choice or expertise.

peak organization   Umbrella organization formed by the association of a number of **pressure groups** (e.g. the TUC).

peer   Member of the House of Lords.

peer group   Body of individuals equal in some significant respect (age, rank, status etc.).

pluralism   Theory of politics seeing **pressure groups** as central to the political process; generally holds their effect to be benign and democratic.

pluralist stagnation   Right-wing explanation for Britain's post-war economic failure claiming that too many **pressure groups** were being permitted to voice their demands.

police complaints procedure   System for handling complaints against the police.

police culture   Characteristic set of attitudes held by the police.

police state   Totalitarian state where police are under control of the government.

Policy Cabinet   A small **Cabinet** of about five, the members of which are concerned with the whole area of government policy, rather than being responsible for specific departments. Has never really been tried.

policy implementation   Carrying out government policy; formally the task of the **bureaucracy**.

policy-making   Essential act of **government** in the modern state. The extent to which government is free to make policy is a matter of debate.

policy networks   Loosely knit and changing complexes of interest groups, politicians and officials brought together, sometimes in harmony sometimes in conflict, over policy issues.

polis   Ancient Greek term for city.

political culture   Set of ideas and attitudes held towards the **political system**.

political party   Group formed for the purpose of gaining political office, usually through winning elections.

political philosophy   Generalized answers to fundamental questions such as the nature of justice.

political science   May loosely be used to denote the study of politics generally, or more rigorously to indicate the application of scientific method.

political socialization   Social process through which individuals develop an awareness of political values, norms and processes; continues throughout life.

political system   A whole consisting of institutions of **government** and the society they serve, a concept stressing the **holistic** nature of politics; no part can be properly understood without reference to its place in the whole.

political theory   Theories about political institutions, law, **constitutions**, **democracy**, etc.

political thought   Corpus of theories whereby people have sought to explain political behaviour, values, and mechanisms and institutions of **political systems**.

politicization   Process whereby an institution may become actively involved in politics (e.g. the **civil service** and police).

politics–administration dichotomy   Long-standing distinction between making policy and carrying it out; underlies **separation of powers** between **executive** and **legislature**.

polity   The political organization of a state.

poll tax   Tax placed on all citizens equally regardless of ability to pay; imposed in 1381 (causing Peasants' Revolt) and as community charge in late 1980s.

polyarchy   Robert Dahl's term for a form of **pluralism** seeing in groups a more effective balance of power than in the **constitution**.

populism   Form of **government** supposed to enshrine the will of the people. Some political leaders have an instinctively populist appeal. Presidents, where directly elected, may claim populist mandate.

positive law Law believed to have been made by applying human reason rather than by some metaphysical power such as God; *see also* **natural law**.

postmodernism A vaguely defined stage beyond the modernism of the **Enlightenment**.

power Key concept in the study and practice of politics; the ability to achieve some desired effect regardless of opposition. May take many forms.

power-sharing executive An **executive** formed to reflect both majority and minority interests.

preferential voting System that permits voters to indicate alternative preferences.

presidential government System of **government** by one person, usually elected directly by the people.

press baron **Capitalist** owner of large-circulation newspapers; today empires extend into the media and entertainments industry, hence **media mogul**.

pressure group Association wishing to influence government policy.

primary elections Elections held before the real elections to choose the candidates.

private members' bills Bills introduced into Parliament by MPs in their personal capacity rather than by the government; rarely get onto the statute book.

privatization Transfer of state-owned assets into private hands.

proletariat Marx's term for the working class.

promotional group Pressure group concerned with promoting an ideal rather than the self-interest of its members (e.g. RSPCA).

proportional representation Electoral system intended to create an assembly that accurately reflects the level of support for the parties in the country.

psephology Study of elections and electoral behaviour.

public choice theory Theory seeking to explain and analyse politics on the basis of the **individualist** premises of classical economics.

public corporation Body created by government in the image of a private company but owned by the state, rather than private shareholders.

public expenditure State expenditure by the state, including redistribution through transfer payments.

public inquiry Official inquiry into some matter of public concern.

public interest Vague term meaning the collective interest of society. What is, or is not, in the public interest is often a matter of judgement. In the Ponting case, the judge denied the right of a citizen to make up his own mind on the matter, declaring that only the government could decide.

public order Well-regulated civic life.

public sector borrowing requirement (PSBR) Amount of money government wishes to borrow in any year.

qualified majority vote Vote in which more than a simple majority is required for success.

quango Quasi-Autonomous Non-Government Organization.

Queen's Speech Great day in the ceremonial calendar of British politics, marking the annual opening of Parliament and outlining the government's proposed programme for the year.

Question Time One-hour period in the Parliamentary timetable when MPs address questions to ministers.

racism Attribution of characteristics of superiority and inferiority to members of particular races.

rational decision-making Making a decision on the basis of reason rather than self-interest, political advantage or prejudice.

rationalism Faith in reason, as opposed to religion or superstition.

redress of grievance Means taken to right a wrong (often inflicted by the state on a citizen).

referendum Popular vote on a particular

issue rather than to choose a representative; being used increasingly in Britain.

regionalism   Giving political power to geographical regions of the state; *see also* **devolution**.

regulation   A major government role; instead of providing a service, exerts control over those that do (often through agencies).

representative government   Form of **government** in which a minority acts on behalf of the rest of the population.

republic   State in which supreme power rests with the people; contrasted with **monarchy**.

royal prerogative   Set of special privileges enjoyed exclusively by the monarch since medieval times; today many of the most important are effectively held by the PM.

rule of law   Constitutional doctrine that the ultimate source of **authority** in the state is the law; kings and governments are themselves subject to it.

sectional group   **Pressure group** composed of members of society from some sectional interest.

sectoral cleavage   An alternative to class as an explanation of voting behaviour.

security services   State agencies concerned with espionage (MI5 and MI6).

select committee   Committee of MPs established to undertake some particular task on behalf of Parliament and scrutinize the **executive**.

selective incentive   Inducement made by a **pressure group** or **political party** to recruit and retain members.

separation of powers   Constitutional doctrine in which the various functions of **government** (rule-making, rule execution and judging) are placed with separate institutions in order to check each other and prevent despotism.

separatism   Desire to be governed as a separate state; *see also* **devolution**.

sexism   Attitudes falsely ascribing certain attributes to one sex, usually to justify inequality.

Shadow Cabinet   Opposition front-bench team.

single currency   The result of a joining together of currencies of different states as in the creation of the Euro.

single-party system   **Political system** in which one party dominates; under totalitarian regimes may actually eliminate its rivals by force.

sleaze   Term increasingly used to describe corrupt or dubious behaviour by politician.

social class   *See* **class**.

social democracy   Ideology of moderate **socialism**, mixed economy, welfare state, etc.

socialism   Egalitarian **ideology** under which the state actively cares for citizens. Reformist socialism aims to achieve this by reform of liberal institutions rather than violent confrontation (*see also* **Fabianism**); revolutionary socialism aims to overthrow capitalism by force.

sovereignty   Concept of the ultimate source of **power** within the state.

'special relationship'   Britain's view of its relationship with the US.

spin doctor   Politician's aide concerned with **news management**.

spoils system   System of **patronage** in which election victors distribute offices to those who have assisted them.

sponsorship   Relationship of MPs to various non-party organizations (e.g. some Labour MPs are sponsored by trade unions).

standing committees of Parliament   Committees of MPs considering **bills** during their process through Parliament (the committee stage).

state   In simple terms, a sovereign community, within a defined territory.

state of nature   A condition imagined by some philosophers (Hobbes, Locke, Rousseau) as a basis for determining what the role of **government** should be.

statute law   Laws made by Parliament.

structural explanation   Explanation of political behaviour seeing it as determined by the structure in which it takes place (e.g. the **capitalist** economy).

subgovernment   Community formed by

those concerned with policy in a certain area (**insider pressure groups, civil service**, the specialist press, ministers, etc.); sometimes termed a policy community.

subsidiarity Principle that the powers of different levels of government should always be placed as low (that is as close to the people) as is compatible with efficiency.

subversion Attempt to overthrow the government by unlawful means.

suffragette Woman active in the cause of women's voting rights.

supragovernmental organizations International authorities standing above national governments.

system Set of elements interacting together to constitute a larger whole.

tabloid Popular newspapers; also called 'redtops' or 'the gutter press'.

tactical voting Behaviour designed to keep out a disliked candidate by supporting the rival most likely to defeat him or her.

tendency Used in politics to designate sections within parties (e.g. Militant Tendency).

territorial management Government role in balancing the **devolutionary** claims of different regions.

Thatcherism Neoliberalism as espoused by Margaret Thatcher.

think-tank Body of intellectuals set up privately or by government to consider public policy alternatives.

'third way' Ideological position espoused by New Labour (and others) claiming to be between **social democracy** and **neoliberalism**.

transnational corporation Private company operating in the global economy and not located within any particular country.

tripartism Form of **corporatism** developed in Britain in the immediate post-war decades involving government, employers and unions.

two-party system **Political system** in which two equal parties monopolize in terms of votes and parliamentary seats.

tyranny Oppressive rule.

ultra vires Legal principle restraining public bodies within a framework of powers prescribed by the **sovereign** body.

underclass Disadvantaged class developing during the 1980s (unemployed, ethnic minorities, etc.).

unitary system **Local government** areal structure without subdivisions.

utilitarianism Moral philosophy preached by Bentham, J. S. Mill and others; sees the maximization of utility (happiness) as the basis for all law, morality, political institutions and right behaviour.

variable geometry Term used to describe a process whereby groups of members move towards integration at differing speeds (applied to EU).

violence, state Legitimate use of force against citizens (e.g. police).

voluntarism View that humans control their own actions, rather than acting as the system forces them to do.

welfare statism A social democratic kind of ideology.

West Lothian question Term used to describe the problem of Scottish MPs being able to vote on certain English matters at Westminster while English MPs cannot vote on issues coming before the Scottish Parliament.

whip MP charged with maintaining **party discipline** in Parliament.

white paper Document published by government to outline and explain its policy; *see also* **green paper**.

world economy The idea that all countries are interlocked through trade.

xenophobia Fear (and often hatred) of foreigners.

Bibliography

Adonis, A. (1993) *Parliament Today*, Manchester, Manchester University Press.

Adonis, A. and Pollard, S. (1997) *A Class Act: The Myth of Britain's Classless Society*, London, Hamish Hamilton.

Alderman, K. (1998) 'The Conservative Party leadership election of 1997', *Parliamentary Affairs* 51(1), 1–16.

Alderman, K. and Carter, N. (1994) 'The Labour Party and the trade unions: loosening the ties', *Parliamentary Affairs*, 47(4), 321–37.

Alderson, J. (1994) *A New Cromwell: The Centralisation of the Police*, London, Charter 88.

Almond, G. A. and Verba, S. (1963) *The Civic Culture*, Princeton, NJ, Princeton University Press.

Almond, G. A. and Verba, S. (eds) (1980) *The Civic Culture Revisited*, Boston, MA, Little Brown.

Althusser, L. (1969) *For Marx* (transl. B. Brewster), Harmondsworth, Penguin.

Amery, L. S. (1947) *Thoughts on the Constitution*, London, Oxford University Press.

Arblaster, A. (1984) *The Rise and Decline of Western Liberalism*, Oxford, Blackwell.

Armstrong, P., Glyn, A. and Harrison, J. (1984) *Capitalism since World War II*, London, Fontana.

Armstrong, P., Glyn, A. and Harrison, J.

(1991) *Capitalism Since 1945*, Oxford, Blackwell.

Audit Commission (1990) *We Can't Go On Meeting Like This*, Abingdon, Audit Commission Publications.

Audit Commission (1993a) *Passing the Buck: The Impact of Standard Spending Assessments on Economy, Efficiency and Effectiveness*, London, HMSO.

Audit Commission (1993b) *Realising the Benefits of Competition: The Client Role for Contracted Services*, London, HMSO.

Auerback, M. M. (1959) *The Conservatism Illusion*, New York, Columbia University Press.

Bagehot, W. (1963) *The English Constitution*, London, Fontana (first published 1867).

Baggott, R. (1995a) 'From confrontation to consultation: pressure groups from Thatcher to Major', *Parliamentary Affairs*, 48(3), 484–502.

Baggott, R. (1995b) *Pressure Groups Today*, Manchester, Manchester University Press.

Bains, M. A. (chairman) (1972) *The New Local Authorities: Management and Structure*, London, HMSO.

Baird, V. (1998) 'Money, markets and madness', *New Internationalist*, no. 306 (Oct.), 7–8.

Baker, K. (1993) *Turbulent Years: My*

Life in Politics, London, Faber.

Baldwin, R. and Kinsey, R. (1982) *Police Powers and Politics*, London, Quartet.

Balogh, T. (1968) 'The apotheosis of the dilettante: the establishment of mandarins', in Thomas, H. (ed.) *Crisis in the Civil Service*, London, Anthony Blond.

Bannister, N. (1993) 'Clean water challenge', *Guardian* (14 July).

Banton, M. (1985) *Promoting Racial Harmony*, Cambridge, Cambridge University Press.

Bar Council (1989) *Quality of Justice: The Bar's Response*, London, Bar Council.

Barberis, P. (ed.) (1996) *The Whitehall Reader*, Buckingham, Open University Press.

Barker, R. (1994) *Politics, Peoples and Government*, Basingstoke, Macmillan.

Barnett, A. (1982) *Iron Britannia*, London, Allison and Busby.

Barnett, A., Ellis, C. and Hirst, P. (1993) *Debating the Constitution*, Cambridge, Polity.

Barron, J., Crawley, G. and Wood, T. (1991) *Councillors in Crisis*, Basingstoke, Macmillan.

Batty, K. and George, B. (1985) 'Finance and facilities for MPs', in Norton, P. (ed.) *Parliament in the 1980s*, Oxford, Basil Blackwell, pp. 169–81.

Baxter, J. and Koffman, L. (eds) (1985) *Police, the Constitution and the Community*, Abingdon, Professional Books.

Beer, S. H. (1956) 'Pressure groups and parties in Britain', *American Political Science Review*, 50(1), 1–23.

Beer, S. H. (1965) *Modern British Politics*, London, Faber.

Beer, S. H. (1982) *Britain Against Itself*, London, Faber.

Bell, Daniel (1960) *The End of Ideology*, Glencoe, IL, Free Press.

Bellamy, R. and Castiglione, D. (1996) 'Introduction: constitutions and politics', *Political Studies,* 44, 413–16.

Benn, M. (1985) 'Policing women', in Baxter and Koffman (eds).

Benn, M. et al. (1983) *The Rape Controversy*, London, National Council for Civil Liberties.

Benn, T. (1979) *Arguments for Socialism*, Harmondsworth, Penguin.

Benn, T. (1980) 'Manifestos and Mandarins', in *Policy and Practice: the Experience of Government*, London, Royal Institute of Public Administration.

Bentley, A. F. (1967) *The Process of Government*, Cambridge, MA, Harvard University Press (first published 1908).

Bentley, M. (1984) *Politics Without Democracy, 1815–1914*, London, Fontana.

Berlin, I. (1970) 'Two concepts of liberty', in Berlin, I., *Four Essays on Liberty*, Oxford, Oxford University Press.

Beveridge, W. (chairman) (1942) *Social Insurance and Allied Services*, Cmd 6404, London, HMSO.

Bhavnani, K. K. and R. (1985) 'Racism and resistance in Britain', in Coates et al. (eds), pp. 147–59.

Birch, A. H. (1959) *Small Town Politics*, Oxford, Oxford University Press.

Birkinshaw, P. (1988) *Freedom of Information: The Law, The Practice and the Ideal*, London, Weidenfeld and Nicolson.

Birkinshaw, P. (1991) *Reforming the Secret State*, Buckingham, Open University Press.

Birkinshaw, P. (1997) 'Freedom of information', *Parliamentary Affairs*, 50(1), 164–81.

Bishop, M., Kay, J. and Mayer, C. (eds) (1995) *The Regulatory Challenge*, Oxford, Oxford University Press.

Blake, R. (1985) *The Conservative Party from Peel to Thatcher*, London, Fontana.

Boaden, N. (1971) *Urban Policy Making*, Cambridge, Cambridge University Press.

Boateng, P. (1985) 'Crisis in accountability', in Baxter and Koffman (eds), pp. 237–45.

Boddy, M. and Fudge, C. (eds) (1984) *Local Socialism: the Way Ahead*, London, Macmillan.

Bogdanor, V. (1981) *The People and the*

Party System, Cambridge, Cambridge University Press.

Bogdanor, V. (1996a) 'The monarchy and the constitution', *Parliamentary Affairs*, 49(3), 407–22.

Bogdanor, V. (1996b) *Politics and the Constitution: Essays on British Government*, Aldershot, Dartmouth.

Bogdanor, V. (1997a) 'Let the people come to the aid of the parties', *Observer* (13 April).

Bogdanor, V. (1997b) 'Ministerial accountability', *Parliamentary Affairs*, 50(1), 71–83.

Bogdanor, V. (1997c) *The Monarchy and the Constitution*, Oxford, Oxford University Press.

Bottomore, T. (1964) *Elites in Society*, Harmondsworth, Penguin.

Bower, T. (1988) *Maxwell: The Outsider*, London, Aurum Press.

Box, S. (1971) *Deviance, Reality and Society*, London, Holt, Rinehart and Winston.

Brand, J. (1992) *British Parliamentary Parties: Policy and Power*, Oxford, Oxford University Press.

Brazier, C. (1997) 'State of the world report', *New Internationalist*, no. 287 (Jan./Feb.), 4–9.

Brett, E. A. (1985) *The World Economy Since the War: The Politics of Uneven Development*, Basingstoke, Macmillan.

Brittan, L. (1993) 'Time to retune to Emu harmony', *Financial Times* (27 Oct.).

Brittan, S. (1983) 'Privatisation: a new approach', *Financial Times* (17 Nov.).

Brown, J. A. (1992) 'The Major effect: changes in party leadership and party popularity', *Parliamentary Affairs*, 45(4), 545–64.

Bruce-Gardyne, J. (1984) *Mrs Thatcher's First Administration*, London, Macmillan.

Bull, H. (1977) *The Anarchical Society*, London, Macmillan.

Bunyan, A. (1977) *The History and Practice of the Political Police in Britain*, London, Quartet.

Burch, M. and Holliday, I. (1996) *The British Cabinet System*, Hemel Hempstead, Prentice Hall/Harvester Wheatsheaf.

Burke, E. (1782) *Reform of Representation in the House of Commons*, in *Works* (1861, vol. VI), London, Bohn.

Burley, A. and Mattli, W. (1993) 'Europe before the Court: a political theory of legal integration', *International Organization*, 47 (Winter), 41–76.

Burnham, J. (1942) *The Managerial Revolution*, London, Putnam.

Burnham, J., Jones, G. W. and Elgie, R. (1995) 'The parliamentary activity of John Major, 1990–94', *British Journal of Political Science*, 25(4), 551–63.

Butler, D. (1960) 'The paradox of party difference', *American Behavioural Scientist*, 4(3).

Butler, D. (1995) *British General Elections since 1945*, Oxford, Blackwell.

Butler, D. and Butler, G. (1994) *British Political Facts, 1900–1994*, Basingstoke, Macmillan.

Butler, D. and Kavanagh, D. (eds) (1987) *The British General Election of 1987*, Basingstoke, Macmillan.

Butler, D. and Kavanagh, D. (eds) (1992) *The British General Election of 1992*, Basingstoke, Macmillan.

Butler, D. and Kavanagh, D. (eds) (1997) *The British General Election of 1997*, Basingstoke, Macmillan.

Butler, D. and Rose, R. (1960) *The British General Election of 1959*, London, Macmillan.

Butler, D. and Stokes, D. (1969) *Political Change in Britain*, London, Macmillan.

Butler, D. E., Adonis, A. and Travers, T. (1994) *Failure in British Government: The Politics of the Poll Tax*, Oxford, Oxford University Press.

Butler, M. (1986) *Europe: More than a Continent*, London, Heinemann.

Cabinet Office (1991) *The Citizen's Charter: Raising the Standard*, Cm 1599, London, HMSO.

Cabinet Office (1993) *Open Government*, Cm 2290, London, HMSO.

Cabinet Office (1994a) *The Civil Service: Continuity and Change*, Cm 2627, London, HMSO.

Cabinet Office (1994b) *Review of Fast Stream Recruitment,* London, HMSO.

Cabinet Office (1996) *Development and Training for Civil Servants: A Framework for Action,* Cm 3321, London, Stationery Office.

Cahanum, S. (1997) 'Finishing school: Asian girls in the British educational system', in Giddens (1997b), pp. 344–7.

Callaghan, J. (1987) *Time and Chance,* London, Collins.

Callaghan, J. (1997) *Great Power Complex,* London, Pluto.

Camilleri, J. A. and Falk, J. (1992) *The End of Sovereignty?* Aldershot, Edward Elgar.

Campbell, D. (1980) 'Society under surveillance', in Hain et al. (eds), pp. 65–150.

Cannadine, D. (1992) *The Decline and Fall of the British Aristocracy,* London, Picador.

Castells, M. (1977) *The Urban Question,* London, Edward Arnold.

Castle, B. (1980) *The Castle Diaries, 1974–6,* London, Weidenfeld and Nicolson.

Cawson, A. (1986) *Corporatism and Political Theory,* Oxford, Basil Blackwell.

Cecil, H. (1912) *Conservatism,* London, Thornton Butterworth.

Chandler, J. A. (1988) *Public Policy-Making for Local Government,* London, Croom Helm.

Chandler, J. A. (1996) *Local Government Today,* 2nd edn, Manchester, Manchester University Press.

Chapman, R. A. (1996) 'Tragedy and farce: the decision to privatise the RAS agency', *Public Policy and Administration,* 11(1), 1–7.

Chapman, R. A. and O'Toole, B. J. (1995) 'The role of the civil service: a traditional view in a period of change', *Public Policy and Administration,* 10(2), 3–20.

Charmley, J. (1998) 'The Conservative defeat: an historical perspective', *Political Quarterly,* 69(2), 118–25.

Checkland, S. G. and E. O. A. (eds)

(1974) *The Poor Law Report of 1834,* Harmondsworth, Penguin.

Chittenden, M. (1988) 'Freemasonry "rife" among top police', *Sunday Times* (10 April).

Chittenden, M. and Grice, A. (1995) 'The new gravy train', *Sunday Times* (14 May).

Chomsky, N. (1997) *World Orders, Old and New,* London, Pluto.

Chrimes, S. B. (1967) *English Constitutional History,* 4th edn, London, Oxford University Press.

Clarke, H. D. and Stewart, M. C. (1995) 'Economic evaluations, prime ministerial approval and governing party support: rival models reconsidered', *British Journal of Political Science,* 25(2), 145–70.

Clifford, P. and Heath, A. (1994) 'The election campaign', in Heath et al. (eds), pp. 7–23.

Coates, D., Johnson, G. and Bush, R. (1985) *A Socialist Anatomy of Britain,* Cambridge, Polity.

Cockburn, C. (1977) *The Local State,* London, Pluto Press.

Cockerell, M., Hennessy, P. and Walker, P. (1984) *Sources Close to the Prime Minister: Inside the Hidden World of the News Manipulators,* London, Macmillan.

Cohen, B. J. (1995) 'Towards a mosaic economy: economic relations in the post-cold-war era', in Freiden, J. A. and Lake, D. A. (eds), *International Political Economy: Perspectives on Global Power and Wealth,* London, Routledge, pp. 519–31.

Cohen, N. (1997) 'All Tory candidates will be subject to editing', *Observer* (12 April).

Commission for Local Democracy (1995) *Taking Charge: The Rebirth of Local Democracy, Final Report,* London, Municipal Journal.

Committee on Standards in Public Life (1995) *First Report of the Committee on Standards in Public Life* (chaired by Lord Nolan), Cm 2850-I, London, HMSO.

Conservative and Unionist Party (1997) *Our Party: Blueprint for Change,*

London, Conservative and Unionist Party.

Cornford, F. M. (ed. and translator) (1941) *The Republic of Plato*, Oxford, Clarendon Press.

Cosgrave, P. (1978) *Margaret Thatcher: A Tory and Her Party*, London, Hutchinson.

Cowling, M. (ed.) (1987) *Conservative Essays*, London, Cassell.

Crewe, I. (1983) 'Representation and ethnic minorities in Britain', in Glazer, N. and Young, K. (eds) *Ethnic Pluralism and Public Policy: Achieving Equality in the United States and Britain*, London, Heinemann.

Crewe, I. (1988) 'Has the electorate become Thatcherite?', in Skidelsky, R. (ed.) *Thatcherism*, London, Chatto and Windus.

Crewe, I. (1992) 'A nation of liars? Opinion polls and the 1992 election', *Parliamentary Affairs*, 45(4), 475–95.

Crewe, I. (1993) 'Voting and the electorate', in Dunleavy et al. (eds), pp. 92–122.

Crewe, I. (1997) 'The opinion polls: confidence restored?', *Parliamentary Affairs*, 50(4), 569–85.

Crewe, I. and King, A. (1994) 'Did Major win? Did Kinnock lose?' in Heath et al. (eds), pp. 125–47.

Crewe, I. and King, A. (1997) *SDP: The Birth, Life and Death of the Social Democratic Party*, Oxford, Oxford University Press.

Crick, B. (1964) *In Defence of Politics*, Harmondsworth, Penguin.

Crick, B. (1987) *Socialism*, Buckingham, Open University Press.

Crick, B. (ed.) (1991) *National Identities: The Constitution of the United Kingdom*, Oxford, Blackwell.

Criddle, B. (1997a) 'MPs and candidates', in Butler and Kavanagh (eds), pp. 186–209.

Criddle, B. (1997b) 'New intake marked by the stamp of the professional', *Financial Times* (3 May).

Crosland, A. (1956) *The Future of Socialism*, London, Jonathan Cape.

Cross, C. (1963) *The Liberals in Power 1905–1914*, London, Pall Mall Press.

Crossman, R. H. S. (1963) 'Introduction', in Bagehot, W., *The English Constitution*, London, Fontana.

Crossman, R. H. S. (1975–7) *Diaries of a Cabinet Minister*, 3 vols, London, Jonathan Cape.

Crouch, C. (1979) *State and Economy in Contemporary Capitalism*, London, Croom Helm.

Curtice, J. (1996) 'What future for the opinion polls?', in Rallings, C. et al. (eds), *British Elections and Parties Yearbook 1995*, London, Frank Cass, pp. 139–56.

Curtice, J. (1997) 'Anatomy of a non-landslide', *Politics Review*, 7(1) 2–8.

Curtice, J. and Semetko, H. (1994) 'Does it matter what the papers say?' in Heath et al. (eds), pp. 43–63.

Curtice, J. and Steed, M. (1987) 'Analysis', in Butler and Kavanagh (eds), pp. 316–62.

Curtice, J. and Steed, M. (1992) 'Appendix: the results analysed', in Butler and Kavanagh (eds), pp. 322–62.

Daalder, H. (1964) *Cabinet Reform in Britain, 1914–63*, Stanford, CA, Stanford University Press.

Dahl, R. (1956) *A Preface to Democratic Theory*, Chicago, IL, University of Chicago Press.

Dahl, R. (1985) *A Preface to Economic Democracy*, Cambridge, Polity.

Dahl, R. and Lindblom, C. E. (1976) *Politics, Economics and Welfare*, New York, Harper.

Davies, B. (1972) *Variations in Children's Services among British Urban Authorities*, London, Bell.

de Jonquieres, G. (1983) 'The BT sale: why are the stakes so high?', *Financial Times* (3 May).

Deane, P. (1963) *The First Industrial Revolution*, Cambridge, Cambridge University Press.

Dearlove, J. (1973) *The Politics of Policy in Local Government*, London, Cambridge University Press.

Denemark, D. (1996) 'Thinking ahead to mixed-member proportional representation', *Party Politics*, 2(3),

409–20.

Denver, D. (1998) 'The British electorate in the 1990s', *West European Politics*, 21(1), 197–217.

Denver, D. (1994) *Elections and Voting Behaviour in Britain*, 2nd edn, Hemel Hempstead, Philip Allan.

Denver, D. (1997) 'Turnout', *Parliamentary Affairs*, 50(4), 720–32.

Denver, D., Norris, P., Broughton, D. and Rallings, C. (eds) (1993) *British Elections and Parties Yearbook, 1993*, Hemel Hempstead, Harvester Wheatsheaf.

Department of the Environment (1983) *Streamlining the Cities*, Cmnd 9063, London, HMSO.

Department of the Environment (1991) *The Internal Management of Local Authorities*, London, HMSO.

Department of the Environment (1993) *Community Leadership and Representation: Report of the Working Party on the Internal Management of Local Authorities*, London, HMSO.

Department of the Environment, Transport and the Regions (1998a) *Modern Local Government: In Touch With the People*, London, Stationery Office.

Department of the Environment, Transport and the Regions (1998b) *Modernising Local Government: Local Democracy and Community Leadership*, London, Stationery Office.

Deutsch, K. W. (1964) *The Nerves of Government*, Glencoe, IL, Free Press.

Devine, F. (1997) *Social Class in America and Britain*, Edinburgh, Edinburgh University Press.

Dicey, A. V. (1959) *An Introduction to the Study of the Law of the Constitution*, 10th edn, London, Macmillan (first published 1885).

Doig, A. (1984) 'Public service and private gain', *Public Money*, 4(3).

Doig, A. (1995) 'Continuing cause for concern? Probity in local government', *Local Government Studies*, 21(1), 99–114.

Dorey, P. (1995) *British Politics since 1945*, Oxford, Blackwell.

Dowding, K. (1995) *The Civil Service*, London, Routledge.

Downs, A. (1957) *An Economic Theory of Democracy*, New York, Harper and Row.

Downs, D. (1997) 'What should the next government do about crime?' *Howard Journal of Criminal Justice*, 36(1), 1–13.

Draper, D. (1997) *Blair's 100 Days*, London, Faber.

Drewry, G. and Butcher, T. (1991) *The Civil Service Today*, 2nd edn, Oxford, Blackwell.

Drucker, H. et al. (eds) (1986) *Developments in British Politics 2*, London, Macmillan.

Duff, A. (1997) *The Treaty of Amsterdam*, London, The Federal Trust.

Dunleavy, P. (1980) *Urban Political Analysis*, London, Macmillan.

Dunleavy, P. (1981) *The Politics of Mass Housing in Britain: Corporate Power and Professional Influence in the Welfare State*, Oxford, Clarendon Press.

Dunleavy, P. (1991) *Democracy, Bureaucracy and Public Choice*, Hemel Hempstead, Harvester Wheatsheaf.

Dunleavy, P. (1993) 'The political parties', in Dunleavy et al., pp. 123–53.

Dunleavy, P. and Husbands, C. T. (1985) *British Democracy at the Crossroads: Voting and Party Competition in the 1980s*, London, George Allen & Unwin.

Dunleavy, P. and Jones, G. W., with Burnham, J., Elgie, R. and Fysh, P. (1993) 'Leaders, politics and institutional change: the decline of prime ministerial accountability to the House of Commons, 1868–1990', *British Journal of Political Science*, 23(2), 267–98.

Dunleavy, P. and Rhodes, R. A. W. (1990) 'Core executive studies in Britain', *Public Administration*, 68(1), 3–28.

Dunleavy, P., Gamble, A., Holliday, I. and Peele, G. (1993) *Developments in British Politics 4*, Basingstoke, Macmillan.

Dunleavy, P., Gamble, A., Holliday, I. and Peele, G. (1997a) *Developments in British Politics 5*, Basingstoke, Macmillan.

Dunleavy, P., Margetts, H., O'Duffy, B. and Weir, S. (1997b) *Making Votes Count*, Democratic Audit Paper 11, Colchester, University of Essex, Democratic Audit.

Dutt, M. (1995) 'God's guerillas', *New Internationalist*, no. 270 (Aug.), 7–10.

Duverger, M. (1966) *The Idea of Politics*, London, Methuen.

Dyer, C. (1995) 'And the verdict m'lud?', *Guardian* (7 April).

Easton, D. (1953) *The Political System*, New York, Knopf.

Eckstein, H. (1960) *Pressure Group Politics*, London, George Allen & Unwin.

Ecologist (1992) 'Whose common future?', special issue of *The Ecologist*, 22(4).

Efficiency Unit (1988) *Improving Management in Government: The Next Steps* (the Ibbs Report), London, HMSO.

Efficiency Unit (1993) *Career Management and Succession Planning Study* (the Oughton Report), London, HMSO.

Elcock, H. (1991) *Change and Decay: Public Administration in the 1990s*, Harlow, Longman.

Elcock, H. (1994) *Local Government*, 2nd edn, London, Routledge.

Elcock, H. (1995) 'Leading people: some issues of local government leadership in Britain and America', *Local Government Studies*, 21(4), 546–67.

Elcock, H. (1997) 'The north of England and a Europe of the regions, or, when is a region not a region?', in Keating and Loughlin (eds), pp. 422–35.

Eldridge, J. (ed.) (1993) *Getting the Message: News, Truth and Power*, London, Routledge.

Elkington, J. and Burke, T. (1989) *The Green Capitalists*, London, Gollancz.

Elshtain, J. B. (1981) *Public Man, Private Woman*, Princeton, NJ, Princeton University Press.

Enthoven, A. (1985) *Reflections on the Management of the National Health Service*, London, Nuffield Provincial Hospitals Trust, Occasional Paper 5.

Evans, G. (1993) 'Class conflict and inequality', in Jowell, R. et al., *International Social Attitudes: The 10th British Social Attitudes Report*, Aldershot, Dartmouth, pp. 123–41.

Evans, M. (1995) *Charter 88: A Successful Challenge to the British Tradition?* Aldershot, Dartmouth.

Evans, P. (1986a) 'Police are all too often a target of those frustrated by society', *The Times* (10 Nov.).

Evans, P. (1986b) 'The low profile policy', *The Times* (11 Nov.).

Ewing, K. D. and Gearty, C. A. (1990) *Freedom under Thatcher: Civil Liberties in Modern Britain*, Oxford, Clarendon Press.

Eysenck, H. J. (1951) 'Primary social attitudes', *British Journal of Sociology*, 2, 198–209.

Farnham, D. (1996) 'New Labour, the new unions and the new labour market', *Parliamentary Affairs*, 49(4), 584–98.

Farrell, D. (1997) *Comparing Electoral Systems,* London, Prentice Hall.

Finer, S. E. (1956) 'The individual responsibility of ministers', *Public Administration*, 34, 377-96.

Finer, S. E. (1968) *Anonymous Empire*, London, Pall Mall.

Fisher, J. (1994) 'Political donations to the Conservative Party', *Parliamentary Affairs*, 47(1), 61–72.

Fisher, J. (1997) 'Donations to political parties', *Parliamentary Affairs*, 50(2), 235–45.

Forbes, I. (1996) 'The privatisation of sex equality policy', *Parliamentary Affairs*, 49(1), 143–60.

Fox, J. (1975) 'The brains behind the throne', in Herman and Alt (eds), pp. 277–92.

Franks, O. (1957) *Report of the Committee on Administrative Tribunals and Inquiries*, Cmnd 218, London, HMSO.

Franks, Lord O. (1972) *Departmental Committee on Section 2 of the Official Secrets Act 1911*, Cmnd 5104,

London, HMSO.

Friedman, M. and R. (1985) *The Tyranny of the Status Quo*, Harmondsworth, Penguin.

Fry, G. K. (1986) 'Inside Whitehall', in Drucker et al. (eds).

Fry, G. K. (1995) *Policy and Management in the British Civil Service*, Hemel Hempstead, Prentice Hall/Harvester Wheatsheaf.

Fryer, P. (1988) *Black People in the British Empire*, London, Pluto.

Fukuyama, F. (1992) *The End of History and the Last Man*, London, Hamish Hamilton.

Fulton, Lord (1968) *The Civil Service, Vol. 1: Report of the Committee*, Cmnd 3638, London, HMSO.

Galbraith, J. K. (1993) *The Culture of Contentment*, London, Penguin.

Gallup (1976) 'Voting behaviour in Britain, 1945–1974', in Rose, R. (ed.) *Studies in British Politics*, 3rd edn, Basingstoke, Macmillan.

Gamble, A. (1981) *An Introduction to Modern Social and Political Thought*, Basingstoke, Macmillan.

Gamble, A. (1988) *The Free Economy and the Strong State*, Basingstoke, Macmillan.

Gamble, A. (1990) *Britain in Decline*, 3rd edn, Basingstoke, Macmillan.

Gamble, A. (1993) 'Shaping a new world order, political capacities and policy challenges', *Government and Opposition*, 25(3), 325–38.

Gamble, A. and Wright, T. (1997) 'New Labour and old left', *Political Quarterly*, 68(2), 125–7.

Gamble, A. and Wright, T. (1998) 'The Conservative predicament', *Political Quarterly*, 69(2), 107–9.

Game, C. (1997) 'How many, where and how? Taking stock of local government reorganisation', *Local Government Policy Making*, 23(4), 3–23.

Garnett, M. and Gilmour, I. (1998) 'The lessons of defeat', *Political Quarterly*, 69(2), 126–32.

Garnsey, E. (1982) 'Women's work and theories of class stratification', in Held, D. and Giddens, A. (eds) *Classes, Power and Conflict*, London, Macmillan.

Gavin, N. T. (1996) 'Class voting and the Labour Party in Britain', *Electoral Studies*, 15(3), 311–26.

George, Stephen (1991) *Politics and Policy in the European Community*, Oxford, Oxford University Press.

George, Stephen (1994) *An Awkward Partner: Britain in the European Community*, 2nd edn, Oxford, Oxford University Press.

George, Susan (1991) *The Debt Boomerang*, London, Pluto.

Gibb, F. (1988) 'Justice by lottery?', *The Times* (25 Oct.).

Gibb, F. (1994) 'Judicious adverts set new benchmark', *The Times* (27 Sept.).

Giddens, A. (1973) *The Class Structure of the Advanced Societies*, London, Hutchinson.

Giddens, A. (1979) *The Class Structure of the Advanced Societies*, 2nd edn, London, Hutchinson.

Giddens, A. (1990) *The Consequences of Modernity*, Cambridge, Polity.

Giddens, A. (1997a) *Sociology*, 3rd edn, Cambridge, Polity.

Giddens, A. (1997b) *Sociology: Introductory Readings*, Cambridge, Polity.

Giddens, A. (1998) *The Third Way: The Renewal of Social Democracy*, Cambridge, Polity.

Giddings, P. and Drewry, G. (1996) *Westminster and Europe: The Impact of the European Union on the Westminster Parliament*, Basingstoke, Macmillan.

Gladden, E. N. (1967) *Civil Services of the United Kingdom*, London, Frank Cass.

Glasgow University Media Group (1976) *Bad News*, (1980) *More Bad News*, (1982) *Really Bad News*, London, Routledge and Kegan Paul.

Gold, M. (ed.) (1993) *The Social Dimension: Employment Policy in the European Community*, Basingstoke, Macmillan.

Goldsmith, E. (1972) *A Blueprint for Survival*, Harmondsworth, Penguin.

Goldthorpe, J. (1982) 'On the service

class: its formation and future', in Giddens, A. and MacKenzie, G. (eds), *Social Class and the Division of Labour: Essays in Honour of Ilya Neustadt*, Cambridge, Cambridge University Press.

Goldthorpe, J. (1987) *Social Mobility and Class Structure in Modern Britain*, 2nd edn, Oxford, Clarendon Press.

Goodin, R. (1986) 'The principle of voluntary agreement', *Public Administration*, 64(4), 435–44.

Goodin, R. (1992) *Green Political Theory*, Cambridge, Polity.

Goodman, A., Johnson, P. and Webb, S. (1997) *Income Inequality in the UK*, Oxford, Oxford University Press.

Gordon, P. (1984) 'Community policing: towards the local police state', *Critical Social Policy*, 4(1), 39–58.

Gordon, P. and Klug, F. (1986) *New Right, New Racism*, London, Searchlight Publications.

Gough, I. (1979) *The Political Economy of the Welfare State*, London, Macmillan.

Gould, B. (1978) 'The MP and constituency cases', in Mackintosh, J. P. (ed.) *People and Parliament*, Farnborough, Saxon House, pp. 84–94.

Grahl, J. and Teague, P. (1990) *1992: The Big Market*, London, Lawrence and Wishart.

Gramsci, A. (1971) *Selections from Prison Notebooks*, London, Lawrence and Wishart.

Grant, W. (1984) 'The role and power of pressure groups', in Borthwick, R. L. and Spence, J. E. (1984) *British Politics in Perspective*, Leicester, Leicester University Press, pp. 123–44.

Grant, W. (1987) *Business and Politics*, London, Macmillan.

Grant, W. (1993) *The Politics of Economic Policy*, Hemel Hempstead, Harvester Wheatsheaf.

Grant, W. (1995) *Pressure Groups, Politics and Democracy*, 2nd edn, Hemel Hempstead, Harvester Wheatsheaf.

Grant, W. and MacNamara, A. (1995) 'When policy communities intersect:

the case of agriculture and banking', *Political Studies*, 43(3), 509–15.

Grant, W. and Marsh, D. (1977) *The CBI*, London, Hodder and Stoughton.

Gray, J. (1995) *Enlightenment's Wake: Politics and Culture at the Close of the Modern Age*, London, Routledge.

Gray, J. (1998) *False Dawn: The Utopia of the Global Free Market*, London, Granta (revised edn 1999 entitled *False Dawn: the Delusions of Global Capitalism*).

Greenwood, J. and Wilson, D. (1994) 'Toward the contract state: CCT in local government', *Parliamentary Affairs*, 47(3), 405–19.

Greer, G. (1970) *The Female Eunuch*, London, MacGibbon & Kee.

Grice, A. (1997) 'Don't mention the party', *Sunday Times* (23 March).

Griffith, J. A. G. (1981) *The Politics of the Judiciary*, London, Fontana.

Griffith, J. A. G. (1991) *The Politics of the Judiciary*, 4th edn, London, Fontana (5th edn 1994).

Groom, I. (1997) 'If at first you don't succeed', *Financial Times* (11 Sept.).

Gunn, S. (1988) 'Reining in the peers', *Marxism Today*, 32 (June), 3.

Guttsman, W. S. (1963) *The British Political Elite*, London, MacGibbon & Kee.

Hailsham, Lord (1978) *The Dilemma of Democracy*, London, Collins.

Hain, P. et al. (eds) (1980) *Policing the Police*, London, Calder.

Halford, A. (1993) *No Way Up the Greasy Pole*, London, Constable.

Hall, W. and Weir, S. (1996) *The Untouchables: Power and Accountability in the Quango State*, Colchester, University of Essex, Democratic Audit and London, Charter 88.

Hambleton, R. (1996) 'Reinventing local government: lessons from the USA', *Local Government Studies*, 22(1), 93–112.

Hamilton, S. and Rufford, N. (1996) 'Party funding touches a raw labour nerve', *Sunday Times* (6 Oct.).

Hampsher-Monk, I. (1987) *The Political Philosophy of Edmund Burke*,

Harlow, Longman.

Hampton, W. (1970) *Democracy and Community*, London, Oxford University Press.

Hansard Society (1993) *Making the Law: Report of the Commission on the Legislative Process*, London, Hansard Society.

Harden, I. and Lewis, N. (1986) *The Noble Lie*, London, Hutchinson.

Harris, P. (1997) *An Introduction to the Law*, 5th edn, London, Weidenfeld.

Harrison, B. (1996) *The Transformation of British Politics 1860–1995*, Oxford, Oxford University Press.

Harrison, D. (1993) 'Who pays for the party?' *Observer* (20 June).

Harrison, M. (1985) *TV News: Whose Bias?*, Hermitage, Policy Journals.

Harrison, M. (1987) 'Broadcasting', in Butler and Kavanagh (eds), pp. 139–62.

Harrison, M. (1992) 'Politics on the air', in Butler and Kavanagh (eds), pp. 155–79.

Harrop, M. and Scammell, M. (1992) 'The tabloid war', in Butler and Kavanagh (eds), pp. 180–210.

Harvey, D. (1989) *The Condition of Postmodernity*, Oxford, Blackwell.

Harvie, C. (1991) 'English regionalism: the dog that never barked', in Crick (ed), pp. 105–18.

Hattersley, R. (1996) *Who Goes Home? Scenes from Political Life*, London, Little, Brown.

Hawley, J. S. (ed.) (1984) *Fundamentalism and Gender*, Oxford, Oxford University Press.

Heath, A. and Park, A. (1998) 'Thatcher's children?' in Jowell et al., pp. 1–22.

Heath, A., Jowell, R. and Curtice, J. (1987) 'Trendless fluctuation: a reply to Crewe', *Political Studies*, 35(2), 256–77.

Heath, A., Jowell, R. and Curtice, J. (with Taylor, B.) (eds) (1994) *Labour's Last Chance? The 1992 Election and Beyond*, Aldershot, Dartmouth.

Heath, E. (1972) *My Style of Government*, London, Evening Standard Publications.

Heclo, H. and Wildavsky, A. (1974) *The Private Government of Public Money*, London, Macmillan.

Heffer, S. (1988) 'Labour brings the House down on its own head', *Daily Telegraph* (8 April).

Heffernan, R. and Marcusee, M. (1992) *Defeat from the Jaws of Victory: Inside Kinnock's Labour Party*, Oxford, Blackwell.

Held, D. (1987) *Models of Democracy*, Cambridge, Polity.

Held, D. (1989) 'The decline of the nation state' in Hall, S. and Jacques, M. (eds), *New Times*, London, Lawrence and Wishart, pp. 191–204.

Held, D. and McGrew, A. (1993) 'Globalisation and the liberal democratic state', *Government and Opposition*, 28(2), 261–88.

Held, D., McGrew, A., Goldblatt, D. and Perraton, J. (1999) *Global Transformations*, Cambridge, Polity.

Hencke, D. (1992) 'More Whitehall staff face market test for jobs', *Guardian* (21 July).

Hennessy, P. (1985) 'The megaphone theory of "Yes Minister"', *Listener* (19 and 26 Dec.).

Hennessy, P. (1986) *Cabinet*, Oxford, Basil Blackwell.

Hennessy, P. (1990) *Whitehall*, London, Fontana.

Hennessy, P. (1992) *Never Again: Britain 1945–1951*, London, Jonathan Cape.

Hennessy, P. (1994) 'The throne behind the power', *The Economist* (24 Dec.).

Hennessy, P. (1995) *The Hidden Wiring: Unearthing the British Constitution*, London, Cassell.

Hennessy, P. (1998) 'The Blair style of government', *Government and Opposition*, 33(1) 3–20.

Henney, A. (1984) *Inside Local Government: a Case for Radical Reform*, London, Sinclair Browne.

Herman, V. and Alt, J. E. (eds) (1975) *Cabinet Studies*, Basingstoke, Macmillan.

Heseltine, M. (1986) 'Deliberate attempt made to avoid discussion of issues', *The Times* (10 Jan.).

Hewart, Lord (1929) *The New Despotism*, London, Ernest Benn.

Heywood, A. (1994) *Political Ideas and Concepts*, Basingstoke, Macmillan.

Hill, D. (1974) *Democratic Theory and Local Government*, London, George Allen & Unwin.

Hills, J. (1981) 'Britain', in Lovenduski, J. and Hills, J. (eds), *The Politics of the Second Electorate: Women and Public Participation*, London, Routledge and Kegan Paul, pp. 8–32.

Himmelweit, H., Humphreys, P. and Jaeger, M. (1985) *How Voters Decide*, Milton Keynes, Open University Press.

Hirst, P. (1995) 'Quangos and democratic government', *Parliamentary Affairs*, 48(2) 341–59.

Hirst, P. and Thompson, G. (1966) *Globalization in Question*, Cambridge, Polity.

Hobbes, T. (1985) *Leviathan* (ed. C. B. Macpherson), Harmondsworth, Penguin (first published 1651).

Hobsbawm, E. (1990) *Nations and Nationalism since 1780*, Cambridge, Cambridge University Press.

Hobsbawm, E. (1992) 'Today's crisis of ideologies', *New Left Review*, no. 192 (March/April), 55–62.

Hobsbawm, E. (1995) *Age of Extremes*, London, Abacus.

Hoggart, R. (1958) *The Uses of Literacy*, Harmondsworth, Penguin.

Hogwood, B. W. (1997) 'The machinery of government, 1979–97', *Political Studies*, 45(4), 704–15.

Holden, A. (1997) 'Royal blues', *Red Pepper* (Oct.).

Holland, P. (1978) *The Quango Explosion*, London, Conservative Political Centre.

Holland, P. (1981a) *The Governance of Quangos,* London, Adam Smith Institute.

Holland, P. (1981b) *Quango, Quango, Quango*, London, Adam Smith Institute.

Holliday, I. (1993) 'Organised interests after Thatcher', in Dunleavy et al. (eds), pp. 307–20.

Hollingsworth, M. (1986) *The Press and Discontent: A Question of Censorship*, London, Pluto.

Hollingsworth, M. (1997) 'Get out of

this one, Mr Spin', *Observer Review* (16 Feb.).

Holme, R. and Elliot, M. (eds) (1988) *1688–1988: Time for a New Constitution*, London, Macmillan.

Home, Lord (1976) *The Way the Wind Blows*, London, Collins.

Home Office (1993*) Police Reform: A Police Service for the Twenty-first Century,* Cm 2281, London, HMSO.

Hood, C. (1979) 'Keeping the centre small: explanations of agency type', *Political Studies*, 26(1), 30–46.

Hood Phillips, O. (1987) *Constitutional and Administrative Law*, 7th edn, London, Sweet and Maxwell.

Hoogvelt, A. (1997) *Globalisation and the Postcolonial World*, Basingstoke, Macmillan.

Horsman, M. and Marshall, A. (1994) *After the Nation State*, London, HarperCollins.

Hoskyns, Sir J. (1984) 'Conservatism is not enough', *Political Quarterly*, 55(1), 3–16.

House of Commons Expenditure Committee (1977) *The Civil Service: Eleventh Report and Volumes of Evidence, 1976/7, Vols. I–III*, HC 535, London, HMSO.

House of Commons Foreign Affairs Committee (1996) *The Future Role of the Commonwealth*, Cm 3303, London, Stationery Office.

House of Commons Home Affairs Committee (1988) *Parliamentary Accountability of the Police Complaints Authority, Fourth Report*, Session 1987/8, London HMSO.

House of Commons Home Affairs Committee (1993) *Accountability of the Security Service*, HC 270, Session 1992/3, London, HMSO.

House of Commons Public Accounts Committee (1994) *The Proper Conduct of Public Business,* HC 154, Session 1993/4, London, HMSO.

House of Commons Public Service Committee (1996) *Ministerial Accountability and Responsibility*, HC 313-I, Session 1995/6, London, Stationery Office.

House of Commons Treasury and Civil

Service Committee (1994) *The Role of the Civil Service*, HC 27-I, Session 1993/4, London, HMSO.

Howe, G. (1994) *Conflict of Loyalty*, Basingstoke, Macmillan.

Hume, D. (1882) 'That politics may be reduced to a science', reprinted in Dahl, R. and Neubauer, D. E. (1968) *Readings in Modern Political Analysis*, Englewood Cliffs, NJ, Prentice Hall.

Hunt, D. (1995) 'Accountability in the NHS', *Parliamentary Affairs*, 48(2), 297–305.

Hunter, F. (1953) *Community Power Structure*, Chapel Hill, NC, University of North Carolina Press.

Hutton, W. (1986) *The Revolution that Never Was*, London, Longman.

Hutton, W. (1996) *The State We're In*, London, Vintage.

Hutton, W. (1998) 'What is Power?', *Observer* (1 Nov.).

Illich, I. (1975) *Medical Nemesis*, London, Calder and Boyars.

Ingham, B. (1991) *Kill the Messenger*, London, Fontana.

Jackson, R. M. (1960) *The Machinery of Justice in England*, Cambridge, Cambridge University Press.

Jacobs, M. (1996) *The Politics of the Real World*, London, Earthscan.

Jaggar, A. (1983) *Feminist Politics and Human Nature*, Brighton, Harvester.

James, B. (1987) 'The coup that never was . . .', *The Times* (7 Aug.).

James, S. (1994) 'The cabinet system since 1945: fragmentation and integration', *Parliamentary Affairs*, 47(4), 613–29.

Jenkins, S. (1995) *Accountable to None: The Tory Nationalisation of Britain*, Harmondsworth, Penguin.

Jennings, I. (1959) *Cabinet Government*, 3rd edn, Cambridge, Cambridge University Press.

Jennings, I. (1966) *The British Constitution*, 5th edn, Cambridge, Cambridge University Press.

John, P. (1994a) 'Central–local government relations in the 1980s and 1990s: towards a policy learning approach', *Local Government Studies*, 20(3), 412–36.

John, P. (1994b) *The Europeanisation of British Local Government: New Management Strategies*, York, Joseph Rowntree Foundation.

Johnson, N. (1998) 'The judicial dimension of British politics', *West European Politics*, 21(1), 148–66.

Johnson, R. W. (1985) *The Politics of Recession*, London, Macmillan.

Johnston, R. J. and Pattie, C. J. (1996) 'The strength of party identification among the British electorate', *Electoral Studies*, 15(3), 295–309.

Johnston, R. J. and Pattie, C. J. (1997) 'Towards an understanding of turnout in British general elections', *Parliamentary Affairs*, 50(2), 280–91.

Johnston, R. J., Pattie, C. J. and Allsopp, J. G. (1988) *A Nation Dividing? The Electoral Map of Great Britain 1979–87*, Harlow, Longman.

Johnston, R. J., Pattie, C. J., Rossiter, D., Dorling, D., Tunstall, H. and McAllister, I. (1998) 'Anatomy of a Labour landslide: the constituency system and the 1997 general election', *Parliamentary Affairs*, 50(2), 131–48.

Jones, B. (1997) 'Wales: a developing political economy', in Keating and Loughlin (eds).

Jones, G. W. (1983) 'Prime ministers' departments really do create problems: a rejoinder to Patrick Weller', *Public Administration*, 61(1), 79–84.

Jones, G. and Stewart, J. (1995) 'Key questions, open debate', *Local Government Chronicle* (17 March).

Jones, R. A. (1996) *The Politics and Economics of the European Union*, Cheltenham, Edward Elgar.

Jones, T. and Newburn, T. (1995) 'Local government and policing: arresting the decline of local influence', *Local Government Studies*, 21(3), 448–60.

Jordan, G. (1991) *The Commercial Lobbyists: Politics for Profit in Britain*, Aberdeen, Aberdeen University Press.

Jowell, R., Curtice, J., Park, A., Brook, L., Thompson, K. and Bryan, C. (1998) *British Social Attitudes: The 14th Report. The End of Conservative Values?* Aldershot, Ashgate.

Judge, D. (ed.) (1983) *The Politics of*

Parliamentary Reform, London, Heinemann.

Kairys, P. (ed.) (1982) *The Politics of Law: A Progressive Critique*, London, Pantheon.

Kavanagh, D. (1980) 'Political culture in Britain: the decline of the civic culture', in Almond and Verba (eds).

Kavanagh, D. (1995) *Election Campaigning: The New Marketing of Politics*, Oxford, Blackwell.

Kavanagh, D. (1996) 'British party conferences and the political rhetoric of the 1990s', *Government and Opposition*, 31(1), 27–44.

Kavanagh, D. (1997a) 'The Labour campaign', *Parliamentary Affairs*, 50(4), 533–41.

Kavanagh, D. (1997b) *The Reordering of British Politics: Politics After Thatcher*, Oxford, Oxford University Press.

Kavanagh, D. (1998) 'Power in the parties: R. T. McKenzie and after', *West European Politics*, 21(1), 28–43.

Kay, J. (1993) *The Foundations of Corporate Success*, Oxford, Oxford University Press.

Kearney, H. (1990) *The British Isles: A History of Four Nations*, Cambridge, Cambridge University Press.

Keating, M. and Loughlin, J. (eds) (1997) *The Political Economy of Regionalism*, London, Frank Cass.

Keegan, W. (1984) *Mrs Thatcher's Economic Experiment*, Harmondsworth, Penguin.

Keen, P. and Travers, T. (1994) *Implementing the Council Tax*, York, Joseph Rowntree Foundation.

Kellas, J. (1975) *The Scottish Political System*, Cambridge, Cambridge University Press.

Kellner, P. (1997) 'Why were the Tories trounced?' *Parliamentary Affairs*, 50(4), 616–30.

Kellner, P. (1998) 'What Blair must do next', *Evening Standard* (27 July).

Kellner, P. and Crowther-Hunt, Lord (1980) *The Civil Servants: An Enquiry into Britain's Ruling Class*, London, Macdonald.

Kennedy, H. (1992) *Eve was Framed*, London, Chatto and Windus.

Kenny, M. and Smith, M. J. (1997) '(Mis)understanding Blair', *Political Quarterly*, 68(3) 220–30.

King, A. (ed.) (1985) *The British Prime Minister*, 2nd edn, Basingstoke, Macmillan.

King, A. et al. (1993) *Britain at the Polls 1992*, Chatham, NJ, Chatham House.

King, D. (1993) 'Government beyond Whitehall', in Dunleavy et al. (eds), pp. 194–218.

Kingdom, J. (1991) *Local Government and Politics in Britain*, Hemel Hempstead, Philip Allan.

Kingdom, J. (1992) *No Such Thing as Society*, Buckingham, Open University Press.

Kingdom, J. (1996) 'Citizen or state consumer: a fistful of charters', in Chandler, J. A. (ed.), *The Citizen's Charter*, Aldershot, Dartmouth, pp. 7–23.

Kirchheimer, O. (1966) 'The transformation of West European Party Systems', in LaPalombara, J. and Weiner, M. (eds), *Political Parties and Political Development*, Princeton, NJ, Princeton University Press, pp. 177–200.

Klare, M. T. (1992) 'US military policy in the post-cold-war era', in Miliband and Panitch (eds), pp. 131–42.

Klein, R. (1989) *The Politics of the NHS*, 2nd edn, Harlow, Longman.

Klug, F. (1997) 'Can human rights fill Britain's morality gap?' *Political Quarterly*, 68(2), 143–52.

Klug, F., Starmer, K. and Weir, S. (1996) 'Civil liberties and the parliamentary watchdog: the passage of the Criminal Justice and Public Order Act 1994', *Parliamentary Affairs*, 49(4), 536–49.

Knightly, P. (1986) *The Second Oldest Profession: The Spy as Bureaucrat, Fantasist and Whore*, London, André Deutsch.

Koffman, L. (1985) 'Safeguarding the rights of the citizen', in Baxter and Koffman (eds), pp. 11–37.

Lacey R. (1997) 'Ministry of Agriculture: Ministry of Truth', *Political Quarterly*, 68(3), 245–54.

Lambert, A. (1988) 'Who should police

the police?', *Independent* (10 Sept.).

Langdon, J. (1998) 'The making of Mo Mowlam', *Daily Mail* (25 May).

Laski, H. J. (1938) *Parliamentary Government in England*, London, George Allen & Unwin.

Lasswell, H. D. (1936) *Politics: Who Gets What, When, How?*, New York, McGraw Hill (reprinted 1958).

Lasswell, H. D. and Kaplan, A. (1950) *Power and Society*, New Haven, CT, Yale University Press.

Lawrence, D. H. (1950) 'Nottingham and the mining country', in *Selected Essays*, Harmondsworth, Penguin.

Lawson, N. (1993) *The View from Number 11: Memoirs of a Tory Radical*, London, Corgi.

Lea, J. et al. (1986) 'The fear and loathing at Broadwater Farm', *Guardian* (4 June).

Leach, R. (1998) 'Local government reorganisation RIP?' *Political Quarterly*, 69(1), 31–40.

Leach, S. and Stewart, J. (1992) *The Politics of Hung Authorities*, Basingstoke, Macmillan.

Lee, S. (1988) *Judging Judges*, London, Faber and Faber.

Leftwich, A. (1984) *What is Politics? The Activity and its Study*, Oxford, Blackwell.

Lehmbruch, G. and Schmitter, P. (eds) (1982) *Patterns of Corporatist Policy-Making*, London, Sage.

Leigh, D. and Lashmar, P. (1987) 'MI5 wanted ITN man as media spy', *Observer* (4 Oct.).

Lester, Lord (1994) 'European rights and the British constitution', in Jowell, J. and Oliver, D. (eds) *The Changing Constitution*, 3rd edn, Oxford, Oxford University Press.

Levy, R. (1992) 'The Scottish Constitutional Convention, nationalism and the Union', *Government and Opposition*, 27(2), 222–34.

Leys, C. (1998) 'Controlling the waves', *Red Pepper* (April).

Lijphart, A. (1994) *Electoral Systems and Party Systems: A Study of Twenty-Seven Democracies 1945–1990*, Oxford, Oxford University Press.

Lijphart, A. (1996) 'The Framework proposal for Northern Ireland and the theory of power sharing', *Government and Opposition*, 31(3), 267–74.

Lindblom, C. E. (1959) 'The science of muddling through', *Public Administration Review*, 19, 79–88.

Lively, J. (1978) 'Pluralism and consensus', in Birnbaum, P., Lively, J. and Parry, G. (eds) *Democracy, Consensus and Social Contract*, London, Sage.

Lockwood, D. (1966) 'Sources of variation in working class images of society', *Sociological Review*, 14, 249–67.

Lodge, J. (ed.) (1993) *The European Community and the Challenge of the Future*, London, Pinter.

Lord Chancellor's Department (1989) *Legal Services: A Framework for the Future*, Cm 740, London, HMSO.

Louis, W. R. and Bull, H. (eds) (1986) *The Special Relationship: Anglo-American Relations Since 1945*, Oxford, Oxford University Press.

Loveday, B. (1994) 'The competing role of central and local agencies in crime prevention strategies', *Local Government Studies*, 20(3), 361–73.

Loveday, B. (1996) 'Business as usual? The new police authorities and the Police and Magistrates' Courts Act', *Local Government Studies*, 22(2), 22–39.

Lovelock, J. E. (1979) *Gaia: A New Look At Life on Earth*, Oxford, Oxford University Press.

Lovenduski, J. (1996) 'Sex, gender and British politics', *Parliamentary Affairs*, 49(1) 1–16.

Lovenduski, J. (1997) 'Gender politics: a breakthrough for women', *Parliamentary Affairs*, 50(4), 708–19.

Lovenduski, J. and Norris, P. (1994) 'Labour and the unions: after the Brighton conference', *Government and Opposition*, 29(3), 201–17.

Lovenduski, J. and Norris, P. (eds) (1996) *Women in Politics*, Oxford, Oxford University Press.

Lowe, P. and Goyder, J. (eds) (1983)

Environmental Groups in Politics, London, Allen and Unwin.

Lowndes, V. (1997) 'Change in public service management: new institutions and new managerial regimes', *Local Government Studies*, 23(2), 42–66.

McAllister, I. (1997) 'Regional voting', *Parliamentary Affairs*, 50(4), 641–57.

McAllister, I. (1998) 'The Welsh devolution referendum', *Parliamentary Affairs*, 51(2), 149–65.

McAlpine, A. (1997) *Once a Jolly Bagman*, London, Weidenfeld and Nicolson.

McGarry, J. and O'Leary, B. (1997) *Explaining Northern Ireland: Broken Images*, Oxford, Blackwell.

McIntosh, R. (chairman) (1976) *A Study of the UK Nationalised Industries*, London, HMSO.

MacIver, D. (ed.) (1996) *The Liberal Democrats*, Hemel Hempstead, Prentice Hall/Harvester.

McKenzie, R. (1967) *British Political Parties*, 2nd rev. edn, London, Heinemann.

McKenzie, R. and Silver, A. (1968) *Angels in Marble*, London, Heinemann.

Mackenzie, W. J. M. (1969) *Politics and Social Science*, Harmondsworth, Penguin.

McKie, D. (1994) 'Uncivil servants sign off', *Guardian* (23 April).

McKinstry, L. (1998) 'The man we should really thank for peace in Northern Ireland', *Daily Mail* (25 May).

Maddock, S. (1993) 'Barriers to women are barriers to local government', *Local Government Studies*, 19(3), 341–50.

Madgewick, P. and Woodhouse, D. (1995) *The Law and Politics of the Constitution*, Brighton, Harvester Wheatsheaf.

Magdoff, H. (1992) 'Globalisation: to what end?' in Miliband and Panitch (eds), pp. 44–75.

Magnus, P. (1963) *Gladstone*, London, Murray.

Mahl (pseud.) (1995) 'Women on the edge of time', *New Internationalist*,

no. 270 (Aug.), 7–10.

Mair, L. (1970) *Primitive Government*, Harmondsworth, Penguin.

Mallalieu, J. P. W. (1941) *Passed to You Please*, London, Victor Gollancz.

Mandel, E. (1983) 'Economics', in McLellan, D., (ed.) *Marx: The First Hundred Years*, London, Fontana, pp. 189–238.

Mandelson, P. and Liddle, R. (1996) *The Blair Phenomenon: Can New Labour Deliver?* London, Faber.

Mansfield, M. (1997) 'Justice for all', *Red Pepper* (April).

Mark, R. (1978) *In the Office of Constable*, London, Collins.

Marquand, D. (1988) *The Unprincipled Society*, London, Fontana.

Marr, A. (1992) *The Battle for Scotland*, Harmondsworth, Penguin.

Marr, A. (1995) *Ruling Britannia*, Harmondsworth, Penguin.

Marsh, A. (1978) *Protest and Political Consciousness*, London, Sage.

Marsh, D. (1992) *The New Politics of British Trade Unionism*, Basingstoke, Macmillan.

Marsh, D. (1993) 'The media and politics', in Dunleavy et. al. (eds), pp. 332–49.

Marsh, D. and Locksley, G. (1987) 'The influence of business', in *British Politics: A Reader*, Manchester, Manchester University Press, pp. 215–26.

Marsh, D. and Rhodes, R. A. W. (1992) (eds) *Implementing Thatcherite Policies: Audit of an Era*, Buckingham, Open University Press.

Marshall, G. (1997) 'The referendum: what, when, how?', *Parliamentary Affairs*, 50(2), 307–13.

Martin, S. and Pearce, G. (1994) 'The demise of the lone ranger: prospects for unitary authorities in the "New Europe"', *Local Government Policy Making*, 20(5), 14–20.

Marwick, A. (1982) *British Society Since 1945*, Harmondsworth, Penguin.

Maud, Sir J. (chairman) (1967) *Management of Local Government*, London, HMSO.

Mazey, S. and Richardson, J. (1993)

Lobbying in the European Community, Oxford, Oxford University Press.

Meadows, D. H., Meadows, D. L., Randers, J. and Behrens, W. III (1972) *The Limits to Growth*, London, Earth Island.

Mercer, P. (1994) *The Directory of British Political Organisations*, Harlow, Longman.

Michels, R. (1962) *Political Parties*, New York, Collier (first published 1920).

Middlemass, K. (1979) *Politics in Industrial Society*, London, André Deutsch.

Miles, R. (1996) 'Small investors who made big killings', *Guardian* (23 Nov.).

Miliband, R. (1961) *Parliamentary Socialism*, London, Merlin.

Miliband, R. (1984) *Capitalist Democracy in Britain*, Oxford, Oxford University Press.

Miliband, R. and Panitch, L. (eds) (1992) *New World Order: Socialist Register 1992*, London, Merlin.

Miller, J. B. D. (1962) *The Nature of Politics*, Harmondsworth, Penguin.

Miller, W. (1991) *Media and Voters*, Oxford, Clarendon Press.

Mills, C. W. (1959) *The Power Elite*, New York, Oxford University Press.

Milne, A. (1988) *DG: Memoirs of a British Broadcaster*, London, Hodder and Stoughton.

Minkin, L. (1980) *The Labour Party Conference*, Manchester, Manchester University Press.

Mirrlees-Black, C., Mayhew P. and Percy, A. (1996) *The 1996 British Crime Survey*, London, Home Office Statistical Bulletin 19/96.

Mitchell, A. (1994) 'Backbench influence: a personal view', *Parliamentary Affairs*, 47(4), 687–704.

Mitchell, D. (1982) 'Intervention, control and accountability: the National Enterprise Board', *Public Administration Bulletin*, 38, 40–65.

Mitchell, J., Denver, D., Pattie, C. and Bochek, H. (1998) 'The 1997 devolution referendum in Scotland', *Parliamentary Affairs*, 51(2), 166–81.

Modelski, G. (1972) *Principles of World Politics*, New York, Free Press.

Monks, J. (1993) 'A change of mood is in the air', *New Statesman and Society Guide to the Trade Unions and Labour Movement* (Sept.).

Moore, J. (1985) Treasury press release, 17 July.

Morgan, J. (1987) *Conflict and Order: the Police and Labour Disputes in England and Wales 1900–1939*, Oxford, Clarendon Press.

Morgan, K. and Roberts, E. (1993) *The Democratic Deficit: A Guide to Quangoland*, Papers in Planning Research, University of Wales.

Morley, J. (1903) *Life of William Ewart Gladstone, Vol. I*, London, Macmillan.

Morrison, H. (1933) *Socialism and Transport*, London, Constable.

Mountfield, R. (1997) 'The new senior civil service: managing the paradox', *Public Administration*, 75(2), 307–12.

Mugham, A. (1993) 'Party leaders and presidentialism in the 1992 election: a post war perspective', in Denver et al. (eds), pp. 193–204.

Mullard, M. (1993) *The Politics of Public Expenditure*, London, Routledge.

Mullard, M. (1997) 'The politics of public expenditure control: a problem of politics or language games', *Political Quarterly*, 68(3), 266–75.

Muller, W. D. (1977) *The Kept Men*, Hassocks, Harvester.

National Audit Office (1996) *The Work of the Directors General of Telecommunications, Gas Supply, Water Services and Electricity Supply*, HC 645, Session 1995/6, London, HMSO.

Navarro, V. (1974) *Medicine under Capitalism*, London, Croom Helm.

Newburn, T. (1995) *Crime and Criminal Justice Policy*, Harlow, Longman.

Newton, K. (1976) *Second City Politics*, Oxford, Clarendon Press.

Newton, K. (1986) 'Mass media', in Drucker et al. (eds), pp. 313–28.

Newton, K. (1993) 'Economic voting in the 1992 general election', in Denver et al. (eds), pp. 158–76.

Newton, K. (1998) 'Politics and the news media: mobilisation or political malaise?' in Jowell et al., pp. 151–68.

Nicholson, E. (1996) *Secret Society*, London, Indigo.

Nicoll, W. and Salmon, C. (1990) *Understanding the New European Community*, Hemel Hempstead, Harvester Wheatsheaf.

Nicolson, N. (1958) *People and Parliament*, London, Weidenfeld and Nicolson.

Niskanen, W. A. (1973) *Bureaucracy: Servant or Master?*, London, Institute of Economic Affairs.

Norris, P. (1993) 'The gender-generation gap', in Denver et al., pp. 129–42.

Norris, P. (1996a) *Electoral Change since 1945*, Oxford, Blackwell.

Norris, P. (1996b) 'The Nolan Committee: financial interests and constituency service', *Government and Opposition*, 31(4), 441–8.

Norris P. (1996c) 'Women politicians: transforming Westminster', *Parliamentary Affairs*, 49(1), 89–102.

Norris, P. and Lovenduski, J. (1994) *Political Recruitment: Gender, Race and Class in the British Parliament*, Cambridge, Cambridge University Press.

Norton, P. (1978) *Conservative Dissidents: Dissent Within the Conservative Party 1970–74*, London, Maurice Temple Smith.

Norton, P. (1993a) 'The Conservative Party from Thatcher to Major', in King et al., pp. 29–69.

Norton, P. (1993b) *Does Parliament Matter?* Hemel Hempstead, Harvester Wheatsheaf.

Norton, P. (1994) 'The growth of the constituency role of the MP', *Parliamentary Affairs*, 47(4), 705–20.

Norton, P. (ed.) (1996) *The Conservative Party*, Hemel Hempstead, Prentice Hall/Harvester.

Norton, P. (1997) 'The United Kingdom: restoring confidence', *Parliamentary Affairs*, 50(3), 357–72.

Norton, P. and Aughey, A. (1981) *Conservatives and Conservatism*, London, Temple Smith.

Norton-Taylor, R., Lloyd, M. and Cook, S. (1996) *Knee Deep in Dishonour: The Scott Report and its Aftermath*, London, Gollancz.

Nugent, N. (1994) *The Government and Politics of the European Community*, 3rd edn, Basingstoke, Macmillan.

Oakeshott, M. (1962) *Rationalism in Politics and Other Essays*, London, Methuen.

O'Connor, J. (1973) *The Fiscal Crisis of the State*, New York, St Martin's Press.

O'Leary, B. (1989) 'The limits to coercive consociationalism in Northern Ireland', *Political Studies*, 37, 562–88.

Oliver, I. (1987) *Police, Government and Accountability*, London, Macmillan.

Olson, M. (1982) *The Rise and Decline of Nations*, New Haven, CT, Yale University Press.

Olson, M. (1968) *The Logic of Collective Action*, New York, Schocken.

Osborne, D. and Gaebler, T. (1992) *Reinventing Government*, Reading, MA, Addison-Wesley.

Ostrogorski, M. (1902) *Democracy and the Organisation of Political Parties*, London, Macmillan.

Oxfam (1998) *Small Arms, Wrong Hands*, Oxford, Oxfam.

Painter, C. (1994) 'Public service reform: reinventing or abandoning government', *Political Quarterly*, 95(2), 242–62.

Paley, W. (1842) *Works*, London, Bohn (first published 1785).

Panitch, L. and Miliband, R. (1992) 'The new world order and the socialist agenda', in Miliband and Panitch (eds), pp. 1–25.

Parkin, S. (1988) 'Green strategy', in F. Dodds (ed.), *Into the 21st Century: An Agenda for Political Realignment*, Basingstoke, Green Print.

Pateman, C. (1983) 'Feminism and democracy', in Duncan, G. (ed.), *Democratic Theory and Practice*, Cambridge, Cambridge University Press.

Pattie, C. J. and Johnston, R. J. (1996) 'Paying their way: local associations, the constituency quota scheme and Conservative Party finance', *Political*

Studies, 44, 921–35.

Pattie, C. J., Johnston, R. and Fieldhouse, E. (1993) '*Plus ça change*? The changing electoral geography of Britain, 1979–1992', in Denver et al. (eds), pp. 85–99.

Pattie, C. J., Fieldhouse, E. and Johnston, R. J. (1994) 'The price of conscience', *British Journal of Political Science*, 24, 359–80.

Pattie, C. J., Fieldhouse, E. A. and Johnston, R. J. (1995) 'Individual vote choices and constituency economic conditions at the 1992 British general election', *Electoral Studies*, 14(4), 399–415.

Paxman, J. (1991) *Friends in High Places*, London, Penguin.

Peele, G. (1986) 'The state and civil liberties', in Drucker et al. (eds), pp. 144–74.

Peele, G. (1991) *British Party Politics: Competing for Power in the 1990s*, Hemel Hempstead, Philip Allan.

Peele, G. (1998) 'Towards "New Conservatives?" Organisational reform and the Conservative Party', *Political Quarterly*, 69(2), 141–7.

Pelling, H. (1968) *A Short History of the Labour Party*, 3rd edn, London, Macmillan.

Pelling, H. and Reid, A. J. (1997) *A Short History of the Labour Party*, 11th edn, Basingstoke, Macmillan.

Perrigo, S. (1985) 'The women's movement: patterns of oppression and resistance', in Coates et al. (eds), pp. 124–45.

Perrigo, S. (1996) 'Women and change in the Labour Party 1979–1995', *Parliamentary Affairs*, 49(1), 116–29.

Pienaar, J. (1987) 'Contemptible smear by Livingstone', *Independent* (10 July).

Pienaar, J. (1988) 'A cabinet exile reflects on the cravings of power', *Independent* (15 Sept.).

Pilger, J. (1998) *Hidden Agendas*, London, Vintage.

Pimlott, B. (1992) *Harold Wilson*, London, HarperCollins.

Pimlott, B. (1996) *The Queen: A Biography of Elizabeth II*, London, HarperCollins.

Pinto-Duschinsky, M. (1972) 'Central Office and power in the Conservative Party', *Political Studies*, 20(1), 1–16.

Pinto-Duschinsky, M. (1997) 'Tory troops are in worse state than feared', *The Times* (6 June).

Pliatzky, L. (1980) *Report on Non-Departmental Public Bodies*, Cmnd 7797, London, HMSO.

Plowden, W. (1994) *Ministers and Mandarins*, London, IPPR.

Ponting, C. (1986) *Whitehall: Tragedy and Farce*, London, Hamish Hamilton.

Porritt, J. and Winner, D. (1988) *The Coming of the Greens*, London, Fontana.

Poulantzas, N. (1973) *Political Power and Social Classes*, London, New Left Books.

Preston, P. (1997) 'Party free or parti pris?' *Observer* (2 March).

Prosser, T. (1996) 'Understanding the British constitution', *Political Studies*, 44(3), 473–87.

Punnett, R. M. (1975) 'Her Majesty's shadow government', in Herman and Alt (eds), pp. 140–56.

Raab, C. D. (1994) 'Open government: policy information and information policy', *Political Quarterly*, 65(3), 340–7.

Rallings, C. and Thrasher, M. (1994) *Explaining Electoral Turnout: A Secondary Analysis of Local Election Statistics*, London, HMSO.

Rallings, C. and Thrasher, M. (1996) *Enhancing Local Electoral Turnout: A Guide to Current Practice and Future Reform*, York, Joseph Rowntree Foundation.

Rallings, C. and Thrasher, M. (1997) 'Strong case for second place', *Local Government Chronicle*, 9 May.

Ramphal, S. (1997) 'The Commonwealth in the global neighbourhood', *The Round Table*, no. 342, 175–85.

Randall, V. (1982) *Women and Politics*, Basingstoke, Macmillan.

Rau, C. B. (1996) 'United Nations at 50: retrospect and prospect', *Round Table*, no. 337, 25–62.

Rawlings, H. F. (1986) 'Judicial review and the "control of government"',

Public Administration, 64(2), 142–3.

Redcliffe-Maud, Lord (chairman) (1969) *Royal Commission on Local Government in England 1966–69, Vol. I*, Cmnd 4040, London, HMSO.

Redlich, J. and Hirst, F. W. (1970) *Local Government in England, Vol. II* (ed. Keith-Lucas, B.), London, Macmillan (first published 1903).

Reiner, R. (1982) 'Who are the police?', *Political Quarterly*, 53(2), 469–71.

Reiner R. (1993) *The Politics of the Police*, 2nd edn, Hemel Hempstead, Harvester Wheatsheaf.

Reiner R. (1996a) 'Criminal investigation', *Guardian* (16 Oct.).

Reiner R. (ed.) (1996b) *Policing*, Aldershot, Dartmouth.

Rhodes, R. A. W. (1981) *Control and Power in Central–Local Government Relations*, Farnborough, Gower.

Rhodes, R. A. W. (1988) *Beyond Westminster and Whitehall: the Sub-central Government of Britain*, London, George Allen & Unwin.

Rhodes, R. A. W. (1994) 'The hollowing out of the state: the changing nature of the public service in Britain', *Political Quarterly*, 65(2), 138–51.

Rhodes, R. A. W. and Dunleavy, P. (1995) *Prime Minister, Cabinet and Core Executive*, Basingstoke, Macmillan.

Rhodes, R. A. W. and Marsh, D. (1992) *Policy Networks in British Government*, Oxford, Oxford University Press.

Rhodes, R. A. W., Hardy, D. and Pudney, K. (1983) *Corporate Bias in Central–Local Relations: A Case Study of the CCLGF*, Colchester, University of Essex, Department of Government.

Richards, D. (1996) 'Recruitment to the highest grades in the civil service: drawing the curtains open', *Public Administration*, 74(4), 657–77.

Richards, P. G. (1970) *Parliament and Conscience*, London, George Allen & Unwin.

Richardson, J. J. and Jordan, A. G. (1979) *Government under Pressure*, Oxford, Martin Robertson.

Riddell, P. (1985) *The Thatcher Government*, Oxford, Basil Blackwell.

Riddell, P. (1993) *Honest Opportunism: The Rise of the Career Politician*, London, Hamish Hamilton.

Riddell, P. (1997) 'Cracks in the Cabinet cement', *The Times* (10 Nov.).

Ridley, F. F. and Wilson, D. (1995) *The Quango Debate*, Oxford, Oxford University Press.

Ridley, N. (1988) *The Local Right*, London, Centre for Policy Studies.

Robertson, G. (1997) 'Justice in all fairness', *Guardian* (30 April).

Robson, W. A. (1966) *Local Government in Crisis*, London, George Allen & Unwin.

Rogaly, J. (1997) 'If television rescues Major it will be a miracle', *Financial Times* (18 March).

Rogers, A. (1997) *Secrecy and Power in the British State*, London, Pluto.

Rollo, J. (1980) 'The Special Patrol Group', in Hain (ed.), pp. 153–208.

Rose, R. (1964) 'Parties, factions and tendencies in British politics', *Political Studies*, 12(1), 33–46.

Rose, R. and McAllister, I. (1986) *Voters Begin to Choose: From Closed Class to Open Elections*, Beverly Hills, CA, Sage.

Rosenberg, J. (1997) *Trial of Strength*, London, Richard Cohen.

Roth, A. (1981) *The Business Backgrounds of MPs*, London, Parliamentary Profiles.

Rousseau, J. J. (1913) *The Social Contract,* London, Dent (first published 1762).

Rowan, D. (1998) 'Meet the new world government', *Guardian* (22 Feb.).

Rowbotham, S. (1973) *Woman's Consciousness, Man's World*, Harmondsworth, Penguin.

Royal Commission on the Distribution of Income and Wealth (1976) *Report No. 3: Higher Incomes from Employment*, London, HMSO.

Rutherford, A. (1996) 'Short sharp shambles', *Guardian* (27 Aug.).

Ryle, M. (1988) *Ecology and Socialism*, London, Radius.

Saggar, S. (1992) *Race and Politics in Britain*, Hemel Hempstead, Harvester

Wheatsheaf.

Saggar, S. (1997) 'Racial politics', *Parliamentary Affairs*, 50(4), 691–707.

Salisbury, R. H. (1969) 'An exchange theory of interest groups', *Midwest Journal of Political Science*, 13, 1–32.

Sampson, A. (1992) *The Essential Anatomy of Britain: Democracy in Crisis*, London, Hodder and Stoughton.

Sanders, A. and Young, R. (1995) 'The PACE regime for suspects detained by the police', *Political Quarterly*, 66(2), 126–40.

Sanders, D. (1993) 'Why the Conservative Party won – again', in King et al., pp. 171–213.

Saunders, P. (1980) *Urban Politics: a Sociological Interpretation*, Harmondsworth, Penguin.

Saunders, P. (1984) 'Rethinking local politics', in Boddy and Fudge (eds), pp. 22–48.

Saunders, P. (1995) 'Privatization, share ownership and voting' *British Journal of Political Science*, 25(1), 131–7.

Scammell, M. (1995) *Designer Politics: How Elections are Won*, Basingstoke, Macmillan.

Scarman, Lord (1974) *English Law: the New Dimension*, London, Stevens.

Scarman, Lord (1981) *The Brixton Disorders, 10–12 April 1981: Report of an Inquiry*, Cmnd 8427, London, HMSO (reprinted by Penguin 1982).

Scattschneider, E. E. (1960) *The Semi-Sovereign People*, New York, Holt, Rinehart and Winston.

Scharpf, F. (1988) 'The joint decision trap: lessons from German federalism and European integration', *Public Administration*, 66, 239–78.

Schmitter, P. (1974) 'Still the century of corporatism', *Review of Politics*, 36, 85–131.

Scott, J. (1985) 'The British upper class', in Coates et al. (eds), pp. 29–54.

Scott, J. (1991) *Who Rules Britain?* Cambridge, Polity.

Scruton, R. (1980) *The Meaning of Conservatism*, Harmondsworth, Penguin.

Seaton, J. and Pimlott, B. (eds) (1987) *The Media in British Politics*, Aldershot, Avebury.

Sedgemore, B. (1980) *The Secret Constitution*, London, Hodder and Stoughton.

Select Committee on Defence (1982) *The Handling of Press and Public Information during the Falklands Conflict: First Report*, HC 17-1, London, HMSO.

Self, P. and Storing, H. (1962) *The State and the Farmer*, London, George Allen & Unwin.

Seltman, C. (1956) *Women in Antiquity*, London, Pan.

Semetko, H., Scammell, M. and Goddard, P. (1997) 'Television', *Parliamentary Affairs*, 50(4), 609–15.

Seyd, P. and Whiteley, P. (1992) *Labour's Grass Roots*, Oxford, Clarendon Press.

Seymour-Ure, C. (1997) 'Editorial opinion and the national press', *Parliamentary Affairs*, 50(4), 586–608.

Shaw, E. (1996) *The Labour Party since 1945: Old Labour, New Labour*, Oxford, Blackwell.

Shell, D. (1992) *The House of Lords*, Hemel Hempstead, Harvester Wheatsheaf.

Shell, D. (1994) 'The House of Lords: time for a change?', *Parliamentary Affairs*, 47(4), 721–37.

Simhony, A. (1991) 'On forcing individuals to be free: T. H. Green's liberal theory of positive freedom', *Political Studies*, 39(2), 303–20.

Simon, H. A. (1947) *Administrative Behaviour*, London, Macmillan.

Sivanandan, V. (1981) 'From resistance to rebellion', *Race and Class*, 23 (Autumn).

Skelcher, C. (1995) 'Reforming the quangos', *Political Quarterly*, 69(1), 41–7.

Skelcher, C. and Davies, H. (1996) 'Understanding the new magistracy: a study of characteristics and attitudes', *Local Government Studies*, 22(2), 8–21.

Small, N. (1989) *Politics and Planning in the National Health Service*, Buckingham, Open University Press.

Smith, D. J. and Gray, J. (1985) *Police and People in London*, Aldershot, Gower.

Smith, M. (1993) *Pressure Power and Policy: State Autonomy and Policy Networks in Britain and the United States*, Hemel Hempstead, Harvester Wheatsheaf.

Smith, M. (1995) 'Utilities row as profits hit £7.7 billion', *Observer* (2 April).

Smith, M. (1999) *The Core Executive in Britain*, Basingstoke, Macmillan.

Sperling, L. (1997) 'Quangos: political representation and women consumers of public services', *Policy and Politics*, 25(2), 119–28.

Spretnack, C. and Capra, F. (1986) *Green Politics: The Global Promise*, London, Collins.

Stanworth, P. and Giddens, A. (eds) (1974) *Elites and Power in British Society*, Cambridge, Cambridge University Press.

Steel, D. (1984) 'Managing health authorities: one member's view', *Public Money*, 4(1), 37–40.

Stenton, F. M. (1941) *Anglo-Saxon England*, Oxford, Clarendon Press.

Stevenson, J. (1993) *Third Party Politics since 1945*, Oxford, Blackwell.

Stewart, J. (1992) 'The rebuilding of public accountability', paper presented at European Policy Forum, December.

Stewart, J. (1995) 'Appointed boards and local government', *Parliamentary Affairs*, 48(2), 226–41.

Steyn, Lord (1997) 'The weakest and least dangerous department of government', *Public Law*, Spring, 84–5.

Stoker, G. (1993) 'Introduction: local government reorganisation as a garbage can process', *Local Government Policy Making*, 19(4), 3–5.

Strange, S. (1992) 'States, firms and diplomacy', *International Affairs*, 68(1), 1–15.

Stuart, C. (ed.) (1975) *The Reith Diaries*, London, Collins.

Studlar, D. T. (1983) 'The ethnic vote 1983: problems of analysis and interpretation', *New Community*,

9(1–2), 92–100.

Tarling, R. and Dowds, L. (1998) 'Crime and punishment', in Jowell et al., pp. 197–214.

Taylor, A. J. P. (1965) *English History 1914–1945*, London, Oxford University Press.

Taylor, S. (1982) *The National Front in English Politics*, Basingstoke, Macmillan.

Thain, C. and Wright, M. (1995) *The Treasury and Whitehall: the Planning and Control of Public Expenditure 1976–1993*, Oxford, Clarendon.

Thatcher, M. (1998) 'Regulating the regulators: the regulatory regime for the British privatised utilities', *Parliamentary Affairs*, 51(2), 209–22.

Theakston, K. (1995) *The Civil Service since 1945*, Oxford, Blackwell.

Theakston, K. and Fry, G. K. (1989) 'Britain's administrative elite: permanent secretaries 1900–1986', *Public Administration*, 67(2), 129–48.

Thomas, H. (ed.) (1959) *The Establishment*, London, Anthony Blond.

Thompson, B. (1997) 'Conclusion: judges as trouble-shooters', *Parliamentary Affairs*, 50(1), 182–9.

Thompson, E. P. (1975) *Whigs and Hunters*, London, Allen Lane.

Thompson, E. P. (1980) 'The logic of exterminism', *New Left Review*, no. 121 (May–June), 3–32.

Thompson, E. P. (1982) 'The heavy dancers of the air', *New Society* (11 Nov.), 244.

Thompson, J. B. (1995) *The Media and Modernity: A Social Theory of the Media*, Cambridge, Polity.

Tickle, A. and Welsh, I. (eds) (1998) *Environment and Society in Eastern Europe*, Harlow, Addison Wesley Longman.

Timmins, N. and Kampfner, J. (1997) 'New tricks for old dogs', *Financial Times* (18 March).

Todd, J. and Butcher, B. (1982) *Electoral Registration in 1981*, London, Office of Population Census and Surveys.

Travers, T. (1996) 'Town hall turns red', *Guardian* (11 Dec.).

Travis, T. (1996) 'Carey attacks "prison works" policies', *Guardian* (10 May).

Treasury (1991) *Competing for Quality: Buying Better Public Services*, Cm 1730, London, HMSO.

Treasury (1997) *Public Expenditure: Statistical Analysis 1997–98*, Cm 3601, London, Stationery Office.

Treasury (1998) *Financial Statement and Budget Report*, London, Treasury.

Tunstall, J. (1970) *The Westminster Lobby Correspondents*, London, Routledge and Kegan Paul.

Turner, D. R. (1969) *The Shadow Cabinet in British Politics*, London, Routledge and Kegan Paul.

Turner, R. (1995) *The British Economy in Transition*, London, Routledge.

Unseem, M. (1984) *The Inner Circle: Large Corporations and the Rise of Business Political Activity in the US and the UK*, Oxford, Oxford University Press.

Urban, M. (1997) *UK Eyes Alpha: The Inside Story of British Intelligence*, London, Faber.

Urry, J. (1985) 'The class structure', in Coates et al. (eds).

Urwin, D. (1989) *Western Europe since 1945*, 4th edn, Harlow, Longman.

Urwin, D. (1997) *A Political History of Western Europe since 1945*, Harlow, Addison Wesley Longman.

Van der Gaag, N. (1995) 'Women: still something to shout about' *New Internationalist*, no. 270 (Aug.), 7–10.

Vidal, J. (1996) 'Happy birthday Friends of the Earth', *Earthmatters*, no. 30, 4–5.

Vidal, J. (1997) *McLibel: Burger Culture on Trial*, Basingstoke, Macmillan.

Vincent, A. (1992) *Modern Political Ideologies*, Oxford, Blackwell.

Von Bertallanfy, L. (1952) *General Systems Theory*, New York, Harper.

Wagstyl, S. (1996) 'Nice work if you can get it', *Financial Times* (18 Dec).

Walker, P. G. (1972) *The Cabinet*, London, Fontana.

Walkland, S. A. and Ryle, M. (eds) (1981) *The Commons Today*, London, Fontana.

Waller, R. and Criddle, B. (1997)

Almanac of British Politics, London, Routledge.

Wallerstein, I. (1979) *The Capitalist World Economy*, Cambridge, Cambridge University Press.

Walles, G. (1948) *Human Nature in Politics*, London, Constable.

Walvin, J. (1984) *Passage to Britain*, Harmondsworth, Penguin.

Ward, G. (1993) 'Reforming the public sector: privatisation and the role of advisers', *Political Quarterly*, 94, 298–305.

Wass, Sir D. (1984) *Government and the Governed* (BBC Reith Lectures), London, Routledge and Kegan Paul.

Wass, Sir D. (1986) 'Foreword', in Harden and Lewis, pp. ix–xiii.

Watts, D. (1997) *Political Communication Today*, Manchester, Manchester University Press.

Wayne, M. (1998) *Dissident Voices: The Politics of Television and Cultural Change*, London, Pluto.

Weber, M. (1978) *Economy and Society, Vol. II*, Berkeley, CA, University of California Press (first published 1922).

Webster, P. and Bowditch, G. (1997) 'White Paper becomes a best seller', *The Times* (25 July).

Weir, S. (1995) 'Quangos: questions of democratic accountability', *Parliamentary Affairs*, 48(2), 307–22.

Weir, S. and Boyle, K. (1997) 'Human rights in the UK: introduction to the special issue', *Political Quarterly*, 68(2), 128–34.

Weir, S. and Hall, W. (eds) (1994) *Ego Trip: Extra-Governmental Organisations in the United Kingdom and their Accountability*, London, Charter 88 Trust.

Whiteley, P. (1997) 'The Conservative campaign', *Parliamentary Affairs*, 50(4), 542–54.

Whiteley, P. and Winyard, S. (1984) 'The origins of the "New Poverty Lobby"', *Public Administration*, 61(1), 32–54.

Whiteley, P., Seyd, P. and Richardson, J. (1994) *True Blues: The Politics of Conservative Party Membership*, Oxford, Clarendon Press.

Whyatt, J. (1961) *The Citizen and the*

Administration, London, Justice.

Widdicombe, D. (1977) *Our Fettered Ombudsman*, London, Justice.

Widdicombe, D. (1986a) *The Conduct of Local Authority Business*, Cmnd 9797, London, HMSO.

Widdicombe, D. (1986b) *Research Volume 1: The Political Organisation of Local Authorities*, Cmnd 9798, London, HMSO.

Wilkenson, H. (1995) *No Turning Back: Generations and the Genderquake*, London, Demos.

Willetts, D. (1996) *Blair's Gurus*, London, Centre for Policy Studies.

Willetts, D. (1998) 'Conservative renewal', *Political Quarterly*, 69(2), 110–17.

Williams, F. (1969) 'A prime minister remembers: the war and post-war memories of the Rt. Hon. Earl Attlee', in King, A. (ed.) *The British Prime Minister*, Basingstoke, Macmillan.

Williamson, N. (1995) 'Civil service ready for Blair, says Sir Robin', *The Times* (20 Nov.).

Wilson, H. (1974) *The Labour Government 1964–70*, Harmondsworth, Penguin.

Wilson, H. H. (1961) *Pressure Group: the Campaign for Commercial Television*, Harmondsworth, Penguin.

Wilson, D. (1994) 'Facing up to the "democratic deficit"', *Local Government Studies*, 20(7), 193–201.

Wilson, D. (1996) 'Structural "solutions" for local government: an exercise in chasing shadows', *Parliamentary Affairs*, 49(3), 441–54.

Wilson, D. and Game, C., with Leach, S. and Stoker, G. (1994) *Local Government in the United Kingdom*, Basingstoke, Macmillan.

Wilson, D. and Game, C. (1997) *Local Government in the United Kingdom*, Basingstoke, Macmillan.

Wilson, E. (1992) *A Very British Miracle*, London, Pluto.

Wilson, T. (1966) *The Downfall of the Liberal Party 1914–1935*, London, Collins.

Winter, M. (1996) 'Intersecting departmental responsibilities, administrative confusion and the role of science in government: the case of BSE', *Parliamentary Affairs*, 49(4), 550–65.

Wintour, P. and Pallister, D. (1995) 'Revelations that led to sleaze inquiry', *Guardian* (12 May).

Woodhouse, D. (1995) 'Politicians and the judiciary: a changing relationship', *Parliamentary Affairs*, 48(3) 401–18.

Woodhouse, D. (1996) 'Politicians and the judges: a conflict of interest', *Parliamentary Affairs*, 49(3), 423–40.

Woodhouse, D. (1998) 'The Parliamentary Commissioner for Standards: lessons from the "Cash for Questions" inquiry', *Parliamentary Affairs*, 51(1), 51–61.

Wraith, R. E. and Lamb, G. B. (1971) *Public Inquiries as Instruments of Government*, London, George Allen & Unwin.

Wright, E. O. (1985) *Classes*, London, Verso.

Wright, P. (1987) *Spycatcher*, New York, Viking.

Wyatt, W. (1973) 'Parliament the waste land', *Sunday Times* (4 Nov.).

Young, H. (1989) *One of Us*, London, Macmillan.

Young, H. (1998) *This Blessed Plot: Britain and Europe from Churchill to Blair*, Basingstoke, Macmillan.

Zander, M. (1969) 'Who goes to solicitors?', *Law Society's Gazette*, no. 66.

Index

Note: The index is arranged in word-by-word order, ignoring words such as 'and', 'in' and 'by' (and treating hyphens as spaces). Page numbers in *italics* refer to diagrams and illustrations. The index enables you to locate both broad topics and specific items and you should normally search by looking for the most specific term possible. For example, to find out about the alternative vote system, you can go directly to that term, rather than to the more general 'electoral system'. For reasons of space, individuals mentioned only briefly in the text are not included. However, these may be tracked down by looking up the event or institution with which they are associated. Remember to consult the Glossary for brief definitions. Note also that material in the Chronology is not included in the index.

*Index compiled by
Ann Barham*